Child Development

An Introduction

Fourth Edition

Child Development

An Introduction

John W. Santrock
University of Texas at Dallas

Steve R. Yussen
University of Wisconsin-Madison

wcb
Wm. C. Brown Publishers
Dubuque, Iowa

Book Team

Editor *Michael Lange*
Developmental Editor *Sandra E. Schmidt*
Production Editor *Kevin Campbell/Vickie Putman Caughron*
Designer *K. Wayne Harms*
Photo Editor *Michelle Oberhoffer*
Permissions Editor *Carrie Husemann*
Visuals Processor *Jodi Wagner*

wcb group

Chairman of the Board *Wm. C. Brown*
President and Chief Executive Officer *Mark C. Falb*

wcb

Wm. C. Brown Publishers, College Division

President *G. Franklin Lewis*
Vice President, Editor-in-Chief *George Wm. Bergquist*
Vice President, Director of Production *Beverly Kolz*
Vice President, National Sales Manager *Bob McLaughlin*
Director of Marketing *Thomas E. Doran*
Marketing Communications Manager *Edward Bartell*
Marketing Manager *Kathy Law Laube*
Production Editorial Manager *Colleen A. Yonda*
Production Editorial Manager *Julie A. Kennedy*
Publishing Services Manager *Karen J. Slaght*
Manager of Visuals and Design *Faye M. Schilling*

Cover photo © 1988 Tony Caputo, Los Angeles, CA

Children's art in cover photo by Hoover Elementary School, Dubuque, IA.

The credits section for this book begins on page 549, and is considered an extension of the copyright page.

Library of Congress Catalog Card Number: 88–72247

ISBN 0–697–05951–0 (Paper)
ISBN 0–697–11057–5 (Cloth)

Printed in the United States of America by Wm. C. Brown Publishers
2460 Kerper Boulevard, Dubuque, IA 52001

10 9 8 7 6 5 4 3 2

With special appreciation to our wives
Mary Jo and Suzann and to our children
Jennifer and Tracy, David and Elayna

Brief Contents

Contents

SECTION
1

The Nature of Child Development

SECTION
2

Biological and Perceptual Development

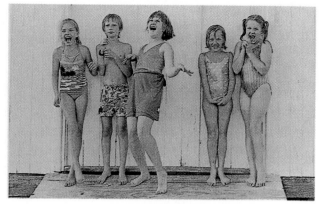

SECTION
3

Cognitive Development

SECTION
4

Social and Personality Development

SECTION
5

Abnormal Behavior, Stress, and Health

Concept Tables

Perspective on Child Development Boxes

Preface

Some fourteen years ago we agreed to write the first edition of *Child Development*. We wanted to develop a book that would portray the scientific study of child development in an enthusiastic manner. The fourth edition of *Child Development* continues our effort to both inform and excite the reader. Because ours is a field of rapidly changing knowledge with extensive research on children being conducted throughout the world, the second and third editions of *Child Development* represented substantial changes from their predecessors. The fourth edition of *Child Development* continues the tradition of extensive research updating. The fourth edition also continues to present child development in a topical manner.

The Research System

Beginning with the first edition and continuing through the present edition, *Child Development* is above all else an extremely up-to-date presentation of research in the three primary domains of development: biological processes, cognitive processes, and social processes. Research on biological, cognitive, and social processes continues to represent the core of *Child Development*. This core includes both classic and cutting edge research. *Child Development* includes more than 400 references from 1986 to 1989, with 175 of those coming from 1988, 1989, or those still "in press." Scientific knowledge about child development is expanding on many frontiers, and we have tried in each chapter to capture the excitement of these new discoveries while also presenting the classic studies that are the foundation of the discipline.

The basic *topical, process-oriented* focus of *Child Development* has not changed. Why is *Child Development* written this way? By means of this process-oriented perspective, students can see how developmental processes reflect fundamental changes in the childhood years. To this end, separate sections focus on biological and perceptual development, cognitive development, social and personality development and abnormal behavior, stress, and health. In addition, the first section of the book provides an insightful introduction to the field of child development, explaining its history, research issues, and methods of study.

New content in the fourth edition of *Child Development* includes considerably increased coverage of prenatal and infant development, pubertal processes, motivation, stress, and health. In addition, *Child Development* now concludes with an epilogue, The Odyssey of Childhood. This concluding section helps students to weave together the developmental themes they have studied into a chronological sequence. Many books simply end with little or no integrative effort. Too often students are left with no sense of conclusion as they finish the last words of the book. We hope this new addition helps to provide a solution to this problem and gives students an overall developmental perspective they can carry with them as they finish the course.

The Writing System

In addition to continuing our strategy of providing extensive updating and coverage of cutting edge research, we asked ourselves what else we could do to improve the fourth edition of *Child Development*. Easily the most dramatic change in the fourth edition of *Child Development* is the *improved readability*. Those familiar with the earlier editions will notice this change after spending only a few minutes with the fourth edition. To accomplish the goal of making the text even more readable, we went over the third edition of *Child Development* with a fine-toothed comb, adding, subtracting, integrating, and simplifying. We examined various ways to present ideas and asked college students to give us extensive feedback on which ways were most effective. Virtually every sentence, every paragraph, and every section of the book were rewritten with these goals uppermost in our minds. We think you will be pleasantly surprised if you are familiar with the first three editions of the book.

Most authors with successful editions of a book only make cosmetic changes in the fourth edition. Why spend so much time rewriting, adding, subtracting, integrating, and simplifying in the fourth edition? Although the third edition provided a solid scientific overview of child development, a new edition offers the opportunity for improvement and fine-tuning throughout. For example, when a concept is introduced it is followed by a comprehensible definition and either research or personal examples, or sometimes both. Noticeable in the fourth edition is an increased use of examples taken from the lives of children as they experience their world.

The Learning System

A carefully designed, refined learning system has been built into the fourth edition of *Child Development*. Critical to this framework are the **Concept Tables** that appear several times in each chapter. The concept tables help students to organize theoretical material and to see the relationships between various concepts. They are designed to activate the student's memory and comprehension of major topics or key concepts that have been discussed to that point. Concept tables provide a visual picture, or cognitive framework, of the most important information in each section.

In addition, **Chapter Outlines** at the beginning of each chapter show the overall organization of material. An imaginative, high-interest piece follows—it focuses on a topic related to the chapter's contents. For example, chapter 3, Prenatal Development and Birth, begins with an interesting account of a baby weighing less than two pounds at birth. Chapter 11, Perspectives on Socialization, begins with a description of several children who grew up in virtually complete social isolation. Chapter 16, Moral Development, begins with a discussion of children who are asked to pretend that they had traveled to a make-believe planet and to give their judgments of what rules and regulations would have to be developed on the planet. **Perspective on Child Development** boxes appear several times in each chapter. A brief glimpse through any chapter reveals their special appeal. For example, chapter 2, Biological Beginnings, includes the box, "Doran, Dr. Graham, and the Repository for Germinal Choice," which is about a Nobel-Prize winners' sperm bank and its ethical issues; chapter 7, Cognitive Development and Piaget's Theory, includes a box, "Where Pelicans Kiss Seals, Cars Float on Clouds, and Humans Are Tadpoles," which focuses on the symbolic world of young children's minds and drawings; and chapter 13 includes a box, "Beyond the Zoo," which evaluates the critera for effective middle schools.

At the end of the chapter, a detailed **Summary** in outline form provides a helpful review. **Key Terms** are boldfaced in the text, listed with page references at the end of each chapter, and defined in a page-referenced **Glossary** at the end of the book. An annotated list of **Suggested Readings** also appears at the end of each chapter. Finally, at the book's end, students will find an **Epilogue** that reviews and integrates the main themes of children's development from a chronological perspective.

Teaching and Learning Aids

The publisher and the ancillary team have worked together to produce an outstanding integrated teaching package to accompany *Child Development*. The authors of the teaching supplements are all experienced teachers of the child development course. The supplements have been designed to make it as easy as possible to customize the entire package to meet the unique needs of individual professors and their students.

The **Instructor's Course Planner** includes the Instructor's Manual, the Test Item File, and the Transparency Set. It is conveniently packaged in a three-ring binder so that lecture notes or classroom material can be added. Adopters will receive a loose-leaf copy of the text so that teaching materials and textbook pages can be easily integrated. This unique system enables instructors to customize their courses and class plans.

The **Instructor's Manual** includes, for each chapter, an annotated chapter outline; page-referenced learning objectives and a list of key terms; a Student Research Project with data record forms, essay questions, and a new feature, "Classroom Activities to Encourage Critical Thinking." In addition, the Instructor's Manual includes a comprehensive film list and an essay on "Ethics, Human Subjects, and Informed Consent."

The comprehensive **Test Item File** has been prepared by Michael Boyes, University of Calgary. The Test Item File consists of two separate test banks. Each test item is referenced to both text page and learning objective, and is identified as factual, conceptual, or applied.

The **Transparency Set** features many acetate transparencies in full color and includes graphics from both the text and outside sources. These transparencies have been designed to help in classroom teaching and lecture organization.

A **Student Study Guide** by Debra Clark and Melvyn King, State University of New York-Cortland, includes the following for each chapter: page-referenced learning objectives, key terms exercise, guided review, student test questions, and a set of "Critical Thinking" questions that go beyond the text, asking students to think critically about issues raised in the chapter and to apply chapter material to real-life circumstances.

wcb TestPak is the free, computerized testing service available to adopters of *Child Development*. All questions in the Test Item File are available on TestPak. Two options are available. The call-in/mail-in TestPak service guarantees that we will put in the mail to you a test master, a student answer sheet, and an answer key within two working days of receiving your request. Call-in hours are 8:30–1:30, Central Time, Monday–Thursday. **wcb** TestPak is also available for instructors who want to use their IBM® PC or their Apple® IIe, IIc, or Macintosh to create their own tests. Upon request, adopters of *Child Development* will receive the Test Item File, program diskettes, and user's guide. With these, the instructor can create tests, answer sheets, and answer keys. The program permits adding, deleting, or modifying test questions. No programming experience is necessary.

wcb QuizPak, the interactive self-testing, self-scoring quiz program, will help your students to review text material from any chapter by testing themselves on an Apple® IIe, IIc, or Macintosh, or an IBM® PC. Adopters will receive the QuizPak program, question disks, and an easy-to-follow user's guide. QuizPak may be used at a number of workstations simultaneously and requires only one disk drive.

Acknowledgments

A project of this magnitude requires the efforts of many people. We owe special thanks to Sandy Schmidt, basic books editor, who guided the extensive revision with both competence and cheer. Kevin Campbell, production editor, efficiently and swiftly moved the book through production to its present attractive state. Wayne Harms, designer, provided creative touches that make the book appealing. Michelle Oberhoffer deserves special credit for tracking down elusive photographs. Carrie Husemann efficiently obtained permissions. Special thanks go to Debra E. Clark and Melvyn B. King, who prepared the excellent Instructor's Manual and Student Study Guide, and to Michael Boyes, who prepared the comprehensive Test Item File.

We also continued to benefit from the contributions in the third edition of *Child Development* by James C. Bartlett, University of Texas at Dallas.

We have benefited enormously from the ideas and insights of many colleagues. We would like to thank the following individuals for their feedback on earlier editions of *Child Development:* Ruth L. Ault, Davidson College; Debra E. Clark, SUNY—Cortland; Roger W. Coulson, Iowa State University; Dennis T. Farrell, Luzerne County Community College; Robert A. Haaf, University of Toledo; Daniel W. Kee, California State University at Fullerton; Melvyn B. King, SUNY—Cortland; Daniel K. Lapsley, University of Notre Dame; Jose E. Nanez, University of Minnesota; Daniel J. O'Neil, Bristol Community College; Ed Scholwinski, Southwest Texas State University; Matthew J. Sharps, University of Colorado; Mark S. Strauss, University of Pittsburgh; E. Audrey Clark, California State University, Northridge; Robert C. Coon, Louisiana State University; Diane C. Draper, Iowa State University; Irma Galejs, Iowa State University; Margaret J. Gill, Kutztown State College; John W. Kulig, Northern Illinois University; Dalton Miller-Jones, Northeast Foundation for Children; Bill M. Seay, Louisiana State University; and Douglas B. Sawin, University of Texas at Austin.

We also express our gratitude to the following professors who provided in-depth reviews of the chapters for the current edition of *Child Development:*

Ruth Ault
Davidson College

Michael Bergmire
Jefferson College

Susan Bland
Niagara County Community College

Maureen Callahan
Webster University

R. Daniel DiSalvi
Kean College

Stanley Hensen
Arkansas Technical University

Seth Kalichman
University of South Carolina

Kenneth Kallio
SUNY-Geneseo

Daniel Lapsley
University of Notre Dame

Carolyn Meyer
Lake Sumter Community College

Robert Pasnak
George Mason University

Marilyn Shea
University of Maine—Farmington

A final note of thanks goes to our families. Mary Jo Santrock and Suzann Yussen have lived through four editions of *Child Development*. We appreciate the support and encouragement they have given to our writing. Our children, Tracy and Jennifer Santrock and Elayna and David Yussen, have provided us with firsthand experiences at watching children develop. Tracy was 7, Jennifer was 5, Elayna was just being born, and David had not yet been born when the first edition of *Child Development* was published. Now Tracy is 22, Jennifer is 19, Elayna is 14, and David is 10. Through these fourteen years they have helped us render a treatment of children's development that captures the complexity, the subtlety, and the humanness of it.

The Nature of Child Development

In every child who is born, under no matter what circumstances, and of no matter what parents, the potentiality of the human race is born again.

—James Agee

Introduction

We reach backward to our parents and forward to our children and through their children to a future we will never see, but about which we need to care.

—Carl Jung

W hy study children? Perhaps you are or will be a parent or teacher. Responsibility for children is or will be a part of your everyday life. The more you learn about children, the better you can deal with them. Perhaps you hope to gain some insight into your own history—as an infant, as a child, and as an adolescent. Or perhaps you just stumbled onto this course thinking that it sounded interesting and that the topic of child development would raise some provocative and intriguing issues about how human beings grow and develop. Whatever your reasons, you will discover that the study of child development *is* provocative, *is* intriguing, and *is* filled with information about who we are and how we grew to be this way.

As you might imagine, understanding children's development, and our own personal journey through childhood, is a rich and complicated undertaking. You will discover that different experts approach the study of children in many different ways and ask many different questions. Amidst this richness and complexity we seek a simple answer: To understand how children change as they grow up and the forces that contribute to this change.

What are some of these changes? Children grow in size and weight. They learn to stand and walk and run. They learn language, picking up words as pigeons pick up peas. They learn to read, to write, and to solve math problems. They learn behaviors and roles that society considers acceptable for "boys" and for "girls" and for "men" and for "women." They learn the necessity of curbing their will and develop an understanding of what is morally acceptable and unacceptable. They learn how to communicate and to get along with many different people. Their families—parents and siblings—are very important influences in their lives, but their growth also is shaped by successive choirs of friends, teachers, and strangers. In their most pimply and awkward moments as adolescents, they become acquainted with sex and try on one face after another searching for an identity they can call their own. These are but a few of the fascinating changes that take place as children develop—many more await you in this text.

In some sense, then, the modern study of child development is not exotic. It is concerned with the same matters that you and I, as ordinary, everyday people might want to understand if and when we raise our own sons and daughters, we teach children in school, or try to get along with children as brothers or sisters or aunts and uncles. Whatever the context, though, it will help us immensely to know and understand precisely how children change.

In this chapter you will be introduced to some contemporary concerns about child development and to a historical perspective on child development. You will learn what development is, what issues are raised by a developmental perspective on children, and what methods are used to study child development.

Child Development—Today and Yesterday

Everywhere an individual turns in contemporary society, the development and well-being of children capture public attention, the interest of scientists, and the concern of policymakers. Through history, though, interest in the development of children has been uneven.

Some Contemporary Concerns

Consider some of the topics you read about in newspapers and magazines every day: educational reform, contemporary changes in family structure and work, the impact of computers on children, and caring for mentally retarded children, for example. What the experts are discovering in each of these areas has direct and significant consequences for understanding children and on our decisions as a society for how children are treated. Let's examine these issues further.

During the past several years, our educational system has come under attack (Kearns, 1988). A national commission, appointed by the Office of Education, concluded that our children are poorly prepared for the increasingly complex future they will be asked to face in our society. The problems are legion—declining skills of those entering the teaching profession, adolescents graduating from high school with primary grade level reading and mathematics skills, a shortage of qualified mathematics and science teachers, less and less time being spent by students in engaging academic work in their classrooms, an absence of any real signs of challenge and thinking required by the school curriculum, and an unfortunately high dropout rate over the four years of high school. Solutions to these problems are not easy. However, in searching for solutions, policymakers will repeatedly find themselves turning to experts in the field of child development, because to design an engaging curriculum, a planner must know what engages and motivates children. To improve our national effort in teaching thinking skills, the planner must understand what thinking is and how it changes across the school years. And to understand the roots of the social difficulties encountered by so many of today's adolescents, difficulties that lead them to drop out of school in droves, the planner needs to understand the nature of the socialization processes involved in the transition to adolescence and the ways in which schools fail to address them.

We hear a great deal from experts and popular writers about pressures on the contemporary family. The number of families in which both parents work is increasing, while at the same time the number of one-parent families has increased over the past two decades as a result of a climbing divorce rate. With more children raised by single parents or by parents who are both working, the time parents have to spend with their children is being squeezed and the quality of child care is of concern to many. Are working parents better using the decreased time with their children? Do day-care arrangements provide quality alternatives for parents? How troubled should we be about the increasing number of latchkey children—those at home alone after school, waiting for their parents to return from work? Answers to these questions can be formed by several different kinds of information obtained by experts in child development. These include studies of the way working parents use time

How well are our children being prepared for the increasingly complex tasks they will face in the future? What can be done to improve their preparation?

with their children and the nature of their parenting approaches and behaviors, studies of the way various day-care arrangements influence children's social and intellectual growth in relation to home-care arrangements, and examination of the consequences of a child being without adult supervision for hours every day after school (Corsini, Wisensale, & Caruso, 1988).

We are now and for the foreseeable future will be in the information age. Increasingly, our economy and our lives are dependent upon the quality, speed, and availability of information. Advances in the field of computing have brought this about, and nowhere is the trend more apparent than in the explosion of the use of computers in business, at home, and in schools. Computing power, available only to large corporations in the 1960s, is now in the hands of four- and five-year-olds. How will this change the nature of children's learning and development in the future? Futurists have many ideas about this, but no one really knows. The nature of the change, however, must be reckoned with on several different fronts. From our perspective as developmentalists, we must ask a number of questions. How do family members interact when extensive time is spent with computers? How are television time and school work influenced? How do children's social interaction patterns with other children change because of exposure to computers, the tendency to associate with other "hackers," and the discovery of the computer as companion, babysitter, or mentor? Finally, how will exposure to computers and programming alter the very nature of thinking, learning, and reasoning, the way these activities must surely have been altered forever when humans learned to read and write and use mathematics to understand the world many years ago? Psychologists are addressing these questions, but as you might expect, the evidence is still quite sketchy (Glasser & Bassok, 1989).

Parents and educators must face the challenging task of helping many mentally retarded children grow and adapt in a world that is beyond their easy comprehension and intellectual pace. How are they to do this most effectively? What experiences and social groupings will yield the best results? Should these children be tracked separately in school or "mainstreamed," that is, joined with their nonretarded age peers in school? The answers are not easy but surely depend on the type of retardation, the knowledge we have acquired about the nature of children's learning and cognitive development, and practical attempts to train retarded children to master a number of intellectual and practical living skills (Zigler, 1987).

This survey of contemporary social issues has purposefully been brief. You will hear more about them in later chapters. In the meantime, we hope your appetite has been whetted for this exciting field of study. Now we turn back the clock and study the history of interest in child development.

Child Development and History

> At first, the infant,
> Mewling and puking in the nurse's arms,
> Then the whining schoolboy, with his satchel
> And shining morning face, creeping like a snail.

While Shakespeare was a man for all seasons and all ages in many respects, he often defined children in terms of such qualities as foolishness, emotionality, innocence, impotence, and need for discipline from adults (Borstelmann, 1983). But the history of interest in children goes back much farther in time than Shakespeare's late sixteenth- and early seventeenth-century portrayals.

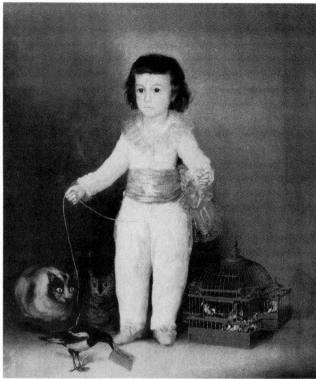

Historical Accounts of Childhood

Childhood has become such a distinct period it is hard to imagine that it was not always thought of in that way. But Philip Aries (1962) suggested that childhood was not a distinctive period during much of history. Aries presented samples of art along with some available publications to conclude that development was divided into infancy—which lasted for many years—and adulthood—which extended somewhere from what we now call middle childhood to postadolescence (figure 1.1 shows the artistic representation of children during the Middle Ages).

A reawakening of interest in the study of children through history, though, casts doubt on Aries' conclusions, which seem to be overdrawn, reflecting artistic style, aristocratic subjects and artists, and an idealization of society at the time. In ancient Egypt, Greece, and Rome, rich conceptions of children's development were presented, for example (Borstelmann, 1983).

During the Renaissance, from the fourteenth to seventeenth centuries, philosophers speculated at length about the nature of children and how they should be reared. During the Middle Ages, the goal of child rearing was salvation—the purpose of parenting was to remove sin from the child's life. This perspective, called the **original sin** perspective, stated that children are born bad; only through the constraints of parenting or salvation would children become competent adults.

Two contrasting views about the nature of the child emerged during the Renaissance—the **tabula rasa** and **innate goodness** views. Near the end of the seventeenth century, John Locke argued that children are not innately bad, but instead they are like a "blank tablet," a *tabula rasa* as he called it. Locke believed that childhood experiences are important in determining adult characteristics; he advised parents to spend time with their children and to help

Figure 1.1
Aries argued that our present concept of childhood is a recent one. He stressed that in the past, children were viewed as miniature adults; however, Aries' writings may have been too stereotypical.

them become contributing members of society. During the eighteenth century, Jean-Jacques Rousseau agreed with Locke that children are not basically bad, but he did not think they were a blank tablet either. Rousseau said children are inherently good and because of their innate goodness, they should be permitted to grow naturally with little parental monitoring or constraint.

In the past century and a half, our view of children has changed dramatically. We now conceive of childhood as a highly eventful and unique period of life that lays an important foundation for the adult years and is highly differentiated from them. In most approaches to childhood, distinct periods are identified in which special skills are mastered and new life tasks are confronted. Childhood is no longer seen as an inconvenient "waiting" period during which adults must suffer the incompetencies of the young. We now value childhood as a special time of growth and change, and we invest great resources in caring for and educating our children. We protect them from the excesses of the adult work world through tough child labor laws; we treat their crimes against society under a special system of juvenile justice; and we have governmental provisions for helping children when ordinary family support systems fail or when families seriously interfere with the child's well-being.

Sociopolitical events and issues have spurred interest in children (Alexander, 1987; White, 1985; Zigler, 1987). Research flourishes when there is substantial national activity on behalf of children and families. The war on poverty in the 1960s led to the formation of Project Head Start, designed to give children from low-income families an opportunity to learn. In the 1980s the changing nature of society motivated research interest in the effects of divorce on children, working mothers and day care, and gender.

The Modern Study of Child Development

The modern era of studying children has a history that spans only a little more than a century (Cairns, 1983). This era begins with some important developments in the late 1800s and extends to the current period of the 1990s. Why is this past century so special? During the past century the study of child development has developed into a sophisticated science. We have a number of major theories that help to organize our thinking about children's development, along with elegant techniques and methods of study. And, new knowledge about children—based on direct observation and testing—is accumulating at a breathtaking pace.

During the last quarter of the nineteenth century, a major shift took place—from viewing human psychology from a strictly philosophical perspective to one that includes direct observation and experimentation. Most of the influential early psychologists were trained either in the natural sciences (such as biology or medicine) or in philosophy. In the field of child development this was true of such influential thinkers as Charles Darwin, G. Stanley Hall, James Mark Baldwin, and Sigmund Freud. The natural scientists, even then, underscored the importance of conducting experiments and collecting reliable observations of what they studied. This approach had advanced the state of knowledge in physics, chemistry, and biology; however, these scientists were not at all sure that people, much less children or infants, could be profitably studied in this way. Part of their hesitation was that no examples to follow with children existed. In addition, philosophers of the time debated, on both intellectual and ethical grounds, whether the methods of science were appropriate for studying people.

Figure 1.2
Gesell is inside his photographic dome with an infant. Cameras rode on metal tracks at the top of the dome and were moved as needed to record the child's activities. Others could observe from outside the dome without being seen by the child.

The deadlock was broken when some daring and entrepreneurial thinkers began to study infants, children, and adolescents, trying out new methods of study. For example, near the turn of the century, French psychologist Alfred Binet invented many tasks to study attention and memory. With them he studied his own daughters, normal children, retarded children, extremely gifted children, and adults. Eventually, he collaborated in the development of the first modern test of intelligence, which is named after him (the Binet). At about the same time, G. Stanley Hall pioneered the use of questionnaires with large groups of children and popularized the findings of earlier psychologists, who he encouraged to do likewise. In one investigation, Hall tested 400 children in the Boston schools to find out how much they "knew" about themselves and the world, asking them such questions as, "Where are your ribs?"

Later, during the 1920s, a large number of child development research centers were created (Cairns, 1983; Senn, 1975), and their professional staffs began to chart and observe a myriad of behaviors in infants and children. The Universities of Minnesota, Iowa, California at Berkeley, and Columbia, where these centers were located, became famous for their investigations of children's play, friendship patterns, fears, aggression and conflict, and sociability. This work became closely associated with the so-called child study movement, and a new organization, The Society for Research in Child Development, was formed at about the same time.

Another ardent observer of children was Arnold Gesell. With his photographic dome, Gesell (1928) could systematically observe children's behavior without interrupting them (figure 1.2). The direct study of children, in which investigators directly observe children's behavior, conduct experiments, or obtain information about children by questioning their parents and teachers, had an auspicious start in the work of these child study experts. The flow of information about children, based on the direct study of them, has not slowed since that time.

Gesell not only developed sophisticated observational strategies for studying children, but he also had some provocative views on the nature of children's development. He theorized that certain characteristics of children simply "bloom" with age because of a biological, maturational blueprint. Gesell strived for preciseness in charting what a child is like at a specific age. Gesell's views, as well as G. Stanley Hall's, were strongly influenced by Charles Darwin's evolutionary theory (interestingly, Darwin had made the scientific study of children respectable when he developed a baby journal for recording systematic observations of children). Hall (1904) believed that child development follows a natural evolutionary course that can be revealed by child study. He also theorized that child development unfolds in a stagelike fashion, with distinct motives and capabilities at each stage. Hall had much to say about adolescence, arguing that it is full of "storm and stress."

Sigmund Freud's psychoanalytic theory was prominent in the early part of the twentieth century. Freud believed that children are rarely aware of the motives and reasons for their behavior, and that the bulk of their mental life is unconscious. His ideas were compatible with Hall's, emphasizing conflict and biological influences on development, although Freud did stress that a child's experiences with parents in the first five years of life are important determinants of later personality development. Freud envisioned the child moving through a series of psychosexual stages, filled with conflict between the child's biological urges and the environmental demands placed on the child by society. Freud's theory has had a profound influence on the study of children's personality development and socialization, especially in the areas of gender differences, morality, family processes, and problems and disturbances.

During the 1920s and 1930s, John Watson's (1928) theory of behaviorism influenced thinking about children. Watson proposed a view of children very different from Freud, arguing that children can be shaped into whatever society wishes by examining and changing the environment. One element of Watson's view, and behaviorism in general, was a strong belief in the systematic observation of children's behavior under controlled conditions. Watson had some provocative views about child rearing as well. He stressed that parents were too soft on children; quit cuddling and smiling at babies so much, he told parents.

While John Watson was observing the environment's influence on children's behavior and Sigmund Freud was probing the depths of the unconscious mind to discover clues about our early experiences with our parents, others were more concerned about the development of children's conscious thoughts, that is, the thoughts of which they are aware. Even as early as the 1880s, James Mark Baldwin touted the framework of this theory with the imposing name of **genetic epistemology.** The term "genetic" at that time was a synonym for "development," and the term "epistemology" means the nature or study of knowledge. Taken together, then, the terms refer to how knowledge changes over the course of the child's development. Later, in the twentieth century, the Swiss psychologist Jean Piaget picked up many of Baldwin's themes, elaborating on them, keenly observing the development of thoughts in his own children, and devising clever experiments to investigate how children think. Piaget was to become a giant in developmental psychology. Many of you, perhaps, are already familiar with his view that children pass through a series of cognitive or thought stages from infancy through adolescence. For Piaget, children think in a qualitatively different manner than do adults.

Our introduction to several influential and diverse theories of children's development has been brief, designed to give you a glimpse of some of the different ways children have been viewed as the study of child development unfolded. You will read more about the three main theoretical perspectives later in the text—psychoanalytic theory (Freud's view) in chapter 11, behaviorism (Watson's view) in chapters 6 and 11, and cognitive-developmental theory (Piaget's view) in chapter 7.

The Nature of Development

Each of us develops like all other individuals, like some other individuals, and like no other individual. Most of the time our attention is directed to an individual's uniqueness. But child developmentalists are drawn to children's commonalities as well as their idiosyncrasies. As children, each of us traveled some common paths. Each of us—Leonardo da Vinci, Joan of Arc, George Washington, Martin Luther King, Jr., your authors, and you—walked at about the age of one, talked at about the age of two, engaged in fantasy play as a young child, and became independent as an adolescent.

Just what do we mean when we speak of a child's development? We use the term **development** to mean a pattern of movement or change that begins at conception and continues throughout the life cycle. Most development involves growth, although it can consist of decay (as in death). The pattern of movement is complex because it is the product of several processes—biological, cognitive, and social.

Biological, Cognitive, and Social Processes

Biological processes involve changes in the individual's physical nature. Genes inherited from parents, the development of the brain, height and weight gains, motor skills, and the hormonal changes of puberty all reflect the role of biological processes in development. Section 2 of this text provides extensive coverage of biological processes in children's development.

Cognitive processes involve changes in the child's thought, intelligence, and language. Watching a colorful mobile swinging above the crib, putting together a two-word sentence, memorizing a poem, solving a math problem, and imagining what it would be like to be a movie star all reflect cognitive processes in children's development. Section 3 describes cognitive processes in children's development.

Social processes involve changes in the child's relationships with other people, emotions, and personality. An infant's smile in response to her mother's touch, a young boy's aggressive attack on a playmate, a girl's development of assertiveness, and an adolescent's joy at the senior prom all reflect social processes in development. Section 4 emphasizes social processes in children's development.

Remember as you read about biological, cognitive, and social processes that they are intricately interwoven. You will read about how social processes shape cognitive processes, how cognitive processes promote or restrict social

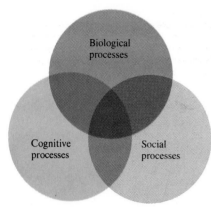

Figure 1.3
Changes in development are the result of biological, cognitive, and social processes. These processes are interwoven in the development of the individual throughout the human life cycle.

processes, and how biological processes influence cognitive processes, for example. While it is helpful to study the different processes involved in children's development in separate sections, keep in mind that you are studying the development of an integrated human child who has only one mind and one body (figure 1.3).

Periods of Development

For the purposes of organization and understanding, we commonly describe children's development in terms of periods. The most widely used classification of periods of children's development involve the following sequence: prenatal period, infancy, early childhood, middle and late childhood, and adolescence. Approximate age bands are placed on the periods to provide a general idea of when a period first appears and when it ends.

The **prenatal period** is the time from conception to birth. It is a time of tremendous growth—an organism complete with brain and behavioral capabilities is produced from a single cell in approximately a nine-month period. Chapter 3 provides a detailed biological timetable of the prenatal period, along with information about environmental hazards that can significantly alter the entire course of the life cycle.

Infancy extends from birth to eighteen or twenty-four months. Infancy is a time of extreme dependence on adults. Many psychological activities are just beginning—language, symbolic thought, sensorimotor coordination, and social learning, for example.

Early childhood, which extends from the end of infancy to about five or six years, roughly corresponds to the period in which the child prepares for formal schooling. The early childhood years sometimes are referred to as the preschool years. During this time the young child learns to be more self-sufficient and to care for herself, develops school readiness skills (following instructions, identifying letters), and spends many hours in play and with peers. First grade typically marks the end of this period.

Middle and late childhood extends from about six to eleven years of age, approximately corresponding to the elementary school years; sometimes this period is called the elementary school years. The fundamental skills of reading, writing, and arithmetic are mastered. Formal exposure to the larger world and its culture takes place. Achievement becomes a more prominent theme of the child's world and self-control increases.

Adolescence is the period of transition from childhood to early adulthood, entered approximately at ten to twelve years of age and ending at eighteen to twenty-two years of age. Adolescence begins with rapid physical change—dramatic gains in height and weight, changes in body contour, and the development of sexual characteristics such as the enlargement of the breasts, the appearance of pubic and facial hair, and a deepening of the voice. At this point in development the individual pushes for independence and pursues an identity. Thought is more logical, abstract, and idealistic. More and more time is spent outside of the family during this period.

Today, developmentalists do not believe that change ends with adolescence. Remember in our definition of development we described development as a lifelong process. However, the purpose of this text is to describe the changes in development that take place from conception through adolescence.

The periods of development from conception through adolescence are shown in figure 1.4 along with the processes of development—biological, cognitive, and social. As figure 1.4 shows, the interplay of biological, cognitive, and social processes produces the periods of development.

The Nature of Child Development

Periods of development

Adolescence

Middle
and late
childhood

Figure 1.4
Development moves through (a) prenatal,
(b) infancy, (c) early childhood, (d) middle and
late childhood, and (e) adolescence periods.
Development is a continuous creation of
increasingly complex forms.

Processes of development

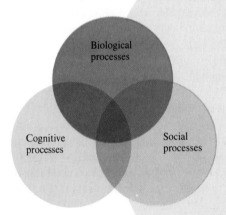

Early
childhood

Infancy

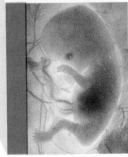

Prenatal
period

Figure 1.5
Continuity and discontinuity in development. Is development like a seedling gradually growing into a giant oak or like a caterpillar suddenly becoming a butterfly?

Maturation and Experience

We can think of development not only as the result of the interplay of biological, cognitive, and social processes but also of the interplay of maturation and experience. **Maturation** is the orderly sequence of changes dictated by the genetic blueprint we each have. Just as a sunflower grows in an orderly way—unless flattened by an unfriendly environment—so does a human being grow in an orderly way, according to the maturational view. The range of environments can be vast but the maturational approach argues that the genetic blueprint produces communalities in our growth and development. We walk before we talk, we speak one word before two words, we grow rapidly in infancy and less so in early childhood, we experience a rush of sexual hormones in puberty after a lull in childhood, we reach the peak of our physical strength in late adolescence and early adulthood and then decline, and so on. The maturationists acknowledge that extreme environments—those that are psychologically barren or hostile—can depress development, but they believe basic growth tendencies are genetically wired into the human.

By contrast, other psychologists emphasize the importance of experiences in development. Experiences run the gamut from the individual's biological environment—nutrition, medical care, drugs, and physical accidents—to the social environment—family, peers, schools, community, media, and culture.

The debate about whether development is influenced primarily by maturation or by experience is another version of the **nature-nurture controversy,** which has been a part of psychology throughout its history. The "nature" proponents claim that biological and genetic factors are the most important determinants of development; the "nurture" proponents claim that environment and experience are most important.

Ideas about the nature of child development have been like a pendulum, swinging between nature and nurture. Today we are witnessing a surge of interest in the biological underpinnings of development, probably because the pendulum had swung too far in the direction of thinking that development was due exclusively to environmental experiences (Hinde & Stevenson-Hinde, 1987). But while nature has grown in popularity recently, all psychologists today believe that both nature *and* nurture are responsible for development; the key to development is the interaction of nature and nurture rather than either factor alone. For example, an individual's cognitive development is the result of heredity-environment interaction, not heredity or environment alone. Much more about the importance of heredity-environment interaction appears in chapter 2.

Continuity and Discontinuity

Think about your development for a moment. Did you gradually grow to become the person you are, like the slow, cumulative growth of a seedling into a giant oak? Or did you experience sudden, distinct changes in your growth, like a caterpillar changing into a butterfly (figure 1.5)? For the most part, developmentalists who emphasize experience describe development as a gradual, continuous process; those who emphasize maturation describe development as a series of distinct stages.

The Nature of Child Development

"Well, whatever it is we change into, it can't come soon enough for me."

Drawing by D. Reilly; © 1973 The New Yorker Magazine, Inc.

Some developmentalists emphasize the **continuity of development,** stressing a gradual, cumulative change from conception to death. A child's first word, while seemingly an abrupt, discontinuous event, is viewed as the result of weeks and months of growth and practice. Puberty, while also seemingly an abrupt, discontinuous occurrence, is viewed as a gradual process occurring over several years.

Other developmentalists emphasize the **discontinuity of development,** stressing distinct stages in the life span. Each of us is described as passing through a sequence of stages in which change is qualitatively rather than quantitatively different. As the oak moves from seedling to giant oak it is *more* oak—its development is continuous. As the caterpillar changes into a butterfly, it is not just more caterpillar, it is a *different kind* of organism—its development is discontinuous. At some point a child moves from not being able to think abstractly about the world to being able to do so. This is a qualitative, discontinuous change in development, not a quantitative, continuous change.

Another aspect of the continuity-discontinuity issue is whether development is best described by *stability* or *change*. Will the shy child who hides behind the sofa when visitors arrive be the wallflower at high school dances, or will this child become a sociable, talkative individual? Will the fun-loving, carefree adolescent have difficulty holding down a nine-to-five job as an adult or become a straight-laced, serious conformist? The **stability-change issue** basically addresses whether we become older renditions of our early selves or whether we can develop into someone different from who we were at an earlier point in development. Today most developmentalists believe that some change is possible throughout the life cycle, although scholars disagree, sometimes vehemently, about just how much change can take place, and how much stability there is.

At this point you should be getting a feel for the developmental perspective in studying children. You have read about some contemporary interests, the historical background, and the nature of development. To help you remember the main points of our discussion so far turn to Concept Table 1.1.

Concept	Processes/Related Ideas	Characteristics/Description
Child development—today and yesterday	Contemporary concerns	Today, the well-being of children is a prominent concern in our culture—four such concerns are educational reform, changes in family structure and work, the impact of computers on children, and caring for mentally retarded children.
	Child development and history	The history of interest in children is long and rich. In the Renaissance, philosophical views were important, including original sin, *tabula rasa*, and innate goodness. We now conceive of childhood as highly eventful. The modern era of studying children spans a little more than a century, an era in which the study of child development has developed into a sophisticated science. Methodological advances in observation and theoretical views—among them psychoanalytic, behavioral, and cognitive-developmental—characterized this scientific theme.
The nature of development	What is development?	Development is the pattern of movement or change that occurs throughout the life cycle.
	Biological, cognitive, and social processes	Development is influenced by an interplay of biological, cognitive, and social processes.
	Periods of development	Development is commonly divided into the following periods from conception through adolescence: prenatal, infancy, early childhood, middle and late childhood, and adolescence.
	Maturation and experience	Development is influenced by the interaction of maturation and experience. The debate of whether development is due primarily to maturation or to environment is another version of the nature-nurture controversy.
	Continuity-discontinuity	Some psychologists describe development as continuous (gradual, cumulative change); others describe it as discontinuous (abrupt, distinct stages). Another aspect of the continuity-discontinuity issue is whether development is best described by stability or change.

The Science Base of Child Development

Some individuals have difficulty thinking of child development as a science in the same way physics, chemistry, and biology are sciences. Can a discipline that studies how babies develop, how parents nurture children, how peers interact, and how children think be equated with disciplines that investigate how gravity works and the molecular structure of a compound? Science is not defined by *what* it investigates but by *how* it investigates. Whether you are studying photosynthesis, butterflies, Saturn's moons, or human development, it is the way you study that makes the approach scientific or not.

Theory and the Scientific Method

In the words of Henri Poincaré, "Science is built of facts the way a house is built of bricks, but an accumulation of facts is no more a science than a pile of bricks a house." Science *does* depend on the raw material of data or facts, but as Poincaré indicated, science is more than just facts. The nature of theory and the scientific method illustrate Poincaré's point.

Theories are general beliefs that help us to explain the data or facts we have observed and make predictions. A good theory has **hypotheses,** which are assumptions that can be tested to determine their accuracy. For example, a

good theory of children's aggression would explain our observations of aggressive children and predict why children become aggressive. We might predict that children become aggressive because of the coercive interchanges they experience and observe in their families. This prediction would help to direct our observations by telling us to look for coercive interchanges in families.

To obtain accurate information about development it is important to adopt the **scientific method.** To do this, we must follow a number of steps: identify and analyze the problem, collect data, draw conclusions, and revise theories. For example, you decide that you want to help aggressive children control their aggression. You have identified a problem, which does not seem like a difficult task. But as part of the first step, you need to go beyond a general description of the problem by isolating, analyzing, narrowing, and focusing on what you hope to investigate. What specific strategies do you want to use to reduce children's aggression? Do you want to look at only one strategy, or several strategies? What aspect of aggression do you want to study—its biological, cognitive, or social characteristics? Gerald Patterson and his colleagues (Patterson, 1982, 1986; Patterson, Reid, & Dishon, in press) argue that parents' failure to teach reasonable levels of compliance sets in motion coercive interchanges with family members. In this first step in the scientific method, a problem was identified and analyzed.

After we identify and analyze the problem, the next step is to collect information (data). Psychologists observe behavior and draw inferences about thoughts and emotions. For example, in the investigation of children's aggression, we might observe how effectively parents teach reasonable compliance levels to their children and the extent coercive exchanges take place among family members.

Once data have been collected, psychologists use statistical procedures to understand the meaning of quantitative data. They then try to draw conclusions. In the investigation of children's aggression, statistics would help the researchers determine whether or not their observations were due to chance. After data have been collected, psychologists compare their findings with what others have discovered about the same issue.

The final step in the scientific method is revising theory. Psychologists have developed a number of theories about children's development; they also have developed a number of theories about why children become aggressive. Data such as those collected by Patterson and his colleagues force us to study

Science is not defined by what it studies but by how it investigates. Whether you are studying butterflies or children's social relationships, it is the way you study that makes the approach scientific or not.

existing theories of aggression to see if they are accurate. Over the years some theories of children's development have been discarded and others revised. Theories are an integral part of understanding the nature of children's development. They will be weaved through our discussion of children's development throughout the remainder of the text.

Collecting Information about Children's Development

Systematic observations can be conducted in a number of ways. For example, we can watch behavior in the laboratory or in a more natural setting such as a school, a home, or a neighborhood playground. We can question children using interviews and surveys, develop and administer standardized tests, conduct case studies, or carry out physiological research. To help you understand how developmentalists use these methods, we will continue to draw examples from the study of children's aggression.

Observation

Sherlock Holmes chided Watson, "You see but you do not observe." We look at things all the time, but casually watching a mother and her infant is not scientific observation. Unless you are a trained observer and practice your skills regularly, you may not know what to look for, you may not remember what you saw, what you are looking for may change from one moment to the next, and you may not communicate your observations effectively.

For observations to be effective, we have to know what we are looking for, who we are observing, when and where we will observe, how the observations will be made, and in what form they will be recorded. That is, our observations have to be made in some *systematic* way. Consider aggression. Do we want to study verbal or physical aggression, or both? Do we want to study younger or older children, or both? Do we want to evaluate them in a university laboratory, at school, at home, at a playground, or at all of these locations. A common way to record our observations is to write them down, using shorthand or symbols. However, tape recorders, video cameras, special coding sheets, and one-way mirrors are used increasingly to make observations more efficient.

When we observe, frequently it is necessary to *control* certain factors that determine children's behavior but are not the focus of our inquiry. For this reason much research on children's development is conducted in a **laboratory,** that is, a controlled setting in which many of the complex factors of the "real world" are removed. For example, Albert Bandura (1965) brought children into a laboratory and had them observe an adult repeatedly hit an inflated plastic Bobo doll about three feet tall. Bandura wondered to what extent the children would imitate the adult's aggressive behavior. The children's imitation of the adult model's aggressive actions was pervasive.

Conducting laboratory research, though, can be costly. First, it is virtually impossible to conduct without the participants knowing that they are being studied. Second, the laboratory setting may be *unnatural* and therefore cause *unnatural* behavior on the part of the children. Children usually show less aggressive behavior in the laboratory than in a more familiar natural setting, such as in a park or at home. They also show less aggression when they are aware that they are being observed. Third, some aspects of children's lives are difficult if not impossible to produce in the laboratory. Certain types of stress are difficult (and unethical) to investigate in the laboratory, for example, recreating the circumstances that stimulate marital conflict or physically punishing the child. In **naturalistic observation,** then, developmentalists observe

behavior in real-world settings and make no effort to manipulate or control the situation. Naturalistic observations have been conducted at hospitals, day-care centers, schools, parks, homes, shopping malls, dances, and other places where children and families live and frequent. Figure 1.6 shows what you might see if you were observing aggression in a naturalistic context.

Interviews and Questionnaires

Sometimes the best and quickest way to get information from children is to ask them for it. Psychologists use interviews and questionnaires to find out about the experiences and attitudes of children. Most **interviews** are conducted face to face, although they may take place over the telephone. An experienced interviewer knows how to put children at ease and get them to open up. A competent interviewer is sensitive to the way children respond to questions and often probes for more information. Care needs to be exercised that interview questions are at a level the child can understand.

Just as observations can take place in different settings, so can interviews. An interview might occur at a university, in a child's home, or at a child's school. For example, Brenda Bryant (1985) developed "The Neighborhood Walk," an interview conducted with a child while walking through the child's neighborhood. Bryant found this type of interview especially worthwhile in generating information about the support systems available to children.

Interviews are not without problems. Perhaps the most critical of these problems is the response set of "social desirability," in which children or adults tell the interviewer what they think is most socially desirable rather than what they truly think or feel. When asked about conflict in their families, children and their parents may not want to disclose that arguments have been frequent in recent months. Skilled interviewing techniques and questions to eliminate such defenses are critical in obtaining accurate information.

Psychologists also question children and adults using questionnaires or surveys. A **questionnaire** is similar to an interview except that children read the question and mark their answer on paper rather than verbally responding to the interviewer. One major advantage of questionnaires is that they can be given to large numbers of individuals easily. Questions on surveys should be concrete, specific, and unambiguous, and an assessment of the authenticity of the replies should be made (Agnew, 1987). Of course, questionnaires are inappropriate for young children because they lack reading skills; even with older children and adolescents, researchers need to monitor whether the individuals have the language and cognitive skills to understand the questions (Weaver, 1988).

Case Studies

A **case study** is an in-depth look at an individual. Case studies are used when the unique aspects of an individual's life cannot be duplicated, either for practical or ethical reasons, yet they have implications for understanding development. A case study provides information about an individual's hopes, fears, fantasies, traumatic experiences, family relationships, health, or anything that will help the psychologist understand children's development. Some vivid case studies appear at different points in this text, among them one about a modern-day wild child named Genie, who lived in near isolation during her childhood (chapter 9).

Standardized Tests

Standardized tests require that the child answer a series of written or oral questions. Two distinctive features of standardized tests are that the child's answers usually are tallied to yield a single score, or a set of scores, that reflects something about the child, and that the child's score is compared with a large group of similar children to determine how the child responded *relative* to others. Scores often are described in percentiles. For example, perhaps a child scored in the ninety-second percentile of the Stanford-Binet Intelligence Test. This method informs us how much lower or higher the child scored than the large group of children who had taken the test previously.

To continue our look at how different measures are used to evaluate aggression, consider the Minnesota Multiphasic Personality Inventory (MMPI), which includes a scale to assess delinquency or antisocial tendencies. The items on this scale ask you to respond whether or not you are rebellious, impulsive, and have trouble with authority figures. This part of the MMPI might be given to adolescents to determine their delinquent and antisocial tendencies.

Physiological Research

Psychologists also can use physiological methods to obtain information about children's development. Increased research into the biological basis of children's development has produced remarkable insights. For example, researchers discovered that an infant's sex seems to be fixed by a single gene in the seventh week of prenatal development—more about this fascinating discovery appears in chapter 2 (Page & others, 1987). And, researchers discovered that higher concentrations of some hormones are associated with delinquent behavior in male adolescents—more about this research appears in chapter 5 (Susman & others, 1987).

Multimeasure, Multisource, Multicontext Approach

Methods have their strengths and weaknesses. Direct observations are extremely valuable tools for obtaining information about children. But there are some things we cannot observe in children—their moral thoughts, their inner feelings, the arguments of their parents, how they acquire information about sex, and so on. In such instances, other measures, such as interviews, questionnaires, and case studies may be valuable. Because virtually every method has limitations, many investigators use multiple measures in assessing children's development. For example, a researcher might ask children about their aggressive behavior, check with their friends, observe them carefully at home and in the neighborhood, interview their parents, observe the children at school

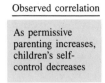

Observed correlation

As permissive parenting increases, children's self-control decreases

Possible explanations for this correlation

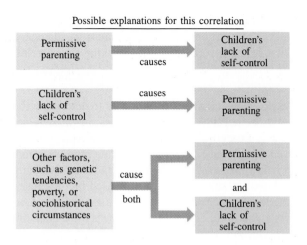

Permissive parenting → causes → Children's lack of self-control

Children's lack of self-control → causes → Permissive parenting

Other factors, such as genetic tendencies, poverty, or sociohistorical circumstances → cause both → Permissive parenting and Children's lack of self-control

Figure 1.7
The correlation between permissive parenting and children's self-control. An observed correlation between two events does not mean that one event causes a second event. The second event could cause the first, or a third event could cause the correlation between the first two events.

during recess, and ask teachers to rate the children's aggression. Researchers hope that the convergence of multimeasure, multisource, and multicontext information provides a more comprehensive and valid assessment of children's development.

Strategies for Setting Up Research Studies

How can we determine if a pregnant mother's cigarette smoking affects her offspring's attentional skills? How can we determine if responding nurturantly to an infant's cries increases attachment to the caregiver? How can we determine if day care is damaging to the child's development? How can we determine if listening to rock music lowers an adolescent's grades in school? When designing a research study to answer such questions the investigator must decide whether to use a correlational or an experimental strategy.

Correlational Strategy

One goal of child development research is to describe how strongly two or more events or characteristics are related. When a researcher has this goal, a **correlational strategy** is used. This is a beneficial strategy because the more strongly two events are correlated (related, associated), the more we can predict one from the other. For example, if we find that as parents use more permissive ways to deal with their children the children's self-control decreases, this does not mean that the parenting style caused the lack of self-control. It could mean that, but also it could mean that the children's lack of self-control stimulated the parents to simply throw up their arms in despair and give up trying to control the obstreperous children's behavior. Or it could mean that other factors might cause this correlation, such as genetic background, poverty, and sociohistorical conditions (several decades ago a permissive parenting strategy was widely advocated but today it no longer is in vogue). Figure 1.7 portrays these possible interpretations of correlational data.

Researchers often use a **correlation coefficient** to describe the degree of association between two variables. The correlation coefficient ranges from -1.00 to $+1.00$. A negative number means an inverse relation. For example, today we often find a *negative* correlation between permissive parenting and children's self-control. And we often find a *positive* correlation between a parent's involvement and monitoring of a child's life and the child's self-control. The higher the correlation coefficient (whether positive or negative), the stronger the association between the two variables. A correlation of 0 means

How might an experimental strategy be used to study whether caffeine intake during pregnancy affects the development of the infant?

that there is no association between the variables. A correlation of −.40 is a stronger correlation than +.20 because we disregard the negative or positive nature of the correlation in determining the correlation's magnitude.

Experimental Strategy

The **experimental strategy** allows us to determine the causes of behavior precisely. The psychologist accomplishes this task by performing an *experiment,* which is a carefully regulated setting in which one or more of the factors believed to influence the behavior being studied is manipulated and all others are held constant. If the behavior under study changes when a factor is manipulated, we say that the manipulated factor causes the behavior to change. Experiments are used to establish cause and effect between events, something correlational studies cannot do. *Cause* is the event being manipulated and *effect* is the behavior that changes because of the manipulation. Remember that in testing correlation, nothing is manipulated; in an experiment, the researcher actively changes an event to see the effect on behavior.

The following example illustrates the nature of an experiment. The problem to be studied is whether caffeine intake during pregnancy affects the development of the infant. We decide that to conduct our experiment we need one group of pregnant women who will ingest caffeine and another that will not. We randomly assign our subjects to these two groups. *Random assignment* reduces the likelihood that the experiment's results will be due to some preexisting differences in the two groups. For example, random assignment greatly reduces the probability that the two groups will differ on such factors as prior use of caffeine, health problems, intelligence, alertness, social class, age, and so forth.

The subjects who take the caffeine are called the **experimental group,** that is, the group whose experience is manipulated. The subjects who do not take the caffeine are the **control group,** that is, a comparison group treated in every way like the experimental group except for the manipulated factor. The control group serves as a baseline against which the effects found in the manipulated condition can be compared.

After the pregnant women in the experimental group ingest caffeine and their babies are born, the behavior of the offspring of the two groups is compared. We choose to study the heart rate and sleeping patterns of the infants. When we analyze the results, we discover that the infants in the experimental group had a faster heart rate and more irregular sleep patterns than the infants in the control group. We conclude that ingestion of caffeine by pregnant women increases the arousal state of the newborn.

In an experiment, the manipulated, or influential, factor is called the **independent variable.** The label *independent* is used because this variable can be changed independently of other factors. In the caffeine experiment, the ingestion of caffeine was the independent variable. The experimenter manipulated the subjects' caffeine ingestion independently of all other factors. In an experiment, the researcher determines what effect the independent variable has on the **dependent variable.** The label *dependent* is used beause this variable depends on what happens to the subjects in the experiment. In the caffeine experiment, the dependent variable was the heart rate and sleeping patterns of the infants. The infants' responses on these measures depended on the influence of the independent variable (whether or not caffeine was taken). An

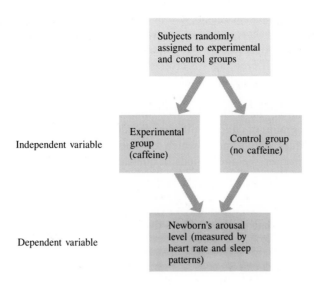

Figure 1.8
Principles of the experimental strategy
applied to a study of the effects of caffeine
ingestion by pregnant women on arousal of
their newborn children.

illustration of the nature of the experimental strategy, applied to the caffeine study, is shown in figure 1.8.

It might seem as if we should always choose an experimental strategy over a correlational strategy, since the experimental strategy gives us a better sense of one variable's influence over another. Are there instances when a correlational strategy might be preferred? Three such instances are (1) when the focus of the investigation is so new that we have little knowledge of which factors to manipulate (for example, factors associated with AIDS), (2) when it is physically impossible to manipulate the variables (for example, suicide), and (3) when it is impractical or unethical to manipulate the variables (for example, determining the link between parenting strategies and children's competence).

Time Span of Inquiry

A special concern of developmentalists is the time span of a research investigation. Studies that focus on the relation of age to some other variable are common in the field of child development. We have several options—we can study different children of different ages and compare them, we can study the same individuals as they grow older, or we can use some combination of these two approaches. We consider each of these in turn.

Cross-Sectional Approach

In the **cross-sectional approach,** children of different ages are compared at one time. In a typical study of children's memory, learning, or peer group interaction, we might test a group of four-year-olds, a group of eight-year-olds, and a group of twelve-year-olds with some procedure designed to elicit information about each of these topics. Notice that the children tested are of different ages and different groups, they were born at different times, they may have experienced different types of parenting and schooling, and they may have been influenced by different trends in dress, television, and play materials.

"That's my dad when he was 10 . . . He was in some sort of cult."

© 1986: Reprinted courtesy of Bill Hoest and *Parade Magazine*.

A cross-sectional design is valuable because it can be conducted in a relatively short period of time. This enables us to get an answer to an important question quickly. Most research in child development that contrasts children of different ages is cross-sectional in nature. However, you may already have anticipated some problems with cross-sectional research. Since different groups of children are tested, it is not "logical" to talk about how "individual children" have changed over time. We can only draw inferences about how the groups of children differed. In addition, group differences may have many sources, only some of which are due to normative features of their development over the age periods in question. For example, the different parenting and school practices that might have been in effect when each group of children was very young could explain some of the differences. Such differences, linked to when the children were born and grew up, are commonly called **cohort effects,** that is, those effects due to a child's time of birth or generation but not to age.

Longitudinal Approach

The second option is to examine the same group of children repeatedly over some extended period of time. This option is called the **longitudinal approach.** In a typical longitudinal study of the same topics discussed with the cross-sectional approach, we might structure a test that we administer to children once a year when they are four, eight, and twelve years old. In this example the same children would be studied over an eight-year time span, allowing us to examine patterns of change within each individual child. One of the great values of the longitudinal approach is that we can evaluate how individual children change as they grow up.

Fewer longitudinal than cross-sectional studies are conducted because they are so time consuming and costly. A close examination of the longitudinal approach reveals some additional problems: (1) When children are examined over a long period of time, some drop out because they lose interest or move away and cannot be recontacted by the investigator. A fairly common finding is that the remaining children represent a slightly biased sample, in that they tend to be psychologically superior to those who dropped out on almost every dimension (intelligence, motivation, and cooperativeness, for example) that the investigator checks. (2) With repeated testing, individual children may become more "testwise," which may increase their ability to perform "better" or "more maturely" the next time the investigator interacts with them. (3) Finally, although cohort effects may not be obvious in a longitudinal approach, they may exist. A group of children born at a particular time may look like they are changing and developing as a result of general maturation. But, in fact, some of the change may be due to special experiences the children encountered during this period of time that were not encountered by children a decade earlier. Perspective on Child Development 1.1 provides such an example. It considers the rather rapid introduction of computers into the lives of children during the 1980s. The computer vocabulary and skill development of young children growing up in the 1970s was essentially nonexistent. By comparison, the computer skills of children growing up in the 1990s make them look like budding Albert Einsteins.

The Nature of Child Development

New Technology and Children's Learning

or some time educators have been interested in teaching school-age children basic information about computers and how to use them. The programming language BASIC, which was invented in the 1960s, is one of the tools many experts feel they can teach young children. Imagine a study that was completed with a group of elementary school children, designed to determine just how much of this language children can learn. Following is a brief summary of this hypothetical investigation.

In 1975, a large group of children in grades one through five (roughly six to ten years of age) was randomly selected from two schools in the same school district of a small city. They were given ten hours of instruction about the BASIC programming language, including the definition and use of elementary programming commands in the language (such as PRINT, HOME, REMARK, = , LET, FOR, NEXT, ":", GO TO, and END) and the rules for how to write and sequence simple lines of programming code, such as:

```
10 PRINT "HELLO, STUDENTS"
20 PRINT "DO YOU LIKE THIS CLASS"
30 END
```

At the end of their instruction, they were given a standard test to determine how many commands they knew and how well they could correct errors in simple programs. Table 1.A shows how many of thirty questions children at each grade correctly answered.

Fifteen years later, in 1990, the same instructional study is repeated with children randomly sampled from the same schools. The researchers check the backgrounds of this new sample of children and discover that they are equivalent to the 1975 sample in terms of their average ability levels, their achievement in school, and their socioeconomic backgrounds. Table 1.B shows how this new sample of children performed on the same test given to the children in 1975. Take a careful look at the results for these two samples. What do you see?

In 1975, the youngest children were able to correctly answer five to six questions, with a modest increase in average performance of fifth graders to eight to nine correct answers. But, in 1990, the youngest children correctly answered more than twice as many questions as their earlier counterparts and actually outperformed the fifth graders tested a decade and a half earlier. And, again, in 1990, we see an increase in children's average level of performance across the elementary school grades.

This hypothetical study is a classic example of a cohort effect. Children born in one era perform differently than children born in another era. And, it does not take much imagination to arrive at a plausible explanation of the cohort effect. An elementary analysis of major historical events between 1975 and 1990 would show that millions of home-

Today's children are experiencing a computer revolution. What are some ways developmentalists could study the effects of computers on children?

Table 1.A
Children's Knowledge of BASIC in 1975

	Grade				
	1	2	3	4	5
Number of programming commands known	5.5	5.3	6.8	7.0	8.8

Table 1.B
Children's Knowledge of BASIC in 1990

	Grade				
	1	2	3	4	5
Number of programming questions answered correctly out of 30	12.5	13.0	15.2	18.5	20.0

owners purchased computers during this time. Most of those homeowners used their computers for word processing and for playing skill and adventure games. And, they made modest efforts to learn simple programming with the BASIC programming language.

So the children tested in 1990 were not necessarily better learners than those tested in 1975. They simply knew more to begin with—before instruction began—than the children from a decade and a half earlier. We are not aware of any investigation of children's development that documents such a dramatic cohort effect, although if someone had had the foresight to envision the modern computer revolution we are confident that results such as these would be easily found.

		Cohort		
		1982	1984	1986
Time of testing	1986	4 years old	2 years old	Newborn
	1988	6 years old	4 years old	2 years old
	1990	8 years old	6 years old	4 years old

Sequential Approach

Developmentalists also combine the cross-sectional and longitudinal approaches in their effort to learn more about development; the combined cross-sectional, longitudinal design is called the **sequential approach.** In most instances, this approach starts with a cross-sectional study that includes children of different ages. A number of months or years after the initial assessment, the same children are tested again—this is the longitudinal aspect of the design. At this later time, a new group of children is assessed at each age level. The new groups at each level are added at a later time to control for changes that might have taken place in the original group of children—some may have dropped out of the study or retesting might improve their performance, for example. The sequential approach is complex, time consuming, and expensive, but it does provide information that is not possible to obtain from the cross-sectional or longitudinal approaches alone. The sequential approach has been especially beneficial in calling attention to cohort effects in development (Baltes, 1973; Schaie, 1965). Figure 1.9 shows an example of a sequential design.

We have covered many ideas about the science base of child development. To help you remember the main points of this discussion turn to Concept Table 1.2.

Ethics in Research on Child Development

Increasingly, child developmentalists recognize that considerable caution must be taken to ensure the well-being of children when they are involved in a research study. Today colleges and universities have review boards that evaluate the ethical nature of research conducted at their institutions. Proposed research plans must pass the scrutiny of an ethics research committee before the research can be initiated. In addition, the American Psychological Association (APA) has developed guidelines for its members' ethics.

The code of ethics adopted by APA instructs researchers to protect their subjects from mental and physical harm. The best interests of the subjects must be kept foremost in the researcher's mind. All subjects, if they are old enough, must give their informed consent to participate in a research study. This requires that subjects know what their participation will entail and any risks that might develop. For example, subjects in an investigation of the effects of divorce on children should be told beforehand that interview questions might stimulate thought about issues they might not anticipate. The subjects should also be informed that in some instances a discussion of the family's experiences might improve family relationships, while in other instances it might bring up issues that bring the child unwanted stress. After informed consent is given, the subjects reserve the right to withdraw from the study at any time.

Concept Table 1.2		
The Science Base of Child Development		
Concept	**Processes/Related Ideas**	**Characteristics/Description**
Theory and the scientific method	Theories	Theories are general beliefs that help us to explain what we observe and make predictions. A good theory has hypotheses, which are assumptions that can be tested.
	Scientific method	The scientific method involves a series of procedures (identifying and analyzing a problem, collecting data, drawing conclusions, and revising theory) to obtain accurate information.
Collecting information about children's development	Observation	Observation is a key ingredient in child development research and includes laboratory and naturalistic observation.
	Interviews and questionnaires	Interviews and questionnaires are used to assess perceptions and attitudes. Social desirability is a special problem with their use.
	Case studies	Case studies provide an in-depth look at an individual. Caution in generalizing is warranted.
	Standardized tests	Standardized tests assess an individual's characteristics relative to those of a large group of similar individuals.
	Physiological research	Physiological research focuses on the biological dimensions of the child.
	Multimeasure, multisource, multicontext approach	Increasingly researchers study children using different measures, obtaining information from different sources, and observing children in different contexts.
Strategies for setting up research studies	Correlational strategy	A correlational strategy describes how strongly two or more events or characteristics are related. It does not allow causal statements.
	Experimental strategy	An experimental strategy involves manipulation of influential factors, the independent variables, and measurement of their effect on the dependent variables. Subjects are randomly assigned to experimental and control groups in many studies. The experimental strategy can reveal the causes of behavior and tell us how one event influences another.
Time span of inquiry	Cross-sectional approach	Individuals of different ages are compared at one time using the cross-sectional approach.
	Longitudinal approach	The same individuals are studied over a period of time, usually several years or more, using the longitudinal approach.
	Sequential approach	The sequential approach is a combined cross-sectional, longitudinal approach that highlights the importance of cohort effects in development.

Special ethical concerns govern the conduct of research with children. First, if children are to be studied, informed consent from parents or legal guardians must be obtained. Parents have the right to a complete and accurate description of what will be done with their children and may refuse to let them participate. Second, children have rights too. The psychologist is obliged to explain precisely what the child will experience. The child may refuse to participate, even after parental permission is given. If so, the researcher must not test the child. Also, if a child becomes upset during the research study, it is the psychologist's obligation to calm the child. Failing to do so, the activity must be discontinued. Third, the psychologist must always weigh the potential for harming children against the prospect of contributing some clear benefits to them. If there is the chance of harm—as when drugs are used, social deception takes place, or the child is treated aversively (that is, punished or reprimanded)—the psychologist must convince a group of peers that the benefits of the experience clearly outweigh any chance of harm. Fourth, since children are in a vulnerable position and lack power and control when facing an adult, the psychologist should always strive to make the professional encounter a positive and supportive experience.

Summary

I. Child Development—Today and Yesterday

Today, the well-being of children is a prominent concern in our culture—four such concerns are educational reform, changes in family structure and work, the impact of computers on children, and caring for mentally retarded children. The history of interest in children is long and rich. In the Renaissance, philosophical views were important, including original sin, *tabula rasa,* and innate goodness. We now conceive of childhood as highly eventful. The modern era of studying children spans a little more than a century, an era in which the study of child development has developed into a sophisticated science. Methodological advances in observation and theoretical views—among them psychoanalytic, behavioral, and cognitive-developmental—characterized this scientific theme.

II. The Nature of Development

Development is the pattern of movement or change that occurs throughout the life cycle. It is influenced by an interplay of biological, cognitive, and social processes. Development is commonly divided into the following periods from conception through adolescence: prenatal, infancy, early childhood, middle and late childhood, and adolescence. Development is influenced by the interaction of maturation and experience. The debate of whether development is due primarily to maturation or to environment is another version of the nature-nurture controversy. Some psychologists describe development as continuous (gradual, cumulative change); others describe it as discontinuous (abrupt, distinct stages). Another aspect of the continuity-discontinuity issue is best described by stability or change.

III. Theory and the Scientific Method

Theories are general beliefs that help us to explain what we observe and make good predictions. A good theory has hypotheses, which are assumptions that can be tested. The scientific method involves a series of procedures (identifying and analyzing a problem, collecting data, drawing conclusions, and revising theory) to obtain information.

IV. Collecting Information about Children's Development

Observation is a key ingredient in child development research and includes laboratory and naturalistic observation. Interviews and questionnaires are used to assess perceptions and attitudes. Social desirability of responses is a special problem with their use. Case studies provide an in-depth look at an individual. Caution in generalizing is warranted. Standardized tests assess an individual's characteristics relative to those of a large group of similar individuals. Physiological research focuses on the biological dimensions of the child. Increasingly researchers study children using different measures, obtaining information from different sources, and observing children in different contexts.

V. Strategies for Setting Up Research Studies

The correlational strategy involves describing how strongly two or more events or characteristics are related. It does not allow causal statements. The experimental strategy involves manipulation of influential factors, the independent variables, and measurement of their effect on the dependent variables. Subjects are randomly assigned to experimental and control groups in many studies. The experimental strategy can reveal the causes of behavior and tell us how one event influences another.

VI. Time Span of Inquiry

In the cross-sectional approach, individuals are compared at one time. In the longitudinal approach, the same individuals are studied over a period of time, usually several years or more. The sequential approach is a combined cross-sectional, longitudinal approach that highlights the importance of cohort effects in development.

VII. Ethics in Research on Child Development

Researchers must ensure the well-being of subjects in child development research. The risk of mental and physical harm must be reduced, and informed consent must occur. Special ethical concerns govern the conduct of research with children.

Key Terms

original sin 9
tabula rasa 9
innate goodness 9
genetic epistemology 12
development 13
biological processes 13
cognitive processes 13
social processes 13
prenatal period 14
infancy 14
early childhood 14
middle and late childhood 14
adolescence 14
maturation 16
nature-nurture controversy 16
continuity of development 17
discontinuity of development 17
stability-change issue 17
theories 18

hypotheses 18
scientific method 19
laboratory 20
naturalistic observation 20
interviews 21
questionnaire 21
case study 22
standardized tests 22
correlational strategy 23
correlation coefficient 23
experimental strategy 24
experimental group 24
control group 24
independent variable 24
dependent variable 24
cross-sectional approach 25
cohort effects 26
longitudinal approach 26
sequential approach 28

Suggested Readings

Borstelmann, L. J. (1983). Children before psychology: Ideas about children from antiquity to the late 1800s. In P. H. Mussen (Ed.), *Handbook of Child Psychology* (4th ed., Vol. 1). New York: John Wiley & Sons.
A comprehensive treatment of the historical conception of children from ancient times up to the twentieth century.

Brim, O. G., & Kagan, J. (Eds.). (1980). *Constancy and change in human development.* Cambridge, MA: Harvard University Press.
A number of developmental experts contributed articles to this book, which focuses on how stable or changeable children's lives are.

Child Development and *Developmental Psychology*
These are two of the leading research journals in the field of children's development. Go to your library and leaf through the issues of the last several years to get a feel for the research interests of developmentalists.

Kessen, W. (1979). The American child and other cultural inventions. *American Psychologist, 34,* 815–820.
An intriguing essay describing how childhood has come to be understood and viewed in contemporary America. Contrasts this conception with conceptions of children at other times in history.

Biological and Perceptual Development

What endless questions vex the thought, of whence and whither, when and how.

—Sir Richard Burton
Kasidah

CHAPTER

2

Biological Beginnings

How can identical twins be studied to evaluate heredity's influence on development?

Jim Springer and Jim Lewis are identical twins. They were separated at the age of four weeks and did not see each other again until they were thirty-nine years old. Both worked as part-time deputy sheriffs, both vacationed in Florida, both drove Chevrolets, both had dogs named Toy, and both married and divorced women named Betty. One twin named his son James Allan, and the other named his son James Alan. Both liked math but not spelling, enjoyed carpentry and mechanical drawing, chewed their fingernails down to the nubs, had almost identical drinking and smoking habits, had hemorrhoids, put on ten pounds at about the same point in development, first suffered headaches at the age of eighteen, and had similar sleep patterns.

But Jim and Jim had some differences. One wore his hair over his forehead, the other slicked back with sideburns. One expressed himself better orally, the other was more proficient in writing. But for the most part their profiles were remarkably similar.

Another pair, Daphne and Barbara, were called the "giggle sisters" because they were always making each other laugh. A thorough search of their adoptive families' histories revealed no gigglers. And the identical sisters handled stress by ignoring it, avoided conflict and controversy whenever possible, and showed no interest in politics.

Two other female identical twin sisters were separated at six weeks and reunited in their fifties. Both had nightmares, which they describe in hauntingly similar ways—both dreamed about doorknobs and fishhooks in their mouths as they smothered to death! The nightmares began during early adolescence and stopped in the last ten to twelve years. Both were bedwetters until about twelve to thirteen years of age and they reported educational and marital histories that were remarkably similar.

These sets of twins are part of the Minnesota Study of Twins Reared Apart, directed by Thomas Bouchard and his colleagues. They bring identical (identical genetically because they come from the same egg) and fraternal (dissimilar genetically because they come from two eggs) twins from all over the world to Minneapolis to investigate their lives. For example, the twins are given a number of personality tests and detailed medical histories are obtained, including information about diet, smoking, exercise habits, chest X rays, heart stress tests, and EEGs (brain wave tests). The twins are interviewed and asked more than 15,000 questions about their family and childhood environment, personal interests, vocational orientation, values, and aesthetic judgments. They also are given ability and intelligence tests (Bouchard & others, 1981; Lykken, 1982; Tellegen & others, in press).

The examples of Jim and Jim, the giggle sisters, and the identical twins who had the same nightmares stimulate us to think about our genetic heritage and the biological foundations of our existence. Organisms are not like billiard balls, moved by simple, external forces to predictable positions on life's pool table. Environmental experiences *and* biological foundations work together to make us who we are. Our coverage of life's biological beginnings focuses on genetics, heredity's influence on development, and the nature of heredity-environmental interaction.

Biological and Perceptual Development

Genetics

No matter what the species, there must be a mechanism for transmitting characteristics from one generation to the next. This mechanism is explained by the principle of genetics. Each of us carries a genetic code that we inherited from our parents. Physically, this code is located within every cell in our bodies. Our genetic codes are alike in one important way—they all contain the *human* genetic code. Because of the human genetic code, a fertilized human egg cannot grow into an eel, an egret, or an elephant.

What Are Genes?

We each began life as a single cell weighing about one twenty-millionth of an ounce! This tiny piece of matter housed our entire genetic code—the information about who we would become. These instructions orchestrated growth from that single cell to a person made of trillions of cells, each containing a perfect replica of the original genetic code.

The nucleus of each human cell contains forty-six **chromosomes,** which are threadlike structures that come in structurally similar pairs. You inherited twenty-three chromosomes from your mother and another twenty-three chromosomes from your father. Chromosomes are composed of the remarkable substance deoxyribonucleic acid, or **DNA.** DNA is a molecule arranged in a "double helix" shape that looks like a spiral staircase (figure 2.1). **Genes,** the units of hereditary information, are short segments of the DNA "staircase." Genes act as blueprints for cells to reproduce themselves and manufacture the proteins that maintain life. Chromosomes, DNA, and genes can be mysterious. To help you turn mystery into understanding see figure 2.2.

Genes are transmitted from parents to offspring by means of **gametes,** or sex cells, which are created in the testes of males and in the ovaries of females. Gametes are formed by the splitting of cells. This process is called **meiosis.** In meiosis, each pair of chromosomes in the cell separates, and one member of each pair goes into each gamete, or daughter cell. Thus, each human gamete has twenty-three unpaired chromosomes. **Reproduction** takes place when a female gamete (ovum) is fertilized by a male gamete (sperm) to create a single-celled **zygote** (figure 2.3). In the zygote, two sets of unpaired chromosomes combine to form one set of paired chromosomes, one member of each pair being from the mother and the other member being from the father. In this manner, each parent contributes 50 percent of the offspring's heredity.

There is more to know about reproduction. The ovum is about 90,000 times larger than a sperm. Thousands of sperm must combine to break down the ovum's membrane barrier and allow even a single sperm to penetrate the

Our genetic codes are alike in one important way—they all possess the human genetic code. Because of the human genetic code, a fertilized human egg cannot grow into an eel, an egret, or an elephant.

Figure 2.1
A DNA molecule. The horizontal bars are the important bases or "rungs" of the DNA ladder. The sequence of these bases plays a key role in scientists' efforts to locate the identity of a gene.

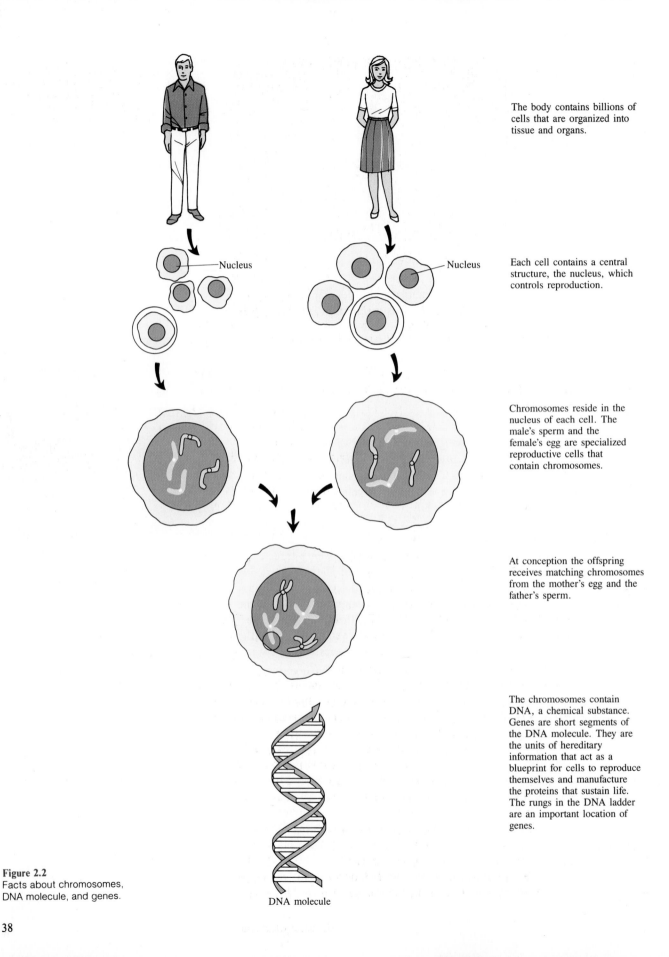

The body contains billions of cells that are organized into tissue and organs.

Each cell contains a central structure, the nucleus, which controls reproduction.

Nucleus

Nucleus

Chromosomes reside in the nucleus of each cell. The male's sperm and the female's egg are specialized reproductive cells that contain chromosomes.

At conception the offspring receives matching chromosomes from the mother's egg and the father's sperm.

The chromosomes contain DNA, a chemical substance. Genes are short segments of the DNA molecule. They are the units of hereditary information that act as a blueprint for cells to reproduce themselves and manufacture the proteins that sustain life. The rungs in the DNA ladder are an important location of genes.

Figure 2.2
Facts about chromosomes, DNA molecule, and genes.

DNA molecule

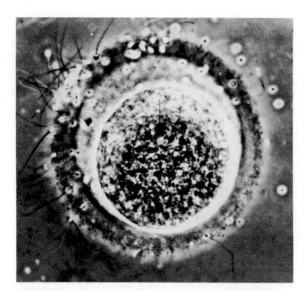

Figure 2.3
An ovum ready for release has been extracted and put into a nutritive solution together with a drop of specially treated seminal fluid. The sperm are eagerly striving toward the ovum. Notice the difference in size.

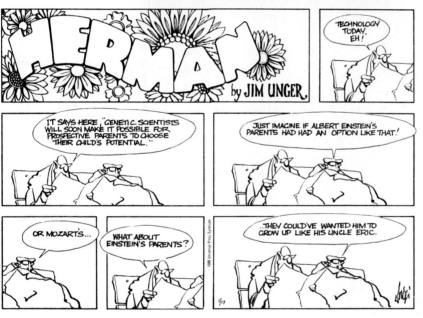

Drawing by Ziegler; © 1985 The New Yorker Magazine, Inc.

barrier. So, a low sperm count does matter. If sperm count is too low, the barrier won't be penetrated. Ordinarily, females have two X chromosomes, males one X and one Y chromosome. Since the Y chromosome is smaller and lighter than the X chromosome, Y-bearing sperm can be separated from X-bearing sperm by a centrifuge. This raises the possibility that the offspring's sex can be controlled. Not only are the Y-bearing sperm lighter but they are more likely than the X-bearing sperm to coat the ovum. This results in 120 to 150 males being conceived for every 100 females. But males are more likely to die (spontaneously abort) at every stage in prenatal development, so only about 106 are born for every 100 females.

The fascinating moments of reproduction have been made even more intriguing in recent years. Consider the following situation. The year is 1978. One of the most dazzling occurrences of the 1970s is about to unfold. Mrs. Brown is infertile, but her physician informs her of a new procedure that could enable her to have a baby. The procedure involves removing the mother's ovum

surgically, fertilizing it in a laboratory medium with live sperm cells obtained from the father or a male donor, storing the fertilized egg in a laboratory solution that substitutes for the uterine environment, and finally implanting the egg in the mother's uterus. The procedure is called **in vitro fertilization.** In the case of Mrs. Brown, the procedure was successful, and nine months later, her daughter Louise was born (figure 2.4).

Since the first in vitro fertilization in the 1970s, variations of the procedure have brought hope to childless couples. A woman's egg can be fertilized with the husband's sperm, or the husband and wife may contribute their sperm and egg with the resulting embryo carried by a third party, who essentially is donating her womb. A summary of nature's way of reproduction and new ways of creating babies is presented in figure 2.5.

Abnormalities in Genes and Chromosomes

Geneticists and psychologists have identified a range of problems caused by some major gene or chromosome defect. In the **PKU syndrome** (phenylketonuria), the problem resides in a genetic code that fails to produce an enzyme necessary for metabolism. In the absence of this enzyme, the cells fail to break down an amino acid, phenylalanine, interfering with metabolic processes and generating a poisonous substance that enters the nervous system. Mental functioning rapidly deteriorates if the enzyme deficiency is not treated shortly after

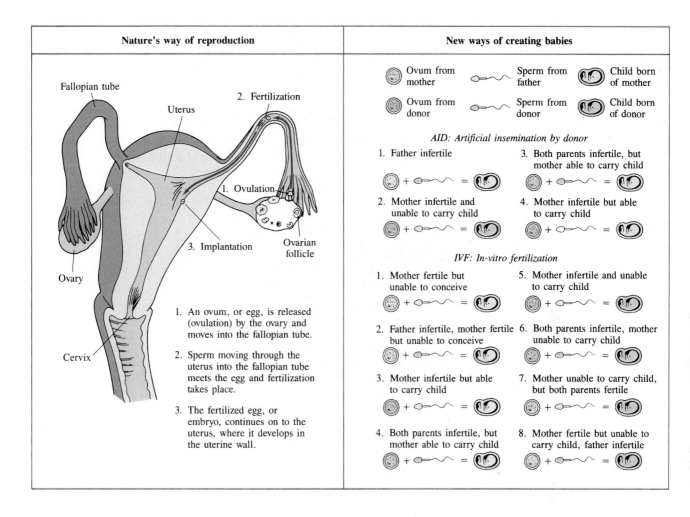

Nature's way of reproduction	New ways of creating babies

Nature's way of reproduction

Fallopian tube
Uterus
2. Fertilization
1. Ovulation
Ovarian follicle
3. Implantation
Ovary
Cervix

1. An ovum, or egg, is released (ovulation) by the ovary and moves into the fallopian tube.

2. Sperm moving through the uterus into the fallopian tube meets the egg and fertilization takes place.

3. The fertilized egg, or embryo, continues on to the uterus, where it develops in the uterine wall.

New ways of creating babies

Ovum from mother   Sperm from father   Child born of mother
Ovum from donor   Sperm from donor   Child born of donor

AID: Artificial insemination by donor

1. Father infertile
2. Mother infertile and unable to carry child
3. Both parents infertile, but mother able to carry child
4. Mother infertile but able to carry child

IVF: In-vitro fertilization

1. Mother fertile but unable to conceive
2. Father infertile, mother fertile but unable to conceive
3. Mother infertile but able to carry child
4. Both parents infertile, but mother able to carry child
5. Mother infertile and unable to carry child
6. Both parents infertile, mother unable to carry child
7. Mother unable to carry child, but both parents fertile
8. Mother fertile but unable to carry child, father infertile

Figure 2.5
Reproduction variations.

birth. Fortunately, the absence of this enzyme can be detected early and treated by diet to keep the phenylalanine at a very low level so that normal metabolism can proceed and the poisonous substance is not generated. The genetic code that fails to produce the enzyme involves a recessive gene. The PKU syndrome only occurs about once every 10,000 to 20,000 live births, but it accounts for about 1 percent of institutionalized mentally retarded individuals. It occurs primarily in whites.

The most common genetically transmitted form of mental retardation is **Down's syndrome.** The Down's child has a flattened skull, an extra fold of skin over the eyelid, and a protruding tongue. Among other characteristics are a short, thin body frame and retardation of motor abilities. The cause of Down's syndrome is an extra chromosome—Down's syndrome children have forty-seven chromosomes instead of the usual forty-six. It is not known why the extra chromosome occurs, but it may involve the health of the female ovum or the male sperm. Women in the eighteen- to thirty-eight-year-old age range are less likely to give birth to a Down's syndrome child than younger or older women. Down's syndrome appears approximately once every 700 live births. Black children rarely are born with Down's syndrome.

Sickle-cell anemia is another genetic disorder. It is a disease of the red blood cells and is a common disorder among blacks. One in 400 black babies is affected. One in 10 black Americans is a carrier as is 1 in 20 Latin Americans (Whaley & Wong, 1989). A red blood cell is usually shaped like a disk but a change in a recessive gene modifies its shape to a hook-shaped "sickle." These cells die quickly, causing anemia and early death because of their failure to carry oxygen to the body's cells.

Other disorders are associated with sex chromosome abnormalities. Remember that normal males have an X and a Y chromosome and that normal females have two X chromosomes. However, in **Klinefelter's syndrome,** males have an extra X chromosome (making them XXY instead of just XY); they have undeveloped testes and usually become tall and thin with enlarged breasts. This disorder occurs in approximately 1 in 800 male live births.

In **Turner's syndrome,** women are minus an X chromosome—they are X0 instead of XX. These women are short in stature with a webbing of the neck. They may be mentally retarded and sexually underdeveloped. This disorder occurs in approximately 1 in every 3,000 female live births.

Another sex chromosome abnormality has been given considerable attention in the last several decades—the **XYY syndrome.** Early interest in this syndrome suggested that the Y chromosome found in males contributed to male aggression and violence; the extra Y chromosome was said to be responsible for excessive aggression and violence. More recent research, however, indicates that XYY males are no more likely to commit crimes than XY males (Witkin & others, 1976).

Each year in the United States approximately 100,000 to 150,000 infants with a genetic disorder or malformation are born. These infants make up about 3 to 5 percent of the three million births and account for at least 20 percent of infant deaths. Increasingly, prospective parents are turning to genetic counselors to learn their risk of having a child born with a genetic defect or malformation. To learn more about genetic counseling turn to Perspective on Child Development 2.1.

Some Genetic Principles

Genetic determination is a complex affair and little is known about how genes work. But a number of genetic principles have been discovered, among them dominant-recessive genes, sex-linked genes, polygenically inherited characteristics, reaction range, and canalization.

The important principle of **dominant-recessive genes** was developed by Gregor Mendel with a simple form of life—peas. Mendel found that when he combined round pea plants with wrinkled pea plants, the next generation consistently came out round. The gene for round pea plants was *dominant* and the gene for wrinkled pea plants was *recessive* (tending to go back or recede).

What is the color of your parents' hair? If they both have brown hair, you probably have brown hair. If one of your parents has brown hair and the other has blond hair, you still probably have brown hair because brown hair is controlled by a dominant gene; blond hair is controlled by a recessive gene. But if both of your parents have blond hair, then you probably have blond hair because there is no dominant gene to interfere with the appearance of blond hair. Examples of other dominant gene-linked characteristics are brown eyes, farsightedness, and dimples; examples of recessive gene-linked characteristics are blue eyes, normal vision, and freckles.

For thousands of years individuals have wondered what determines whether an offspring will be male or a female. Aristotle believed that the father's degree of arousal during intercourse determined the offspring's sex. The more excited the father was, the more likely the offspring would be a male, he reasoned. In the 1920s, researchers confirmed the existence of human sex

Genetic Counseling

Bob and Mary Sims have been married for several years. They would like to start a family, but they are frightened. The newspapers and popular magazines are full of stories about infants born prematurely who don't survive, infants with debilitating physical defects, and cases of congenital mental retardation. The Simses feel that to have such a child would create a social, economic, and psychological strain on them and on society.

Accordingly, the Simses turn to a genetic counselor for help. Genetic counselors are usually physicians or biologists who are well versed in the field of medical genetics. They are familiar with the kinds of problems that can be inherited, the odds for encountering them, and helpful measures for offsetting some effects. The Simses tell their counselor that there is a history of mental retardation in Bob's family. Bob's younger sister was born with Down's syndrome, a form of mental retardation. Mary's older brother has hemophilia, a condition in which bleeding is difficult to stop. They wonder what the chances are that a child of theirs might also be retarded or have hemophilia and what measures they can take to reduce their chances of having a mentally or physically handicapped child.

The counselor probes more deeply because she understands that these facts in isolation do not give her a complete picture of the possibilities. She learns that no other relatives in Bob's family are retarded and that Bob's mother was in her late forties when his younger sister was born. She concludes that the retardation was due to the age of Bob's mother and not to some general tendency for members of his family to inherit retardation. It is well known that women over forty have a much higher probability of giving birth to retarded children than do younger women. Apparently the ova (egg cells) are not as healthy in older women as in women under forty.

In Mary's case the counselor determines that there is a small but clear possibility that Mary may be a carrier of hemophilia and transmit that condition to a son. Otherwise, the counselor can find no evidence from the family history to indicate genetic problems. The decision is then up to the Simses. In this case, the genetic problem will probably not occur, so the choice is fairly easy. But what should parents do if they face the strong probability of having a child with a major birth defect? Ultimately, the decision depends on the couple's ethical and religious beliefs. They must decide how to balance these against the quality of their child's life.

The moral dilemma is even more acute, of course, once a pregnancy has begun. **Amniocentesis** is a test that can detect more than 100 birth defects. It is performed in the fourteenth to sixteenth weeks of pregnancy. A long, thin needle is inserted into the abdomen to extract a sample of amniotic fluid, the liquid that cushions the fetus (figure 2.A). Fetal cells in the fluid are grown in the laboratory for

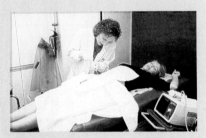

Figure 2.A
Amniocentesis being performed on a pregnant woman.

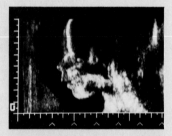

Figure 2.B
An ultrasound sonography record taken at four months into prenatal development.

two to four weeks and then studied for the presence of defects. The later amniocentesis is performed, the better the diagnostic potential. But the earlier it is performed, the more useful it can be in deciding whether a pregnancy should be terminated.

Another type of prenatal assessment that is frequently used when a structural malformation is suspected is **ultrasound sonography** (figure 2.B). High-frequency sound waves are directed into the pregnant woman's abdomen. The echo from the sounds is transformed into a visual representation of the fetus's inner structures. This technique has been beneficial in detecting such disorders as microencephaly, a form of mental retardation involving an abnormally small brain.

As scientists have searched for more accurate, safe assessments of high-risk prenatal circumstances, they have developed the **chorionic villus test.** Available since the mid-1980s, this test involves removing a small sample of the placenta nine to ten weeks into pregnancy. It takes two to three weeks to diagnose the sample. The chorionic villus test allows a decision about abortion to be made near the end of the first trimester of pregnancy, a point when abortion is safer and less traumatic than after amniocentesis in the second trimester. These techniques provide valuable information about the presence of birth defects, but they also raise moral issues pertaining to whether an abortion should be obtained if birth defects are present.

Figure 2.6
The genetic difference between males and females: (a) the chromosome structure of a male and (b) the chromosome structure of a female. The twenty-third pair is shown in the bottom right box of each; notice that the Y chromosome of the male is smaller. To obtain this chromosomal picture, a cell is removed from the individual's body, usually from the inside of the mouth. The chromosomes are magnified extensively and then photographed.

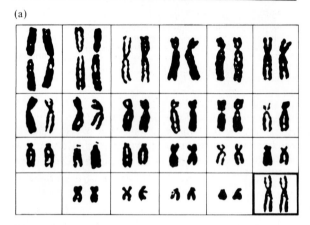

(a)

(b)

chromosomes, two of the forty-six chromosomes humans normally carry. Ordinarily, females have two X chromosomes, men have an X and Y (figure 2.6 shows the chromosome makeup of a male and a female). However, it still was not clear whether the "switch" consisted of one gene or many.

To discover how sexual differentiation takes place, David Page and his colleagues (1987) decided to study the sex chromosomes of individuals who are genetically abnormal: men with two X chromosomes and women with an X and a Y chromosome. Despite the genetic reversal, the XX men and XY women, while infertile, appeared normal. The researchers showed that one X chromosome in these men had a tiny bit of Y attached, while the women's Y chromosomes failed to have that tiny bit. They figured that a critical gene must be contained in that fragment, which sometimes breaks off from the Y.

Finding the suspect gene was a lengthy process involving several years of painstaking analysis. The researchers call the gene **testis determining factor, or TDF,** and it does appear to fix the infant's sex. To confirm their findings, Page and his co-workers plan to insert the TDF gene in a fertilized mouse egg to see if it will transform a female embryo into a male.

Another important genetic principle is **polygenic inheritance.** Genetic transmission is usually more complex than the simple examples we just examined. Few psychological characteristics are the result of the actions of single gene pairs. Most are determined by the interaction of many different genes. There are 50,000 or more genes, so you can imagine that the possible combinations of these are staggering. Traits produced by this mixing of genes are said to be polygenically determined.

Biological and Perceptual Development

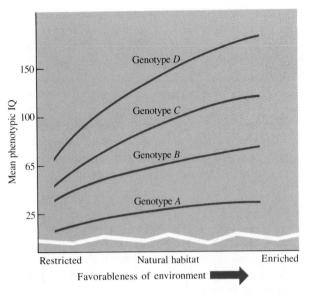

Figure 2.7
Hypothetical set of reaction ranges of intellectual development of several genotypes under environmental conditions that range from poor to good. Although each genotype responds favorably to improved environments, some are more responsive to environmental deprivation and enrichment than others.

No one possesses all the characteristics that our genetic structure makes possible. The actual combination of genes produces what is known as the **genotype.** However, not all of this genetic material is apparent in our observed and measurable characteristics. These observed and measurable characteristics, called **phenotypes,** include physical traits—such as height, weight, eye color, and skin pigmentation—and psychological characteristics—such as intelligence, creativity, personality, and social tendencies.

For each genotype, a range of phenotypes can be expressed. Imagine that we could identify all the genes that would make a child introverted or extraverted. Would measured introversion-extraversion be predictable from knowledge of the specific genes? The answer is no, because even if our genetic model was adequate, introversion-extraversion is a characteristic shaped by experience throughout life. For example, parents may push an introverted child into social situations and encourage the child to become more gregarious.

To understand how introverted an individual is, think about a series of genetic codes that predispose the child to develop in a particular way and imagine environments that are responsive or unresponsive to this development. For example, the genotype of some individuals may predispose them to be introverted in an environment that promotes a turning inward of personality, yet in an environment that encourages social interaction and outgoingness, these individuals may become more extraverted. However, it would be unlikely for the individual with this introverted genotype to become a strong extravert. The term **reaction range** is used to describe the range of phenotypes for each genotype, suggesting the importance of an environment's restrictiveness or enrichment (figure 2.7).

Sandra Scarr (1984) explains reaction range this way: Each of us has a range of potential. For example, an individual with "medium-tall" genes for height who grows up in a poor environment may be shorter than average. But in an excellent nutritional environment, the individual may grow taller than average. However, no matter how well fed the individual is, an individual with "short" genes will never be taller than average. Scarr believes that characteristics such as intelligence and introversion work the same way. That is, there is a range within which the environment can modify intelligence, but intelligence is not completely malleable. Reaction range gives us an estimate of how modifiable intelligence is.

Genotypes, in addition to producing many phenotypes, may show the opposite track for some characteristics—those that are somewhat immune to extensive changes in the environment. These characteristics seem to stay on track—on a particular developmental course—regardless of the environmental assaults on them (Waddington, 1957). *Canalization* is the term that describes the narrow path or developmental course that certain characteristics take. Apparently, preservative forces help to protect or buffer an individual from environmental extremes. For example, Jerome Kagan (1984) points to his research on Guatemalan infants who had experienced malnutrition as infants, yet showed normal social and cognitive development later in childhood. And, some abused children do not grow up to be abusers themselves.

Methods Used by Behavior Geneticists

Behavior genetics is concerned with the degree and nature of behavior's hereditary basis. Behavior geneticists assume that behaviors are jointly determined by the interaction of heredity and environment. To study heredity's influence on development, behavior geneticists often use either the adoption study or the twin study.

In the **adoption study,** researchers compare correlations between children's characteristics and those of their biological and adoptive parents. Adopted children share half their genes with each biological parent but do not share an environment with them. In contrast, they share an environment with their adopted parents but not their genes.

In the **twin study,** identical (called **monozygotic**) twins and fraternal (called **dizygotic**) twins are compared. Identical twins are born when a fertilized egg divides into two parts that then develop into two separate embryos. Since the twins come from the same fertilized egg, they share all of their genes. In contrast, fraternal twins develop when a woman's ovaries release two eggs instead of one and each egg is fertilized by different sperm. Fraternal twins share the same womb but they are no more alike genetically than any two siblings, and they may be of different sexes. By comparing groups of identical and fraternal twins, psychologists capitalize on the basic knowledge that identical twins are genetically more similar than fraternal twins. Several problems arise, though, when the twin study method is used. Adults may stress the similarities of identical twins more than those of fraternal twins. And identical twins may perceive themselves as a "set" and play together more than fraternal twins. If so, observed similarities in identical twins could be environmentally influenced.

The concept of **heritability** is used in many adoption and twin studies. Heritability is a statistical estimate of the degree to which physical, cognitive, and social characteristics among individuals are due to their genetic differences. It is measured by the use of correlational statistical procedures. The highest degree of heritability is 1.00. A heritability quotient of .80 suggests a strong genetic influence, one of .50 a moderate genetic influence, and one of .20 a much weaker, but nonetheless perceptible, genetic influence.

Although heritability values may vary considerably from one study to the next, it is possible to determine the average magnitude of a particular characteristic's quotient. For some kinds of mental retardation, the average heritability quotient approaches 1.00. That is, the environment makes almost no contribution to the characteristic's variation. This is not the same as saying the environment has no influence; the characteristic could not be expressed without the environment.

	Concept Table 2.1	
	Genetics	
Concept	**Processes/Related Ideas**	**Characteristics/Description**
What are genes?	Genes and chromosomes	The nucleus of each human cell contains forty-six chromosomes, which are composed of DNA. Genes are short segments of DNA and act as a blueprint for cells to reproduce and manufacture the proteins that maintain life.
	Reproduction	Genes are transmitted from parents to offspring by gametes, or sex cells. Gametes are formed by the splitting of cells, a process called meiosis. Reproduction takes place when a female gamete (ovum) is fertilized by a male gamete (sperm) to create a single-celled zygote. In vitro fertilization has helped to solve some infertility problems.
Abnormalities in genes and chromosomes	The range of problems	A range of problems are caused by some major gene or chromosome defect, among them the PKU syndrome, Down's syndrome, sickle-cell anemia, Klinefelter's syndrome, Turner's syndrome, and the XYY syndrome.
	Genetic counseling and tests	Genetic counseling has increased in popularity, as couples desire information about their risk of having a defective child. Amniocentesis, ultrasonic sonography, and the chorionic villus test are used to determine the presence of defects once pregnancy has begun.
Some genetic principles	Their nature	Genetic transmission is complex but some principles have been discovered, among them dominant-recessive genes, testis determining factor, polygenic inheritance, genotype-phenotype distinction, reaction range, and canalization.
	Methods used by behavior geneticists	Behavior genetics is the field concerned with the degree and nature of behavior's hereditary basis. Among the most important methods used by behavior geneticists are the twin study and the adoption study. The concept of heritability is used in many of the twin and adoption studies. The heritability index is not without its flaws.

The heritability index is not a flawless measure of heredity's contribution to development. It is only as good as the information fed into it and the assumptions made about genetic-environmental interaction. First, it is important to consider how varied the environments are that are being sampled. The narrower the range of environments, the higher the heritability index; the broader the range of environments, the lower the heritability index. Another important consideration is the reliability and validity of the measures being used in the investigation. That is, what is the quality of the measures? The weaker the measure, the less confidence we have in the heritability index. A final consideration is that the heritability index assumes that heredity and environment can be separated; information can be quantitatively added to arrive at a discrete influence for each. In reality, heredity and environment interact; their interaction is often lost when the heritability index is computed.

So far our coverage of the biological beginnings of the life cycle have taken us through some important aspects of heredity. A summary of these ideas is presented in Concept Table 2.1. Now let's turn our attention to some aspects of development influenced by heredity.

Heredity's Influence on Development

What aspects of development are influenced by genetic factors? They all are. However, behavior geneticists are interested in more precise estimates of the variation in a characteristic accounted for by genetic factors. Intelligence and temperament are among the most widely investigated aspects of heredity's influence on development.

Intelligence

Arthur Jensen (1969) sparked a lively and at times hostile debate when he presented his thesis that intelligence is primarily inherited. Jensen believes that environment and culture play only a minimal role in intelligence. He examined a number of studies of intelligence, many of which involved comparisons of identical and fraternal twins. Remember that identical twins have identical genetic endowments so their IQs should be similar. Fraternal twins and ordinary siblings are less similar genetically so their IQs should be less similar. Jensen found support for his argument in these studies. Studies with identical twins produced an average correlation of .82; studies with ordinary siblings produced an average correlation of .50. Note the difference of .32. To show that genetic factors are more important than environmental factors, Jensen compared identical twins reared together with those reared apart; the correlation for those reared together was .89 and for those reared apart it was .78 (a difference of .11). Jensen argued that if environmental influences were more important than genetic influences, then siblings reared apart, who experienced different environments, should have IQs much farther apart.

Many scholars have criticized Jensen's work. One criticism concerns the definition of intelligence itself. Jensen believes that IQ as measured by standardized intelligence tests is a good indicator of intelligence. Critics argue that IQ tests tap only a narrow range of intelligence. Everyday problem solving, work, and social adaptability, say the critics, are important aspects of intelligence not measured by the traditional intelligence tests used in Jensen's sources. A second criticism is that most investigations of heredity and environment do not include environments that differ radically. Thus, it is not surprising that many genetic studies show environment to be a fairly weak influence on intelligence.

Jensen places the importance of heredity's influence on intelligence at about 80 percent (Jensen, 1969). Jensen is such a strong advocate of intelligence that he believes we can breed for intelligence. Just such an effort—the Repository for Germinal Choice—is being made today. To read more about the Nobel Prize sperm bank for breeding intelligence, turn to Perspective on Child Development 2.2. Intelligence *is* influenced by heredity, but most developmentalists do not put the figure this high. Other reviews estimate heredity's influence on intelligence as being in the 30- to 60-percent range (e.g., Henderson, 1982).

Temperament

Temperament is another widely studied aspect of human development, especially in infancy. Some infants are extremely active, moving their arms, legs, and mouths incessantly; others are tranquil. Some children explore their environment eagerly for great lengths of time; others do not. Some infants respond warmly to people; others fuss and fret. All of these behavioral styles represent an individual's temperament.

Biological and Perceptual Development

Doran, Dr. Graham, and the Repository for Germinal Choice

Doran (a name from the Greek word meaning "gift") learned all of the elements of speech by two years of age. An intelligence test showed that at the age of one his mental age was four (figure 2.C). Doran was the second child born through the Nobel Prize sperm bank, which came into existence in 1980. The sperm bank was founded by Robert Graham in Escondido, California, with the intent of producing geniuses (figure 2.D). Graham collected the sperm of Nobel Prize-winning scientists and offered it free of charge to intelligent women of good stock whose husbands were infertile.

One of the contributors to the sperm bank is physicist William Shockley, who shared the Nobel Prize in 1956 for inventing the transistor. Shockley has received his share of criticism for preaching the genetic basis of intelligence. Two other Nobel Prize winners have donated their sperm to the bank, but Shockley is the only one who has been identified.

More than twenty children have been sired through the sperm bank. Are the progeny prodigies? It may be too early to tell. Except for Doran, little has been revealed about the children. Doran's genetic father was labeled "28 Red" in the sperm bank (the color apparently has no meaning). He is listed in the sperm bank's catalog as handsome, blond, and athletic, with a math SAT score of 800 and several prizes for his classical music performances. One of his few drawbacks is that he passed along to Doran an almost one-in-three chance of developing hermorrhoids. Doran's mother says that her genetic contribution goes back to the royal court of Norway and to the poet William Blake.

The odds are not high that a sperm bank will yield that special combination of factors required to produce a creative genius. George Bernard Shaw, who believed that heredity's influence on intelligence is strong, once told a story about a beautiful woman who wrote him saying that with her body and his brain they could produce marvelous offspring. Shaw responded by saying that unfortunately the offspring might get his body and her brain.

Not surprisingly, the Nobel Prize sperm bank is heavily criticized. Some say that brighter does not mean better. They also say that IQ is not a good indicator of social competence or human contribution to the world. Other critics say that intelligence is an elusive concept to measure and that it cannot reliably be reproduced like the sperm bank is trying to do. Visions of the German gene program of the 1930s and 1940s are created. The German Nazis believed that certain traits were superior and tried to breed children with such traits and killed people without these traits.

While Graham's Repository for Germinal Choice (as the Nobel Prize sperm bank is formally called) is strongly criticized, consider its possible contributions. The repository

Figure 2.C
Doran, the second offspring produced by the Repository for Germinal Choice.

Figure 2.D
Robert Graham, founder of the Repository for Germinal Choice, shown with frozen sperm containers.

does provide a social service for couples who cannot conceive a child, and individuals who go to the sperm bank probably provide an enriched environment for the offspring. To once childless parents, the offspring produced by the sperm bank, or any of the new methods of conception available, are invariably described as a miracle (Garelik, 1985).

Table 2.1
Dimensions and Clusters of Temperament in Chess and Thomas's Research

Temperament dimension	Description	Temperament cluster		
		Easy child	*Difficult child*	*Slow-to-warm-up child*
Rhythmicity	Regularity of eating, sleeping, toileting	Regular	Irregular	
Activity level	Degree of energy movement		High	Low
Approach-withdrawal	Ease of approaching new people and situations	Positive	Negative	Negative
Adaptability	Ease of tolerating change in routine plans	Positive	Negative	Negative
Sensory threshold	Amount of stimulation required for responding			
Predominant quality of mood	Degree of positive or negative affect	Positive	Negative	
Intensity of mood expression	Degree of affect when pleased, displeased, happy, sad	Low to moderate	High	Low
Distractibility	Ease of being distracted			
Attention span/persistence				

Alexander Chess and Stella Thomas (Chess & Thomas, 1977; Thomas & Chess, 1987; Thomas, Chess, & Birch, 1970) define temperament broadly in terms of an individual's behavioral style. They developed nine dimensions of temperament that fall into three clusters. The nine dimensions are rhythmicity of biological functions, activity level, aproach to or withdrawal from new stimuli, adaptability, sensory threshold, predominant quality of mood, intensity of mood expression, distractibility, and persistence/attention span. The three temperamental clusters are "easy," "difficult," and "slow-to-warm-up." These clusters seemed to be moderately stable across the childhood years. Table 2.1 lists the nine different temperaments, their descriptions, and the three temperamental clusters; the table also shows which of the nine dimensions were critical in spotting a cluster and what the level of responsiveness was for a critical feature. A blank space indicates that the dimension was not strongly related to cluster.

Other researchers suggest different basic dimensions of temperament. Arnold Buss and Robert Plomin (1984, 1987) believe that infants differ on three basic dimensions.

Emotionality is the tendency to be distressed. It reflects the arousal of the individual's sympathetic nervous system. Distress develops during infancy into two separate emotional responses—fear and anger. Fearful infants try to escape something that is unpleasant; angry ones protest it. Buss and Plomin argue that children are labeled "easy" or "difficult" on the basis of their emotionality.

Sociability is the tendency to prefer the company of others to being alone. This matches up with a tendency to respond warmly to others.

Activity involves tempo and vigor of movement. Some children walk fast, are attracted to high-energy games, and jump or bounce around a lot; others are more placid.

A number of scholars, including Chess and Thomas, conceive of temperament as a stable characteristic of newborns that comes to be shaped and modified by the child's later experiences (Goldsmith, 1988; Goldsmith & others, 1987; Thomas & Chess, 1987). This raises the question of heredity's

Biological and Perceptual Development

role in temperament. Twin and adoption studies have been conducted to answer this question (e.g., DeFries & others, 1981; Matheny, Dolan, & Wilson, 1976; Plomin, 1987). The researchers found a heritability index in the range of .50 to .60, suggesting a moderate influence of heredity on temperament. However, the strength of the association usually declines as infants become older (Goldsmith & Gottesman, 1981). This finding supports the belief that temperament becomes more malleable with experience. Alternatively, it may be that as the child becomes older, behavioral indicators of temperament may be more difficult to spot. The biological basis of the temperament of inhibition or shyness and its developmental course is currently the interest of Jerome Kagan (1987a & b) and Stephen Suomi (1987). To learn about the stability of our tendency to be shy and how much it can be modified, turn to Perspective on Child Development 2.3.

The consistency of temperament depends in part on the "match" or "fit" between the child's nature and the parents' (Chess & Thomas, 1986; Plomin, DeFries, & Fulker, 1988; Plomin & Thompson, 1987; Rothbart, in press). Imagine a high-strung parent with a child who is difficult and sometimes slow to respond to the parent's affection. The parent may begin to feel angry or rejected. A father who does not need much face-to-face social interaction will find it easy to manage a similarly introverted baby, but he may not be able to provide an extraverted baby with sufficient stimulation. Parents influence infants, but infants also influence parents. Parents may withdraw from difficult children, or they may become critical and punish them; these responses may make the difficult child even more difficult. A more easygoing parent may have a calming effect on a difficult child or may continue to show affection even when the child withdraws or is hostile, eventually encouraging more competent behavior.

Heredity-Environmental Interaction and Development

Both genes and environment are necessary for an organism—from amoeba to human—to even exist. Heredity and environment operate—or cooperate—to produce an individual's intelligence, temperament, height, weight, ability to pitch a baseball, career interests, and so on. No genes, no organism; no environment, no organism (Scarr & Weinberg, 1980). If an attractive, popular, intelligent girl is elected as president of the student body, would we conclude that her success is due to environment or to heredity? Of course, it is both. Because the environment's influence depends on genetically endowed characteristics, we say that the two factors *interact*.

But as we have seen, developmental psychologists probe further to determine more precisely the influence of heredity and environment on development. What do we know about heredity-environment interaction? According to Sandra Scarr and Kenneth Kidd (1983), we know that literally hundreds of disorders appear because of miscodings in DNA. We know that abnormalities in chromosomal number adversely influence the development of physical, intellectual, and behavioral features. We know that genotype and phenotype do not correlate in a one-to-one fashion. We also know that it is very difficult to distinguish between genetic and cultural transmission. There usually is a familial concentration of a particular disorder, but familial patterns are considerably different from what would be precisely predicted from simple modes of inheritance. We know that when we consider the normal range of variation, the stronger the genetic resemblance, the stronger the behavioral

Born to Be Shy?

Each of you has seen a shy toddler—the one who clings to a parent and only reluctantly ventures into an unfamiliar place. Faced with a stranger, the shy toddler freezes, becomes silent, and stares fearfully. The shy toddler seems visibly tense in social situations; parents of such children often report that their children always seem to have been that way.

Despite parents' comments that shy children seem to have been shy virtually from birth, psychologists have resisted the notion that such characteristics are inborn, focusing instead on the importance of early experience. Both the research of Jerome Kagan with extremely shy children and the research of Stephen Suomi with "uptight" monkeys supports the belief that shyness is a part of an individual's basic temperament.

Kagan (1987a & b, 1988), collaborating with Steven Resnick and Nancy Snidman, followed the development of extremely inhibited and uninhibited two- to three-year-old children for six years. They evaluated the children's heart rates and other physiological responses. They also observed their behavior in novel circumstances. After six years, the very inhibited children no longer behave exactly as they did when they were two, but they still reveal the pattern of very inhibited behavior combined with intense physiological responsiveness to mild stress. Very uninhibited children typically speak within the first minute when they are observed in a social situation, but very inhibited children will sometimes wait as long as twenty minutes before they say anything (figure 2.E).

Suomi (1987) has discovered that uptight monkeys, like Kagan's inhibited children, do not easily outgrow their intense physiological response to stress and their frozen behavioral responses to social situations (figure 2.F). Even as late as adolescence—which is four to five years of age in monkeys—those who were uptight at birth continued to respond in intense ways to stress, but at this point they became hyperactive. As adults, they seemed to regress in the face of stress, revealing the shy, inhibited behavior seen in infancy.

Kagan says that the proper environmental context can change the tendency to be shy. But if parents let their children remain fearful for a long time, it becomes harder to modify the shyness. Kagan discovered that 40 percent of the originally inhibited children—mainly boys—became much less inhibited by five and one-half years, while less than 10 percent became more timid. Based on parent interviews, parents helped their children overcome their shyness by bringing other children into the home and by encouraging the child to cope with stressful circumstances.

Figure 2.E
Shy children are a special concern of developmentalists. How stable is their behavior through childhood? What might parents do to facilitate their children's social interaction?

Figure 2.F
"Uptight" infant monkeys show some of the same shy, inhibited behaviors as their human counterparts.

The modifications of shyness in some cases can be extreme. Some shy individuals even become performers. Celebrities such as Johnny Carson, Carol Burnett, Barbara Walters, and Michael Jackson have strong tendencies toward shyness, but even with the biological underpinnings loaded against them, they turned the tables on heredity's influence (Asher, 1987).

| Concept Table 2.2 |||
| Heredity's Influence on Development and Heredity-Environmental Interaction and Development |||
Concept	Processes/Related Ideas	Characteristics/Description
Heredity's influence on development	Its scope	All aspects of development are influenced by heredity.
	Intelligence	Jensen's argument that intelligence is primarily due to heredity sparked a lively and at times bitter debate. Intelligence is influenced by heredity but not as strongly as Jensen envisioned.
	Temperament	Temperament refers to behavioral style; it has been studied extensively in infancy. Chess and Thomas developed nine temperament dimensions and three temperament clusters. Temperament is influenced strongly by biological factors in early infancy but becomes more malleable with experience. An important consideration is the fit of the infant's temperament with the parents' temperament.
Heredity-environmental interaction and development	Its nature	No genes, no organism; no environment, no organism. Because the environment's influence depends on genetically endowed characteristics, we say that the two factors interact.

resemblance. This holds more strongly for intelligence than personality or interests. The influence of genes on intelligence is present early in children's development and continues through the late adulthood years. And finally, we also know that being raised in the same family accounts for some portion of intellectual differences among individuals, but common rearing accounts for little of the variation in personality or interests. One reason for this discrepancy may be that families place similar pressures on their children for intellectual development in the sense that the push is clearly toward the highest level, while they do not direct their children toward similar personalities or interests, in which extremes are not especially desirable. That is, virtually all parents would like their children to have above-average intellect, but there is much less agreement about whether a child should be highly extraverted.

What do we need to know about the role of heredity-environmental interaction in development? Scarr and Kidd (1983) commented that we need to know the pathways by which genetic abnormalities influence development. The PKU success story is but one such example. Scientists discovered the genetic linkage of the disorder and subsequently how the environment could be changed to reduce the damage to development. We need to know more about genetic-environmental interaction in the normal range of development. For example, what accounts for the difference in one individual's IQ of 95 and another individual's IQ of 125? The answer requires a polygenic perspective and information about cultural and genetic influences.

We also need to know about heredity's influence across the entire life cycle. For instance, puberty is not an environmentally produced accident; neither is menopause. While puberty and menopause can be influenced by such environmental factors as nutrition, weight, drugs, and health, the basic evolutionary and genetic program is wired into the species. It cannot be eliminated, nor should it be ignored. This evolutionary and genetic perspective gives biology its appropriate role in our quest to better understand human development through the life cycle. A summary of the main ideas in our discussion of heredity's influence on development and heredity-environmental interaction is presented in Concept Table 2.2.

Summary

I. What Are Genes?

The nucleus of each human cell contains forty-six chromosomes, which are composed of DNA. Genes are short segments of DNA and act as a blueprint for cells to reproduce and manufacture the proteins that maintain life. Genes are transmitted from parents to offspring by gametes, or sex cells. Gametes are formed by the splitting of cells, a process called meiosis. Reproduction takes place when a female gamete (ovum) is fertilized by a male gamete (sperm) to create a single-celled zygote. In vitro fertilization has helped solve some infertility problems.

II. Abnormalities in Genes and Chromosomes

A range of problems are caused by some major gene or chromosome defect, among them the PKU syndrome, Down's syndrome, sickle-cell anemia, Klinefelter's syndrome, and the XYY syndrome. Genetic counseling has increased in popularity, as couples desire information about their risk of having a defective child. Amniocentesis and the chorionic villus test are used to determine the presence of defects once pregnancy has begun.

III. Some Genetic Principles

Genetic transmission is complex but some principles have been discovered, among them dominant-recessive genes, testis determining factor, polygenic inheritance, genotype-phenotype distinction, reaction range, and canalization.

IV. Methods Used by Behavior Geneticists

Behavior genetics is the field concerned with the degree and nature of behavior's heredity basis. Among the most important methods used by behavior geneticists are the twin study and the adoption study. The concept of heritability is used in many of the twin and adoption studies. The heritability index is not without its flaws.

V. Heredity's Influence on Development

All aspects of development are influenced by heredity. Jensen's argument that intelligence is primarily influenced by heredity sparked a lively and at times bitter debate. Intelligence is influenced by heredity but not as strongly as Jensen envisioned. Temperament refers to behavioral style; it has been studied extensively in infancy. Chess and Thomas developed nine temperament dimensions and three temperament clusters. Temperament is strongly influenced by biological factors in early infancy but becomes more malleable with experience. An important consideration is the fit of the infant's temperament with the parents' temperament.

VI. Heredity-Environmental Interaction and Development

No genes, no organism; no environment, no organism. Because the environment's influence depends on genetically endowed characteristics, we say that the two factors interact.

Key Terms

chromosomes 37
DNA 37
genes 37
gametes 37
meiosis 37
reproduction 37
zygote 37
in vitro fertilization 40
PKU syndrome 40
Down's syndrome 41
sickle-cell anemia 41
Klinefelter's syndrome 42
Turner's syndrome 42
XYY syndrome 42
dominant-recessive genes 42
amniocentesis 43

ultrasound sonography 43
chorionic villus test 43
testis determining factor, or TDF 44
polygenic inheritance 44
genotype 45
phenotypes 45
reaction range 45
behavior genetics 46
adoption study 46
twin study 46
monozygotic 46
dizygotic 46
heritability 46

Suggested Readings

Chess, S., & Thomas, A. (1986). *Temperament in clinical practice.* New York: Guilford.
Details of Chess and Thomas's classical longitudinal study of temperament are provided; applications to clinical problems are described.

Gould, S. (1983). *Hen's teeth and horse's toes; Reflections on natural history.* New York: Norton.
A collection of fascinating articles by a biologist interested in evolution. The essays originally were published in the magazine *Natural History.*

Lewontin, R. C., Rose, S., & Kamin, L. J. (1984). *Not in our genes.* New York: Pantheon.
Argues for an environmental view of development and provides many reasons as to why heredity's role is overestimated.

Plomin, R., DeFries, J. C., & McClearn, G. E. (1980). Behavioral genetics: A primer. San Francisco: W. H. Freeman.
A good introduction to research on genes and behavior by leading behavior geneticists.

Watson, J. D. (1968). *The double helix.* New York: New American Library.
A personalized account of the research leading up to one of the most provocative discoveries of the twentieth century—the DNA molecule. Reading like a mystery novel, it illustrates the exciting discovery process in science.

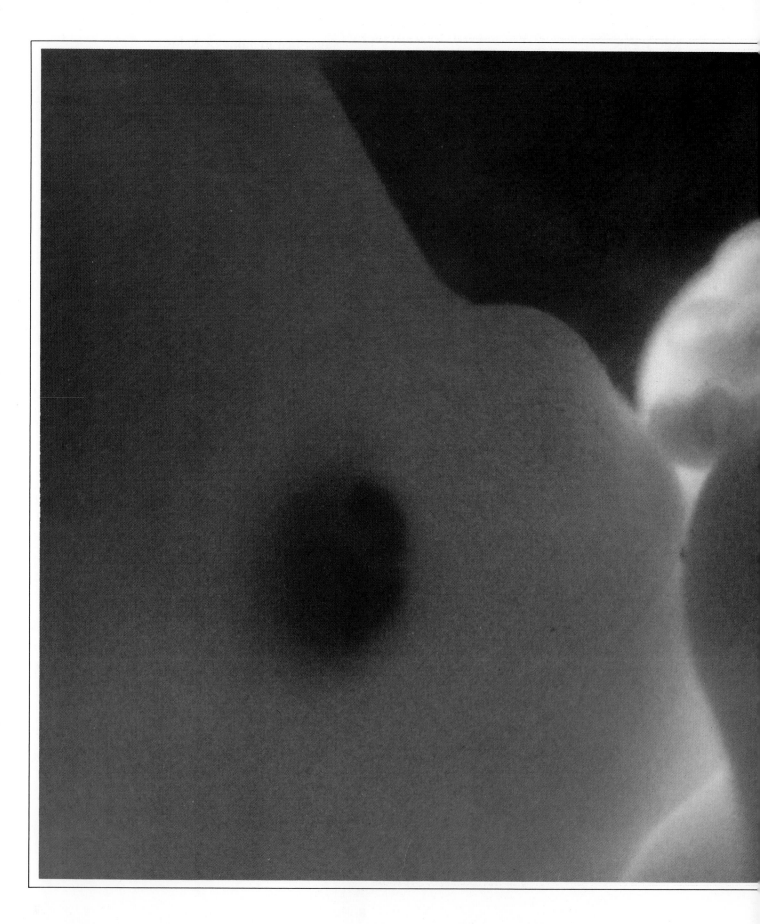

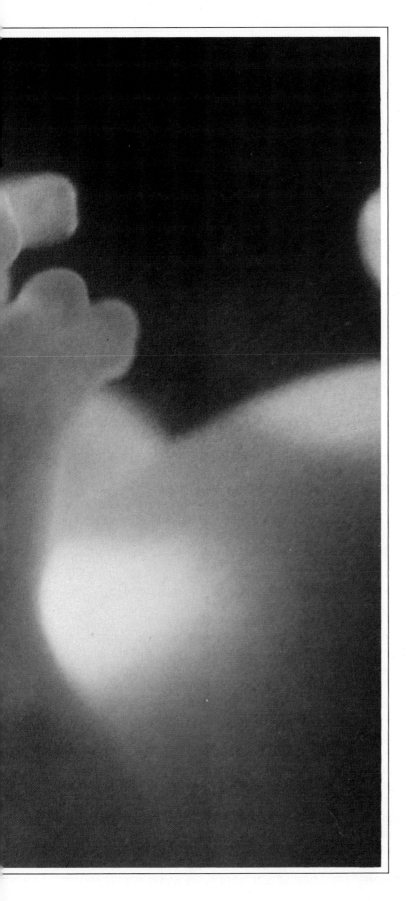

Prenatal Development and Birth

The history of man for nine months preceding his birth would, probably, be far more interesting, and contain events of greater moment than all three score and ten years that follow it.

Samuel Taylor Coleridge

eresa Block's second pregnancy was difficult—a rupture of the amniotic sac, an infection that sent her temperature skyrocketing, and an exhausting breech delivery. Robert weighed just less than two pounds at birth. His mother said she couldn't imagine a baby looking so tiny. The first time his mother saw him he was lying on his back attached to a respirator and wires were connected all over his body. Robert stayed at the hospital until two weeks before his originally projected birth date, at which time he weighed four pounds eight ounces. Teresa and her husband lived in a small town sixty miles from the hospital; they commuted each day to spend time with Robert and brought their other child along with them when it was practical.

A decade later Robert is still at the bottom of the weight chart but he is about average in height and virtually the only physical residue of his early birth difficulties is a "lazy eye." He has 20/20 vision in his good eye but 20/200 in the other. He is doing special exercises for the bad eye and the doctor thinks he is not far from the day he can go without glasses. Robert is on the soccer team and the swim team (Fincher, 1982).

Considering his circumstances, Robert had a relatively uncomplicated stay at the hospital. Not all children born so frail survive, and those that do sometimes show the consequences many years into the future.

At one time you were an organism floating around in a sea of fluid inside your mother's womb. From the moment you were conceived until the moment you were born, some astonishing developments took place. This chapter chronicles the truly remarkable developments that occur from conception to birth and the nature of the birth process itself.

Prenatal Development

Imagine how you came to be. Out of thousands of eggs and millions of sperm, one egg and one sperm united to produce you. Had the union of sperm and egg come a day or even an hour earlier or later, you might have been very different—maybe even the opposite sex.

The Course of Prenatal Development

Remember from chapter 2 that conception occurs when a single sperm cell from the male unites with the ovum (egg) in the female's fallopian tube in a process called fertilization. The fertilized egg is called a **zygote.** By the time the zygote ends its three- to four-day journey through the fallopian tubes and reaches the uterus, it has divided into approximately twelve to sixteen cells.

The period from conception until about twelve to fourteen days later is called the **germinal period;** it includes the creation of the zygote, continued cell division, and attachment of the zygote to the uterine wall. Approximately one week after conception—when the zygote is composed of 100 to 150 cells—it is called the **blastula.** Differentiation of cells has already commenced in the blastula as inner and outer layers are formed. The inner layer of the blastula is called the **blastocyst,** which later develops into the embryo. The outer layer is called the **trophoblast,** which later provides nutrition and support for the embryo. At about ten days after conception, a major milestone in the germinal period takes place: **implantation.** This refers to the attachment of the zygote to the uterine wall.

During the **embryonic period,** the embryo differentiates into three layers and life support systems develop. As the zygote attaches to the uterine wall, its cells form two layers; it is at this time that the mass of cells changes names from zygote to embryo. The embryonic period lasts from about two weeks to eight weeks after conception. The inner layer of cells is called the **endoderm;** this will develop into the digestive and respiratory systems. The outer layer of cells is divided into two parts. The outermost layer—the **ectoderm**—will become the nervous system, sensory receptors (ear, nose, and eyes, for example), and skin parts (hair and nails, for example). The middle layer—the **mesoderm**—will become the circulatory system, bones, muscle, excretory system, and reproductive system. Every body part eventually develops from these three layers—the endoderm primarily produces internal body parts, the mesoderm primarily produces parts that surround the internal areas, and the ectoderm primarily produces surface parts.

As the embryo's three layers are formed, life support systems for the embryo mature and develop rapidly; these include the placenta, umbilical cord, and the amnion. The **placenta** is a disk-shaped group of tissues in which small blood vessels from the mother and the offspring intertwine but do not join. The **umbilical cord** contains two arteries and one vein, connecting the baby to the placenta. Very small molecules—oxygen, water, salt, food from the mother's blood, and carbon dioxide and digestive wastes from the embryo's blood—pass back and forth between the mother and infant. Large molecules cannot pass through the placental wall—red blood cells and harmful substances such as most bacteria, maternal wastes, and hormones, for example. The mechanisms that govern transfer of substances across the placental barrier are complex and still not entirely understood (Rosenblith & Sims-Knight, 1985). The **amnion,** a sort of bag or envelope that contains a clear fluid in which the developing embryo floats, is another important life support system of the embryo. It provides an environment that is temperature and humidity controlled, as well as shockproof.

Before most women even know they are pregnant, some other important embryonic developments take place. In the third week, the neural tube that eventually becomes the spinal cord forms. At about twenty-one days, eyes begin to appear, and by twenty-four days, the cells for the heart begin to differentiate. During the fourth week, the first appearance of the urogenital system is apparent, and arm and leg buds emerge. Four chambers of the heart take shape and blood vessels surface (figure 3.1 shows a four-week-old embryo). From the fifth to eighth weeks, arms and legs differentiate further; at this time the face starts to form but still is not very recognizable. The intestinal tract develops and the facial structures fuse. At eight weeks, the developing organism weighs about one-thirtieth of an ounce and is just over one inch long.

The first eight weeks of development are a time when many body systems are being formed. When body systems are forming, they are especially vulnerable to environmental changes. This process of organ formation is called **organogenesis;** it characterizes the first two months of development after conception. Later in the chapter we detail the environmental hazards that are especially harmful during organogenesis.

"My Mom says I come from Heaven. My Dad says he can't remember an' Mr. Wilson is positive I came from Mars!"

DENNIS THE MENACE® used by permission of Hank Ketcham and © by North America Syndicate.

Figure 3.1
At four weeks, the embryo is about .2 inches long, and the head, eyes, and ears begin to show. The head and neck are half the body length; the shoulders will be located where the whitish arm buds are attached.

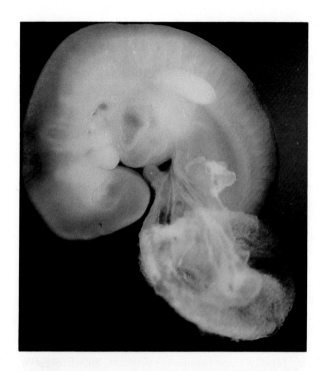

Figure 3.2
Fetus at eight weeks, the beginning of the fetal period.

The **fetal period** begins eight weeks after conception and lasts for seven months on the average. Growth and development continue their dramatic course during this time frame (figure 3.2 shows a fetus at eight weeks after conception). Three months after conception the fetus is about three inches long and weighs about one ounce. It has become active, moving its arms and legs, opening and closing its mouth, and moving its head. The face, forehead, eyelids, nose, and chin are distinguishable, as are the upper arms, lower arms, hands, and lower limbs. The genitals can be identified as male or female. By the end of the fourth month, the fetus has grown to six inches in length and weighs four to seven ounces. At this time a growth spurt occurs in the body's lower parts.

Prenatal reflexes are stronger—arm and leg movements can be felt for the first time by the mother, for example. Figure 3.3 shows the fetus at four and one-half months; notice the sucking reflex.

By the end of the fifth month, the fetus is about twelve inches long and weighs close to a pound. Structures of the skin have formed—toenails and fingernails, for example. The fetus is more active, showing a preference for a particular position in the womb. By the end of the sixth month, the fetus is about fourteen inches long and already has gained another pound. The eyes and eyelids are completely formed. A fine layer of hair covers the head. A grasping reflex is present and irregular breathing occurs. By the end of the seventh month, the fetus is about sixteen inches long and has gained another pound, now weighing about three pounds. During the eighth and ninth months, the fetus grows longer and gains substantial weight—about four pounds. At birth, the average American baby weighs seven pounds and is twenty inches long. In these last two months, fatty tissues develop and the functioning of various organ systems—heart and kidneys, for example—is stepped up.

Miscarriage and Abortion

A miscarriage, or spontaneous abortion, happens when pregnancy ends before the developing organism is mature enough to survive outside of the womb. This happens when the embryo separates from the uterine wall and is expelled by the uterus. Estimates indicate that about 15 to 20 percent of all pregnancies end in a spontaneous abortion, most in the first two to three months. Many spontaneous abortions occur without the mother's knowledge and many involve an embryo or fetus that was not developing normally.

Early in history it was believed that a woman could be frightened into a miscarriage by loud thunder or a jolt in a carriage. Today we recognize that this occurrence is highly unlikely; the developing organism is well protected. Abnormalities of the reproductive tract and viral or bacterial infections are more likely candidates for causes of spontaneous abortions. In some cases, severe traumas may be at fault.

Deliberate termination of pregnancy is a complex issue, medically, psychologically, and socially. Possibly carrying the baby to term will affect the mother's health, possibly her pregnancy resulted from rape or incest, or possibly she is unmarried, poor, and wants to continue her education. Abortion is

Ethics and the Medical Use of Fetal Tissue

The increased medical uses for tissue from aborted fetuses opens up a new debate about medical technology and the beginnings of life, adding a new dimension to the long-standing controversy over abortion. Evidence is increasing that the special properties of fetal tissue might make it useable for tissue transplants to treat Parkinson's disease, Alzheimer's disease, and other disorders. Most medical researchers believe it is only a matter of time until fetal tissue is routinely used. Scientists expect fetal tissue to be especially valuable in implant treatments because it grows faster than adult tissue, it is more adaptable, and it causes less immunological rejection. One of the most troubling possibilities is that some women will conceive children with the intent of aborting them, either to aid a family member or to sell them for their tissue.

The laws governing organ donations require the consent of the donor, or the donor's next of kin. In the case of fetuses, tissue may be donated with the consent of the pregnant woman. Many states have laws restricting experiments on fetuses, which may interfere with the new medical uses of fetal tissue. A recent panel on biomedical ethics at Case Western Reserve University in Cleveland made recommendations about the use of fetal tissue. First, the doctors involved in decisions regarding the abortion should not conduct the procedures using fetal tissue. Second, anonymity should be maintained between the donor and recipient, and donors and recipients should not be related. Almost everyone concerned with the use of fetal tissue agrees it is morally wrong, although not illegal, to become pregnant for the sole purpose of aborting a fetus to obtain certain tissues. As this text went to press, the United States Department of Health and Human Services placed a moratorium on certain fetal tissue research until the ethical issues involved in fetal research are resolved (United States Public Health Service, 1988). Specifically, research on induced abortions, but not spontaneous abortions or stillbirths, is banned. Prior to the announcement by the Department of Health and Human Services, some ethics committees had already shut down this type of fetal research until the ethical issues could be evaluated further (Burtchaell, in press).

Biomedical ethicists say there is a big difference between taking advantage of a death to harvest tissue and creating a life just to abort it. When an abortion is planned anyway, some ethicists say that donating the fetal tissue may help to relieve some of the sadness surrounding the decision. Donating tissue to help someone else can benefit the process of grieving or bereavement, say some ethicists. The National Right-to-Life Committee, however, says the idea is morally repulsive. They point out that people who kill tiny developing babies lose any moral right to use those tissues. They also believe that the medical use of fetal tissue offers an additional rationale to some individuals who defend abortion. As can be seen, the use of fetal tissue is a debate that probably will be with us for some time (Lewin, 1987).

again legal in the United States; in 1973, the Supreme Court ruled that any woman could obtain an abortion during the first six months of pregnancy. This decision continues to generate ethical objections from those opposed to induced abortion, especially advocates of the Right-to-Life movement. The United States Supreme Court has ruled that abortion in the first trimester is solely the decision of the mother and her doctor. Specific cases have added the point that the father and the parents of minor girls do not have any say during this time frame. In the second trimester, states can legislate the time and method of abortion to protect the mother's health. In the third trimester, the fetus's right to life is the primary concern.

An unwanted pregnancy is stressful for a woman regardless of how she resolves the problem—ending the pregnancy, giving the child up for adoption, or keeping the child and raising it. Depression and guilt are common reactions of a woman, both before and after an induced abortion. If an abortion is performed, it should not only involve competent medical care, but the woman's psychological needs also should be considered. Yet another ethical issue related to abortion is the medical use of tissues from aborted fetuses. To learn more about this ethical issue turn to Perspective on Child Development 3.1.

Teratology and Hazards to Prenatal Development

Some expectant mothers tiptoe about in the belief that everything they do and feel has a direct effect on their unborn child. Others behave casually, assuming that their experiences have little impact on the unborn child. The truth lies somewhere between these two extremes. Although the fetus lives in a protected, comfortable environment, it is not totally immune to the larger environment surrounding the mother. The environment can affect the child in a number of well-documented ways. Thousands of babies are born deformed or mentally retarded every year as a result of events as early as one or two months prior to conception.

Teratology

The field of study that investigates the causes of congenital (birth) defects is called **teratology.** Any agent that causes birth defects is called a *teratogen* (from the Greek word *tera,* meaning "monster"). A specific teratogen (such as a drug) usually does not cause a specific birth defect (such as malformation of the legs). Virtually every fetus is exposed to at least some teratogens, so many exist. For this reason it is difficult to determine which teratogen causes which birth defect. In addition, it may take a long time for the effects of a teratogen to show up—only about half are present at birth.

Despite the many unknowns about teratogens, scientists have discovered the identity of some of these hazards to prenatal development and the particular point of fetal development at which they do their greatest damage (figure 3.4). As figure 3.4 shows, sensitivity to teratogens occurs about three weeks after conception. Early in the embryonic period, the probability of a structural defect is greatest because this is when organs are being formed. After organogenesis is complete, teratogens are less likely to cause anatomical defects. Exposure later during the fetal period is more likely to stunt growth or to create problems in the way organs function. The preciseness of organogenesis is evident when teratologists point out that vulnerability of the brain is greatest at fifteen to twenty-five days after conception, the eyes at twenty-four to forty days, the heart at twenty to forty days, and the legs at twenty-four to thirty-six days.

In the following sections, we explore how certain environmental agents influence prenatal development. That is, we examine how maternal diseases and conditions as well as drugs influence the embryo or fetus.

Maternal Diseases and Conditions

Maternal diseases or infections can produce birth defects by crossing the placental barrier, or they can cause damage during the birth process itself.

Rubella (German measles) and syphilis (a sexually transmitted disease) are two maternal diseases that can damage prenatal development. A rubella outbreak in 1964–65 produced 30,000 prenatal and neonatal (newborn) deaths, and more than 20,000 infants were born with malformations, including mental retardation, blindness, deafness, and heart problems. The greatest damage occurs when mothers contract rubella in the third and fourth weeks of pregnancy, although infection during the second month is also damaging. Elaborate efforts ensure that rubella will never again have the same disastrous effects as it did in the mid-1960s. A vaccine that prevents German measles is routinely administered to children, and mothers who plan to have children should have a blood test before they become pregnant to determine if they are immune to the disease.

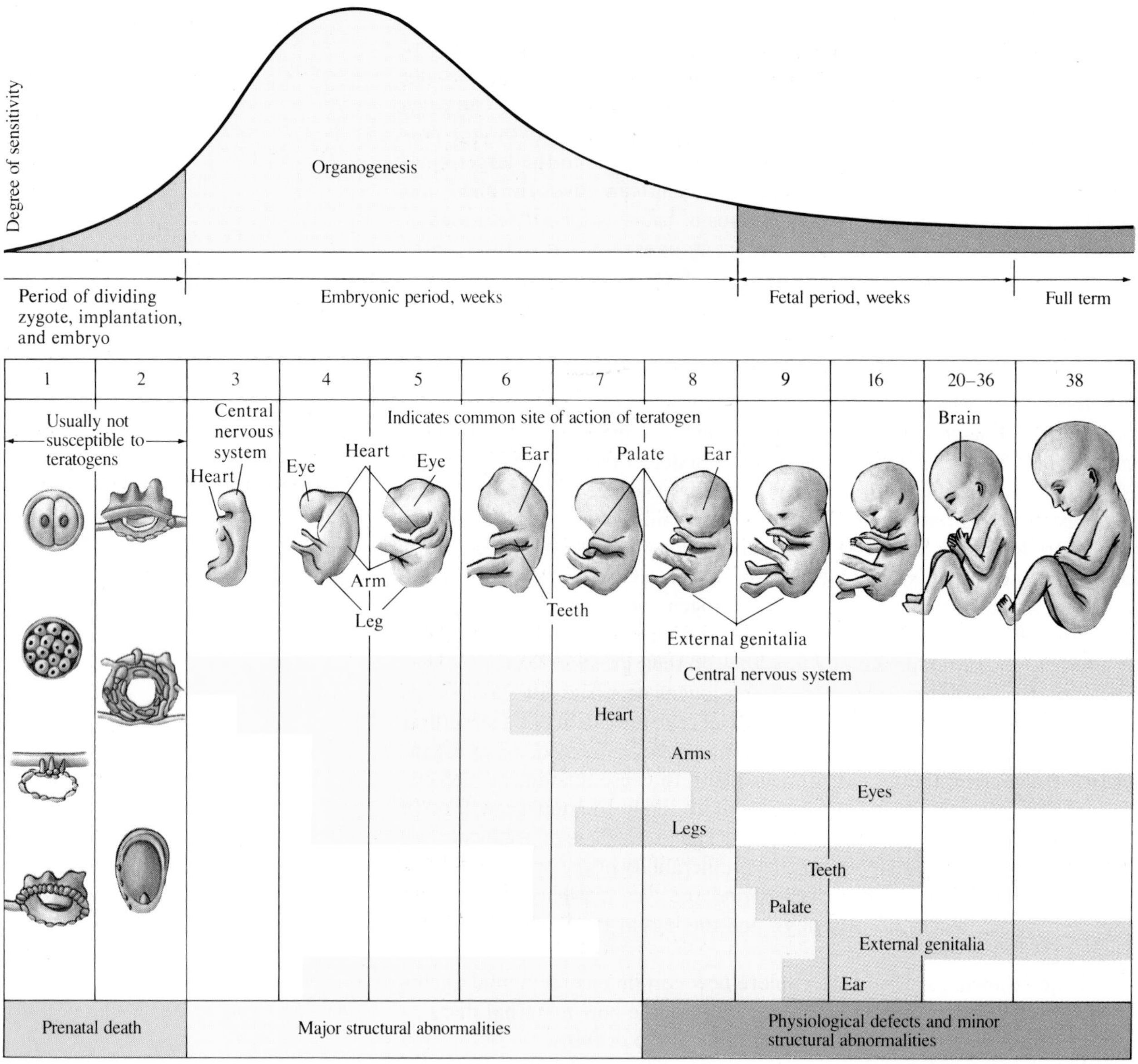
Degree of sensitivity
Organogenesis
Period of dividing zygote, implantation, and embryo
Embryonic period, weeks
Fetal period, weeks
Full term
1
2
3
4
5
6
7
8
9
16
20–36
38
Usually not susceptible to teratogens
Central nervous system
Heart
Indicates common site of action of teratogen
Eye
Heart
Eye
Ear
Palate
Ear
Brain
Arm
Leg
Teeth
External genitalia
Central nervous system
Heart
Arms
Eyes
Legs
Teeth
Palate
External genitalia
Ear
Prenatal death
Major structural abnormalities
Physiological defects and minor structural abnormalities

Figure 3.4
Teratogens and the timing of their effects on prenatal development. The danger of structural defects caused by teratogens is greatest early in embryonic development. This is the period of organogenesis and it lasts for several months. Damage caused by teratogens during this period is represented by the dark-colored bars. Later assaults by teratogens typically occur during the fetal period and, instead of structural damage, are more likely to stunt growth or cause problems of organ function.

Syphilis is more damaging later in prenatal development—four months or more after conception. Rather than affecting organogenesis like rubella does, syphilis damages organs after they already are formed. Damage includes eye lesions, which can cause blindness, and skin lesions. When syphilis is present at birth, other problems involving the central nervous system and gastrointestinal tract can develop. Most states require that a pregnant woman be given a blood test to detect the presence of syphilis.

Another infection that has received widespread attention recently is genital herpes. Increased numbers of newborns contract this virus when they are delivered through the birth canal of a mother with genital herpes. About one-third of babies delivered through an infected birth canal will die; another one-fourth become brain damaged. If a pregnant woman detects an active case of genital herpes close to her delivery date, a cesarean section can be performed (in which the infant is delivered through the mother's abdomen) to keep the virus from infecting the newborn (Rice, 1989).

The Mother's Age

When the mother's age is considered in terms of possible harmful effects on the fetus and infant, two time periods are of special interest—adolescence and the thirties and beyond. Approximately one in every five births is to an adolescent; in some urban areas, the figure reaches as high as one in every two births. Infants born to adolescents are often premature. The mortality rate of infants born to adolescent mothers doubles that of infants born of mothers in their twenties (Graham, 1981). While such figures probably reflect the mother's immature reproductive system, they also may involve poor nutrition, lack of prenatal care, and low socioeconomic status. Prenatal care decreases the probability that a child born to an adolescent girl will have physical problems. However, adolescents are the least likely of all age groups to obtain prenatal assistance from clinics, pediatricians, and health services (Blum & Goldhagen, 1981; Timberlake & others, 1987; Worthington, 1988).

Increasingly, women seek to establish a career before beginning a family, delaying childbearing until their thirties (figure 3.5). Down's syndrome, a form of mental retardation, is related to the mother's age. A baby with Down's syndrome rarely is born to a mother under the age of thirty, but the risk increases after the mother reaches thirty. The risk also increases prior to age eighteen. By age forty, the probability is slightly over 1 in 100, and by age fifty, it is almost 1 in 10.

Women also have more difficulty becoming pregnant after the age of thirty. In one investigation (Schwartz & Mayaux, 1982), the clients of a French fertility clinic all had husbands who were sterile. To increase their chances of having a child, they were artificially inseminated once a month for one year. Each woman had twelve chances to become pregnant. Seventy-five percent of the women in their twenties became pregnant, 62 percent of the women thirty-one to thirty-five years old became pregnant, and only 54 percent in the group over thirty-five years old became pregnant.

We still have much to learn about the role of the mother's age in pregnancy and childbirth. As women become more active, exercise regularly, and are careful about their nutrition, their reproductive systems may remain healthier longer. Indeed, as we see next, the mother's nutrition influences prenatal development.

Nutrition

The developing fetus completely depends on the mother for its nutrition, which comes from the mother's blood. Nutritional state is not determined by any specific aspect of diet; among the important factors are the total number of calories and appropriate levels of protein, vitamins, and minerals. The mother's nutrition even influences her ability to reproduce. In extreme instances of malnutrition, women stop menstruating, thus precluding conception. And children born to malnourished mothers are more likely to be malformed (Hurley, 1980).

One investigation of Iowa mothers documents the importance of nutrition in prenatal development and birth (Jeans, Smith, & Stearns, 1955). The diets of 400 pregnant women were studied and the status of the newborns was assessed. The mothers with the poorest diets were more likely to have offspring who weighed the least, had the least vitality, were born prematurely, and who died. Diet supplements given to malnourished mothers during pregnancy improved the performance of offspring during the first three years of life in one investigation (Werner, 1979).

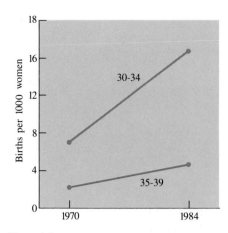

Figure 3.5
Birth rates for women aged thirty to thirty-nine years of age.

Source: National Center for Health Statistics.

Emotional State and Stress

Tales abound about how a mother's emotional state affects the fetus. For centuries it was thought that frightening experiences—a severe thunderstorm or a family member's death—would leave birthmarks on the child or affect the child in more serious ways. Today, we believe that the mother's stress can be transmitted to the fetus, although we have gone beyond thinking that these happenings are somehow magically produced. We now know that when a pregnant woman experiences intense fear, anxiety, and other emotions, physiological changes occur—heart rate, respiration, and glandular secretions among them. For example, the production of adrenaline in response to fear restricts blood flow to the uterine area and may deprive the fetus of adequate oxygen.

The mother's emotional state during pregnancy can influence the birth process as well. An emotionally distraught mother might have irregular contractions and a more difficult labor. This may cause irregularities in the baby's oxygen supply, or it may lead to irregularities after birth. Babies born after extended labor may adjust more slowly to their world and be more irritable. One investigation revealed a connection between the mother's anxiety during pregnancy and the newborn's condition (Ottinger & Simmons, 1964). In this study, mothers answered a questionnaire about their anxiety every three months during pregnancy. When the babies were born, the babies' weights, activity levels, and crying were assessed. The babies of the more anxious mothers cried more before feedings and were more active than the babies born to the less anxious mothers.

Drugs

How might drugs affect prenatal development? Some pregnant women take drugs, smoke tobacco, and drink alcohol without thinking about the possible effects on the fetus. Occasionally, a rash of deformed babies are born, bringing to light the damage drugs can have on the developing fetus. This happened in 1961 when many pregnant women took a popular tranquilizer called thalidomide to reduce their morning sickness. In adults, the effects of thalidomide are mild; in embryos, they are devastating. Not all infants were affected in the same way. If the mother took thalidomide on day twenty-six (probably before she knew she was pregnant), an arm might not grow. If she took the drug two days later, the arm might not grow past the elbow. The thalidomide tragedy shocked the medical community and parents into the stark realization that the mother does not have to be a chronic drug user for the fetus to be harmed. Taking the wrong drug at the wrong time is enough to physically handicap the offspring for life.

Heavy drinking by pregnant women also can be devastating to an offspring. A cluster of characteristics called **fetal alcohol syndrome (FAS)** identifies children born to mothers who are heavy drinkers; it includes a small head (called microencephaly) as well as defective limbs, face, and heart. Most of these children are below average in intelligence. While no serious malformations such as those found in FAS are found in infants born to mothers who are moderate drinkers, in one investigation infants whose mothers drank moderately during pregnancy (for example, one to two drinks a day) were less attentive and alert, with the effects present at four years of age (Streissguth & others, 1984).

Cigarette smoking by a pregnant woman also can adversely influence prenatal development, birth, and infant development. Fetal and neonatal deaths are higher among smoking mothers; also prevalent are higher preterm births

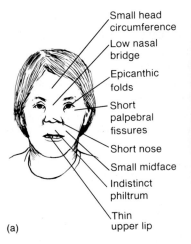

Small head circumference
Low nasal bridge
Epicanthic folds
Short palpebral fissures
Short nose
Small midface
Indistinct philtrum
Thin upper lip

(a)

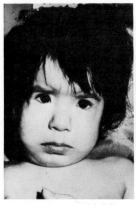 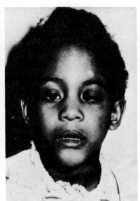 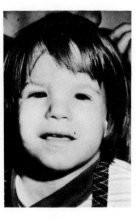

(b)

Children of different racial backgrounds, diagnosed with fetal alcohol syndrome.

and lower birth weights. In one investigation (Landesman-Dwyer & Sackett, 1983), 271 infant-mother pairs were studied during the infant's eighth, twelfth, and sixteenth weeks of life by having each mother keep a diary of her infant's activity patterns. The infants of mothers who smoked during pregnancy were awake on a more consistent basis, a finding one might expect since the active chemical ingredient in cigarettes—nicotine—is a stimulant. Respiratory problems and sudden infant death syndrome (also known as crib death) are more common among the offspring of mothers who smoke. Evidence suggests that intervention programs to help pregnant women stop smoking are successful in reducing some of the negative effects of cigarette smoking on offspring, especially in raising infants' birth weights (Sexton & Hebel, 1984; Vorhees & Mollnow, 1987).

It is well documented that infants whose mothers are addicted to heroin show a number of behavioral difficulties (Hutchings & Fifer, 1986). The young infant of these mothers is addicted and shows withdrawal symptoms characteristic of opiate abstinence, such as tremors, irritability, abnormal crying, disturbed sleep, and impaired motor control. Often, behavioral problems are still present at the first birthday and attention deficits may appear later in the child's development.

With the increased use of cocaine in the United States, there is growing concern regarding its effects on the fetuses and neonates of pregnant cocaine abusers (Howard, 1988). In one investigation, infants whose mothers were cocaine abusers during pregnancy showed less social interaction and more poorly organized responses to environmental stimuli than their counterparts whose mothers were not cocaine abusers (Chasnoff, Burns, & Burns, 1987).

At this point we have discussed a number of ideas about prenatal development. A summary of the main points in this discussion is presented in Concept Table 3.1. Next, we turn to the study of the birth process itself.

The Birth Process

Delivery can be as difficult for the baby as for the mother, lasting anywhere from four to twenty-four hours. The newborn emerges splattered with the mother's blood and a thick, greasy, white material called vernix, which aids movement through the birth canal. The newborn's head is not the most attractive in the world; it may be swollen at the top because of pressure against the pelvic outlet during the last hours of labor. The baby's face may be puffy

Concept Table 3.1
Prenatal Development

Concept	Processes/Related Ideas	Characteristics/Description
The course of prenatal development	Germinal period	The period from conception to about ten to fourteen days later. The fertilized egg is called a zygote. The period ends when the zygote attaches to the uterine wall.
	Embryonic period	The period that lasts from about two weeks to eight weeks after conception. The embryo differentiates into three layers, life support systems develop, and organ systems form (organogenesis).
	Fetal period	The period that lasts from about two months after conception until nine months or when the infant is born. Growth and development continue their dramatic course and organ systems mature to the point where life can be sustained outside the womb.
Miscarriage and abortion	Its nature and ethical issues	A miscarriage, or spontaneous abortion, happens when pregnancy ends before the developing organism is mature enough to survive outside of the womb. Estimates indicate that about 15 to 20 percent of all pregnancies end this way, many without the mother's knowledge. Induced abortion is a complex issue, medically, psychologically, and socially. An unwanted pregnancy is stressful for the woman regardless of how it is resolved. A recent ethical issue focuses on the use of fetal tissue in transplant operations.
Teratology and hazards to prenatal development	Teratology	Teratology is the investigation of causes of congenital (birth) defects. Any agent that causes birth defects is called a teratogen.
	Maternal diseases and conditions	Maternal diseases and infections can cause damage by crossing the placental barrier, or they can be destructive during the birth process itself. Among the maternal diseases and conditions believed to be involved in possible birth defects are rubella, syphilis, genital herpes, the mother's age, nutrition, and emotional state and stress.
	Drugs	Thalidomide was a tranquilizer given to pregnant mothers to reduce morning sickness. In the early 1960s, thousands of babies were malformed as a consequence of their mothers taking this drug. Alcohol, cigarette smoking, heroin, and cocaine are other drugs that can adversely affect prenatal and infant development.

and bluish; her ears may be pressed against her head in a bizarre position—matted forward on her cheeks, for example. Her nose may be flattened and skewed to one side by the squeeze through the pelvis. The baby may be bow-legged and her feet may be pigeon-toed from being up beside her head for so long in the mother's womb. They can be flexed and put in a normal position at birth. How stunning it must be to be thrust suddenly into a new, bright, airy world so totally different from the dark, moist warmth of the womb. Despite the drama of human birth, newborns who have had a comfortable stay in the womb and are born when due are well equipped by nature to withstand the birth process. Among the intriguing questions about the birth process are, What kinds of childbirth strategies are available? What are the stages of birth and what delivery complications can arise? What are preterm infants like? How can we measure the newborn's health and social responsiveness? How crucial is bonding? We consider each of these in turn.

Childbirth Strategies

Controversy exists over how childbirth should proceed. Some critics argue that the standard delivery practices of most hospitals and physicians need to be overhauled; others suggest that the entire family—especially the father—should be more involved in childbirth; and others argue that procedures that ensure mother-infant bonding should be followed.

Biological and Perceptual Development

In the standard childbirth procedure that was practiced for many years—and the way you probably were delivered—the expectant mother was taken to a hospital, where a doctor was responsible for the baby's delivery. The pregnant woman was prepared for labor by having her pubic hair shaved and by having an enema. She then was placed in a labor room often filled with other pregnant women, some of whom were screaming. When she was ready to deliver, she was taken to the delivery room, which looked like an operating room, and laid on the table with her legs in the air. The physician, along with an anesthetist and a nurse, delivered the baby.

What could be wrong with this procedure? Critics list three things: (1) Individuals important to the mother are excluded from the birth process. (2) The mother is separated from her infant in the first minutes and hours after birth. (3) Giving birth is treated like a disease and a woman is thought of as a sick patient (Rosenblith & Sims-Knight, 1985). As we see next, some alternative procedures differ radically from this standard procedure.

The **Leboyer method,** developed by French obstetrician Frederick Leboyer, makes the birth process less stressful for infants. Leboyer's procedure is referred to as "birth without violence." He describes standard childbirth as torture (Leboyer, 1975). Leboyer vehemently objects to holding newborns upside down and slapping or spanking them, putting silver nitrate into their eyes, separating them immediately from their mothers, and scaring them with bright lights and harsh noises in the delivery room. He also criticizes the traditional habit of cutting the umbilical cord as soon as the infant is born, a situation that forces the infant to immediately take in oxygen from the air to breathe. Leboyer believes that the umbilical cord should be left intact for several minutes to allow the newborn a chance to adjust to breathing air. In the Leboyer method, the baby is placed on the mother's stomach immediately after birth so the mother can caress the infant. Then the infant is placed in a bath of warm water to relax.

While most hospitals do not use the soft lights and warm baths for the newborn suggested by Leboyer, they sometimes do place the newborn on the mother's stomach immediately after birth, believing that it will stimulate bonding between the mother and the infant.

Another well-known birth procedure that deviates markedly from the standard practice is the **Lamaze method,** a form of prepared or natural childbirth developed by Fernand Lamaze, a pioneering French obstetrician. The Lamaze method is widely accepted in the medical profession and involves helping the pregnant mother cope with the pain of childbirth in an active way to avoid or reduce medication. Lamaze classes are available on a widespread basis in the United States, usually consisting of six weekly classes. In these classes, the pregnant woman learns about the birth process and is trained in breathing and relaxation exercises.

As the Lamaze method grew in popularity, it became more common for the father to participate in the exercises and to assist in the birth process. To learn more about the father's role in the Lamaze method and his participation in the birth process, turn to Perspective on Child Development 3.2.

Medical doctors provide most maternity care in the United States. However, in many countries of the world, midwives are the primary caregiver for pregnant and laboring women. In the United States, midwives are not as well established, although all states have provisions for their practice. The emphasis of the midwife's training is that birth is a normal physiological event. Midwives support and promote the woman's physical and emotional well-being. Midwives do not care for women with complications of pregnancy. In the United

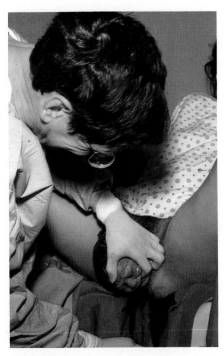

Birth marks a dramatic transition for the fetus. The baby is on a threshold, between two worlds.

A Father in the Delivery Room: "It Was Out of This World!"

A n interesting historical accident led to one of the major components of Lamaze training as it is now practiced in the United States. In France, trained women assist a woman in labor. Since such assistants are not available in the United States, fathers assumed the assistant's function. Fathers attend childbirth classes with their wives, learn the strategies required, and assist in timing contractions, massaging the mother, and giving psychological support.

The father's participation in the birth process may help to stengthen his relationship with his wife and increase the probability that he will develop a strong bond with the infant. Data supporting the belief that the father's participation in Lamaze classes and in the birth process benefits the infant's long-term development have not been generated. However, there is something intuitively positive about the father's involvement in the birth process, if he is motivated to participate. It may increase the family's sense as a cohesive, interdependent unit that does things together. One survey indicated that the father's presence in the delivery room is a positive experience (Pawson & Morris, 1972). Only 1 of the 544 fathers sampled said that he regretted participating in the birth process. While most fathers who participate in the delivery room process provide glowing reports about the experience, many fathers feel uncomfortable and anxious about delivery room participation and have no desire to be involved.

What are some reactions of fathers who have participated in Lamaze natural childbirth classes and in the birth process in the delivery room? More than twenty years ago, I was allowed in the delivery room by a progressive physician at a hospital that did not permit such practices. I still have a vivid image of those moments, moments that truly inspire a sense of awe and excitement in a father when he sees his child being born.

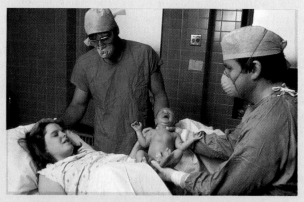

Do you think fathers should be encouraged to participate in the birth process? How might our society increase the father's participation in the delivery room?

One father who participated in natural childbirth classes proudly described how he felt at his accomplishments and his sense of involvement in sharing the birth of the baby with his wife:

It made me feel good to be able to help out. I know it was a painful experience, and I wanted to make it as easy as possible for her. She was willing to have the baby and go through nine months of carrying it around. The least I could do was go to the childbirth classes once a week and give her my support. There were times during her pregnancy when she did not feel well. I know she appreciated my willingness to assist her in the baby's birth. Then, in the delivery room itself—what a great, uplifting feeling. It was out of this world! I would not have missed that moment when the baby first came out for the world.

States, certified nurse-midwives are the most numerous. They generally work in close cooperation with physicians in hospitals, in homes, or in birthing centers.

Most births in the United States take place in a hospital. In recent years, hospitals have offered more comfortable, homelike rooms for birth. Many hospitals now have birthing rooms—where the mother can labor, give birth, and spend time with her newborn.

Birthing centers also have emerged as an alternative setting to hospitals if the pregnant woman is healthy and no complications are foreseen. Birthing centers provide a sense of community and learning with social gatherings and classes often held there.

Stages of Birth and Delivery Complications

The birth process occurs in three stages. The first stage lasts an average of twelve to twenty-four hours for a woman having her first child—it is the longest of the three stages. In the first stage, uterine contractions are fifteen to twenty minutes apart at the beginning and last up to a minute. These contractions cause the woman's cervix to stretch and open. As the first stage progresses, the contractions come closer together, appearing every two to five minutes. Their intensity increases as well. By the end of the first birth stage, contractions dilate the cervix to an opening of about four inches so that the baby can move from the uterus to the birth canal.

The second birth stage begins when the baby's head starts to move through the cervix and the birth canal and ends when the baby completely emerges from the mother's body. This stage lasts for approximately one and one-half hours. With each contraction, the mother bears down hard to push the baby out of her body. By the time the baby's head is out of the mother's body, the contractions come almost every minute and last for about one minute.

The third birth stage—known as **afterbirth**—involves the detachment and expelling of the placenta, umbilical cord, and other membranes. This final stage is the shortest of the three birth stages, lasting only several minutes.

Complications can accompany a baby's delivery. When the baby moves through the birth canal too rapidly, the delivery is called **precipitate.** A precipitate delivery is one that takes the baby less than ten minutes to be squeezed through the birth canal. This deviation in delivery can disturb the infant's normal flow of blood and the pressure on the infant's head can cause hemorrhaging. If the delivery takes very long, brain damage can occur because of **anoxia,** meaning that insufficient oxygen is available to the infant.

Another delivery complication involves the baby's position in the uterus. Normally, the crown of the baby's head comes through the vagina first. But in one of every twenty-five births, the head does not come through first. Some come with their buttocks first—called the **breech position.** A breech baby has difficulties because his head is still in the uterus when the rest of the body is out, which can cause respiratory problems. Some breech babies cannot be passed through the cervix and must be delivered by cesarean section.

The Use of Drugs during Childbirth

Drugs can be used to relieve pain and anxiety and to speed up delivery during the birth process. The widest use of drugs during delivery is to relieve the expectant mother's pain or anxiety. A wide variety of tranquilizers, sedatives, and analgesics are used for this purpose. Researchers are interested in the effects of these drugs because they can cross the placental barrier and because their use is so widespread. One survey of hospitals found that only 5 percent of deliveries involved no anesthesia, for example (Brackbill, 1979).

One drug that has been widely used to speed up delivery is **oxytocin,** a hormone that stimulates uterine contractions. Controversy surrounds the use of this drug. Some physicians argue that it can save the mother's life or keep the infant from being damaged. They also stress that using the drug allows the mother to be well rested and prepared for the birth process. Critics argue that babies born to mothers who have taken oxytocin are more likely to have jaundice, that induced labor requires more painkilling drugs, and that greater medical care is required after the birth, resulting in the separation of the infant and the mother.

What are some of the conclusions that can be reached based on research about the influence of drugs during delivery? Four such conclusions are as follows (Rosenblith & Sims-Knight, 1985).

1. Research studies are few in number and those that have been completed often have methodological problems. However, it can be said that all drugs do not have similar effects. Some drugs—tranquilizers, sedatives, and analgesics, for example—do not seem to have long-term effects. Other drugs—oxytocin, for example—are suspected of having long-term effects.
2. The degree to which a drug influences an infant is usually small. Birth weight and social class, for instance, are more powerful predictors of infant difficulties than drugs.
3. A specific drug may affect some infants but not others. And in some cases, the drug may have a beneficial effect, while in others, it may have a harmful effect.
4. The overall amount of medication may be an important factor in understanding drug effects on delivery.

Preterm Infants and Age-Weight Considerations

A full-term infant is one who has grown in the womb for the full thirty-eight to forty-two weeks between conception and delivery. A **preterm infant** (also called a premature infant) is one who is born prior to thirty-eight weeks after conception. Infants born after a regular *gestation period* (the length of time between conception and birth) of thirty-eight to forty-two weeks, but who weigh less than five and one-half pounds, are called **low-birth-weight infants.** Both preterm and low-birth-weight infants are considered high-risk infants. In one investigation (Milham & others, 1983), children were assessed at least once per year through the first four years of life. The most severe cognitive deficits appeared among those who were preterm or low-birth-weight babies and who came from an impoverished rather than a middle-class background.

A short gestation period does not necessarily harm the infant; it is distinguished from retarded prenatal growth, in which the fetus has been damaged in some way (Kopp, 1983, 1987). The neurological development of the short gestation infant continues after birth on approximately the same timetable as if the infant still were in the womb. For example, consider an infant born after a gestation period of thirty weeks. At thirty-eight weeks, approximately two months after birth, this infant shows the same level of brain development as a thirty-eight week fetus who is yet to be born. Some infants are born early and have a precariously low birth weight. To learn more about these so-called kilogram kids, turn to Perspective on Child Development 3.3.

Preterm infants do have a different profile than full-term infants. For instance, Tiffany Field (1979) found that four-month-old preterm infants vocalized less, fussed more, and avoided eye contact more than their full-term counterparts. Other researchers have found differences in the information-processing skills of preterm and full-term infants. In one investigation, Susan Rose and her colleagues (1988) found that seven-month-old high-risk preterm infants were less visually attentive to novelty and showed deficits in visual recognition memory when compared with full-term infants.

Without doubt, preterm infants are perceived differently by the adults in their world. Consider the medical community—they know a great deal about the problems confronting preterm infants. The staff-patient ratio of preterm infants is often one of the most favorable in the hospital. And the preterm infant is immersed in an exotic environment of high-technology life support

Kilogram Kids

K ilogram Kids'' weigh less than 2.3 pounds (which is 1 kilogram or 1,000 grams) and are very premature. The task of saving one is not easy. At the Stanford University Medical Center in Palo Alto, California, 98 percent of the preterm babies survive; however, 32 percent of those between 750 and 1,000 grams do not and 76 percent of those below 750 grams do not. Approximately 250,000 preterm babies are born in the United States each year and 15,000 to 20,000 of these weigh less than 1,000 grams.

Neonatal intensive care units report not only increased survival rates but decreases in the severity of the handicaps of those babies who suffer handicaps. In the neonatal intensive care units banks of blipping lights, blinking numbers, and beeping alarms stand guard over the extreme preterm infant. He lies on a water bed that gently undulates; the water bed is in an incubator controlled for temperature and humidity by the baby's own body. So many electronic machines and computerized devices incessantly monitor, report, and sound warnings on such vital signs as brain waves, heartbeat, blood gases, and respiratory rate that a team of technicians is needed to service them around the clock. All of this can be very expensive— five to six months can run as high as $200,000, although it usually is within five figures.

Kilogram babies are by definition not flawed but merely perilously ahead of schedule. After its size and sex, the question parents of a preterm infant ask is, "What is wrong with my baby?" The baby is normal. His form, his needs, how he is behaving—everything is precisely normal for his current stage of development.

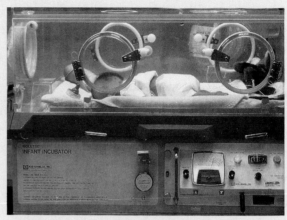

A "kilogram kid." How might the kilogram kid's development be different from that of a full-term infant?

Preterm infants—even the kilogram kids—are no more sick than you are. But the kilogram kid is as close to death as you would be if you were quickly transported to the moon's surface or the ocean's bottom. Being on the moon or the ocean floor is not a disease, but it certainly is life threatening. The kilogram kid has been taken from an environment to which he is beautifully adapted to one that can be deadly. Without an amniotic sac to protect him, without a placenta to feed him, breathe for him, oxygenate his blood, and eliminate his waste, he needs a space suit with all kinds of tubes and waves and needles (Fincher, 1982).

---

equipment (Als, 1988). Parents undoubtedly also perceive their preterm infant differently than the parents of full-term infants. Parents know that their preterm infant is different and have reasonable fears about the infant's health and future. Preterm infants frequently remain in the hospital for a long time, making the parent's role as a competent caregiver difficult. Parents must cope with uncertainty for a lengthy period of time.

How do parents actually deal with their preterm infants? Before the newborn goes home from the hospital, mothers show less confidence in dealing with their preterm infant than the mothers of full-term infants. And they are less likely to hold the baby close, cuddle, and smile at the infant than the mothers of full-term infants. Possibly such mothers feel awkward or perceive the preterm baby as more fragile than a full-term baby. Anticipated interaction with the infant may be frustrated and a close attachment bond shut off (Campos & others, 1983).

Because parents have to deal with infants who are physically and behaviorally different from full-term infants, possibly the differences in the way

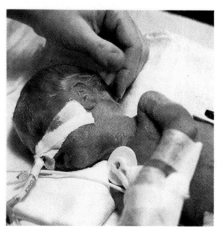

Preterm infants are often hooked up to electronic machines and computerized devices that constantly monitor vital signs.

mothers handle preterm infants are based on their sincere motivation to negotiate this infant difference. One program to facilitate maternal adjustment to the care of a low-birth-weight infant was successful (Rauh & others, 1988). The mothers developed more self-confidence and satisfaction with mothering, as well as more favorable perceptions of their infant's temperament. Other research indicates that by the beginning of the preschool years many of the early differences between preterm and full-term infants have diminished, both in terms of the child's skills and parenting behavior (Greenberg & Crnic, 1988; Siegel, 1984).

Conclusions about Preterm Infants

What conclusions can we draw from research on preterm infants? Four such conclusions seem appropriate at this time (Kopp, 1983, 1987).

1. As intensive-care technology has improved, there have been fewer serious consequences of preterm births. For instance, from 1961 to 1965, the manner of feeding preterm infants changed and intravenous fluid therapy came into use. From 1966 to 1968, better control of hypoxemia (oxygen deficiency) resulted. In 1971, artificial ventilation was introduced. And in the mid-1970s, neonatal support systems became less intrusive and damaging to the infant.
2. Infants born with an identifiable problem are likely to have a poorer developmental future than infants born without a recognizable problem. For instance, extremely sick or extremely tiny babies are less likely to survive than healthy or normal weight babies.
3. Social class differences are associated with the preterm infant's development. Put simply, the higher the socioeconomic status, the more favorable is the developmental outcome for a newborn. Social class differences are tied to a number of other differences. For example, quality of environment, cigarette and alcohol consumption, IQ, and knowledge of competent parenting strategies are associated with social class; less positive characteristics are associated with lower-class families.
4. We do not have solid evidence that preterm infants, as a rule, have difficulty later in school. Nor is there good evidence that these preterm children perform poorly on IQ and information-processing tests. Such claims to the contrary were made just one or two decades ago.

Measures of Neonatal Health and Responsiveness

For many years, the **Apgar scale,** shown in table 3.1, has been used to assess the newborn's health. One minute and five minutes after birth, the obstetrician or nurse gives the newborn a reading of zero, one, or two on each of five signs: heart rate, respiratory effort, muscle tone, body color, and reflex irritability. A high total score of seven to ten indicates that the newborn's condition is good, a score of five indicates that there may be developmental difficulties, and a score of three or below signals an emergency and indicates that survival may be in doubt.

While the Apgar Scale is used immediately after birth to identify high-risk infants who need resuscitation, another scale is used for long-term neurological assessment—the **Brazelton Neonatal Behavioral Assessment Scale**

Table 3.1
The Apgar Scale

	Score		
	0	1	2
Heart rate	Absent	Slow—less than 100 beats per minute	Fast—100–140 beats per minute
Respiratory effort	No breathing for more than one minute	Irregular and slow	Good breathing with normal crying
Muscle tone	Limp and flaccid	Weak, inactive, but some flexion of extremities	Strong, active motion
Body color	Blue and pale	Body pink, but extremities blue	Entire body pink
Reflex irritability	No response	Grimace	Coughing, sneezing, and crying

From V. A. Apgar, "A Proposal for a New Method of Evaluation of a Newborn Infant" in *Anesthesia and Analgesia: Current Researches 32*: 260–267. Copyright © 1953 International Anesthesia Research Society, Cleveland, OH. Reprinted by permission.

Table 3.2
The Twenty-Six Categories on the Brazelton Neonatal Behavioral Assessment Scale

1. Response decrement to repeated visual stimuli
2. Response decrement to rattle
3. Response decrement to bell
4. Response decrement to pinprick
5. Orienting response to inanimate visual stimuli
6. Orienting response to inanimate auditory stimuli
7. Orienting response to animate visual stimuli—examiner's face
8. Orienting response to animate auditory stimuli—examiner's voice
9. Orienting responses to animate visual and auditory stimuli
10. Quality and duration of alert periods
11. General muscle tone—in resting and in response to being handled, passive and active
12. Motor activity
13. Traction responses as he or she is pulled to sit
14. Cuddliness—responses to being cuddled by examiner
15. Defensive movements—reactions to a cloth over his or her face
16. Consolability with intervention by examiner
17. Peak of excitement and capacity to control self
18. Rapidity of buildup to crying state
19. Irritability during the examination
20. General assessment of kind and degree of activity
21. Tremulousness
22. Amount of startling
23. Lability of skin color—measuring autonomic lability
24. Lability of states during entire examination
25. Self-quieting activity—attempts to console self and control state
26. Hand-to-mouth activity

From *Cultural Perspective on Child Development* by Daniel A. Wagner and Harold W. Stevenson. Copyright © 1982 W. H. Freeman and Company. Reprinted by permission.

(Brazelton, 1973, 1984, 1988; Brazelton, Nugent, & Lester, 1987). This scale includes an evaluation of the newborn's reactions to people. The Brazelton Scale usually is given on the third day of life and then repeated several days later. Twenty reflexes are assessed along with reactions to various circumstances, such as the neonate's reaction to a rattle. The examiner rates the newborn on each of twenty-six different categories (table 3.2). As an indication

Table 3.3

The Assessment of Cuddliness on the Brazelton Neonatal Behavioral
Assessment Scale

Score	Infant behavior
1	The infant resists being held and continually pushes away, thrashes, and stiffens.
2	The infant resists being held most of the time.
3	The infant does not resist but does not participate either, acting like a rag doll.
4	The infant eventually molds into the examiner's arms after considerable nestling and cuddling efforts by the examiner.
5	The infant usually molds and relaxes when initially held, nestling into the examiner's neck or crook of the elbow. The infant leans forward when held on the examiner's shoulder.
6	The infant always molds at the beginning, as described above.
7	The infant always molds initially with nestling and turns toward body and leans forward.
8	The infant molds and relaxes, nestles and turns head, leans forward on the shoulder, fits feet into cavity of other arm, and all of the body participates.
9	All of the above take place, and in addition, the infant grasps the examiner and clings.

From *In The Beginning: Development in the First Two Years*, by J. E. Rosenblith and J. E. Sims-Knight. Copyright © 1985 by Wadsworth, Inc. Reprinted by permission of Brooks/Cole Publishing Company, Pacific Grove, CA 93950.

of how detailed the ratings are, consider item 14 in table 3.2—cuddliness. As shown in table 3.3, nine categories are involved in assessing this item, with infant behavior scored on a continuum that ranges from the infant being very resistant to being held to the infant being extremely cuddly and clinging. The Brazelton Scale not only is used as a sensitive index of neurological integrity in the week after birth but it also is used widely as a measure in many research studies on infant development. In recent versions of scoring the Brazelton Scale, Brazelton and his colleagues (1987) categorize the twenty-six items into four different categories—physiological, motoric, state, and interaction. They also classify the baby in global terms such as worrisome, normal, or superior, based on these categories.

A very low Brazelton score can indicate brain damage. But if the infant merely seems sluggish in responding to social circumstances, parents are encouraged to give the infant attention and to undergo **Brazelton training,** which involves using the Brazelton Scale to show parents how their newborn responds to people (Brazelton, 1979, 1987). As part of the training, parents are shown how the neonate can respond positively to people and how such responses can be stimulated. Brazelton training has improved the social interaction of high-risk infants and the social skills of healthy, responsive infants (Widmayer & Field, 1980; Worobey & Belsky, 1982). Considerable interest has been generated in increasing the caregiver's recognition and management of stress in the neonatal period (Gorski, 1988; Klauss, 1988).

Bonding

Perhaps the most controversial strategy focused on the mother's role in the newborn's life involves what is called **bonding.** Advocates of bonding argue that long-term consequences for the infant's development are set in motion during the first minutes, hours, or days of the newborn's interaction with the social world. Situations surrounding delivery may prevent or make difficult the occurrence of an emotional bond between the infant and mother. For example, preterm infants are isolated from their mothers to an even greater degree

Biological and Perceptual Development

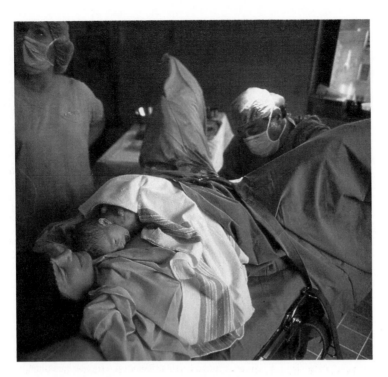

than full-term infants. In many hospitals it is common to give the mother drugs to make the delivery less painful. The drugs may make the mother drowsy and may interfere with her ability to respond to and stimulate the newborn.

Many pediatricians have been adamant about the importance of bonding during the initial hours and days of the newborn's life. In particular, Marshall Klaus and John Kennell (1976) influenced the introduction of bonding in many hospitals. They argue that the first few days of life are a critical period in development. During this period, close contact, especially physical contact, between the newborn and the mother is believed to create an important emotional attachment that provides a foundation for optimal development for years to come.

Is there evidence that such close contact between the mother and the newborn is absolutely critical for optimal development later in life? While some research supports the bonding hypothesis (Klaus & Kennell, 1976), a growing body of research challenges the significance of the first few days of life as a critical period (Bakeman & Brown, 1980; Rode & others, 1981). Indeed, the extreme form of the bonding hypothesis—that the newborn must have close contact with the mother in the first few days of life to develop optimally—simply is not true.

Nonetheless, the weakness of the maternal-infant bonding research should not be used as an excuse to keep motivated mothers from interacting with their infants in the postpartum period because such contact brings pleasure to many mothers. In the case of some mother-infant pairs—preterm infants, adolescent mothers, or mothers from disadvantaged circumstances— the practice of bonding may set in motion a climate for improved mother-infant interaction after the mother and infant leave the hospital (Maccoby & Martin, 1983).

We have discussed a number of dimensions of the birth process. To help you remember the main points of this discussion turn to Concept Table 3.2.

Concept Table 3.2
The Birth Process

Concept	Processes/Related Ideas	Characteristics/Description
Childbirth strategies	Their nature	Controversy exists over how childbirth should proceed. Standard childbirth has been criticized and the Leboyer and Lamaze methods have been developed as alternatives. Medical doctors deliver most babies in the United States, but midwives sometimes are used. Most babies in the United States are delivered in hospitals, but birthing centers also may be used.
Stages of birth and delivery complications	Stages	Three stages of birth have been defined—the first lasts about twelve to twenty-four hours for a woman having her first child and the cervix dilates to about four inches; the second stage begins when the baby's head moves through the cervix and ends with the baby's complete emergence; the third stage is afterbirth.
	Complications	A baby can move through the birth canal too rapidly or too slowly. A delivery that is too fast is called precipitate; when delivery is too slow anoxia may result.
The use of drugs during childbirth	Drugs used to relieve pain and anxiety and to speed up delivery	A wide variety of tranquilizers, sedatives, and analgesics are used to relieve the expectant mother's pain and anxiety, while oxytocin is used to speed up delivery. It is hard to make general statements about drug effects, but it is known that birth weight and social class are more powerful predictors of problems than drugs. A specific drug can have mixed effects and the overall amount of medication needs to be considered.
Preterm infants and age-weight considerations	Types	Preterm infants are those born prior to thirty-eight weeks after conception. Infants born after a regular gestation period of thirty-eight to forty-two weeks but who weigh less than five and one-half pounds are called low-birth-weight infants.
	Conclusions	As intensive-care technology has improved, preterm babies have benefited considerably. Infants born with an identifiable problem have a poorer developmental future than those born without a recognizable problem. Social class differences are associated with the preterm infant's development. There is no solid evidence that preterm infants perform more poorly than full-term infants when they are assessed years later in school.
Measures of neonatal health and responsiveness	Types	For many years the Apgar Scale has been used to assess the newborn's health. A more recently developed test—the Brazelton Neonatal Behavioral Assessment Scale—is used for long-term neurological assessment. It not only assesses the newborn's neurological integrity but also social responsiveness. If the newborn is sluggish, Brazelton training is recommended.
Bonding	Its nature	There is evidence that bonding—establishment of a close mother-infant bond in the first hours or days after birth—is not critical for optimal development, although for some mother-infant pairs it may stimulate interaction after they leave the hospital.

Summary

I. The Course of Prenatal Development

Prenatal development is divided into three periods. The germinal period lasts from conception to about ten to fourteen days later. The fertilized egg is called a zygote. The period ends when the zygote attaches to the uterine wall. The embryonic period lasts from two weeks to eight weeks after conception. The embryo differentiates into three layers, life support systems develop, and organ systems form (organogenesis). The fetal period lasts from two months after conception until nine months or when the infant is born. Growth and development continue their dramatic course and organ systems mature to the point where life can be sustained outside the womb.

II. Miscarriage and Abortion

A miscarriage, or spontaneous abortion, happens when pregnancy ends before the developing organism is mature enough to survive outside of the womb. Estimates indicate that about 15 to 20 percent of all pregnancies end this way, many without the mother's knowledge. Induced abortion is a complex issue—medically, psychologically, and socially. An unwanted pregnancy is stressful for the woman regardless of how it is resolved. A recent ethical issue focuses on the use of fetal tissue in transplant operations.

III. Teratology and Hazards to Prenatal Development

Teratology is the field that investigates the causes of congenital (birth) defects. Any agent that causes birth defects is called a teratogen. Maternal diseases and infections can cause damage by crossing the placental barrier, or they can be destructive during the birth process itself. Among the maternal diseases and conditions believed to be involved in possible birth defects are rubella, syphilis, genital herpes, the mother's age, nutrition, and emotional state and stress. Thalidomide was a tranquilizer given to pregnant mothers to reduce morning sickness. In the early 1960s, thousands of babies were malformed as a consequence of their mothers taking this drug. Alcohol, cigarette smoking, heroin, and cocaine are other ways drugs can adversely affect prenatal and infant development.

IV. Childbirth Strategies

Controversy exists over how childbirth should proceed. Standard childbirth has been criticized and the Leboyer and Lamaze methods have been developed as alternatives. Medical doctors deliver most babies in the United States, but midwives sometimes are used. Most babies in the United States are born in hospitals, but birthing centers also may be used.

V. Stages of Birth and Delivery Complications

Three stages of birth have been defined—the first lasts about twelve to twenty-four hours for a woman having her first child and the cervix dilates to about four inches; the second stage begins when the baby's head moves through the cervix and ends with the baby's complete emergence; the third stage is afterbirth. A baby can move through the birth canal too quickly or too slowly. A delivery that is too fast is called precipitate; when delivery is too slow anoxia may result.

VI. The Use of Drugs during Childbirth

A wide variety of tranquilizers, sedatives, and analgesics are used to relieve the expectant mother's pain and anxiety, while oxytocin is used to speed up delivery. It is hard to make general statements about drug effects, but it is known that birth weight and social class are more powerful predictors of problems than drugs. A specific drug can have mixed effects and the overall amount of medication needs to be considered.

VII. Preterm Infants and Age-Weight Considerations

Preterm infants are those born prior to thirty-eight weeks after conception. Infants born after a regular gestation period of thirty-eight to forty-two weeks but who weigh less than five and one-half pounds are called low-birth-weight infants. As intensive-care technology has improved, preterm babies have benefited considerably. Infants born with an identifiable problem have a poorer developmental future than those born without a recognizable problem. Social class differences are associated with the preterm infant's development. There is no solid evidence that preterm infants perform more poorly than full-term infants when they are assessed years later in school.

VIII. Measures of Neonatal Health and Responsiveness

For many years the Apgar Scale has been used to assess the newborn's health. A more recently developed test—the Brazelton Neonatal Behavioral Assessment Scale—is used for long-term neurological assessment. It not only assesses the newborn's neurological integrity but also social responsiveness. If the newborn is sluggish, Brazelton training is recommended.

IX. Bonding

There is evidence that bonding—establishment of a close mother-infant bond in the first hours or days after birth—is not critical for optimal development, although for some mother-infant pairs it may stimulate interaction after they leave the hospital.

Key Terms

zygote 58
germinal period 58
blastula 58
blastocyst 59
trophoblast 59
implantation 59
embryonic period 59
endoderm 59
ectoderm 59
mesoderm 59
placenta 59
umbilical cord 59
amnion 59
organogenesis 59
fetal period 60

teratology 63
fetal alcohol syndrome (FAS) 66
Leboyer method 69
Lamaze method 69
afterbirth 71
precipitate 71
anoxia 71
breech position 71
oxytocin 71
preterm infant 72
low-birth-weight infants 72
Apgar Scale 74
Brazelton Neonatal Behavioral Assessment Scale 74
Brazelton training 76
bonding 76

Suggested Readings

Brazelton, T. B., & Lester, B. M. (1982). *New approaches to developmental screenings of infants.* New York: Elsevier.
A group of experts on infant development relate new developments in the assessment of newborns.

Falkner, F., & Macy, C. (1980). *Pregnancy and birth.* New York: Harper & Row.
An easy-to-read description of experiences during pregnancy and the nature of childbearing.

Goldberg, S., & Devitto, B. A. (1983). *Born too soon: Preterm birth and early development.* San Francisco: W. H. Freeman.
Gives recent information about the nature of preterm infants and ways to socially interact with them.

Nilsson, L, (1966). *A child is born.* New York: Delacourt.
Contains an abundance of breathtaking photographs that take you inside the mother's womb to see the development of the zygote, embryo, and fetus.

Physical, Motor, and Perceptual Development

he creature has poor motor coordination and can move itself only with great difficulty. Its general behavior appears to be disorganized, and though it cries when uncomfortable, it has few other vocalizations. In fact, it sleeps most of the time, about sixteen to seventeen hours a day. You are curious about this creature and want to know more about what it can do. You think to yourself, "I wonder if it can see? How could I find out?"

You obviously have a communication problem with the creature. You must devise a way that will allow the creature to "tell" you that it can see. While examining the creature one day, you make an interesting discovery. When you move a large object toward it, it moves its head backward, as if to avoid a collision with the object. The creature's head movement suggests that it has at least some vision.

In case you haven't already guessed, the creature you have been reading about is the human infant and the role you played from outer space is that of a developmentalist interested in devising techniques to learn about the infant's visual perception. After years of work, scientists have developed research tools and methods sophisticated enough to examine the subtle abilities of infants and to interpret their complex actions. Videotape equipment makes it possible to investigate elusive behaviors and high-speed computers make it possible to perform complex data analysis in minutes instead of months and years. Other sophisticated equipment is used to monitor respiration, heart rate, body movement, visual fixation, and sucking behavior, which provide clues to what is going on inside of the infant.

Among the first things developmentalists were able to demonstrate was that infants have highly developed perceptual motor systems. Until recently even nursery personnel in maternity hospitals often believed that newborns were blind at birth, and they told mothers this. And most parents were told that their newborns could not taste, smell, or feel pain. As you will discover later in this chapter, we now know that newborns can see (although their visual perception is fuzzy), that they can taste, that they can smell, and that they can feel pain. Before we turn to the fascinating world of the infant's perception, though, we will discuss a number of ideas about physical development.

Physical Growth and Development in Infancy

How do infants respond to their world? What is the developmental course of emotions in infancy? What are the infant's states like? We consider each of these questions in turn.

Reflexes

The newborn is not an empty-headed organism. Among other things, it has some basic reflexes that are genetically carried survival mechanisms. For example, the newborn has no fear of water. It will naturally hold its breath and contract its throat to keep water from rushing in.

Reflexes govern the newborn's movements, which are automatic and beyond the newborn's control. For example, if you stroke the newborn's hand or foot on the back or top, the whole arm or leg withdraws slightly and the hand or foot flexes and then returns so that fingers or toes may grasp your finger. This withdrawal reflex only exists until the baby begins to use his limbs in a different way—legs for standing and stepping, arms for reaching.

The newborn has many other reflexes. If you hold the infant in a standing position and gently press the sole of one foot and then the other to the bed, the infant will draw up each leg successively as if walking. The newborn actually can "walk" across a bed. Almost a year after the newborn's walk reflex vanishes, it reappears as the voluntary, complex art of walking.

One of the most frequent and dramatic reflexes of the newborn is the **Moro reflex,** a vestige from our primate ancestory. If infants are handled roughly, hear a loud noise, see a bright light, or feel a sudden change of position, they startle, arch their backs, and throw their heads back. At the same time, they fling out their arms and legs, then rapidly close them to the center of their bodies, and then flex as if they were falling. As they cry, they startle, then cry because of the startle. This reflex—normal in all newborns—tends to disappear at three to four months of age. Steady pressure on any part of the infant's body calms the infant. If you hold the infant's arm flexed at her shoulder, she will quiet even though undressed and free of restraints. Table 4.1 presents additional information about the newborn's repertoire of reflexes. Some reflexes are important in the baby's life—crying in response to pain and sucking, for example. Although the usefulness of many neonatal reflexes is unclear, if some relexes—such as the Moro reflex—are weak, brain damage may be indicated. Reflexes are tested in the newborn as a way of discovering whether the nervous system is working properly.

Physical, Motor, and Perceptual Development

Table 4.1
The Newborn's Reflex Repertoire

If you	Then the baby's
Tap the bridge of the nose, shine a bright light suddenly into the eyes, clap hands about eighteen inches from the infant's head, or touch the white of the eye with cotton	Eyes close tightly.
Make sudden contact or noise	Head drops backward, neck extends, arms and legs fling outward and back sharply (Moro reflex).
Extend forearms at elbow	Arms flex briskly.
Lightly prick soles of feet	Knee and foot flex.
Stand infant; press foot to bed	Feet step.
Pull baby to sit	Eyes snap open, shoulders tense. Baby tries unsuccessfully to right head (China doll reflex).
Pull baby on tummy on flat surface	Head turns to side and lifts. Baby crawls, lifts self with arms.
Support chest on water surace	Arms and legs "swim."
Place baby on back and turn head to side	Body arches away from face side; arm on face side extends, leg draws up; other arm flexes (tonic neck reflex).
Stroke foot or hand on top	Limb withdraws, arches, returns to grasp.
Stroke palm or sole at base of digits	Limb grasps.
Stroke outside of sole	Toes spread, large toe sticks up.
Tap upper lips sharply	Lips protrude.
Stroke cheek or mouth	Mouth roots; head turns and tongue moves toward stroking object; mouth sucks.
Stroke cheek or palm	Mouth roots; arm flexes; hand goes to open mouth.
Place object over nose and mouth.	Mouth works vigorously; head twists, arms fling across face.
Stroke leg, upper part of body	Opposite leg or hand crosses to push your hand away; withdraws.
Rotate baby to side	Head turns, eyes precede direction of rotation.
Suspend by legs	Body curls to upside-down ball, legs extend, arms drop into straight line; neck arches backward.

Some reflexes present in the newborn—such as coughing, blinking, and yawning—persist throughout our lives. They are important for the adult just as they are for the infant. Other reflexes, though, disappear in the several months following birth as the infant's brain functions mature and voluntary control over many behaviors develops. Let's look at three reflexes in greater detail—sucking, crying, and smiling.

Sucking

Sucking is an important means of obtaining nutrition and it also is an enjoyable, soothing activity. An investigation by T. Berry Brazelton (1956) involved observations of infants for more than one year to determine the incidence of their sucking when they were not nursing and how their sucking changed as they grew older. More than 85 percent of the infants engaged in considerable sucking behavior unrelated to feeding. They sucked their fingers, their fists, and pacifiers. By one year old, most had stopped the sucking behavior.

Parents should not worry when infants suck their thumbs, fist, or even a pacifier. Many parents, though, do begin to worry when thumb sucking persists into the preschool and elementary school years. As many as 40 percent of children continue to suck their thumbs after they have started school (Kessen,

Haith, & Salapatek, 1970). Most developmentalists do not attach a great deal of significance to this behavior and are not aware of parenting strategies that might have contributed to it. Individual differences in children's biological makeup to some degree may be involved in the continuation of sucking behavior.

Infant researchers are interested in nonnutritive sucking for another reason. **Nonnutritive sucking** is used as a measure in a large number of research studies with young infants beause young infants quit sucking when they attend to something, such as a picture or a vocalization. Nonnutritive sucking is one of the ingenius ways developmentalists, then, study the young infant's attention and learning.

Nutritive sucking is the infant's route to nourishment. Neonates' sucking capabilities vary considerably—some newborns are efficient at forceful sucking and getting milk while others are not so adept and also get tired before they are full. It takes most newborns several weeks to establish a sucking style that is coordinated with the way the mother is holding the infant, the way milk is coming out of the bottle or breast, and the infant's speed and temperament.

Crying and Smiling

Crying and smiling are emotional behaviors that are important in the infant's communication with the world. Crying is the infant's first emotional or affective behavior. Newborns spend 6 to 7 percent of their day crying, although some infants cry more, others less (Korner & others, 1981). Infants' earliest cries are reflexive reactions to discomfort. The cries may signify information about the infant's biological state and possibly indicate distress. They are highly differentiated and have different patterns of frequency, intensity, and pause.

Most adults can determine whether the infant's cries signify anger or pain. Even for brief segments of infant crying, adults can distinguish between aversive and arousing cries (more distressful) and those indicating hunger (less distressful). Even shortly after birth, then, infants' cries communicate information (Zeskind, 1987; Zeskind & Marshall, 1988).

Should a crying infant be given attention and be soothed, or does such parental behavior spoil the infant? Many years ago, John Watson (1928) argued that parents spend too much time responding to the infant's crying and as a consequence reward the crying and increase its incidence. By contrast, more recent arguments by ethologists such as Mary Ainsworth (1979) stress that it is difficult to respond too much to the infant's crying. Ainsworth views a caregiver's responsiveness to infant crying as contributing to the formation of a secure attachment between the infant and the caregiver. One investigation (Bell & Ainsworth, 1972) found that mothers who responded quickly to their infant's crying at three months of age had infants who cried less when assessed later in the first year of life. Other research by behaviorists (e.g., Gewirtz, 1977) suggests that a quick, soothing response by a caregiver to crying increases the infant's subsequent crying. Controversy, then, still surrounds the issue of when and how caregivers should respond to infant crying.

Smiling is another important communicative behavior of the infant. Two kinds of smiling can be distinguished in infants—one reflexive, the other social. At some point in the first month after birth, an expression appears on the infant's face that adults call a smile; this is a **reflexive smile** because it does not occur in response to external stimuli. The reflexive smile occurs most often during irregular patterns of sleep and does not appear when the infant is in an alert state. A **social smile,** which typically occurs in response to a face, usually does not occur until two to three months of age (Emde, Gaensbauer,

& Harmon, 1976). Others, however, feel that social smiling appears earlier than two months of age, arguing that an infant grins in response to voices as early as three weeks of age (Stroufe & Waters, 1976). The power and importance of the infant's smiles were appropriately summed up by the famous attachment theorist John Bowlby (1969): "Can we doubt that the more and better an infant smiles the better is he loved and cared for? It is fortunate for their survival that babies are so designed by Nature that they beguile and enslave mothers." Much more about Bowlby's fascinating ideas on attachment appear in chapter 12.

Emotions

If you cannot name an emotion, it does not exist. That was the dominant view of infant emotions for much of this century. But now a different picture has emerged, one that recognizes the infant's repertoire of emotions. Just as you will discover later in the chapter that seeing and hearing are more highly developed in infancy than was originally believed, we now know that interest, distress, and disgust are present early in infancy and can be communicated to parents. Much earlier than the arrival of language, infants add other emotions such as joy, anger, surprise, shyness, and fear to their capabilities.

What are the functions of emotions in infancy? Emotions are adaptive and promote survival, they serve as a form of communication, and they provide regulation (Barrett & Campos, 1987; Bretherton & others, 1986; Izard and Malatesta, 1987). For example, various fears—such as fear of the dark and fear of sudden changes in the environment—are adaptive because there are clear links between such events and possible danger. Infants also use emotions to inform others about their feelings and needs. The infant who smiles probably is telling others that she is feeling pleasant; the infant who cries probably is communicating that something is unpleasant. And infants use emotions to increase or decrease the distance between themselves and others. The infant who smiles may be encouraging someone to come closer; the infant who displays anger may be suggesting that an intruder should go away. Emotions influence the information the infant selects from the perceptual world and the behaviors the infant displays.

How can we find out if an infant is displaying emotion? Psychologist Carol Izard and his colleagues (Izard, 1982; Izard & Malatesta, 1987; La Barbera & others, 1976) have developed a system for decoding the emotional expressions on infants' faces. Izard wanted to discover which emotions were inborn, which emerged later, and under which conditions they were displayed. The conditions included being given an ice cube, having tape put on the backs of their hands, being handed a favorite toy and then having it taken away, being separated from and reunited with their mothers, being approached by a stranger, having their heads gently restrained, having a ticking clock held next to their ears, having a balloon popped in front of their faces, and being given camphor to sniff and lemon rind and orange juice to taste.

Izard's system for coding emotions has the imposing name Maximally Discriminative Facial Movement Coding System—or MAX for short. The coder, using MAX, watches slow-motion and stop-action videotapes of the infant's facial reactions to the circumstances described. Anger, for example, is indicated when the brows are sharply lowered and drawn together, the eyes are narrowed or squinted, and the mouth is open in an angular, squarelike shape. The key elements of emotional facial codes in infants are shown in figure 4.1 and the developmental timetable of their emergence in infancy is shown in table 4.2.

Figure 4.1
Facial expressions of emotions and their characteristics.

Joy
Mouth forms smile, cheeks
lifted, twinkle in eyes.

Anger
Brows drawn together and downward,
eyes fixed, mouth squarish.

Interest
Brows raised or knit, mouth
softly rounded, lips pursed.

Disgust
Nose wrinkled, upper lip
raised, tongue pushed outward.

Surprise
Brows raised, eyes widened,
mouth rounded in oval shape.

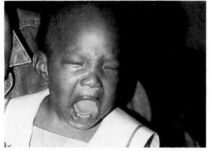

Distress
Eyes tightly closed, mouth, as
in anger, squared and angular.

Sadness
Brows' inner corners raised,
drawn out and down.

Fear
Brows level, drawn in
and up, eyelids lifted,
mouth retracted.

Physical, Motor, and Perceptual Development

Table 4.2
The Development Course of Infants' Emotions

Emotional Expression	Approximate Time of Emergence
Interest	Present at birth
Neonatal smile (a sort of half smile that appears spontaneously for no apparent reason)*	
Startle response*	
Distress*	
Disgust	
Social smile	4 to 6 weeks
Anger	3 to 4 months
Surprise	
Sadness	
Fear	5 to 7 months
Shame/shyness	6 to 8 months
Contempt	Second year of life
Guilt	

*The neonatal smile, the startle response, and distress in response to pain are precursors of the social smile and the emotions of surprise and sadness, which appear later. No evidence exists to suggest that they are related to inner feelings when they are observed in the first few weeks of life.

States

To chart and understand the infant's development, developmentalists have constructed different classification schemes of the infant's states (Berg & Berg, 1987; Brown, 1964; Prechtl, 1965; Wolff, 1966). One classification scheme (Brown, 1964) describes seven infant states.

1. *Deep sleep.* The infant lies motionless with eyes closed, has regular breathing, shows no vocalization, and does not respond to outside stimulation.
2. *Regular sleep.* The infant moves very little, breathing might be raspy or involve wheezing, and respirations may be normal or move from normal to irregular.
3. *Disturbed sleep.* There is a variable amount of movement, the infant's eyelids are closed but might flutter, breathing is irregular, and there may be some squawks, sobs, and sighs.
4. *Drowsy.* The infant's eyes are open or partly open and appear glassy, there is little movement (although startles and free movement may occur), vocalizations are more regular than in disturbed sleep, and some transitional sounds may be heard.
5. *Alert Activity.* This is the state most often viewed by parents as being awake. The infant's eyes are open and bright, a variety of free movements are shown, fretting may occur, skin may redden, and there may be irregular breathing when the infant feels tension.
6. *Alert and focused.* This kind of attention is often seen in older children but is unusual in the neonate. The child's eyes are open and bright. Some motor activity may occur, but it is integrated around a specific activity. This state may occur when focusing on some sound or visual stimulus.
7. *Inflexibly focused.* In this state, the infant is awake but does not react to external stimuli—two examples are sucking and wild crying. During wild crying the infant may thrash about, but the eyes are closed as screams pour out.

On the 1 to 7 classification scheme of sleeping-waking described in the text, what rating would you give to this infant?

Using classification schemes such as the one just described, researchers have identified many different aspects of the infant's development. One such aspect is the sleeping-waking cycle. Each night, something lures us from our work, our play, our loved ones—the sandman's spell claims more of our time than any other pursuit. As an infant, sleep consumed even more of our time than it does now. Newborns sleep for sixteen to seventeen hours a day, although some sleep more, others less. The range is from a low of about ten hours to a high of about twenty-one hours (Parmalee, Wenner, & Schulz, 1964). The longest period of sleep is not always between 11 P.M. and 7 A.M. While total sleep remains somewhat consistent for young infants, the patterns of sleep during the day do not always follow a rhythmic pattern—an infant might change from sleeping several long bouts of seven or eight hours to three or four shorter sessions only several hours in duration. By about one month of age, most infants have begun to sleep longer at night, and by about four months of age, they usually have moved closer to adultlike sleep patterns, spending their longest span of sleep at night and their longest span of waking during the day (Coons & Guilleminault, 1982, 1984).

Researchers also are intrigued by different forms of infant sleep. This intrigue focuses on how much of the infant's sleep is **REM sleep**—rapid eye movement sleep (Berg & Berg, 1987) (figure 4.2). Children and adults who have been awakened in sleep laboratories during REM sleep frequently report that they were dreaming (Webb, 1975). Most adults spend about one-fifth of their night in REM sleep; their REM sleep usually appears about one hour after non-REM sleep. However, about half of an infant's sleep is REM sleep; infants often begin their sleep cycle with REM rather than non-REM sleep. By the time infants reach three months of age, the percentage of time spent

Figure 4.2
During REM sleep, our eyes move rapidly as if we were observing the images we see moving in our dreams. During REM sleep, dreams increase dramatically. About one-half of an infant's sleep is REM sleep. What might be the functions of REM sleep in the infant's development?

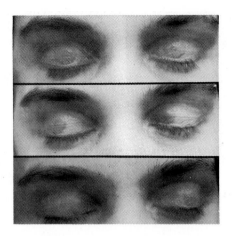

in REM sleep falls to about 40 percent and REM sleep no longer begins the sleep cycle. The large amount of time spent in REM sleep may provide young infants with added self-stimulation since they spend less time awake than older infants. REM sleep also may promote the brain's development.

Physical Growth and Motor Development

Physically, newborns are admittedly limited. Newborns are tiny—from head to heels, they are about twenty inches long and weigh seven pounds. They are bound by where they are put, and they are at the mercy of their bodily needs. Their heart beats twice as fast as an adult's—120 beats a minute—and they breathe twice as fast as an adult does—about thirty-three times a minute. They urinate as many as eighteen times and move their bowels from four to seven times in twenty-four hours. On the average, they are alert and comfortable for only about thirty minutes in a four-hour period.

The infant's pattern of physical development in the first two years of life is exciting. At birth, the neonate has a gigantic head (relative to the rest of the body) that flops around in uncontrollable fashion; she possesses reflexes that are dominated by evolutionary movements. In the span of twelve months, the infant becomes capable of sitting anywhere, standing, stooping, climbing, and probably walking. During the second year, growth decelerates, but rapid increases in such activities as running and climbing take place.

Among the important changes in growth are those involving the cephalocaudal and proximodistal sequences, gross and fine motor skills, rhythmic motor behavior, and the brain. We examine each of these in turn.

Cephalocaudal and Proximodistal Sequences

The **cephalocaudal pattern** means that the greatest growth always occurs at the top of the individual—the head—with physical growth in size, weight, and feature differentiation gradually working its way down from top to bottom (for example, neck, shoulders, middle trunk, and so on). This same pattern occurs in the head area because the top parts of the head—the eyes and brain—grow faster than the lower parts—such as the jaw. This pattern is illustrated in figure 4.3. As shown in the figure, an extraordinary proportion of the total body is occupied by the head at birth, but by the time the individual reaches maturity, this proportion is almost cut in half.

In a second pattern of development—the **proximodistal pattern**—growth starts at the center of the body and moves toward the extremities. An example of this is the early maturation of muscular control of the trunk and arms as compared with that of the hands and fingers.

Biological and Perceptual Development

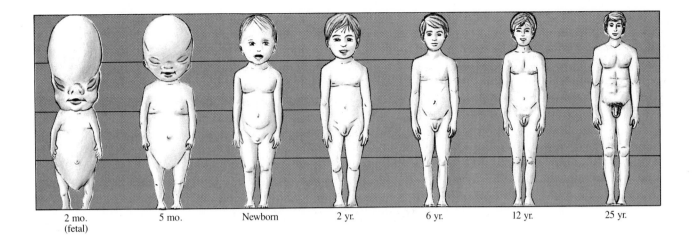

2 mo.
(fetal)　　　　5 mo.　　　　Newborn　　　　2 yr.　　　　6 yr.　　　　12 yr.　　　　25 yr.

Figure 4.3
Changes in body form and proportion during prenatal and postnatal growth.

Gross Motor and Fine Motor Skills

In addition to cephalocaudal and proximodistal growth patterns, we also can describe growth in terms of **gross motor skills**—those skills involving large muscle activities like moving one's arms and walking—and **fine motor skills**—those involving more fine-grained movements like finger dexterity.

At birth, the infant has no appreciable coordination of the chest or arms. By about four months of age, however, two striking accomplishments occur in turn. The first is the infant's ability to hold the chest up in a facedown position (at about two months). The other is the ability to reach for objects placed within the infant's direct line of vision, without, of course, making any consistent contact with the objects (because the two hands don't work together and the coordination of vision and grasping is not yet possible) (at about three to four months of age). A little later, there is further progress in motor control. By five months, the infant can sit up with some support and grasp objects. By six months, the infant can roll over when lying down in a prone position.

At birth, the newborn is capable of supporting some weight with the legs. This is proven by formal tests of muscular strength. These tests use a specially constructed apparatus to measure the infant's leg resistance as the foot is pulled away by a calibrated spring device. This ability is also evidenced by the infant's partial support of its own weight when held upright by an adult. If the infant is given enough support by the adult, some forward movement is seen in a built-in stepping reflex, which disappears in a few months. Each leg is lifted, moved forward, and placed down, as if the infant were taking a series of steps. However, the sequence lasts only two to three steps, and, of course, the infant does not have sufficient balance or strength to execute the movement independently.

It is not until eleven months of age that the infant can walk with limited help from an adult. Sometime later (at about twelve to fourteen months), the infant can pull up to a standing position, then stand alone, and then finally walk (at about fifteen months). The actual age at which some milestone occurs may vary by as much as two to four months, especially among older infants. What remains fairly uniform, however, is the sequence of accomplishments. The remarkable achievement of posture and locomotion in infants is summarized in figure 4.4. An important implication of these motor achievements of infants is the increasing degree of independence that children accomplish. They can explore their environment more extensively and initiate social interaction with caregivers and peers.

Based on our discussion of locomotor achievements in the text, how old would you estimate this infant to be?

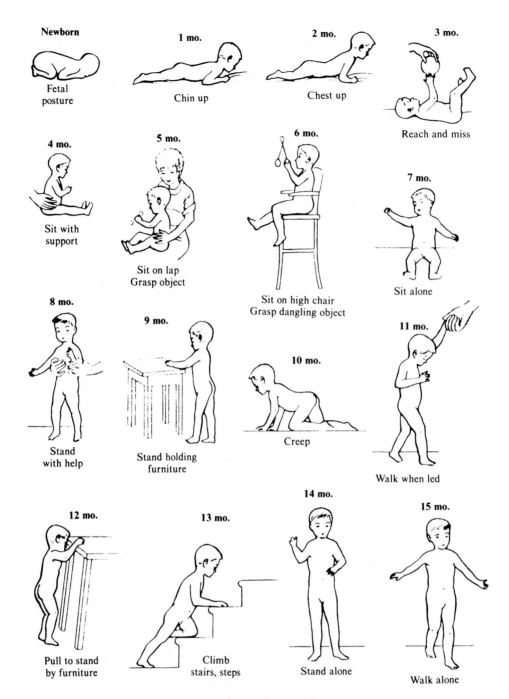

Newborn

Fetal
posture

1 mo.

Chin up

2 mo.

Chest up

3 mo.

Reach and miss

4 mo.

Sit with
support

5 mo.

Sit on lap
Grasp object

6 mo.

Sit on high chair
Grasp dangling object

7 mo.

Sit alone

8 mo.

Stand
with help

9 mo.

Stand holding
furniture

10 mo.

Creep

11 mo.

Walk when led

12 mo.

Pull to stand
by furniture

13 mo.

Climb
stairs, steps

14 mo.

Stand alone

15 mo.

Walk alone

Figure 4.4
The development of posture and locomotion
in infants.

Rhythmic Motor Behavior

During the first year of life, repetitious movement of the limbs, torso, and head
is common. Such **rhythmic motor behavior**—kicking, rocking, waving,
bouncing, banging, rubbing, scratching, swaying—has intrigued developmentalists for many years. These infant motor behaviors stand out not only
because they occur frequently but also because of the pleasure infants seem
to derive from performing them.

Explanations of rhythmic motor behavior are numerous. Arnold Gesell
(1954) saw rocking as a specific stage of development but warned that persistent rhythmic motor behavior was a sign of developmental delay or an impoverished environment. Jean Piaget (1967) referred to kicking and waving

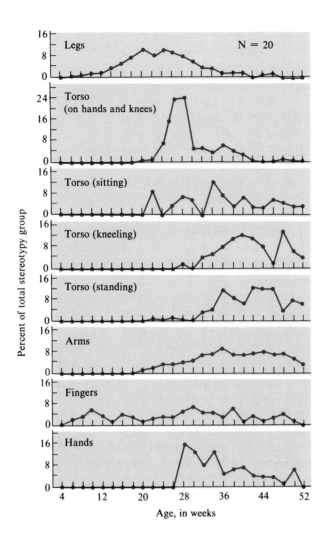

Figure 4.5
Frequency of rhythmic motor behavior in the first year of life. Frequencies are expressed as a percentage of the total bouts of rhythmical behavior observed at each age. The bouts are grouped by body parts.

as a stage of sensorimotor development when infants try to repeat a behavior that has an interesting effect on the environment. Psychoanalytic theorists interpret rocking as the infant's attempt to establish relations with an aloof mother. And pediatricians suggest that head banging is due to a bad temper.

More recently, Esther Thelen (1981, 1987) argued that rhythmic motor behavior serves an important adaptive function for infants in the first year of life. She believes it is an important transition between uncoordinated activity and complex, coordinated motor behavior. She conducted extraordinarily detailed observations of twenty normal infants from the time they were four weeks old until they were one year old. More than 16,000 bouts of rhythmic behavior were observed. Infants spent about 5 percent of their time in rhythmic motor behavior, although some infants at some ages spent as much as 40 percent of the time they were observed in rhythmic motor behavior. The forty-seven distinct movements observed included variations of kicking, waving, bouncing, scratching, banging, rubbing, thrusting, swaying, and twisting. When stereotyped movements were grouped by body part and posture, their frequencies showed certain developmental profiles over the first year, as shown in figure 4.5. Rhythmic leg behavior gradually increased at about one month, peaked at five to six months, and then declined, for example. If all rhythmic cycles are summed, the age of peak frequency was six to seven months, with a small decline in the last few months of the first year.

Figure 4.6
The development of dendritic spreading at birth, three months, six months, and twenty-four months in the cerebral cortex of the human infant. Note the increase in connectedness between neurons over the course of the first two years of life.

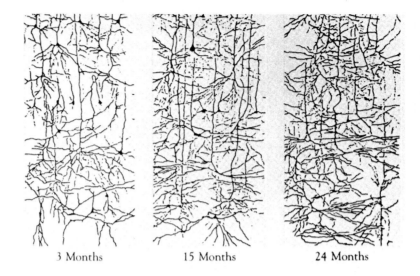

3 Months   15 Months   24 Months

A dramatic confirmation of the developmental importance of rhythmic motor behavior was documented by Selma Fraiberg (1977) with blind infants. Motor development in blind infants was characteristically uneven. Blind infants attained postural milestones such as sitting alone, "bridging" on hands and knees, and standing at ages comparable to sighted infants. Their loco-motor development was severely delayed, however, probably due to a lack of visual motivation to move forward. In normal infants, crawling follows soon after the infant assumes the hands and knees posture, for example. In blind infants, there may be four or more months delay between these events. None-theless, all the infants rocked vigorously in sitting, hands and knees, and standing postures; but unlike in normal infants, this rocking did not disappear. In Fraiberg's own words,

> In the blind infant, rhythmic activity may be more prolonged because, at each point along the gross motor sequence, the self-initiated mobility that should follow upon the new posture is delayed. Thus, a child with good control of his trunk in a bridging posture, with "readiness" we would say for creeping, might be observed on all fours, rocking steadily, "ready to go" with "no place to go." The motor impetus, which normally leads mobility was exercised in a vacuum. Again typically, when mobility was achieved, the stereotyped rocking was extinguished. (pp. 217, 218)

The Brain

As the infant walks, talks, runs, shakes a rattle, smiles, and frowns, changes in the brain occur. Consider that the infant began life as a single cell and that in nine months is born with a brain and nervous system that contains some 10 to 100 billion nerve cells. Indeed, at birth, the infant probably has all of the nerve cells—called neurons—it is going to have in its entire life. But at birth and in early infancy, the connectedness of all of these neurons is impoverished. As shown in figure 4.6, as the infant moves from birth to two years of age, the interconnections of neurons increase dramatically as the dendrites (the receiving part) of neurons branch out.

Undoubtedly, neurotransmitters change during the prenatal period and the infant years too—these are the tiny chemical substances that carry information across gaps from one neuron to the next. Little is known about neuro-transmitter changes in infancy, although changes in one important neurotransmitter—dopamine—has been documented in monkeys (Golman-Rakic &

Biological and Perceptual Development

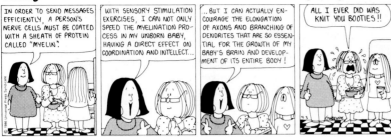

others, 1983). The concentration of dopamine in the prefrontal lobe—the area of the brain involved in higher cognitive functions such as problem solving—peaks at five months of age, declines until about eighteen to twenty-four months, and then increases again at two to three years of age. These changes in dopamine concentration may reflect a switch from growth and nutritional functions to the neurotransmitter function for this substance. Such speculation only scratches the surface of the important role neurotransmitter substances might play in the brain's early development.

At this point we have discussed many ideas about physical development in infancy. A summary of the main points in this discussion is presented in Concept Table 4.1. Next, we explore the infant's fascinating sensory and perceptual development.

Sensory and Perceptual Development in Infancy

At the beginning of this chapter, you read about how the newborn comes into the world equipped with sensory capacities. But what are sensation and perception anyway? Can a newborn see, and if so, what can it perceive? And what about the other senses—hearing, smell, taste, touch, and pain? What are they like in the newborn? These are among the intriguing questions we now explore.

What Are Sensation and Perception?

How does a newborn know that his mother's skin is soft rather than rough? How does a five-year-old know what color her hair is? How does an eight-year-old know that summer is warmer than winter? How does a ten-year-old know that a firecracker is louder than a cat's meow? Infants and children "know" these things because of their senses. All information comes to the infant through the senses. Without vision, hearing, touch, taste, smell, and other senses, the infant's brain would be isolated from the world; the infant would live in dark silence—a tasteless, colorless, feelingless void.

Sensation occurs when information contacts sensory receptors—the eyes, ears, tongue, nostrils, and skin. The sensation of hearing occurs when waves of pulsating air are collected by the outer ear and transmitted through the bones of the inner ear to the auditory nerve. The sensation of vision occurs as rays of light contact the two eyes and become focused on the retina. **Perception** is the interpretation of what is sensed. The information about physical events that contacts the ears may be interpreted as musical sounds, for example. The physical energy transmitted to the retina may be interpreted as a particular color, pattern, or shape.

Concept Table 4.1
Physical Growth and Development in Infancy

Concept	Processes/Related Ideas	Characteristics/Description
Reflexes	Their nature	The newborn is no longer viewed as a passive, empty-headed organism. Physically, newborns are limited, though, and reflexes—automatic movements—govern the newborn's behavior.
	Sucking	Sucking is an important means of obtaining nutrition, as well as a pleasurable, soothing activity for infants. Nonnutritive sucking is of interest to researchers because it provides a means of evaluating attention.
	Crying and smiling	Crying and smiling are emotional behaviors that are important in the infant's communication with the world.
Emotions	Their nature and development	Emotions in infancy are adaptive and promote survival, they serve as a form of communication, and they provide regulation. Izard developed the MAX system for coding infant facial expressions of emotion. Using this system, it was found that interest and disgust are present in the newborn, and that a social smile, anger, surprise, sadness, fear, and shame/shyness develop in the first year while contempt and guilt develop in the second year.
States	Classification	Researchers have put together different classification systems; one classification involved seven infant state categories, including deep sleep, drowsy, alert and focused, and inflexibly focused.
	The sleeping-waking cycle	Newborns usually sleep sixteen to seventeen hours a day. By four months, they approach adultlike sleeping patterns. REM sleep, during which children and adults are most likely to dream, occurs more often in early infancy than in childhood and adulthood. The high percentage of REM sleep—about half of neonatal sleep—may be a self-stimulatory device, or it may promote brain development.
Physical growth and motor development	Cephalocaudal and proximodistal sequences	The cephalocaudal pattern is growth from the top down; the proximodistal pattern is growth from the center out.
	Gross motor and fine motor skills	Gross motor skills involve large muscle activity as in walking; fine motor skills involve more fine-grained activities like manual dexterity. Both gross and fine motor skills undergo extensive change in the first two years of development.
	Rhythmic motor behavior	During the first year rhythmic motor behavior, involving rapid, repetitious movement of the limbs, torso, and head is common; it seems to represent an important adaptive transition in development.
The Brain		There is a great deal of brain growth in infancy as well as in prenatal development. Dendritic spreading is dramatic in the first two years. Some important changes in neurotransmitters probably take place, although these changes are just beginning to be charted.

Developmental Theories of Perception

As with most aspects of development, theories have been proposed to explain the development of perception. Two prominent theories of perceptual development are the **ecological view** of Eleanor and James Gibson and the **constructivist view** of Jean Piaget.

Eleanor Gibson (1969, 1986, in press) and James J. Gibson (1979) argue that the invariants—those aspects of the environment that do not change—in stimulation of the infant's world provide rich information. These aspects of the environment involve places (a room), objects (a face), and pictures (a picture of a face). Since these things are actually in the world, and since perceptual invariants specify their properties, the ecological theorists believe the infant only has to attend to the appropriate information; she does not have to build up internal representations to see them.

An important assumption of the ecological view is that even complex things—such as the spatial layout of a room—can be perceived "directly" by picking up the invariants rather than engaging in any complex constructive mental activity. This important dimension of the ecological view has led it to also be labeled the *direct perception* view. If complex things can be perceived directly, perhaps they can be perceived at young ages, maybe even by young

Biological and Perceptual Development

Ecological or direct perception view

Constructivist view

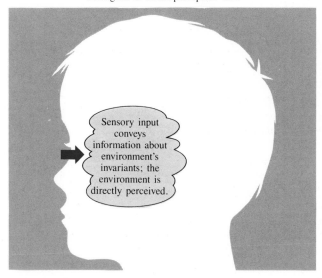
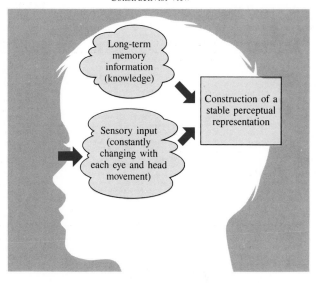

Figure 4.7
Comparison of the ecological or direct perception view and the constructivist view of how an infant perceives the world.

infants. This possibility has inspired investigators to search for the competencies of very young infants (Aslin, 1987; Bower, 1982; Kagan, 1987). The advocates of the ecological or direct perception view do not deny that perception develops as infants and children grow. In fact, they assume that as perceptual processes mature a child becomes more efficient at discovering the environment's invariant properties that are available to the senses.

By contrast, the constructivist view advocated by Jean Piaget stresses that perceiving the world is more than merely picking up information about its invariant properties. Piaget says that perception is a mental construction based on sensory input from the eyes or other sensory receptors plus information retrieved from memory. It is a kind of *representation* of the world that builds up in the mind. This view suggests that many changes in perception reflect changes in how the infant or child constructs a representation of the world. As the child's memory develops, changes in long-term memory knowledge play an important role in how the child perceives the world. Figure 4.7 compares the ecological and constructivist views.

In the next chapter we explore the exciting question of whether young infants have memory, and if so, when it emerges. Much more about Piaget's theory of development appears in the next chapter.

Visual Perception

How do we see? Anyone who has ever taken photographs on a vacation appreciates the miracle of perception. The camera is no match for it. Consider a favorite scenic spot that you visited and photographed sometime in the past. Compare your memory of this spot to your snapshot. Although your memory may be faulty, there is little doubt that the richness of your perceptual experience is not captured in the picture. The sense of depth you felt at this spot probably is not conveyed, nor is the subtlety of the colors you perceived or the intricacies of textures and shapes. Human vision is complex, as is its development.

Psychologist William James (1890) called the newborn's perceptual world a blooming, buzzing confusion. Was James right? A century later we can safely say that he was wrong. We can sum up the research on infant perception with one simple statement: Infants' perception of visual information is *much* more advanced than previously thought.

Figure 4.8
The "looking chamber" has been used to study visual preference in infants.

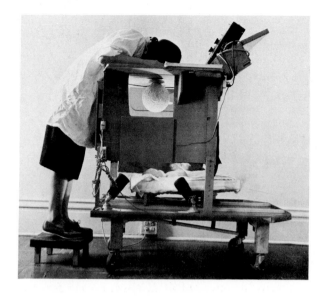

Figure 4.9
Schematic drawing of an infant's eye as seen by the experimenter in the test chamber when the infant has been visually exposed to checked and plain squares. The more the target reflection overlays the pupil, the greater the degree of fixation.

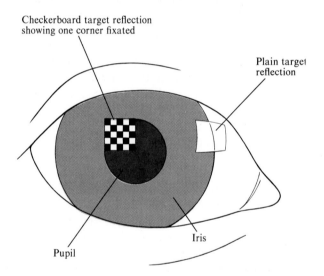

Checkerboard target reflection showing one corner fixated

Plain target reflection

Iris

Pupil

Our tour of visual perception begins with the pioneering work of Robert Fantz (1958, 1961). Fantz placed infants in a "looking chamber," which had two visual displays on the ceiling of the chamber above the infant's head (figure 4.8). An experimenter viewed the infant's eyes by looking through a peephole. If the infant was fixating on one of the displays, the experimenter could see the display's reflection in the infant's eyes (figure 4.9). This allowed the experimenter to determine how long the infant looked at each display. The findings were simple: When presented with a pair of visual displays, an infant looked longer at one than the other. For instance, an infant looked longer at a display of stripes than a display of a solid gray patch. This demonstrates that newborns can see and also that they can tell the difference between two dissimilar objects. The newborn's visual world is not the blooming, buzzing confusion James envisioned.

Just how well can infants see? The newborn's vision is about 20/600 on the well-known Snellen chart that you are tested with when you have your eyes examined; this is about thirty times lower than normal adult vision (20/20). But by six months of age, vision is 20/100 or better (Banks & Salapatek, 1983).

Biological and Perceptual Development

Figure 4.10
A child's depth perception is tested on the visual cliff. The apparatus consists of a board laid across a sheet of heavy glass, with a patterned material directly beneath the glass on one side and several feet below it on the other.

The human face is perhaps the most important visual pattern for the newborn to perceive. The infant masters a sequence of steps in progressing toward full perceptual appreciation of the face (Gibson, 1969). At about three and one-half weeks the infant is fascinated with the eyes, perhaps because the infant notices simple perceptual features such as dots, angles, and circles. At one to two months of age, the infant notices and perceives contour. At two months and older, the infant begins to differentiate facial features: the eyes are distinguished from other parts of the face, the mouth is noticed, and movements of the mouth draw attention to it. By five months of age, the infant has detected other facial features—its plasticity, its solid, three-dimensional surface, the oval shape of the head, the orientation of the eyes and the mouth. Beyond six months of age, the infant distinguishes familiar faces from unfamiliar faces—mother from stranger, masks from real faces, and so on.

How early can infants perceive depth? To investigate this question, Eleanor Gibson and Richard Walk (1960) conducted a classic experiment. They constructed a miniature cliff with a drop-off covered by glass. The motivation for this experiment happened when Gibson was eating a picnic lunch on the edge of the Grand Canyon. She wondered if an infant looking over the canyon's rim would perceive the dangerous drop-off and back up. In their laboratory, Gibson and Walk placed infants on the edge of a visual cliff and had their mothers coax them to crawl out on the glass (figure 4.10). Most infants would not crawl out on the glass, choosing instead to remain on the shallow side, indicating that they could perceive depth. Because the six- to fourteen-month-old infants had extensive visual experience, this research did not answer the question of whether depth perception is innate.

Exactly how early in life does depth perception develop? Since younger infants do not crawl, this question is difficult to answer. Research with two- to four-month-old infants shows differences in heart rate when the infants are placed directly on the deep side of the visual cliff versus the shallow side of the cliff (Campos, Langer, & Krowitz, 1970). However, an alternative interpretation is that young infants respond to differences in some visual characteristic of the deep and shallow cliffs, with no actual knowledge of depth.

We have discussed a good deal of research on visual perception in infancy. Many fundamental aspects of vision are in working order by birth, and many others are present by several months of age. Yet, perception is not complete by one or two years of age. Many aspects of perception continue to grow more efficient and accurate during the childhood years (Bornstein, 1988).

The Fetus and *The Cat in the Hat*

T he fetus can hear sounds in the last few months of pregnancy—the mother's voice, music, loud sounds from television, the roar of an airplane, and so on. Given that the fetus can hear sounds, two psychologists wanted to find out if listening to Dr. Seuss's classic story, *The Cat in the Hat,* while they were still in the mother's womb would produce a preference for hearing the story after they were born (Spence & DeCasper, 1982). Sixteen pregnant women read *The Cat in the Hat* to their fetuses twice a day over the last six weeks of their pregnancies. When the babies were born, they were given a choice of sucking on either of two nipples. Sucking on one nipple produced a recording of their mothers reading *The King, the Mice and the Cheese,* a story with a different rhyme and pace to it. Sucking on the other nipple produced a recording of their mothers reading *The Cat in the Hat.* The newborns preferred listening to *The Cat in the Hat,* which they had heard frequently as a fetus.

Two important conclusions can be drawn from this investigation. First, it reveals how ingenious scientists have become at assessing the development not only of infants

What ingenious method did researchers develop to discover whether the fetus could hear its mother reading The Cat in the Hat?

but fetuses as well, in this case discovering a way to "interview" newborn babies who cannot yet talk. Second, it reveals the remarkable ability of the brain to learn even before the infant is born.

Hearing

Immediately after birth, infants can hear, although their sensory thresholds are somewhat higher than those of adults. That is, a stimulus must be louder to be heard by a newborn than by an adult. Not only can a newborn hear, but the possibility has been raised that the fetus can hear as it nestles within its mother's womb. To learn more about this possibility, read Perspective on Child Development 4.1.

Smell

Infants can smell soon after birth. In one investigation (Lipsitt, Engen, & Kaye, 1963), infants less than twenty-four hours old made body and leg movements and showed changes in breathing when they were exposed to asafetida, a bitter and offensive odor. An infant's sense of smell is not just for unpleasant odors. They apparently can recognize the smell of their mother's breasts, which presumably is pleasant. In one study (MacFarlane, 1975), two- to seven-day-old infants were exposed to two breast pads, one to their right and one to their left. One of these breast pads had been used by the infant's mother, the other was clean. The infants were more likely to turn toward their mother's breast pad than toward the clean breast pad. Infants this young, though, may not respond to their mother's breast pad but to any mother's breast pad. To test this, MacFarlane replaced the clean breast pad with another mother's breast pad. Two-day-old infants showed no preference; it may not be until several weeks of age that infants recognize their own mother's smell.

Taste

Sensitivity to taste may be present prior to birth. When saccharin was added to the amniotic fluid of a near-term fetus, increased swallowing was observed (Windle, 1940). Sensitivity to sweetness is clearly present in the newborn. When sucks on a nipple are rewarded with a sweetened solution, the amount of sucking increases (Lipsitt & others, 1976). In another investigation (Steiner, 1979), newborns showed a smilelike expression after being stimulated with a sweetened solution but pursed their lips after being stimulated with a sour solution.

Touch

Just as newborns respond to taste, they also respond to touch. A touch to the cheek produces a turning of the head, while a touch to the lips produces sucking movements. An important ability that develops in infancy is to connect information about vision with information about touch. One-year-olds clearly can do this and it appears that six-month-olds also can (Acredelo & Hake, 1982). Whether still younger infants can coordinate vision and touch is yet to be determined.

Pain

If and when you have a son and need to consider whether he should be circumcised, the issue of an infant's pain perception probably will become important to you. Circumcision is usually performed on young boys about the third day after birth. Will your young son experience pain if he is circumcised when he is three days old? Increased crying and fussing occurs during the circumcision procedure, suggesting the three-day-old infant experiences pain (Anders & Chalemian, 1974; Gunnar, Malone, & Fisch, 1987; Porter, Porges, & Marshall, 1988).

In an investigation by Megan Gunnar and her colleagues (1987), the healthy newborn's ability to cope with stress was evaluated. Newborn infant males cried intensely during the circumcision, indicating that it was stressful. The researchers pointed out that it is rather remarkable the newborn infant does not suffer serious consequences from the surgery. Rather, the circumcised infant displays amazing resiliency and ability to cope. Within several minutes after the surgery, the infant can nurse and interact in a normal manner with his mother. And, if allowed, the newly circumcised newborn drifts into a deep sleep that seems to serve as a coping mechanism. As shown in figure 4.11, the percent of time spent in deep sleep was greater 60 to 240 minutes after the circumcision than prior to the circumcision.

For many years, doctors have performed operations on newborns without anesthesia. The accepted standard medical practice was followed because of the dangers of anesthesia and the supposition that newborns do not feel pain. Recently, as researchers have convincingly demonstrated that newborns feel pain, the long-standing medical practice of operating on newborns without using anesthesia is being challenged.

Bimodal Perception

Is the young infant competent enough to relate and integrate information from several sensory modalities? The ability to relate and integrate information about two sensory modalities—such as vision and audition (hearing)—is called **bimodal perception.** An increasing number of developmentalists believe the young

Yellow Kangaroos, Gray Donkeys, Thumps, Gongs, and Four-Month-Old Infants

Imagine yourself playing basketball or tennis. There are obviously many visual inputs: the ball coming and going, other players moving around, and so on. But there also are many auditory inputs: the sound of the ball bouncing or being hit and the grunts, groans, and curses emitted by yourself and others. There is also good correspondence between much of the visual and auditory information: when you see the ball bounce, you hear a bouncing sound; when a player leaps, you hear a groan.

We live in a world of objects and events that can be seen, heard, and felt. When mature perceivers look and listen to an event simultaneously, they experience a unitary episode. All of this is so commonplace that it scarcely seems worth mentioning. But consider the task of the very young infant with little practice at perceiving. Can she put vision and sound together as precisely as adults?

To test bimodal perception, Elizabeth Spelke (1979) performed three experiments with the following structure: Two simple films were shown side by side in front of a four-month-old infant. One film showed a yellow kangaroo

bouncing up and down, and the other showed a gray donkey bouncing up and down. There also was an auditory sound track—a repeating thump or gong sound. A number of measures assessed the infant's tendency to look at one film versus the other.

In experiment 1, the animal in one of the films bounced at a slower rate than the animal in the other. And the sound track was synchronized either with the film of the slow-bouncing animal or with the film of the fast-bouncing animal. Infants' first looks were toward the film that was specified by the sound track. Experiments 2 and 3 explored two components of the relation between the sound track and the matching film: common tempo and simultaneity of sounds and bounces. The findings indicated that the infants were sensitive to both of these components.

Spelke's clever demonstration suggests that infants only four months old do not experience a world of unrelated visual and auditory dimensions; they can perceive these as unitary.

Figure 4.11
Percentage of time spent in deep sleep by male newborns before and after circumcision.

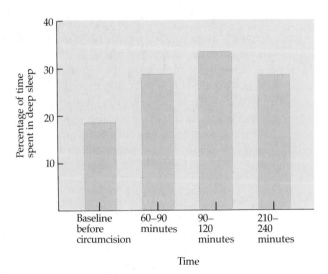

infant experiences a related visual and auditory world (Bahrick, 1988; Gibson & Spelke, 1983; Kagan, 1987; Rose & Ruff, 1987). This remains a controversial view. For example, in one recent investigation of six-month-old infants, the auditory sense dominated the visual sense, restricting bimodal perception (Lewkowicz, 1988). To learn more about bimodal perception, read Perspective on Child Development 4.2.

The claim that the young infant can relate information from one sensory dimension to another has important theoretical ties. The constructivist view of perception—reflected in Piaget's theory—argues that the main perceptual

	Concept Table 4.2	
	Perceptual Development in Infancy	

Concept	Processes/Related Ideas	Characteristics/Description
What are sensation and perception?	Sensation	Sensation occurs when information contacts sensory receptors—eyes, ears, tongue, nostrils, and skin.
	Perception	Perception is the interpretation of what is sensed.
Developmental theories of perception	Ecological or direct perception view	The view developed by the Gibsons that the infant perceives the world by picking up perceptual invariants in the environment.
	Constructivist view	The view developed by Piaget that what the infant perceives is a construction based on a combination of sensory input and information retrieved from memory.
Visual perception	The newborn's visual world	William James called the newborn's world, a blooming, buzzing confusion; he was wrong. The newborn's perception is more advanced than we previously thought.
	Visual preferences	Fantz's research, which showed that infants prefer striped to solid patches demonstrated that newborns can see.
	Quality of vision	The newborn is about 20/600 on the Snellen chart; by six months vision has improved to at least 20/100.
	The human face	Is an important visual pattern for the newborn. The infant gradually masters a sequence of steps in perceiving the human face.
	Depth perception	A classic study by Gibson and Walk demonstrated through the use of the visual cliff that six-month-old infants can perceive depth.
Other senses	Hearing	The fetus can hear several weeks before birth; immediately after birth newborns can hear, although their sensory threshold is higher than for adults.
	Smell, taste, touch, and pain	Each of these senses is present in the newborn. Research on circumcision shows that three-day-old males experience pain and have the ability to adapt to stress.
Bimodal perception	Its nature	Considerable interest focuses on the infant's ability to relate information across perceptual modalities; the coordination and integration of perceptual information across two modalities—such as the visual and the auditory senses—is called bimodal perception. Research indicates that infants as young as four months of age have bimodal perception.

abilities—visual, auditory, and tactile, for example—are completely uncoordinated at birth, and further that young infants do not have bimodal perception. According to Piaget, it is only through months of sensorimotor interactions with the world that bimodal perception is possible. By contrast, the ecological or direct perception view—reflected in the Gibsons' theory—stresses that infants are born with some bimodal perceptual abilities or predispositions that enable them to develop these abilities early in infancy.

Pushing back the age barriers of when an infant can coordinate information from different senses has found support in research such as that conducted by Elizabeth Spelke (1979) and others (Rose & Ruff, 1987). This research supports the ecological view of the Gibsons. Still, there are enough inconsistencies and methodological problems in this research to keep alive the debate on the degree to which such complex perceptual capabilities are inborn or are constructed over a longer period of time through interaction with the world. Nonetheless, if research in bimodal perception continues to be verified with young infants, the ecological interpretation will be difficult to refute. What we do know is that when newborns emerge into this world, they know a lot more than we used to think. They see more and hear more than we believed was possible.

In our tour of the infant's perceptual world, we discussed a number of senses—vision, hearing, smell, taste, touch, and pain. A summary of the main ideas about these aspects of perceptual development is presented in Concept Table 4.2.

Table 4.3
Physical Growth, Ages Three to Six (50th Percentile)

Age	Height (inches) Boys	Height (inches) Girls	Weight (pounds) Boys	Weight (pounds) Girls
3	38	37¾	32¼	31¾
3½	39¼	39¼	34¼	34
4	40¼	40½	36½	36¼
4½	42	42	38½	38½
5	43¼	43	41½	41
5½	45	44½	45½	44
6	46	46	48	47

From George H. Lowrey, *Growth and Development of Children*, 7th ed. Copyright © 1978 Year Book Medical Publishers, Chicago, IL. Reproduced with permission.

Physical and Perceptual Motor Development in Childhood

Remember from earlier in the chapter that the infant's growth in the first year of life is extremely rapid. During the infant's second year, the growth rate begins to slow down, but both gross and fine motor skills progress rapidly. What are some important physical, as well as perceptual motor, changes during childhood?

Early Childhood

The growth rate continues to slow down in early childhood; otherwise we would be a species of giants. Continuing the theme of cephalocaudal development, the brain is closer to full growth than the rest of the child's body, attaining 75 percent of its adult weight by the age of three. The average child grows two and one-half inches in height and gains five to seven pounds a year during early childhood. As the preschool child grows older, the percentage of increase in height and weight decreases with each additional year of age. Table 4.3 shows the average height and weight of children as they age from three to six years. Girls are only slightly smaller and lighter than boys during this age period, a difference that continues until puberty. In early childhood, both boys and girls slim down as the trunks of their bodies become longer. Although their heads are still somewhat large for their bodies, by the end of early childhood, most children have lost their top-heavy look.

Growth patterns vary individually, though. Think back to your preschool years. This probably was the first time you noticed that some children were taller than you, some shorter; that some were fatter, some thinner; that some were stronger, some weaker. Much of the variation is due to heredity, but environmental experiences are involved to some degree. A review of the heights of preschool children around the world concluded that the two most important contributors to height differences are ethnic origin and nutrition (Meredith, 1978). Urban, middle-class, and first-born children were taller than rural, lower-class, and later-born children—probably because the former get better health care and nutrition. Children whose mothers smoked during pregnancy were one-half inch shorter than children whose mothers did not smoke during pregnancy. In the United States, black children are taller than white children.

Building towers with blocks . . . running as fast as you could, falling down, getting right back up, and running just as fast again . . . scribbling, scribbling, and then scribbling some more on lots of pieces of paper . . . cutting paper with scissors—during the preschool years you probably developed all of these motor activities. Table 4.4 summarizes how a number of gross and fine motor skills change during the preschool years.

Table 4.4
Motor and Perceptual Development in Early Childhood

The following tasks are reasonable to expect in 75 to 80 percent of the children of the indicated ages. Children should be tested individually. The data upon which this is based have been collected from children in white middle-class neighborhoods.
A child failing to master four to six of the tasks for his or her age probably needs (a) a more thorough evaluation and (b) some kind of remedial help. Various sex differences are indicated.

Two to three years	Yes	No	Five to five-and-a-half	Yes	No
1. Displays a variety of scribbling behavior	____	____	1. Runs thirty yards in just over eight seconds	____	____
2. Can walk rhythmically at an even pace	____	____	2. Balances on one foot (girls six to eight seconds) (boys four to six seconds)	____	____
3. Can step off low object, one foot ahead of the other.	____	____	3. Child catches large playground ball bounced to him or her chest-high from fifteen feet away four to five times out of five	____	____
4. Can name hands, feet, head, and some face parts	____	____	4. Rectangle and square drawn differently (one side at a time)	____	____
5. Opposes thumb to fingers when grasping objects and releases objects smoothly from finger-thumb grasp	____	____	5. Can high-jump 8 inches or higher over bar with simultaneous two-foot takeoff	____	____
6. Can walk a two-inch wide line placed on ground, for ten feet	____	____	6. Bounces playground ball, using one or two hands, a distance of 3 to 4 feet	____	____

Four to four-and-a-half	Yes	No	Six to six-and-a-half	Yes	No
1. Forward broad jump, both feet together and clear of ground at the same time	____	____	1. Can block-print first name in letters 1½ to two inches high	____	____
2. Can hop two or three times on one foot without precision or rhythm	____	____	2. Can gallop, if it is demonstrated	____	____
3. Walks and runs with arm action coordinated with leg action	____	____	3. Can exert six pounds or more of pressure in grip strength measure	____	____
4. Can walk a circular line a short distance	____	____	4. Can walk balance beam two inches wide, six inches high, and ten to twelve inches long	____	____
5. Can draw a crude circle	____	____	5. Can run sixty feet in about five seconds	____	____
6. Can imitate a simple line cross using a vertical and horizontal line	____	____	6. Can arise from ground from back lying position, when asked to do so as fast as he or she can, in two seconds or under	____	____

From B. Cratty, *Psychomotor Behavior in Education and Sport*, 1974. Courtesy of Charles C. Thomas Publishers, Springfield, Illinois.

The large muscles of preschool children develop extensively, especially those in the arms and legs. For this reason, daily exercise is recommended. Sedentary periods should be brief and few. Although fine motor skills also increase during the preschool years, they grow more rapidly during the elementary school years (Robinson, 1977).

How do developmentalists measure motor development? One widely used measure is the **Denver Developmental Screening Test;** it was devised to be a simple, inexpensive, and fast way to diagnose developmental delay in children from birth through six years of age. The test is individually administered and includes an evaluation of language and personal-social ability in addition to separate assessments of gross and fine motor skills. Among the gross motor skills that are measured are the child's ability to sit, walk, broad jump, pedal a tricycle, throw a ball overhand, catch a bounced ball, hop on one foot, and balance on one foot. Fine motor skills that are measured include the child's ability to stack cubes, reach for objects, and draw a person.

Another important development in early childhood is how children perceive the space in which they live. If you are sitting in the bedroom and the door is shut, can you identify what lies beyond each wall? Can you point toward the television in the living area or the stove in the kitchen? Can you sketch a map showing the location of your house, your school, and the downtown area of the city where you live? Chances are that you can perform all of these tasks with some degree of accuracy. But some of us—those with a "good sense of direction"—are much better at such tasks than others. The rest of us—those

with a mediocre or poor sense of direction—generally regard this as a significant failing. Studying the development of "mapping" in young children may help us to discover why individual differences in sense of direction occur. Mapping in children is important in its own right—how many cases of children getting lost are due to the child's inability to map large-scale spaces (those too large to be seen all at once)? Research reveals that three-year-old children have deficiencies in mapping large-scale spaces, but what perhaps is more surprising is that children as young as three years old learn such layouts as well as they do. In one experiment (Hazen, Lochman, & Pick, 1978), three five-year-old children were led on a route through four rooms, each containing a toy. After training in identifying which doors to use and which toys would be present in successive rooms, the children were given a reversed route test. All of the children showed some ability to choose which doors to go through and to identify toys that would be present when they took the reverse route. However, younger children made more errors.

Middle and Late Childhood

During the elementary school years, children grow an average of two to three inches per year until—at about the age of eleven—the average girl is four feet ten inches tall and the average boy is four feet nine and one-half inches tall. Weight increases range from three to five pounds per year until—at the age of eleven—the average girl weighs eighty-eight and one-half pounds and the average boy weighs eighty-five and one-half pounds (Krogman, 1970).

In middle and late childhood, children's legs become longer and their trunks slimmer, and they are steadier on their feet. Fat tissue develops more rapidly than muscle tissue (which increases substantially in adolescence). Children who have a rounded, somewhat "chubby" body build—referred to as **endomorphic**—have noticeably more fat tissue than muscle tissue. The reverse is true of children with athletic, muscular body builds—referred to as **mesomorphic.** Other children have a skinny, thin body build—they are referred to as **ectomorphic.**

During middle and late childhood, children's motor development becomes much smoother and more coordinated than in early childhood. For example, only one child in a thousand can hit a tennis ball over the net at the age of four; most children, though, can learn to play this sport by the age of eleven. In the early elementary school years, children become competent at running, throwing, climbing, catching, swimming, skipping a rope, bicycle riding, and skating, to name just a few of the physical skills that, when mastered, are sources of pleasure and accomplishment. There usually are marked sex differences in these gross motor skills, with boys outperforming girls handily. However, in fine motor skills—drawing and penmanship, for example—girls usually outperform boys.

During middle and late childhood, sensory mechanisms continue to mature. Early farsightedness is overcome, binocular vision becomes well developed, and hearing acuity increases. Children of this age also have fewer illnesses than younger children, especially fewer respiratory and gastrointestinal problems.

Physical development, of course, does not stop with middle and late childhood. In the next chapter we chronicle the dramatic growth spurt that characterizes puberty.

Summary

I. Reflexes

The newborn is no longer viewed as a passive, empty-headed organism. Physically, newborns are limited, though, and reflexes—automatic movements—govern the newborn's behavior. Sucking is an important means of obtaining nutrition, as well as a pleasurable, soothing activity for infants. Nonnutritive sucking is of interest to researchers because it provides a means of evaluating attention. Crying and smiling are affective behaviors that are important in the infant's communication with the world.

II. Emotions

Emotions in infancy are adaptive and promote survival, they serve as a form of communication, and they provide regulation. Izard developed the MAX system for coding infant facial expression of emotion. Using this system, it was found that interest and disgust are present in the newborn, and that a social smile, anger, surprise, sadness, fear, and shame/shyness develop in the first year while contempt and guilt develop in the second year.

III. States

Researchers have put together different classification systems; one classification involved seven infant state categories, including deep sleep, drowsy, alert and focused, and inflexibly focused. Newborns usually sleep sixteen to seventeen hours a day. By four months, they approach adultlike sleeping patterns. REM sleep, during which children and adults are most likely to dream, occurs more often in early infancy than in childhood or adulthood. The high percentage of REM sleep—about half of neonatal sleep—may be a self-stimulatory device, or it may promote brain development.

IV. Physical Growth and Development in Infancy

The cephalocaudal pattern is growth from the top down; the proximodistal pattern is growth from the center out. Gross motor skills involve large muscle activity as in walking; fine motor skills involve more fine-grained activities like manual dexterity. Both gross and fine motor skills undergo extensive change in the first two years of development. During the first year, rhythmic motor behavior—involving rapid, repetitive movement of the limbs, torso, and head—is common; it seems to represent an important adaptive transition in development.

V. The Brain

There is a great deal of brain growth in infancy as well as in prenatal development. Dendritic spreading is dramatic in the first two years. Some important changes in neurotransmitters probably take place, although these changes are just beginning to be charted.

VI. What Are Sensation and Perception?

Sensation occurs when information contacts sensory receptors—eyes, ears, tongue, nostrils, and skin. Perception is the interpretation of what is sensed.

VII. Developmental Theories of Perception

The ecological or direct perception view—developed by the Gibsons—says that the infant perceives the world by picking up perceptual invariants in the environment. The constructivist view—developed by Piaget—says that what the infant perceives is a construction based on a combination of sensory input and information retrieved from memory.

VIII. Visual Perception

William James said that the newborn's perceptual world was like a blooming, buzzing confusion; he was wrong. The newborn's perception is more advanced than previously was thought. Fantz's research, which showed that infants prefer stripes to solids, demonstrated that newborns can see. The newborn is about 20/600 on the Snellen chart; by six months vision has improved to at least 20/100. The human face is an important visual pattern for the newborn. The infant gradually masters a sequence of steps in perceiving the human face. A classic study by Gibson and Walk demonstrated through the use of the visual cliff that six-month-old infants can perceive depth.

IX. Other Senses

The fetus can hear several weeks before birth; immediately after birth newborns can hear, although their sensory threshold is higher than for adults. Smell, taste, touch, and pain are present in the newborn. Research on circumcision shows that three-day-old males experience pain and have the ability to cope with stress.

X. Bimodal Perception

Considerable interest focuses on the infant's ability to relate information across perceptual modalities; the coordination and integration of perceptual information across two modalities—such as the visual and auditory senses—is called bimodal perception. Research indicates that infants as young as four months of age have bimodal perception.

XI. Early Childhood

Growth is slower in early childhood than in infancy. The average child grows two and one-half inches and gains between five and seven pounds a year during early childhood. Both genetic and environmental circumstances contribute to growth. Ethnic origin and nutrition are important influences on height. Considerable progress in gross motor skills takes place in early childhood, especially in the arms and legs. Children's ability to map large-scale spaces markedly improves during this period of development as well.

XII. Middle and Late Childhood

Growth is slow and consistent in middle and late childhood—the calm before the rapid spurt of adolescence. With regard to body build, children can be classified as ectomorphs, mesomorphs, and endomorphs. Motor and sensory development becomes smoother and sensory mechanisms continue to mature.

Key Terms

Moro reflex 83
nonnutritive sucking 85
reflexive smile 85
social smile 85
REM sleep 89
cephalocaudal pattern 90
proximodistal pattern 90
gross motor skills 91
fine motor skills 91
rhythmic motor behavior 92

sensation 95
perception 95
ecological view 96
constructivist view 96
bimodal perception 101
Denver Developmental
Screening Test 105
endomorphic 106
mesomorphic 106
ectomorphic 106

Suggested Readings

Banks, M. S., & Salapatek, P. (1983). Infant visual
perception. In P. E. Mussen (Ed.), *Handbook of child
psychology* (4th ed.), Vol. 2. New York: John Wiley &
Sons.
This authoritative version of research on infant perception
covers in great detail the topics discussed in this chapter.
Bower, T. G. R. (1977). *The perceptual world of the child.*
Cambridge, MA: Harvard University Press.
A scholarly introduction to the study of infant perception,
including the topics of space perception, distance
perception, and size constancy.
Caplan, F. (1981). *The first twelve months of life.* New York:
Bantam.
An easy-to-read, well-written account of each of the first
twelve months of life.
Lamb, M. E., & Bornstein, M. C. (1987). *Development in
infancy.* New York: Random House.
This portrayal of the infant by two leading researchers
includes individual chapters on perceptual development as
well as the ecology of the infant's development.
Osofsky, J. D. (1987). *Handbook of infant development,* 2d
ed. New York: John Wiley & Sons.
Leading experts in the field of infant development have
contributed chapters on a far-ranging set of topics about
infants.

CHAPTER
5

Puberty

If we listen to boys and girls at the very moment when they seem most pimply, awkward and disagreeable, we can partly penetrate a mystery most of us felt heavily within us, and now have forgotten. This mystery is the very process of creation of man and woman.

Colin Mcinnes
The World of Children

I am pretty confused. I wonder whether I am weird or normal. My body is starting to change but I sure don't look like a lot of my friends. I still look like a kid for the most part. My best friend is only thirteen but he looks like he is sixteen or seventeen. I get nervous in the locker room during PE class because when I go to take a shower I'm afraid somebody is going to make fun of me since I'm not as physically developed as some of the others.

—Robert, age twelve

I don't like my breasts. They are too small and they look funny. I'm afraid guys won't like me if they don't get bigger.

—Angie, age thirteen

I can't stand the way I look. I have zits all over my face. My hair is dull and stringy. It never stays in place. My nose is too big. My lips are too small. My legs are too short. I have four warts on my left hand and people get grossed out by them. So do I. My body is a disaster.

—Ann, age fourteen

The comments of these three adolescents in the midst of pubertal change underscore the dramatic upheaval in our bodies following the calm, consistent growth of middle and late childhood. The changes puberty brings are perplexing to adolescents as they go through them. While these changes are perplexing and confusing, bringing forth doubts, questions, fears, and anxieties, most of us survive them quite well. Our journey through the fascinating moments of puberty explores its nature, psychological dimensions, and sexuality.

The Nature of Puberty

Ideas about the nature of puberty focus on defining its boundaries and determinants, hormonal changes, physical changes, and individual variation. We evaluate each of these in turn.

The Boundaries and Determinants of Puberty

Puberty can be distinguished from adolescence. For most of us, puberty ended long before adolescence was exited, although puberty is the most important marker of the beginning of adolescence. What is puberty? **Puberty** is a rapid change to physical maturation involving hormonal and bodily changes that take place primarily during early adolescence.

Imagine a toddler displaying all the features of puberty—a three-year-old girl with fully developed breasts or a boy just slightly older with a deep male voice. That is what we would see by the year 2250 if the age at which puberty arrives continued to decrease at its present pace. In Norway, **menarche**—the girl's first menstruation—occurs at just over thirteen years of age,

Puberty involves a dramatic upheaval in bodily change. Young adolescents develop an acute concern about their bodies. Columnist Bob Greene (1988) recently dialed a party line in Chicago called Connections, to discover what young adolescents were saying to each other. The first thing the boys and girls asked—after first names—was physical descriptions. The idealism of the callers was apparent. Most of the girls described themselves as having long blond hair, five feet five inches tall, and weighing about 110 pounds. Most of the boys described themselves as having brown hair, said they lifted weights, were six feet tall, and weighed about 170 pounds.

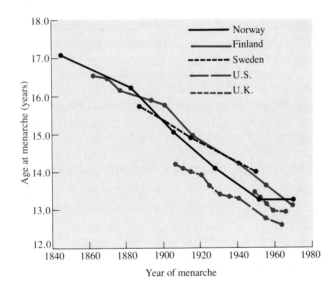

Figure 5.1
Age at menarche in selected northern European countries and the United States from 1845 to 1969.

compared to seventeen years of age in the 1840s. In the United States—where children mature up to a year earlier than children in European countries— the average age of menarche has been declining an average of about four months per decade for the past century (figure 5.1). Fortunately, however, we are unlikely to see pubescent toddlers, since what has happened in the past century is special. The best guess is that the something special is a higher level of nutrition and health. The available information suggests that menarche began to occur earlier at about the time of the Industrial Revolution, a period associated with increased standards of living and advances in medical science (Petersen, 1979).

Genetic factors also are involved in puberty. Puberty is not simply an environmental accident. As we indicated in chapter 2, nutrition, health, and other factors affect the timing of puberty and variations in its makeup, but the basic genetic program is wired into the species (Scarr & Kidd, 1983).

From *Penguin Dreams and Stranger Things* by Berke Breathed. Copyright © 1985 by The Washington Post Writers Group. By permission of Little, Brown and Company and The Washington Post Writers Group.

Another key factor in the occurrence of puberty is weight (Frisch & Revelle, 1970). For example, menarche occurs at a relatively consistent weight in girls. A body weight approximating 106 ± 3 pounds signals menarche and the end of the adolescent growth spurt. And for menarche to begin and continue, fat must make up 17 percent of the girl's body weight. Both teenage anorexics whose weight drops dramatically and female athletes in certain sports (such as gymnastics) may become amenorrheic (absence or suppression of menstrual discharge).

In summary, the determinants of puberty include nutrition, health, heredity, and weight. So far our discussion of puberty has emphasized its dramatic changes. Keep in mind, though, that puberty is not a single, sudden event. We know when a young boy or girl is going through puberty but pinpointing its beginning and its end is difficult. Except for menarche, which occurs rather late in puberty, no single marker heralds puberty. For boys, the first whisker or first wet dream are events that could mark its appearance, but both may go unnoticed.

Hormonal Changes

Behind the first whisker in boys and widening of hips in girls is a flood of **hormones,** powerful chemical substances secreted by the endocrine glands and carried through the body by the bloodstream. The concentrations of certain hormones increase dramatically during adolescence. In boys, **testosterone** is associated with the development of external genitals, an increase in height, and voice change. In girls, **estradiol** is associated with breast, uterine, and skeletal development (Dillon, 1980). In one investigation, testosterone levels increased eighteenfold in boys but only twofold in girls during puberty. Estradiol increased eightfold in girls but only twofold in boys (Nottelmann & others, 1987) (figure 5.2).

This same influx of hormones that puts hair on a male's chest and imparts curvature to a female's breasts may contribute to psychological adjustment in adolescence. In one study of 108 normal boys and girls ranging in age from nine to fourteen, a higher concentration of testosterone was present in boys who rated themselves more socially competent (Nottelmann & others, 1987). In another investigation of 60 normal boys and girls in the same age range, girls with higher estradiol levels expressed more anger and aggression (Inoff-Germain & others, 1988).

Biological and Perceptual Development

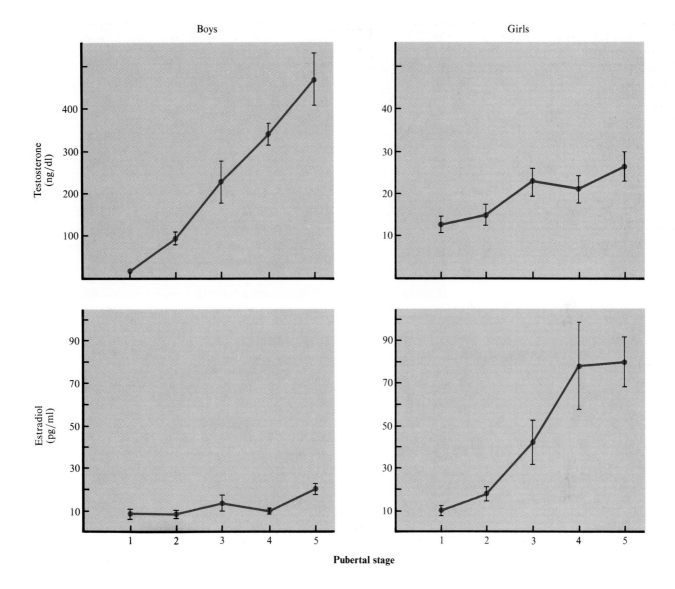

Boys   Girls

Pubertal stage

Before we leave our discussion of the hormones that affect puberty, the powerful role of the pituitary gland needs to be examined. The **pituitary gland** is described as the body's master gland. It is located at the base of the brain and its description as a master gland derives from its regulation of a number of other glands. Not only does the pituitary gland release hormones that stimulate the testes and ovaries, but through interaction with the hypothalamus in the brain, it secretes hormones that influence growth in height and weight (Styne, 1988).

Physical Changes

Among the most noticeable changes during puberty are increases in height and weight and sexual maturation. As indicated in figure 5.3, the growth spurt for girls occurs approximately two years earlier than for boys. The growth spurt in girls begins at approximately ten and one-half years for girls and lasts for about two years. During this time girls increase in height by about three and one-half inches per year. The growth spurt for boys begins at about twelve

Figure 5.2
Changes in testosterone and estradiol in males and females during puberty.
(From Editha D. Nottelmann et al., "Hormone Level and Adjustment and Behavior During Early Adolescence," paper presented at AAAS meeting, Los Angeles, CA, 1985.)

As reflected in the adolescents who are dancing here, females experience pubertal change much earlier than boys, approximately two years on the average.

Figure 5.3
Growth curves for height in boys and girls. These curves represent the rate of growth of typical boys and girls at a given age.

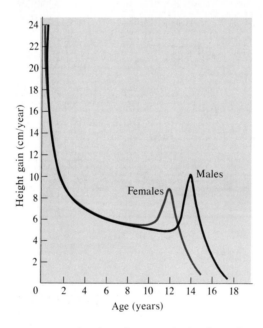

and one-half years of age and also lasts for approximately two years. Boys usually grow about four inches per year during this time frame (Faust, 1977; Tanner, 1970).

Think back to the onset of your puberty. Of the striking changes that were taking place in your body, what was the first change that occurred? Researchers have found that male pubertal characteristics develop in this order: increase in penis and testicle size, appearance of straight pubic hair, minor voice change, first ejaculation (which usually occurs through masturbation or a wet dream), appearance of kinky pubic hair, onset of maximum growth, growth of hair in armpits, more detectable voice changes, and growth of facial hair (Faust, 1977; Garrison, 1968). Three of the most noticeable areas of sexual maturation in boys are penis elongation, testes development, and growth of facial hair. The normal range and average age of development for these sexual characteristics, along with height spurt, is shown in figure 5.4.

Biological and Perceptual Development

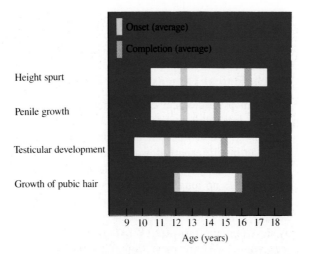

Onset (average)

Completion (average)

Height spurt

Penile growth

Testicular development

Growth of pubic hair

9 10 11 12 13 14 15 16 17 18

Age (years)

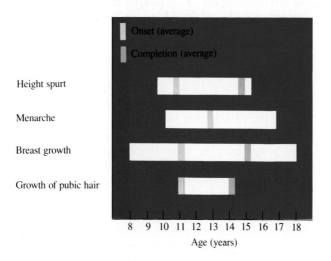

Onset (average)

Completion (average)

Height spurt

Menarche

Breast growth

Growth of pubic hair

8 9 10 11 12 13 14 15 16 17 18

Age (years)

What is the order of appearance of physical changes in females? First, either the breasts enlarge or pubic hair appears. Later hair will appear in the armpits. As these changes occur, the female grows in height and her hips become wider than her shoulders. Her first menstruation comes rather late in the pubertal cycle. Initially her menstrual cycles may be highly irregular. For the first several years she may not ovulate every menstrual cycle. In some instances it is two years after her period begins that she becomes fertile. No voice changes comparable to those in pubertal males take place in pubertal females. By the end of puberty, the female's breasts have become more fully rounded. Two of the most noticeable aspects of the female's pubertal change are pubic hair and breast development. Figure 5.5 shows the normal range and average age of development of these sexual characteristics as well as information about menarche and height gain.

Individual Variation in Puberty

The pubertal sequence may begin as early as ten years of age or as late as thirteen and one-half years of age for most boys. It may end as early as thirteen years or as late as seventeen years of age for most boys. The normal range is wide enough that if we have two boys of the same chronological age, one may complete the pubertal sequence before the other one has begun it. For girls, the age range of the first menstrual period is even wider. Menarche is considered to be within a normal range if it appears between the ages of nine and fifteen (Brooks-Gunn, 1988; Hill, 1980).

Psychological Dimensions of Puberty

A host of psychological changes accompany an adolescent's pubertal development. Imagine yourself as you were beginning puberty. Not only did you probably think of yourself differently, but your parents and peers probably began acting differently toward you. Maybe you were proud of your changing body, even though you were perplexed about what was happening. Perhaps your parents no longer perceived you as someone they could sit in bed with and watch television or as someone who should be kissed goodnight. Among the intriguing questions about the psychological dimensions of puberty posed by developmentalists are: What parts of their body image are adolescents preoccupied with the most? What are the psychological consequences of early and late maturation? How complex is on-time and off-time pubertal development? Are the effects of pubertal timing exaggerated? Let's look further at each of these questions.

Body Image

One thing is certain about the psychological aspects of physical development— adolescents are preoccupied with their bodies and develop individual images of what their bodies are like. Perhaps you looked in the mirror on a daily or sometimes even on an hourly basis to see if you could detect anything different about your changing body. Preoccupation with one's body image is strong throughout adolescence, but it is especially acute during puberty, a time when adolescents are more dissatisfied with their bodies than in late adolescence (Hamburg, 1974).

Being physically attractive and having a positive body image are associated with an overall positive conception of one's self. In one investigation, girls who were judged as being physically attractive and who generally had a positive body image had higher opinions of themselves in general (Lerner & Karabenick, 1974). In another investigation, breast growth in nine- to eleven-year-old girls was associated with a positive body image, positive peer relationships, and superior adjustment (Brooks-Gunn & Warren, in press).

Was there a part of your body you were preoccupied with the most during puberty? In one study, boys and girls did not differ much in their preoccupation with various body characteristics (Lerner & Karabenick, 1974). For both males and females, general appearance, the face, facial complexion, and body build were thought to be the most important characteristics in physical attractiveness. Ankles and ears were thought to be the least important.

Early and Late Maturation

Some of you entered puberty early, others entered late. When adolescents mature earlier or later than their peers, might they perceive themselves differently? Some years ago, in the California Longitudinal Study, early maturing boys perceived themselves more positively and had more successful peer relations than their late maturing counterparts (Jones, 1965). The findings for early maturing girls were similar but not as strong as for boys. When the late maturing boys were studied in their thirties, however, they had developed a stronger sense of identity than the early maturing boys (Peskin, 1967). Possibly this occurred because the late maturing boys had more time to explore

Reprinted with special permission of NAS, Inc.

life's options or because the early maturing boys continued to focus on their advantageous physical status instead of career development and achievement.

More recent research confirms, though, that at least during adolescence, it is advantageous to be an early maturing rather than a late maturing boy (Blyth, Bulcroft, & Simmons, 1981; Petersen, 1987a; Simmons & Blyth, 1987). The more recent findings for girls suggest early adolescence is a mixed blessing: these girls experience more problems in school but also more independence and popularity with boys. When maturational timing is assessed grade level also is a factor. In one investigation, sixth-grade early maturing girls were more satisfied with their figures than sixth-grade late maturing girls, but by the tenth grade late maturing girls were more satisfied (Blyth, Bulcroft, & Simmons, 1981) (figure 5.6). The reason for this is that by late adolescence, early maturing girls are shorter and stockier, late maturing girls are taller and thinner. The late maturing girls in late adolescence possess bodies that more closely approximate the American ideal of feminine beauty—tall and thin.

Complexity of On-Time and Off-Time in Development

Being on-time and off-time in terms of pubertal events is a complex affair. For example, the dimensions may involve not just biological status and pubertal age, but also chronological age, grade in school, cognitive functioning, and social maturity (Petersen, 1987b). Adolescents may be at risk when the demands of a particular social context and the adolescents' physical and behavioral characteristics are mismatched (Lerner, 1987). On-time dancers are one such example. In general peer comparisons, on-time dancers should not show adjustment problems. However, they do not have the ideal characteristics thought to be important in the world of dancers. That is, the ideal characteristics of dancers are generally those associated with late maturity—a thin, lithe body build. The dancers, then, are on-time in terms of their peer group in general, but there is an asynchrony to their development in terms of their more focused peer group—dancers.

A special concern about being off-time in pubertal development focuses on health care. To learn more about the implications for health care of being off-time in pubertal development, turn to Perspective on Child Development 5.1.

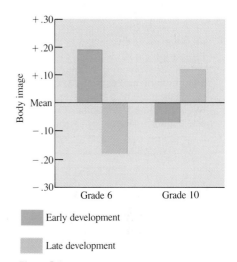

Early development

Late development

Figure 5.6
Early and late maturing adolescent girls' perceptions of body image in early and late adolescence.

Pubertal Timing and Health Care

What can be done to identify off-time maturers who are at risk for problems? Many boys and girls whose development is extremely early or extremely late are likely to come to the attention of a physician—such as a boy who has not had a spurt in height by the age of sixteen or a girl who has not menstruated by the age of fifteen. Girls and boys who are early or late maturers but well within the normal range are less likely to be taken to a physician because of their maturational status. Nonetheless, these boys and girls may have fears and doubts about being normal that they do not raise unless a physician, counselor, or some other health-care provider takes the initiative. A brief discussion outlining the sequence and timing of events and the large individual variations in them may be all that is required to reassure many adolescents who are maturing off-time.

Health-care providers may want to discuss the adolescent's off-time development with parents as well as the adolescent. Information about the peer pressures involved with off-time development can be beneficial. Especially helpful to early maturing girls is a discussion of peer pressures to date and to engage in adultlike behavior at early ages. The transition to middle school, junior high school, or high school may be more stressful for girls and boys who are in the midst of puberty than for those who are not (Brooks-Gunn, 1988).

If pubertal development is extremely late, a physician may recommend hormonal treatment. In one investigation of extended pubertal delay in boys, hormonal treatment worked to increase the height, dating interest, and peer relations in several boys, but little or no improvement resulted in other boys (Lewis, Money, & Bobrow, 1977).

In sum, most early and late maturing individuals weather puberty's challenges and stresses competently. For those who do not, discussions with sensitive and knowledgeable health-care providers and parents can improve the off-time maturing adolescent's coping abilities.

The sexual fantasies of adolescent boys focus specifically on sexual activity.

Concept Table 5.1
The Nature of Puberty and Psychological Dimensions of Puberty

Concept	Processes/Related Ideas	Characteristics/Description
The nature of puberty	Boundaries and determinants	Puberty is a rapid change to physical maturation involving hormonal and bodily changes that takes place primarily during early adolescence. Its determinants include nutrition, health, heredity, and weight.
	Hormonal changes	The endocrine glands secrete hormones. Testosterone is the sex hormone that increases the most in adolescent males. Estradiol is the sex hormone that increases the most in adolescent females. The pituitary gland is the master gland and is involved in puberty through its interconnections with other glands.
	Physical changes	As adolescents undergo a growth spurt, they make rapid gains in height. The spurt occurs approximately two years earlier in girls (ten and one-half) than in boys (twelve and one-half).
	Individual variation	Individual variation is extensive within a wide normal range.
Psychological dimensions of puberty	Body image	Adolescents show a considerable interest in their body images. Young adolescents are more preoccupied and less satisfied with their body images than are late adolescents.
	Early and late maturation	Early maturation favors boys at least during adolescence. As adults, though, late maturing boys may achieve more successful identities. The results are more mixed for girls than for boys.
	On-time and off-time	Being on-time or off-time in pubertal development is complex. Adolescents may be at risk when the demands of a particular context and the adolescent's physical and behavioral characteristics are mismatched.
	Are the effects of puberty exaggerated?	Some scholars have expressed doubt that the effects of puberty on development are as strong as once believed. It is important to keep in mind that adolescent development is influenced by an interaction of biological, cognitive, and social factors.

Are the Effects of Puberty Exaggerated?

Some researchers have begun to question whether the effects of puberty are as strong as once was believed (Lerner, 1988; Petersen, 1987a). How strong are these effects? Have the effects of early and late maturation been exaggerated? Puberty affects some adolescents more strongly than others, and some behaviors more strongly than others. Body image, dating interest, and sexual behavior are quite clearly affected by pubertal change. The recent questioning of the effects of puberty suggests that if we look at overall development and adjustment in the human life cycle, puberty and its variations have less dramatic effects for most individuals than is commonly thought. For some young adolescents the transition through puberty is stormy, but for most it is not. Each period of the human life cycle has its stresses. Puberty is no different. It has newly imposed challenges resulting from emerging developmental changes, but the vast majority of adolescents weather these stresses nicely. In thinking about the effects of puberty also keep in mind that the world of adolescents involves not only biological influences on development, but also cognitive and social, environmental influences. As with all periods of human development, these processes work in concert to produce who we are in adolescence. Singling out biological changes as the dominating change in adolescence is a mistake. As we will see in sections 3 and 4, there are equally impressive changes in cognitive and social development during the adolescent years.

At this point we have discussed a number of ideas about puberty. A summary of these ideas is presented in Concept Table 5.1. Now we turn our attention to more information about one of the hallmarks of puberty—sexuality.

Figure 5.7
Percent of college youth reporting having sexual intercourse at different points in the twentieth century. Two lines are drawn for males and two for females. The lines represent the best two fits through the data for males and the data for females of the many studies surveyed.

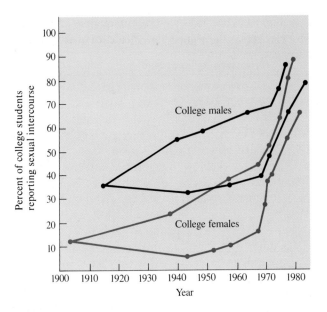

Sexuality

The hormonal and bodily changes associated with puberty generate an almost insatiable curiosity about the mysteries of sexuality. Adolescents continually think about whether they are sexually attractive, whether they will grow more so, whether anyone will ever love them, whether their penis or vagina is too small or oddly shaped, and whether it is normal not to have sex. Sexual identity becomes a major developmental task of adolescence. The majority of adolescents eventually manage to develop a mature sexual identity, but for most of us there are periods of vulnerability along life's sexual journey. Our coverage of adolescent sexuality includes information about sexual attitudes and behavior, sexually transmitted diseases, and pregnancy.

Sexual Attitudes and Behavior

Had you been a college student in 1940 you probably would have had a different attitude toward many aspects of sexuality than you do today, especially if you are female. A review of college students' sexual practices and attitudes from 1900 to 1980 reveals two important trends (Darling, Kallen, & VanDusen, 1984). First, the percent of youth reporting that they have had sexual intercourse has dramatically increased. Second, the percent of females reporting that they have had sexual intercourse has increased more rapidly than for males, although the initial base for males was greater (figure 5.7). These changes suggest movement away from a double standard that says it is more appropriate for males than females to have sexual intercourse.

At age sixteen, slightly more than 40 percent of males and between 30 to 40 percent of females have had sexual intercourse (Dreyer, 1982). The pressure on males to have sexual intercourse is reflected in more than twice as many males (12 percent) reporting having had sexual intercourse than females (5 percent) at age thirteen, even though male adolescents enter puberty on the average two years later than female adolescents. Recent data indicate that in some areas of the country, sexual experiences of young adolescents may even be greater. In an inner city area of Baltimore, at age fourteen, 81 percent

Biological and Perceptual Development

of the males said they already had engaged in sexual intercourse. Other surveys in inner city, low-income areas also reveal a high incidence of early sexual intercourse (Clark, Zabin, & Hardy, 1984).

While sexual intercourse can be a meaningful experience for older, more mature adolescents, many of us are ill-equipped to handle sexual experiences, especially in early adolescence. Adolescents may attempt sexual intercourse without really knowing what to do or how to satisfy their partner, leading to frustration and a sense of sexual inadequacy. And many are poorly informed about contraception or fail to use contraceptives.

As we explore our sexual identities we often engage in sexual scripts (Gagnon & Simon, 1973; Gordon & Gilgun, 1987). Differences in the way we are socialized as males and females are involved in these sexual scripts. Discrepancies in male-female scripting can produce confusion and problems for adolescents as they work out their sexual identities. Adolescent girls have learned to link sexual intercourse with love. Female adolescents often rationalize their sexual behavior by telling themselves that they were swept away by love. A number of investigations reveal that adolescent females, more than adolescent males, report being in love as a primary reason for being sexually active (e.g., Cassell, 1984). Far more females than males engage in intercourse with partners they love and would like to marry. Other reasons for engaging in sexual intercourse include giving in to male pressure, gambling that sex is a way to get a boyfriend, curiosity, and sexual desire unrelated to loving and caring. Adolescent males may be aware that their female counterparts have been socialized into a love ethic. They also may know the pressure many of them feel to have a boyfriend. Two classic male lines show how males understand female thinking about sex and love: "You would if you loved me," and "If you really loved me, you would have sex with me." The female adolescent who says, "If you really loved me, you would not put so much pressure on me," reflects insight about male sexual motivation.

Some experts on adolescent sexuality, though, believe we are moving toward a new norm suggesting that sexual intercourse is acceptable but mainly within the boundary of a loving and affectionate relationship (Dreyer, 1982). As part of this new norm, promiscuity, exploitation, and unprotected sexual intercourse are more often perceived as unacceptable by adolescents. One variation of the new norm is that intercourse is acceptable in a nonlove relationship but physical or emotional exploitation of the partner is not (Darling, Kallen, & VanDusen, 1984). The new norm suggests that the double standard does not operate as it once did, that is, physical and emotional exploitation of adolescent females by males is not as strong today as in prior decades.

Other experts on adolescent sexuality are not so sure the new norm has arrived (Gordon & Gilgun, 1987; Morrison, 1985). They argue that remnants of the double standard unfortunately still flourish. In most investigations, about twice as many boys as girls report positive feelings about sexual intercourse. Females are more likely to report guilt, fear, and hurt. Adolescent males feel considerable pressure from their peers to experience sexual intercourse and to be sexually active. I remember vividly the raunchy conversations that filled our basketball locker room in junior high school. By the end of the ninth grade, I was sure that I was the only virgin on the fifteen-member team, but of course, there was no way I let my teammates know that. As one young adolescent recently remarked, "Look, I feel a lot of pressure from my buddies to go for the score." Further evidence for the male's physical and emotional exploitation

How do the sexual scripts of adolescent males and females differ in the American culture?

of the female was found in a survey of 432 fourteen- to eighteen-year-olds (Goodchilds & Zellman, 1984). Both male and female adolescents accepted the right of the male adolescent to be sexually aggressive but left matters up to the female to set the limits for the male's sexual overtures. Another attitude related to the double standard was the belief that females should not plan ahead to have sexual intercourse but be swept up in the passion of the moment, not taking contraceptive precautions. Unfortunately, while we may have chipped away at some parts of the sexual double standard, other aspects still remain.

Both the early and more recent surveys of sexual choice indicate that about 4 percent of males and about 3 percent of females are exclusively homosexual (Hunt, 1974; Kinsey, Pomeroy, & Martin, 1948). As many as 10 percent of adolescents worry about whether or not they are lesbian or gay (Gordon & Gilgun, 1987). At least until several years ago, attitudes toward homosexuality were becoming increasingly permissive. But with the threat of AIDS, future surveys probably will indicate reduced acceptance of homosexuality.

Adolescence may play an important role in the development of homosexuality. In one investigation, participation in homosexual behavior and sexual arousal by same-sex peers in adolescence was strongly related to an adult homosexual orientation (Bell & others, 1981). When interest in the same sex is intense and compelling, an adolescent often experiences severe conflict (Boxer, 1988; Irvin, 1988). The American culture stigmatizes homosexuality—negative labels such as "fags" and "queers" are given to male homosexuals and "lessies" and "dykes" are given to female homosexuals. The sexual socialization of adolescent homosexuals becomes a process of learning to hide (Herdt, 1988). Some gay males wait out their entire adolescence, hoping that heterosexual feelings will develop. Many female adolescent homosexuals have similar experiences, although same-sex genital contact is not as common as among males. Many adult females who identify themselves as homosexuals considered themselves predominantly heterosexual during adolescence (Bell & others, 1981).

Why do some individual's become homosexual and others do not? Speculation on this question has been extensive, but no firm answers are available. Heredity, hormonal imbalance, family processes, and chance learning are among the factors that have been proposed to cause homosexuality. Concerning family processes, it has been argued that a dominant mother and a weak father promote homosexuality. The evidence is far from clear about this proposal. Concerning chance learning, someone may be seduced by an individual of the same sex and subsequently develop a homosexual preference. The most widely adopted view is that there are a number of ways to become homosexual, including any of the aforementioned biological and environmental reasons (McWhirter, Reinsch, & Sanders, in press; Money, 1987).

Yet another important dimension of adolescent sexual attitudes and behavior is masturbation, the most frequent sexual outlet for many adolescents. In one investigation, masturbation was commonplace among adolescents (Haas, 1979). More than two-thirds of the boys and half of the girls masturbated once a week or more. Adolescents today do not feel as guilty about masturbation as they once did, although they still feel embarrassed and defensive about it (Sorensen, 1983). In past eras masturbation was touted as causing everything from warts to insanity. Today, as few as 15 percent of adolescents attach any stigma to masturbation (Hyde, 1988).

Sexually Transmitted Disease

Formerly called venereal disease (or VD), sexually transmitted disease is transmitted primarily through sexual intercourse although it can be transmitted orally. Sexually transmitted disease is fairly common among today's adolescents. The most common sexually transmitted diseases that adolescents are likely to encounter are chlamydia, gonorrhea, venereal warts, and herpes, although the greatest scare in recent years has become the epidemic of AIDS (Belfer, Kerner, & Miller, 1988; Brookman, 1988).

Chlamydia affects as many as 10 percent of all college students. The disease, which is named for the tiny bacterium that causes it, appears in both males and females. Males experience a burning sensation during urination and a mucoid discharge, while females experience painful urination or a vaginal discharge. These signs often mimic gonorrhea; however, while penicillin is prescribed for the gonorrhealike symptoms, the problem does not go away, as it would if gonorrhea were the culprit. If left untreated, chlamydia can infect the entire reproductive tract. Scar tissue may be produced, preventing the female from becoming pregnant. Drugs have been developed to treat this very common sexually transmitted disease and they are very effective.

Another major sexual problem in recent years has focused on a virus called genital herpes. While this disease is more common among young adults (estimates range to as high as one in five sexually active adults), as many as one in thirty-five adolescents have genital herpes (Oppenheimer, 1982). The first herpes symptom is a vague itching or burning sensation in or near the genital area. Two or three days later, the burning usually turns into a more painful feeling. Shallow, fluid-filled blisters appear on the shaft or tip of the penis in males and on the outer genitalia, vagina, or cervix in females. The first attack is usually the most painful, often accompanied by flulike symptoms. The severity of the attacks and whether they recur vary from one individual to another, although approximately 70 percent experience a repeat attack within nine months of the first.

Usually when you catch a virus like measles or chicken pox, your body produces antibodies that try to destroy the invading virus. The antibodies remain in your bloodstream the rest of your life and instantly attack the virus if it reappears. This is the reason we get measles only once. Unfortunately, herpes antibodies do not work this way. Instead, the virus retreats to the nerve cells at the base of the spine, where it can remain dormant anywhere from several weeks to a lifetime. During new attacks, the virus travels down the nerve fibers to the genitalia and produces another crop of painful blisters.

Girls and women with herpes need to be especially cautious, since there is some indication that it is associated with cervical cancer. Females with herpes should have a Pap smear every six months—fortunately, this type of cancer develops slowly and can be detected in an early form. No cure for genital herpes has yet been found. Some of the unanswered questions about herpes are: How is the virus able to persist in the body? Why does it become dormant? What happens when it reactivates? And how does the body finally repress the recurrences?

Far more rare than any other sexually transmitted disease in the adolescent or adult population, **AIDS** (Acquired Immune Deficiency Syndrome) is unrivaled in the fear it has generated among the American public. AIDS is caused by a virus that destroys the body's immune system. Consequently, many germs that would usually not harm someone with a normal immune system can produce devastating results and ultimately death. More about this terrorizing disease and its implications for children and adolescents appears in Perspective on Child Development 5.2.

AIDS, Children, and Adolescents

In 1981, when AIDS was first recognized in the United States, there were fewer than 60 cases. By November 1986, there were 27,000 cases of AIDS and 15,000 deaths from the disease. By March 1987, there were more than 32,000 cases of AIDS and 20,000 deaths. Beginning in 1990, according to Dr. Frank Press, president of the National Academy of Sciences, "We will lose as many Americans each year to AIDS as we lost in the entire Vietnam War." Almost 60,000 Americans died in that war. According to federal health officials, 1 to 1.5 million Americans are now asymptomatic carriers of AIDS—those who are infected with the virus and presumably capable of infecting others but who show no clinical symptoms of AIDS.

In a recent survey of 35,239 high school students in 11 states by the Centers for Disease Control in Atlanta, it was revealed that many adolescents are misinformed about AIDS. More than 50 percent of the adolescents believed that an individual can get AIDS from a blood test; about the same percentage said that AIDS can be contracted from a public toilet. Experts say the disease can only be transmitted by sexual contact, sharing needles, or blood transfusions. More than 90 percent of the adolescents did know that AIDS can be transmitted through sex and through sharing drug needles.

While 90 percent of AIDS cases continue to occur among homosexual males or intravenous drug users, a disproportionate increase among females who are heterosexual partners of bisexual males or of intravenous drug users was noted between 1985 and 1988. This increase suggests that the risk of AIDS may be increasing among heterosexual individuals who have multiple sexual partners (Quinn & others, 1988).

Of special interest to children and adolescents is the controversy surrounding individuals who have contracted the virus. For example, one thirteen-year-old hemophiliac contracted AIDS while receiving injections of a clotting agent. He was barred from resuming his seventh-grade classes. In another case in another school district, school officials and doctors met with more than 800 concerned parents to defend their decision to admit a fourteen-year-old AIDS patient to school. Some parents will not let their children attend schools where an identified AIDS patient is enrolled. Others believe children with the disease should not be society's outcasts based on our current knowledge of how the disease spreads.

AIDS is a lethal threat to adolescents whose sexual activities put them at risk for contracting the disease—especially those who are sexually active with more than one partner and those who are intravenous drug users. Sexually active adolescents—homosexual or heterosexual—can reduce the probability they will contract AIDS by following certain precautions (Nielson, 1987). First, sex with strangers or sex with individuals living in metropolitan locations where AIDS is most prevalent should be engaged in with extreme caution. Second, condoms may provide some protection against the virus, but data are inconclusive on this at this time. Third, a test is now available to determine if an individual has AIDS. Not everyone exposed to the AIDS virus contracts AIDS, but adolescents who test positive for the AIDS virus should refrain from further sexual contacts until their physician informs them otherwise.

Adolescent Pregnancy

Pregnancy is one of the major problems for today's adolescents. The adolescent pregnancy rate is increasing even though the birthrate is decreasing. If current trends continue, four in ten females will become pregnant at least once while they are in adolescence (Alan Guttmacher Institute, 1981). As indicated in figure 5.8, adolescents in the United States have the highest pregnancy rate at all ages when compared with many other industrialized countries. More than one million fifteen- to nineteen-year-old girls become pregnant every year in the United States (Hayes, 1987).

The consequences of our nation's high adolescent pregnancy rate are cause for great concern. Adolescent pregnancy increases the health risk of both the offspring and the mother. Infants born to adolescent mothers are more likely to have low birth weights—a prominent cause of infant mortality as well as neurological problems and childhood illnesses (Hamburg, 1986; Hayes, 1987; Schorr, in press). Approximately 90 percent of adolescent mothers presently keep their babies. They often drop out of school, fail to gain employment, and become dependent on welfare. Adolescent pregnancy rates have reached

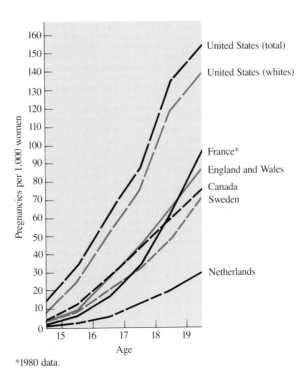

Figure 5.8
Pregnancy rates per 1,000 women by women's age, 1981.

*1980 data.

Note: pregnancies are defined here as births plus abortions; age is the age at outcome.

crisis proportions in our nation. Serious, extensive efforts need to be directed toward helping pregnant adolescents and young mothers stay in or return to school or work, obtain competent day care, and plan for the future (Edelman, 1987; Furstenberg, Brooks-Gunn, & Morgan, 1987). Four recommendations for how we should attack the high rate of adolescent pregnancy were recently offered by John Conger (1988)—sex education and family planning, access to contraceptive methods, the life options approach, and broad community involvement and support—each of which we discuss in turn.

We badly need age-appropriate family life education, including sex education that begins in childhood and continues through adolescence. Currently, almost half of all parents report that substantive sex education is not available in their schools (Hayes, 1987). Surveys of adolescents' sources of sex education indicate that only about 16 percent comes from schools (Thornburg, 1981). The biological aspects of sex are more likely to be taught than the social aspects. The most likely place and time an adolescent will be exposed to sex education is in biology class during the tenth grade. While 85 percent of all parents nationwide favor sex education in the schools, sex education continues to be a highly controversial topic.

An important missing ingredient in the fight against adolescent pregnancy is greater participation of parents in the sex education of their children and adolescents. The majority of adolescents say that they cannot talk freely with their parents about sexual matters. Surveys indicate that about 17 percent of adolescents' sex education comes from mothers and only about 2 percent comes from fathers (Thornburg, 1981). While parents, especially fathers, have been infrequent sources of sex education for adolescents, adolescents report that when they can talk with parents openly and freely about sex they are *less* likely to be involved in sexual intercourse. Contraceptive use by female adolescents also increases when adolescents report that they can communicate with their parents about sexual matters (Fisher, 1987).

Knowledge about contraceptive use is a major need among today's adolescents. These needs can often be fulfilled through adolescent clinics that provide comprehensive, high-quality health services.

127

Concept Table 5.2 Sexuality		
Concept	**Processes/Related Ideas**	**Characteristics/Description**
Sexual attitudes and behavior	Heterosexual trends	There has been a major increase in the number of adolescents reporting intercourse, and the proportion of females engaging in intercourse has increased more rapidly than that of males. National data indicate that at age sixteen roughly one-fourth to one-half of adolescents report having had intercourse. Urban inner city areas report even higher incidences.
	Sexual scripts	As we develop our sexual identities we often follow sexual scripts, which are different for males and females. While some aspects of the sexual double standard have been reduced, others are still rampant.
	Homosexual	Homosexuality is not widespread in adolescence. For many years homosexual behavior was increasingly accepted by adolescents, but because of the AIDS epidemic we can expect lower acceptance rates in the future. A number of factors may cause homosexuality.
	Masturbation	Masturbation is a frequent sexual outlet for many adolescents. It is no longer as widely stigmatized as it once was.
Sexually transmitted diseases	Its nature	A number of diseases may accompany sexual intercourse among adolescents, just as they do sexual intercourse among adults. These include chlamydia, gonorrhea, venereal warts, herpes, and AIDS.
Adolescent pregnancy	Trends	Even though the birthrate is decreasing in the United States, adolescent pregnancy rates are increasing.
	Prevention	Prevention includes sex education and family planning, access to contraceptive methods, life options, and broad community involvement and support.

In addition to age-appropriate family life and sex education, sexually active adolescents need access to contraceptive methods (Rickel, 1989). These needs often can be fulfilled through adolescent clinics that provide comprehensive, high-quality health services. At four of the nation's oldest adolescent clinics in St. Paul, Minnesota, the overall annual rate of first-time pregnancies has dropped from 80 per 1,000 to 29 per 1,000 (Schorr, in press). An important aspect of the adolescent clinics, whether they are in or out of a school context, is their provision for overall health services and sex education by providers trained to understand the special needs and confusions of this age group.

Better sex education, family planning, and access to contraceptive methods alone will not remedy the adolescent pregnancy crisis, especially for high-risk adolescents. Adolescents have to become *motivated* to reduce their pregnancy risk. This motivation only will come when adolescents look to the future and see that they have an opportunity to become self-sufficient and successful (Edelman, 1987). Adolescents need opportunities to improve their academic and career-related skills and their job opportunities. They need more life planning consultation and extensive health and mental health services.

Finally, for adolescent pregnancy prevention ultimately to succeed we need broad community involvement and support. This support has emerged as a major reason for the success of pregnancy prevention efforts in other developed nations where adolescent pregnancy rates, abortion, and childbearing are much lower than ours despite similar levels of sexual activity (Jones & others, 1985).

At this point we have discussed a number of ideas about adolescent sexuality. A summary of these ideas is presented in Concept Table 5.2.

Biological and Perceptual Development

Summary

I. The Boundaries and Determinants of Puberty
Puberty is a rapid change to physical maturation involving hormonal and bodily changes that takes place primarily during early adolescence. Its determinants include nutrition, health, heredity, and weight.

II. Hormonal and Physical Changes
The endocrine glands secrete hormones. Testosterone is the sex hormone that increases the most in adolescent males. Estradiol is the sex hormone that increases the most in adolescent females. The pituitary gland is the master gland and is involved in puberty through its interconnections with other glands. As adolescents undergo a growth spurt, they make rapid gains in height. The spurt occurs approximately two years earlier in girls (ten and one-half) than boys (twelve and one-half). Within a wide normal range, there is extensive individual variation in the changes brought on by puberty.

III. Body Image
Adolescents show a considerable interest in their body images. Young adolescents are more preoccupied and less satisfied with their body images than are late adolescents.

IV. Early and Late Maturation
Early maturation favors boys at least during adolescence. As adults, though, late maturing boys achieve more successful identities. The results are more mixed for girls than for boys. Being on-time or off-time in pubertal development is a complex affair. Adolescents may be at risk when the demands of a particular context and the adolescent's physical and behavioral characteristics are mismatched. Recently some scholars have expressed doubt that the effects of puberty are as strong as once believed. It is important to keep in mind that adolescent development is influenced by an interaction of biological, cognitive, and social factors.

V. Heterosexual Trends in Adolescence
There has been a major increase in the number of adolescents reporting intercourse, and the proportion of females engaging in intercourse has increased more rapidly than in the case of males. National data indicate that roughly one-fourth to one-half of adolescents report having had intercourse. Urban inner city areas report even higher incidences.

VI. Sexual Scripts
As we develop our sexual identities we often follow sexual scripts, which are different for males and females. While some aspects of the sexual double standard have been reduced, others are still rampant.

VII. Homosexuality and Masturbation
Homosexuality is not widespread in adolescence. For many years homosexual behavior was increasingly accepted by adolescents, but because of the AIDS epidemic we can expect lower acceptance rates in the future. A number of factors may cause homosexuality. Masturbation is a frequent sexual outlet for adolescents. It is no longer as widely stigmatized as it once was.

VIII. Sexually Transmitted Disease
A number of diseases may accompany sexual intercourse among adolescents, just as they do sexual intercourse among adults. These include chlamydia, gonorrhea, venereal warts, herpes, and AIDS.

IX. Adolescent Pregnancy
Even though the birthrate is decreasing in the United States, adolescent pregnancy rates are increasing. Prevention of adolescent pregnancy focuses on sex education and family planning, access to contraceptive methods, life options, and community involvement and support.

Key Terms

puberty 112	estradiol 114
menarche 112	pituitary gland 115
hormones 114	chlamydia 125
testosterone 114	AIDS 125

Suggested Readings

Brooks-Gunn, J. (1988). Antecedents and consequences of variations in girls' maturational timing. In M. D. Levine & E. R. McAnarney (Eds.), *Early adolescent transitions*. Lexington, MA: Lexington Books.
An authoritative review of what we know about the young adolescent girl's pubertal transitions.

Early adolescent sexuality: Resources for parents, professionals, and young people. (1983). Chapel Hill, NC: Center for Early Adolescence, University of North Carolina.
This compendium of resources provides an excellent annotated bibliography of a wide variety of topics related to sexuality in early adolescence.

Lerner, R. M., & Foch, T. T. (Eds.) (1987). *Biological-psychological interactions in early adolescence*. Hillsdale, NJ: Erlbaum.
Includes articles on a wide range of topics related to pubertal changes and their effects on development.

McCoy, K., & Wibbelsman, C. (1987). *The teenage body book*. Los Angeles, CA: The Body Press.
An award-winning book for youth. Includes extensive questions and answers adolescents have about their bodies and pubertal transitions.

Pierce, C., & VanDeVeer, D. (1988). *AIDS*. Belmont, CA: Wadsworth.
An excellent collection of essays on AIDS is presented, including a general overview of what is known about AIDS and information about ethical issues and public policy involved in AIDS.

Cognitive Development

Our life is what our thoughts make it.

—Marcus Aurelius, *Meditations,* 121–186 A.D.

CHAPTER
6

Learning and Motivation

Learning is an ornament in prosperity, a refuge in adversity.

Aristotle

Cora is in the fifth grade and enjoying her school year immensely. Her teacher, Ms. Greene, is energetic and uses a variety of teaching techniques each school day. The children seem to like the variation and richness of her teaching style. As we eavesdrop on the class one Tuesday morning, we see Cora begin her day's schoolwork by taking out a notebook and writing for fifteen minutes. The class has a standing assignment to begin each day by writing a journal entry of what they did in their free time the day before. Ms. Greene feels that the assignment helps to settle the children down immediately, to get them to reflect on their experiences, and to practice writing everyday. The teacher observes Cora finish, praises her in front of the class ("I'm happy to see you complete your writing assignment for today, Cora. Good job!"), and records a check next to Cora's name on a large class roster prominently displayed in the front of the room. Ms. Greene does this, in turn, for each of the children who finish. Each child who completes the writing assignment for every school day of the month is promised a spaghetti dinner at Ms. Greene's house.

Later in the day, we observe Ms. Greene instructing the children in mathematics. She shows the children, step by step, how to complete long division problems such as 21 divided into 446 and 18 divided into 3,641, emphasizing the testing of multiples, bringing intermediate products down, keeping columns in line, and recording remainders correctly (e.g., for the first problem the answer is 21 R. 5). As she works each example problem, she asks the children to copy her work from the blackboard and to study the steps. She answers several questions the children have and then gives them several problems to try on their own. Cora works diligently and since her penmanship isn't especially strong, she devotes attention to the mechanics of getting columns lined up and writing intermediate products and answers in the right places.

This real-life example illustrates two important concepts in learning that are pervasive in the lives of children throughout the world—reinforcement (or reward) and imitation, respectively. **Reinforcement** (or **reward**) is a consequence that increases the probability that a behavior will recur. When Cora and her classmates complete their daily journal entries, Ms. Greene provides immediate, but modest, verbal reinforcement with a concrete record or symbolic token (the check marks) that subsequently is converted into a large concrete reward (the spaghetti dinner). The larger reward is given only after a substantial period of time so that children learn to delay gratification. In her math instruction, Ms. Greene demonstrates, or models, some techniques for completing a basic task in mathematics. In this situation, the children learn through imitation of an expert model (Ms. Greene) and practice the imitated behaviors. **Imitation** (or **modeling**) takes place when children learn new behaviors by watching someone else perform the behaviors. We will have much more to say about these two powerful learning processes—reinforcement and imitation—later in the chapter.

This chapter is about children's learning and motivation—about the hows and whys of children's behavior, respectively. Among the questions we evaluate are: What are learning and motivation? What are the different ways children learn? What are different ways we can motivate children? What is the nature of children's achievement motivation?

The Nature of Learning and Motivation

The term **learning** is used extensively in our everyday conversation. As a result, most of us have fairly rich ideas about what it means to learn and a number of concrete experiences we can call to mind to illustrate actual cases of learning. We might associate learning with what takes place in school, with the conscious efforts of a parent to "teach" a child something, with the outcome of a child exploring a new place or a new object, with the practice of some physical or athletic skill, and so forth. Although many of these examples may indeed involve learning, in psychology, we try to be more formal and precise about the definition of learning. So, we say that learning occurs only when certain features of situations are evident.

One feature that shows evidence of learning is *change*. When a parent shows a child how to hold a spoon, when a teacher shows a child how to use a computer keyboard, or when a child attempts to head a soccer ball, the child probably does not perform these feats appropriately at first. For example, the spoon may be held backwards, the keys of the keyboard stroked randomly, and the soccer ball missed or struck with the face. But, at a later point, the child does complete these behaviors appropriately—in effect changing from not being able to respond correctly to being able, clearly, to respond correctly.

A second feature that shows evidence of learning is the *relative permanence* of the change in responding. Consider the examples given. We can presume that most children will continue to hold spoons, stroke keyboards, and head soccer balls correctly for a considerable time to come, once they have mastered these feats. These actions have become relatively permanent in the child's repertoire of behavior and skills.

A third feature of learning is the central role of *experience*. Roughly speaking, experience is the opportunity to repeatedly practice or observe events and actions. The infant may repeatedly try to grasp the spoon, the child may practice at the keyboard, and the soccer novice will repeatedly try to head the ball accurately (although perhaps not too often, since excessive heading hurts). The actual practice may be combined with time spent observing skilled adults do these things.

To summarize, then, learning is defined as a relatively permanent change in behavior that occurs through some form of experience. This definition helps us to distinguish between behaviors that the child acquires through learning as opposed to behaviors that originate primarily in some other way. For example, if a child is physically ill, drugged, or injured, she may talk and act in unusual and distinct ways that never occurred before and never occur in normal states. Ordinarily, we would not say that the child has learned new behaviors as a result of the illness, drug state, or injury. But we might well waive this disclaimer for children whose "distressed" condition lasts for a long time. Because then, indeed, the behaviors may be practiced to the extent that they become relatively permanent. Another example is that many behaviors develop in children through maturational processes, primarily, and learning processes only secondarily. For example, children learn to walk and talk and

The behavior of the girls in this elementary school classroom indicates a motivation for achievement. What do we mean by the concept of motivation, or that a child is motivated to do something?

adolescents experience intense interest in members of the opposite sex. These behaviors are heavily influenced by biological processes. A child learns to walk and talk as part of the natural process of maturation, although we know that practice helps to shape these behaviors. An adolescent's interest in members of the opposite sex is largely caused by the physical and hormonal changes occurring at the same time.

As with learning, the concept of **motivation** is loaded with many meanings from our everyday experiences and conversations. We can easily imagine activities we enjoy doing, occasions when we feel especially productive, individuals who work harder than others, pep talks from significant others, and attractive things we admire and covet. Although these examples indeed involve motivation, we need to be more formal and precise about the definition and meaning of motivation.

Motivation is wrapped up in the question of "why" children behave, think, and feel the way they do. Why is a child hungry? Why is a child studying so hard? Why is a child going to a party? Two important dimensions of the "whys" of children's behavior involve the *activation* of behavior and the *direction* of behavior. First, when children are motivated they do something. Their behavior is activated or energized. If children are hungry, they might go to the refrigerator for a snack. If they are motivated to get a good grade on a test, they might study hard. Second, when children are motivated, their behavior is directed. Why does one child behave one way when there are several options available? For example, if a father reprimands his daughter for failing to clean her room before going out to play, one child might seem to ignore the reprimand, another child might hurry to clean the room before departing, and a third child might start a verbal argument. Motivation, thus, involves an attempt to explain how children direct their behavior or, put another way, to explain the specific behaviors they select in certain situations but not others. To summarize, motivation focuses on the question of "why" children behave, think, and feel the way they do with special consideration of the activation and the direction of their behaviors.

How are learning and motivation connected? Why have we chosen to discuss these two topics together? The answer is at once simple and complicated. The simple answer is that learning and motivation are inextricably linked—much (but not all) learning occurs in the presence of forces that activate and direct behavior, in other words, factors that motivate the learning. And, conversely, much of human motivation is learned—we were not born predisposed to act a particular way, we acquired the motivation through learning. The more complicated answer is that we are not always sure just how learning and motivation are related. For example, we sometimes cannot decide whether or not a particular learned behavior requires some motivational push or pull to take place. Did a child learn in some class out of a strong need for achievement or a strong affinity for the teacher, for example?

Learning

What are the major ways children learn? In this section, we discuss the major, traditional forms of learning that psychologists have used to describe a wide range of changes. These include classical conditioning, operant conditioning, habituation, imitation, and cognitive learning. There are other forms of learning to be sure. Some of these are described in the chapters on cognitive development and Piaget's theory (chapter 7), information processing (chapter 8), and

Cognitive Development

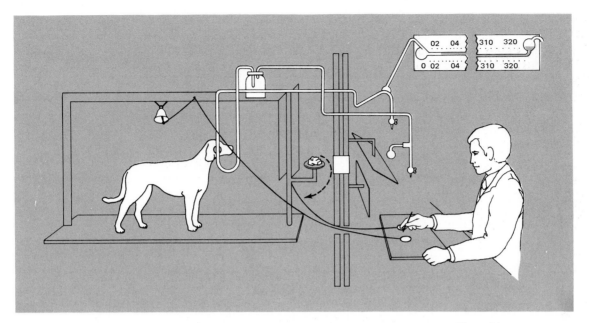

Figure 6.1
A modern apparatus for Pavlov's experiment in classical conditioning.

language (chapter 9). The forms of learning described here are especially useful when the change in question involves an easily observed behavior that is shaped by experiences and is relatively easy to define (e.g., smiling, crying, hitting). Other behaviors that involve a considerable amount of mental activity and organization (e.g., talking) and biological supports are best described by other forms of learning.

Classical Conditioning

It is a nice spring day. A father takes his baby out for a walk. The baby reaches over to touch a pink flower and is badly stung by a bumble bee sitting on the petals. Several weeks later, the baby's mother brings home some pink flowers. She removes a flower from the arrangement and takes it over for her baby to smell. The baby cries loudly as soon as she sees the pink flower. The baby's panic at the sight of the pink flower illustrates the learning process of **classical conditioning.**

How Classical Conditioning Works

The principle of classical conditioning was discovered by the Russian physiologist Ivan Pavlov (1927) while he was investigating the way the body digests food. In his study of the digestive system, Pavlov implanted a tube in a dog's salivary gland so he could measure the amount of saliva the dog secreted under various conditions. One day as Pavlov approached the dog with a tray of powdered meat, the dog began to salivate. Previously the saliva had flowed only when the dog was eating (see figure 6.1 to observe Pavlov's experimental setting). This aroused Pavlov's curiosity. Why did the dog salivate *before* eating the meat powder? He began putting together the pieces that complete the puzzle of classical conditioning.

Pavlov sensed that the dog's behavior included both unlearned and learned components. He called the food an **unconditioned stimulus (UCS)** and defined it as a stimulus that causes reflexive, or unlearned, behavior. The saliva that flowed from the dog's mouth in response to the food was called an **unconditioned response (UCR).** The unconditioned response is not learned. The

This infant looks calm and curious. Imagine that a bee comes by and lands on the flower. The infant touches the bee, gets stung, and cries. What components of classical conditioning do the bee sting and crying represent? Can you think of other circumstances in children's lives that might involve classical conditioning?

Figure 6.2
Diagram of the classical conditioning procedure. At the start of conditioning, the UCS will evoke the UCR, but the CS does not have this capacity. During conditioning, the CS and UCS are paired so that the CS comes to elicit the response. The key learning ingredient is the association of the UCS and CS.

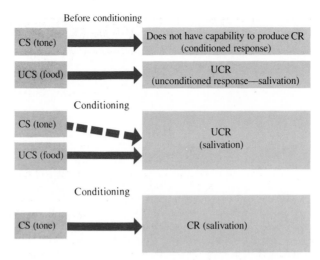

UCS and UCR automatically become associated. In the case of the baby and the flower, the baby's learning and experience did not cause her to cry when the bee stung her. Her crying was unlearned and occurred automatically. The bee's sting was the UCS and the crying was the UCR.

The more Pavlov showed food to the dog, the more the dog salivated. Pavlov then rang a bell immediately before giving the meat powder to the dog. Until then, ringing the bell did not have a particular effect on the dog, except perhaps to wake the dog from a nap. The bell was a neutral stimulus. But the dog began to associate the sound of the bell with the food and salivated when the bell was sounded. The bell had become a **conditioned** (learned) **stimulus (CS)** and the salivation a **conditioned response (CR).** Before conditioning (or learning), the bell and the food were not related. After their association, the conditioned stimulus (the bell) produced a conditioned response (salivation). In the case of the baby, the pink flower (the conditioned stimulus) elicited crying (the conditioned response) because of its association with the bee. Figure 6.2 provides a summary of how classical conditioning works.

Classical Conditioning with Children

Since Pavlov's experiments, children have been conditioned to respond to the sound of a buzzer, a glimpse of light, the touch of a hand. Classical conditioning has a great deal of survival value for children. Because of classical conditioning, children jerk their hands away before they are burned by fire and they move out of the way of a rapidly approaching truck before it hits them. Classical conditioning is at work in words that serve as important signals. A boy walks into an abandoned house with a friend and yells, "Snake!" The friend bolts out the door. An adolescent imagines a peaceful, tranquil scene—an abandoned beach with waves lapping onto the sand—and relaxes as if she were actually lying on the beach.

Phobias are irrational fears, which many psychologists believe are caused by classical conditioning. The famous behaviorist John Watson conducted an experiment to demonstrate this (Watson & Raynor, 1920). A little boy named Albert was shown a white laboratory rat to see if he was afraid of it. He was not. As Albert played with the rat a loud noise was sounded behind his head. As you might imagine, the noise caused little Albert to cry. After only seven pairings of the loud noise with the white rat, Albert began to fear the rat even when the noise was not sounded. Albert's fear was generalized to a rabbit, a dog, and a sealskin coat. Today we could not ethically conduct this experiment.

The toddler shown backing away from the dog has a phobia about dogs. How do phobias develop? How might they be eliminated?

Cognitive Development

Fear, Excitement, and Salivation

Martha, a third grader, is accompanying her mother on a business errand. The two are walking down a hall in their town's City-County Building. As they pass an office, a clerk inside suddenly opens the door and Martha notices a pale green wall and smells the strong odor of an alcohol-based disinfectant. (Someone inside is wiping off his desk top with a cleaning solution.) Suddenly Martha is overcome with apprehension, her heart rate increases, and her palms begin to sweat. On further investigation, we discover that Martha had a serious illness when she was five and spent a number of painful and uncomfortable days in a hospital bed. Guess what color the hospital walls were? And what do you suppose was a frequent odor in the hospital environment?

Jim, a seventh grader, is taking a leisurely bath. He is lying on his back—relaxing, listening to rock music on his shower radio, and generally unconcerned with anything going on around him. A few minutes go by before he remembers to take his wristwatch off—it isn't water resistant—and reaches over for a bar of soap to begin washing himself. The song on the radio has a momentary silence, followed by the unmistakable sound of a handgun being fired. Jim becomes excited, crouches, and begins a motion resembling the block-start dive at the outset of a swimming race. Jim is a competitive swimmer who has participated in the sport for six years. What cues might have triggered this highly trained response in him—the water, the pistol firing, taking off his wristwatch, or some combination of them?

Sally, like many four-year-olds, is a junk-a-holic. You name a sweet or a candy, and Sally would be happy to consume a truckload of it for you—just say the word. As she watches the world go by in the front seat of her Dad's car one day as the two of them are traveling about Sally spies an M&Ms sign on the window of a convenience store. Her eyes grow big, she begins to salivate, and she beckons her father to head to the convenience store.

In each anecdote described, see if you can offer a plausible analysis of the four key elements of the classical conditioning paradigm—that is, the UCS, the CS, the UCR, and the CR. If you can, chances are you grasp the essence of classical conditioning.

Especially noteworthy is the fact that Watson and Raynor did not remove Albert's fear of rats, so presumably this phobia remained with him after the experiment.

If we can produce fears by classical conditioning, we should be able to eliminate them. **Counterconditioning** is a procedure for weakening a CR by associating the stimulus to a new response incompatible with the CR. Though Watson did not eliminate little Albert's fear of white rats, an associate of Watson's, Mary Cover Jones (1924), did eliminate the fears of a three-year-old boy named Peter. Peter had many of the same fears as Albert; however, Peter's fears were not produced by Jones. Among Peter's fears were white rats, fur coats, frogs, fish, and mechanical toys. To eliminate these fears, a rabbit was brought into Peter's view but kept far enough away that it would not upset him. At the same time the rabbit was brought into view, Peter was fed crackers and milk. On each successive day the rabbit was moved closer to Peter as he ate crackers and milk. Eventually Peter reached the point where he would eat the food with one hand and pet the rabbit with the other.

Evaluating Classical Conditioning

Pavlov described all learning in terms of classical conditioning. In reality children learn in many other ways. Still, classical conditioning helps children to learn about their environment and has been successful in eliminating children's fears. More about the role of classical conditioning in children's everyday lives appears in Perspective on Child Development 6.1. However, a view that

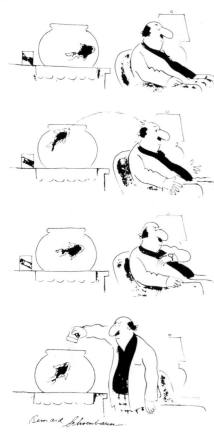

Drawing by Bernard Schoenbaum; © 1987 The New Yorker Magazine, Inc.

describes children as *responding* to the environment fails to capture the *active* nature of children and their influence on the environment. Next, we study a major form of learning that places more emphasis on children's activity in the environment—operant conditioning.

Operant Conditioning

What is operant conditioning? What are some different features of reinforcement? What is punishment and does it work? What are some practical applications of operant conditioning? We consider each of these in turn.

Operant Conditioning Defined

B. F. Skinner (1938, 1953) describes the way behavior is controlled in the following way. The child *operates* on the environment to produce a change that will lead to a reward. A baby cries and gets attention from its mother. As this sequence is repeated, the baby will learn to cry a lot. A child works diligently in school and receives praise from the teacher. If the hard work is repeatedly praised, the child will consistently display exemplary work habits in school. Skinner chose the term *operants* to describe the responses that are actively emitted because of the consequences for the child. The consequences— rewards or punishments—are *contingent,* or dependent, on the child's behavior. For example, the baby's crying is contingent on the mother's attention, and the child's work is contingent on the teacher's praise. In sum, **operant conditioning** is a form of learning in which the consequences of behavior lead to changes in the probability of that behavior's occurrence.

More needs to be said about the nature of reinforcement and punishment. *Reinforcement* (or reward) is a consequence that increases the probability a behavior will occur. By contrast, **punishment** is a consequence that decreases the probability a behavior will occur. For example, if a child meets an adult who smiles and the two continue to talk for some time, the adult's smile has reinforced the child's talking. However, if the child meets an adult who frowns and the child quickly leaves the situation, the frown has punished the child's talk with the adult.

Although Skinner began his work, as did Pavlov, with laboratory studies of animals whose environments could be carefully and extensively controlled, operant conditioning has been applied extensively to the lives of infants, children, and adults for the last fifty years. There is literally a cast of thousands of professionals who have used techniques based on operant conditioning both to study behavioral changes and to help individuals lead more adaptive lives. In the discussion that follows we highlight some of the techniques and concepts of this approach.

The Flow of Events

Operant psychologists often chart the course of behavioral change in individual children by dividing their observations into three categories. During a **baseline** period, we assume that the behavior in question has no consequences effecting it and that it is at a relatively low level of occurrence. To document this belief, we count the number of times the behavior occurs for some well-defined period of time. For example, suppose we wished to follow the progress of an unruly child—Richard—who rarely stays on task in school. We create an observational sampling procedure where we observe and record how many times Richard stays in his seat and focuses on his assigned work. For example,

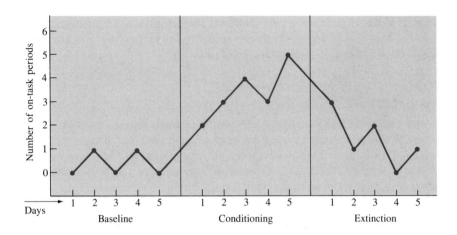

Figure 6.3
Baseline, conditioning, and extinction of Richard's on-task behavior.

we might record how many blocks of time (perhaps in five-minute intervals) he is on task during two designated hours of the school day for a continuous week. We discover, at most, one such interval each day and record it on a chart (figure 6.3).

Next, during a **conditioning** period, we institute a program to change Richard's unruly behavior. Everyone is instructed to ignore Richard when he is out of his seat. When he is at his seat working, the teacher praises him and the other children smile at him. We record the number of blocks of time Richard is on task as before, using the same sampling scheme for the next continuous week. We discover that he has from two to five such intervals per day during the week (figure 6.3).

Finally, during an **extinction** period, we remove the consequences for Richard's on-task behavior so that the teacher and other students in the class treat him just as they did in the baseline period. There is no praise from the teacher or smiling faces from the students when Richard is on task. We repeat the recording procedure for another week and discover that Richard is on task anywhere from zero to three such intervals on any given day (figure 6.3).

So, what have we learned about Richard? We objectively documented that he had a low level of academic behavior at the start of the procedure. Then, when we introduced two reinforcers—teacher's praise and classmates' smiles—Richard's academic behavior increased measurably over the week. So, these reinforcers were effective in changing Richard's academic behavior. Finally, when we withdrew the reinforcers, Richard's academic behavior gradually decreased, although not to the same low level before the conditioning.

By using this procedure it is possible to follow the effects of particular reinforcing events on behavior change. Notice that we chart the behavior change over time in an individual child, that we make our observational scheme as simple and objective as possible, and that we focus on easily observable behaviors such as whether or not a child is sitting at his seat focusing on his schoolwork. These are the hallmarks of operant methodology. They have proven to be powerful observational tools and insightful logical devices for explaining behavior change. In practice, operant experiments like this are often more complex: there may be several different conditioning phases in which slightly different consequences (contingencies) are used to change behavior; observers might be asked to record the occurrences of several different aspects of behavior at the same time; and the procedure is often tried with a number of subjects at about the same time. However, the complexity does not alter the power of this type of design—only the amount of work the investigators must do to collect, record, and analyze the information.

Arrangements for Reinforcement

Our definition of reinforcement was rather simple—a behavior is strengthened by the consequences that follow it. Notwithstanding, it turns out that there are many details about the arrangement of behavior and its consequences that influence the effectiveness of reinforcement. Among these details are consideration of shaping, schedules of reinforcement, primary and secondary reinforcement, the child's reinforcement history, and naturalistic settings.

A child who enters a new learning situation may not have the slightest inclination to behave in a way that is appropriate for the setting. On the first day of school she may walk around the room and talk incessantly, not realizing that generally, one of the first requirements in school is to sit quietly at one's desk. A boy whose mother asks for some help baking a cake hasn't the slightest inkling of what to do first. An autistic child initially does not speak at all. In each case *shaping* is required to develop the desired response.

Skinner first showed that such zero-level entry behavior can be shaped gradually through *successive approximations* to produce the final, desired response (Skinner, 1938). The child may gradually learn to sit quietly at her desk by first being reinforced for a distantly related response, such as approaching the desk to sit down, and then a closer response, such as sitting down for a moment, and so on, until the final behavior appears. The boy's mother may first reward him for selecting a baking utensil, then for mixing some ingredients, and so on, until all components of the task have been mastered. A therapist may first reward the autistic child for a sound faintly resembling speech, then for a word, a phrase, and finally, whole sentences. O. Ivar Lovaas (1977; Lovaas, Koegel, & Schreibman, 1979) has had some success with this procedure.

In most of life's experiences, children are not reinforced every time they make a response. A student is not patted on the back every time she solves a problem, for example. This type of reinforcement is called **partial reinforcement** (or intermittent reinforcement), which simply means that the child's responses are not reinforced every time they occur. Various types of partial reinforcement have been identified, each with rules that determine the occasion when a response will be reinforced. These **schedules of reinforcement** are based on time (*interval schedule*) and frequency of the specific behaviors (*ratio schedule*).

First, let's examine an example of an interval schedule. Consider the example given of Richard, our unruly elementary school child. The teacher decides that she would like Richard to be cooperative throughout the day, and that it is difficult to pay attention to him continuously given her other responsibilities. So, instead of praising Richard each time he is sitting at his seat, she arranges to praise him every other hour (9 A.M., 11 A.M., 1 P.M., 3 P.M.) if she has seen him engaged in work for an agreed-upon period of time (e.g., five minutes) just before the hour in question. She institutes a reward schedule throughout the week, using this same schedule each day.

To illustrate a ratio schedule, we can modify the example. Suppose the teacher found the reinforcement schedule to be ineffective. Richard did not respond. In fact, his behavior may have actually deteriorated in the face of

infrequent attention from the teacher. The teacher decides that her initial intuition is still correct. It would be advantageous not to reinforce Richard every time he is on task academically—with the goal being to extend the length and frequency of his on-task behavior throughout the day. So, she tries another reinforcement schedule. She decides that she will keep track of each on-task period that Richard displays. But, she will only reinforce him after he has displayed three on-task periods—each, say, five minutes long. So, in effect, for each set of three behaviors Richard displays, he will receive reinforcement. As before, the reward schedule is instituted each day throughout the week.

Both of these schedules are *intermittent,* that is, the teacher has chosen to reward the child on an occasional, as opposed to continuous, basis. The usual technique in operant conditioning is to start off conditioning by shaping a behavior, then reinforcing the behavior continuously, and finally adopting some form of intermittent schedule. Often, but not always, an intermittent schedule of reinforcement will produce a more stable and long-lasting behavioral change.

Reinforcement also can be classified in terms of **primary and secondary reinforcement,** which focuses on the distinction between inborn and unlearned and learned aspects of behavior. Primary reinforcers are innately satisfying; that is, it does not take any learning on the organism's part to make them positive, only experience for them to shape up particular behaviors to desired levels. Food, water, and sexual satisfaction are primary reinforcers.

Secondary reinforcers acquire their positive value through experience. Hundreds of secondary reinforcers penetrate our lives. For example, social reinforcers include praise, smiles, and a pat on the back. When a student is given $25 for the A on her report card, the $25 is a secondary reinforcer. It is not innate, and it increases the probability that the student will work to get another A in the future. Money often is referred to as a *token reinforcer.* When an object can be exchanged for some other reinforcer, the object may have reinforcing value itself, thus, it is called a token reinforcer. Gift certificates and poker chips are other token reinforcers.

Another consideration in the reinforcement of learning is the child's reinforcement history. Each child has a unique history of previous reinforcement; an event that is reinforcing for one child may well not be reinforcing for another. A child who works to learn a response for the reward of a toy may not work for the reward of new clothes or social praise. Some children are more likely to learn a response when the event that follows the response is social in nature, for example, verbal praise and social attention. Other children are more likely to work for material rewards like toys, candies, and treats.

One way to find out what is the most effective reinforcing event for a child is by scaling the value of different objects. For example, Sam Witryol (1971) and his colleagues developed a technique whereby young children are asked to judge which of two objects they prefer. The objects were drawn from toys, edibles, and other attractive objects, and all possible pairs were presented to the children. From the pattern of preferences that emerged, Witryol was able to describe a hierarchy of incentive values for the items. For example, most children preferred a piece of bubble gum to a marble and a marble to a paper clip. Other objects shown to them included a penny, a toy cow, an M&M candy, and a metal washer.

An important question in reinforcement is the degree to which the processes of learning we have been describing apply in the natural world of the child. Many psychologists have shown that young children frequently can and

Children's out-of-control behavior may be on any of a number of schedules of reinforcement. If we said this boy's out-of-control behavior in the classroom is on an interval schedule of reinforcement, what do we mean?

do reward one another in the preschool setting (Fagot, 1977; Hartup, 1983; Lamb & Roopnarine, 1979). By doing so, children dramatically alter one another's behavior. The demonstration has proven especially powerful in increasing or decreasing the likelihood children will engage in gender-stereotyped behaviors and activities. Little girls, for instance, will be more likely to engage in artistic activities if their friends applaud their efforts. Little boys will be more likely to perform high-energy physical activities if their peers praise them for doing so.

Punishment

Earlier in the chapter we indicated that *punishment* decreases the probability a behavior will occur. That is, if a punishing stimulus follows a behavior, the behavior is less likely to recur. The use of punishment is pervasive in our world. Consider Mark, who asks Valerie for a date and hears, "Are you kidding? Me go out with you!" Mark does not ask Valerie out again. Also consider a one-year-old whose mother spanks him for playing with an electrical socket. After the spanking, the infant does not go near the socket again. For ethical reasons, psychologists do not go around spanking infants to see whether such a stimulus decreases behavior. However, a number of laboratory experiments on punishment have been conducted with lower animals, and some modified versions of punishment experiments with animals have been conducted with humans. Psychologists have made recommendations about the effective use of punishment and decisions about when it might be called for in human behavior.

First, punishment may lead to escape or avoidance. Second, when a response is successfully reduced or eliminated by punishment and no appropriate alternative behavior is strengthened, other undesirable behaviors may take the place of the punished behavior. Third, a person who administers punishment is serving as an aggressive model, possibly inadvertently modeling how to behave in an aggressive, punishing manner. Fourth, desirable behaviors may be eliminated along with undesirable ones. For example, a child may stop interacting with other children altogether when he is slapped for biting another child. Because punishment has so many side effects, are there circumstances when it is called for? There may be some circumstances when punishment is beneficial. For example, when positive reinforcement has not been found to work, punishment can be considered. And when the behavior that is being punished is considered more destructive than the punishment itself, the process may be justified. For example, some children engage in behavior that is very dangerous to their well-being, such as head banging. In such cases, the use of punishment, even electric shock, may reduce the injurious behavior. Nonetheless, as punishment is reduced, it is always wise to reinforce an alternative behavior so that undesirable behavior does not replace the punished response.

Applications of Operant Conditioning

A preschool child repeatedly throws down his glasses and breaks them. A young girl feels depressed. An adolescent mother lacks appropriate parenting skills. Operant conditioning has helped individuals such as these adapt more effectively and cope with their problems. Using operant conditioning to change behavior in everyday life is often called **behavior modification.**

The main goal of behavior modification is to replace unacceptable, maladaptive responses with acceptable, adaptive ones. Consequences for behavior are established to ensure that acceptable responses are reinforced and unacceptable ones are not. Advocates of behavior modification believe that without adequate response consequences, children may develop emotional and mental problems (Kanfer & Schefft, 1987; O'Leary & Wilson, 1987). The child who throws down his glasses and breaks them may be receiving too much attention from his teacher and peers for his behavior, thus, an unacceptable behavior is unwittingly reinforced. In this instance, parents and the teacher would be instructed to remove attention from the destructive behavior and transfer it to more constructive behavior such as working quietly and playing cooperatively (Harris, Wolf, & Baer, 1964). Behavior modification also is used to teach fathers to engage in more effective caregiving with their infants, to encourage mentally retarded children to be less aggressive, to decrease children's consumption of caffeine drinks, to increase autistic children's social skills, to help obese children lose weight, and to increase the assertiveness of adolescents (Dachman & others, 1986; Koegel, Dyer, & Bell, 1987; Masters & others, 1988; O'Leary & Wilson, 1987). And as described in Perspective on Child Development 6.2, behavior modification can be used to increase the probability children will "buckle up for safety" in automobiles.

Habituation

Another form of learning has been especially interesting in recent years to researchers who study infant development. If a stimulus—a sight or a sound—is presented to infants several times in a row, they usually pay less attention to it each time, suggesting that they are bored with it. This is the process of **habituation**—repeated presentation of the same stimulus, which causes reduced attention to the stimulus. If a different stimulus is then presented, infants perk up and pay attention to it, suggesting they can discriminate between the two—this is the process of **dishabituation.** Among the measures researchers have used to study whether habituation or dishabituation is occurring are heart rate and respiration rate, sucking behavior (sucking stops when the young infant attends to an object), and the length of time the infant looks at an object. Newborn infants can habituate to repetitive stimulation in virtually every sensory modality—vision, audition, touch, and so on (Rovee-Collier, 1987). However, habituation becomes more acute over the course of the first three months of life. The extensive assessment of habituation in recent years has resulted in its use as a measure of the infant's maturity and well-being. Infants who have brain damage or have suffered birth traumas—such as a lack of oxygen—do not habituate well and may have developmental and learning problems later in life.

A knowledge of habituation and dishabituation can benefit parent-infant interaction. Infants respond to changes in stimulation. If stimulation is repeated often, the infant's response will decrease to the point that the infant no longer responds to the parent. In parent-infant interaction, it is important for parents to do novel things and to repeat them often until the infant stops responding. The wise parent senses that the infant shows an interest and that many repetitions of the stimulus may be necesary for the infant to process the information. The parent stops or changes behavior when the infant redirects her attention (Rosenblith & Sims-Knight, 1985).

Getting Children to "Buckle Up"

E ach year more American children are injured or die as a result of automobile accidents than as a result of any other type of accident or disease. According to recent statistics from the National Safety Council, about 1,500 deaths and 125,000 injuries occur each year in children fourteen years or younger. There seems to be a strong consensus that safety belts and child safety seats, if used properly, could eliminate about half of these deaths and injuries.

In the face of such evidence one natural question is, How can we get children to use safety belts consistently? For those children old enough to understand and take responsibility for themselves, how can we make "buckling up" a high frequency operant response when the youngsters get into an automobile?

A recent study by Karen Sowers-Hoag, Bruce Thyer, and Jon Bailey (1987) offers a simple, but powerful, answer. The authors first reviewed what other experts had tried. Many of these efforts, not unexpectedly, were directed toward adults. Typical intervention programs included reminder flyers placed on automobile windshields, safety-belt lotteries, dashboard reminder stickers, and "flash-for-life" cards used as prompts for unbuckled drivers. Only modest gains were observed in the number of individuals buckling up in these programs.

The researchers thought that it was important to direct efforts at children themselves, to try to invent a program that would get large percentages of children buckling up, and to demonstrate the lasting effects of the behavior change. They identified sixteen children ranging from 4.8 to 7.1 years, all of whom attended an after-school program, and none of whom buckled up at all when they drove home with their parents at the end of the school day.

Following a baseline period of observing the children, the behavior modification program consisted of four parts. First, one of the authors presented educational facts about the use of safety belts and discussed famous role models known to use safety belts, such as airline and jet fighter pilots, race car drivers, and well-known movie stars. Second, the same author taught children how to be assertive about the use of seat belts by role playing a number of situations children might encounter. Third, the children

What techniques can be used to get children to buckle up their seatbelts with more regularity?

engaged in behavioral rehearsal during which they went to the school parking lot and practiced getting into and out of the front and back seats of several cars, buckling the seat belts in the cars and practicing to accomplish this quickly. Finally, a lottery was set up and any child observed buckling up on the after-school trip home was eligible to win a prize in the next day's lottery. Half of the children won prizes in this lottery, including stickers, toy cars, and coloring books. The lottery part of the study had

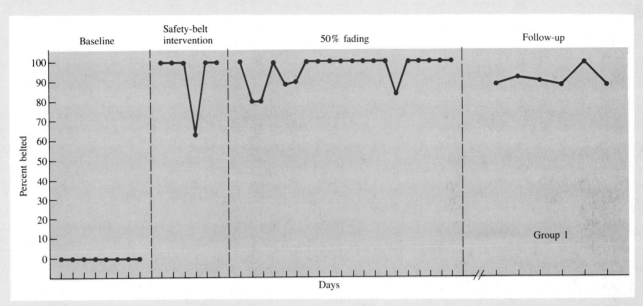

Figure 6.A
Percent of safety-belt use by eight children.

two phases. The first phase lasted several days until the children's buckling-up behavior increased. The second phase involved changing the behavioral criterion so that children became eligible for the lottery only if they had buckled up for two consecutive days (remember our discussion of intermittent interval schedules earlier in the chapter). The results for half of the children are shown in figure 6.A. (The results for the other half of the children are similar but are not included to avoid confusion—these other children received the different parts of the training at different points.)

As shown in figure 6.A, during the baseline period, lasting seven days, none of the eight children buckled up on the way home. During the four-part training (safety-belt intervention), the children all buckled up on five of the six days, a significant improvement. When the behavioral criterion increased to two days (in figure 6.A., this is reported

as 50 percent fading), most of the children continued to buckle up during the three weeks their behaviors were observed. Notice that on many days all the children (100 percent) buckled up. Finally, the authors conducted follow-up observations, beginning one month after the lottery ended (60 days). The children were observed periodically over another month and a half (until day 102). In this follow-up period, a high percentage of the children were still using their safety belts. To confirm that the children were buckling up at other times, the children's parents were interviewed. Apparently the training program was successful because the parents reported that the children consistently buckled up on other occasions as well.

We think these findings are important because they report a relatively simple educational technique that takes only a few hours to implement and because the results may save a child's life someday.

Concept Table 6.1
The Nature of Learning and Motivation, Classical Conditioning, Operant Conditioning, and Habituation

Concept	Processes/Related Ideas	Characteristics/Description
The nature of learning and motivation	Learning	Learning is a relatively permanent change in behavior that occurs through some form of experience.
	Motivation	Motivation focuses on the question of "why" children behave the way they do with special consideration of the activation and the direction of their behaviors.
Classical conditioning	How classical conditioning works	Pavlov discovered that the organism learns the association between an unconditioned stimulus (UCS) and a conditioned stimulus (CS). The UCS automatically produces the unconditioned response (UCR). After conditioning (CS-UCS pairing), the CS elicits the conditioned response (CR) by itself.
	Classical conditioning with children	Classical conditioning has survival value for children, for example, when they develop a fear of hazardous conditions. Irrational fears are explained by classical conditioning. Counterconditioning has been used to eliminate children's fears.
	Evaluating classical conditioning	Classical conditioning is important in explaining how some learning occurs, but it is certainly not the predominant way children learn because it misses the active nature of the child.
Operant conditioning	Defined	It is a form of learning in which the consequences of the child's behavior lead to changes in the probability of its occurrence. Reinforcement (reward) is a consequence that increases the probability a behavior will occur. Punishment is a consequence that decreases the probability a behavior will occur.
	The flow of events	Researchers often set up experiments on operant conditioning by establishing a baseline, then instituting conditioning, and finally setting up extinction of the learned behavior.
	Arrangements for reinforcement	These include shaping, schedules of reinforcement, primary and secondary reinforcement, the child's reinforcement history, and naturalistic settings.
	Punishment	Reasoning is often more effective than high-intensity punishment. Experts recommend that alternatives to punishment be explored before punishment is used.
	Applications	Using operant conditioning to change everyday behaviors is called behavior modification, which is designed to reduce maladaptive behavior and to promote adaptive behavior.
Habituation	Its nature	Habituation occurs when the repeated presentation of the same stimulus causes reduced attention to the stimulus. If a different stimulus is presented and the infant pays attention to it, dishabituation has occurred. Newborn infants can habituate although habituation becomes more acute over the first three months of infancy.

We have discussed a number of ideas about the nature of learning and motivation and the learning processes of classical conditioning, operant conditioning, and habituation. A summary of these ideas is presented in Concept Table 6.1. Now we turn our attention to another important learning process—imitation—and cognitive factors involved in children's learning.

Imitation and Cognitive Learning

When children learn, they often cognitively represent or transform their experiences. So far we have had little to say about these cognitive processes. In the operant view of Skinner and the classical conditioning view of Pavlov, no room is given to the possibility that cognitive factors such as memory, thinking, planning, and expectations might be important in learning. Skinnerians point out that they do not deny the existence of thinking, but since they cannot observe thinking they do not believe it is an important factor in the scientific study of learning. Many contemporary learning experts, though, advocate the importance of cognitive factors in learning. Albert Bandura has been a pioneer in promoting the role of cognition in learning. First we describe his important thoughts and research on imitation and then turn to his recently developed model of learning.

Imitation

Would it make sense to put a fifteen-year-old boy behind the wheel of a car and turn him loose with no driver's training? Should we ask him to drive down the road and then reward his positive behaviors? Not many of us would want to be on the road when some of his disastrous mistakes occur. Albert Bandura (1971, 1986) believes that if we learned in such a trial-and-error fashion, it would be an exceedingly laborious and at times hazardous undertaking. Instead, many of children's complex behaviors are due to their exposure to competent models who display appropriate behavior in solving problems and coping with their world.

Recall from our description earlier in the chapter that *imitation,* or modeling, occurs when children learn new behaviors by watching someone else perform the behaviors. The capacity to learn behavior patterns by observation eliminates tedious trial-and-error learning. In many instances imitation takes less time than operant conditioning.

The following experiment by Bandura (1965) illustrates how imitation can occur by watching a model who is neither reinforced nor punished. The only requirement for learning is that the child be connected in time and space with the model. The experiment also illustrates an important distinction between learning and performance.

An equal number of boys and girls of nursery school age watched one of three films in which an individual beat up an adult-sized plastic Bobo doll (figure 6.4). In the first film, the aggressor was rewarded with candy, soft drinks, and praise for aggressive behavior; in the second film, the aggressor was criticized and spanked for the aggressive behavior; and in the third film, there were no consequences to the aggressor for the behavior. Subsequently, each child was left alone in a room filled with toys, including a Bobo doll. The child's behavior was observed through a one-way mirror. As shown in figure 6.5, children who watched the aggressor be reinforced or suffer no consequences for aggressive behavior imitated the aggressive behavior more than the children who watched the aggressor be punished. As might be expected, boys were more aggressive than girls. The important point about these results is that imitation occurred just as extensively when modeled aggressive behavior was not reinforced as when it was reinforced.

A second important point focuses on the distinction between learning and performance. Just because a person does not *perform* a response does not mean it was not *learned.* When children were offered rewards (in the form of decals and fruit juice) for imitating the model's behavior, the differences in imitative behavior among the children in the three situations disappeared. In this experiment, all of the children *learned* about the model's behavior, but the *performance* of the behavior did not occur for some children until reinforcement was presented. Bandura believes that when the child observes behavior but makes no observable response, the child still may have acquired the modeled response in cognitive form.

Since his early experiments, Bandura (1986) has focused on some specific processes that influence an observer's behavior following exposure to a model. One of these is **attention.** Before the child can reproduce a model's

Figure 6.4
Children imitate aggression. An adult model aggressively attacks a Bobo doll. The preschool-aged girl who has observed the adult model's aggressive actions follows suit.

Figure 6.5
Results of Bandura's experiment on imitation and children's aggression.

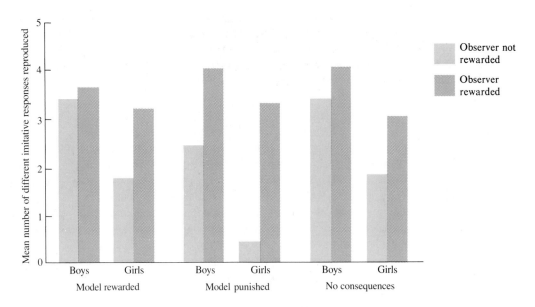

Figure 6.6
Bandura's model of imitation.

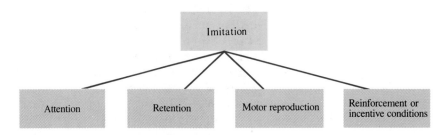

action, she must attend to what the model is saying or doing. A child may not hear what a teacher is saying if another child in the next aisle is always talking, for example. Attention to the model is influenced by a host of characteristics. For example, warm, powerful, atypical individuals command children's attention more than do cold, weak, typical individuals.

The next consideration is the child's **retention.** To reproduce a model's actions, the child must code the information and keep it in memory so that it can be retrieved. A simple verbal description or a vivid image of what the model did assists retention. Memory is such an important cognitive process we will consider it in much greater detail in chapter 8.

Another process in imitation is **motor reproduction.** A child may attend to a model and code in memory what he has seen, but because of limitations in motor development the child may not be able to reproduce the model's actions. A five-year-old may observe a teacher make the letter *A* on the blackboard but not have sufficient fine motor skills to reproduce the *A,* for example.

A final process in Bandura's conception of imitation involves **reinforcement or incentive conditions.** On many occasions children attend to what a model says or does, retain the information in memory, and possess the motor capabilities to perform the action, yet they fail to repeat the behavior because adequate reinforcement is not present. This was demonstrated in Bandura's study (1965) when those children who had seen a model punished for aggression reproduced the model's aggression only when they were offered an incentive to do so. A summary of Bandura's view of imitation is presented in figure 6.6.

Cognitive Development

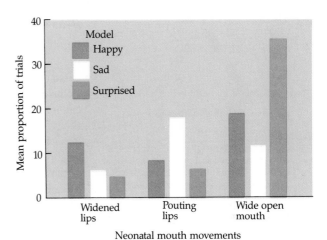

Figure 6.8
Imitation of adult emotions by thirty-six-hour-old newborns.

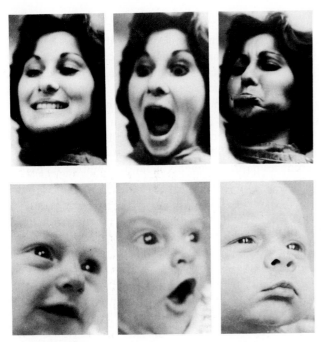

Figure 6.7
Sample photographs of a model's happy, surprised, and sad expressions and an infant's corresponding expressions.

Bandura views imitation as an information-processing activity. As the child observes, information about the world is transformed into cognitive representations that serve as guides to action. An interesting question is whether young infants can engage in imitation. Can a young infant imitate someone else's emotional expressions? If an adult smiles, will the baby follow up with a smile? If an adult protrudes her lower lip, wrinkles her forehead, and frowns, will the baby show a saddened look? If an adult opens her mouth, widens her eyes, and raises her eyebrows as though startled, will the baby follow suit? Could infants only one day old do these things?

Tiffany Field and her colleagues (1982) explored these questions with newborns only thirty-six hours after birth. The model held the newborn's head upright with the model's and the newborn's faces separated by ten inches. The newborn's facial expressions were recorded by an observer who stood behind the model. The observer could not see which facial expressions the model was showing. The model expressed one of three emotions: happiness, sadness, or surprise (figure 6.7). Infants were most likely to imitate the model's display of surprise by widely opening their mouths. When the infants observed a happy mood, they frequently widened their lips. When the model expressed sadness, the infants followed with lips that reflected pouting (figure 6.8). Other research supports the belief that young infants can imitate an adult's emotional expressions (Meltzoff, 1987, 1988; Meltzoff & Moore, 1977). Still other research suggests that while newborns can imitate an adult's tongue protrusion, they cannot imitate their emotional expressions (Kaitz & others, 1988). It also is open to interpretation whether imitation in young infants is innate or learned (Wolff, 1987).

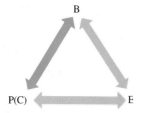

Figure 6.9

Bandura's model of the reciprocal influence of behavior (B), personal and cognitive factors P(C), and environment (E). The arrows reflect how relations between these factors are reciprocal rather than unidirectional.

Behavior, Person (Cognition), and Environment

Bandura's most recent model of learning and development involves behavior, the person (cognition), and the environment. Behavior, cognitive and other personal factors, and environmental factors operate interactively (figure 6.9). Behavior can influence cognition and vice versa, the child's cognitive activities can influence the environment, environmental influences can change the child's thought processes, and so on.

Let's consider how Bandura's model might work in the case of a seventh-grade girl's achievement behavior. As the girl diligently studies and gets good grades, her behavior produces positive thoughts about her abilities. As part of her effort to make good grades, she plans and develops a number of strategies to make her studying more efficient. In these ways her behavior has influenced her thought and her thought influenced her behavior. At the beginning of the school year, her school district made a special effort to involve students in a study skills program. Her success, along with that of other students who were involved in the program, led to the expansion of the program the next year. In these ways, environment influenced behavior, and behavior changed the environment. And the expectations of the school administrators that the study skills program would work made it possible in the first place. The program's success spurred expectations that this type of program could work in other school systems. In these ways cognition changed the environment and the environment changed cognition. Expectations are an important process in Bandura's model. In this example, we focused on a seventh-grade girl's achievement behavior. Achievement will be one of the most important topics in our discussion of children's motivation.

Motivation

Remember from our description early in the chapter that *motivation* focuses on the question of "why" children behave the way they do with special consideration of the activation and direction of their behaviors. First, we consider some ideas about the "whys" of children's behavior, and second, we extensively discuss an important dimension of children's lives—their achievement motivation.

Some Ideas about the "Whys" of Children's Behavior

Ten-year-old Robert has already made $3,000 this year mowing lawns and doing cleanup work. Fourteen-year-old Richard has aleady gone steady with four different girls. What motivated Robert to work so hard and make so much money? What motivated Richard to go with so many different girls? Psychologists have offered a number of ideas to account for why children behave the way they do.

Biological motives are patterns built into the child's central nervous system at birth. Put another way, all human beings inherit these patterns because they are human. Humans are born with **fixed-action patterns.** In contrast to reflexes, which are usually simple responses triggered by specific events, fixed-action patterns are more complex. As the name suggests, they are actually a series of responses chained together in a stereotyped fashion. Examples are moving away from someone when they get too close, holding and exploring a soft, graspable object like a human body or a terry cloth doll, and ending a fight with someone by turning away and falling to the ground. These examples illustrate, respectively, instinctual behavior related to personal space, touch, and retreat from aggression. Notice that for each example, there are many different events that could trigger the behaviors and that the behaviors themselves consist of several different actions.

Another type of biological motive is drive. A **drive** is an aroused state that occurs because of a physiological **need.** A child might have a need for water or for food. The need for food, for example, arouses the child's hunger drive. This motivates the child to do something—get her parents to take her to McDonald's for a Big Mac, for example—to reduce the drive and satisfy the need. As a drive becomes stronger, the child is motivated to reduce it. This action is known as **drive-reduction theory.**

An important concept in motivation and one that is important in understanding drives is **homeostasis**—the tendency to maintain equilibrium, or a steady state. Literally hundreds of biological states in children's bodies must be maintained within a certain range: temperature, blood-sugar level, potassium and sodium levels, oxygen, and so on. When a child dives into an icy swimming pool, his body heats up. When a child walks out of an air-conditioned room into the heat of a summer day, her body begins to cool down. These changes occur automatically in an attempt to restore children's bodies to their optimal state of functioning.

Homeostatis is used to explain both physiological imbalances and psychological imbalances. For example, if a child has not been around friends for a long time, he may be motivated to seek their company. If a child has not studied hard for a test in some months, she may be aroused to put in considerably more study time. The concepts of drive and homeostasis have played important roles in understanding children's motivation.

However, psychologists became disenchanted with drive-reduction theory as a comprehensive theory of motivation when it became apparent that children and adults are not always motivated to reduce a need. In the 1950s, experiments began to show that in many instances individuals are motivated to seek stimulation (e.g., Butler, 1953). Rather than always being motivated to reduce biological needs, R. W. White (1959) said that children have **competence motivation** (also called mastery or effectance motivation), which is the motivation to deal effectively with the environment, to do well what is attempted, to process information efficiently, and to make the world a better place. White said we do these things not because they serve biological needs but because we have an intrinsic (internal) motivation to effectively interact with our environment. Closely related to this idea is the motivation for achievement, which we discuss in a few moments.

In recent years there has been a flourish of interest in children's motivation for competence (Harter, 1980; MacTurk & others, 1987; Messer & others, 1987; Wachs, 1987). Why has competence motivation generated this interest among developmentalists? One attraction is that the concept pulls together many different aspects of children's development under a single theme. Another attraction is that findings indicate that the assessment of mastery motivation in infancy may provide a better basis for predicting later competence than do scores on developmental tests (Messer, Yarrow, & Vietze, 1982; Yarrow & others, 1983). And researchers are beginning to show that intervention programs with developmentally delayed children are especially beneficial when children are given the opportunity to become effective agents, that is, when they are given the opportunity for self-determination and self-responsibility in effectively interacting and controlling the environment (Brinker & Lewis, 1982).

How might the concept of drive and homeostasis be involved in the third grade child's motivation to study harder?

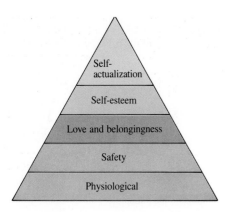

Figure 6.10
Maslow's hierarchy of needs.

As psychologists recognized the importance of competence motivation and the environment's role in motivation, they began to describe a number of learned motives in humans. These include the motivation for achievement, the motivation for power, the motivation for affiliation, the motivation for identity, and the motivation for self-actualization. As we see next, self-actualization is viewed as the highest form of motivation in one well-known theory of motivation.

Is getting an A in school more important to a child than eating? If the girl of an adolescent boy's dreams told him that he was marvelous would that motivate him to throw himself in front of a car for her safety? According to Abraham Maslow (1954, 1971), basic motives have to be satisfied before higher motives can be satisfied. Based on Maslow's **hierarchy of motives**, we would conclude that in most instances children need to eat before they can achieve and that they need to satisfy their safety motives before their love motives. Maslow believes that humans have five basic motives, which unfold in the following sequence: physiological, safety, love and belongingness, self-esteem, and self-actualization (figure 6.10). It is the motive for self-actualization that Maslow has described in the greatest detail. Self-actualization includes everything an individual is capable of being. According to Maslow, self-actualization is possible only after the other motives in the hierarchy are met. Obviously, children cannot be everything they are capable of being if they are hungry all the time. Among the characteristics of self-actualization are finding self-fulfillment and peace with one's life, realizing one's full potential, and feeling content with that. A self-actualized individual has an open manner, is not defensive, loves himself or herself, feels no need to manipulate others or be aggressive toward them, acts in ways to promote moral and ethical principles in society, and is creative, curious, and spontaneous in interchanges with others.

The idea that humans have a hierarchy of motives is an appealing one. Maslow's theory stimulates us to think about the ordering of the motives in children's lives. Not everyone agrees on the order in which children satisfy their needs, though. In some instances the order may be different than Maslow envisioned.

Achievement

Children are motivated to do well at what they attempt, to gain mastery over the world in which they live, to explore with enthusiasm and curiosity unknown environments, and to achieve the heights of success. When Vince Lombardi was coach of the Green Bay Packers, in his customary intense manner, he said, "Winning isn't everything, it is the *only* thing." A less intense promotion of achievement was offered by Henry Wadsworth Longfellow: "Let us be up and doing with a heart for any fate; still achieving, still pursuing."

Children live in an achievement-oriented world with standards that tell them success is important. These standards suggest that success requires a competitive spirit, a desire to win, a motivation to do well, and the wherewithal to cope with adversity and persist until obstacles are overcome. Some developmentalists, though, believe we are a nation of hurried, wired people who are raising our children to become the same way—too uptight about success and failure and far too worried about what we accomplish in comparison to others (Elkind, 1981). It was in the 1950s that an interest in achievement began to flourish. The interest initially focused on the need for achievement.

Need for Achievement

Think about yourself and your friends for a moment. Are you more achievement oriented than they are or less so? If we asked you and your friends to tell stories about achievement-related themes could we accurately determine which of you is more achievement oriented?

David McClelland (1955) stressed that individuals vary in their motivation for achievement and that we can measure these differences. McClelland referred to achievement motivation as *n achievement* (need for achievement), meaning the individual's motivation to overcome obstacles, desire for success, and effort expended to seek out difficult tasks and do them well as quickly as possible. To measure achievement, children were shown ambiguous pictures that were likely to stimulate achievement-related responses. Then they were asked to tell a story about the picture. Their comments were scored according to how strongly they reflected achievement (McClelland & others, 1953).

A host of studies have correlated achievement-related responses with different aspects of children's experiences and behavior. The findings are diverse, but they do suggest that achievement-oriented children have a stronger hope for success than fear of failure, are moderate rather than high or low risk takers, and persist for appropriate lengths of time in solving difficult problems (Atkinson & Raynor, 1974). Early research indicated that independence training by parents promoted children's achievement, but more recent research reveals that parents need to set high standards for achievement, model achievement-oriented behavior, and reward their children for their attempts to increase achievement (Huston-Stein & Higgens-Trenk, 1978).

Intrinsic and Extrinsic Motivation

As part of their interest in achievement motivation, psychologists have focused on the internal and external factors that contribute to such motivation. Considerable enthusiasm has greeted the issue of whether we should emphasize intrinsic or extrinsic motivation. Imagine that you must teach children about the addition and subtraction of fractions and help them practice these problems. One possibility would be to develop a simple "drill-and-practice" exercise that provides each child with a sequence of problems and praise after each correct answer. Such programs, indeed, are widespread. An alternative approach might be to present the same sequence of problems in the form of an instructional computer game specifically tailored to enhance the child's motivation. These programs are becoming available but they are less common than the drill-and-practice type. "Fractions Basketball" is one example developed by the PLATO Project at the University of Illinois (Dugdale & Kibbey, 1980). Figure 6.11 shows how the drill-and-practice program and the computer game strategy vary (Lepper, 1985).

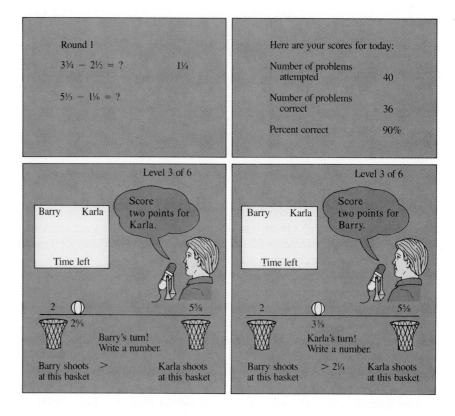

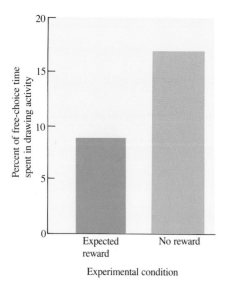

Figure 6.12
Time spent in a drawing activity under expected reward and no-reward conditions. Students with a strong interest in art spent more time drawing when no reward was mentioned than when they expected a reward for the participation.

The interest in intrinsic motivation comes from ideas about motivation for challenge, competence, effectiveness, and mastery (Harter, 1981; White, 1959); curiosity, incongruity, complexity, and discrepancy (Berlyne, 1960); and perceived control and self-determination (Deci, 1975). **Intrinsic motivation** involves an underlying need for competence and self-determination. By contrast, **extrinsic motivation** involves external factors in the environment, especially rewards. If you work hard in school because a personal standard of excellence is important to you, intrinsic motivation is involved. But if you work hard in school because you know it will bring you a higher paying job when you graduate, extrinsic motivation is at work.

An important consideration when motivating a child to do something is whether or not to offer an incentive (Pittman & Heller, 1987). If a child is not doing competent work, is bored, or has a negative attitude, it may be worthwhile to consider incentives to improve motivation. However, there are times when external rewards can get in the way of motivation. In one investigation, children with a strong interest in artistic work spent more time in a drawing activity when they expected no reward than their counterparts who knew that they would be rewarded (figure 6.12) (Lepper, Greene, & Nisbett, 1973).

Intrinsic motivation implies that internal motivation should be promoted and external factors deemphasized. In this way, children learn to attribute the causes of their successes and failures to themselves, especially how much effort they expend. But in reality, achievement is motivated by both internal *and* external factors. Children are never divorced from their external environment. Some of the most achievement-oriented children are those who have *both* a high personal standard for achievement and are also highly competitive. In one investigation, low-achieving boys and girls who engaged in individual goal

Cognitive Development

Sandra Graham, shown here talking with a group of young boys about motivation, has conducted important research showing that middle-class black children—like their middle-class white counterparts—have high achievement expectations and understand that their failure is often due to lack of effort rather than to lack of luck.

setting *and* were given comparative information about peers worked more math problems and got more of them correct than their counterparts who experienced either condition alone (Schunk, 1983). Other research suggests that social comparison—by itself—is not a wise strategy (Nicholls, 1984). The argument is that social comparison puts the child in an ego-involved, threatening, self-focused state rather than a task-involved, effortful, strategy-focused state.

Achievement in Minority-Group Children

One of the primary limitations of existing research on minority-group achievement is that there has been so little of it. The research literature on achievement has focused heavily on white males. And too often research on minority groups has been interpreted as "deficits" by middle-class, white standards. Rather than characterizing individuals as *culturally different,* many conclusions unfortunately characterize the cultural distinctiveness of blacks, Hispanics, and other minority groups as deficient in some way.

Much of the research on minority-group children is plagued by a failure to consider socioeconomic status (determined by some combination of education, occupation, and income). In many instances, when race *and* socioeconomic status (also called social class) are investigated in the same study, social class is a far better predictor of achievement orientation than race (Graham, 1986). Middle-class individuals fare better than their lower-class counterparts in a variety of achievement-oriented circumstances—expectations for success, achievement aspirations, and recognition of the importance of effort, for example (McAdoo & McAdoo, 1985).

Sandra Graham has conducted a number of investigations that reveal not only stronger social-class than racial differences but also the importance of studying minority-group motivation in the context of general motivational theory (Graham, 1984, 1986, 1987). Her inquiries focus on the causes blacks give for their achievement orientation—why they succeed or fail, for example. She is struck by how consistently middle-class black children do not fit our stereotypes of either deviant or special populations. They—like their middle-class white counterparts—have high expectations and understand that failure is often due to lack of effort rather than to luck.

Achievement in Math Requires Time and Practice— Comparisons of Children in the United States and Japan

arold Stevenson and his colleagues (1986) recently conducted a detailed investigation of math achievement in first- and fifth-grade children from the United States and Japan. The final sample included 240 first graders and 240 fifth graders from each country. Extensive time was spent developing the math test that was given to the children, the children were observed in their classrooms, and additional information was obtained from mothers, teachers, and the children themselves. The Japanese children clearly outscored the American children on the math test in both the first and fifth grades (table 6.A) And, by the fifth grade, the highest average score of any of the American classrooms fell *below* the worst performing score of the Japanese classrooms.

What are some reasons for these dramatic differences between American and Japanese children's math achievement? Curriculum did not seem to be a factor. Neither was the educational background of the children's parents. And neither was intelligence—the American children sampled actually scored slightly higher than the Japanese children on such components of intelligence as vocabulary, general information, verbal ability, and perceptual speed. Possibly the Japanese teachers had more experience? Apparently, this was not the case since no differences were found in terms of educational degrees and years of teaching experience.

The amount of time spent in school and in math classes probably was an important factor. The Japanese school year consists of 240 days of instruction and each school week is 5½ days; the American school year consists of 178 days of instruction and each school week is 5 days. In the fifth grade, Japanese children were in school an average of 37.3 hours per week and American children only 30.4 hours. Observations in the children's classrooms re-

Average Mathematics Achievement Scores by Japanese and American Children

Country	Boys	Girls
Grade 1		
Japan	20.7	19.5
United States	16.6	17.6
Grade 5		
Japan	53.0	53.5
United States	45.0	43.8

Adapted with permission from *Child Development and Education in Japan* by Harold Stevenson et al. Copyright © 1986 W. H. Freeman and Company.

vealed that Japanese teachers spent far more time teaching math than did American teachers: approximately one-fourth of total classroom time in the first grade was spent in math instruction in Japan; approximately one-tenth of total classroom time was spent in the United States. Observations also indicated that the Japanese children attended more efficiently to what the teacher was saying than did American children. And Japanese children spent far more time doing homework than American children— on weekends, sixty-six minutes versus eighteen minutes, respectively.

The conclusion: Learning requires time and practice. When either is reduced, learning is impaired. Such seems to be the case in American children's poor math achievement in comparison to Japanese children.

Not only can we compare the achievement orientation of children from different ethnic groups and social classes, but we also can compare the achievement orientation of children in different countries. Quite clearly, American children are more achievement oriented than children in many countries. However, there recently has been concern about the achievement American children display in comparison to children in other countries that have developed strong educational orientations—Russia, China, and Japan, for example (McKnight & others, 1987; Uttal, Lummis, & Stevenson, 1988). To learn more about the achievement orientation of American children compared to Japanese children, turn to Perspective on Child Development 6.3.

We have discussed a number of ideas about imitation and cognitive factors involved in learning as well as the nature of motivation. A summary of these ideas is presented in Concept Table 6.2.

Concept Table 6.2
Imitation and Cognitive Learning and Motivation

Concept	Processes/Related Ideas	Characteristics/Description
Imitation and cognitive learning	Imitation	Imitation, also called modeling, occurs when children learn new behaviors by watching someone else perform the behaviors. Bandura believes imitation involves attention, retention, motor reproduction, and reinforcement or incentive conditions. Many researchers believe that young infants can imitate an adult's emotional expressions.
	Cognitive learning	Many psychologists recognize the importance of studying how cognitive factors mediate environment-behavior connections. Bandura's contemporary model emphasizes reciprocal connections between behavior, person (cognition), and environment.
Some ideas about the "whys" of behavior	Biological motives	Fixed-action patterns and drive-reduction theory have been proposed as explanations for children's biological motives. Homeostasis is an important concept in drive-reduction theory and in understanding motivation. It describes the motivation for equilibrium.
	Competence motivation	As psychologists recognized there was more to motivation than drive reduction, they turned to the concept of competence motivation, first described by R. W. White. Also called mastery motivation, this involves the motivation to deal effectively with the environment.
	Learned motives	Interest in competence motivation and the environment's role in motivation led to the description of learned motives, including achievement, power, affiliation, identity, and self-actualization.
	Hierarchy of motives	Maslow believed some motives need to be satisfied before others; self-actualization is given special importance.
Achievement	Need for achievement	McClelland argued that we can measure individual differences in achievement motivation, or *n* achievement. The need for achievement is the motivation to overcome obstacles, the desire for success, and effort expended to seek out difficult tasks and to do them well. Achievement motivation is associated with a number of aspects of children's experiences and behavior.
	Intrinsic and extrinsic motivation	Intrinsic motivation involves an underlying need for competence and self-determination; extrinsic motivation involves external factors in the environment, especially rewards. Many of the most achievement-oriented children have both a high personal standard of achievement and are highly competitive. Social comparison by itself is not a wise strategy.
	Achievement in minority-group children	There has been too little research on minority-group children's achievement. When race and social class are investigated, social class is a better predictor of children's achievement than race.

Summary

I. The Nature of Learning and Motivation
Learning is a relatively permanent change in behavior that occurs through some form of experience. Motivation focuses on the question of "why" children behave the way they do with special consideration of the activation and the direction of their behaviors.

II. Classical Conditioning
Pavlov discovered that the organism learns the association between an unconditioned stimulus (UCS) and a conditioned stimulus (CS). The UCS automatically produces the unconditioned response (UCR). After conditioning (CS-UCS pairing), the CS elicits the conditioned response (CR) by itself. Classical conditioning has survival value for children, for example, when they develop a fear of hazardous conditions. Irrational fears have been explained by classical conditioning. Counterconditioning has been used to alleviate children's fears. Classical conditioning is important in explaining how some learning occurs, but it is certainly not the predominant way children learn because it misses the child's active nature.

III. Operant Conditioning
The child operates in the environment to produce change that will lead to reward. Operant conditioning is a form of learning in which the consequences of the

child's behavior lead to changes in the probability of its occurrence. Reinforcement (reward) is a consequence that increases the probability a behavior will occur. Punishment is a consequence that decreases the probability a behavior will occur. Researchers often set up experiments on operant conditioning by establishing a baseline, then instituting conditioning, and finally setting up extinction of the learned behavior. Arrangements for reinforcement include shaping, schedules of reinforcement, primary and secondary reinforcement, the child's reinforcement history, and naturalistic settings. Consideration of punishment suggests that reasoning is often more effective than high-intensity punishment. Experts recommend that alternatives to punishment be explored before punishment is used. Operant conditioning has been used in many circumstances to reduce maladaptive behavior and to promote adaptive behavior. This use is often referred to as behavior modification.

IV. Habituation

Habituation occurs when repeated presentation of the same stimulus causes reduced attention to the stimulus. If a different stimulus is presented and the infant pays attention to it, dishabituation has occurred. Newborn infants can habituate although habituation becomes more acute over the first three months of life.

V. Imitation and Cognitive Learning

Imitation, also called modeling, occurs when children learn new behaviors by watching someone else perform the behaviors. Bandura believes imitation involves attention, retention, motor reproduction, and incentive or reinforcement conditions. Many researchers believe that young infants can imitate an adult's emotional expressions. Many psychologists also recognize the importance of studying how cognitive factors mediate environment-behavior connections. Bandura's contemporary model emphasizes reciprocal connections between behavior, person (cognition), and environment.

VI. Some Ideas about the "Whys" of Behavior

Understanding motivation involves knowledge of biological motives, competence motivation, learned motives, and the hierarchy of motives. Fixed-action patterns and drive-reduction theory have been proposed as explanations for children's biological motives. Homeostasis is an important concept in drive-reduction theory and in understanding children's motivation. It describes the motivation for a balanced equilibrium. As psychologists recognized there was more to motivation than drive reduction, they turned to the concept of competence motivation, first described by R. W. White. Also called mastery motivation, this involves the motivation to deal effectively with the environment.

Interest in competence motivation and the environment's role in motivation led to the description of learned motives, including achievement, power, affiliation, identity, and self-actualization. Maslow described the hierarchy of motives—the idea that some motives need to be satisfied prior to others. Self-actualization is given special importance in his view.

VII. Achievement

McClelland argued that we can measure individual differences in achievement motivation, or *n* achievement. The need for achievement is the motivation to overcome obstacles, the desire for success, and effort expended to seek out difficult tasks and to do them well. Achievement motivation is associated with a number of aspects of children's experiences and behaviors. Intrinsic motivation involves an underlying need for competence and self-determination; extrinsic motivation involves external factors in the environment, especially rewards. Many of the most achievement-oriented children have both a high personal standard for success and are highly competitive. Social comparison by itself is not a wise strategy. There has been too little research on minority-group children's achievement. When race and social class are investigated, social class is a better predictor of children's achievement than race.

Key Terms

reinforcement (reward) 134
imitation (modeling) 134
learning 135
motivation 136
classical conditioning 137
unconditioned stimulus (UCS) 137
unconditioned response (UCR) 137
conditioned stimulus (CS) 138
conditioned response (CR) 138
phobias 138
counterconditioning 139
operant conditioning 140
punishment 140
baseline 140
conditioning 141
extinction 141
partial reinforcement 142
schedules of reinforcement 142

primary and secondary reinforcement 143
behavior modification 144
habituation 145
dishabituation 145
attention 149
retention 150
motor reproduction 150
reinforcement or incentive conditions 150
fixed-action patterns 152
drive 153
need 153
drive-reduction theory 153
homeostasis 153
competence motivation 153
hierarchy of motives 154
n achievement 155
intrinsic motivation 156
extrinsic motivation 156

Suggested Readings

Axelrod, S., & Apsche, J. (Eds.)
(1983). *The effects of punishment on human behavior.*
New York: Academic Press.
An up-to-date, authoritative volume on how punishment
can be used effectively to control behavior. Considerable
detail about reducing the negative side effects of
punishment and a full consideration of the ethical issues
involved in the use of punishment are included.

Bandura, A. (1986). *Social foundations of thought and
action.* Englewood Cliffs, NJ: Prentice-Hall.
This book presents Bandura's cognitive view of learning,
including the importance of considering reciprocal
connections between behavior, environment, and
cognition. An extensive discussion of observational
learning is included.

Masters, J. C., Burish, T. G., Hollow, S. D., & Rimm, D. C.
(1988). *Behavior therapy.* San Diego: Harcourt Brace
Jovanovich.
This leading textbook on behavior therapy provides
numerous examples of behavior modification with
children.

McAdoo, H. P., & McAdoo, J. L. (1985). *Black children:
Social, educational, and parental environments.* Beverly
Hills, CA: Sage.
This book provides a contemporary look at the nature of
achievement orientation in black children. Included are
chapters written by leading experts in the field of
minority-group motivation.

Mook, D. G. (1987). *Motivation.* New York: W. W. Norton.
A textbook on motivation that covers the topics in this
chapter, plus many more aspects of motivation. Includes
detailed looks at contemporary theorizing about the
nature of human motivation.

CHAPTER 7

Cognitive Development and Piaget's Theory

*The thirst to know and understand . . .these are the goods in
life's rich hand.*

Sir William Watson, 1905

An amazing thing happened when Jean was only ten years old. He wrote an article about the rare albino sparrow, an article that was published in the *Journal of the Natural History of Neuchâtel.* The article was so brilliant that the curators of the Geneva Museum of Natural History, who had no idea the article had been written by a ten-year-old, offered the pre-adolescent boy a job as a curator of the museum. The heads of the museum quickly withdrew their offer when they found out that Jean was only ten years old.

Jean is Jean Piaget, born August 9, 1896, in Neuchâtel, Switzerland. His father was an intellectual who taught young Jean to think systematically. Jean's mother also was very bright and strongly religious as well. His father seemed to maintain an air of detachment from his mother, who has been described by Piaget as prone to frequent outbursts of neurotic behavior.

In his autobiography, Piaget (1952a) detailed why he chose to pursue the study of cognitive development rather than emotional development.

> I started to forego playing for serious work very early. Indeed, I have always detested any departure from reality, an attitude which I relate to . . . my mother's poor mental health. It was this disturbing factor which at the beginning of my studies in psychology made me keenly interested in psychoanalytic and pathological psychology. Though this interest helped me to achieve independence and to widen my cultural background, I have never since felt any desire to involve myself deeper in that particular direction, always much preferring the study of normalcy and of the workings of the intellect to that of the tricks of the unconscious. (p. 238)

Piaget's interest in zoology continued through his adolescent years and culminated in his doctoral dissertation on the behavior of mollusks in 1918 at the University of Neuchâtel. During his adolescence, though, Piaget was not just interested in zoology. Philosophy and psychology books filled his room, and he spent much of his spare time reading Kant, Durkheim, and James (philosopher, sociologist, and psychologist, respectively).

While his studies had taken him in the direction of biology and other intellectual pursuits, the deteriorating health of Piaget's mother had an important impact on his first job after he completed his doctorate degree. In 1918 Piaget took a position at Bleuler's psychiatric clinic in Zurich, where he learned about clinical techniques for interviewing children. Then, still at the young age of twenty-two, he went to work in the psychology laboratory at the University of Zurich, where he was exposed to the insights of Alfred Binet, who developed the first intelligence test. By the time Piaget was twenty-five, his experience in varied disciplines had helped him see important links between philosophy, psychology, and biology.

This chapter is about Jean Piaget, a true giant in the field of child development—about the man, about his masterful view of children's cognitive development, about the stages of thought children move through, and about the processes responsible for the cognitive stages.

Jean Piaget and His Place in Child Psychology

Discussing Sigmund Freud's contribution to psychology, Edwin Boring (1950) remarked that it is not likely the history of experimental psychology can be written in the next three centuries without mention of Freud's name and still claim to be a general history of psychology. Indeed, the best criterion of greatness may be posthumous fame. Four decades after Boring published his book, it seems likely that his judgment was accurate—Freud is still a dominating presence in psychology. Piaget's contribution to developmental psychology may be as important as Freud's contribution to personality and abnormal behavior. Piaget's death was a rather recent event (he died in 1980), so it may be too early to judge. But certainly for the foreseeable future Piaget's contributions will be strongly felt. He truly is a giant in the field of developmental psychology.

Shortly after Piaget's death, John Flavell (1980), a leading Piagetian scholar, described what we owe Piaget:

> First, we owe him a host of insightful concepts of enduring power and fascination . . . concepts of object permanence, conservation, assimilation, accommodation, and decentration, for example. Second, we owe him a vast conceptual framework that has highlighted key issues and problems in human cognitive development. This framework is the now-familiar vision of the developing child, who, through its own active and creative commerce with its environment, builds an orderly succession of cognitive structures enroute to intellectual maturity. These two debts add up to a third, more general one: We owe him the present field of cognitive development. . . . Our task is now to extend and go beyond what he began so well. (p. 1)

From J. H. Flavell, "A Tribute to Piaget" in *Society for Research in Child Development Newsletter*, Fall 1980. Copyright © The Society for Research in Child Development, Chicago, IL. Reprinted by permission.

Jean Piaget.

Cognitive Developmental Theory, Processes, and Stages

What is the basic nature of cognitive developmental theory? How does it differ from the learning perspective described in chapter 6? What cognitive processes are responsible for changes in the child's development? What stages of cognitive development does the child move through?

Cognitive Developmental Theory

Cognitive developmental theory emphasizes the developing child's rational thinking and stages of thought. Environmental experiences are important in the cognitive developmental view, but from Piaget's perspective they are mainly the "food" for children's cognitive machinery. In the cognitive learning perspective described in chapter 6, cognitive processes were seen as important mediators in linking environmental experiences to children's behavior. In Piaget's view, thoughts are more than mediators of environment-behavior connections. Rather, thoughts are the central focus of development, the primary determinants of children's actions.

Cognitive Processes

Piaget emphasized that cognitive changes in children's development can be explained by the processes of adaptation (assimilation, accommodation), organization, and equilibration. We consider each of these in turn.

If children are to develop normally, they have to interact effectively with the environment. Effective interaction is called **adaptation.** For Piaget the interaction is a cognitive one. It involves the child's use of thinking skills. Adaptation is subdivided into **assimilation** and **accommodation,** which usually

Figure 7.1
Piaget's mechanisms of cognitive change.

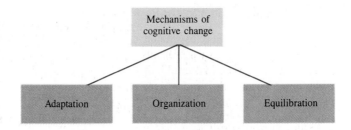

occur together. In assimilation, the child tries to incorporate features of the environment into already existing ways of thinking about them. In accommodation, the child tries to incorporate new features of the environment into his or her thinking by slightly modifying existing modes of thought. An example may help to clarify these terms.

A young girl is presented with a hammer and nails to use in hanging a picture on her bedroom wall. She has never had the opportunity to use a hammer before. From experience and observation, however, she realizes that a hammer is an object to be held, that it is swung by the handle to strike the nail, and that it is swung repeatedly. Realizing each of these things, she incorporates her behavior into a conceptual framework that already exists (assimilation). But the hammer is heavy, so she must hold it near the top. As she swings too hard, the nail bends, so she must adjust the pressure of her taps. These adjustments show her sensitivity to the need to alter the concept slightly (accommodation).

Piaget thought that assimilation and accommodation operate even in the young infant's life. Newborns reflexively suck everything that touches their lips (assimilation), but after several months of experience, they construct their understanding of the world differently. Some objects, such as fingers and the mother's breast, can be sucked, and others, such as fuzzy blankets, should not be sucked (accommodation).

A second mechanism of change is **organization,** that is, the tendency of isolated behaviors or thoughts to be grouped into a higher-order, more smoothly functioning system. Every level of thought is organized in some fashion. Continual refinement of this organization is an inherent part of development. The girl who has only a vague idea about how to use a hammer may also have a vague idea about how to use other tools. After learning how to use each one, she must interrelate these uses, or organize her knowledge, if she is to become skilled in using tools. In the same way, the child continually integrates and coordinates the many other branches of knowledge that often develop independently. Organization occurs within stages of development as well as across them.

Equilibration is a third mechanism invoked to explain how a child shifts from one stage to the next. The goal of better organization is to reach a more lasting state of balance in thought. This goal is achieved as thought becomes more logical and abstract. But before a new stage of thought can be reached, the child must face the inadequacy of the current one. He must experience cognitive conflict, or uncertainty. If a child believes that an amount of liquid is changed simply because it was poured into a container with a different shape, he might be puzzled by such issues as where the "extra" liquid came from and whether there is actually more liquid to drink. These puzzles will eventually be resolved as thought becomes concrete. In the everyday world the child is constantly faced with such counterexamples and inconsistencies. Let's now look at these stages of cognitive development that we have been mentioning. Piaget's mechanisms of change are shown in figure 7.1.

Piaget's Stages of Cognitive Development

Piaget (1952b) also believed that we go through four stages in understanding the world. Each of the stages is age-related and consists of distinct ways of thinking. It is the *different* way of understanding the world that makes one stage more advanced than another; knowing *more* information does not make the child's thinking more advanced in the Piagetian view. This is what Piaget meant when he said that the child's cognition is *qualitatively* different in one stage compared to another (Ginsburg & Opper, 1988). What are Piaget's four stages of cognitive development like?

In the **sensorimotor stage,** which lasts from birth to about two years of age, the infant constructs an understanding of the world by coordinating sensory experiences (such as seeing and hearing) with physical, motoric actions—hence the term *sensorimotor.* At the beginning of this stage, the newborn has little more than reflexive patterns with which to work; at the end of the stage, the two-year-old has complex sensorimotor patterns and is beginning to operate with primitive symbols.

In the **preoperational stage,** which lasts from approximately two to seven years of age, the child begins to represent the world with words, images, and drawings; symbolic thought goes beyond simple connections of sensory information and physical action. But while the preschool child can symbolically represent the world, according to Piaget, she still cannot perform **operations,** that is, mental operations that are reversible. This is why Piaget (1967) said children two to seven years of age were in the preoperational stage of thought.

In the **concrete operational stage,** which lasts from approximately seven to eleven years of age, the child can use operations—she can mentally reverse an amount of liquid from one beaker to another and understand that the volume is the same even though the beakers are different in height and width. Logical reasoning replaces intuitive thought as long as the principles can be applied to specific or *concrete* examples. Concrete operational thinkers are capable of understanding such mathematical operations as addition and substraction, which involve being able to mentally reverse numbers, but they are not capable of imagining the steps necessary to complete an algebraic equation, which involves more abstract concepts.

In the **formal operational stage,** which appears between the ages of eleven and fifteen, the adolescent moves beyond the world of actual, concrete experiences and thinks in abstract and more logical terms. As part of thinking more abstractly, the adolescent develops images of ideal circumstances. He may think about what an ideal parent is like and compare his parents with this ideal standard. He begins to entertain possibilities for the future and is fascinated with what he can be. In solving problems, the adolescent is more systematic, developing hypotheses about why something is happening the way it is; then he may test these hypotheses in a deductive fashion. Piaget's stages are summarized in table 7.1. Now we turn to a deeper understanding of each of Piaget's stages of cognitive development.

Sensorimotor Thought

Poet Nora Perry once asked, "Who knows the thoughts of the child?" As much as anyone, Piaget knew. Through careful, inquisitive interviews and observations of his own three children—Laurent, Lucienne, and Jacqueline—Piaget changed our thinking about the way infants think about their world.

Table 7.1
Piaget's Stages of Cognitive Development

Stage	Description	Age range
Sensorimotor	The infant progresses from reflexive instinctual action at birth to the beginning of symbolic thought. The infant constructs an understanding of the world by coordinating sensory experiences with physical actions.	Birth to 2
Preoperational	The child begins to represent the world with words and images; these words and images reflect increased symbolic thinking and go beyond the connection of sensory information and physical action.	2 to 7
Concrete operational	The child now can reason logically about concrete events and can mentally reverse information.	7 to 11
Formal operational	The adolescent reasons in more abstract, idealistic, and logical ways.	11 to 15

Basic Features of Sensorimotor Thought

Two of the most important features of sensorimotor thought involve the co-ordination of sensation and action and nonsymbolic aspects of the period.

The sensorimotor stage lasts from birth to about two years of age, corresponding to the period known as infancy. During this time the infant develops the ability to organize and coordinate her sensations and perceptions with her physical movements and actions. This coordination of sensation with action is the source of the term *sensorimotor*. The stage begins with the newborn, who has little more than reflexes to coordinate her senses with actions. The stage ends with the two-year-old, who has complex sensorimotor patterns and is beginning to adopt a primitive symbol system. For example, the two-year-old can imagine looking at a toy and manipulating it with her hands before she actually does so. The child can also use simple sentences—for example, "Mommy, jump"—to represent a sensorimotor event that has just occurred.

Think about your dog or cat and the kind of intelligence that the animal possesses. Although many of us brag about the intelligence of our pets, realistically we realize that their cognitive abilities are limited. Piaget would argue that their abilities are limited in a quite specific way: they are bound up with the animal's behavior. They are not reflective or contemplative abilities, and they do not provide for conscious thinking about things that are not perceptually available. In a word, these abilities are not symbolic.

Think about your own cognition when you are engaged in behavior that is well practiced—something such as driving home from work or mowing your lawn. There is a kind of intelligence in such behavior. You show tremendous physical coordination and timing and must continuously monitor perceptual information. You also must make many small adjustments and compensations, even some low-level decisions (e.g., to change lanes in preparation for an upcoming turn or to stop when the light turns yellow). Yet, while accomplishing all of these complex behaviors, you may have been thinking about entirely different things (problems at work or with a personal relationship). And your subsequent ability to remember these behaviors probably is quite meager. Piaget would argue that the intelligence you use in such well-practiced behaviors is similar to that of your dog or cat—it is a nonsymbolic sensorimotor intelligence.

Nonsymbolic, sensorimotor intelligence is what Piaget claimed for the very young infant, up until about one and a half years or so. Thus, the most critical aspect of Piaget's sensorimotor stage is that it is nonsymbolic throughout most of its duration (Flavell, 1985; Piaget, 1970).

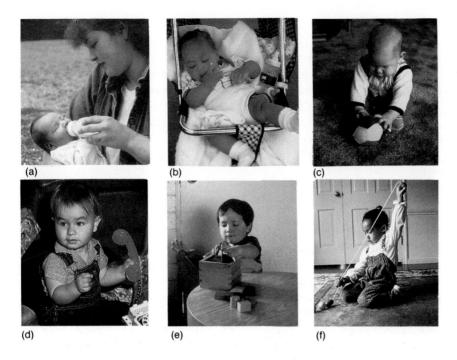

Piaget's substages of sensorimotor thought, which describe qualitative changes in sensorimotor organization (a) Substage 1, simple reflexes—the two-week-old infant's sucking is a reflex that was present at birth; (b) Substage 2, first habits and primary circular reactions—the three-month-old infant's thumb sucking occurs even when no bottle is present; (c) Substage 3, secondary circular reactions—the six-month-old infant's fascination with the multicolored ball shows how object-oriented he has become; (d) Substage 4, coordination of secondary reactions—the eleven-month-old infant's handling of the telephone reflects her ability to combine previously learned schemes in a coordinated way; (e) Substage 5, tertiary circular reactions, novelty, and curiosity—the sixteen-month-old boy purposely explores new possibilities with this box of blocks; (f) Substage 6, internalization of schemes— this twenty-month-old girl symbolically mimicks her mother's behavior of slipping spools onto a rope.

Additional arguments for the nonsymbolic nature of thought in early infancy concern the solving of problems through internal reflection or insight. Problem solving occurs quite early in life, perhaps by twelve months of age. But Piaget claimed that until about one and a half to two years of age, this problem solving is of the trial-and-error variety, devoid of an internal, symbolic component. For example, one of Piaget's daughters insightfully discovered how to get a matchbox open; looking at the slightly open matchbox, she began opening and closing her mouth. Only after making a few such movements did she reach for the matchbox and pull out its drawer with her hands. Piaget interpreted the moving-mouth behavior as reflecting internal, symbolic operations, which emerge only at the end of the sensorimotor stage.

The Substages of Sensorimotor Thought

The sensorimotor stage is divided into six substages, which describe qualitative changes in sensorimotor organization. Within a given substage there may be different schemes—sucking, rooting, and blinking in substage 1, for example. The term *scheme* refers to the basic unit for an organized pattern of sensorimotor functioning. In substage 1, schemes are basically reflexive in nature. From substage to substage, the organization of the schemes changes. The six substages of sensorimotor development are: (1) simple reflexes; (2) first habits and primary circular reactions; (3) secondary circular reactions; (4) coordination of secondary, circular reactions; (5) tertiary circular reactions, novelty, and curiosity; and (6) internalization of schemes.

In substage 1, **simple reflexes,** which corresponds to the first month after birth, the basic means of coordinating sensation and action is through reflexive behaviors—such as rooting and sucking—which the infant has at birth. In substage 1, the infant exercises these reflexes. More importantly, the infant develops an ability to produce behaviors that resemble reflexes in the absence of obvious reflexive stimuli. The newborn may suck when a bottle or nipple is only nearby, for example. The bottle or nipple would have produced the sucking pattern only when placed directly in the newborn's mouth or touched to the newborn's lips when the baby was just born. Reflexlike action in the absence of a triggering stimulus is evidence that the infant is initiating action and is actively structuring experiences in life's first month.

In substage 2, **first habits and primary circular reactions,** which develops between one and four months of age, the infant learns to coordinate sensation and types of schemes or structures, that is, habits and primary circular reactions. A *habit* is a scheme based on a simple reflex, such as sucking, that has become completely divorced from its eliciting stimulus. For example, an infant in substage 1 might suck when orally stimulated by a bottle or when visually shown the bottle, but an infant in substage 2 might exercise the sucking scheme even when no bottle is present.

A **primary circular reaction** is a scheme based on the infant's attempt to reproduce an interesting or pleasurable event that initially occurred by chance. In a popular Piagetian example, a child accidentally sucks his fingers when they are placed near his mouth. Later, he searches for his fingers to suck them again, but the fingers do not cooperate in the search because the infant cannot coordinate visual and manual actions. Habits and circular reactions are stereotyped in that the infant repeats them the same way each time. The infant's own body remains the center of attention. There is no outward pull by environmental events.

In substage 3, **secondary circular reactions,** which develops between four and eight months of age, the infant becomes more object oriented or focused on the world, moving beyond preoccupation with the self in sensorimotor interactions. The chance shaking of a rattle, for example, may fascinate the infant, and the infant will repeat this action for the sake of experiencing fascination. The infant imitates some simple actions of others, such as the baby talk or burbling of adults, and some physical gestures. However, these imitations are limited to actions the infant is already able to produce. Although directed toward objects in the world, the infant's schemes lack an intentional, goal-directed quality.

In substage 4, **coordination of secondary reactions,** which develops between eight and twelve months of age, several significant changes take place. The infant readily combines and recombines previously learned schemes in a *coordinated* way. She may look at an object and grasp it simultaneously or visually inspect a toy, such as a rattle, and finger it simultaneously in obvious tactile exploration. Actions are even more outwardly directed than before. Related to this coordination is the second achievement—the presence of *intentionality,* the separation of means and goals in accomplishing simple feats. For example, the infant might manipulate a stick (the means) to bring a desired toy within reach (the goal). She may knock over one block to reach and play with another one.

In substage 5, **tertiary circular reactions, novelty, and curiosity,** which develops between twelve and eighteen months of age, the infant becomes intrigued by the variety of properties that objects possess and by the multiplicity of things she can make happen to objects. A block can be made to fall, spin, hit another object, slide across the ground, and so on. *Tertiary circular reactions* are schemes in which the infant purposely explores new possibilities with objects, continually changing what is done to them and exploring the results. Piaget says that this stage marks the developmental starting point for human curiosity and interest in novelty. Previous circular reactions have been devoted exclusively to reproducing former events, with the exception of imitation of novel acts, which occurs as early as substage 4. The tertiary circular act is the first to be concerned with novelty.

In substage 6, **internalization of schemes,** which develops between eighteen and twenty-four months, the infant's mental functioning shifts from a purely sensorimotor plane to a symbolic plane and the infant develops the ability to use primitive symbols. For Piaget, a *symbol* is an internalized sensory image or word that presents an event. Primitive symbols permit the infant to think about concrete events without directly acting them out or perceiving them. Moreover, symbols allow the infant to manipulate and transform the represented events in simple ways. As we mentioned earlier, in a favorite Piagetian example, his young daughter saw a matchbox being opened and closed. Sometime later she mimicked the event by opening and closing her mouth. This was an obvious expression of her image of the event. In another example, a child opened a door slowly to avoid disturbing a piece of paper lying on the floor on the other side. Clearly, the child had an image of the unseen paper and what would happen to it if the door opened quickly. Recently, however, developmentalists have debated whether two-year-olds really have such representations of action sequences at their command (Corrigan, 1981; Escalona, 1988).

Object Permanence

One of the infant's most significant accomplishments is the development of object permanence (Flavell, 1985). **Object permanence** is the ability to understand that objects and events continue to exist even though the infant is not in direct contact with them. Imagine what thought would be like if you could not distinguish between yourself and your world. Your thought would be chaotic, disorderly, and unpredictable. This is what the mental life of the newborn is like. There is no self-world differentiation and no sense of object permanence (Piaget, 1952b). By the end of the sensorimotor period, however, both are clearly present. The transition between these states is not abrupt. It is marked by qualitative changes that reflect movement through each of the substages of sensorimotor thought.

The principal way that object permanence is studied is by watching the infant's reaction when an attractive object or event disappears. If the infant shows no reaction, it is assumed that he believes it no longer exists. By contrast, if the infant is surprised at the disappearance and searches for the object, it is assumed that he believes it continues to exist. According to Piaget, six distinct substages characterize the development of object permanence. Table 7.2 shows how these six substages reflect Piaget's substages of sensorimotor development.

Although Piaget's stage sequence is the best summary of what might happen as the infant fathoms the permanence of things in the world, some contradictory findings have emerged. Piaget's stages broadly describe these interesting changes reasonably well, but the infant's life is not so neatly packaged into distinct organizations as Piaget believed. And some of Piaget's explanations for the causes of change are debated (Wellman, Cross, & Bartsch, 1986).

For example, Piaget claimed that certain processes are crucial in stage transitions. The data do not always support his explanations, however. According to Piaget, the critical requirement for the infant to progress into sensorimotor substage 4 is the coordination of vision and the sense of touch, or hand-eye coordination. Another important feature involved in the progress into substage 4 for Piaget is the infant's inclination to search for an object hidden in a familiar location rather than looking for the object in a new location. If new locations serve as hiding places, the infant progressing into substage 4

One of Piaget's important contributions to understanding infant development was his conceptualization of object permanence. The infant shown here indicates an awareness of object permanence by reaching for the disappearing object. Object permanence is typically investigated by observing an infant's reaction when an attractive object disappears. The infant's surprise at the disappearance of the object and the infant's search for the object signifies the presence of object permanence.

Table 7.2
The Six Substages of Object Permanence

Stage	Behavior
Sensorimotor substage 1	There is no apparent object permanence. When a spot of light moves across the visual field, the infant follows it but quickly ignores its disappearance.
Sensorimotor substage 2	A primitive form of object permanence develops. Given the same experience, the infant looks briefly at the spot where the light disappeared, with an expression of passive expectancy.
Sensorimotor substage 3	The infant's sense of object permanence undergoes further development. With the newfound ability to coordinate simple schemes, the infant shows clear patterns of searching for a missing object, with sustained visual and manual examination of the spot where the object apparently disappeared.
Sensorimotor substage 4	The infant actively searches for a missing object in the spot where it disappeared, with new actions to achieve the goal of searching effectively. For example, if an attractive toy has been hidden behind a screen, the child may look at the screen and try to push it away with a hand. If the screen is too heavy to move or is permanently fixed, the child readily substitutes a secondary scheme—for example, crawling around it or kicking it. These new actions signal that the infant's belief in the continued existence of the missing object is strengthening.
Sensorimotor substage 5	The infant now is able to track an object that disappears and reappears in several locations in rapid succession. For example, a toy may be hidden under different boxes in succession in front of the infant, who succeeds in finding it. The infant is apparently able to hold an image of the missing object in mind longer than before.
Sensorimotor substage 6	The infant can search for a missing object that disappeared and reappeared in several locations in succession, as before. In addition, the infant searches in the appropriate place even when the object has been hidden from view as it is being moved. This activity indicates that the infant is able to "imagine" the missing object and to follow the image from one location to the next.

should make frequent mistakes, selecting the familiar hiding place (A) instead of the new location (B). This occurrence is called the **A-B error,** or perseveration. But researchers find that the A-B error does not show up consistently (Corrigan, 1981; Harris, 1975; Sophian, 1985). Sometimes it occurs, sometimes it does not. There also is accumulating evidence that A-B errors are sensitive to the delay between hiding an object at B and the infant's attempt to find it (Diamond, 1985). Thus, the A-B error might be partly due to the failure of memory.

At this point we have discussed a number of important ideas about Piaget's theory of cognitive development, especially chronicling the stage of sensorimotor thought. A summary of these ideas is presented in Concept Table 7.1.

Preoperational Thought

What kinds of changes take place in the preoperational stage of thought? Since this stage is called preoperational, it would seem that not much of importance occurs until full-fledged operational thought appears. Not so. The preoperational stage stretches from approximately the age of two to the age of seven—it is a time when stable concepts are formed, mental reasoning emerges, egocentrism is stronger in the beginning and then weakens, and magical beliefs are constructed. Preoperational thought is anything but a convenient waiting period for concrete operational thought, although the label "preoperational"

Cognitive Development

Concept Table 7.1
Piaget's Theory and Sensorimotor Thought

Concept	Processes/Related Ideas	Characteristics/Description
Cognitive developmental theory, processes, and stages	Cognitive developmental theory	Cognitive developmental theory emphasizes the child's rational thinking and stages of cognitive development.
	Cognitive processes	According to Piaget, the cognitive processes responsible for change are adaptation (assimilation, accommodation), organization, and equilibration.
	Piaget's stages	Piaget believed that children go through four qualitatively different stages of thought: sensorimotor, preoperational, concrete operational, and formal operational.
Sensorimotor thought	Basic features	Sensorimotor thought involves the infant's ability to organize and coordinate sensations with physical movements. The stage lasts from birth to about two years of age and is nonsymbolic through most of its duration.
	Substages of sensorimotor thought	Sensorimotor thought has six substages: simple reflexes; first habits and primary circular reactions; secondary circular reactions; coordination of secondary circular reactions; tertiary circular reactions, novelty, and curiosity; and internalization of schemes.
	Object permanence	Object permanence refers to the ability to understand that objects and events continue to exist even though the infant no longer is in contact with them. Piaget believed this ability develops over the course of the six substages of sensorimotor thought.

emphasizes that the child at this stage does not yet think in an operational way. As we indicated earlier, operations are sets of actions that allow the child to do mentally what before was done physically. They are highly organized and conform to certain rules and principles of logic. The operations appear in one form in concrete operational thought and in another form in formal operational thought. Thought in the preoperational stage is still flawed and not well organized. Preoperational thought is the beginning of the ability to reconstruct at the level of thought what has been established in behavior and is a transition from primitive to more sophisticated use of symbols. Preoperational thought can be divided into two substages—the symbolic function substage and the intuitive thought substage.

Symbolic Function Substage

The **symbolic function substage** of preoperational thought occurs roughly between the ages of two and four years. By two years of age, the child has the ability to mentally represent an object. At this point the child has begun to use symbols to represent objects that are not present. The ability to engage in such symbolic thought is referred to as symbolic function, and it vastly expands the child's mental world during this age period. Young children use shapes and scribbles to represent people, houses, cars, clouds, animals, and so on. More on young children's scribbles and art is presented in Perspective on Child Development 7.1. Other examples of symbolism in early childhood are the prevalence of pretend play, which will be discussed in chapter 13, and language, more about which appears later in this chapter and in chapter 9. In sum, during this early substage of preoperational thought, the ability to think symbolically and represent the world mentally predominates. However, while the young child makes distinct progress during the symbolic function substage, her thought still has several important limitations, two of which are egocentrism and animism.

Where Pelicans Kiss Seals, Cars Float on Clouds, and Humans Are Tadpoles

A t about three years of age and sometimes even at two, children's spontaneous scribbles begin to resemble pictures. One three and one-half-year-old child looked at the scribble he had just drawn and said it was a pelican kissing a seal (figure 7.A). At about three to four years of age, children begin to create symbols of humans. Invariably the first symbols look curiously like tadpoles; see the circle and two lines in figure 7.B—the circle represents a head and the two lines are legs.

These observations of children's drawings were made by Denise Wolf, Carol Fucigna, and Howard Gardner at Harvard University. They point out that many people think young children draw a human in this rather odd way because it is the best they can do. Piaget said children intend their drawings to be realistic. They draw what they know rather than what they see. So the tadpole with its strange exemptions of trunk and arms might reflect a child's lack of knowledge of the human body and how its parts fit together. However, children know more about the human body than they are capable of drawing. One three-year-old child drew a tadpole but described it in complete detail, pointing out where the feet, chin, and neck were. When three- and four-year-old children are asked to draw someone playing ball, they produce symbols of humans that include arms, since the task implicitly requires arms (figure 7.C).

Possibly because preschool children are not very concerned about reality, their drawings are fanciful and inventive (figure 7.D). Suns are blue, skies are yellow, and cars float on clouds in the preschool child's symbolic world. The symbolism is simple but strong, not unlike the abstractions found in some contemporary art. In the elementary school years, the child's symbols become more realistic, neat, and precise (figure 7.E). Suns are yellow, skies are blue, and cars are placed on roads.

A child's ability to symbolically represent the world on paper is related to the development of perceptual motor skills. But once such skills are developed, some artists revert to the style of young children's drawings. As Picasso once commented, "I used to draw like Raphael but it has taken me a whole lifetime to learn to draw like children" (Winner, 1986).

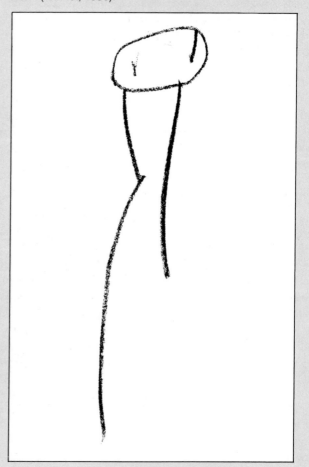

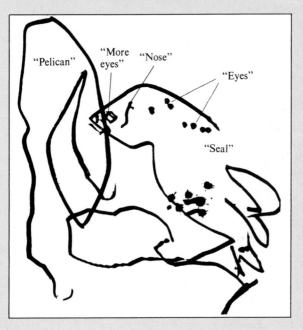

Figure 7.A
Halfway into this drawing, the three and one-half-year-old artist said it was "a pelican kissing a seal."

Figure 7.B
The three-year-old's first drawing of a person: a "tadpole" consisting of a circle with two lines for legs.

Figure 7.C
A young child, asked to draw people playing ball, includes only a single arm on the figures playing ball; the fourth figure, an observer, is armless.

Figure 7.D
This six-year-old's drawing is free, fanciful, and inventive.

Figure 7.E
An eleven-year-old's drawing is neater and more realistic than the six-year-old's drawing, but it is also less inventive.

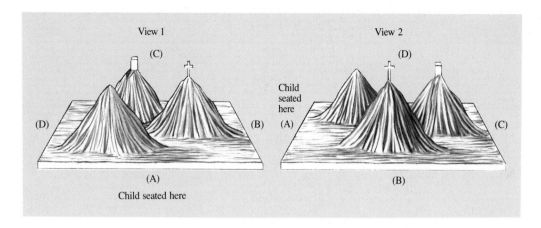

View 1

(C)

(D)   (B)

(A)
Child seated here

View 2

Child
seated
here

(D)

(A)   (C)

(B)

Figure 7.2
The three mountains task devised by Piaget and Inhelder. View 1 shows the child's perspective from where he or she is sitting. View 2 is an example of the photograph the child would be shown mixed in with others from different perspectives. For the child to correctly identify this view, he or she has to take the perspective of a person sitting at spot (B). Invariably the preschool child who thinks in a preoperational way cannot perform this task. When asked what the perspective or view of the mountains will look like from position (B), the child selects a photograph taken from location (A), the view he or she has at the time.

Egocentrism is a salient feature of preoperational thought—it is the inability to distinguish between one's own perspective and someone else's perspective. The following telephone conversation between four-year-old Mary, who is at home, and her father, who is at work, typifies Mary's egocentric thought:

Father: Mary, is Mommy there?
Mary: (Silently nods)
Father: Mary, may I speak to Mommy?
Mary: (Nods again silently)

Mary's response is egocentric in the sense that she fails to consider her father's perspective before replying. A nonegocentric thinker would have responded verbally.

Piaget and Barbara Inhelder (1969) initially studied young children's egocentrism by devising the three mountains task (figure 7.2). The child walks around the mountains and becomes familiar with what the mountains look like from different perspectives. The child can see that there are different objects on the mountains as well. The child then is seated on one side of the table on which the mountains are placed. The experimenter takes a doll and moves it to different locations around the table, at each location asking the child to pick one photo from a series of photos that most accurately reflects the view the doll is seeing. Children in the preoperational stage often pick the view they have from where they are sitting rather than the view that the doll has. Perspective taking does not seem to develop uniformly in the preschool child, who frequently shows perspective skills on some tasks but not others (Rubin, 1978; Shantz, 1983).

Animism is another facet of preoperational thought—the belief that inanimate objects have "lifelike" qualities and are capable of action. The young child might say, "That tree pushed the leaf off, and it fell down," or "The sidewalk made me mad; it made me fall down," revealing animism. The young child who uses animism fails to distinguish the appropriate occasions for using human and nonhuman perspectives. Some developmentalists, though, believe that animism represents incomplete knowledge and understanding, not a general conception of the world (Dolgin & Behrend, 1984; Bullock, 1985). And other developmentalists believe that preschool children have a more elaborate and coherent knowledge of animals and inanimate objects than Piaget envisioned (Massey & Gelman, 1988).

Intuitive Thought Substage

As the preschool child becomes older, she moves from the symbolic thought substage to an inner world of thinking that is more intuitive, that is, knowing without the use of rational thinking. The preoperational stage of thought continues until about seven years of age for most children—the **intuitive thought substage** stretches from approximately four to seven years of age. During this time, the child begins to reason primitively and wants to know the answers to all sorts of questions. Children's thinking in this substage is prelogical. While reasoning and a search for many answers are present, the reasoning is highly imperfect compared to adult standards. Piaget referred to this period as *intuitive* because, on the one hand, young children seem so sure about their knowledge and understanding, yet on the other hand, they are so unaware of how they know what they know.

An example of the young child's reasoning ability is the difficulty she has putting things into their correct classes. Faced with a random collection of objects that can be grouped together on the basis of two or more properties, the preoperational child is seldom capable of using these properties consistently to sort the objects into appropriate categories. For example, look at the collection of objects in figure 7.3. An older child would respond to the direction, "Put the things together that you believe belong together" by sorting the characteristics of size and shape together. The older child's sorting might look something like that shown in figure 7.4, but the younger, preoperational child cannot accomplish this sorting. In the social realm, the five-year-old girl might be given the task of dividing her peers into groups according to whether they are friends and whether they are boys or girls. She would be unlikely to arrive at the following classification: friendly boys, friendly girls, unfriendly boys, unfriendly girls. Another example of classification shortcomings involves the

Figure 7.3
A random array of objects.

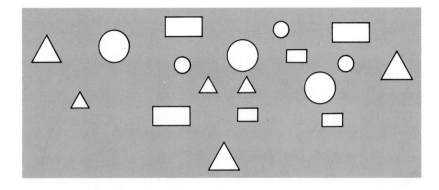

Figure 7.4
An ordered array of objects.

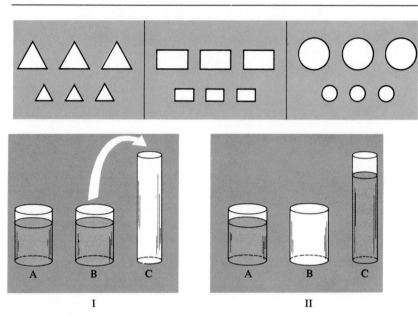

Figure 7.5
Piaget used the beaker task to determine whether children had conservation of liquid. In I, two identical beakers (A and B) are presented to the child; then the experimenter pours the liquid from B into beaker C, which is taller and thinner than A and B. The child is asked if beakers B and C have the same amount of liquid. The preoperational child says no, responding that the taller, thinner beaker (C) has more.

preoperational child's understanding of religious concepts (Elkind, 1976). When asked, "Can you be a Protestant and an American at the same time?" six- and seven-year-olds usually say no: nine-year-olds are likely to say yes, understanding that objects can be cross-classified simultaneously.

Many of these examples reveal a characteristic of preoperational thought called **centration**—the focusing, or *centering,* of attention on one characteristic to the exclusion of all others. Centration is most clearly evidenced in the young child's lack of **conservation**—the idea that an amount stays the same, or is conserved, regardless of how shape changes. To adults, it is obvious that a certain amount of liquid stays the same regardless of a container's shape. But this is not obvious at all to young children. Instead they are struck by the height of the liquid in the container. In this task—Piaget's most famous—the child is presented with two identical beakers, each filled to the same level with liquid (figure 7.5). The child is asked if these beakers have the same amount of liquid, and she usually says yes. Then, the liquid from one beaker is poured into a third beaker, which is taller and thinner than the first two. The child is now asked if the amount of liquid in the tall, thin beaker is equal to that which remains in one of the original beakers. If the child is less than seven or eight years old, she usually says no and justifies her answer in terms of the differing height or width of the beakers. Older children usually answer yes and justify their answers appropriately (e.g., "If you poured the milk back, it would show that the amount is the same").

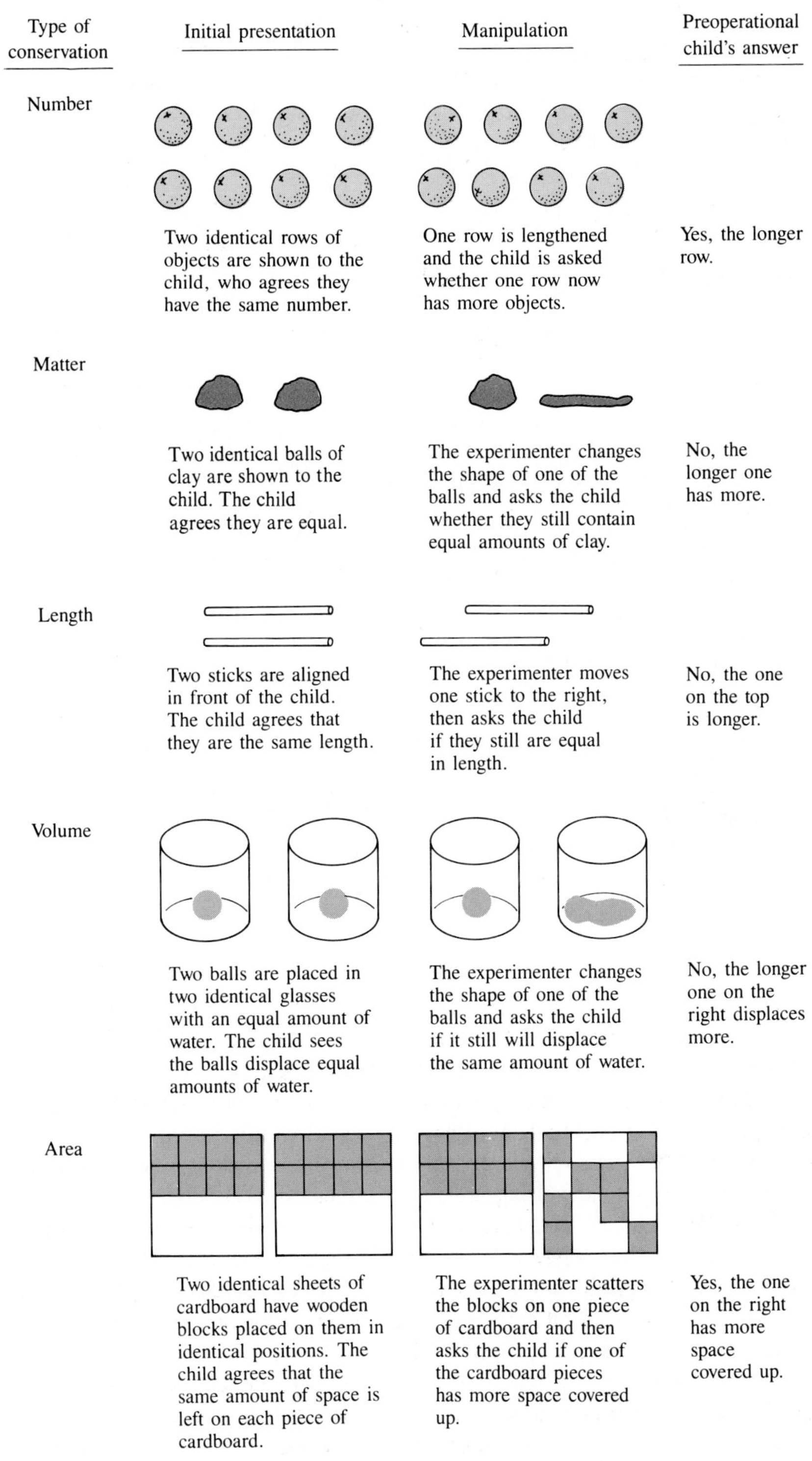

Figure 7.6
The domains of conservation.

Type of conservation	Initial presentation	Manipulation	Preoperational child's answer
Number	Two identical rows of objects are shown to the child, who agrees they have the same number.	One row is lengthened and the child is asked whether one row now has more objects.	Yes, the longer row.
Matter	Two identical balls of clay are shown to the child. The child agrees they are equal.	The experimenter changes the shape of one of the balls and asks the child whether they still contain equal amounts of clay.	No, the longer one has more.
Length	Two sticks are aligned in front of the child. The child agrees that they are the same length.	The experimenter moves one stick to the right, then asks the child if they still are equal in length.	No, the one on the top is longer.
Volume	Two balls are placed in two identical glasses with an equal amount of water. The child sees the balls displace equal amounts of water.	The experimenter changes the shape of one of the balls and asks the child if it still will displace the same amount of water.	No, the longer one on the right displaces more.
Area	Two identical sheets of cardboard have wooden blocks placed on them in identical positions. The child agrees that the same amount of space is left on each piece of cardboard.	The experimenter scatters the blocks on one piece of cardboard and then asks the child if one of the cardboard pieces has more space covered up.	Yes, the one on the right has more space covered up.

In Piaget's theory, failing the conservation of liquid task is a sign that a child is at the preoperational stage of cognitive development, while passing this test is a sign that he is at the concrete operational stage. In Piaget's view, the preoperational child not only fails to show conservation of liquid, but also number, matter, length, volume, and area (see figure 7.6). We have discussed a number of Piaget's ideas about preoperational thought, among them egocentrism, animism, and conservation. To learn more about these fascinating aspects of the preschool child's thoughts, turn to Perspective on Child Development 7.2, where you will discover how these concepts were included in the story of *Winnie-the-Pooh*.

Some developmentalists do not believe Piaget was entirely correct in his estimate of when children's conservation skills emerge (Bjorklund, 1989). For example, Rochel Gelman (1969, 1979; Gelman & Baillargeon, 1983) has shown that by improving the child's attention to relevant aspects of the conservation task, the child is more likely to conserve. And she has demonstrated that attentional training on one type of task, such as number, improves the preschool child's performance on another type of task, such as mass. Thus, Gelman believes that conservation appears earlier than Piaget thought and that the process of attention is especially important in explaining conservation.

Yet another characteristic of the preoperational child is the barrage of questions that they ask. The child's earliest questions appear around the age of three, and by the age of five, the child has just about exhausted the adults around with "why" questions. These questions yield clues about mental development and reflect the child's intellectual curiosity. They also signal the emergence of the child's interest in reasoning and figuring out why things are the way they are. The following are examples of questions children ask during the period of four to six years of age (Elkind, 1976).

"What makes you grow up?"
"What makes you stop growing?"
"Why does a lady have to be married to have a baby?"
"Who was the mother when everybody was a baby?"
"Why do leaves fall?"
"Why does the sun shine?"

Concrete Operational Thought

Remember that, according to Piaget, concrete operational thought is made up of operations—mental actions or representations that are reversible. In the well-known test of reversibility of thought involving conservation of matter, the child is presented with two identical balls of clay. The experimenter rolls one ball into a long, thin shape; the other remains in its original ball shape. The child is then asked if there is more clay in the ball or in the long, thin piece of clay. By the time children reach the age of seven or eight, most answer that the amount of clay is the same. To answer this problem correctly, children have to imagine that the clay ball is rolled out into a long, thin strip and then returned to its original round shape—imagination that involves a reversible mental action. Thus, a concrete operation is a reversible mental action on real, concrete objects. Concrete operations allow the child to coordinate several characteristics rather than focusing on a single property of an object. In the clay example, the preoperational child is likely to focus on height *or* width; the concrete operational child coordinates information about both dimensions. We can get a better understanding of concrete operational thought by considering further ideas about conservation and the nature of classification.

Conservation

We already have highlighted some of Piaget's basic ideas on conservation in our discussion of preoperational children's failure to correctly answer questions about such circumstances as the beaker task. Remember that conservation involves the recognition that the length, number, mass, quantity, area,

Piglet, Pooh, and Piaget

According to psychologist Dorothy Singer (1972), if Piaget had opened the pages of *Winnie-the-Pooh*, he would have discovered how A. A. Milne used some of the same concepts he believed were so prominent in the preschool child's thought. Milne's psychological insight gives life and meaning to a little story about an imaginary forest, peopled with animals from the nursery (figure 7.F).

We first meet Edward Bear as he is being dragged down the stairs on the back of his head. "It is, as far as he knows, the only way of coming down the stairs." This example of egocentrism sets the tone for the rest of the book. The narrator tells us that Edward's name is Winnie-the-Pooh. When asked if Winnie is not a girl's name, Christopher replies with a second example of egocentrism. "He's Winnie-ther-Pooh. Don't you know what *ther* means?" Again, an example of egocentrism. Christopher knows, so no further explanation is necessary, or forthcoming. Piglet, an egocentric friend of Pooh who is a weak and timid pig, is certain that everyone knows when he is in distress. But Pooh is just as egocentric when he interprets a note. Pooh only recognizes the letter "P" and each "P" convinces him further that "P" means "Pooh" so "it's a very important Missage to me." In a later chapter, Pooh eats a jar of honey that he had intended to give to everyone else on his birthday. In egocentric form, though, Pooh rationalizes his gluttony and decides to give everyone the empty jar: "It's a very nice pot. Everyone could keep things in it."

Milne recognized the pervasiveness of animism in young children's thought. Each of the imaginary characters displays a talent for animism. In the first chapter, Pooh develops an elaborate plan to steal some honey from a bee's hive. He disguises himself as a cloud in a blue sky. He rolls over and over in the mud until he is as dark as a thundercloud. He borrows a sky-blue balloon from Christopher and floats off into the sky, singing as he goes. The singing cloud is an example of animism.

Milne's story of Eeyore's (the cynical and pessimistic donkey) birthday illustrates the principle of conservation. Piglet plans to give Eeyore a large red balloon. On the way, Piglet catches his foot in the rabbit's hole and falls down. When he recovers, he finds out to his dismay that the balloon has burst. All that he has left is a small piece of a

Figure 7F

A young girl, shown reading *Winnie-the-Pooh*. How are Piaget's ideas incorporated into A. A. Milne's famous book?

damp rag. Nevertheless, Piglet is determined to give a present to Eeyore. When he finally reaches Eeyore, the conversation goes like this:

"Yes, Eeyore, I brought you a balloon."

"*Balloon,*" said Eeyore, . . . "one of those big coloured things you blow up? Gaiety, song-and-dance, here we are and there we are?"

"Yes . . . but I fell down . . . and I burst the balloon."

"My birthday balloon?"

"Yes, Eeyore," said Piglet, sniffing a little. "Here it is. With—many happy returns of the day. . . ."

"My present?"

Piglet nodded again.

"The balloon?"

"Yes."

"Thank you, Piglet," said Eeyore. "You don't mind my asking," he went on, "but what color was this balloon when it—when it *was* a balloon?"

Poor Eeyore cannot understand that red remains red even when the balloon is small and no longer round or full.

weight, and volume of objects and substances do not change by transformations that alter their appearance. An important point that needs to be made about conservation is that children do not conserve all quantities or on all tasks simultaneously. The order of their mastery is: number, length, liquid quantity, mass, weight, and volume. Piaget used the term *horizontal décalage* to describe how similar abilities to conserve different quantities do not appear at the same time. For example, an eight-year-old child may know that a long stick of clay can be rolled back into a ball but not understand that the ball and stick weigh the same. At about nine years of age the child will recognize

Figure 7.7
A family tree of four generations, (I) to (IV).
The preoperational child has trouble
classifying the members of the four
generations; the concrete operational child
can classify the members vertically,
horizontally, and obliquely (up and down and
across).

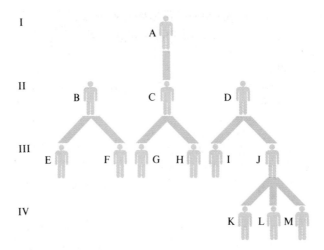

that they weigh the same and eventually at about eleven to twelve years of age the child will understand that the clay's volume is unchanged by rearranging it. Children initially master tasks in which the dimensions are more salient and visible, only later mastering those not as visually apparent, such as volume.

Classification

Many of the concrete operations identified by Piaget focus on the way children reason about the properties of objects. One important skill that characterizes the concrete operational child is the ability to classify or divide things into different sets or subsets and to consider their interrelationships. An example of the concrete operational child's classification skills involves a family tree of four generations (figure 7.7) (Furth & Wachs, 1975). This family tree suggests that the grandfather (A) has three children (B, C, & D), each of whom has two children (E through J), and that one of these children (J) has three children (K, L, & M). A child who comprehends this classification system can move up and down a level (vertically), across a level (horizontally), and up and down and across (obliquely) within the system. The concrete operational child understands that person J can at the same time be father, brother, and grandson, for example.

While concrete operational thought is more advanced than preoperational thought, it has its limitations. Logical reasoning replaces intuitive thought as long as the principles can be applied to specific or *concrete* examples. For example, the concrete operational child cannot imagine the steps necessary to complete an algebraic equation, which is too abstract for thinking at this stage of cognitive development.

Piaget's ideas have been applied extensively to the education of elementary school children. A summary of these applications is presented in Perspective on Child Development 7.3.

Formal Operational Thought

Adolescents' developing power of thought opens up new cognitive and social horizons. Thought becomes more abstract, logical, and idealistic. Adolescents become more capable of examining their own thoughts, others' thoughts, and what others are thinking about them.

Cognitive Development

Applying Piaget to Education

Americans—interested in improving children's intellects—moved swiftly to embrace Piaget and apply his ideas to children's education (Murray, 1978). Two social crises, the proliferation of behaviorism, and the psychometric, IQ approach to intelligence made the adoption of Piaget's theory inevitable. The first social crisis was the post-Sputnik concern of a country preoccupied with its deteriorating position as the world's leader in engineering and science, and the second was the need for compensatory education for minority groups and the poor. Curriculum projects that soon came into being after these social crises included the "new math," Science Curriculum Improvement Study, Project Physics, and Man: A Course of Study. All of these projects were based on Piaget's notion of cognitive developmental changes. Piaget's theory contains information about the child's reasoning in the areas of math, science, and logic—information not found anywhere else in developmental psychology.

Piaget was not an educator and never pretended to be. But he did provide a sound conceptual framework from which to view educational problems. What are some of the principles in Piaget's theory of cognitive development that can be applied to children's education? David Elkind (1976) described three. First, the foremost issue in education is *communication*. In Piaget's theory, the child's mind is not a blank slate. To the contrary, the child has a host of ideas about the physical and natural world, but these ideas differ from those of adults. We must learn to comprehend what children are saying and to respond in the same mode of discourse that children use. Second, the child is always unlearning and relearning in addition to acquiring knowledge. Children come to school with their own ideas about space, time, causality, quantity, and number. Third, the

While Piaget was not an educator and never intended to be, his ideas have been prolifically applied to children's education. How might Piaget's ideas about cognitive development be applied to improving the education of these minority group children?

child is by nature a knowing creature, motivated to acquire knowledge. The best way to nurture this motivation for knowledge is to allow the child to spontaneously interact with the environment. Education needs to ensure that it does not dull the child's eagerness to know by providing an overly rigid curricula that disrupts the child's own rhythm and pace of learning.

Piaget believed that formal operational thought came into play between the ages of eleven and fifteen. Formal operational thought is more *abstract* than a child's thinking. The adolescent is no longer limited to actual concrete experience as the anchor of thought. Instead, she may conjure up make-believe situations, hypothetical possibilities, or purely abstract propositions and reason about them. The adolescent increasingly thinks about thought itself. One adolescent pondered, "I began thinking about why I was thinking what I was. Then I began thinking about why I was thinking about why I was thinking about what I was." If this sounds abstract, it is, and it characterizes the adolescent's increased interest in thought itself and the abstractness of thought.

Accompanying the abstract nature of adolescent thought is the quality of idealism. Adolescents begin to think about ideal characteristics pertaining to themselves and others and compare themselves and others in terms of these

". . . and give me good abstract-reasoning ability, interpersonal skills, cultural perspective, linguistic comprehension, and a high sociodynamic potential."

Drawing by Ed Fisher; © 1981 The New Yorker Magazine, Inc.

Table 7.3
An Example of Hypothetical Deductive Reasoning

A common task for all of us is to determine what can logically be inferred from a statement made by someone else. Young children are often told by teachers that, if they work hard, they will receive good grades. Regardless of the empirical truth of the claim, the children may believe that good grades are the result of hard work, and that if they do not get good grades, they did not work hard enough. (Establishing the direction of the relationship between variables is an important issue.)

Children in the late concrete operational stage, too, are concerned with understanding the relations between their behavior and their teachers' grading practices. However, they are beginning to question the ''truths'' of their childhood. First, they now know that there are four possible combinations if two variables are dichotomized (work hard—not work hard; good grades—not good grades):

Behavior	Consequences
1 Work hard	Good grades
2 Work hard	Not good grades
3 Not work hard	Good grades
4 Not work hard	Not good grades

Two combinations are consistent with the hypothesis that a student's hard work is necessarily related to good grades: (1) they work hard and get good grades, and (4) they do not work hard and do not get good grades. When the presumed ''cause'' is present, the effect is present; when the cause is absent, the effect is absent. There are also two combinations that do not fit the hypothesis of a direct relation between hard work and good grades: (2) they work hard and do not get good grades, and (3) they get good grades without working hard.

The adolescent's notion of possibility allows him or her to take this analysis of combinations one important step further. Each of the four basic combinations of binary variables may be true or it may not. If 1, 2, 3, or 4 are true alone or in combination, there are 16 possible patterns of truth values:

1 or 2 or 3 or 4 is true	4 patterns
1–2 or 1–3 or 1–4 or 2–3 or 2–4 or 3–4 are true	6 patterns
1–2–3 or 1–2–4 or 1–3–4 or 2–3–4 are true	4 patterns
All (1–2–3–4) are true	1 pattern
All are false	1 pattern
Total	16 patterns

The list is critically important because each pattern leads to a different conclusion about the possible relation between two variables.

From ''An Example of Hypothetical Deductive Reasoning,'' from *Piaget with Feeling* by Philip A. Cowan, copyright © 1978 by Holt, Rinehart and Winston, Inc., reprinted by permission of the publisher.

---

ideal standards. In contrast, children think more in terms of what is real and what is limited. During adolescence, thoughts often take fantasy flights into the future. It is not unusual for the adolescent to become impatient with these newfound ideal standards and to be perplexed over which of many ideal standards to adopt.

At the same time an adolescent thinks more abstractly and idealistically than a child, she also thinks more logically. The adolescent begins to think like a scientist in the sense of devising a plan to solve a problem and systematically testing solutions. This kind of problem solving has an imposing name: **hypothetical deductive reasoning.** The adolescent develops hypotheses, or best guesses, about ways to solve a problem, such as an algebraic equation. She then deduces, or concludes, which is the best path to follow in solving the equation. By contrast, a child is more likely to solve the problem in a trial-and-error fashion. See table 7.3 for one example of hypothetical deductive reasoning.

As the adolescent's thought becomes more abstract and logical, the use of language also changes. This development includes changes in the use of satire and metaphor, in writing skills, and in conversational skills.

A junior high school student is sitting in school making up satirical labels for his teachers. One he calls "the walking wilt Wilkie and his wilking waste." Another he describes as "the magnificent Manifred and his manifest morbidity." The use of nicknames increases during early adolescence as does their

Cognitive Development

abstractness—"stilt," "spaz," "nerd," and "marshmallow mouth," for example. These examples reflect the aspect of language known as **satire,** which refers to irony, wit, or derision used to expose folly or wickedness. Adolescents use and understand satire more than children (Demorest & others, 1984). The satire of *Mad* magazine, which relies on double meaning, exaggeration, and parody to highlight absurd circumstances and contradictory happenings, finds a more receptive audience among thirteen- to fourteen-year-olds than eight- to nine-year-olds (figure 7.8).

Figure 7.8
The satire of *Mad* magazine is more popular among thirteen- to fourteen-year-olds than eight- to nine-year-olds.

Another aspect of language that comes into use in adolescence is **metaphor.** A metaphor is an implied comparison between two ideas that is conveyed by the abstract meaning contained in the words used. For example, a person's faith and a piece of glass are alike in that they both can be shattered. A runner's performance and a politician's speech are alike in that they both are predictable. Children have a difficult time understanding metaphorical comparisons; adolescents are better able to understand their meaning.

The increased abstractness and logical reasoning of the adolescent's cognition can be witnessed in improved writing ability (Scardamalia, Bereiter, & Goelman, 1982). Organizing ideas is critical to good writing. Logical thinking helps the writer develop a hierarchical structure, which helps the reader understand which ideas are general, which are specific, and which are more important than others. Researchers have discovered that children are poor at organizing their ideas prior to writing and have difficulty detecting the salient points in prose passages (Brown & Smiley, 1977). While adolescents are not yet Pulitzer Prize-winning novelists, they are better than children at recognizing the need for making both general and specific points in their writing. The sentences adolescents string together make more sense than those constructed by children. And adolescents are more likely than children to include an introduction, several paragraphs that represent a body, and concluding remarks when writing an essay (Fischer & Lazerson, 1984).

Most adolescents also are better conversationalists than are children. Adolescents are better at letting individuals take turns in discussions instead of everyone talking at once; they are better at using questions to convey commands ("Why is it so noisy in here?"); they are better at using words like *the* and *a* in ways that enhance understanding ("He is *the* living end! He is not just *a* person); they are better at using polite language in appropriate situations (when a guest comes to the house, for example); and they are better at telling stories that are interesting, jokes that are funny, and lies that convince.

Another intriguing change in thought during adolescence is the appearance of a curious sort of egocentrism. David Elkind (1978) believes **adolescent egocentrism** has two parts: an imaginary audience and a personal fable. The **imaginary audience** is the adolescent's belief that others are as preoccupied with her as she herself is. Attention-getting behavior, so common in adolescence, reflects egocentrism and the desire to be on stage, noticed, and visible. Imagine the eighth-grade boy who thinks he is an actor and all others the audience as he stares at the small spot on his trousers. Imagine the seventh-grade girl who thinks that all eyes are riveted on her complexion because of her tiny blemish.

Jennifer converses with her best friend, Anne, about something she has just heard. "Anne, did you hear about Barbara. You know she fools around a lot. Well, the word is that she is pregnant. Can you believe it? That would never happen to me." Later in the conversation, Anne tells Jennifer, "I really like Bob, but sometimes he is a jerk. He just can't understand me. He has no

How might the concept of an imaginary audience be wrapped up in this young adolescent girl's mirror watching?

How might the personal fable be involved in these adolescents' drinking and driving?

clue about what my personal feelings are." The **personal fable** refers to the adolescent's sense of personal uniqueness and indestructibility, reflected respectively in Jennifer's and Anne's comments. In their efforts to maintain a sense of uniqueness and indestructibility, adolescents sometimes create a fictitious story, or a fable. Imagine a girl who is having difficulty getting a date. She may develop a fictitious account of a handsome boy living in another part of the country who is madly in love with her.

While Elkind's ideas about egocentrism seem to capture the flavor of the young adolescent's self-centeredness, adequate measures to evaluate the imaginary audience and personal fable have not been devised, nor have longitudinal data been collected to support the developmental emergence and course of egocentrism (Lerner, 1988). Current controversy about the nature of egocentrism also focuses on whether it emerges because of formal operational thought (Elkind, 1985) or because of perspective taking and interpersonal understanding (Lapsley & Murphy, 1985; Lapsley & others, 1986).

Are most adolescents formal operational thinkers as Piaget envisioned? There is more individual variation in formal operational thought than Piaget believed. Research indicates that some adolescents are formal operational thinkers but many are not (Niemark, 1982). And some adolescents may think in more formal operational ways in some domains but not others. For example, a fourteen-year-old boy may reason at the formal operational level when it comes to analyzing an algebraic equation but not be able to do so in verbal problem solving or interpersonal relations.

At this point we have discussed a number of ideas about preoperational, concrete operational, and formal operational thought. A summary of these ideas is presented in Concept Table 7.2.

Piagetian Contributions and Criticisms

Piaget was a genius when it came to observing children, and his insights are often surprisingly easy to verify. Piaget showed us some important things to look for in development, including the shift from preoperational to concrete operational thought. He also showed us how we must make experiences fit our cognitive framework, yet simultaneously adapt our cognitive orientation to experience. Piaget also revealed how cognitive change is likely to occur if the situation is structured to allow gradual movement to the next higher level.

But Piaget's view has not gone unquestioned. Four types of findings question the Piagetian approach to cognitive development (Gelman & Baillargeon, 1983; Inhelder, De Caprona, & Cornu-Wells, in press; Kuhn, 1984). First, Piaget conceived of stages as unitary structures of thought, so his theory assumes that there is synchrony in development; that is, various aspects of a stage should emerge at about the same time. However, several concrete operational concepts do not appear in synchrony—for example, children do not learn to conserve at the same time they learn to cross-classify. Second, small changes in the procedures involved in a Piagetian task sometimes have significant effects on a child's cognition. Third, in some cases, children who are at one cognitive stage—such as preoperational thought—can be trained to reason at a higher cognitive stage—such as concrete operational thought. Piaget argued that such training only works on a superficial level and is ineffective unless the child is at a transitional point from one stage to the next. Fourth, some cognitive abilities emerge earlier than Piaget believed and their subsequent development may be more prolonged than he thought. Conservation of

Cognitive Development

Concept Table 7.2 Preoperational, Concrete Operational, and Formal Operational Thought		
Concept	**Processes/Related Ideas**	**Characteristics/Discussion**
Preoperational thought	Basic nature	This stage marks the beginning of the ability to reconstruct at the level of thought what has been established in behavior and a transition from primitive to more sophisticated symbol use. The child does not yet think operationally.
	Symbolic function and initiutive thought substages	The symbolic function substage occurs roughly between two and four years of age. The ability to think symbolically and represent the world mentally develops. Thought still has several limitations, two being egocentrism and animism. The intuitive thought substage occurs roughly between four and seven years of age. It is called intuitive because, on the one hand, children are so sure about their knowledge, yet on the other hand, they are so unaware of how they know what they know. The preoperational child lacks conservation. One important reason children cannot conserve is centration. The preoperational child also asks a barrage of questions.
Concrete operational thought	Its nature	Concrete operational thought is made up of operations—mental actions or representations that are reversible. The concrete operational child shows conservation and classification skills. Conservation involves a horizontal décalage. Concrete operational thought is limited by the inability to reason abstractly about objects.
Formal operational thought	Its nature	Piaget believed that formal operational thought comes into play between eleven and fifteen years of age. Formal operational thought is more abstract, idealistic, and logical than concrete operational thought. Piaget believed that adolescents become capable of using hypothetical deductive reasoning. Language changes that accompany formal operational thought include an increased understanding of satire and metaphor, improved writing ability, and superior conversation skills. Adolescents develop a curious type of egocentrism that involves an imaginary audience and a personal fable about being unique and indestructible. There is more individual variation in formal operational thought than Piaget envisioned.

number has been demonstrated in children as young as three years of age, although Piaget did not believe it came about until seven years of age. Some aspects of formal operational thought that involve abstract reasoning do not consistently appear as early in adolescence as Piaget believed.

Summary

I. Cognitive Developmental Theory, Processes, and Stages

Cognitive developmental theory emphasizes the child's development of rational thinking and stages of cognitive development. According to Piaget, the cognitive processes responsible for change are adaptation (assimilation, accommodation), organization, and equilibration. Piaget believed that children go through four qualitatively different stages of thought: sensorimotor, preoperational, concrete operational, and formal operational.

II. Sensorimotor Thought

Sensorimotor thought involves the infant's ability to organize and coordinate sensations with physical movements. The stage lasts from birth to about two years of age and is nonsymbolic through most of its duration. Sensorimotor thought has six substages: simple reflexes; first habits and primary circular reactions; secondary circular reactions; coordination of secondary circular reactions; tertiary circular reactions, novelty, and curiosity; and internalization of schemes. Object permanence refers to the ability to understand that objects and events continue to exist even though the infant no longer is in contact with them. Piaget believed this ability develops over the course of the six substages of sensorimotor thought.

III. Preoperational Thought: Basic Features

Preoperational thought involves the beginning of the ability to reconstruct at the level of thought what has been established in behavior and a transition from primitive to more sophisticated symbol use. The child does not yet think operationally. The symbolic function substage occurs roughly between two and four years of age. The ability to think symbolically and represent the world mentally develops. Thought still has several limitations, two being egocentrism and animism. The intuitive thought substage occurs roughly between four and seven years of age. It is called intuitive because on the one hand, children are so sure of their knowledge, yet on the other hand, they are so unaware of how they know what they know. The preoperational child lacks conservation. One important reason children cannot conserve is centration. The preoperational child asks a barrage of questions.

IV. Concrete Operational Thought

Concrete operational thought is made up of operations—mental actions or representations that are reversible. The concrete operational child shows conservation and classification skills. Concrete operational thought is limited by the inability to reason abstractly about objects. Concrete operational thought involves a horizontal décalage.

V. Formal Operational Thought

Piaget believed that formal operational thought comes into play between eleven and fifteen years of age. Formal operational thought is more abstract, idealistic, and logical than concrete operational thought. Piaget believed that adolescents become capable of using hypothetical deductive reasoning. Language changes that accompany formal operational thought include an increased understanding of satire and metaphor, improved writing ability, and superior conversation skills. Adolescents develop a curious type of egocentrism that involves an imaginary audience and a personal fable about being unique and indestructible. There is more individual variation in formal operational thought than Piaget envisioned.

VI. Piagetian Contributions and Criticisms

Piaget was a genius at observing children; he showed us some important things to look for and mapped out some general cognitive changes. Criticisms of his theory focus on such matters as stages, which are not as unitary as he believed and do not follow the timetable he envisioned.

Key Terms

adaptation 165
assimilation 165
accommodation 165
organization 166
equilibration 166
sensorimotor stage 167
preoperational stage 167
operations 167
concrete operational stage 167
formal operational stage 167
simple reflexes 169
first habits and primary circular reactions 170
primary circular reaction 170
secondary circular reactions 170
coordination of secondary reactions 170
tertiary circular reactions, novelty, and curiosity 170

internalization of schemes 171
object permanence 171
A-B error 172
symbolic function substage 173
egocentrism 176
animism 176
intuitive thought substage 177
centration 178
conservation 178
hypothetical deductive reasoning 184
satire 185
metaphor 185
adolescent egocentrism 185
imaginary audience 185
personal fable 186

Suggested Readings

Cowan, P. A. (1978). *Piaget with feeling: Cognitive, social, and emotional dimensions*. New York: Holt, Rinehart, & Winston.
  Philip Cowan, a clinical psychologist at the University of California, Berkeley, like many clinicians, believes Piaget has more to tell us about socioemotional development than Piaget himself thought.

Flavell, J. H. (1985). *Cognitive development* (2nd ed.). Englewood Cliffs, NJ: Prentice-Hall.
  An excellent statement of contemporary thinking about children's cognitive development by one of the leading scholars in the field. Although inspired by Piaget's work, the author goes well beyond it, offering new insights, critical evaluations, and reflections about his own research.

Furth, H. G., & Wachs, H. (1975). *Thinking goes to school*. New York: Oxford University Press.
  An intriguing application of Piaget's ideas to education. Includes 179 thinking games that can be incorporated into the everyday teaching of children.

Ginsburg, H., & Opper, S. (1988). *Piaget's theory of intellectual development* (3rd ed.). Englewood Cliffs, NJ: Prentice-Hall.
  One of the best explanations and descriptions of Piaget's theory of development.

Piaget, J. (1987). (Translated from the French by Helga Feider). *Possibility and necessity*. Minneapolis: University of Minnesota Press.
  Children's understanding of possibility and how they learn to choose among alternatives was a major interest of Piaget late in his life. This book describes a number of problems Piaget devised to assess these possibilities and choices.

Information Processing

The mind is an enchanting thing.

Marianne Moore
Collected Poems, 1944

S am Winters, a fifth-grade student, left his book on the dining room table and went off to school. It was a popular novel, written for nine- to twelve-year-olds, describing how a friendship is struck up between two children in a rural elementary school in contemporary Maryland. The book is entitled *Bridge to Terabithia.* The author, Katherine Paterson, won a Newbery Award for one of her children's novels in 1981.

Sam's three-year-old sister, Nancy, spied the inviting cover of the book shortly after Sam left, swooped it up, and headed to her room to "read" it. Nancy stared at the book's cover drawing of two children for a while and then turned the book upside down to contemplate what the drawing looked like from that perspective. A few moments later, Nancy was poring over the story. A quick "reader," Nancy finished the entire 128-page book in about six minutes. In that six minutes she studied each of the twelve drawings in the book and thought to herself what each drawing represented. Nancy also picked out several capital letters she knew (B, A, D, Z, M, N, C, Y) and spotted some familiar numbers on different pages (0, 1, 3, 6). She returned the book to the dining room table when she finished.

Sam came home from school at noon to have lunch. After wolfing down his hamburger, he decided to spend a little time reading and picked up *Bridge to Terabithia* to read. He sat quietly for fifteen minutes and read the eight pages of chapter 2, which introduced a new character, Leslie—a bright eleven-year-old female. A few of the words in the chapter were unfamiliar, but Sam got the idea that Leslie was an unusual girl, she looked like a boy, said whatever she pleased, and knew a lot about everything. The other character in the story, Jess, sort of liked her and Sam figured that the rest of the book would be about the two of them.

Nancy, still eating lunch, hollered over to Sam, "Did you finish the book? I did!"

Sam smiled. "You can't read this book, Nancy. You're just a little kid."

Their mother intervened to prevent a predictable fight. "Well, tell us what you read Nancy."

"A boy . . . um . . . a girl . . . a little dog house . . . a 'B', a '6'."

Sam laughed and Mrs. Winters complimented Nancy for reading so well. After Sam was comfortably off to school and Nancy was occupied with her crayons and coloring book, Mrs. Winters sat down with *Bridge to Terabithia* herself to see what she could learn about the novel. She skimmed the book in twenty minutes, forming a general idea of the plot outline. As she read, she made some mental notes about words and concepts she'd discuss at a later time with Sam, because she was fairly certain he didn't know them. She also considered whether the book was a good selection for Sam. Was the book's difficulty level about right given her assessment of his reading skills and would Sam assimilate the moral lessons the author was trying to communicate?

When we read, we process information and interpret it. So reading serves as a practical and simple example to introduce and illustrate the topic of information processing in childhood, which is the focus of this chapter. The study of information processing is concerned with how children analyze the many sources of physical information available to them in the environment and make sense of these experiences. When we read, for example, we have available to our senses a rich and complex set of visual symbols. The symbols are associated with sounds, the sounds are combined to form words, and the words and larger units that contain them (phrases, sentences, paragraphs) have conventional meanings.

To read effectively, we have to perceive and attend to these symbols. Notice that while Sam and Mrs. Winters attend to words and sentences, Nancy primarily attends to pictures, letters of the alphabet, and printed numbers. Another process in reading is holding the information we attend to in memory, while new information is taken in. Notice that Mrs. Winters, because she can read so much faster than Sam, is able to hold meanings "skimmed" from the entire novel in mind during a twenty-minute reading session, while Sam only holds the meanings from one chapter in memory.

The study of children's information processing is concerned with basic processes such as perception (which we discussed in chapter 4), attention, memory, and thinking. In this chapter, we consider these processes and other aspects of information processing, beginning with an overview of information processing. Then follows a description of three major facets of information processing—elementary processes, higher-order processes, and role of knowledge.

The Nature of Information Processing

Information processing is at once a framework for thinking about children's development and a facet of that development. As a framework, information processing includes certain ideas about how people's minds work and the best methods for studying this. As a facet of development, we can think of the different aspects of information processing that change as the child matures. For example, changes in children's attention and memory capabilities, are, in effect, changes in information-processing capabilities. In the discussion that follows, we turn our attention first to information processing as a framework.

Framework

For many experts, the **information-processing approach** is a framework for understanding how children learn and think. (Siegler, 1983, in press). It assumes that to understand children's learning and thinking, we need to analyze the way children take in information (sights, sounds, smells, etc.), how they store the information, and the way they evaluate it for some clearly defined purposes and goals. But we already have discussed learning in chapter 6 and Piaget's theory of cognitive development in chapter 7. So what else is there to say about these topics? Quite a lot. Concepts of learning, if you remember from chapter 6, focus on behaviors and the events in the environment that change these behaviors. Traditional principles of learning do little to explain what is going on in a child's mind, however. Piagetian theory, on the other hand, has quite a lot to say about the child's mind. For example, Piaget described the different ways a child structures thought at different ages; these are the stage descriptions of sensorimotor, concrete, and formal operational thought. But the Piagetian description is general—it doesn't tell us much about how the child reads, solves mathematical problems, learns new scientific facts, or composes an essay. It leaves out a lot of important details about how our

minds actually work on specific kinds of tasks like reading, writing, arithmetic, and solving a variety of problems. The information-processing framework attempts to correct the shortcomings of traditional learning theory and Piagetian ideas about development. It describes mental processes and it offers specific details about how these processes work in concrete situations. Where possible these descriptions include analyses of all the steps needed to complete some task, the specific mental processes needed to complete these steps, and precise mathematical estimates of how "hard" or how "long" the mind had to work to execute these steps. Often, the information-processing psychologist tries to write a computer program to represent the steps needed to solve the problem. Computer "models" of how something is done force the scientist to be precise. Computers are basically "dumb" machines. They do only what you tell them to do. If a dumb machine can be made to complete some task, so goes the reasoning, we will have an exhaustive understanding of everything that might possibly be needed to complete the task by a person. In practice, it is not really possible to list every step for complex activities like reading and writing. But, what we can do is study particular features of these activities and try to understand them in great detail (Anderson, 1988).

To summarize, then, information processing, as a framework for studying children's development, attempts to be very detailed about the mental processes underlying learning and thinking in very specific situations and, where possible, to model the specific steps needed to complete a task using computer programs and mathematical estimates of mental activities.

Let's consider an example to illustrate how the information-processing approach differs from the learning and Piagetian approaches. Suppose we observe a third-grade student attempting to perform some subtraction problems, for example, 176 minus 47, 395 minus 46, and 272 minus 34, written out in the usual form:

$$
\begin{array}{ccc}
176 & 395 & 272 \\
-\ \ 47 & -\ \ 46 & -\ \ 34 \\
\end{array}
$$

The student calculates the answers to be 21, 241, and 132, respectively. It will help you to write out these problems on a piece of paper, calculate the correct answers, and then note the incorrect answers provided by our hypothetical third-grader. Can you figure out the errors made by the student? Why were these errors made?

Cognitive Development

Learning theory might explain these mistakes by arguing that the child has not yet learned the correct "behavior" of "borrowing" numbers. There has been insufficient practice, modeling, and/or reinforcement for the child. Piagetian theory would have little to say about this problem. Information-processing theory, on the other hand, would give a detailed description of all the steps needed to solve these arithmetic problems (e.g., Brown & Burton, 1978) and predict precisely when a child would and would not have difficulty based on an explanation of the child's flaws. What are the steps? A partial list includes: (1) recognizing that this is a subtraction problem, (2) understanding which number is to be subtracted from which other number, (3) beginning to subtract the right-most digit on the bottom from the corresponding top digit, (4) realizing that step 3 cannot be done immediately, (5) borrowing ten from the ten's column, (6) marking the new value of the ten's column, (7) marking "one" to represent the borrowed "ten" near the top of the digit's column, (8) performing the new subtraction, (9) repeating the process for the ten's column, and so on.

What are the flaws present in this child's subtraction? There seem to be two problems or "bugs" as they sometimes have been called (Brown & Burton, 1978). First, even though the child may borrow from the ten's column, he still performs the first (digit's column) subtraction incorrectly—ignoring the borrowed number and choosing to subtract the smaller digit's value number on top from the larger one on the bottom. The ten's column subtraction is performed correctly, because the higher and lower numbers are in the locations that the child would expect (top and bottom, respectively). The second "bug" occurs when we move to the hundredth's column. The child has incorrectly continued to borrow and reduced the value of the hundredth's digit, when no borrowing was necessary.

The value of this information-processing analysis, even though it becomes tedious when it is spelled out in such great detail is that it forces us to consider exactly what the child may be doing and exactly what his procedural "bugs" are. If you know exactly how children think about this task, you have a good beginning point for trying to change and improve their thinking (Morris, 1988).

Earlier we indicated that the information-processing psychologist may try to write a computer program to represent the steps needed to solve a problem. Indeed, information-processing psychologists sometimes rely on computers to tell them something about the way children's cognition works. **Artificial intelligence,** the branch of computer science devoted to creating computers capable of handling complicated tasks that require some "thinking," has been given special attention. Since true "thinking" is usually considered to be a "human" activity, when computers play chess, solve math problems, create designs, guide industrial robots, and "see" enemy aircraft approaching, the computer thought is dubbed "artificial." What is artificial about it? Well, computers do not have human brains and a central nervous system. So, physically, computers operate differently than people. Human beings also do not think in a strictly logical fashion; they are intuitive and emotional, even when working on the logical types of problems of physics and math. As you might be aware, debate rages as to whether computers will ever achieve the powers of human thought (Dreyfus & Dreyfus, 1986). Some computer scientists feel that the best computers already have accomplished this goal. Critics argue that the highest forms of human intelligence have not been created and simply cannot be modeled in a machine. More about this fascinating issue appears in Perspective on Child Development 8.1.

According to the information-processing perspective, if you know exactly how a child is thinking about this subtraction task, you have an excellent starting point for trying to improve his ability to perform subtraction problems.

"Ask If the Computer Ever Eats Breakfast"

W ithout exactly trying to settle the computer-human debate, Richard Lehrer and Steven Yussen (1988) conducted an investigation with children and adults to discover what ideas these everyday "experts" have about the similarities and differences between human thought and intelligence and the everyday intelligence present in typical computers. Children in the third, fifth, eighth, eleventh, and twelfth grades and university students were asked to respond to a series of questions, such as What is intelligence? Are computers and people intelligent in the same way, or are they different? Do computers think about what they are doing, for example, whether or not they are solving a problem correctly, like people do? Do computers have many different feelings like people do, such as happy, sad, excited, tired, bored? What question could you ask where you would be sure to get a different (kind of) answer from a person and a computer?

The elementary school children frequently cited physical differences between people and computers. For example, their responses included: "Computers can't see!" "Ask if it ever eats breakfast. A computer will have to say no. But a person will have to say yes," and "Ask if it swims." Although these children generally regarded computers as nonfeeling things, they did believe that computers could feel certain emotions, such as "excited" and "tired." The children explained that a computer might get excited if it figured out a hard problem and tired if it was on for a long time.

The adolescents and adults were more likely to distinguish between computers and humans on the basis of internal, mental properties. For example, they frequently mentioned the extraordinary speed and memory capacities of computers (e.g., "Computers can do things much faster than people," and "If you gave it a problem like 3,688 times 4,266, a computer could get it right"). They also commented on the computer's lack of flexibility in problem solving and the stereotyped responses it would give in response to a question. And, they strongly stated that a computer could not experience any type of emotion.

The differences between natural and artificial intelligence and thought, then, are interpreted in different ways depending on age. We hasten to add that we are not suggesting that any one set of ideas about this distinction is necessarily the correct one. Rather this concept, like many others we have studied, changes with development and experience.

Developmental Change

In general, then, what aspects of information processing change as children mature? How can these changes be described? There are two equally good answers. One is of the "life just is not simple" variety; that is, there are no compelling general changes. The nature of information processing is such that to understand how younger children differ from older children, we have to examine specific processes (such as attention and memory) and tasks (such as reading, writing, and communicating), observing how children differ on each of them. Much of the remainder of this chapter details this answer, process by process.

You might have anticipated the second answer. It is exactly the opposite of the first and goes something like this. Sure, information processing is complicated, but there are some general features of it that readily distinguish the ways children at different ages perform a variety of mental processes and tasks. So, it is possible to offer a modest and general description of developmental changes in information processing without getting bogged down in details. What are these general features? Three important ones are processing speed, processing capacity, and automaticity, each of which we consider in turn.

Processing Speed

Many things children do are constrained by how much time is available. A child is told to finish writing a letter in five minutes so the family can leave. A phone message must be written down before the message is forgotten. The teacher gives children five minutes to finish a series of arithmetic problems. There is abundant evidence that the speed with which such tasks is completed improves dramatically across the childhood years (Kail, in press; Stigler, Nusbaum, & Chalip, in press). In fact, it is difficult to find any cognitive tasks where there is *not* some striking developmental change. The causes of the change are not always clear, however. Is a seven-year-old slower to write down a phone message than a thirteen-year-old because of limitations in the physical act of writing or because of other, more mental limitations such as the time needed to think of how to spell words correctly or to summarize a message briefly? And, are such differences readily overcome by some concentrated practice? Or will such age differences persist despite practice, suggesting some maturational, central nervous system differences in maturity?

Processing Capacity

Information-processing capacity can be viewed as a type of mental energy needed to perform mental work. The difficulty we have in dividing attention to two things at once is attributed to limits on capacity. So also is the trouble we have performing complex tasks (such as mentally working complicated arithmetic problems). Although capacity is believed to be limited at all ages, there is no generally accepted measure of a child's capacity, and thus findings are ambiguous. For example, it is possible that capacity does not change with age but that young children must spend more capacity on lower-level processes (such as identifying stimuli), leaving less capacity for higher-level processes (such as dividing attention or performing complex computations).

Automaticity

Some activities are completed with little thought or effort. A bright four-year-old picks up some crayons and quickly labels them—"yellow," "green," "brown," "blue," and "red." An able ten-year-old zips through a practice list of single-digit addition problems (e.g., 5 + 8) with little conscious effort. An adult picks up the newspaper and quickly reads a lead paragraph that reveals the results of an important basketball game held the previous evening. Each of these examples illustrates relatively automatic information processing. By comparison, imagine a four-year-old trying to sound out the words in a primer, a ten-year-old doing long division with three to five digit numbers, or an adult trying to decipher the meaning of a lead news paragraph in a foreign language studied years ago in high school. These activities require considerable mental processing and effort. And, while automatic processing can probably be performed at the same time the individual is completing some other (parallel) activity, effortful tasks such as these demand single-minded direction and focus. For any given task, such as calculating, reading, or writing, children's automaticity—the ability to perform automatically with little or no effort—improves dramatically as they get older (e.g., Brown & others, 1983; Siegler, 1986, 1987). Automaticity is clearly linked to speed and processing capacity. As an activity is completed faster, it requires less processing capacity. And as processing capacity increases, it becomes easier to complete tasks that were previously considered to be difficult.

Elementary Processes

What are the elementary processes necessary for children to process information about their world? They are attention and memory, each of which we consider in turn.

Attention

"Pay attention" is a phrase children hear all of the time. Just what is attention? **Attention** can be defined as the focusing of perception to produce increased awareness of a stimulus. Remember from chapter 6 that attention was discussed in the context of habituation, which is something like being bored in the sense that the infant becomes disinterested in a stimulus and no longer attends to it. The importance of these aspects of attention in infancy for later development was underscored by research indicating that both decrement and recovery of attention—when measured in the first six months of life—were associated with higher intelligence toward the end of the preschool years (Bornstein & Sigman, 1986).

While the infant's attention has important implications for cognitive development in the preschool years, significant changes in a child's ability to pay attention take place during this time (Pillow, 1988). The toddler wanders around, shifting attention from one activity to another, usually seeming to spend little time focused on any one object or event. By comparison, the preschool child might be observed watching television for a half hour.

The changes in ability to pay attention continue beyond the preschool years into the elementary school years. In the classroom children are able to observe the teacher for extended periods of time, and they can pour over their books in long hours of independent study. These demands on attention exceed what was required of the preschooler, who is generally free to move about in various play activities. These apparent changes in attention have a dramatic influence on children's learning (Stevenson, 1972).

The development of strategic use of attention is aptly shown in a study of visual scanning (Vurpillot, 1968). Children were shown two similar pictures and asked to judge whether the two were identical (figure 8.1). To perform well on this task, children have to systematically scan the pictures, comparing them feature by feature. Observation of six- and nine-year-old children's eye movement patterns suggested they were systematically scanning the pictures but observation of four-year-old children suggested they were not.

One deficit in attention during the preschool years concerns those dimensions that stand out or are *salient* compared to those that are relevant to solving a problem or performing well on a task. For example, a problem might have a flashy, attractive clown that presents the directions for solving a problem. Preschool children are influenced strongly by the features of the task that stand out—such as the flashy, attractive clown. After the age of six or seven, children attend more efficiently to the dimensions of the task that are relevant—such as the directions for solving a problem. Developmentalists believe this change reflects a shift to cognitive control of attention so that children act less precipitously and reflect more (Paris & Lindauer, 1982).

Developmentalists also study children's divided attention and selective attention. Children are constantly bombarded by stimuli. Although they cannot possibly handle all of these stimuli, children often are interested in handling more than just one. Thus there are two different types of attention tasks that children frequently face: selective attention and divided attention. **Selective**

Figure 8.1
Sample of the stimuli used in Vurpillot's study: a pair of identical houses and a pair of different houses.

attention is the ability to focus and concentrate on a narrow band of information. The child has the problem of ignoring some stimuli while focusing on others more relevant to her goals (Posner, 1987). For example, a child may need to ignore the blaring sound of a television set while studying for a test. A number of clever experiments have shown that as children get older they become more efficient at performing selective attention (Higgins & Turnure, 1984; Sexton & Geffen, 1979).

In **divided attention,** the child has the problem of handling two or more information "channels" at once. For example, the child might be listening to what the teacher is saying while also listening to what a friend is whispering to him. Following the content of these messages is bound to be difficult. Older children are considerably better at divided attention than younger children (Guttentag, 1984; Schiff & Knopf, 1985).

Memory

There are few moments when children's lives are not steeped in memory. Memory is at work with each step children take, each thought they think, and each word they utter. **Memory** is the retention of information over time. It is central to mental life and to information processing. To successfully learn and reason, children need to hold on to information and to retrieve the information

Selective attention means that the individual has the problem of ignoring some stimuli while focusing on others more relevant to her goals. How does this adolescent girl's behavior reflect selective attention? Can you think of other examples of selective attention?

Figure 8.2
Memory span increased from about two digits in two- to three-year-old children to about five digits in seven-year-old children. Between seven and thirteen years of age, memory span only increased by one and one-half digits. The solid line represents developmental differences and the dashed lines represent individual differences.

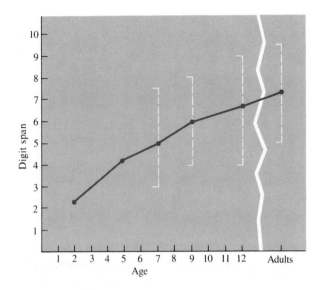

they have tucked away. In **short-term memory** we retain recently encountered information or information retrieved from long-term memory for a brief time, usually fifteen to thirty seconds. In **long-term memory** we retain information for an indefinite period of time and the information can be used over and over again.

Short-Term Memory

As a child listens to instructions from her mother, to directions from a teacher, or to a story on television, information that is encountered lasts for a short while. For this information to last longer, it has to be elaborated or transformed in some fashion, so that it can move into long-term memory, which may last for years. A child's short-term memory is severely limited, as is the short-term memory of an adult. Only a handful of "bits" of information can be handled. Many years ago, George Miller (1956) suggested that the limit is seven plus or minus two bits of information. If too much information is encountered, some of the information circulating in short-term memory is displaced and may be lost forever.

One way to illustrate this is to present a list of items to children to remember, perhaps the most common method for studying short-term memory in psychology (Case, 1985). A task that has been used in this manner is the memory span task. If you have taken an IQ test, you probably were exposed to one of these tasks. A short list of stimuli—usually digits—are presented at a rapid pace (e.g., one per second). Then you are asked to repeat the digits back. Research with the memory span task suggests that short-term memory increases during early childhood. For example, in one investigation memory span increased from about two digits in two- to three-year-old children to about five digits in seven-year-old children; yet between seven and thirteen years of age, memory span only increased by one and one-half digits (Dempster, 1981) (figure 8.2). Keep in mind, though, that memory is affected by individual differences, which is why IQ and various aptitude tests are used.

Why are there age differences in memory span? Rehearsal of information seems important—older children rehearse the digits more than younger children. Also important are the speed and efficiency of information processing, especially the speed with which memory items can be identified. For

Cognitive Development

example, in one investigation (Case, Kurland, & Goldberg, 1982), children were tested on their speed of repeating auditorially presented words. Speed of repetition strongly predicted memory span using these same words. Indeed, when speed of repetition was controlled, the six-year-olds' memory spans were equal to those of young adults!

Long-Term Memory

Remember that long-term memory is information we retain indefinitely—it can be used over and over again. Is the same pattern of developmental change found for short-term memory also found for long-term memory? Long-term memory shows a different developmental pattern: long-term memory increases with age during middle and late childhood. If we know anything at all about long-term memory, it is that long-term memory depends on the learning activities individuals engage in when learning and remembering information (Siegler, in press). Most learning activities fit under the category of effortful **control processes.** These activities are under the learner's conscious control. They are appropriately referred to as *strategies*. Four important control processes involved in children's memory are rehearsal, organization, semantic elaboration, and imagery.

Rehearsal is extended repetition of material after it has been presented—as when a child is trying to remember a phone number, for example. If someone tells a child to remember a phone number, how might the child remember it more effectively? A classic study by John Flavell and his colleagues (Flavell, Beach, & Chinsky, 1966) illustrates the importance of rehearsal and developmental changes in its use. Children from five to ten years old were given the task of remembering the names of a set of two to five pictures for fifteen seconds. The novel feature of the experiment was that the experimenter was a trained lip-reader. Some of the children made lip movements showing rehearsal of names and pictures. The percentage of children making lip movements increased with age—10 percent of the five-year-olds, 60 percent of the seven-year-olds, and 85 percent of the ten-year-olds. In a later study of six-year-olds, the research team found that children who rehearsed showed better recall than those who did not. And if nonrehearsers were taught to rehearse, their performance rivaled that of the spontaneous rehearsers (Keeney, Cannizzo, & Flavell, 1967).

More recent investigations make the interesting point that rudimentary, rehearsal-like processes begin to appear at very young ages (DeLoache, Cassidy, & Brown, 1985; Wellman, Ritter, & Flavell, 1985). In one study, three- and four-year-old children watched a toy dog being hidden under one of three cups. Instructed to remember where the dog was hidden, the children looked at, pointed to, and touched the appropriate cup (Wellman, Ritter, & Flavell, 1985).

Organization is the tendency to group or arrange items into categories. The use of organization improves long-term memory. Children show increased organization in middle and late childhood. In one investigation (Moely & others, 1969), children were presented with a circular array of pictures from four different categories: clothing, furniture, animals, and vehicles. The children were told to study the pictures so that later they could say their names back to the experimenter. They also were told they could move the pictures around to remember them better. The ten- and eleven-year-olds performed

Figure 8.3
The keyword method is used to help children remember the state capitals. A special component of this method is the use of mental imagery, which is stimulated by the presentation of a vivid visual image, such as the one shown here of two apples being married. The strategy is to help children associate *apple* with Annapolis and *marry* with Maryland.

such groupings, the younger children did not. Importantly, when younger children were put through a brief training procedure that encouraged grouping, they were able to follow this strategy. And their memory for the pictures improved.

Semantic elaboration is making something more meaningful by associating it with other ideas. Semantic elaboration increases in middle and late childhood and is important in long-term memory. Research on children's memory for meaningful sentences is informative. In experiments by Scott Paris and his colleagues (Paris & Lindauer, 1976; Paris, Lindauer, & Cox, 1977), children heard sentences that implied but did not actually mention certain tools or instruments. One of the sentences was, "Her friend swept the floor." This sentence clearly implies but does not actually mention the instrument "broom." The critical question in the experiments was this: If a child hears a sentence such as "Her friend swept the floor," will the child spontaneously infer that a broom was used? If so, we can predict that a word like *broom* should be a good cue for reminding the child of the sentence. The results of these experiments supported the prediction for eleven-year-olds but not for seven-year-olds. This indicates that spontaneous inferencing increased over the course of the elementary school years.

Imagine walking up the sidewalk to your house, opening the door, and going inside. What do you see when you are standing inside the door? Now mentally walk through the house to the room in the back and form a picture of what this room is like. Now picture your bedroom in the house. Where is your bed in relation to the door? Imagining these things is reasonably easy for most adults and children. **Imagery** refers to sensations without the presence of an external stimulus (Paivio, 1971, 1986). It is another control process that enables children to improve their memory. A powerful imagery strategy is the **keyword method,** which has been used to practical advantage by teaching children how to rapidly master new information such as foreign vocabulary words, the states and capitals of the United States, and the names of the presidents of the United States. For example, in remembering that Annapolis is the capital of Maryland, children were taught the keywords for the states, such that when a state was given (*Maryland*) they could supply the keyword (*marry*) (Levin, 1980). Then, children were given the reverse type of keyword practice with the capitals. That is, they had to respond with the capital (*Annapolis*) when given a keyword (*apple*). Finally, an illustration was provided (figure 8.3). The keyword strategy's use of vivid mental imagery—such as the image in figure 8.3, was effective in increasing children's memory of state capitals. Developmentalists today encourage the use of imagery in our nation's schools, believing it helps to increase the child's memory (McDaniel & Pressley, 1987).

At this point we have discussed a number of ideas about the nature of the information-processing approach and about the elementary processes of attention and memory. A summary of these ideas is presented in Concept Table 8.1.

Higher-Order Processes

Attention and memory may occur rather quickly as children examine information or attempt to complete some task. Children may devote little effort and complete the new activity quickly. By contrast, a variety of activities usually occur over an extended period of time and require the mobilization of considerable cognitive resources on the part of children. When children read or write, for example, the activity usually extends over a period of time. And

Cognitive Development

Concept Table 8.1
The Nature of Information Processing and Elementary Processes

Concept	Processes/Related Ideas	Characteristics/Description
The nature of information processing	Framework	The information-processing approach attempts to be very detailed about the mental processes underlying learning and thinking in specific situations and, where possible, to model the specific steps needed to complete a task using computer programs and mathematical estimates of mental activities.
	Development	Information processing emphasizes that with age children's processing speed, processing capacity, and automaticity increase.
Elementary processes	Attention	Attention is the focusing of perception to produce increased awareness of a stimulus. Children's attention increases dramatically in the preschool years and becomes even more efficient in the elementary school years. During the elementary school years, scanning of visual patterns, attention to relevant dimensions, selective attention, and divided attention improve.
	Memory	Memory is the retention of information over time. Two important dimensions are short-term memory—information held for about fifteen to thirty seconds—and long-term memory—information held indefinitely. Short-term memory has a limited capacity. Several control processes or strategies facilitate long-term memory, among them rehearsal, organization, semantic elaboration, and imagery. There is evidence that short-term memory improves most in the preschool years, and long-term memory improves most in the elementary school years.

when children encounter some difficulty or lapse of attention, they must overcome the temporary impasse and get back on track. Two themes in children's information processing illuminate the ability to guide and take control of activity: cognitive monitoring and problem solving, each of which we consider in turn.

Cognitive Monitoring

Cognitive monitoring is the process of taking stock of what you are currently doing, what you will do next, and how effectively the mental activity is unfolding. When children engage in an activity like reading, writing, or solving a math problem, they are repeatedly called on to take stock of what they are doing and what they plan to do next (e.g., Baker & Brown, 1984; Bereiter & Scardamalia, 1982). For example, when children begin to solve a math problem—especially one that might take awhile to finish—they must figure out what kind of problem they are working on and what would be a good approach to take in solving it. And once they undertake a problem solution, it is helpful to check on whether the solution seems to be working or whether some other approach would be better.

The source of much cognitive monitoring for young children is other people—especially parents and teachers. Adults provide a lot of guidance and direction for children's activities and they tell children what specific strategies to use to complete different cognitive tasks (Wertsch, 1985; Yussen, 1985). They suggest when children should start an activity, they intervene at points when they think children might encounter difficulty (e.g., to explain difficult words, how to get started writing on a topic, a strategy for looking at math problems, a good study strategy), and they check children's progress and understanding (e.g., giving oral spelling quizzes, asking for explanations, holding

What is the source of cognitive monitoring in many children? How might this father cognitively monitor his daughter's homework?

Reciprocal Teaching

One of the most intractable problems for teachers is to help children, diagnosed as learning disabled, to improve significantly in school. By the time these children have been in school for five or six years, they have experienced almost as many years of "failing" to keep up in their schoolwork, they have frustrated parents and teachers who are dissatisfied with them, they have a great sense of personal guilt and low self-esteem, and they have a perceived hopelessness about ever succeeding in school. Many techniques and approaches have been tried to make a difference in these children's academic lives, and many have failed. One approach that seems to work is an instructional procedure first described by Annemarie Palincsar and Ann Brown (1984) called **reciprocal teaching.**

The instruction involves a small group of students, often working with an adult leader, actively discussing a short text, with the goal of *summarizing* it, asking *questions* to promote understanding, offering *clarifying* statements for difficult or confusing words and ideas, and *predicting* what will come next. The procedure involves children in an active way, it teaches them some techniques to reflect about their own understanding, and the group interaction is highly motivating and engaging. It is one of the most thoughtful and useful instructional techniques based on "metacognitive" principles. Table 8.A provides the transcript from a reciprocal dialogue involving a group of seventh-grade students who were poor at reading comprehension. The children had to read a paragraph, explain its main idea to each other, clarify points, elaborate on its meaning, and predict what came next.

Table 8.A
An Example of Reciprocal Teaching

Text:		Can Snakes Sting With Their Tongues? No—snakes' tongues are completely harmless. They're used for feeling things and for sharpening the snakes' sense of smell. Although snakes can smell in the usual way, the tongue flickering in the air picks up tiny particles of matter. These particles are deposited in two tiny cavities at the base of the nostrils to increase the snake's ability to smell.
1.	A:	Do snakes' tongues sting?
2.	K:	Sometimes.
3.	A:	Correct. This paragraph is about do snakes sting with their tongue, and different ways that the tongue is for and the senses of smell.
4.	*T:	Are there any questions?
5.	C:	Snakes' tongues don't sting.
6.	*T:	Beautiful! I thought, boy, I must have been doing some fast reading there because I missed that point. A___ , could you ask your question again?

*Indicates turns taken by the adult teacher (T). Other letters stand for student names. This reciprocal dialogue occurred from an early session in a group of students poor at comprehending information.

From A. L. Brown and A. S. Palincsar, 1987. "Reciprocal Teaching of Comprehension Strategies: A Natural History of One Program for Enhancing Learning." In J. Borkowski and J. D. Day (eds.), Intelligence and Cognition in Special Children: Comparative Studies of Giftedness, Mental Retardation and Learning Disabilities (pp. 81–132). New York: Ablex.

discussions). An important aspect of children's progress in cognitive monitoring as they mature, then, is their abilities to take independent control of their own cognitive activities and to develop the knowledge base to permit significant, strategic performances.

One trend in education that may help to foster this transition is cooperative learning groups in schools (e.g., Slavin, 1987). One of the by-products of cooperative learning arrangements is to place cognitive monitoring in the hands of other children. That is, instead of adults telling children what to do and checking their performance, this chore is performed by other children. For a good example of this, see Perspective on Child Development 8.2, which highlights the technique of reciprocal teaching in reading. Are cooperative groups effective? There is some evidence that they are (e.g., Slavin, 1987, 1988). But are children capable of offering the same level of cognitive monitoring to other children as adults can provide? There is no clear evidence

Table 8.A Continued

7.	A:	Do snakes' tongues really sting?			used for smell? O.K.?
8.	*T:	Now, A_ , since you have asked the question, can you find in that paragraph where the question is answered?	20.	B:	They are used for feeling things for sharpening snakes' sense of smell.
9.	A:	No, snakes' tongues are completely harmless.	21.	*T:	O.K. They are used for sharpening the snakes' sense of smell. Are they used for smelling? That's the point we aren't clear on.
10.	*T:	So we'll try it again. Can you generate another question that you think a teacher might ask?	22.	L:	In my answer I said it is for the sense of smell.
11.	A:	What are the tongues used for?	23.	*T:	That is fine; this is what the technique is all about. What it means is not that you are right or wrong or good or bad. What it says is that we have just read something and have had a disagreement about what it says. We need to work it out.
12.	*T:	Good!			
13.	L:	The sense of smell.			
14.	*T:	Is that correct? A___ , do you disagree? Yes.			
15	A:	That answer was right, but there are other things that the tongue can do.	24.	A:	My prediction is that they will now talk about the different things about snakes. Where they live, and what they eat and stuff like that.
16.	L:	But she only said tell one, she didn't say tell all of them.			
17.	*T:	O.K.	25.	*T:	O.K. Good, What do you think they eat?
18.	B:	It is used to pick up tiny particles.	26.	A:	Animals.
19.	*T:	O.K. I think that this is an important point. You have the basic concept which is correct, O.K., but what the question really is saying, is is it	27.	A:	Deserts.
			28.	C:	I challenge. Snakes, all of them, don't live in the desert. They live in the woods and in swamp areas.

about this, but we would guess that the answer is mixed. Children in cooperative groups probably provide rather simple advice and guidance (which sometimes might even be very wrong). On the other hand, children may listen to and follow the advice offered by peers in give-and-take, shared activities.

What evidence is there that young children need advice to help them monitor their cognitive activities? Plenty! Developmentalists have accumulated a vast amount of information about what children do and do not know about how to remember (Brown & others, 1983; Kreutzer, Leonard, & Flavell, 1975), how to read effectively (Baker & Brown, 1984; Garner, 1987), how to compose and write (Bereiter & Scardamalia, 1982), and how to solve problems (Mayer, 1987).

An example involving understanding messages is illuminating. In a classic study, Ellen Markman (1977) asked individual elementary school children in the first through the third grades to help her determine the adequacy of instructions written to teach other children how to play games and perform magic

Cooperative learning contexts have increased in our nation's schools. Can you think of circumstances in which cooperative learning might be more effective than other methods?

tricks. She then read each child a standard set of instructions supposedly explaining how to play a special "card game" and how to perform a particular "magic trick." The instructions for the card game were (after showing the children a set of alphabet cards and dividing them equally between the child and the experimenter):

We each put our cards in a pile. We both turn over the top card in our pile. We look at cards to see who has the special card. Then we turn over the next card in our pile to see who has the special card this time. In the end, the person with the most cards wins the game.

Notice that there was no mention of what the special card might be. So there is information missing without which children could not possibly understand how to play the game. Did they realize something was amiss with these instructions? To find out, Markman probed the children's thoughts with a series of questions, beginning with a vague statement, ("That's it. Those are my instructions.") and continuing with increasingly specific probes designed to elicit the child's awareness of the flawed instructions ("What do you think?" "Do you have any questions?" "Did I tell you everything you need to know to play the game?" and so on).

Markman found with the card game as well as with the magic trick that the first-grade children did not spontaneously notice the problem. It took a lot of probes before they spotted something wrong with the instructions. By contrast, third graders detected the flaws in the instructions by the second or third general probe ("What do you think?" "Do you have any questions?").

Other research such as this—sometimes called error detection—reveals that the failure to detect problems with oral messages and written text continues to be a problem for elementary school children even in later grades and for those who are poor readers (Baker, 1984; Garner, 1987; Markman, 1979). However, children do not always perform poorly. In particular, if they have some idea of what kind of problem will occur, they are more likely to spot it. Among the problems that might occur in short texts like these are contradictions, meaningless words, and violations of common sense.

Problem Solving

Just what is problem solving? **Problem solving** is an attempt to find an appropriate way of attaining a goal when the goal is not readily available. We face many problems in our everyday lives—trying to figure out why our car won't start, planning how to get enough money to buy a stereo, or estimating our chances of winning at blackjack. Children also face many problems in their everyday lives—working a jigsaw puzzle, doing math homework, or getting some money that is out of reach, for example.

With children, a common tactic has been to formulate a problem that requires them to apply some newly learned academic skills in a practical context. Word problems in mathematics have been a popular topic of study (e.g., Carpenter, Moser, & Romberg, 1982; Hiebert & Wearne, 1988). For example, consider the following word problems.

1. Marie has nine fish. Her sister Jill has fourteen fish. How many more fish does Jill have than Marie?
2. Fred has eight M&Ms. How many more M&Ms does he have to put with them so he has thirteen M&Ms altogether?
3. There are five jars of paint. Three jars are red and the rest are blue. How many blue jars of paint are there?

Also try to solve the following problem: If a human being has an inoperable stomach tumor, how can the tumor be removed by rays that destroy organic tissue at sufficient intensity without destroying the healthy tissue surrounding it? (Duncker, 1945). The question has been posed to many generations of college students to illustrate how they proceed to think through alternative solutions (the answer to the tumor problem appears at the end of the chapter).

How do children and adults go about solving these and other problems? What accounts for change in problem-solving ability as children mature? There seem to be at least four important parts involved—problem finding and goal setting, planning the approach, monitoring progress, and checking solutions.

First, we have to figure out what the problem is precisely and set one or more goals. This has sometimes been referred to as *problem finding* and *goal setting*. The examples of problems given are reasonably well defined. The creators of these problems have taken pains to set up the context and to tell us what they want us to find. In everyday problem solving, however, we often have to find out what the problem is and what, precisely, we have to do, ourselves. For example, if a child is asked to clean her room, she must first figure out what must be done. What must the room look like when she is completed and what currently is out of order?

Once the problem and goal have been defined, a second step is to *plan the approach* to solving the problem. Planning may involve isolating the correct pieces to the puzzle and working out the general pattern to solve the problem with these pieces. For example, in Duncker's tumor-removal problem, the student would have to isolate these crucial elements: a tumor is to be destroyed with an intense ray, the tumor is in the stomach, no tissue around the tumor can be destroyed. The plan then becomes to devise ways to make the ray intensely focused on the tumor but not anywhere else. By brainstorming and calling upon popular knowledge about technology and physics, a number of ideas may be tried out and discarded as impractical, until a single elegant solution suggests itself. With arithmetic word problems, a similar phenomenon of planning may occur for younger children. In the third word problem, for example, the child must recognize that there are five jars of paint, three of a certain color, and the remaining ones of a different color. The plan is to figure out how many remaining ones there are.

A third step is to *monitor the progress* of the problem-solving activity, a topic we already have discussed. Basically, this involves taking stock of how the solution process is faring, which is a kind of self-assessment in midstream. As ideas for solving the tumor problem come forth, for example, the student may stop to ponder whether a given idea is an improvement over the preceding one and/or whether he is still keeping the correct problem elements and goal in mind. As another example, younger children working out the arithmetic problems may wonder if they are proceeding smoothly. There are several common approaches taken by first and second graders to solve these problems. Some count on their fingers, some rely on number facts in their heads, and some use counting props made available by the experimenter. The monitoring activity, then, may consist of children's self-assessments of the viability of the counting technique each has chosen.

The fourth and final step is to *check solutions*. Whereas monitoring focuses on the progress of problem-solving efforts, this final step occurs when individuals feel they have completed their tasks. Simply put, it is to check the solution in whatever way possible. In the tumor problem the student may compare the final solution offered against the initial criteria that had to be met,

The information-processing perspective has increasingly been applied to children's education. What are some examples of its application to education?

against the solutions that other classmates have thought up, or against published accounts of its ideal solution. Children solving the arithmetic problems may recheck their adding and subtracting or check the internal consistency of answers (e.g., by seeing in the third problem if the number of jars of blue paint computed, when added to the three jars of red paint, yields five).

So far, we have learned a great deal about how children process information about their world. We have studied how children attend to information, how they perceive it, retain it over time, engage in cognitive monitoring, and solve problems. Recently, ways that information processing might be applied to children's education have been considered (Gagne, 1985; White, in press). To learn more about this application, turn to Perspective on Child Development 8.3.

But it is important to keep in mind that information processing does not occur in the absence of knowledge: we need to have something to think about (Sternberg, 1987). Next, we turn to the nature of children's knowledge and expertise.

Knowledge and Expertise

As we study changes in children's information-processing skills, it does not take long to realize that specific processes such as memory depend on what children already know. It seems obvious that most of what children try to remember and understand in everyday activities depends on the children's knowledge about people, places, and things (Neisser, 1982). If a child makes a trip to a toy store, her ability to recount what was seen is largely governed by what the child knows about toy stores and the things found there, for example. With little knowledge about what is usually found in a toy store, the child would have a much harder time recounting what was there. If prior knowledge proves helpful in this way, it can also be distorting. For example, in an investigation by Ann Brown and her colleagues (1977), third-, fifth-, and seventh-grade children heard the following story with either George or Galen as the main character.

The Fugitive

Galen (George) was alone. He knew they would soon be here. They were not far behind him when he left the village, hungry and cold. He dare not stop for food or shelter for fear of falling into the hands of his pursuers. There were many of them; they were strong and he was weak. Galen (George) could hear the noise as the uniformed band beat its way through the trees not far behind him. The sense of their presence was everywhere. His spine tingled with fear. Eagerly he awaited darkness. In darkness he would find safety.

Children who heard the story about Galen immediately assumed that the vignette was about a popular character in the television show "Planet of the Apes." In recalling the story later, they inferred that the character was an ape, that the pursuers were apes, that his "fur" tingled, and that the pursuers made their way using trees rather than walking among them. Those who read about George had no such "intrusions" in their memories.

As we evaluate the contribution of knowledge to children's information processing, in succeeding sections we will explore the different kinds of knowledge children acquire, the different ways the knowledge is put to use, and how experts differ from others in the kind of knowledge they have and the way they use it.

Cognitive Development

Information Processing, the Information Age, and Children's Education

When you were in elementary school, did any teacher at any time work with you on improving your memory strategies? Did any of your teachers work with you on your reading skills after the first and second grade? Did any of your teachers discuss with you ways in which imagery could be used to enhance your processing of information? If you are like most individuals, you spent little or no time in elementary school on improving these important processes involved in our everyday encounters with the world.

Why is it important to have an educational goal of improving the information-processing skills of children? Think for a moment about yourself and the skills necessary for you to be successful in adapting to your environment and for improving your chances of getting a good job and having a successful career. To some extent, knowledge itself is important; more precisely, content knowledge in certain areas is important. For example, if you plan to become a chemical engineer, a knowledge of chemistry is required. Our schools have done a much better job of imparting knowledge than in instructing students how to process information.

Another important situation in your life where instruction in information processing would have helped you tremendously was when you took the SAT or ACT test. SAT cram courses are popping up all over the United States, in part because schools have not done a good job of developing information-processing skills. For example, is speed of processing information important on the SAT? Most of you probably felt that you did not have as much time as you would have liked to handle difficult questions. Are memory strategies important on the SAT? You had to read paragraphs and hold a considerable amount of information in your mind to answer some of the questions. And you certainly had to remember how to solve a number of math problems. Didn't you also have to remember the definitions of a large number of vocabulary words? And what about problem solving, inferencing, and understanding? Remember the difficult verbal problems you had to answer and the inferences you had to make when reasoning was required?

The story of information processing is one of attention, perception, memory (especially the control processes in memory), and thinking. These information-processing skills become even more crucial in education when we consider that we are now in the midst of a transition from an industrial to a postindustrial information society, with approximately 65 to 70 percent of all workers involved in service industries. The information revolution in our society has placed strains on workers who are called on daily to process huge amounts of information in a rapid fashion, to have efficient memories, to attend to relevant details, to reason logically about difficult issues, and to make inferences about information that may be fuzzy or unclear. Students graduate from high school, college, or postgraduate work and move into jobs requiring information-processing skills, yet they have had little or no instruction in improving these skills.

At this time, we do not have a specified curriculum of information processing that can be taught in a stepwise, developmental fashion to our nation's children. We also do not have the trained personnel for this instruction. Further, some information-processing experts believe that processes such as attention and memory cannot be trained in a general way. Rather, they argue that information processing is domain- or content-specific; that is, we should work on improving information-processing skills that are specific to math or specific to history. They do believe, though, that an infusion of the information-processing approach into all parts of the curriculum would greatly benefit children (Dillon & Sternberg, 1988; Lorden & Falkenberg, 1988).

Researchers are beginning to study the importance of information-processing skills for school learning. Ellen Gagne (1985) provided a menu of information-processing skills that need to be given attention when instructing children in specific content areas—reading, writing, math, and science, for example. Her review concludes that successful students—those who get better grades and higher achievement test scores—are better at information-processing skills such as focusing attention, elaborating and organizing information, and monitoring their study strategies. As yet, though, we do not know the extent these information-processing skills can be taught. Nonetheless, in one investigation, Gagne and her colleagues (in press) demonstrated that children can be taught effective ways to elaborate information so that it can be remembered more efficiently. Elaboration refers to more extensive processing. Getting the child to think of examples of a concept is a good way to improve the child's memory of the concept; so is getting the child to think about how the concept relates to herself. Other experts in cognitive psychology also believe that information-processing skills can be taught. For example, Joan Baron and R. J. Sternberg (1987) believe we need to teach children to think in less irrational ways; children need to be more critical of the first ideas that pop into their minds. They should be taught to think longer about problems and to search in more organized ways for evidence to support their views.

Knowledge

In our everyday learning and thinking we use many simple concepts to understand and make sense of the world. Words for ordinary objects, people, and places, such as "house," "man," and "street," stand for simple ideas and concepts that are the building blocks for our thought. A **concept** is a category used to group objects, events, and characteristics on the basis of common properties. Why are concepts important? Without concepts, each object in a child's world would be unique. Any kind of generalization would be impossible.

Researchers have been interested in the organization of concepts (e.g., Markman & Callanan, 1983; Mervis & Rosch, 1988). One of the most powerful ideas from this research is that simple concepts are organized into rich patterns called **semantic networks,** which gradually grow in size and complexity. As children mature, the increased size and complexity of semantic networks allow them to connect many ideas quickly and to have all of these ideas in hand to accomplish whatever task is necessary. A good example of a semantic network is provided by an investigation of a four-year-old dinosaur expert (Chi & Koeske, 1983). Like many children his age, this young boy enjoyed hearing stories about dinosaurs and examining picture books of dinosaurs. Unlike most children his age, however, this young boy was able to name at least forty-six distinct dinosaurs and could identify at least one and often many features of each one (e.g., plant eater, flies). The researchers carefully mapped out what the child knew about each dinosaur and how directly each dinosaur name was linked in the child's mind to other dinosaur names. Figure 8.4 shows a complete "mapping" of the boy's semantic dinosaur network. It represents visually how the dinosaurs were linked and the particular features associated with each dinosaur in the child's mind. Although the figure is complicated, some simple points can be learned from it. Each line represents a link, each circled letter represents a dinosaur attribute, and the individual dinosaur names/concepts are included in the rectangular or hexagonal boxes. Notice, first, that some dinosaurs are not linked to many others. This is true of "Dimetrodon" and "Pterodactyl." We would not expect these dinosaurs to be as easily remembered or used compared to others. Notice, second, that among the dinosaurs that are linked, some have more links (e.g., "Styracosaur" has more links than "Ornitholestes"). And notice, third, that some dinosaurs are more centrally located in a network than those surrounding them. We would expect dinosaur names with more links and a more central location in the network to be more salient in the child's mind when he thinks about dinosaurs.

You may be somewhat intimidated by this young child's knowledge. We certainly are. You can get a good personal understanding of semantic networks by creating your own mapping of a domain of concepts familiar to you. Perhaps try one of these: "foods I like to eat," "games I know," or "places I visit."

Another form of knowledge children possess is a **schema** (plural, **schemata**). Piaget used this term to refer to any of the elementary structures of thought in his theory of cognitive operations. So we have sensorimotor schemata such as "sucking," "visual searching," and "eye-hand examination" of objects. In the field of information processing, a schema is defined as an abstract knowledge structure that summarizes or describes a set of related experiences or events (Anderson & Pearson, 1984).

One of your authors (Steven Yussen) has studied one type of schema, that of story schema. Children frequently hear and tell stories. And as they develop the ability to read, they are exposed to many kinds of stories in print.

Cognitive Development

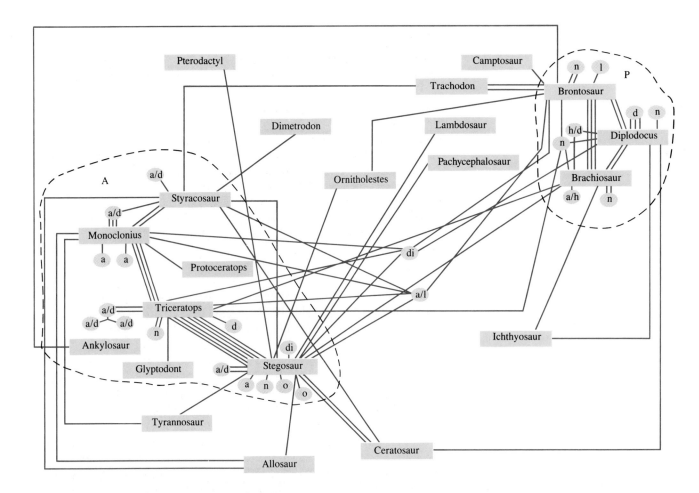

Figure 8.4
A four-year-old dinosaur expert's semantic network.

Simple stories have a structure to them and after hearing enough stories, children develop a strong expectation about what kind of information will be contained in a story. This expectation is a *story schema*. For example, a story tells about what happens in a particular place and circumstance. This content is called the setting. A story will also have at least one main character, the protagonist, who attempts to achieve some purposeful goal for some clear reason. The protagonist's actions are usually captured in one or more episodes of a story, which can be further broken down, depicting a fairly simple, one-episode story (figure 8.5).

A decade of research has shown that children at a very young age are able to use structures like these to fill in missing information, remember better, and tell relatively coherent stories (Ackerman, in press; Buss & others, 1983; Rahman & Bisanz, 1986; Stein & Glenn, 1979; Yussen & others, 1988). Changes occur throughout the childhood years, however, in children's abilities to identify salient events in stories, to unscramble mixed-up stories, and to keep multiple plot lines straight in their minds when facing more complex stories involving several episodes and more than one major character.

A final type of knowledge is a *script*. In ordinary language, a script is the written record that guides the actors who are to perform a play or story. It tells the actors what to say and what to do at each moment in the action. In psychology, the term was popularized by Roger Schank and Philip Abelson (1977) to indicate a type of psychological record that serves a similar purpose.

Figure 8.5
"Albert, the fish," a representative story.

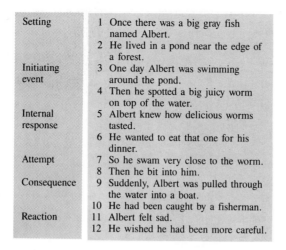

Setting	1	Once there was a big gray fish named Albert.
	2	He lived in a pond near the edge of a forest.
Initiating event	3	One day Albert was swimming around the pond.
	4	Then he spotted a big juicy worm on top of the water.
Internal response	5	Albert knew how delicious worms tasted.
	6	He wanted to eat that one for his dinner.
Attempt	7	So he swam very close to the worm.
	8	Then he bit into him.
Consequence	9	Suddenly, Albert was pulled through the water into a boat.
	10	He had been caught by a fisherman.
Reaction	11	Albert felt sad.
	12	He wished he had been more careful.

A psychological script is a knowledge structure that preserves information about highly familiar events having a stereotyped pattern. Unlike the other knowledge structures we have discussed so far, scripts are concrete rather than abstract because they deal with actions that people frequently take and concrete events that we do and see. Adults frequently go to restaurants, visit the doctor, and play or watch sporting events such as baseball. Children get up in the morning, go to school, take tests, and also visit restaurants and the doctor. All of these events involve scripts. An example of a restaurant script is shown in figure 8.6; it represents the knowledge people have about the ordinary event of going to a restaurant. Notice that this script has information about the different people (roles) encountered at restaurants, the standard things (props) salient in restaurants, the usual conditions for going to a restaurant (entry conditions), and the different things that happen at restaurants (scenes). This script should be useful to us when we are actually in a restaurant or when we need to understand some communication that refers to a person at a restaurant. For example, if you are in a restaurant and a man comes over and lays a piece of paper on your table, your script can tell you he is probably a waiter who is giving you the check (of course, he might be a spy leaving a secret message, but your script lets you make a good first guess).

Children's first scripts appear very early in development, perhaps as early as the first year of life. Children clearly have scripts by the time they enter school. As they develop, their scripts become less crude and more sophisticated. For example, a four-year-old child's script for a restaurant might only include information about sitting down and eating food. By eight to nine years of age, the child will have added information about the types of people who serve food, paying the cashier, and so on to the restaurant script (Bower, Black, & Turner, 1979; Mandler, 1983; Nelson, 1978).

Earlier we addressed the possibility of applying the information-processing approach to children's education. Some educators also believe that a broad base of knowledge, or cultural literacy, is sorely lacking in our nation's children. To learn more about a provocative new concern pertaining to improving children's broad-based knowledge turn to Perspective on Child Development 8.4.

Figure 8.6
A script for a restaurant.

Name:	Restaurant		
Props:	Tables	**Roles:**	Customer
	Menu		Waiter
	Food		Cook
	Bill		Cashier
	Money		Owner
	Tip		
Entry Conditions:	Customer is hungry.	**Results:**	Customer has less money.
	Customer has money.		Owner has more money.
			Customer is not hungry.

Scene 1: *Entering*
Customer enters restaurant.
Customer looks for table.
Customer decides where to sit.
Customer goes to table.
Customer sits down.

Scene 2: *Ordering*
Customer picks up menu.
Customer looks at menu.
Customer decides on food.
Customer signals waitress.
Waitress comes to table.
Customer orders food.
Waitress goes to cook.
Waitress gives food order to cook.
Cook prepares food.

Scene 3: *Eating*
Cook gives food to waitress.
Waitress brings food to customer.
Customer eats food.

Scene 4: *Exiting*
Waitress writes bill.
Waitress goes over to customer.
Waitress gives bill to customer.
Customer gives tip to waitress.
Customer goes to cashier.
Customer gives money to cashier.
Customer leaves restaurant.

Cultural Literacy

We are in the midst of an era of educational reform across the country. State after state is implementing legislated changes at all levels of schooling to try to improve public education. The list of concerns is legion (Bernstein, 1988). Some worry that not enough students are taking mathematics and science classes in high school with the consequence that our country will compete poorly with Japan and Western Europe in future high-technology industries. Others worry that we are not teaching children to read and write very effectively anymore. And undergirding specific curriculum concerns such as these is a basic sense of uneasiness about the quality of people entering the teaching profession. Add to this list a provocative new concern popularized by English professor E. D. Hirsch of the University of Virginia in his book *Cultural Literacy* (1987). We share Hirsch's idea with you because it is receiving a great deal of attention among members of the educational community and because, fundamentally, it is based on a central idea discussed in this chapter.

To have some appreciation of Hirsch's concerns, bear with us and try a little test on yourself. Following is a list of words and terms. Read each one and see if you can silently identify its basic meaning in some way. For example, define it, give an example, or explain its significance, even in a crude way.

1066	Zurich	mainspring	golden fleece
burgher	golden rule	nicotine	probate court

We selected these words at random from several thousand included in a glossary in Hirsch's book that runs over sixty pages in length. It is a provisional list defining what Hirsch calls the knowledge that every literate adult should learn in school in order to function well in our contemporary society. It includes terms drawn from history, literature, government, science, mathematics, art, geography, and other areas of knowledge.

Simplifying the argument, somewhat, here are Hirsch's bold claims.

1. To be a full participant in our modern democratic society, it is necessary to be literate.
2. Stripped of its subtleties, the core of adult literacy is having a broad and wide-ranging base of knowledge.

3. The knowledge he has in mind is *schematic* in nature. It needn't be detailed or complete. If you know that nicotine is an ingredient in cigarettes or that Zurich is a city in Switzerland that is sufficient.
4. American schools used to make students learn more schematic knowledge. The curriculum had substance and factual content. Recently it has slipped, with faddish concerns about "process," "thinking skills," and "developmental curricula."
5. We need to reform the American school curriculum starting at the beginning of elementary school so that more content is present, specifically of the sort outlined in his glossary.
6. To guarantee recommendation 5 is taken seriously, school systems ought to begin immediately creating tests to see whether children's knowledge bases are improving.

What do you think of Hirsch's ideas? Do they make sense to you? Do you accept his arguments? You may well be faced with the consequences of its adoption in some form. If you haven't already done so, we encourage you to read his book and think about it further. Briefly, our own reaction is this: Few educators could or would want to argue against the notion that the accumulation of a broad base of knowledge is important. As we have seen throughout this chapter, a child's general knowledge has repercussions on the success of his or her learning and, we would agree with Hirsch, with the later success the child has as an adult. But, should we be content with "shallow" knowledge of the sort that would be encouraged by a test such as his? And should everyone be expected to be a broad, Renaissance collector of information? Or do we, in our specialized society, need to tolerate the "distortion" of some otherwise well-educated people, becoming narrowly "expert." Also, how will we ever resolve the perpetually thorny issue of who defines what's on the test and whose consensus defines what constitutes contemporary cultural literacy? And shouldn't we also be concerned about improving children's information processing skills?

Expertise

What is an expert? An **expert** is someone who has a great deal of knowledge about a domain of human interest and a great deal of experience performing tasks typical of that domain. These individuals are recognized by others in their fields as having reached the highest levels of knowledge and performance. Examples of experts are easy to offer. Any list would include, but not be limited to, exceptional athletes, talented musicians, acclaimed artists, highly esteemed professionals in medicine and law, highly skilled manual trades people,

and chess masters. Experts are often contrasted with novices, who are just beginning to learn in the domain. A great deal of research has been done in the past two decades to characterize the differences between experts and others. Most, but not all, of this work is with adults (e.g., Glaser & Bassok, in press), an inevitable result of the limited time children have had to become expert at anything.

Our survey of the topic considers why an understanding of expertise is important in the study of children's information processing, some of the differences found between experts and others, and implications for learning and instruction.

Recently, considerable interest has developed in the distinction between experts and novices. What characteristics might qualify this magician as an expert rather than a novice?

Developmental Implications of Expertise

In some ways, young children are universal novices. They perform almost any cognitive task with very little of the knowledge and experience of adults. If adults are not always experts, neither are they rank novices at reading, writing, solving mathematics problems, following travel directions, and so on. But young children are almost always novices at these tasks. There are exceptions, of course. We can find children with high levels of skill in chess, handling an abacus, and dinosaur identification, for example. But, our interest in these forms of childhood expertise is partly a result of the novelty and rarity with which it occurs. And, if we study such forms of childhood expertise carefully we would probably conclude that the children are not really experts at all. Our four-year-old dinosaur "expert" is certainly a wonder, but he hardly has the knowledge of a paleontologist—among whom the real dinosaur experts would be found.

The appeal then is not to make children experts. This is not a feat we're likely to manage with any great success. The attraction, instead, is to understand what an expert does, how the expert got to that level of functioning, and the stages or landmarks that led up to the high level of functioning. With this knowledge in hand, we can have realistic goals about fostering high levels of competence in children and of cultivating expertise in children who seem to have interest and potential in particular fields.

Differences between Experts and Novices

How do experts and novices differ in the way they approach tasks in a particular domain? One difference concerns initial *planning time*. Present a problem to an expert and the expert spends more time, relative to the total time needed to complete the task, than a novice or less experienced person would in thinking about how to go about solving the problem or completing the task. Expert writers spend a great deal of time thinking about what they want to communicate, how to communicate it, and what the parts or units of their written product will look like. Expert computer programmers spend a considerable amount of time describing to themselves what their finished program will accomplish and the form their program will take. And expert athletes spend a great deal of effort planning their approach to conditioning, polishing skills, and choosing competition. Novices, on the other hand, leap right in. They may not have the skill to plan effectively or they may not realize the value of initial planning. This emphasis on planning often surprises people, because a common stereotype of experts is that they know how to do everything in their domain of expertise with relatively little effort.

In fact, if a task is straightforward, and not a "problem" to solve, experts are extremely fast. Their performances seem *automatic* and *effortless*. Having planned an essay, the expert writer may dash off pages of print in just several

Information Processing   215

hours. Having planned a computer program, the programmer writes code at a speed that dazzles beginners. Having prepared physically and mentally for a match, the expert tennis player serves, volleys, and returns ground strokes with speed and grace. The contrasting performance of the novice is one of sluggish fits and starts, conscious thought about what to do, and great effort.

Another feature of expert performance is the tendency to see what might be called the *underlying structure* of the task and to ignore surface details. Faced with a political speech to write, an expert writer will set aside the fact that the speech must be ten pages long and must cover certain current issues. These are less important than to communicate the message, the perspective, and the leadership qualities that the candidate wants to project to the particular audience. These goals define the underlying structure of the writing task. The novice is more likely to focus on the length and topics to be covered; these will be sufficiently challenging, although ultimately not what writing a speech is principally about.

A final characteristic we will consider is the tendency of an expert to use **heuristics** and intuition to complete tasks rather than formal rules and principles. In school we are taught to do things according to formal rules and guidelines. To write a good essay, we need a central thesis and supporting arguments. To do well on an exam, we should review all the material likely to be on a test and distribute our study time over a reasonable period of days and hours. To perform well in an athletic contest, we must remember the fundamentals of the game and concentrate on doing things simply and cleanly. Rules such as these serve most of us, who are not experts, quite well most of the time. And novices need rules to perform tasks with some degree of proficiency. But experts often throw rules and principles out the window when they are functioning at their highest form. They rely, instead, on their own informal rules and intuition. Have you ever read a political essay by Mike Royko? His form is usually meandering, with a tone of outrage and disbelief, in the form of a story. Have you ever watched a chess match among masters? What is the player thinking while waiting to make a move? No, he isn't computing all possible moves, as is commonly thought. Usually he comes up with one or two likely moves very quickly and intuitively (based on experience and a fantastic memory of similar game situations faced before) and spends the rest of the time making sure these are not going to get him in trouble later (in other words, backtracking).

Expertise and Learning and Instruction

Experts are made, not born. It takes a long time and a lot of practice to reach high levels of expertise in most fields of human endeavor. Herbert Simon has estimated that world-class athletes, for example, are the product of ten or more years of continuous training for the equivalent of about eight hours a day. Experts in academic and creative walks of life may likely require much more time than this.

And there are no shortcuts. One simply cannot emulate the characteristics of experts (e.g., spending more time planning, looking for underlying structure, and functioning intuitively) and expect to mimic their levels of performance. If an area of human endeavor holds some appeal to a child, the best advice to the child is to learn patiently, acquire more knowledge and experience, and practice the skills of the discipline.

Concept	Processes/Related Ideas	Characteristics/Description
Higher-order processes	Cognitive monitoring	Cognitive monitoring is the process of taking stock of what one is doing currently, what will be done next, and how effectively the mental activity is unfolding. The source of much cognitive monitoring in young children is other people. With development through the elementary school years, greater independence is achieved. One example of cognitive monitoring is detecting errors in messages.
	Problem solving	The components of problem solving include: problem finding and goal setting, planning the approach to the problem, monitoring the progress of the problem, and checking solutions.
Knowledge and expertise	Knowledge	Information processing at both low and high levels depends on what the child already knows. Kinds of knowledge include elementary concepts, semantic networks, schemata, and scripts.
	Expertise	Expertise is a highly developed knowledge base coupled with a considerable amount of experience in some domain, which permits individuals to perform at very effective levels. Experts are the very best at what they do. They differ from novices in several ways: they plan more, their performances are often automatic and effortless, they search for underlying structure in cognitive tasks, and they use heuristics and intuition.

Experts must be sought out as teachers, because they have insight into what was required to reach high levels of accomplishment. Although instruction in school is a good starting point to build toward an expert level in some domain, school is limited. Usually, expert levels are achieved at some later point in a person's life. If we take Simon's estimate to heart, we see, for example, that in twelve years of public school there is simply not sufficient time for most children to focus on a single area of endeavor for the number of hours necessary to reach a true expert level. The exceptions to this, of course, are some areas of athletics (e.g., swimming and gymnastics) where learning and practice begin very early, where relative "youth" is a necessity for speed, strength, and agility, and where students manage to cram in three to five hours per day of practice.

We have discussed a number of ideas about higher-order processes and about knowledge and expertise. A summary of these ideas is presented in Concept Table 8.2.

Answer to Inoperable Tumor Problem

The solution is to isolate the tumor tissue and focus several rays (e.g., a laser beam) on it through an optical arrangement that guarantees the rays are intensely focused only on one spot. The rays must be too diffuse to harm the surrounding tissue.

Summary

I. The Nature of Information Processing

The information-processing approach attempts to be very detailed about the mental processes underlying learning and thinking in specific situations and, where possible, to model the specific steps needed to complete a task using computer programs and mathematical estimates of mental activities. The development of children's information-processing skills emphasizes that children's processing speed, processing capacity and automaticity increase with age.

II. Attention

Attention is the focusing of perception to produce increased awareness of a stimulus. Children's attention increases dramatically in the preschool years and becomes even more efficient in the elementary school years. During the elementary school years, scanning of visual patterns, attention to relevant dimensions, selective attention, and divided attention improve.

III. Memory

Memory is the retention of information over time. Two important dimensions are short-term memory—information held for about fifteen to thirty seconds—and long-term memory—information held indefinitely. Short-term memory has a limited capacity. Several control processes or strategies facilitate long-term memory, among them rehearsal, organization, semantic elaboration, and imagery. There is evidence that short-term memory improves most in the preschool years, and long-term memory improves most in the elementary school years.

IV. Higher-Order Processes

Cognitive monitoring involves taking stock of what one is currently doing, what will be done next, and how effectively the mental activity is unfolding. The source of much cognitive monitoring in young children is other people. With development through the elementary school years, greater independence is achieved. One example of cognitive monitoring is detecting errors in messages. The components of problem solving include: problem finding and goal setting, planning the approach to the problem, monitoring the progress of the problem, and checking solutions.

V. Knowledge and Expertise

Information processing at both low and high levels depends on what the child already knows. Kinds of knowledge include elementary concepts, semantic networks, schemata, and scripts. Expertise is a highly developed knowledge base coupled with a considerable amount of experience in some domain, which permits individuals to perform at very effective levels. Experts are the very best at what they do. They differ from novices in several ways: they plan more, their performances are often automatic and effortless, they search for underlying structure in cognitive tasks, and they use heuristics and intuition.

Key Terms

information-processing approach   193
artificial intelligence   195
attention   198
selective attention   198
divided attention   199
memory   199
short-term memory   200
long-term memory   200
control processes   201
rehearsal   201
organization   201
semantic elaboration   202
imagery   202
keyword method   202
cognitive monitoring   203
reciprocal teaching   204
problem solving   206
concept   210
semantic networks   210
schema (schemata)   210
expert   214
heuristics   216

Suggested Readings

Baron, J. B., & Sternberg, R. J. (Eds.). (1987). *Teaching thinking skills: Theory and practice.* New York: W. H. Freeman.
This book presents essays by ten eminent psychologists, educators, and philosophers that describe ways to improve critical thinking skills. It offers various strategies and exercises for children and adults.

Dreyfus, H. L., & Dreyfus, S. E. (1986). *Mind over machine.*
New York: Free Press.
A thought-provoking analysis of the differences between
human thinking and computer thought. The authors
criticize the claim of some computer scientists that
computers have already achieved high levels of cognitive
performance rivaling that of humans and develop an
interesting stage model of human expertise.

Hirsch, E. D., (1987). *Cultural literacy: What every
American needs to know.* Boston: Houghton Mifflin.
An easy-to-read and engaging critique of school practices.
Hirsch reviews schema theory from a broad perspective,
considers the nature of national culture, and concludes
with arguments supporting the adoption of a national test
for literacy.

Kail, R. (1984). *The development of memory in children.* San
Francisco: W. H. Freeman.
A readable overview of developmental changes in
children's memory. Includes information about many of
the aspects of memory considered in this chapter
including short-term and long-term memory, rehearsal,
and organization.

Papert, S. (1980). *Mindstorms.* New York: Basic Books.
This author invented a computer language for children,
LOGO, which is taught extensively and has some unique
consequences for children's thinking processes. The
author offers an easy-to-understand introduction to
LOGO as he explains his philosophy of educating the
mind.

Siegler, R. S. (1986). *Children's thinking.* Englewood Cliffs,
NJ: Prentice-Hall.
An authoritative and relatively complete treatment of
cognitive development. It features a comparison of
Piaget's approach with information processing and
descriptions of the major theories of information-
processing and the specific task analysis and computer
modeling techniques used in information processing.

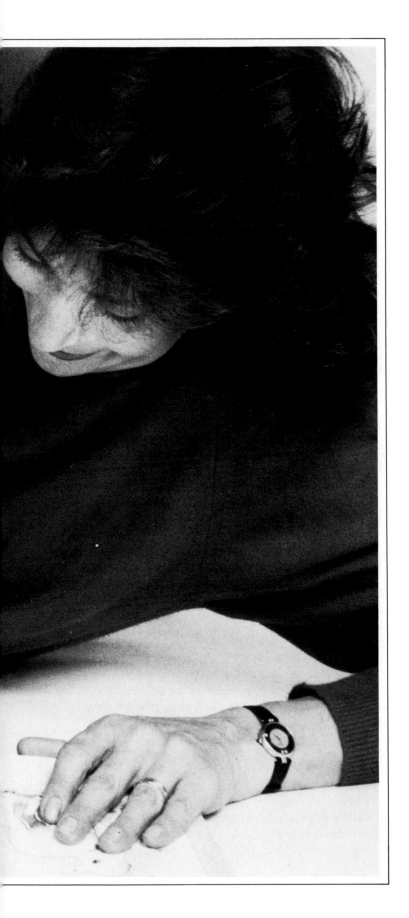

Language Development

Children pick up words as pigeons pick up peas.

John Ray
English Proverbs, 1670

You are an intelligent young girl who has been captured by a group of some rather bizarre creatures, members of a highly advanced species who interact with all sorts of complex devices, drape unusual garments all over themselves, frequently emit long sequences of sound, and in general behave in complex and mysterious ways. You have no idea where these creatures came from or what they want with you. On the bright side, they appear to be friendly, even affectionate, and give you plenty of good food, including lots of chocolate, which you love. But they won't let you go. And they insist on you playing some sort of weird game they have invented.

They started the game one day at your snack time. You expected some fruit, and one of your captors came with a banana. However, instead of giving the banana to you, he placed it where you could see it but could not get to it. Then he gave you a small plastic object, a pink square to be exact, and a small board. Not knowing what else to do, you took the pink square and placed it on the board. It stuck in place. Your captor then made some very strange excited sounds and gave you the banana.

Your captors repeated this game again and again. After a time they started using fruits other than just bananas. It soon became obvious that for you to get different fruits, you had to put different pieces of plastic on the board. For example, to get an apple, you had to put a blue triangle on the board. If you put the pink square on the board, your captors made some of their very strange sounds, but the apple stayed where it was—out of reach.

Different chips for different foods was only the start of the complexity that followed. Before long, getting some food depended not only on you sticking the corresponding chip on the board; in addition, you had to put a special chip above it. This chip was a funny-looking six-sided thing. And the order was important. If you put the six-sided shape below the chip instead of above it, you did not get your food.

After awhile the captors taught you a plastic "name" for yourself, as well as a name for each of them and for each of your fellow prisoners (you were not the only prisoner they had). If you wanted one of your captors to give you an apple, you had to put his plastic name at the top of the board, put the six-sided chip below it, put the blue-triangle chip (for apple) below that, and finally, put your own plastic name at the bottom. So much work for an apple?

Later, your captors taught you ways of asking and answering questions and of making strange deals. For example, one of your captors wrote to you on the board, "If you pick up the apple, you will get some chocolate; if you pick up the banana, you will get no chocolate." You picked up the apple, and sure enough, they gave you chocolate!

What could this game be about? Who are these creatures and why are they interested in you? These creatures are psychologists who are studying language. You are one of their nonhuman subjects, a chimpanzee named Sarah. They are interested in you because they want to find out if nonhuman species can learn simple languages.

In this chapter we tell the elegant story of children's language development. Among the questions we explore are, What is language? What are language's rule systems? What is language's biological heritage (including the question of whether chimpanzees can learn language)? What is language's environmental heritage? What is cognition's role in language? What is the course of children's language development? How should reading be taught to children? What issues are involved in bilingualism?

What Is Language?

Every human society has language. There are thousands of human languages, and they differ so dramatically that many individuals despair of ever mastering more than one. Yet all human languages have some things in common—if not, we would not call them all language. What are these characteristics that all human languages share?

Language has been defined by one expert as a sequence of words (Miller, 1981). This definition describes language as having two different characteristics—the presence of words and sequencing. It might seem obvious that all languages have *words,* but think for a minute about what words are. We produce and perceive words every day—yet words have an almost magical property: They stand for or symbolize things other than themselves. We use our words to refer to things, things like objects, people, actions, events, and even abstract ideas. What a word refers to is arbitrary in the sense that it is based on convention—a word refers to something commonly agreed upon by a group of language users. To understand this point, consider the fact that different languages have different names for the same thing. What we call a house is also called *casa* (in Spanish) and *maison* (in French). Since different languages have different words, we are forced to conclude that words are linked arbitrarily and by convention to their referents.

Although words are important in language, the mere presence of words is not enough to make a language. Sequencing of the words also is required. Can you imagine a language with only one-word utterances? True, a thirteen-month-old infant may use one-word utterances, but as we will see later in the chapter experts argue that the infant has whole sentences in mind when the single word is uttered. Adults the world over speak in sequences of words called sentences.

Why is sequencing important for language? The answer leads us to a third characteristic of language—**infinite generativity.** Sequencing allows a finite number of individual words to be combined in an infinite number of sentences. Thus, language has a creative aspect. We say things never said before by anyone else.

Yet another characteristic of language is **displacement.** This means that we can use language to communicate information about another place and time, although we also use language to describe what is going on in our immediate environment. Anyone hooked on light fiction can attest to the power of displacement in language. But reading light fiction is just one example of how language gives secondhand experience. Language contributes to the transmission of knowledge from one individual to another and from one generation to the next (Brown, 1986).

Figure 9.1
Language's rule systems.

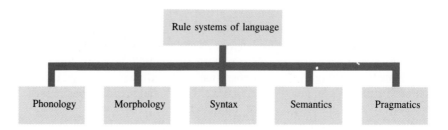

A final aspect of language is that it has different levels of rule systems. Thus, we can now define **language** as a sequence of words that involves infinite generativity, displacement, and different levels of rule systems. The rule systems include phonology, morphology, syntax, semantics, and pragmatics, which we now discuss in turn (figure 9.1).

Language's Rule Systems

When Emerson said, "The world was built in order and the atoms march in tune," he must have had language in mind. The truly elegant system of language is highly ordered and organized. What is this order and organization like?

Phonology

Language is comprised of basic sounds or **phonemes.** In the English language there are approximately thirty-six phonemes. The study of language's sound system is called **phonology;** phonological rules ensure that certain sound sequences occur (e.g., *sp, ar, ba*) and others do not (e.g., *zx, qp*). A good example of a phoneme in the English language is /k/, the sound represented by the letter *k* in the word *ski* and by the letter *c* in the word *cat*. While the /k/ sound is slightly different in these two words, the variation is not distinguished and the /k/ sound is viewed as a single phoneme.

Imagine what language would be like if there were no phonology. Each word in the language would have to be represented by a signal—a sound, for example—that differed from the signals of all other words. The obvious consequence is that the number of words could be no larger than the number of different signals that an individual could efficiently produce and perceive. We do not know precisely what that number is but we do know that it is very small, especially in the case of speech, in contrast to the tens or even hundreds of thousands of words that commonly comprise a language.

What phonology does is to provide a basis for constructing a large and expandable set of words—all that are or ever will be—out of two-to-three dozen signal elements. We do not need five hundred thousand. All we need is two-to-three dozen (Liberman, 1987).

Morphology

Language also is characterized by a string of sounds that give meaning to what we say and hear. The string of sounds is a **morpheme; morphology** refers to the rules for combining morphemes. Every word in the English language is made up of one or more morphemes. Not all morphemes are words, however (e.g., *pre-, -tion,* and *-ing*). Some words consist of a single morpheme (e.g., *help*); other words are made up of more than one morpheme (e.g., *helper,* which has two morphemes, *help +er,* with the morpheme *er* meaning "one

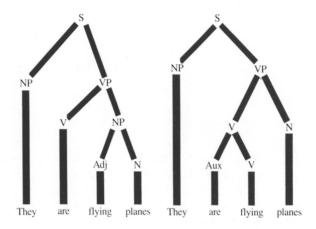

Figure 9.2
Two deep structures for a single ambiguous
sentence ("Adj" stands for adjective and
"Aux" stands for auxiliary verb).

who," in this case, "one who helps"). Just as phonemes ensure that certain sound sequences occur, morphemes ensure that certain strings of sounds occur in particular sequences. For example, we would not reorder helper to *erhelp*. Morphemes have fixed positions in the English language, and these morphological rules ensure that some sequences appear in words (e.g., *combining, popular,* and *intelligent*) and others do not (e.g., *forpot,* and *skiest*).

Syntax

Syntax involves the way words are combined to form acceptable phrases and sentences. Because you and I share the same syntactic understanding of sentence structure, if I say to you, "Bob slugged Tom, and "Bob was slugged by Tom," you know who did the slugging and who was slugged in each case. You also understand that the sentence, "You didn't stay, did you?" is a grammatical sentence but that "You didn't stay, didn't you?" is unacceptable and ambiguous.

A concept closely related to syntax is **grammar**—the formal description of syntactical rules. In elementary school and high school most of us learned rules about sentence structure. Linguists devise rules of grammar that are similar to those you learned in school but are much more complex and powerful. Many contemporary linguists distinguish between the "surface" and "deep" structure of a sentence. **Surface structure** is the actual order of words in a sentence. **Deep structure** is the syntactic relation of the words in a sentence. By applying syntactic rules in different ways, one sentence (the surface structure) can have two very different deep structures. For example, consider this sentence: "Mrs. Smith found drunk on her lawn." Was Mrs. Smith drunk or did she find a drunk on the lawn? Either interpretation fits the sentence, depending on the deep structure applied. Another example of deep-structured ambiguity can be found in the sentence, "They are flying planes." The two deep structures for this sentence are presented in figure 9.2.

"If you don't mind my asking, how much does a sentence diagrammer pull down a year?"

Reprinted by permission of UFS, Inc.

Semantics

Semantics refers to the meaning of words and sentences. Every word has a set of semantic features. Girl and woman, for example, share the same semantic features as the words female and human but differ in regard to age. Words have semantic restrictions on how they can be used in sentences. The sentence, "The bicycle talked the boy into buying a candy bar" is syntactically correct but semantically incorrect. The sentence violates our semantic knowledge— bicycles do not talk.

What kind of pragmatic rules might be involved in this communication?

Pragmatics

A final set of language rules involves **pragmatics**—the ability to engage in appropriate conversation. The domain of pragmatics is broad, covering such circumstances as: (a) taking turns in discussions instead of everyone talking at once; (b) using questions to convey commands ("Why is it so noisy in here?" "What is this, Grand Central Station?"); (c) using words like *the* and *a* in a way that enhances understanding ("I read *a* book last night. *The* plot was boring."); (d) using polite language in appropriate situations (e.g., when talking to one's teacher), and (e) telling stories that are interesting, jokes that are funny, and lies that convince.

Pragmatic rules can be complex and they may differ from one culture to another. If you ever study the Japanese language, you come face to face with countless pragmatic rules about conversing with individuals of various social levels and with various relationships to you. Some of these pragmatic rules concern ways of saying thank you (table 9.1). Indeed, the pragmatics of saying thank you are complex even in our own culture. Preschoolers' use of this term varies with sex, socioeconomic status, and the age of the individual they are addressing. Through pragmatics children learn to convey meaning

Cognitive Development

Table 9.1
Different Ways of saying "Thank You" in Japanese (with Romanized Spelling)

Expression	Context	Expression	Context
Dōmo	Used with a social "inferior" who has served you in some way (e.g., a servant who has brought some tea).	Dōmo arigatō	Used with a social "equal" who has done a small favor for you (e.g., held open a door).
Arigatō	A more formal expression used in similar situations as *Domo* (tourists are advised to use this word after being served in a store or shop).	Arigatō gozaimasu	Used with a social "superior" in a polite or a formal situation (e.g., a "greeter" in a department store might say this as you leave the store with packages).
		Dōmo arigatō gozaimasu	Used with a "superior" in a very formal situation (e.g., your boss has just given you a gift).

with words, phrases, and sentences. Pragmatics helps children to communicate more smoothly with others (Bates, O'Connell, & Shore, 1987; Hay, 1987; Nelson, 1978).

Is this ability to generate rule systems for language, and then to use them to create an almost infinite number of words, learned or is it the product of biology and evolution?

Language's Biological and Environmental Heritage

In 1882, two-year-old Helen Keller was left deaf, blind, and mute by a severe illness. By the time she was seven years old, she feared the world she could not see or hear. Alexander Graham Bell suggested to her parents that they hire a tutor named Anne Sullivan to help Helen overcome her fears (figure 9.3). By using sign language Anne was able to teach Helen a great deal about language. Helen Keller became an honors graduate of Radcliffe College and had this to say, "Whatever the process, the result is wonderful. Gradually from naming an object we advance step by step until we have traversed the vast distance between our first stammered syllable and the sweep of thought in a line of Shakespeare."

What is the process of learning language like? Helen Keller had the benefit of a marvelous teacher, which suggests that experience is important in learning language. But might there have been biological explanations for her language capabilities?

The Biological Story

Newborn birds come into the world ready to sing the song of their species. They listen to their parents sing the song a few times and then they have learned it for the rest of their lives. Noam Chomsky (1957) believes that the language of humans works in much the same way. He says we are biologically predisposed to learn language at a certain time and in a certain way. Chomsky's ideas prompted David McNeil (1970) to propose that the child comes into the world with a **language acquisition device (LAD)** that is wired to detect certain language categories—phonology, syntax, and semantics, for example. McNeil also believes that we are able to detect deep and surface structures in language.

The contemporary view of language continues to stress that biology plays a very strong role in language (Bates, O'Connell, & Shore, 1987; Miller, 1981; Pinker, 1984). For example, George Miller (1981) argues that biology is far

Figure 9.3
Anne Sullivan was able to use sign language to teach Helen Keller about language.

more important than environment in determining the nature of language. In his view, the fact that evolution shaped humans into linguistic creatures is undeniable.

Both physical and cultural evolution help to explain the development of language skills. The brain, nervous system, and vocal system changed over hundreds of thousands of years. Prior to *Homo sapiens,* the physical equipment to produce language was not present. Then social evolution occurred as humans, with their newly evolved language capacity, had to generate a way of communicating. *Homo sapiens* went beyond the groans and shrieks of their predecessors with the development of abstract speech. Estimates vary as to how long ago humans acquired language—from about 20,000 to 70,000 years ago. That means language is a recent acquisition in evolutionary time. The role of language in human evolution stimulated psychologists to think about the possibility that animals have language.

In 1914 in what is now Addo Park in South Africa a hunter was asked to exterminate a herd of 140 elephants. He killed all but 20, and those elephants were so clever at hiding that he abandoned the effort to find them. In 1930 the area became a wild game preserve and the elephants have been protected since that time. Elephants four generations removed from the time the hunter killed most of the herd remain curiously nocturnal and shy. Somehow the elephants must have communicated from one generation to the next the hazards they might encounter, possibly through trumpeting calls that tell other elephants to avoid humans (Gould, 1983).

No one doubts that animals of many different species have wondrous and ingenious communication systems and that their communication is adaptive in signaling danger, food, and sex. Indeed, some of these communication systems are complex. For example, the female of one firefly species has learned to imitate the flashing signal of another species to lure the aliens into her territory. Then she eats them. But are such communications language in the human sense?

Let's think about some of the important characteristics of human language that make it unique. There are at least four such characteristics. First, human language is productive—remember our comments about the infinite generativity of language. Second, human language is structured at different levels—remember that language begins with phonemes and ends with the more complex levels of syntax, semantics, and pragmatics. Third, the sounds of human language are arbitrary—languages around the world use words that sound different for the same thing. Fourth, all human languages make some use of sequencing to reveal variations in meaning—remember that "Bob slugged Tom" means something very different than "Bob was slugged by Tom."

The issue in the animal language controversy is whether these four characteristics of human language are present in animal communication. To learn more about this intriguing issue turn to Perspective on Child Development 9.1, where you will read how scientists teach apes and chimpanzees language. We conclude that animals communicate with each other and that chimpanzees can be trained to use sign language. Whether animals such as chimpanzees possess all of the characteristics of human language (such as the rule systems of phonology, morphology, syntax, semantics, and pragmatics) is still a topic of heated debate.

Another aspect of biology's role in language involves the accumulating evidence that language processing is controlled in the brain's left hemisphere (Sperry, 1974; Gazzaniga, 1986.) Indeed, studies of language in brain-

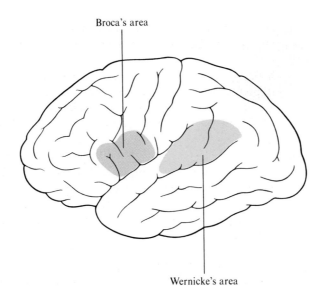

Broca's area

Wernicke's area

Figure 9.4
Speech and language functions are localized in Broca's and Wernicke's areas in the left hemisphere of the human brain.
Adapted with permission from *Language and Speech* by George A. Miller. Copyright © 1981 W. H. Freeman and Company.

damaged individuals pinpoint two areas of the left hemisphere that are especially critical. One of these areas—called **Broca's area**—is important for speech production; the other area—called **Wernicke's area**— is important in speech comprehension (figure 9.4). Damage to these areas of the brain (as a result of a stroke, for example) can seriously interfere with an individual's ability either to produce or to understand speech. Lateralization of language in the human brain is detectable at several months after birth, perhaps even earlier (Entus, 1975). These developmental findings, together with discoveries of Broca's and Wernicke's areas, suggest some inborn capacity to construct language in distinct parts of the brain (Miller, 1981).

In addition to considering the role of evolution, continuities in language between humans and animals, and the left hemisphere's powerful role in language, another biological aspect of language involves the issue of whether there is a critical period for learning language. If you have listened to Henry Kissinger, former secretary of state, speak you have some evidence for the belief that there exists a critical period for learning language. If an individual over twelve years of age emigrates to a new country and then starts to learn its language, the individual probably will speak the language with a foreign accent the rest of his life. Such was the case with Kissinger. But if an individual emigrates as a young child, the accent goes away as the new language is learned (Asher & Garcia, 1969; Oyama, 1973). Similarly, speaking like a native New Yorker is less related to how long you have lived in the city than to the age at which you moved there. Speaking with a New York "dialect" is more likely if you moved there before the age of twelve. Apparently, puberty marks the close of a critical period for acquiring the phonological rules of different languages and dialects.

Eric Lenneberg (1962) speculated that lateralizaion of language in the brain also is subject to a similar critical period. He says that up until about twelve years of age, a child who has suffered damage to the brain's left hemisphere can shift language to the brain's right hemisphere; after this period, the shift is impossible. The idea of a critical period for shifting lateralization is controversial and research on the issue is inconclusive (de Villiers & de Villiers, 1978).

Ape Talk—from Gua to Nim Chimpsky

It is the early 1930s. A seven-month-old chimpanzee named Gua has been adopted by humans (Kellogg & Kellogg, 1933). Gua's adopters want to rear her alongside their ten-month-old son, Donald. Gua was treated much the way we rear human infants today—her adopters dressed her, talked with her, and played with her. Nine months after she was adopted, the project was discontinued because the parents feared that Gua was slowing down Donald's progress.

About twenty years later, another chimpanzee was adopted by humans (Hayes & Hayes, 1951). Viki, as the chimp was called, was only a few days old at the time. The goal was straightforward: teach Viki to speak. Eventually she was taught to say "Mama," but only with painstaking effort. Day after day, week after week, the parents sat with Viki and shaped her mouth to make the desired sounds. She ultimately learned three other words—Papa, cup, and up—but she never learned the meanings of these words and her speech was not clear.

Approximately twenty years later, another chimpanzee named Washoe was adopted when she was about ten months old (Gardner & Gardner, 1971). Recognizing that the earlier experiments with chimps had not demonstrated that apes have language, the trainers tried to teach Washoe the American sign language, which is the sign language of the deaf. Daily routine events, such as meals and washing, household chores, play with toys, and car rides to interesting places provided many opportunities for the use of sign language. In two years Washoe learned 38 different signs and by the age of five she had a vocabulary of 160 signs. Washoe learned how to put signs together in novel ways, such as "you drink" and "you me tickle" (figure 9.A).

Yet another way to teach language to chimpanzees exists. The Premacks (Premack & Premack, 1972) constructed a set of plastic shapes that symbolized different objects and were able to teach the meanings of the shapes

Figure 9.A
Washoe is learning to ask for objects by means of sign language.

to a six-year-old chimpanzee, Sarah. Sarah was able to respond correctly using such abstract symbols as "same as" or "different from." For example, she could tell you that "banana is yellow" is the same as "yellow color of banana." Sarah eventually was able to "name" objects, respond "yes," "no," "same as," and "different from" and tell you about certain events by using symbols (such as putting a banana on a tray). Did Sarah learn a generative language capable of productivity? Did the signs Washoe learned have an underlying system of language rules?

Herbert Terrace (1979) doubts that these apes have been taught language. Terrace was part of a research project designed to teach language to an ape by the name of Nim Chimpsky (named after famous linguist Noam Chomsky) (figure 9.B). Initially, Terrace was optimistic about Nim's ability to use language as humans use it, but after further evaluation he concluded that Nim really did not have language in the sense that humans do. Terrace says that apes do not spontaneously expand on a train-er's statements like humans do; instead, the apes basically just imitate their trainer. Terrace also believes that apes do not understand what they are saying when they speak; rather they are responding to cues from the trainer that they are not aware of.

The Gardners take exception to Terrace's conclusions (Gardner & Gardner, 1986). They point out that chimpanzees use inflections in sign language to refer to various actions, people, and places. They also cite recent evidence that the infant chimp Loulis learned over 50 signs from his adopted mother Washoe and other chimpanzees who used sign language.

The ape language controversy goes on. It does seem that chimpanzees can learn to use signs to communicate meanings, which has been the boundary for language. Whether the language of chimpanzees possesses all of the characteristics of human language such as phonology, morphology, syntax, semantics, and pragmatics is still being argued (Maratsos, 1983; Rumbaugh, 1988).

Figure 9.B
Nim Chimpsky learning sign language.

Modern-Day Wild Child

Genie was found in 1970 in California (figure 9.C). At the time she was thirteen years old and had been reared by a partially blind mother and a violent father. She was discovered because her mother applied for assistance at a public welfare office. At the time Genie could not speak and could not stand erect. She had lived in almost total isolation during her childhood years. Naked and restrained by a harness that her father had fashioned, she was left to sit on her potty seat day after day. She could only move her hands and feet and had virtually nothing to do every day of her life. At night, she was placed in a kind of straight jacket and caged in a crib with wire mesh sides and an overhead cover She was fed, although sparingly. When she made a noise, her father beat her. He never spoke to her with words but growled and made barking sounds toward her.

Genie underwent extensive rehabilitiation and training over a number of years (Curtiss, 1977). During her therapy, Genie learned to walk with a jerky motion and was toilet trained. She learned to recognize many words and to speak. At first she spoke in one-word utterances and eventually began to string together two-word utterances. She began to create some two-word sequences on her own—such as "big teeth," "little marble," and "two hand." Later she was able to put together three words—"small two cup," for example.

But unlike normal children, Genie never learned how to ask questions and she never understood grammar. Even four years after she began to put words together, her speech sounded like a garbled telegram. Genie never understood the differences between pronouns and between passive and active verbs. She continues as an adult to speak in short mangled sentences, such as "father hit leg," "big wood," and "Genie hurt."

Figure 9.C
Artist's drawing of the modern-day wild child, Genie, after she was found.

The experiences of a modern-day wild child named Genie raises further interest in the idea of whether a critical time period for acquiring language exists. To learn more about Genie, turn to Perspective on Child Development 9.2. Such findings confirm the belief that language must be triggered to be learned and that the optimal time for that triggering is during the early years of childhood.

Clearly, biology's role in language is powerful. But, even the most inherited aspects of human development require an environment for their expression.

The Environmental Story

Behaviorists view language as just another behavior, like sitting, walking, or running. They argue that language represents chains of responses (Skinner, 1957) or imitation (Bandura, 1977). But many of the sentences we produce are novel in the sense that we have not heard them or spoken them before. For example, a child hears the sentence, "The plate fell on the floor," and then says, "My mirror fell on the blanket," after she drops the mirror on the blanket. The behavioral mechanisms of reinforcement and imitation cannot completely explain this.

While spending long hours observing parents and their young children, Roger Brown (1973) searched for evidence that parents reinforce their children for speaking grammatically. He found that parents did sometimes smile and praise their children for sentences they liked, but that they also reinforced sentences that were ungrammatical. Brown concluded that no evidence exists to document that reinforcement is responsible for language's rule systems.

Another criticism of the behavioral view is that it fails to explain the extensive orderliness of language. The behavioral view predicts that vast individual differences should appear in children's speech development because of each child's unique learning history. But as we have seen, a compelling fact about language is its structure and ever-present rule systems. All infants coo before they babble. All toddlers produce one-word utterances before two-word utterances and all state sentences in the active form before they state them in the passive form.

However, we do not learn language in a social vacuum. Most children are bathed in language from a very early age. We need this early exposure to language to acquire competent language skills. Genie's language was rudimentary even after a number of years of extensive training.

What are some of the ways the environment contributes to language development? Imitation is one important candidate. A child who is slow in developing her language ability can be helped if parents use carefully selected lists of words and grammatical constructions in their speech to the child (Stine & Bohannon, 1984; Whitehurst, 1985; Whitehurst & Valdez-Ménchaca, 1988). Evidence also suggests that parents provide more corrective feedback for children's ungrammatical utterances than Roger Brown originally thought (Bohannon & Stanowicz, 1988; Penner, 1987). Nonetheless, a number of experts on language believe that imitation and reinforcement facilitate language but are not absolutely necessary for its acquisition (de Villiers & de Villiers, 1978).

One intriguing role of the environment in the young child's acquisition of language involves **motherese,** or the **baby-talk register,** a characteristic way of talking to young language learners. (A *register* is a way of speaking to people (or pets) in a particular category, such as babies or foreigners). Motherese is somewhat of a misnomer because mothers, fathers, and people in general talk to babies this way. If you pay attention to your behavior when you talk to a baby, you will notice some interesting things. Your sentences will be short, you will use exaggerated intonation contours (speaking with great ups and downs in pitch), you will pause for long periods between sentences, and you will place great stress on important words. The baby-talk register is virtually universal. It was documented as early as the first century B.C. and is present in diverse languages (Brown, 1986; Grieser & Kuhl, 1988). When parents are asked why they use baby talk, they point out that it is designed to teach their baby to talk. When children indicate that they do not understand what adults are saying, adults often simplify their speech further (Bohannon & Marquis, 1977). Older peers also talk baby talk to infants, but observations of siblings indicate that the affectional features are dropped when sibling rivalry is sensed (Dunn & Kendrick, 1982).

Most infants are bathed in language at an early age. Mothers often talk to their infants in motherese, also called the baby-talk register. The mother's sentences are short, she uses exaggerated intonation contours, she pauses for long periods between sentences, and she places great stress on certain words.

Other than the baby-talk register, are there other strategies adults use to enhance the child's acquisition of language? Four candidates are recasting, echoing, expanding, and labeling. **Recasting** is phrasing the same or a similar meaning of a sentence in a different way, perhaps turning it into a question. For example, if the child says, "The dog was barking," the adult can respond by asking, "When was the dog barking?" The effects of recasting fit with suggestions that "following in order to lead" helps a child to learn language (Schaffer, 1977); that is, letting a child initially indicate an interest and then proceeding to elaborate that interest—commenting, demonstrating, and explaining—may enhance communication and help language acquisition. In contrast, an overly active, directive approach to communicating with the child may be harmful.

Echoing is repeating what the child says to you, especially if it is an incomplete phrase or sentence. **Expanding** is restating what the child has said in a linguistically sophisticated form. **Labeling** is identifying the names of objects. Young children are forever being asked to identify the names of objects. Roger Brown (1986) identified this as the great word game and claimed that much of the early vocabulary acquired by children is motivated by this adult pressure to identify the words associated with objects. As described in Perspective on Child Development 9.3, this great word game often is ritualized.

At this point we have discussed a number of important ideas about what language is, language's rule systems, and the biological and environmental heritage of language. A summary of these ideas is presented in Concept Table 9.1.

The Role of Cognition in Language

Noam Chomsky's idea of the young language learner as richly endowed with prewired equipment is widely accepted today. But there is a question about just what type of equipment the child possesses. Is the equipment specifically linguistic, like McNeil's (1970) language acquisition device? Or is it more cognitive, being derived from humans' generally high level of intelligence (Maratsos, 1983)? The basic claim of the cognitive theorists is that a child's growing intelligence and desire to express meanings, together with language input from parents, "drive" the acquisition of language. Thus, the focus in the cognitive view is on the semantic and pragmatic levels of language rather than the linguist's focus on the syntactic, morphological, and phonological levels.

One type of evidence for the cognitive view is that children's early utterances seem to indicate knowledge of semantic categories, such as agent and action, rather than linguistic categories, such as noun and verb (Maratsos, 1983). To support this view, it has been found that children can tell that semantically deviant sentences are wrong before they can tell that syntactically deviant sentences are wrong (Washburn & Hakes, 1985). This implies that a five-year-old might detect the unacceptability of the sentence, "The bicycle talked to the boy" (semantically deviant), and yet fail to reject the sentences. "The boy ride the bicycle" and "What you are doing today?" (syntactically deviant).

Evidence that cognition is important for language comes from studies of deaf children. On a variety of thinking and problem-solving skills, deaf children perform at the same level as children of the same age who have no hearing problems. Some of the deaf children in these studies do not even have command of written or sign language (Furth, 1973).

Another argument for a cognitive theory of language concerns what we know about how language evolved. Since a spoken language leaves no physical trace, the age of human language is difficult to determine. But according to

Picture Books, First Words, and Labeling

Anat Ninio and Jerome Bruner (1978) took a close look at the subtle interplay between a mother and her infant son as the two performed the great word game in its quintessential setting—reading picture books and playing with objects. The mother and child were part of a longitudinal study that covered the period of eight months to eighteen months in the child's life. The child was firstborn, and his parents were white, English, and middle class. Labeling was part of the filmed play activity captured in the videotape records, made every two to three weeks in the infant's home.

The investigators uncovered some remarkable findings. Chief among these was the ritualized nature of mother-child labeling activity. It seemed as though labeling of pictures was a highly structured activity that obeyed clear rules and had the texture of a dialogue. A number of scholars have described conversations as having fairly tight patterns in ascribing roles, turn taking, imitating, and responding (e.g., Bruner, 1983; Cherry-Wilkinson, Clevenger, & Dolloghan, 1981; Snow, 1977). So did the labeling activity. Each time mother and child interacted over a picture name, for example, they took about the same number of turns, lasting about the same length of time. And the linguistic forms of the mother's utterances in book reading were very limited. She made repeated use of four key types of statements; (1) "Look!" (to get the child's attention); (2) "What's that?"; (3) "It's an X!" (labeling the picture for the child); and (4) "Yes!" (giving the child feedback on his utterance). These types of statements accounted for virtually all of the language the mother directed toward the child while reading books during the entire period of the study, and they obeyed some simple rules of occurrence. For example, the attention getter "Look!" always preceded the query, "What's that?" or the labeling phrase, "It's an X!" Similarly, the query always preceded the labeling phrase.

At the outset of the study, of course, few of the child's verbal responses to the mother's queries were distinguishable words. At best, the child produced consistent babble. By the end of the period, however, words were present. Associated with this change, the mother dropped the question "What's that?" from the ritual since the child now could produce a word for the picture.

Mothers and children often play the great word game involving mother-child labeling activity. In the great word-labeling game, the mother and child take about the same number of turns, lasting about the same length of time.

Summarizing key points of the study, in the author's own words:

The book reading dialogue seems . . . to be a format well suited to the teaching of labeling. It has few elements and strict ordering rules between them. It is flexible in the sense of accepting a great variety of responses by the child. It is highly repetitive. Not only do the fixed elements ["Look," "What's that?" and "It's a (*label*)"] appear over and over again, with minimal changes in the wording, but the variable elements, the labels themselves, appear repeatedly as well. (Ninio & Bruner, 1978, p. 12)

some estimates, language evolved as recently as 10,000 to 100,000 years ago (Swadesh, 1971), quite recent in evolutionary time, perhaps too recent for a large amount of purely linguistic machinery to have evolved in the brain. From an evolutionary perspective, cognition is much older than human language. For example, tool-making activity—a clear sign of high intellectual functioning—is at least two million years old (Miller, 1981).

Considerations such as these favor the view that language is at least partly a product of cognition, not being solely determined by specific linguistic abilities.

Concept Table 9.1
What Is Language?, Language's Rule Systems, and Biological and Environmental Influences

Concept	Processes/Related Ideas	Characteristics/Description
What is language?	Basic nature	Language is a sequence of words that involves infinite generativity, displacement, and different levels of rule systems.
Language's rule systems	Phonology	Phonology governs the sequencing of phonemes (basic sounds that differ in their distinctive features).
	Morphology	Morphology governs the sequencing of morphemes (the smallest units of language that carry meaning).
	Syntax	Syntax governs the ordering of words within sentences or phrases. These rules apply to deep and surface structures.
	Semantics	Semantics places restrictions on how words must be used to make meaningful sentences.
	Pragmatics	Pragmatics facilitates good communication and good social relations among language users.
Language's biological and environmental heritage	The biological story	Chomsky believes that children are biologically prewired to learn language. McNeil says that we have a language acquisition device that includes wiring for surface and deep structures. The fact that evolution shaped humans into linguistic creatures is undeniable. Animals clearly can communicate and chimpanzees can use sign language. Whether animals have all of the properties of human language is debated. The brain's left hemisphere plays a dominant role in language processing. The experiences of Genie and other children suggest that early childhood is an optimal time to learn language. If exposure to language does not come before puberty, life-long deficits in grammar occur.
	The environmental story	In the behavioral view, language is just another behavior. Behaviorists believe language is learned primarily through reinforcement and imitation, although these processes probably play a facilitative rather than a necessary role. Most children are bathed in language early in their development. Among the ways adults teach language to infants are the baby-talk register, recasting, echoing, expanding, and labeling.

How Language Develops

In the thirteenth century, the Holy Roman Emperor Frederick II had a cruel idea. He wanted to know what language children would speak if no one talked to them. He selected several newborns and threatened the adults who cared for them with their lives if they ever talked to the infants. Frederick never found out what language the children spoke because they all died. As we move toward the twenty-first century, we are still curious about infants' development of language, although our experiments and observations are, to say the least, far more humane than the evil Frederick's.

Language Development in Infancy

When does an infant utter her first word? The event usually occurs at about ten to thirteen months of age, though some infants take longer. Many parents view the onset of language development as coincident with this first word, but some significant accomplishments are attained earlier. Before babies say words, they babble, emitting such vocalizations as "goo-goo" and "ga-ga." Babbling starts at about three to six months of age. The start is determined by biological maturation, not reinforcement or the ability to hear. Even deaf babies babble for a time (Lenneberg, Rebelsky, & Nichols, 1965). Babbling exercises the baby's vocal apparatus and facilitates the development of articulation skills that are useful in later speech (Clark & Clark, 1977). But the purpose of a

Reprinted with special permission of NAS, Inc.

baby's earliest communication is to attract attention from parents and others in the environment. Infants engage the attention of others by making or breaking eye contact, by vocalizing sounds, or by performing manual actions such as pointing. All of those behaviors involve pragmatics.

A child's first words include those that name important people (dada), familiar animals (kittie), vehicles (car), toys (ball), food (milk), body parts (eye), clothes (hat), household items (clock), or greeting terms (bye). These were the first words of babies fifty years ago; they are the first words of babies today (Clark, 1983). At times it is hard to tell what these one-word utterances mean. One possibility is that they stand for an entire sentence in the infant's mind. Because of limited cognitive or linguistic skills, possibly only one word comes out instead of the whole sentence. This is called the **holophrase hypothesis,** that is, a single word is used to imply a complete sentence.

For words that a child uses as nouns, the meanings can be overextended or underextended. Eve Clark (1983) has studied early words and described a number of **overextensions.** For instance, when a child learns to say the word "dada" for father, she often applies the term beyond the individual it was intended to represent, using it for other men, strangers, or boys, for example. With time, such overextension decreases and eventually disappears. **Underextension** occurs when a child fails to use a noun to name a relevant event or

In every culture, individuals are bathed in language from a very early age.

object. For instance, the child may learn to use the word "boy" to describe a five-year-old neighbor but not apply the word to a male infant or a nine-year-old male.

By the time children are eighteen to twenty-four months of age, they usually utter two-word statements. During this two-word stage, they quickly grasp the importance of expressing concepts and the role that language plays in communicating with others. To convey meaning with two-word utterances, the child relies heavily on gesture, tone, and context. The wealth of meaning children can communicate with a two-word utterance includes (Slobin, 1972):

Identification: See doggie.
Location: Book there.
Repetition: More milk.
Nonexistence: Allgone thing.
Negation: Not wolf.
Possession: My candy.
Attribution: Big car.
Agent-action: Mama walk.
Action-direct-object: Give papa.
Action-instrument: Cut knife.
Question: Where ball?

One of the striking aspects of this list is that it is used by children all over the world. The examples are taken from utterances in English, German, Russian, Turkish, and Samoan, but the entire list could be derived from a two-year-old's speech in any language.

A child's two-word utterance differs substantially from adult word combinations. Language usage at this time is called **telegraphic speech.** When we send telegrams to individuals we try to be short and precise, excluding any unnecessary words. As indicated in the examples of telegraphic speech from children around the world, articles, auxiliary verbs, and other connectives usually are omitted. Of course, telegraphic speech is not limited to two-word utterances. "Mommy give ice cream," or "Mommy give Tommy ice cream," also are examples of telegraphic speech.

One- and two-word utterances classify children's language development in terms of the number of utterances. Roger Brown (1973) expanded this concept by proposing that *mean length of utterance (MLU)* is a good index of a child's language maturity. Brown identified five stages based on an estimation of the number of words per sentence that a child produces in a sample of about 50 to 100 sentences. The mean length of utterance for each stage is:

Stage	MLU
1	1 + →2.0
2	2.5
3	3.0
4	3.5
5	4.0

The first stage begins when the child generates sentences consisting of more than one word, such as examples of two-word utterances we gave. The 1 + designation suggests that the average number of words in each utterance is greater than one but not yet two because some of the child's utterances are still holophrases. This stage continues until the child averages two words per utterance. Subsequent stages are marked by increments of 0.5 in mean length of utterance.

Brown's stages are important for several reasons. First, children who vary in chronological age as much as one-half to three-fourths of a year still have similar speech patterns. Second, children with similar mean lengths of utterance seem to have similar rule systems that characterize their language. In some ways, then, MLU is a better indicator of language development than chronological age. Figure 9.5 shows the individual variation in chronological age that characterizes children's MLU.

Language Development in Childhood

What kinds of changes occur in language development during childhood? Language changes continue to obey certain principles, following the rules of phonology, morphology, syntax, semantics, and pragmatics.

Regarding phonology, some preschool children have difficulty speaking in consonant clusters (e.g., "*str*" as in "*string*"). Pronouncing some of the more difficult phonemes is still problematic—*r,* for example—and can continue to be a problem in the elementary school years. Also, some of the phonological rules for pronouncing word endings (in the past tense, for example) are not mastered until children are six to eight years of age.

Regarding morphology, as children move beyond two-word utterances, there is clear evidence that they know morphological rules. Children begin using the plural and possessive forms of nouns (e.g., *dogs* and *dog's*), putting appropriate endings on verbs (e.g., *s* when the subject is third-person singular, *ed* for the past tense, and *ing* for the present progressive tense), using prepositions (*in* and *on*), articles (e.g., *a* and *the*), and various forms of the verb *to be* (e.g., "I was going to the store"). Some of the best evidence for morphological rules appears in the form of *overgeneralizations* of these rules. Have you ever heard a preschool child say "foots" instead of "feet," or "goed" instead of "went?" If you do not remember having heard such things, talk to some parents who have young children—you will hear some interesting errors in the use of morphological rule endings.

In a classic experiment, Jean Berko (1958) presented preschool and first-grade children with cards such as the one shown in figure 9.6. Children were asked to look at the card while the experimenter read the words on the card aloud. Then the children were asked to supply the missing word. This might sound easy, but Berko was interested not just in the children's ability to recall the right word but their ability to say it "correctly" (with the ending that was dictated by morphological rules). "Wugs" would be the correct response for the card in figure 9.6. Although the children were not perfectly accurate, they were much better than chance. Moreover, they demonstrated their knowledge of morphological rules not only with the plural forms of nouns ("There are two wugs") but also with possessive forms of nouns and with the third-person singular and past-tense forms of verbs. What makes the study by Berko impressive is that most of the "words" were fictional; they were created especially for the experiment. Thus, the children could not base their responses on remembering past instances of hearing the words. It seems, instead, that they were forced to rely on *rules.* Their performance suggested that they did so successfully.

Similar evidence that children learn and actively apply rules can be found at the level of syntax. After advancing beyond two-word utterances, the child speaks word sequences that show a growing mastery of complex rules for how words should be ordered. Consider the case of *wh-* questions—for example,"Where is Daddy going?" and "What is that boy doing?" To ask these

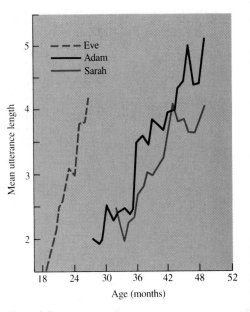

Figure 9.5
The average length of utterances generated by three children who ranged in age from one and one-half to just over four years.

Figure 9.6
In Jean Berko's (1958) study, young children were presented cards such as this one with a "wug" on it. Then the children were asked to supply the missing word; in supplying the missing word, they had to say it correctly too. "Wugs" is the correct response here.

questions properly, the child has to know two important differences between *wh-* questions and simple affirmative statements (e.g., "Daddy is going to work" and "That boy is waiting on the school bus"). First, a *wh-* word must be added at the beginning of the sentence. Second, the auxiliary verb must be "inverted," that is, exchanged with the subject of the sentence. Young children learn quite early where to put the *wh-* word, but they take much longer to learn the auxiliary-inversion rule. Thus, it is common to hear preschool children asking such questions as "Where daddy is going?" and "What that boy is doing?"

As children move into the elementary school years, they become skilled at using syntactical rules to construct lengthy and complex sentences. Sentences such as "The man who fixed the house went home" and "I don't want you to use my bike" are impressive demonstrations of how the child can use syntax to combine ideas into a single sentence. Just how a young child achieves the mastery of such complex rules—while at the same time she may be struggling with relatively simple arithmetic rules—is a mystery we have yet to solve.

Regarding semantics, as children move beyond the two-word utterance stage, their knowledge of meanings also rapidly advances. The speaking vocabulary of a six-year-old child ranges from 8,000 to 14,000 words (Carey, 1977). Assuming that word learning began when the child was twelve months old, this translates into a rate for new word meanings of five to eight words a day between the ages of one and six. After five years of word learning, the six-year-old child does not slow down. According to some estimates, the average child of this age is moving along at the awe-inspiring rate of twenty-two words a day (Miller, 1981)! How would you fare if you were given the task of learning twenty-two new words every day? It is truly miraculous how quickly children learn language (Winner & Gardner, 1988).

Although there are many differences between a two-year-old's language and a six-year-old's language, none is more important than those pertaining to pragmatics, that is, rules of conversation. A six-year-old is simply a much better conversationalist than a two-year-old. What are some of the improvements in pragmatics that are made in the preschool years? At about three years of age, children improve in their ability to talk about things that are not physically present—that is, they improve their command of the characteristic of language known as displacement. One way displacement is revealed is in games of pretend. Although a two-year-old might know the word *table,* he is unlikely to use this word to refer to an imaginary table that he pretends is standing in front of him. But a child over three probably has this ability, even if he does not always use it—there are large individual differences in preschoolers' talk about imaginary people and things.

Somewhat later in the preschool years—at about four years of age—children develop a remarkable sensitivity to the needs of others in conversation (Gleason, 1988). One way in which they show such sensitivity is their use of the articles *the* and *an* (or *a*). When adults tell a story or describe an event, they generally use *an* (or *a*) when they first refer to an animal or an object and then use *the* when referring to it later (e.g., "Two boys were walking through the jungle when *a* fierce lion appeared. *The* lion lunged at one boy while the other ran for cover."). Even three-year-olds follow part of this rule (they consistently use the word *the* when referring to previously mentioned things). However, using the word *a* when something is initially mentioned develops more slowly—although five-year-old children follow this rule on some occasions, they fail to follow it on others.

Another pragmatic ability that appears around four to five years of age involves speech style. As adults we have the ability to change our speech style in accordance with social situations and persons with whom we are speaking. An obvious example is that adults speak in a simpler way to a two-year-old child than to an older child or to an adult. Interestingly, even four-year-old children speak differently to a two-year-old than a same-aged peer (they "talk down" to the two-year-old using shorter utterance lengths). They also speak differently to an adult than to a same-aged peer (using more polite and formal language with the adult (Shatz & Gelman, 1973).

Reading and Bilingualism

As children develop, reading becomes an important aspect of their language competence. Debate still flourishes about the best way to teach reading to children. And as increasing numbers of children in our nation's schools come from homes in which English is not the main language, issues related to bilingualism must be addressed.

Reading

In the history of learning-to-read techniques, three approaches dominate: (1) the **ABC method,** which emphasizes memorization of the names of the letters of the alphabet; (2) the **whole-word method,** which focuses on learning direct associations between whole words and their meanings; and (3) the **phonics method,** which stresses the sounds that letters make when in words—such sounds can differ from the names of these letters (e.g., the sound of the name of the letter *C* is not to be found in *cat*). The ABC method is in ill repute today. Because of the imperfect relation between the names of letters and their sounds in words, the technique is seen as ineffective if not harmful in teaching children to read. Despite its poor reputation, the ABC method was that by which many children (including your authors, and probably your professor in this class) in past generations successfully learned to read.

Most disputes in recent times center on the merits of the whole-word and phonics methods. Although there has been some research comparing these two techniques, the findings have not been conclusive (Crowder, 1982). However, there is evidence that drilling the sounds made by letters in words (part of some phonics methods) improves reading ability (Liberman, 1987; Williams, 1979). In any case, many current techniques of reading instruction incorporate both whole-word and phonics components.

Bilingualism

Octavio's Mexican parents moved to the United States one year before Octavio was born. They do not speak English fluently and have always spoken to Octavio in Spanish. At six years of age, Octavio has just entered the first grade at an elementary school in San Antonio, Texas, and does not speak English. What is the best way to teach Octavio? How much easier would elementary school be for Octavio if his parents had been able to speak to him in Spanish and English when he was an infant?

According to the 1980 census, well over six million children in the United States come from homes where the primary language is not English. Often, like Octavio, they live in a community where this same non-English language is the major means of communication. These children face a more difficult task than most of us—they must master the native tongue of their family to

Well over six million children in the United States come from homes where the primary language is not English. A tripling of their numbers is expected in the twenty-first century. How should language be taught to them when they enter elementary school?

be effective at home and in their own community, and they must also master English to make their way in and contribute to the larger society. The number of bilingual children is expanding at such a rapid rate in our country (some experts, for example, predict a tripling in their numbers by early in the twenty-first century) that they constitute an important subgroup of language learners to be dealt with by society. Although the education of such children in the public schools has a long history, only recently has a national policy evolved to guarantee a quality language experience for them.

Great debates have raged concerning how best to conduct this bilingual education. Does one teach English as a foreign language, adopting the child's native tongue as the language of the classroom, or does one treat English as a second, equal language and strive for balance in usage of English and the native tongue? The answer to this has important consequences for the way in which school curricula and texts are written in cities with large concentrations of Spanish-speaking children (e.g., New York, Miami, San Antonio, and Los Angeles).

Practical educational decisions about bilingual education ideally should rest on a sound understanding of how second-language learning comes about. Research in this area is only beginning, but already we have learned enough to question many previously held beliefs. Barry McLaughlin (1978) considers several popular notions about second-language learning, including the three following:

1. The young child acquires a language more quickly and easily than an adult because the child is biologically programmed to acquire languages, whereas the adult is not.
2. The younger the child, the more skilled in acquiring a second language.
3. Second-language acquisition is a qualitatively different process than first-language acquisition.

Although these ideas sound plausible, it may surprise you to learn that the bulk of research evidence weighs against all three! It certainly is true that young children are impressive at the task of language learning. But so are adults who are highly motivated and are also extensively exposed to a new language. Although college students might feel like morons when trying to learn French, consider the number of hours per day (or week) they actually spend with this language. In contrast, young children learning their first language are almost literally immersed in it, hearing it and trying to use it to communicate every day. Motivation is probably also involved. Although a college student might have difficulty actually opening up that French book, there can be no doubt that young children are simply driven to learn their first language. When studies have controlled these critical variables of exposure time and motivation and have measured language competence by objective criteria, the evidence does not favor superiority of younger children over older children and adults, but rather the reverse. Furthermore, there has been no strong evidence that the basic mechanisms of language learning are different in young children than in older children and adults.

Concept Table 9.2
The Role of Cognition in Language, How Language Develops, and Reading and Bilingualism

Concept	Processes/Related Ideas	Characteristics/Description
The role of cognition in language	Basic nature	Although children have prewired machinery for language, the cognitive view argues that at least some of it is cognitive rather than strictly linguistic.
How language develops	Infancy	Vocalization begins with babbling at about three-to-six months of age. A baby's earliest communication skills are pragmatic. One-word utterances occur at about ten to thirteen months; the holophrase hypothesis has been applied to this. By eighteen to twenty-four months, most infants use two-word utterances. Language at this point is referred to as telegraphic. Brown developed the idea of mean length of utterance (MLU). Five stages of MLU have been identified, providing a valuable indicator of language maturity.
	Childhood	Advances in phonology, morphology, syntax, semantics, and pragmatics continue in childhood.
Reading and bilingualism	Reading	Three main techniques involved in teaching children how to read are the ABC method, the whole-word method, and the phonics method. Most reading instruction today involves some form of either the whole-word or phonics methods, or some combination of the two.
	Bilingualism	An increasing number of children who come from homes in which English is not the primary language are entering our nation's schools. At present, there is no evidence that second-language learning is more successful in younger than in older children, with the exception of phonology prior to puberty.

Of course, the foregoing is not meant to deny that there are benefits to beginning second-language learning early. As McLaughlin (1978) remarks:

> The success of young children in acquiring two languages under such conditions need not be attributed to superior language learning skills. Given the same amount and quality of exposure, an older child (or an adult) would presumably do just as well, most likely better. This, of course, is not to denigrate the young child's achievement or to downgrade the advantages of early introduction to a second language. Older children and adults do not have the amount of time at their disposal for learning a second language that the young child does. There is no reason not to utilize this advantage and to begin language instruction early. The practice of total immersion programs of introducing children to a second language in kindergarten through games, songs, rhymes, and so forth has produced extremely favorable results and is in all likelihood a more pleasant way to acquire a second language for the child than the repetitive drills that often characterize later classroom instruction. (p. 200)

A qualification of McLaughlin's conclusions concerns the phonological level of language. As mentioned earlier, acquiring a new accent after the onset of puberty is extremely difficult. Thus, learning phonemes may indeed be easier for children than for adolescents, perhaps because of a critical period tied to biological maturation.

We have discussed a number of important ideas about the role of cognition in language, children's language development, and reading and bilingualism. A summary of these ideas is presented in Concept Table 9.2.

Summary

I. What Is Language?
Language is a sequence of words that involves infinite generativity, displacement, and different levels of rule systems.

II. Language's Rule Systems
Phonology governs the sequencing of phonemes (basic sounds that differ in their distinctive features). Morphology governs the sequencing of morphemes (the smallest units of language that carry meaning). Syntax governs the ordering of words within sentences or phrases (these rules apply to deep and surface structures). Semantics places restrictions on how words must be used to make meaningful sentences. Pragmatics facilitates good communication and good social relations among language users.

III. Language's Biological Heritage
Chomsky believes that children are biologically prewired to learn language. McNeil says that children have a language acquisition device that includes wiring for surface and deep structures. The fact that evolution shaped humans into linguistic creatures is undeniable. Animals clearly can communicate and chimpanzees can use sign language. Whether animals have all of the properties of human language is debated. The brain's left hemisphere plays a dominant role in language processing. The experiences of Genie and other children suggest that the early years are an optimal time to learn language. If exposure to language does not come before puberty, life-long deficits in grammar occur.

IV. Language's Environmental Heritage
In the behavioral view, language is just another behavior. Behaviorists believe language is learned primarily through reinforcement and imitation, although these processes probably play a facilitative rather than a necessary role. Most children are bathed in language early in their development. Among the ways adults teach language to infants are the baby-talk register, recasting, echoing, expanding, and labeling.

V. The Role of Cognition in Language
Although children have prewired machinery for language, the cognitive view argues that at least some of it is cognitive rather than strictly linguistic.

VI. How Language Develops
Vocalization begins with babbling at about three to six months of age. A baby's earliest communication skills are pragmatic. One-word utterances occur at about ten to thirteen months; the holophrase hypothesis has been applied to this. By eighteen to twenty-four months, most infants use two-word utterances. Language at this point is called telegraphic. Brown developed the idea of mean length of utterance (MLU). Five stages of MLU have been identified, providing a valuable indicator of language maturity. Advances in phonology, morphology, syntax, semantics, and pragmatics take place during childhood.

VII. Reading and Bilingualism
Three main techniques involved in teaching reading to children are the ABC method, the whole-word method, and the phonics method. Most reading instruction today involves some form of either the whole-word method or the phonics method, or some combination of the two. An increasing number of children who come from homes in which English is not the primary language are entering our nation's schools. At present, there is no evidence that second-language learning is more successful in younger than older children, with the exception of phonology prior to puberty.

Key Terms

Suggested Readings

Bruner, J. (1983). *Child talk*. New York: Norton.
A fascinating view of children's language development by one of the leading cognitive theorists.

Crowder, R. G. (1982). *The psychology of reading.* New York: Oxford University Press.
A thorough overview of strategies for teaching children how to read.

Curtiss, S. (1977). *Genie.* New York: Academic Press.
Susan Curtiss tells the remarkable story of Genie, a modern-day wild child and her ordeal of trying to acquire language.

Kessel, F. (Ed.) (1988). *The development of language and language researchers.* Hillsdale, NJ: Erlbaum.
A number of chapters by experts on language development are presented; includes a chapter by Berko-Gleason on language and socialization and Winner and Gardner on creating a world with words.

Maratsos, M. (1983). Some current issues in the study of the acquisition of grammar. In P. H. Mussen (Ed.). *Handbook of child psychology* (4th ed.), vol. 2. New York: John Wiley & Sons.
A thorough, informative review of what we know about language development.

Premack, D. (1986). *Gavagai! The future history of the ape language controversy.* Cambridge, MA: MIT Press.
Premack describes the fascinating ape language controversy and predicts its future directions.

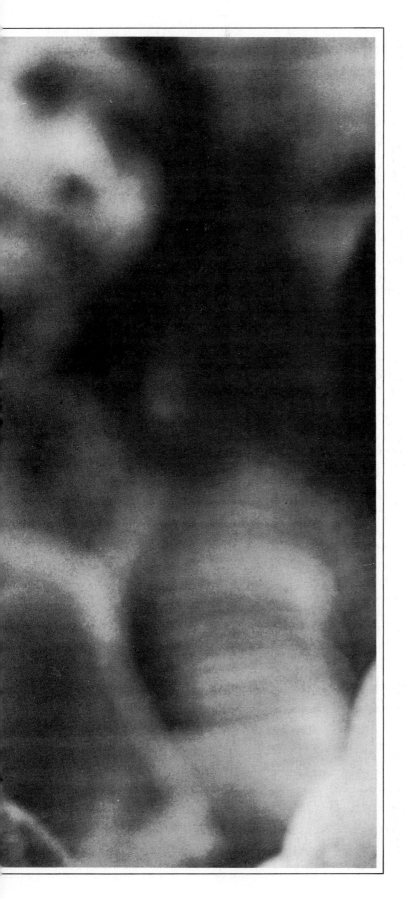

CHAPTER 10

Intelligence

Children are remarkable for their intelligence and ardor, for their curiosity, their intolerance of shams, the clarity of their vision.

Aldous Huxley
Music at Night, 1931

nformation about children's intelligence and intelligence tests frequently makes the news. The following two stories appeared in the *Los Angeles Times:*

IQ testing that leads to the placement of an unusually large number of black children in so-called mentally retarded classes has been ruled unconstitutional by a federal judge. On behalf of five black children, Chief District Court Judge Robert Peckham said the use of standardized IQ tests to place children in educable mentally retarded (EMR) classes violated recently enacted federal laws and the state and federal constitutions. . . . Peckham said the history of IQ testing and special education in California "revealed an unlawful discriminatory intent . . . not necessarily to hurt black children, but it was an intent to assign a grossly disproportionate number of black children to the special, inferior and dead-end EMR classes." (October 18, 1979)
A controversial Escondido sperm bank for superbrains has produced its first baby—a healthy, nine-pound girl born to a woman identified only as a small-town resident in "a sparsely populated state." . . . Founded by inventor Robert K. Graham of Escondido in 1979, the facility contains sperm donated by at least three Nobel Prize winners, plus other prominent researchers. . . .The sperm bank was founded to breed children of higher intelligence. The goal has been denounced by many critics, who say that a child's intelligence is not determined so much by his genes as by his upbringing and environment. (May 25, 1982)

As you might expect, these stories sparked impassioned debate (Kail & Pellegrino, 1985). Some arguments focus on the ethical and moral implications of selective breeding of bright children and selective placement of children in special classes. Other arguments concern the statistical basis of conclusions, such as whether the tests are really biased if the data are analyzed properly. What you hear *less* often but should hear *more* often is a discussion of the construct of intelligence itself (Dwyer, 1987). That is, what is intelligence? How should it be conceptualized?

What Is Intelligence?

Intelligence is a possession most of us value highly, yet it is an abstract concept with few agreed-upon referents. You would agree on referents for such characteristics as children's height, weight, and age, but if asked to agree on referents for something like a child's size, there is less certainty. Size is a more *abstract* notion than height or weight. Also, size is more difficult to measure directly than height or weight. We can only estimate a child's size from a set of empirical measures of height and weight. Measuring a child's intelligence is much the same as measuring a child's size, though *much more* abstract. That is, we believe a child's intelligence exists, but we do not measure a child's intelligence directly. We cannot peel back a child's scalp and observe the child's intellectual processes in action. We can only study these intellectual processes *indirectly,* by evaluating the intelligent acts that a child generates. For the most part, psychologists have relied on intelligence tests to provide an estimate of the child's intellectual processes.

Throughout much of the history of Western civilization, intelligence has been described in terms of knowledge and reasoning (Kail & Pellegrino, 1985). Today, most of us view intelligence in a similar light. In one investigation, individuals were asked to judge which of 250 behaviors were typical of an intelligent individual (Sternberg & others, 1981). Both experts (psychologists researching intelligence) and lay individuals (people of various backgrounds and education) judged the behaviors similarly. The two groups agreed that intelligence can be divided into two main categories. The first is *verbal ability,* reflected in such behaviors as "displays a good vocabulary," "reads with high comprehension," "is knowledgeable about a particular field of knowledge," and "displays curiosity." The second is *problem-solving skills,* reflected in such behaviors as "reasons logically and well," "is able to apply knowledge to problems at hand," and "makes good decisions."

Thus, the primary components of intelligence are very close to the mental processes we discussed in the chapters on language, cognitive development, and information processing. The differences in how we discussed language, cognition, and information processing and how we will discuss intelligence lie in the concepts of individual differences and measurement. **Individual differences** are the stable, consistent ways children are different from each other. The history of the study of intelligence has focused extensively on individual differences and their assessment. We can talk about individual differences in personality or in any other domain of development, but it is in the area of intelligence that the most attention is given to individual differences. For example, an intelligence test will tell us whether a child can reason better than most others who have taken the test.

Psychologists have a name for the field that involves the assessment of individual differences—**psychometrics.** In a few moments we will look at several of the most widely used tests to assess children's intelligence, but first we need to know something very important in the field of psychometrics—how tests are constructed and how they are evaluated.

How Tests Are Constructed and Evaluated

Any good test must meet three criteria—it must be reliable, it must be valid, and it must be standardized. We consider each of these three criteria in turn.

Reliability

If a test that measures some characteristic of a child is a stable and consistent test, the child's scores should not significantly fluctuate because of chance factors, such as how much sleep the child gets the night before the test, who the examiner is, the temperature in the room where the child takes the test, and so on. How consistently a child performs on the test is known as the test's **reliability.**

Reliability can be measured in several different ways. One common method is to give the same child the same test on two different occasions—this is called **test-retest reliability.** Thus, if we gave an intelligence test to a group of elementary school children today and then gave them the same test in six months, the test would be considered reliable if those who scored high

What contributes to the standardization of the test this child is taking?

on the test today scored high on the test in six months. One negative feature of test-retest reliability is that children sometimes do better the second time they take the test because they are more familiar with it.

A second method of measuring reliability is to give alternate forms of the same test on two different occasions. The test items on the two forms are similar but not identical. This strategy eliminates the chance of children doing better due to familiarity with the items, but it does not eliminate a child's familiarity with the procedures and strategies involved in the testing.

A third method of measuring reliability is **split-half reliability.** With this method, test items are divided into halves, such as the odd-numbered items and the even-numbered items. The items are different, and the two scores are compared to determine how consistently the child performed. When split-half reliability is high we say the test is *internally consistent.* For example, if we gave an intelligence test that included vocabulary items on one half of the test and logical reasoning items on the second half of the test, we would expect the total scores of the children taking the test to be similar to their scores on each half of the test.

Validity

A test may consistently measure an attribute such as intelligence, but this consistency does not ensure that we are measuring the attribute we want to measure. A test of children's intelligence might actually measure something else, such as children's anxiety. The test might consistently measure how anxious children are, and thus have high reliability, but not measure children's intelligence, which it purports to measure. **Validity** is the extent a test measures what it is intended to measure.

Like reliability, there are a number of ways to measure validity. One method is **content validity,** which refers to the test's ability to give a broad picture of what is to be measured. For example, a final test in a high school class, if it is comprehensive over an entire textbook, should sample items from each of the chapters rather than just two or three chapters. If an intelligence test purports to measure both children's verbal ability and problem-solving ability, the items should include a liberal sampling of items that reflect both of these domains. The test would not have high content validity if it asked children to define several vocabulary words but did not require them to reason logically in solving a number of problems.

One of the most important methods for measuring validity is **criterion validity,** which is the test's ability to predict other measures, or criteria, of the attribute. For example, a psychologist might validate an intelligence test by investigating how well it predicts children's grades in school. The grades in school are a criterion for measuring intelligence. When the scores on the two measures substantially overlap, we say the test has high criterion validity. We might give the children a second intelligence test, get their teacher's perception of their intelligence, and observe their behavior in problem-solving situations as other ways of establishing an intelligence test's criterion validity.

Criterion validity can follow one of two courses, concurrent or predictive. **Concurrent validity** assesses the relation of a test's scores to a criterion that is presently available (concurrent). For example, a test might assess children's intelligence. Concurrent validity might be established by analyzing how the scores on the intelligence test correspond to the children's grades in school at this time. **Predictive validity** assesses the relation of a test's scores to an individual's performance at some point in the future. For example, scores on an

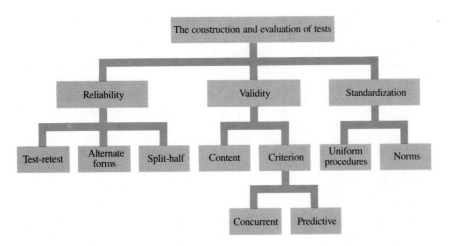

Figure 10.1
Test construction and evaluation.

intelligence test might be used to predict whether the individual will be successful in college. Likewise, the SAT test is used for a similar purpose. Individuals take the test and then at some later time are evaluated to see if indeed the test predicted their performance.

Standardization

Good tests are not only reliable and valid, they are standardized as well. Developing uniform procedures for administering and scoring a test is important in **standardization.** Uniform testing procedures require that the testing environment be as similar as possible for all children. The test directions and the amount of time allowed for children to complete the test should be the same, for example.

The test constructor also develops **norms**—established standards of performance—for the test as part of the standardization process. This is accomplished by giving the test to a large group of children representative of the population for whom the test is intended. This allows the test constructor to determine the distribution of scores. Norms inform us which children's scores are considered high, low, or average. For example, if a child scores 120 on an intelligence test, that number alone has little meaning. The score takes on meaning when we compare it with the other scores. If only 20 percent of the children in the standardized group scored above 120, then we can interpret the child's score as high rather than low or average. Many tests of intelligence were designed for children from diverse groups. So that the tests will be applicable to such different groups, many of them have norms, that is, established standards of performance for children of different ages, social classes, and races. Figure 10.1 summarizes the main points of our discussion of test construction and evaluation.

The Measurement and Nature of Children's Intelligence

Earlier we indicated that often intelligence is defined in terms of verbal ability and problem-solving skills. But we also indicated that intelligence is an abstract concept that is difficult to define. While many psychologists and lay people equate intelligence with verbal ability and problem-solving skills, others prefer to define it as the child's ability to learn from and adapt to the experiences of everyday life. If we were to settle on a definition of children's intelligence based on these criteria it would be that **intelligence** is verbal ability, problem-solving skills, and the ability to learn from and adapt to the experiences of everyday life. As we discuss the most widely used children's intelligence tests and the nature of intelligence, however, you will see that experts still debate what intelligence is.

Alfred Binet and the Binet Tests

In 1904, the French Ministry of Education asked psychologist Alfred Binet to devise a method that would determine which students did not profit from typical school instruction. School officials wanted to reduce overcrowding by placing those who did not benefit from regular classroom teaching in special schools. Binet and his student Theophile Simon developed an intelligence test to meet this request. The test is referred to as the 1905 Scale and consisted of thirty different items ranging from the ability to touch one's nose or ear when asked to the ability to draw designs from memory and define abstract concepts.

Binet developed the concept of **mental age (MA),** which is an individual's level of mental development relative to others. Binet reasoned that a mentally retarded child would perform like a normal child of a younger age. He developed norms for intelligence by testing fifty nonretarded children from three to eleven years of age. Children suspected of mental retardation were given the test and their performance was compared with children of the same chronological age in the normal sample. Average mental-age scores (MA) correspond to chronological age (CA), which is age from birth. A bright child has an MA above CA, a dull child has an MA below CA.

The term **intelligence quotient (IQ)** was devised in 1912 by William Stern. IQ consists of a child's mental age divided by chronological age multiplied by 100:

$$IQ = \frac{MA}{CA} \times 100$$

If mental age is the same as chronological age, then the individual's IQ is 100; if mental age is above chronological age, the IQ is more than 100; if mental age is below chronological age, the IQ is less than 100. Scores noticeably above 100 are considered above average, those noticeably below are considered below average. For example, a six-year-old child with a mental age of eight would have an IQ of 133 while a six-year-old child with a mental age of five would have an IQ of 83.

Over the years extensive effort has been expended to standardize the Binet test, which has been given to thousands of children and adults of different ages, selected at random from different parts of the United States. By administering the test to large numbers of individuals and recording the results, it has been found that intelligence measured by the Binet approximates a **normal distribution** (figure 10.2). This type of distribution is symmetrical, with a majority of cases falling in the middle of the possible range of scores and few scores appearing toward the ends of the range.

The many revisions of the Binet test in the United States are called the Stanford-Binet tests (Stanford University is where the revisions have been done). Many of the revisions were carried out by Lewis Terman, who applied Stern's IQ concept to the test, developed extensive norms, and provided detailed, clear instructions for each problem appearing on the test.

The current Stanford-Binet is given to individuals from the age of two through adulthood. It includes a wide variety of items, some requiring verbal responses, others nonverbal responses. For example, items that characterize a

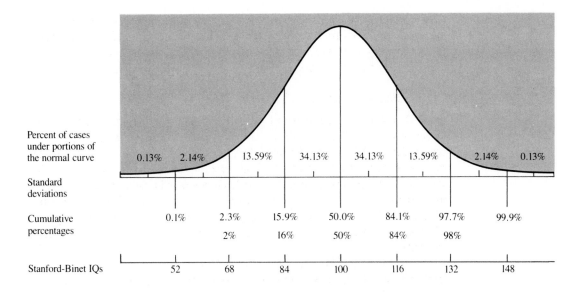

| Percent of cases under portions of the normal curve | 0.13% | 2.14% | 13.59% | 34.13% | 34.13% | 13.59% | 2.14% | 0.13% |

Standard deviations

| Cumulative percentages | 0.1% | 2.3% | 15.9% | 50.0% | 84.1% | 97.7% | 99.9% |
| | | 2% | 16% | 50% | 84% | 98% | |

| Stanford-Binet IQs | 52 | 68 | 84 | 100 | 116 | 132 | 148 |

six-year-old's performance on the test include the verbal ability to define at least six words such as "orange" and "envelope," and the nonverbal ability to trace a path through a maze. Items that reflect the average adult's intelligence include defining such words as "disproportionate" and "regard," explaining a proverb, and comparing idleness and laziness.

The fourth edition of the Stanford-Binet was published in 1985 (Thorndike, Hagan, & Sattler, 1985). One important addition to this version is the analysis of the individual's responses in terms of four content areas: verbal reasoning, quantitative reasoning, abstract/visual reasoning, and short-term memory (Keith & others, 1988). A general composite score also is obtained to reflect overall intelligence. The Stanford-Binet continues to be one of the most widely used individual tests of intelligence.

The Wechsler Scales

Besides the Stanford-Binet, the other most widely used individual intelligence tests are the **Wechsler scales,** developed by David Wechsler. They include the Wechsler Adult Intelligence Scale-Revised (WAIS-R); the Wechsler Intelligence Scale for Children-Revised (WISC-R), for use with children between the ages of six and sixteen; and the Wechsler Preschool and Primary Scale of Intelligence (WPPSI), for use with children from the ages of four to six and a half (Wechsler, 1949, 1955, 1967, 1974, 1981).

The Wechsler scales not only provide an overall IQ score but the items are grouped according to eleven subscales, six of which are verbal and five of which are nonverbal. This allows the examiner to obtain separate verbal and nonverbal IQ scores and to see quickly the areas of mental performance in which the individual is below average, average, or above average. The inclusion of a number of nonverbal subscales makes the Wechsler test more representative of verbal *and* nonverbal intelligence; the Binet-Simon test includes some nonverbal items but not as many as the Wechsler scales. The subscales of the Wechsler Intelligence Scale for Children-Revised (WISC-R) are shown in figure 10.3, along with examples of each subscale.

Figure 10.2
The normal curve and Stanford-Binet IQ scores (Sattler, 1982). The distribution of IQ scores approximates a normal curve. Most of the population falls in the middle range of scores. Notice that extremely high and extremely low scores are very rare. Slightly more than two-thirds of the scores fall between 84 and 116. Only about one in fifty individuals has an IQ of more than 132 and only about one in fifty individuals has an IQ of less than 68.

Figure 10.3
The subtests of the WISC-R and examples of
each subtest.

Verbal subtests

General information
The individual is asked a number of general information questions about experiences
that are considered normal for individuals in our society.
  For example, "How many wings does a bird have?"

Similarities
The individual must think logically and abstractly to answer a number of questions
about how things are similar.
  For example, "In what way are boats and trains the same?"

Arithmetic reasoning
Problems measure the individual's ability to do arithmetic mentally and include
addition, subtraction, multiplication, and division.
  For example, "If two buttons cost 14¢, what will be the cost of a dozen buttons?"

Vocabulary
To evaluate word knowledge, the individual is asked to define a number of words.
This subtest measures a number of cognitive functions, including concept formation,
memory, and language.
  For example, "What does the word *biography* mean?"

Comprehension
This subtest is designed to measure the individual's judgment and common sense.
  For example, "What is the advantage of keeping money in the bank?"

Digit span
This subtest primarily measures attention and short-term memory. The individual
is required to repeat numbers forward and backward.
  For example, "I am going to say some numbers and I want you to repeat them
backward: 4 7 5 2 8."

Performance subtests

Picture completion
A number of drawings are shown, each with a significant part missing. Within a
period of several seconds, the individual must differentiate essential from
nonessential parts of the picture and identify which part is missing. This subtest
evaluates visual alertness and the ability to organize information visually.
  For example, "I am going to show you a picture with an important part missing.
Tell me what is missing."

Picture arrangement
A series of pictures out of sequence are shown to the individual, who is asked to
place them in their proper order to tell an appropriate story. This subtest evaluates
how individuals integrate information to make it logical and meaningful.
  For example, "The pictures below need to be placed in an appropriate order to
tell a meaningful story."

Figure 10.3
Continued

Object assembly
The individual is asked to assemble pieces into something. This subtest measures visual-motor coordination and perceptual organization.
For example, "When these pieces are put together correctly, they make something. Put them together as quickly as you can."

Block design
The individual must assemble a set of multi-colored blocks to match designs that the examiner shows. Visual-motor coordination, perceptual organization, and the ability to visualize spatially are measured.
For example, "Use the four blocks on the left to make the pattern on the right."

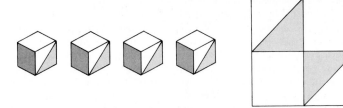

Coding
This subtest evaluates, how quickly and accurately an individual can link code symbols and digits. The subtest assesses visual-motor coordination and speed of thought.
For example, "As quickly as you can, transfer the appropriate code symbols to the blank spaces."

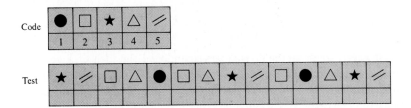

Does Intelligence Have a Single Nature?

Is it more appropriate to think of intelligence as a child's general ability or as a number of specific abilities? Long before David Wechsler analyzed intelligence in terms of general and specific factors (giving the child an overall IQ but also providing information about specific subcomponents of intelligence), Charles Spearman (1927) proposed that intelligence has two factors. Spearman's **two-factor theory** argued that children have both general intelligence, which he called *g*, and a number of specific intelligences, which he called *s*. Spearmen believed that these two factors could account for a child's performance on an intelligence test.

Bird to Beethoven—Seven Frames of Mind

A blond-haired ten-year-old boy springs into motion on the playground in the small town of French Lick, Indiana. Grabbing a rebound, he quickly dribbles the ball the length of the court, all the while processing the whereabouts of his five opponents and four teammates. He throws the ball to an open teammate who scores on an easy lay-up. Years later the young boy had become a six-foot, nine-inch superstar for the Boston Celtics. His name: Larry Bird. Is there intelligence to Bird's movement and perception of the spatial layout of the basketball court?

Now we turn the clock back 200 years. A tiny boy just four years of age is standing on a footstool in front of a piano keyboard practicing. At the age of six the young boy is given the honor of playing concertos and trios at a concert. The young boy is Ludwig von Beethoven, whose musical genius was evident at a young age. Did Beethoven have a specific type of intelligence, one we might call musical intelligence?

Bird and Beethoven are different types of individuals with different types of abilities. Howard Gardner (1983), in his book, *Frames of Mind,* argues that Bird's and Beethoven's talents represent two of seven intelligences that we possess. Beyond the verbal and mathematical intelligences tapped by such tests as the SAT and most traditional intelligence tests, Gardner thinks that we have the ability to spatially analyze the world, movement skills, insightful skills for analyzing ourselves, insightful skills for analyzing others, and musical skills.

Gardner believes that each of the seven intelligences can be destroyed by brain damage, that each involves unique cognitive skills, and that each shows up in exaggerated fashion in both the gifted and *idiots savants* (individuals who are mentally retarded but who have unbelievable skill in a particular domain, such as drawing, music, or computing). I remember vividly an individual from my childhood who was mentally retarded but could instantaneously respond with the correct day of the week (say Tuesday or Saturday) when given any date in history (say June 4, 1926, or December 15, 1746).

Gardner is especially interested in musical intelligence, particularly when it is exhibited at an early age. He points out that musically inclined preschool children not only have the remarkable ability to learn musical patterns easily, but that they rarely forget them. He recounts a story about Stravinsky, who as an adult could still remember the musical patterns of the tuba, drums, and piccolos of the fife-and-drum band that marched outside of his window when he was a young child.

To measure musical intelligence in young children, Gardner might ask a child to listen to a melody and then ask the child to recreate the tune on some bells he provides. He believes such evaluations can be used to develop a profile of a child's intelligence. He also believes that it is during this early time in life that parents can make an important difference in how a child's intelligence develops.

Critics of Gardner's approach point out that we have geniuses in many domains other than music. There are outstanding chess players, prize fighters, writers, politicians, physicians, lawyers, preachers, and poets, for example; yet we do not refer to chess intelligence, prize-fighter intelligence, and so on.

However, some factor approaches abandoned the idea of a general intelligence and searched for specific factors only. L. L. Thurstone (1938) proposed a **multiple-factor theory of intelligence.** Thurstone consistently came up with six to twelve abilities when analyzing large numbers of intelligence test responses. He called these factors primary mental abilities. The seven primary mental abilities that most often appeared in Thurstone's analysis were verbal comprehension, number ability, word fluency, spatial visualization, associative memory, reasoning, and perceptual speed.

One more recent classification, developed by Howard Gardner (1983), also includes seven components of intelligence, although they are not the same as Thurstone's seven factors. By turning to Perspective on Child Development 10.1, you can read about Gardner's seven frames of mind. Clearly, there is disagreement about whether intelligence is a general ability or a number of specific abilities, and if there are specific abilities just what those are.

Larry Bird, NBA superstar of the Boston Celtics. Howard Gardner believes movement skills and spacial perception are forms of intelligence.

Ludwig von Beethoven. Gardner also argues that musical skills, such as those shown by Beethoven, are a form of intelligence.

Two reasons stand out why so much disagreement characterizes the approaches to intelligence (Kail & Pellegrino, 1985). First, there are many ways to analyze the same data. Different apparent solutions, which produce different psychological interpretations, can be obtained from the same data. Second, the data obtained in separate studies differ. The critical data for interpretations of whether intelligence is a general ability or a number of specific abilities involve correlations (recall our discussion of this in chapter 1). The pattern of correlations depends on the group tested (school children, armed service recruits, or criminals, for example), the total number of tests administered, and the specific tests that are included in the battery. The outcome of studies is that the abilities thought to make up the core of intelligence may vary across different investigations. Despite these inconsistencies, evidence suggests that intelligence is *both* a general ability and a number of specific abilities.

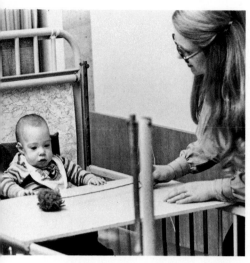

The Bayley Mental and Motor Scales are among the most widely used developmental scales for infants. What should the average baby at six months be able to do on the Bayley scales? The average twelve-month-old?

Infant Intelligence and the Stability of Intelligence

Many standardized intelligence tests do not assess infant intelligence. Intelligence tests that have been created for infants are often called **developmental scales.** What are these tests like? Can we predict a child's or an adolescent's intelligence from the individual's scores on an infant intelligence test? How much do intelligence test scores change as children grow and develop?

Infant Intelligence Tests

It is advantageous to know whether an infant is advancing at a slow, normal, or fast rate of cognitive development. If the infant is advancing at a particularly slow rate, for example, environmental enrichment may be called for. If an infant is progressing at an advanced rate, parents may be advised to provide toys that are designed to stimulate cognitive development in slightly older infants.

One of the most widely used developmental scales is the Bayley Mental and Motor Scales, consisting of a series of items to measure mental skills and to evaluate motor skills. The components of the Bayley Mental Scale were designed to measure the infant's adaptive responses to the environment. They include attention to visual and auditory stimuli; grasping, manipulating, and combining objects; shaking a rattle; and ringing a bell. Items that measure the infant's social and cognitive skills also are included: smiling, cooing, babbling, imitating, and following directions. Showing memory and being aware of object constancy (looking for a hidden toy) are part of the Bayley Mental Scale, as is beginning to understand language. The language items include following directions that involve the use of object names, prepositions, and the concept of "one." The Bayley Motor Scale tests the infant's ability to hold up his or her head, turn over, sit, creep, stand, walk, and go up and down stairs. It also tests manual skills, such as grasping small objects and throwing a ball (Bayley, 1970). According to the Bayley scales, at approximately six months of age the average baby should be able to—

1. accept a second cube—baby holds first cube, while examiner takes second cube and places it within easy reach of the infant;
2. grasp the edge of a piece of paper when it is presented;
3. vocalize pleasure and displeasure;
4. persistently reach for objects placed just out of immediate reach;
5. turn his or her head after a spoon the experimenter suddenly drops on the floor; and
6. approach a mirror when the examiner places it in front of the infant.

At approximately twelve months of age the average baby should be able to—

1. inhibit behavior when commanded to do so; for example, when the infant puts a block in his or her mouth and the examiner says, "no, no," then the infant should cease the activity;
2. repeat an action if he or she is laughed at;
3. imitate words the experimenter says, like "mama," and "dada";
4. imitate actions of the experimenter: for example, if the experimenter rattles a spoon in a cup, then the infant should imitate this action;
5. respond to simple requests, such as "take a drink."

The Stability of Intelligence

In one study conducted by Nancy Bayley, the developer of the Bayley scales, no relation was found between the scales and intelligence as measured by the Stanford-Binet at the ages of six and seven (Bayley, 1943). Another investigation found correlations of only .01 between intelligence measured at three months and intelligence measured at five years of age and .05 between measurement at one year and measurement at five years (Anderson, 1939). These findings indicate virtually no relationship between infant development scales and intelligence at five years of age. Again, it should be remembered that one of the reasons for this finding is that the components of intelligence tested in infancy are not the same as the components of intelligence tested at the age of five.

There is a strong relation between IQ scores obtained at the ages of six, eight, and nine and IQ scores obtained at the age of ten. For example, in one study the correlation between IQ at the age of eight and IQ at the age of ten was .88. The correlation between IQ at the age of nine and IQ at the age of ten was .90. These figures show a very high relation between IQ scores obtained in these years. The correlation of IQ in the preadolescent years and IQ at the age of eighteen is slightly less but still statistically significant. For example, the correlation between IQ at the age of ten and IQ at the age of eighteen was .70 in one study (Honzik, MacFarlane, & Allen, 1948).

What has been said so far about the stability of intelligence has been based on measures of groups of individuals. The stability of intelligence also can be evaluated through studies of individual persons. As we see next, there can be considerable variability in an individual's scores on IQ tests.

Let's look at an example of the absence of a relation between intelligence in infancy and intelligence in later years for two children in the same family. The first child learned to speak at a very early age. She displayed the characteristics of an extravert, and her advanced motor coordination was indicated by her ability to walk at a very early age. The second child learned speech very late, saying very few words until she was two and one-half years old.

Both children were given standardized tests of intelligence during infancy and then later, during the elementary school years. In the earlier test the first child's scores were higher than her sister's. In the later test their scores were reversed. What are some of the possible reasons for the reversal in the IQ scores of the two girls? When the second child did begin to speak, she did so prolifically, and the complexity of her language increased rapidly, undoubtedly as a result of her biological readiness to talk. Her sensorimotor coordination had never been as competent as the first child's, perhaps also accounting in part for her lower scores on the infant intelligence tests. The parents recognized that they had initially given the first child extensive amounts of their time. They were not able to give the second child as much of their time as they had the first, but when the second child was about three years old, they made every opportunity to involve her in physical and academic activities. They put her in a Montessori preschool program, gave her dancing and swimming lessons, and frequently invited other children of her age in to play with her. There may have been other reasons as well for the changes in scores, but these do serve to demonstrate that infant intelligence tests may not be good predictors of intelligence in later years. However, as discussed in Perspective on Child Development 10.2, aspects of the infant's behavior other than performance on infant IQ tests may be linked to later intelligence.

Response to Novel Stimulation in Infancy and Intelligence at Five to Six Years of Age

In contrast to the poor predictive power of infant IQ tests, other aspects of infants' behavior are linked to intelligence at five and six years of age. Specifically, a number of recent studies have suggested that an infant's response to novel stimulation—what we have referred to as dishabituation (chapter 6)—is significantly correlated with later IQ. One impressive study by Susan Rose and Ina Wallace (1985) assessed the amount of time that six-month-old infants spent looking at novel versus previously viewed visual stimuli. "Novelty scores," which measured the preference for viewing novel stimuli, predicted WISC-R IQ scores at six years of age ($r = .56$). Infant preferences for novel auditory stimuli are similarly predictive of later IQ. Mary O'Connor, Sarale Cohen, and Arthur Parmelee (1984) found that four-month-old infants' cardiac (heart rate) responses to repetitive versus novel sounds predicted Stanford-Binet IQ at five years ($r = .60$). These findings are provocative in supporting the claim that the nature of intelligence—if measured appropriately—is fundamentally continuous from infancy through childhood (Fagan, 1985). They also suggest that intelligence may be conceptualized as including the component of responsiveness to novelty (Berg & Sternberg, 1985), not only in infancy but in childhood as well (Marr & Sternberg, 1985). Although some loose ends remain in the data on novelty-intelligence associations (McCall, 1985), the emerging findings promise some important new insights on the emergence and development of intelligence.

Many of the early efforts to relate infant intelligence to intelligence at later points in development were not very successful. Recently, developmentalists have investigated some different aspects of infant intelligence they believe are more likely to be related to intelligence at later developmental points. Especially noteworthy is the link between response to novel stimulation in infancy with intelligence at five to six years of age.

Can you predict what a child's IQ will be when she is ten or eighteen years old from her scores on an IQ test administered when she is two, three, and four years old? IQ tests still do not provide very reliable predictions of this sort. Based on statistical techniques, IQ scores obtained at two and three years of age are related to the IQ scores of the same individuals even at ten and eighteen years, although they are not very strongly related. IQ scores obtained at the age of four are much better at predicting IQ at the age of ten than at the age of eighteen (Honzik, MacFarlane, & Allen, 1948).

Robert McCall and his associates (1973) studied 140 children between the ages of two and one-half and seventeen years of age. They found that the average range of IQ scores was more than twenty-eight points. The scores of one out of three children changed by as much as thirty points and one out of seven by as much as forty points. These data suggest that intelligence test scores can fluctuate dramatically across the childhood years and that intelligence is not as stable as the original intelligence theorists envisioned.

What can we conclude about the nature of stability and change in intelligence in childhood? Children are adaptive beings. They have the capacity for intellectual change but they do not become entirely new intelligent beings. In a sense, children's intelligence changes but has connections to earlier points in development—amidst intellectual change is some underlying coherence and continuity.

At this point we have discussed many ideas about the nature of intelligence, test construction, and intelligence tests. A summary of these ideas is presented in Concept Table 10.1. Now we turn our attention to some controversial issues in intelligence.

Concept	Processes/Related Ideas	Characteristics/Description
What is intelligence?	Its nature	Intelligence is an abstract concept that is measured indirectly. Psychologists rely on intelligence tests to estimate intellectual processes. Verbal ability and problem-solving skills are included in a definition of intelligence. Some psychologists believe intelligence includes an ability to learn from and adapt to everyday life. Extensive effort is given to assessing individual differences in intelligence. This is called psychometrics.
How tests are constructed and evaluated	Reliability	Reliability is how consistently an individual performs on a test. Three forms of reliability are test-retest, alternate forms, and split-half.
	Validity	Validity is the extent to which a test measures what it is intended to measure. Two methods of assessing validity are content validity and criterion validity.
	Standardization	Standardization involves uniform procedures for administering and scoring a test; it also involves norms.
The measurement and nature of intelligence	Alfred Binet and the Binet tests	Alfred Binet developed the first intelligence test, known as the 1905 Scale. He developed the concept of mental age while William Stern developed the concept of IQ. The Binet has been standardized and revised a number of times. The many revisions are called the Stanford-Binet tests. The test approximates a normal distribution. The current test is given to individuals from the age of two through adulthood.
	The Wechsler scales	Besides the Binet, the Wechsler scales are the most widely used intelligence tests. They include the WAIS-R, the WISC-R, and the WPPSI. These tests provide an overall IQ, verbal and performance IQ, and information about subtests.
	Does intelligence have a single nature?	Psychologists debate whether intelligence is a general ability or a number of specific abilities. Spearman's two-factor theory and Thurstone's multiple-factor theory state that a number of specific factors are involved. Current thinking suggests that Spearman's conceptualization of intelligence as both a set of specific abilities and a general ability was right.
Infant intelligence and the stability of intelligence	Infant intelligence tests	Many standardized intelligence tests do not assess infant intelligence. Intelligence tests designed to measure infant intelligence are often referred to as developmental scales, the most widely used being the Bayley scales.
	Stability of intelligence	While intelligence is more stable across the childhood years than many attributes, many children's scores on intelligence tests fluctuate widely.

Controversies and Issues in Intelligence

Intelligence has been one of psychology's concepts that seems to attract controversy. Among the most controversial issues of intelligence are those related to racial differences, heredity-environment determinants, cultural bias in intelligence tests, knowledge versus process, and the uses and misuses of intelligence tests. We consider each of these in turn.

Social Class, Racial, and Ethnic Differences in Intelligence

Some years ago I knocked on the door of a house in a low-income area of the city. The father came to the door and invited me into the living room. It was getting dark outside and no lights were on inside the house. The father excused himself for a minute, then returned with a light bulb, which he screwed into the lamp socket. He said that he could barely pay his monthly mortgage and

Extensive interest has been shown in the possible intelligence differences between blacks and whites. On the average, white American school children score ten to fifteen points higher on standardized intelligence tests than black American schoolchildren. However, keep in mind that these are average scores and that many black children score higher than many white children because the distributions for black and white children overlap. The consensus is that the differences in the intelligence of black and white children are environmentally based.

the electric company had threatened to turn off his electricity so he was carefully monitoring his family's use of electricity. There were seven children in the family ranging in age from two to sixteen. Neither he nor his wife had completed high school. He worked as a brick layer when he could find a job and his wife worked in a laundry ironing clothes. The parents wanted their children to have more opportunities than they themselves had but so far their children were experiencing a life of social disadvantage. Do children from families such as this one perform more poorly on tests of intelligence than their middle-income counterparts? Are there racial and ethnic differences in intelligence as well?

A consistent finding is that children from low-income or lower-class families average ten to twenty points lower than children from middle-income or middle-class families on standardized intelligence tests (Anastasi, 1988). However, it is important to consider the dimensions of intelligence when evaluating social-class differences. Those dimensions related to academic performance, such as verbal, numerical, and spatial abilities, are more likely to reflect social-class differences. Those more closely related to mental abilities, such as memory and reasoning, are less likely to reveal social-class differences (Globerson, 1983).

Racial and ethnic differences in children's performance on intelligence tests also exist. For example, in the United States, children in black and Hispanic families score below children from white families on standardized intelligence tests. The most interest in group differences has focused on black-white comparisons. On the average, white American school children score ten to fifteen points higher on standardized intelligence tests than black American school children (Anastasi, 1988). Keep in mind, though, that we are talking about average scores. Many black children score higher than many white children because the distributions for black and white children overlap. Estimates indicate that 15 to 25 percent of black school children score higher than half of all white school children (Shuey, 1966).

While the greatest interest has been in black-white comparisons, patterns of intelligence in Jewish, Chinese, black, and Puerto Rican children suggest some strengths and weaknesses in children from different ethnic backgrounds (Lesser, Fifer, & Clark, 1965). Jewish children scored higher on verbal abilities, lower on reasoning and numerical abilities, and lower still on spatial abilities. Chinese children scored low on verbal abilities but higher on numerical, spatial, and reasoning abilities. Black children scored higher on verbal abilities and lower on reasoning, spatial, and numerical abilities. Puerto Rican children scored lower on verbal abilities and higher on numerical, spatial, and reasoning abilities.

How extensively are racial and ethnic differences in children's intelligence influenced by heredity and environment? The consensus is that the available data do not support a genetic explanation. For example, in recent decades, as black Americans have experienced improved social, economic, and educational opportunities, the gap between white and black children on standardized intelligence and achievement tests has begun to diminish (Jones, 1984). And when children from disadvantaged black families are adopted by more advantaged middle-class families their scores on intelligence tests more closely resemble national averages for middle-class than lower-class children (Scarr & Weinberg, 1976).

The Heredity-Environment Controversy

Remember our discussion of the heredity-environment controversy from chapter 2 where we discussed Arthur Jensen's argument that intelligence is heavily based on heredity, criticisms of Jensen, and the conclusion that the best way to view the influence of heredity on intelligence is to conceptualize the effects in terms of genetic-environmental interaction. To refresh your memory of the role of heredity in intelligence you might benefit from reviewing our discussion of this topic in chapter 2.

The genes we inherited from our parents make important contributions to our intelligence. But genes alone are an incomplete explanation. What are some of the important environmental contributions to intelligence? We just described how social class is related to intelligence and how educational and social opportunities for black children are leading to improvements in their performances on standardized intelligence tests. Family experiences, the effects of being institutionalized, education, culture, and social class have been among the most widely investigated environmental influences on children's intelligence. Let's look further at the effects of being institutionalized, family structure, and early prevention efforts designed to elevate children's intelligence.

In one well-known study of institutionalization, Harold Skeels (1966) removed children from an unstimulating orphanage and placed them in an institution where they received individual attention. The change in institutions raised their level of intellectual functioning substantially. In this study, children were assigned an "adoptive mother," an older, mentally retarded girl who was given the responsibility of caring for them. At the end of two and one-half years, the children with the mentally retarded "mother" gained an average of thirty-two points in IQ. The children who remained in the inferior institution dropped an average of twenty-one points in IQ.

Many studies of institutionalization have been criticized. For example, some of the early studies (e.g., Spitz, 1945) interpreted the negative effects of institutionalization in terms of a lack of mother love. However, studies of institutionalization do not provide accurate tests of the mother's or the family's role in intelligence. Multiple mothering in the institution, separation from the mother, and such distortions in mothering as rejection and overprotection are possible explanations for the observed effects of institutionalization. Descriptions of several institutions in the Soviet Union support the belief that it is not institutionalization per se that has disastrous effects on intelligence but rather the quality of the institution (Brackbill, 1962; Bronfenbrenner, 1970). Where nurses give considerable individual attention to infants and children and provide them with many visual-motor opportunities, and where children are trained to become self-reliant and to engage in appropriate peer interaction, institutionalized children show normal intellectual patterns.

Families influence their children's intellectual development both genetically and environmentally. Untangling these two sources of influence is a formidable task (Anastasi, 1988). While developmentalists do not know precisely how much of the variance in intellectual development is due to enriched surroundings provided by parents, family structure, and other environmental influences, they do know that these factors are significant. Children from smaller families, those who are firstborn, and those who come from intact families perform better on intelligence tests than their counterparts from larger families, of younger sibling status, and from single-parent families (Santrock, 1972;

One of the most challenging circumstances in the area of intelligence is how to best help parents in high-risk families to provide a more enriched environment for their children. The research by Craig Ramey and his associates in North Carolina suggests that educational day care, medical care, and dietary supplements are likely to benefit the offspring of pregnant women with low IQs.

Zajonc & Marcus, 1975). Nonetheless, many developmentalists believe that the nature of interaction in families, such as how parents socialize their children, parents' involvement with their children, and how much verbal give-and-take occurs, is a better predictor of intelligence than family structure characteristics such as family size, birth order, and intact versus single-parent status (Santrock, in press).

Researchers are increasingly interested in manipulating the environment early in children's lives when they are perceived to be at risk for impoverished intelligence. The new emphasis is on *prevention* rather than remediation (Heinicke, Beckwith, & Thompson, 1988). Prevention means literally to keep something from happening. This suggests that intervention needs to take place in a deliberate and positive way to counteract harmful circumstances before they cause impoverished intellectual functioning (Goldston, 1986). Some parents have difficulty providing an adequate environment for the intellectual needs of their infants. Once these difficulties are a repetitive part of the family system, then change efforts probably will be more difficult and costly. Early intervention in the family system is directed at changing parental adaptive and responsive functioning so that permanent negative effects on children are minimized. A number of early intervention programs have demonstrated that positive effects on the family participants can be achieved (Halpern, 1984; Ramey, Bryant, & Suarez, 1985; Ramey & Haskins, 1981).

In a program conducted in North Carolina by Craig Ramey and his associates, pregnant women with IQs averaging 80 were recruited for an intervention study. After their babies were born, half of the infants were cared for during the day at an educational day-care center and half were reared at home by their mothers. Both groups of children were given medical care and dietary supplements, and their families were given social services if they requested them.

At the age of three, the children who attended the educational day-care center had significantly higher IQs than the home-reared children. This difference seemed to be due to a decline in the IQs of the home-reared children during the twelve- to eighteen-month period. By the time the children were five years old, 39 percent of the home-reared children had IQs below 85 but only 11 percent of the educational day-care children had IQs this low.

A recent review of intervention studies involving the family suggests that intervention is more likely to be successful if the number of contacts between the intervenor and the family is approximately eleven or more, if they begin shortly after birth, and if they extend over a period of at least three months (Heinicke, Beckwith, & Thompson, 1988). While eleven sessions is a somewhat arbitrary number, it does reflect that a certain duration of contact is necessary for the success of the intervention.

Are Intelligence Tests Culturally Biased?

Many of the early intelligence tests were culturally biased, favoring urban children over rural children, middle-class children over lower-class children, and white children over minority children. The norms for the early tests were based almost entirely on white, middle-class children. And some of the items themselves were culturally biased. For example, one item on an early test asked what should be done if you find a three-year-old child in the street; the correct answer was "call the police." Children from impoverished inner-city families might not choose this answer if they have had bad experiences with the police; rural children might not choose it since they may not have police nearby. Such

Cognitive Development

Table 10.1
The Chitling Intelligence Test

1. A "gas head" is a person who has a:
   a. fast-moving car
   b. stable of "lace"
   c. "process"
   d. habit of stealing cars
   e. long jail record for arson
2. "Bo Diddley" is a:
   a. game for children
   b. down-home cheap wine
   c. down-home singer
   d. new dance
   e. Moejoe call
3. If a pimp is uptight with a woman who gets state aid, what does he mean when he talks about "Mother's day"?
   a. second Sunday in May
   b. third Sunday in June
   c. first of every month
   d. none of these
   e. first and fifteenth of every month

4. A "handkerchief head" is:
   a. a cool cat
   b. a porter
   c. an Uncle Tom
   d. a hoddi
   e. a preacher
5. If a man is called a "blood," then he is a:
   a. fighter
   b. Mexican-American
   c. Negro
   d. hungry hemophile
   e. red man, or Indian
6. Cheap chitlings (not the kind you purchase at a frozen-food counter) will taste rubbery unless they are cooked long enough. How soon can you quit cooking them to eat and enjoy them?
   a. forty-five minutes
   b. two hours
   c. twenty-four hours
   d. one week (on a low flame)
   e. one hour

Answers: 1.c 2.c 3.e 4.c 5.c 6.c

Source: Adrian Dove, "Taking the Chitling Test," *Newsweek*, July 15, 1968, pp. 51–52.

items clearly do not measure the knowledge necessary to adapt to one's environment or to be "intelligent" in an inner-city minority neighborhood or in rural America (Scarr, 1984). The contemporary versions of intelligence tests attempt to reduce cultural bias.

Even if the content of test items is made appropriate, another problem may exist with intelligence tests. Since many questions are verbal in nature, minority groups may encounter problems understanding the language of the questions. Minority groups often speak a language that is very different from standard English. Consequently, they may be at a disadvantage when they take intelligence tests oriented toward middle-class, white children. Cultural bias is dramatically underscored by tests like the one shown in table 10.1. The items in this test were developed to reduce the cultural disadvantage black children might experience on traditional intelligence tests.

Culture-fair tests were devised to reduce cultural bias. Two types of culture-fair tests have been developed. The first includes items that are familiar to individuals from all socioeconomic and ethnic backgrounds, or items that at least are familiar to the individuals who are taking the test. For example, a child might be asked how a bird and a dog are different, on the assumption that virtually all children have been exposed to birds and dogs. The second type of culture-fair test has all the verbal items removed. Figure 10.4 shows a sample item from the Raven Progressive Matrices Test, which exemplifies this approach. Even though tests like the Raven Test are designed to be culture fair, individuals with more education score higher on them than those with less education (Anastasi, 1988).

Culture-fair tests remind us that traditional intelligence tests are probably culturally biased, yet culture-fair tests do not provide a satisfactory alternative. Constructing a truly culture-fair test, one that rules out the role of experience emanating from socioeconomic and ethnic background, has been difficult and may be impossible. Consider, for example, that the intelligence of the Iatmul people of Papua, New Guinea, involves the ability to remember the names of some 10,000 to 20,000 clans. By contrast, the intelligence of the islanders in the widely dispersed Caroline Islands involves the talent of navigating by the stars.

Figure 10.4
A sample item from the Raven Progressive
Matrices Test.

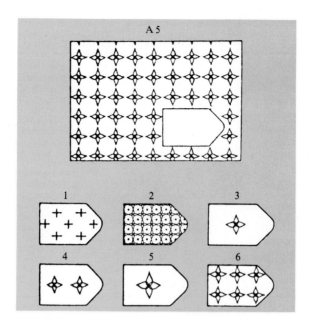

Knowledge versus Process in Intelligence

The information-processing approach we discussed in chapter 9 raises two interesting questions about children's intelligence: What are children's fundamental information-processing abilities? and How do these develop?

Few of us would deny that changes in both processing and knowledge occur as we develop. However, a consensus does not exist on something more fundamental. We accumulate knowledge as we grow from an infant to an adult, but what may be growing is simply a reserve of processing capacity. That is, your greater processing capacity as an adult than as a child might be what allows you to learn more. By contrast, possibly your greater processing capacity as an adult is a consequence of your greater knowledge, which allows you to process information more effectively. It is not easy to choose between these two possibilities, and the issue has been called the great **structure-process dilemma** of intelligence (Keil, 1984). That is, What are the mechanisms of intelligence and how do they develop? Does information-processing ability change or does knowledge and expertise change? Or do both change?

To make the structure-process dilemma more concrete, consider a simple computer metaphor. Suppose we have two computers, each of which is capable of solving multiplication problems (e.g., 13×24, 45×21), but one computer works faster than the other. What is the explanation? One possibility is that the faster computer has a greater capacity—that is, core memory—in which to do mental work. This greater core memory, which psychologists refer to as *working memory,* might allow the computer to work on two or more components of a problem at once. Another explanation is that the faster computer might have a greater store of relevant knowledge. Perhaps it has in its data bank (long-term memory) a complete multiplication table up to 99×99. The slower computer might have a table up to 12×12 (as do most humans). The faster computer need not be fundamentally faster—its subroutines may be relatively slow but it is able to perform the multiplication task because of knowledge, not because of processing capacity.

Explaining intelligence is similar to explaining the difference between the fast and slow computers—is processing or knowledge responsible for how intelligence changes with age? Based on research on memory, it seems likely

Analytical Ann, Insightful Todd, and Street-Smart Art

Every child has three types of intelligence, according to R. J. Sternberg (1985, 1986, 1987, 1988), and he calls this view the **triarchic theory of intelligence.** Consider Ann, who scores high on traditional intelligence tests such as the Stanford-Binet and is a star analytical thinker. Consider Todd, who does not have the best test results but has an insightful and creative mind. And consider Art, a street-smart child who has learned how to deal in practical ways with his world, although his scores on traditional intelligence tests are low.

Sternberg calls Ann's analytical thinking and abstract reasoning *componential intelligence;* it is the closest to what we call intelligence in this chapter and what commonly is measured by intelligence tests. Todd's insightful and creative thinking is called *experiential intelligence* by Sternberg. And Art's street smarts and practical know-how is called *contextual intelligence* by Sternberg (figure 10.A).

In Sternberg's view of componential intelligence, the basic unit of intelligence is a *component,* simply defined as a basic unit of information processing. Sternberg believes that such components include those used to acquire or store information, to retain or retrieve information, to transfer information, to plan, to make decisions, and solve problems, and to carry out problem-solving strategies or translate thoughts into performance.

The second part of Sternberg's model focuses on experience. An intelligent individual has the ability to solve new problems quickly, but she also learns how to solve

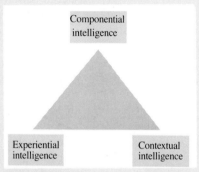

Figure 10.A
Sternberg's triarchic model of intelligence.

familiar problems in an automatic way so that her mind is free to handle problems that require insight and creativity.

The third part of the model involves practical knowledge—such as how to get out of trouble, how to replace a fuse, and how to get along with people. Sternberg calls this practical knowledge *tacit knowledge.* It includes all of the information about getting along in the world that is not taught in school. Sternberg believes that tacit knowledge is more important for success in life than explicit, or "book," knowledge. Once again, we see—in Sternberg's model—the effort to determine the nature of intelligence.

that the answer is both (Zembar & Naus, 1985). If so, the essential task becomes one of determining the ways that processing and knowledge interact in the course of intellectual development.

The modern information-processing approach does not argue that knowledge is unimportant. Rather, many information-processing psychologists believe that attention should be given to the knowledge base generated by intellectual processes. One information-processing approach to intelligence that recognizes the importance of both process and knowledge is R. J. Sternberg's (1986) model. To learn more about Sternberg's view of intelligence, turn to Perspective on Child Development 10.3.

The Use and Misuse of Intelligence Tests

Psychological tests are tools. Like all tools, their effectiveness depends on the knowledge, skill, and integrity of the user. A hammer can be used to build a beautiful kitchen cabinet or it can be used as a weapon of assault. Like a hammer, intelligence tests can be used for positive purposes or they can be badly abused. It is important for both the test constructor and the test examiner to be familiar with the current state of scientific knowledge about intelligence and intelligence tests (Anastasi, 1988).

Even though they have limitations, intelligence tests are among psychology's most widely used tools. To be effective, though, intelligence tests must be viewed realistically. They should not be thought of as a fixed, unchanging indicator of an individual's intelligence. They also should be used in conjunction with other information about the individual and not relied upon as the sole indicator of intelligence. For example, an intelligence test should not be used as the sole indicator of whether a child should be placed in a special education or gifted class. The child's developmental history, medical background, performance in school, social competencies, and family experiences should be taken into account too.

The single number provided by many IQ tests can easily lead to stereotypes and expectations about the individual. Many individuals do not know how to interpret the results of an intelligence test and sweeping generalizations about an individual too often are made on the basis of an IQ score. For example, imagine that you are a teacher in the teacher's lounge on the day after school has started in the fall. You mention a student—Johnny Jones—and a fellow teacher remarks that she had Johnny in class last year; she comments that he was a real dunce and points that his IQ is 78. You cannot help but remember this information and it may lead to thoughts that Johnny Jones is not very bright so it is useless to spend much time teaching him. In this way, IQ scores are misused and stereotypes are formed (Rosenthal & Jacobsen, 1968).

We also have a tendency in our culture to consider intelligence or a high IQ as the ultimate human value. It is important to keep in mind that our value as humans includes other matters—consideration of others, positive close relationships, and competence in social situations, for example. The verbal and problem-solving skills measured on traditional intelligence tests are only one part of human competence.

Despite their limitations, when used judiciously by a competent examiner, intelligence tests provide valuable information about individuals. There are not many alternatives to intelligence tests. Subjective judgments about individuals simply reintroduce the biases the tests were designed to eliminate.

The Extremes of Intelligence

The atypical child has always been of interest to developmentalists. Intellectual atypicality has intrigued many psychologists and drawn them to study the mentally retarded, the gifted, and the creative.

Mental Retardation

The most distinctive feature of mental retardation is inadequate intellectual functioning. Long before formal tests were introduced to assess intelligence, the mentally retarded were identified by a lack of age-appropriate skills in learning and caring for oneself. With the development of intelligence tests more emphasis was placed on IQ as an indicator of mental retardation. But it is not unusual to find two retarded individuals with the same low IQ, one of whom is married, employed, and involved in the community and the other requiring constant supervision in an institution. These differences in social competence led developmentalists to include deficits in adaptive behavior in their definition of mental retardation. The currently accepted definiton of **mental retardation** refers to an individual who has a low IQ, usually below 70 on a traditional intelligence test, and who has difficulty adapting to everyday life. About five million Americans fit this definition of mental retardation (Baumeiser, 1987; Robinson, 1987; Zigler, 1987).

There are different classifications of mental retardation. About 80 percent of the mentally retarded fall into the mild category, with IQs of 50 to 70. About 12 percent are classified as moderately retarded, with IQs of 35 to 49; these individuals can attain a second-grade level of skills and may be able to support themselves as adults through some type of labor. About 7 percent of the mentally retarded fall into the severe category, with IQs of 20 to 34; these individuals learn to talk and engage in very simple tasks, but they require extensive supervision. Only 1 percent of the mentally retarded are classified as profoundly retarded with IQs below 20; they are in constant need of supervision.

What causes retardation? The causes are divided into two categories: organic and cultural-familial. Individuals with **organic retardation** are retarded because of a genetic disorder or brain damage; *organic* refers to the tissues or organs of the body, so there is some physical damage that has taken place in organic retardation. Down's syndrome—a form of organic retardation—occurs when an extra chromosome is present, possibly influenced by the health of the female ovum or the male sperm (figure 10.5). Although those who suffer organic retardation are found across the spectrum of mental retardation IQ distribution, most have IQs between 0 and 50.

Individuals with **cultural-familial retardation** make up the majority of the mentally retarded population; they have no evidence of organic damage or brain dysfunction. Their IQs range from 50 to 70. Developmentalists seek to discover the cause of this type of retardation in the impoverished environments these individuals probably have experienced. Even with organic retardation, though, it is wise to think about the contributions of genetic-environment interaction. Parents with low IQs not only may be more likely to transmit genes for low intelligence to their offspring but also tend to provide them with a less enriched environment.

Giftedness

Conventional wisdom has identified some individuals in all cultures and historical periods as gifted because they have talents not evident in the majority of people. Despite this widespread recognition of the gifted, developmentalists have difficulty reaching a consensus on the precise definition and measurement of giftedness. Some experts view the gifted as the top end of a continuum of intelligence (Humphreys, 1985; Zigler & Farber, 1985). Some of these advocates view this ability as a unitary characteristic that is perhaps hereditary. Others see the gifted as individuals who express specific talents that have been nurtured environmentally (Wallach, 1985). A comprehensive definition of **gifted** is an individual with well-above-average intelligence (an IQ of 120 or more) and/or a superior talent for something. Most school systems emphasize intellectual superiority and academic aptitude when selecting children for special instruction; however, they rarely consider competence in the visual and performing arts (art, drama, dance), psychomotor abilities (tennis, golf, basketball), or other special aptitudes.

A classic study of the gifted was begun by Lewis Terman (1925) more than sixty years ago. Terman studied approximately 1,500 children whose Stanford-Binet IQs averaged 150. His goal was to follow these children through their adult lives—the study will not be complete until the year 2010. The accomplishments of the 1,500 children in Terman's study are remarkable. Of

Figure 10.5
What are the possible causes of this young girl's mental retardation?

"I'm a gifted child."
Drawing by Drucker; © 1981
The New Yorker Magazine, Inc.

the 800 males, 78 have obtained Ph.D.s (they include two past presidents of the American Psychological Association), 48 have earned M.D.s, and 85 have been granted law degrees. Nearly all of these figures are ten to thirty times greater than found among 800 men of the same age chosen randomly from the overall population. These findings challenge the commonly held belief that the intellectually gifted are somehow emotionally or socially maladjusted. This belief is based on striking instances of mental disturbances among the gifted. Sir Isaac Newton, Van Gogh, da Vinci, Socrates, and Poe all had emotional problems. But these are exceptions rather than the rule. No relation between giftedness and mental disturbance in general has been found. Recent studies support Terman's conclusion that—if anything—the gifted tend to be more mature and have fewer emotional problems than others (Janos & Robinson, 1985).

Individuals with exceptional talents as adults were interviewed about what they believe contributed to their giftedness in one investigation (Bloom, 1983). The 120 individuals had excelled in one of six fields—concert pianists and sculptors (arts), Olympic swimmers and tennis champions (psychomotor), and research mathematicians and research neurologists (cognitive). They said the development of their exceptional accomplishments required special environmental support, excellent teaching, and motivational encouragement. Each experienced years of special attention under the tutelage and supervision of a remarkable set of teachers and coaches. They also were given extensive support and encouragement from parents. All of these stars devoted exceptional time to practice and training, easily outdistancing the amount of time spent in all other activities combined.

Creativity

Most of us would like to be gifted *and* creative. Why was Thomas Edison able to invent so many things? Was he simply more intelligent than most individuals? Did he spend long hours toiling away in private? Somewhat surprisingly, when Edison was a young boy his teacher told him that he was too dumb to learn anything! Other examples of famous individuals whose creative genius went unnoticed when they were young include Walt Disney, who was fired from a newspaper job because he did not have any good ideas; Enrico Caruso, whose music teacher told him that his voice was terrible; and Winston Churchill, who failed one year of secondary school. Among the reasons such individuals are underestimated is the difficulty of defining and measuring creativity.

The prevailing belief of experts who study intelligence and creativity is that the two are not the same thing (Monroe, 1988; Wallach, 1985). One distinction is between **convergent thinking,** which produces one correct answer, and **divergent thinking,** which produces many different answers to the same question (Guilford, 1967). For example, this problem-solving task has one correct answer and requires convergent thinking: How many quarters will you get for sixty dimes? But this question has many possible answers and requires divergent thinking: What are some unique things that can be done with a paper clip? A degree of creativity is needed to answer this question. Other examples of divergent thinking are generated by the following: Name words that belong to a particular class. For example, name as many objects as you can that weigh

1. *Sketches:* Add just enough detail to the circle below to make a recognizable object (two examples of acceptable responses are shown).

2. *Word fluency:* Write as many words as you can think of with the first and last letters R_____M ("rim" would be one).

3. *Name grouping:* Classify the following six names in as many different ways as you can (a person might group 1, 3 and 4 together because each has two syllables).
   1. GERTRUDE 2. BILL
   3. ALEX   4. CARRIE
   5. BELLE   6. DON

4. *Making objects:* Using two or more of the forms shown below, make a face. Now make a lamp (examples of good responses are shown).

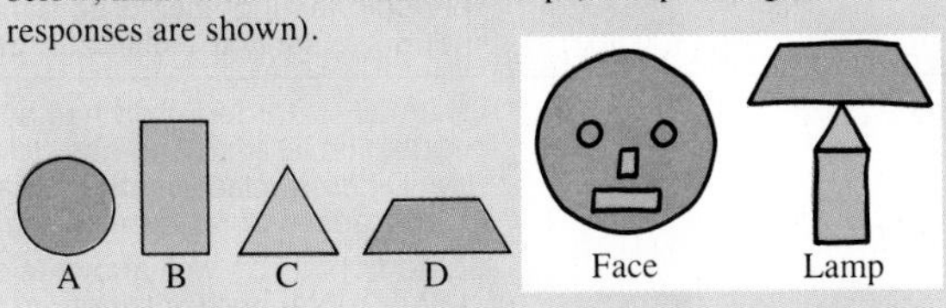

A   B   C   D   Face   Lamp

Figure 10.6
Creativity sample items from Guilford's (1967) Divergent Productions Tests.

less than one pound. Even when you are not asked to, do you give divergent answers? For example, if you are asked what things can be done with a paper clip do you spontaneously generate different categories of use for the paper clip? For more examples of items on tests of creativity turn to figure 10.6.

Creativity is the ability to think about something in a novel way and to come up with unique solutions to problems. When individuals in the arts and sciences who fit this description are asked what enables them to produce their creative works, they say that they generate large amounts of associative content when solving problems and that they have the freedom to entertain a wide range of possible solutions in a playful manner (Wallach & Kogan, 1965).

How strongly is creativity related to intelligence? A certain level of intelligence seems to be required to be creative in most fields, but many highly intelligent individuals (as measured by IQ tests) are not very creative.

Since our last review we have discussed a number of controversies and issues in intelligence and described the extremes of intelligence. A summary of these ideas is presented in Concept Table 10.2.

Controversies and Issues in Intelligence and Extremes of Intelligence

Concept	Processes/Related Ideas	Characteristics/Description
Controversies and issues in intelligence	Social class, racial, and ethnic differences	These differences exist, but the evidence suggests they are not genetically based. Special attention has been given to black-white differences. In recent decades, as blacks have experienced more opportunities, this gap has been diminishing.
	The heredity-environment controversy	Debate flourishes about heredity's and environment's contributions to intelligence. We reviewed this controversy in chapter 2. Institutionalization and early prevention studies support the importance of environmental influences on intelligence.
	Are intelligence tests culturally biased?	Early tests favored middle-class, white, urban children. Current tests try to reduce such bias. Culture-fair tests are an alternative to traditional tests; most psychologists believe they cannot replace the traditional tests.
	Knowledge versus process in intelligence	The mechanisms of intelligence and its development are both those of changing information-processing abilities and changing expertise and knowledge. Sternberg's triarchic model includes an emphasis on both information-processing and knowledge. He believes intelligence comes in three forms: componential, experiential, and contextual.
	The use and misuse of intelligence tests	Despite limitations, when used by a judicious examiner, tests are valuable tools for determining individual differences in children's intelligence. The tests should be used with other information about the child. IQ scores can produce unfortunate stereotypes and expectations. Ability tests can help divide children into homogeneous groups. However, periodic testing should be done. Intelligence or a high IQ is not necessarily the ultimate human value.
The extremes of intelligence	Mental retardation	A mentally retarded child has a low IQ, usually below 70 on a traditional IQ test, and has difficulty adapting to everyday life. Different classifications of retardation exist. The two main causes of retardation are organic and cultural-familial.
	Giftedness and creativity	A gifted child has well-above-average intelligence (an IQ of 120 or more) and/or superior talent for something. Creativity is the ability to think about something in a novel or unusual way and to come up with unique solutions to problems.

Summary

I. What Is Intelligence?

Intelligence is an abstract concept that is measured indirectly; psychologists rely on intelligence tests to estimate intellectual processes. Verbal ability and problem-solving skills are described by both experts and lay people as components of intelligence. Some psychologists believe that the definition of intelligence should include the ability to learn and adapt to experiences in everyday life. Extensive effort has been given to assessing individual differences in intelligence. This field is called psychometrics.

II. How Tests Are Constructed and Evaluated

Three important aspects of test construction are reliability, validity, and standardization. Reliability refers to how consistently an individual performs on a test. Three measures of a test's reliability are test-retest, alternate forms, and split-half. Validity is the extent to which a test measures what it is intended to measure. Two main measures of validity are content validity and criterion validity. Standardization focuses on the development of uniform procedures for administering and scoring a test and norms.

III. The Measurement and Nature of Children's Intelligence

Alfred Binet developed the first intelligence test, known as the 1905 Scale. He developed the concept of mental age while William Stern developed the concept of IQ. The Binet has been standardized and revised a number of times. The many revisions are called the Stanford-Binet tests. The test approximates a normal distribution. The current test is given to individuals from the age of two through adulthood. Besides the Binet, the Wechsler scales are the most widely used intelligence tests. They include the WAIS-R, the WISC-R, and the WPPSI. These tests provide an overall IQ, verbal and performance IQ, and information about subtests. Psychologists debate whether intelligence is a general ability or a number of specific abilities. Spearman's two-factor theory and Thurstone's multiple-factor theory state that a number of specific factors are involved; so does Gardner's theory. Current thinking suggests that intelligence is both a set of specific abilities and a general ability.

IV. Infant Intelligence and the Stability of Intelligence
Many standardized intelligence tests do not assess infant intelligence. Intelligence tests designed to measure infant intelligence are often referred to as developmental scales, the most widely used being the Bayley scales. While intelligence is more stable across the childhood years than most attributes, many children's scores on intelligence tests fluctuate widely.

V. Social Class, Racial, and Ethnic Differences
These differences exist, but the evidence does not favor a genetic interpretation of the differences. Special attention has been given to black-white differences. In recent decades, as blacks have experienced more opportunities, this gap has been diminishing.

VI. The Heredity-Environment Controversy
Debate flourishes about heredity's and environment's contribution to intelligence. We reviewed this controversy in chapter 2. Institutionalization and early prevention studies support the importance of environmental influences on intelligence.

VII. Are Intelligence Tests Culturally Biased?
Early tests favored middle-class, white, urban children. Current tests try to reduce such bias. Culture-fair tests are an alternative to traditional tests; most psychologists believe they cannot replace the traditional tests.

VIII. Knowledge versus Process
The mechanisms of intelligence and its development are both those of changing information-processing abilities and changing expertise and knowledge. Sternberg's triarchic model includes an emphasis on both information processing and knowledge. He believes intelligence comes in three forms: componential, experiential, and contextual.

IX. The Use and Misuse of Intelligence Tests
Despite limitations, when used by a judicious examiner, tests are valuable tools for determining individual differences in children's intelligence. The tests should be used in conjunction with other information about the child. IQ scores can produce unfortunate stereotypes and expectations. Ability tests can help divide children into homogeneous groups. However, periodic testing should be done. Intelligence or a high IQ is not necessarily the ultimate human value.

X. The Extremes of Intelligence
A mentally retarded child has a low IQ, usually below 70 on a traditional IQ test, and has difficulty adapting to everyday life. Different classifications of retardation exist. The two main causes of retardation are organic and cultural-familial. A gifted child has well-above-average intelligence (an IQ of 120 or above) and/or a superior talent for something. Creativity is the ability to think about something in a novel and unusual way and to come up with unique solutions to problems.

Key Terms

individual differences 249
psychometrics 249
reliability 249
test-retest reliability 249
split-half reliability 250
validity 250
content validity 250
criterion validity 250
concurrent validity 250
predictive validity 250
standardization 251
norms 251
intelligence 251
mental age (MA) 252
intelligence quotient (IQ) 252
normal distribution 252

Wechsler scales 253
two-factor theory 255
multiple-factor theory of intelligence 256
developmental scales 258
culture-fair tests 265
structure-process dilemma 266
triarchic theory of intelligence 267
mental retardation 268
organic retardation 269
cultural-familial retardation 269
gifted 269
convergent thinking 270
divergent thinking 270
creativity 271

Suggested Readings

Anastasi, A. (1988). *Psychological testing* (6th ed.). New York: Macmillan.
This widely used text on psychological testing provides extensive information about test construction, test evaluation, and the nature of intelligence testing.

Fancher, R. E. (1985). *The intelligence men: Makers of the IQ controversy.* New York: Norton.
Fancher's book includes an extensive portrayal of the history of intelligence testing—many insights and detailed descriptions of the lives of the intelligence test makers are provided.

Horowitz, F. D., & O'Brien, M. (Eds.). (1985). *The gifted and the talented.* Washington, D.C.: The American Psychological Association.
This volume pulls together what we currently know about the gifted and the talented. Experts have contributed chapters on the nature of the gifted and the diverse topics involved.

Kail, R., & Pellegrino, J. W. (1985). *Human intelligence.* New York: W. H. Freeman.
This book brings together a number of different perspectives on human intelligence; it includes separate chapters on the psychometric and information-processing approaches.

Sattler, J. M. (1982). *Assessment of children's intelligence and special abilities.* Boston: Allyn & Bacon.
Extensive information is provided about the measurement of children's intelligence, both for normal children and those from special populations, such as the mentally retarded.

Social and Personality Development

Children are on a different plane.
They belong to a generation and
a way of feeling properly their own.

George Santayana

CHAPTER

11

Perspectives on Socialization

Our most basic common link is that we all inhabit this planet. We all breathe the same air. We all cherish our children's future.

John F. Kennedy, address, The American University, 1963

The year is 1940 and you are living in a rural village in India. You are walking in an isolated area and feeling very peaceful. Then you hear several howling sounds. You look behind the bushes and see two strange looking animals, or are they children? Their eyes glare like blue lights in the darkened area of the bushes.

One of the girls is about one and a half years old, the other about eight years old. They are the "wolf girls," so-called because it appears that they were reared by wolves. A missionary had heard reports of small, naked children running around on all fours and decided to go and observe the wolf children. In *Wolf Children and Feral Men* (*feral* means wild), the missionary Singh told the story of the two girls who had been reared by wolves. The younger girl learned to walk upright, but she died about a year after she was taken to an orphanage. The older girl never learned to walk upright, although she eventually stopped howling like a wolf and learned to use about fifty words. She died after eight years at the orphanage.

Probably the most famous case of social isolation involves the Wild Boy of Aveyron (Lane, 1976). In 1799 a nude boy was observed running through the woods in France. The boy was eventually captured when he was believed to be about eleven years old. It was thought he had lived in the woods with no human contact for at least six years. Like the wolf girls, he seemed to be more animal than person. Experts examined the boy and proclaimed he was an incurable idiot. However, a young French physician, Jean Itard, believed differently, thinking that the bizarre behavior of the boy was due to his social isolation. Itard named the boy Victor and over a period of five years tried to socialize him.

When Victor was first found he walked more like an animal than a human. When alone, he sat and rocked back and forth. He was unable to focus his eyes on anything for more than a few seconds, and he made no attempt to communicate. After five years with Itard, Victor had not changed very much. He did learn to eat with silverware and sleep in a bed, to wear clothes and focus his eyes, but he never learned to communicate effectively. His social development was very impoverished. Though he seemed to develop some affection for Itard and the woman who cared for him, he never learned to interact with others.

Psychologists have long wondered what people would be like if they were brought up in isolation from other people from the time they were born. Though circumstances such as those experienced by the wolf girls and Victor provide some indication of the outcome, to truly find the answers we would have to randomly assign some children to live in isolation from other people for a number of years and other children to live a "normal" life with parents or caregivers. Of course, we cannot ethically do such a thing, so we try to get

Social and Personality Development

some sense of the importance of social experiences through such naturally occurring situations as those of the wolf girls and Victor, as well as the modern-day socially isolated child, Genie, about whose impoverished language and social development you read in chapter 9.

The experiences of these children provide information about the importance of social conditions in children's development. In impoverished social circumstances, the wolf girls, Victor, and Genie were able to develop some human competencies, but their desolate early experiences seemed to have lasting effects on their development. In this chapter we explore five perspectives on children's social development, perspectives that help us to understand how our social experiences as we are growing determine who we are and what we are all about as people. These five perspectives are the psychoanalytic, the behavioral and social learning, the cognitive, the biological, and the ecological perspectives, each of which we discuss in turn.

The diversity of perspectives makes understanding children's development a challenging undertaking. Just when you think one perspective has the correct explanation of children's development, another perspective crops up and makes you rethink your earlier conclusion. To keep from getting frustrated, remember that children's development is complex and multifaceted, and no single perspective has been able to account for all aspects of children's development. Each perspective has contributed an important piece to the child development puzzle. While the perspectives sometimes disagree about certain aspects of children's development, much of their information is *complementary* rather than contradictory. Together they let us see the total landscape of children's social development in all its richness.

The Psychoanalytic Perspective

For psychoanalytic theorists, children's development is primarily unconscious, beyond awareness, and made up of thought structures heavily colored by emotion. Psychoanalytic theorists believe that children's behavior is merely a surface characteristic and that to truly understand it we have to look at the symbolic meanings of their behaviors and the deep inner workings of their minds. Psychoanalytic theorists also stress that early experiences with parents and underlying sexual tension shape children's development. These characteristics are highlighted in the main psychoanalytic perspective, that of Sigmund Freud.

Freud's Theory

Loved and hated, respected and despised, for some the master, for others misdirected—Sigmund Freud, whether right or wrong in his views, has been one of the most influential thinkers of the twentieth century. Freud was a medical doctor who specialized in neurology. He developed his ideas about psychoanalytic theory from his work with patients with mental problems. He was born in 1856 in Austria and he died in London at the age of eighty-three. Most of his years were spent in Vienna, though he left the city near the end of his career because of the Nazis' anti-Semitism.

Sigmund Freud (1856–1939).

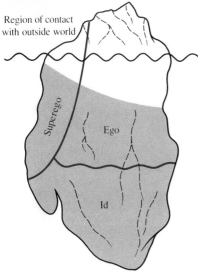

Region of contact with outside world

Superego

Ego

Id

Figure 11.1
Conscious and unconscious processes. Freud believed that most of the important personality processes occurred below the level of conscious awareness. In examining children's conscious thoughts and their behaviors, we can see some reflections of the ego and the superego. But, whereas the ego and superego are partly conscious and partly unconscious, the primitive id is the unconscious, totally submerged part of the "iceberg."

The Structure of Personality

Freud (1917) believed that personality had three structures: the id, the ego, and the superego. One way to understand the three structures is to consider them as three rulers of a country (Singer, 1984). The id is king or queen, the ego is prime minister, and the superego is high priest. The id is an absolute monarch, owed complete obedience; it is spoiled, willful, and self-centered. The id wants what it wants right now, not later. The ego as prime minister has the job of getting things done right; it is tuned into reality and is responsive to society's demands. The superego as high priest is concerned with right and wrong; the id may be greedy and needs to be told that nobler purposes should be pursued.

The **id** is the reservoir of psychic energy and instincts that perpetually press us to satisfy our basic needs—food, sex, and avoidance of pain, for example. In Freud's view, the id is completely unconscious, beyond our awareness; it has no contact with reality. The id works according to the **pleasure principle,** that is, it *always* seeks pleasure and avoids pain. Freud believed the id is the only part of personality present at birth; even in adults the id acts like a selfish infant, demanding immediate gratification.

It would be a dangerous and scary world if our personalities were all id. As the young child develops, he learns that he cannot eat twenty-six popsicles; sometimes he is not even allowed to eat one. He also learns that he has to use the toilet instead of his diaper. As the child experiences the demands and constraints of reality, a new structure of personality is being formed—the **ego.** The ego abides by the **reality principle;** it tries to bring the individual pleasure within the boundaries of reality. Few of us are cold-blooded killers or wild wheeler-dealers. We take into account obstacles to our satisfaction that exist in our world. We recognize that our sexual and aggressive impulses cannot go unrestrained. The ego helps us to test reality—to see how far we can go without getting into trouble and hurting ourselves.

While the id is completely unconscious, the ego is partly conscious. It houses our higher mental functions—reasoning, problem solving, and decision making, for example. For this reason, the ego is referred to as the executive branch of personality; like an executive in a company, it makes the rational decisions that help the company succeed.

The id and the ego have no morality. They do not take into account whether something is right or wrong. This is left to the third structure of personality—the **superego,** which is referred to as the moral branch of personality. Think of the superego as what we often refer to as our "conscience." Like the id, the superego does not consider reality; it doesn't deal with what is realistic, only with whether the id's sexual and aggressive impulses can be satisfied in moral terms. You probably are beginning to sense that both the id and the superego make life rough for the ego. Your ego might say, "I only will have sex occasionally and be sure to take the proper precautions because I don't want the intrusion of a child in the development of my career." But your id is saying, "I want to be satisfied; sex is pleasurable." And your superego is at work too, saying, "I feel guilty about having sex."

Freud considered personality to be like an iceberg; most of personality exists below our level of awareness, just as the massive part of the iceberg is beneath the surface of the water (figure 11.1).

Social and Personality Development

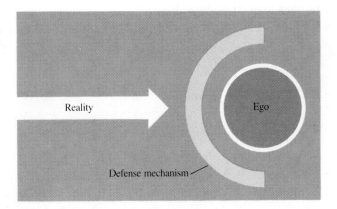

Figure 11.2
The function of an ego defense mechanism. Like a shield, the defense mechanism protects the ego from the harsher aspects of reality.

Defense Mechanisms

How does the ego resolve the conflict between its demands for reality, the wishes of the id, and the constraints of the superego? In Freud's view, the conflicting demands of the personality structures produce anxiety. For example, when the ego blocks the pleasurable pursuits of the id an inner anxiety is felt. This diffuse, distressed state develops when the ego senses that the id is going to cause some harm for the individual. The anxiety alerts the ego to resolve the conflict by means of **defense mechanisms,** which protect the ego and reduce the anxiety produced by the conflict (figure 11.2).

Freud thought that the most powerful and pervasive defense mechanism is **repression;** it works to push unacceptable id impulses out of our awareness and back into our unconscious mind. Repression is the foundation from which all other defense mechanisms work; the goal of every defense mechanism is to *repress* or push threatening impulses out of awareness. Freud said that our early childhood experiences, many of which he believed were sexually laden, are too threatening and conflictual for us to deal with consciously. We reduce the anxiety of this conflict through the defense mechanism of repression.

Among the other defense mechanisms we use to protect the ego and reduce anxiety are sublimation, reaction formation, and regression. **Sublimation** occurs when a socially useful course of action replaces a distasteful one. For example, an individual with strong sexual urges may turn them into socially approved behavior by becoming an artist who paints nudes. **Reaction formation** occurs when we express an unacceptable impulse by transforming it into its opposite. For example, an individual who is attracted to the brutality of war becomes a peace activist. Or an individual who fears his sexual urges becomes a religious zealot. **Regression** occurs when an individual behaves in a way that characterized a previous developmental level. When anxiety becomes too great for us, we revert to an early behavior that gave us pleasure. For example, a woman may run home to her mother every time she and her husband have a big argument.

Two final points about defense mechanisms need to be understood. First, they are unconscious. We are not aware we are using them to protect our ego. Second, when used in moderation or on a temporary basis, defense mechanisms are not necessarily unhealthy. For example, the defense mechanism of denial can help an individual cope with impending death. For the most part, though, we should not let defense mechanisms dominate our behavior and prevent us from facing reality's demands.

(a)

(b)

(c)

(d)

(e)

According to Freud, each of us goes through five stages of psychosexual development: In the oral stage (a), pleasure centers around the mouth. In the anal stage (b), pleasure focuses on the anus—the nature of toilet training is important here. In the phallic stage (c), pleasure involves the genitals—the opposite-sex parent becomes a love object here. In the latency stage (d), the child represses sexual urges—same-sex friendship is prominent. In the genital stage (e), sexual reawakening takes place—the source of pleasure becomes someone outside the family.

The Development of Personality

As Freud listened to, probed, and analyzed his patients, he became convinced that their problems were the result of experiences early in life. Freud believed that we go through five stages of psychosexual development and that at each stage of development we experience pleasure in one part of the body more than others. He called these body parts **erogenous zones** because of their pleasure-giving qualities.

Freud thought that our adult personality was determined by the way conflicts between these early sources of pleasure—the mouth, the anus, and then the genitals—and the demands of reality were resolved. When these conflicts are not resolved, the individual may become fixated at a particular stage of development. **Fixation** is closely linked with the defense mechanism of

Social and Personality Development

Doonesbury

G. B. TRUDEAU

regression. Fixation occurs when an individual's needs are under- or overgratified. For example, a parent may wean a child too early, be too strict in toilet training the child, punish the child for masturbation, or smother the child with warmth. We will return to the idea of fixation and how it may show up in an adult's personality, but first we need to learn more about the early stages of personality development.

During the first twelve to eighteen months of life, the activities that bring the greatest amount of pleasure center around the mouth. In the **oral stage** of development chewing, sucking, and biting are chief pleasure sources. These actions reduce the infant's tension.

The period from about one and a half years to three years of life is called the **anal stage** because the child's greatest pleasure involves the anus, or the eliminative functions associated with it. In Freud's view, the exercise of the anal muscles reduces tension.

The **phallic stage** of development occurs approximately between the ages of three and six; its name comes from the word *phallus,* a label for penis. During the phallic stage, pleasure focuses on the genitals as the child discovers that self-manipulation is enjoyable.

In Freud's view, the phallic stage has special importance because it is during this period that the **Oedipus complex** appears. This name comes from Greek mythology, in which Oedipus, the son of the King of Thebes, unwittingly killed his father and married his mother. In the Oedipus complex, the

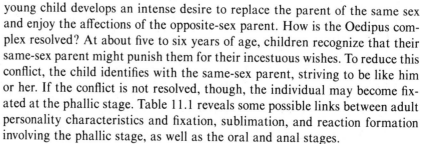

Table 11.1
Possible Links between Adult Personality Characteristics and Fixation at the Oral, Anal, and Phallic Stages

Stage	Adult extensions	Sublimations	Reaction formations
Oral	Smoking, eating, kissing, oral hygiene, drinking, chewing gum	Seeking knowledge, humor, wit, sarcasm, being a food or wine expert.	Speech purist, food faddist, prohibitionist, dislike of milk
Anal	Notable interest in one's bowel movements, love of bathroom humor, extreme messiness	Interest in painting or sculpture, being overly giving, great interest in statistics	Extreme disgust with feces, fear of dirt, prudishness, irritability
Phallic	Heavy reliance on masturbation, flirtatiousness, expressions of virility	Interest in poetry, love of life, interest in acting, striving for success	Puritanical attitude toward sex, excessive modesty

From *Personality* by E. J. Phares. Copyright © 1984 by Scott, Foresman and Company. Reprinted by permission.

young child develops an intense desire to replace the parent of the same sex and enjoy the affections of the opposite-sex parent. How is the Oedipus complex resolved? At about five to six years of age, children recognize that their same-sex parent might punish them for their incestuous wishes. To reduce this conflict, the child identifies with the same-sex parent, striving to be like him or her. If the conflict is not resolved, though, the individual may become fixated at the phallic stage. Table 11.1 reveals some possible links between adult personality characteristics and fixation, sublimation, and reaction formation involving the phallic stage, as well as the oral and anal stages.

In the **latency stage,** occurring between approximately six years of age and puberty, the child represses all interest in sexual urges, showing more interest in developing intellectual and social skills. This activity channels much of the child's energy into emotionally safe areas and aids the child in forgetting the highly stressful conflicts of the phallic stage.

The **genital stage,** which occurs from puberty on, is a time of sexual reawakening; the source of sexual pleasure now becomes someone outside of the family. Freud believed that unresolved conflicts with parents reemerged during adolescence. When resolved, the individual was capable of developing a mature love relationship and functioning independently as an adult. More about adolescent adjustment appears in Perspective on Child Development 11.1.

Because Freud explored so many new and uncharted regions of personality and development, it is not surprising that many individuals thought his views needed to be replaced or revised. One of these individuals, whose theory has become one of the most prominent perspectives on life-span development, was Erik Erikson.

Erik Erikson.

Erikson's Theory

Erik Erikson spent his childhood and adolescence in Europe. After working as a young adult under Freud's direction, Erikson came to the United States in 1933. He became a United States citizen and taught at Harvard University.

Erikson recognized Freud's contributions but he believed Freud misjudged some important dimensions of human development. For one, Erikson

Social and Personality Development

The Role of Defense Mechanisms in Adolescent Adjustment

For Peter Blos (1962, 1985), one of the most well-accepted contemporary psychoanalytic theorists who studies adolescents, regression during adolescence is not defensive at all but rather an integral part of puberty. Such regression, according to Blos, is inevitable and universal. The nature of this regression may vary from one adolescent to the next. It may involve childhood autonomy, compliance, and cleanliness, or it may involve a sudden return to the passiveness that characterized the adolescent's behavior during infancy or early childhood. Blos believes that intrafamilial struggles during adolescence reflect the presence of unresolved conflicts from childhood.

An excellent example of how the psychoanalytic theorist works in tying together adolescent feelings with childhood experiences rests in the work of Joseph Adelson and Margery Doehrman (1980). When their patient, John, was sixteen he entered a group therapy session with other adolescents. At that time he was recovering from severe depression following the break-off of a serious relationship with a girlfriend. The girl's mother actually referred John to the clinic, sensing that John's depression was severe, just as she had earlier detected that his dependency on her daughter was acute. John was a handsome, intelligent, articulate adolescent and a leader at school, hardly the type of person you would think might be deeply and severely depressed.

After a series of sessions with John it became apparent that he kept most girls at a distance, especially when they seemed to want to get seriously involved or to "mother" him. On the other hand, he was attracted to girls who were either aloof or tomboyish. It gradually became clear that John's relationships with girls were characterized by a wish to reestablish a union with his mother and that he had an intense fear of that wish. He was attracted to girls who were standoffish, but once he established a relationship with one of them, he would sink into an uncontrollable dependency on her, to the point of being enthralled by the dependency.

To some degree, then, John's attachments to girls represented a wish to become reunited with his mother. What was John's relationship with his mother like in adolescence? He was often abusive toward her; he complained that she nagged at him all the time; but in truth he was frightened by his regressive feelings toward her, according to Adelson. The regressive feelings came out clearly in group therapy when his intelligent participation would be replaced by sarcasm and then scorn whenever he seemed to be drawn to the "maternal" females in the group. This was especially true with the woman therapist, who was seen as the group's "mother."

Although some psychoanalytic writers, like Blos, consider regression a normal part of adolescent development, for individuals like John the reappearance of unresolved conflicts from early childhood requires therapy. For most individuals, however, the conflicts are not so serious that therapy is warranted. Thus, the intensity and persistence of the regression determine whether it is a healthy or unhealthy part of adolescent development.

Anna Freud (1958, 1966) has developed the idea that defense mechanisms are the key to understanding adolescent adjustment. She believes that the problems of adolescence are not to be unlocked by understanding the id, or instinctual forces, but instead are to be discovered in the existence of "love objects." She argues that the attachment to these love objects, usually parents, is carried forward from the infant years and merely toned down or inhibited during the latency years. During adolescence, these urges may be reawakened, or worse, newly acquired adolescent urges may combine with the urges that developed in early childhood.

Anna Freud goes on to describe how adolescent defense mechanisms are used to ward off these infantile intrusions. Youth may withdraw from their attachment and identification with their parents and suddenly transfer their love to others—to parent substitutes, to leaders who represent ideals, or to peers. Or, rather than transferring the attachment to someone else, adolescents may reverse their feelings toward the attachment figure—replacing love with hate or dependence with rebellion. Finally, the instinctual fears may even generate unhealthy defense solutions. For example, the adolescent may withdraw within himself, which could lead to grandiose ideas of triumph or persecution; or regression could occur. Thus, from Anna Freud's perspective, a number of defense mechanisms are essential to the adolescent's handling of conflicts.

Erik Erikson's theory stresses that the human life cycle consists of eight stages: (a) trust versus mistrust, (b) autonomy versus shame, doubt, (c) initiative versus guilt, (d) industry versus inferiority, (e) identity versus identity confusion, (f) intimacy versus isolation, (g) generativity versus stagnation, and (h) integrity versus despair.

(1950, 1968) says that Freud placed too much emphasis on the sexual basis of development. Erikson thinks that psychosocial development holds the key to understanding life-span development. For another, Erikson says that Freud was wrong in thinking that developmental change does not occur in adulthood. And for yet another, Erikson says that humans have the potential to solve their conflicts and anxieties as they develop, painting a more optimistic picture of development than Freud's pessimistic view of the id's dominance.

For Erikson, the **epigenetic principle** guides our development through the life cycle. This principle states that anything that grows has a ground plan, out of which the parts arise, each having a special time of ascendency, until all of the parts have arisen to form a functioning whole.

In Erikson's theory, eight stages of development unfold as we go through the life cycle. He called these *psychosocial* stages (in contrast to Freud's *psychosexual* stages). The eight stages are shown in figure 11.3. Each stage consists of a unique developmental task that confronts the individual with a crisis that must be faced. For Erikson, the crisis is not a catastrophe, but a turning point of increased vulnerability and enhanced potential. The more the individual resolves the crises successfully the healthier development will be.

Social and Personality Development

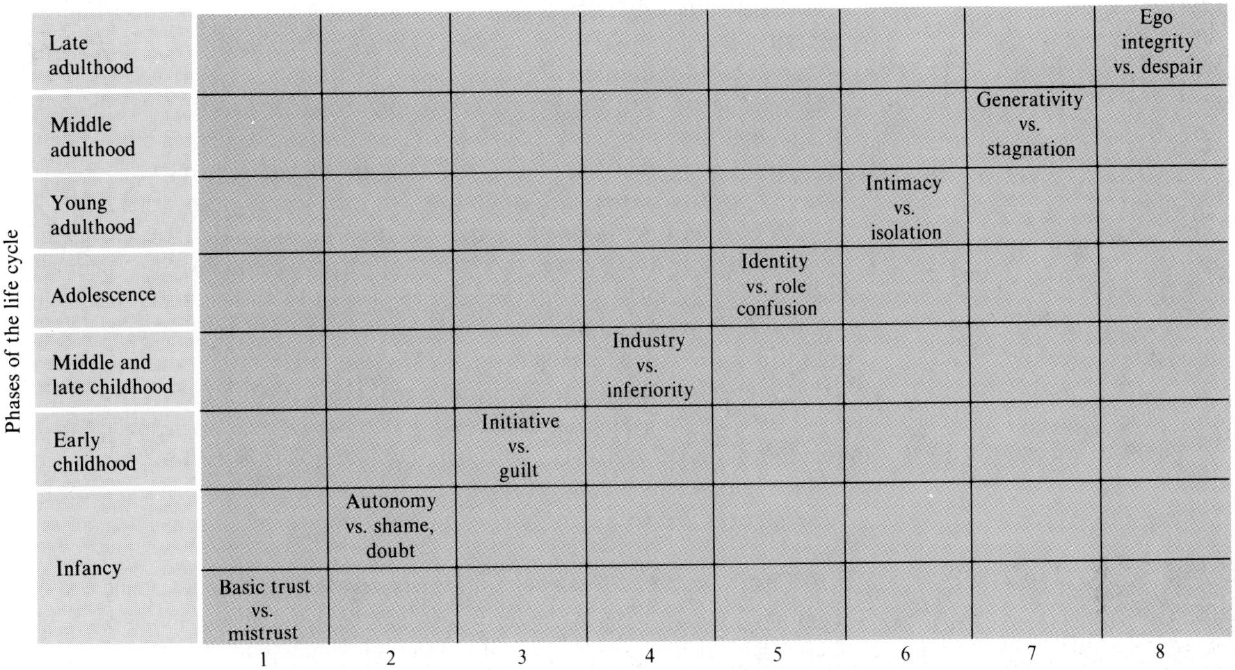

Phases of the life cycle	1	2	3	4	5	6	7	8
Late adulthood								Ego integrity vs. despair
Middle adulthood							Generativity vs. stagnation	
Young adulthood						Intimacy vs. isolation		
Adolescence					Identity vs. role confusion			
Middle and late childhood				Industry vs. inferiority				
Early childhood			Initiative vs. guilt					
Infancy		Autonomy vs. shame, doubt						
Infancy	Basic trust vs. mistrust							

Figure 11.3
Erikson's eight stages of life-span development.

The first stage, **trust versus mistrust,** corresponds to the oral stage in Freud's theory. An infant depends almost exclusively on parents, especially the mother, for food, sustenance, and comfort. Parents are the primary representative of society to the child. If parents discharge their infant-related duties with warmth, regularity, and affection, the infant will develop a feeling of trust toward the world, a trust that someone will always be around to care for one's needs. Alternatively, a sense of mistrust develops if parents fail to provide for the infant's needs in their role as caregivers.

The second stage, **autonomy versus shame and doubt,** corresponds to Freud's anal stage. The infant begins to gain control over eliminative functions and motor abilities. At this point, children show a strong push for exploring their worlds and asserting their wills. Parents who are encouraging and patient allow the child to develop a sense of autonomy, but parents who are highly restrictive and impatient promote a sense of shame and doubt.

The third stage, **initiative versus guilt,** corresponds to Freud's phallic stage and the preschool years. The child's motor abilities continue to expand and mental abilities also become more expansive and imaginative. Parents who allow the child to continue to explore the world's unknowns and encourage symbolic thought and fantasy play promote initiative in their child. Restrictive, punitive parents promote guilt and a passive recipience of whatever the environment brings.

The fourth stage, **industry versus inferiority,** corresponds to Freud's latency stage and the elementary school years. At this time, the child becomes interested in how things work and how they are made. Achievement becomes a more salient part of the child's life. If parents and teachers make work and achievement an exciting and rewarding effort, the child develops a sense of industry. If not, the child develops a sense of inferiority.

The fifth stage, **identity versus identity confusion,** corresponds to the adolescent years. At this time, individuals are faced with finding out who they are, what they are all about, and where they are headed in life. Adolescents are confronted with many new roles and adult statuses—vocational and romantic, for example. Parents need to allow the adolescent to explore many different roles and different paths within a particular role. If the adolescent explores such roles in a healthy manner and arrives at a positive path to follow in life, then a positive identity will be achieved. If an identity is pushed on the adolescent by parents, if the adolescent does not adequately explore many roles, and if a positive future path is not defined, then identity confusion reigns.

The sixth stage, **intimacy versus isolation,** corresponds to the early adulthood years. Early adulthood brings a stronger commitment to an occupation and the opportunity to form intimate relationships with others. Erikson described intimacy as finding oneself yet losing oneself in another. If the young adult forms healthy friendships and an intimate close relationship with another individual, intimacy will be achieved; if not, then isolation will result.

The seventh stage, **generativity versus stagnation,** corresponds to the middle adulthood years. A chief concern of adults is to assist the younger generation in developing and leading useful lives—this is what Erikson meant by *generativity.* The feeling of having done nothing to help the next generation is *stagnation.*

The eighth and final stage, **integrity versus despair,** corresponds to late adulthood. In the later years of life, we look back and evaluate what we have done with our lives. Through many different routes the older individual may have developed a positive outlook in each of the previous stages of development. If so, the retrospective glances reveal a picture of a life well spent, and the individual feels a sense of satisfaction—integrity is achieved. If the older adult resolved one or more of the earlier stages negatively, the retrospective glances may yield doubt or gloom—the despair Erikson talks about.

Erikson does not believe the proper solution to a stage crisis is always completely positive in nature. Some exposure or commitment to the negative end of the individual's bipolar conflict is sometimes inevitable—you cannot trust all people under all circumstances and survive, for example. Nonetheless, in the healthy solution to a stage crisis, the positive resolution dominates.

Evaluating the Psychoanalytic Perspective

While psychoanalytic theories have become heterogeneous, nonetheless, they share some core principles. Our development is determined not only by current experiences but also by those from early in our life. The principles that early experiences are important determinants of personality and that we can better understand personality by examining it developmentally have withstood the test of time. The belief that environmental experiences are mentally transformed and represented in the mind likewise continues to receive considerable attention. Psychoanalytic theorists forced psychologists to recognize that the mind is not all consciousness; our minds have an unconscious portion that influences our behavior. Psychoanalytic theorists' emphasis on the importance of conflict and anxiety requires us to consider the dark side of our existence, not just its bright side. Adjustment is not always easy, and the child's inner world often conflicts with the outer demands of reality.

However, the main concepts of psychoanalytic theories have been difficult to test. Inference and interpretation are required to determine whether psychoanalytic ideas are accurate. Researchers have not successfully investigated such key concepts as represssion in the laboratory. Much of the data used to support psychoanalytic theories come from patients' reconstruction of the past, often the distant past, and are of doubtful accuracy. Other data come from clinicians' subjective evaluations of clients; in such cases it is easy for the clinician to see what she expects because of the theory she holds. Some psychologists object that Freud overemphasized sexuality and the unconscious mind. The psychoanalytic theories also provide a model of the child that is too negative and pessimistic. Children are not born into the world with only a bundle of sexual and aggressive impulses. Their compliance with the external demands of reality does not always conflict with their biological needs.

The Behavioral and Social Learning Perspective

Fifteen-year-old Tom is going steady with fourteen-year-old Ann. Both have warm, friendly personalities and they enjoy being together. Psychoanalytic theorists would say that their warm, friendly personalities are derived from long-standing relationships with their parents, especially their early childhood experiences. They also would argue that the reason for their attraction is unconscious. They are unaware of how their biological heritage and early life experiences have been carried forward to influence their personalities in adolescence.

Psychologists from the behavioral and social learning perspective would observe Tom and Ann and see something quite different. They would examine their experiences, especially their most recent ones, to understand the reason for their attraction. Tom would be described as rewarding Ann's behavior, and vice versa, for example. No reference would be made to unconscious thoughts, the Oedipus complex, defense mechanisms, and so on.

Behaviorists believe we should examine only what can be directly observed and measured. At approximately the same time Freud was interpreting his patients' unconscious minds through early childhood experiences, behaviorists such as Ivan Pavlov and John B. Watson were conducting detailed observations of behavior in controlled laboratory circumstances. Out of the behavioral tradition grew the belief that children's development is observable behavior, learned through experience with the environment. The two versions of the behavioral approach that are prominent today are the view of B. F. Skinner and social learning theory. These views were touched on in our discussion of learning in chapter 6—here we describe their importance for understanding the child's socialization.

Skinner's Behaviorism

Skinner did not need the mind, conscious or unconscious, to explain development. For him, development was the child's behavior. For example, observations of Sam reveal that his behavior is shy, achievement oriented, and caring. Why is Sam's behavior this way? For Skinner, rewards and punishments in Sam's environment have shaped him into a shy, achievement oriented, and caring individual. Because of interactions with family members, friends, teachers, and others, Sam has *learned* to behave in this fashion.

Since behaviorists believe that development is learned and often changes according to environmental experiences, it follows that rearranging experiences can change the child's development. For the behaviorist, shy behavior can be changed into outgoing behavior; aggressive behavior can be shaped into docile behavior; lethargic, boring behavior can be turned into enthusiastic, interesting behavior. Let's briefly review some of Skinner's main concepts of how children learn social behavior.

Skinner describes the way in which behavior is controlled in the following way. The child *operates* on the environment to produce a change that will lead to a reward (Skinner, 1938). Skinner chose the term *operants* to describe the responses that are actively emitted because of the consequences for the child. The consequences—rewards and punishments—are *contingent,* or depend, on the child's behavior. For example, an operant might be pressing a lever on a machine that delivers a candy bar. The delivery of the candy bar is contingent on pressing the lever. In sum, **operant conditioning** is a form of learning in which the consequences of behavior lead to changes in the probability of that behavior's occurrence.

More needs to be said about reinforcement and punishment. **Reinforcement** (or reward) is a consequence that increases the probability a behavior will occur. By contrast, **punishment** is a consequence that decreases the probability a behavior will occur. For example, if someone smiles at you and the two of you continue talking for some time, the smile has reinforced your talking. However, if someone you meet frowns at you and you quickly leave the situation, the frown has punished your talking with the individual. And so it was too when you were a child.

Recall from chapter 6 our description of Richard, whose academic behavior was improved by reinforcement of certain of his behaviors. Some of the first studies of reinforcement with children were conducted with nursery school boys and girls who the teachers agreed needed some shaping up (Harris, Wolf, & Baer, 1964). One boy repeatedly threw his glasses down and broke them; another loved to pinch adults, especially the teacher. One girl spent over 80 percent of her time on the floor; another isolated herself from other children more than 85 percent of the time. It was decided that the teacher's attention might serve as an important reinforcer to change the inappropriate behavior of the children.

The first step is to observe the child without making any changes. This procedure provides a baseline measure of the behavior that needs to be changed. The second step involves following the behavior to be changed with a positive consequence (a reinforcer)—in this case, the teacher's attention. This procedure is often called acquisition—a new response is being acquired or an old one is being strengthened. For example, when the girl isolated herself, the teacher simply gave no attention to her. However, an important part of this second step is for positive consequences to follow desirable behaviors. Thus, when the child was with one or more of the other children, the teacher provided positive reinforcement—the teacher smiled at her, patted her on the back, and commented on how nice it was that she was playing with the other children. This procedure was very effective in increasing the desired behavior (figure 11.4).

In many of these studies a third step follows. It is called extinction and describes a decrease in performance when positive reinforcement is removed from the desired behavior. In the case of the child who isolated herself, the teacher initiated a phase in which the child was ignored when interacting with peers and was given attention when she isolated herself. In a fourth phase the teacher again reinforced peer interaction. The effects of reversal were evident,

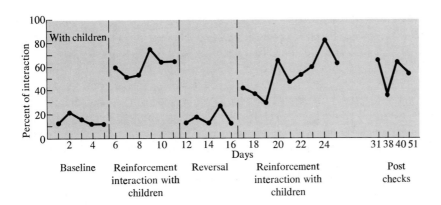

as you can see in figure 11.4. Postchecks (phase 5) were made periodically to determine whether peer interaction was sustained even after the teacher's continued attention had been phased out. Social interaction with peers remained at high levels during this last phase (figure 11.4).

In most instances "acting-out" types of behavior are more difficult to modify than such passive behavior as social isolation. Perhaps the more active behaviors have a payoff in terms of attention (it *is* hard not to say "ouch" when you are pinched). Peer attention to such behaviors is usually high, whereas most peers probably do not pay attention to passive behaviors.

Social Learning Theory

Some psychologists believe the behaviorists basically are right when they say development is learned and is influenced strongly by environmental experiences. But they believe Skinner went too far in declaring that cognition is unimportant in understanding development. **Social learning theory** is the view of psychologists who emphasize behavior, environment, *and* cognition as the key factors in development.

The social learning theorists say that children are not like mindless robots, responding mechanically to others in their environment. Rather, children think, reason, imagine, plan, expect, interpret, believe, value, and compare. When others try to control them, they may resist the control, or even try to control the other individual in return.

Albert Bandura (1977, 1986) and Walter Mischel (1973, 1984) are the main architects of the contemporary version of social learning theory, which was labeled **cognitive social learning theory** by Mischel. You might recall from chapter 6 that Bandura believes much of children's social learning occurs by observing others. Through observational learning (also called modeling or imitation) children cognitively represent others' behavior and then possibly adopt this behavior themselves. For example, a young boy may observe his father's aggressive outbursts and hostile interchanges with people. When observed with his peers, the young boy's style of interaction is curiously like his father's—highly aggressive. Or, a young girl adopts the dominant and sarcastic style of her teacher. When observed interacting with a playmate, the young girl says, "You do this right now. I'm not going to stand for this." Social learning theorists believe children acquire a wide range of such behaviors, thoughts, and feelings through observing others' behavior. These observations are important dimensions of children's development.

Consider the acting-out behavior of these boys in a classroom setting. Why might this type of behavior be more difficult to change than passive behavior, such as social isolation from peers?

Figure 11.5
Bandura's model of reciprocal socialization:
behavior, person (cognition), and
environment.

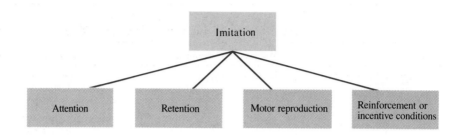

Recall also from chapter 6 that Bandura's most recent model of learning and development involves behavior, the person, and the environment. We repeat Bandura's model in figure 11.5. In this model, the children's social behavior can influence their social thoughts and vice versa, children's thoughts can influence the environment, environmental influences can influence children's thought processes, and so on.

Bandura (1986) recently has emphasized the importance of **self-efficacy**—the belief that one can master a situation and produce positive outcomes—in understanding children's social development. In Bandura's view, the child's expectations of self-efficacy are a critical aspect of positive social development. At each step in development, the child needs to bolster her confidence by telling herself, "I can do this," "I'm going to do it good," and "Way to go, you are improving," for example. As she gains confidence and begins to successfully adapt, the successes become intrinsically rewarding. The self-efficacy statements also are reinforced by the successes they produce. Before long, the child will persist with considerable effort at coping with life's challenges and stresses because of the pleasurable outcomes that were set in motion by self-efficacy.

The behavior and social learning perspective has been widely applied to children's behavior problems. Initially the applications were based almost exclusively on the principles of operant and classical conditioning. In recent years, the applications have become more diversified; as social learning theory grew in popularity and the cognitive approach became more prominent in psychology, cognitive factors were more likely to be included when attempts were made to improve children's adjustment (Fishman, Rotgers, & Franks, 1988; Masters & others, 1988).

Keep in mind that like the behavioral approach of Skinner, the social learning approach emphasizes the importance of empirical research in studying children's development. This research focuses on the processes that explain children's social development—the social and cognitive factors that determine what children are like as they interact with and think about others in their social world.

Evaluating the Behavioral and Social Learning Perspective

The behavioral and social learning theories emphasize that environmental experiences determine development. These approaches have fostered a scientific climate for understanding development that highlights the observation of behavior. Social learning theory emphasizes both environmental influences and cognitive processes in explaining development. This view also suggests children have the ability to control their environment.

The criticisms of the behavioral and social learning theories sometimes are directed at the behavioral view alone and at other times at both approaches. The behavioral view has been criticized for ignoring the importance

| Concept Table 11.1 | | |
| The Psychoanalytic and Behavioral and Social Learning Perspectives | | |

Concept	Processes/Related Ideas	Characteristics/Description
The psychoanalytic perspective	Freud's theory	Freud said that our personality has three structures—id, ego, and superego—which conflict with each other. Most of our thoughts are unconscious in Freud's view and the id is completely unconscious. The conflicting demands of personality structures produce anxiety; defense mechanisms, especially repression, protect the ego and reduce anxiety. Freud was convinced that problems develop because of childhood experiences. He said we go through five psychosexual stages—oral, anal, phallic, latency, and genital. During the phallic stage the Oedipus complex is a main source of conflict.
	Erikson's theory	Erikson developed a theory that emphasizes eight psychosocial stages of development: trust versus mistrust, autonomy versus shame and doubt, initiative versus guilt, industry versus inferiority, identity versus identity confusion, intimacy versus isolation, generativity versus stagnation, and integrity versus despair.
	Evaluating the psychoanalytic perspective	The strengths of the psychoanalytic perspective are an emphasis on the past, the developmental course of personality, mental representation of environment, unconscious mind, and emphasis on conflict. Weaknesses are the difficulty in testing main concepts, lack of an empirical data base and overreliance on past reports, too much emphasis on sexuality and the unconscious mind, and a negative view of human nature.
The behavioral and social learning perspective	Skinner's behaviorism	Skinner emphasizes that cognition is unimportant in development; development is observed behavior, which is influenced by the rewards and punishments in the environment.
	Social learning theory	The environment is an important determinant of development, but so are cognitive processes. We have the capability of controlling our own behavior through thoughts, beliefs, and values. Bandura's emphasis on observational learning exemplifies the social learning approach, as does his model of reciprocal influences of behavior, person (cognition), and environment and also self-efficacy. The contemporary version of social learning theory is called cognitive social learning theory, first described by Walter Mischel.
	Evaluating the behavioral and social learning perspective	The strengths of both theories include emphases on environmental determinants and a scientific climate for investigating development, as well as the focus on cognitive processes and self-control in social learning theory. The behavioral view has been criticized for taking the person out of development and for ignoring cognition. These approaches have not given adequate attention to biological factors and to development as a whole.

of cognition in development and placing too much importance on environmental experiences. Both approaches have been described as too concerned with change and situational influences on development, not paying adequate tribute to the enduring qualities of development. Both views are said to ignore the biological determinants of development. Both are labeled as reductionistic, which means they look at only one or two components of development rather than at how all of the pieces fit together. And critics have charged that the behavioral and social learning theories are too mechanical. By being overly concerned with several minute pieces of development, the most exciting and rich dimensions of development are missed, say the detractors.

At this point we have discussed two important perspectives on children's socialization—psychoanalytic and behavioral and social learning. A summary of the main ideas in these perspectives is presented in Concept Table 11.1.

The Cognitive Perspective

We are in the midst of a cognitive revolution in psychology. Psychology is no longer defined as the science of behavior alone but rather as the science of mind and behavior (Santrock, 1988). This definition underscores the importance of such cognitive processes as thinking, memory, attention, reasoning, and problem solving in understanding the nature of children as well as adults. The cognitive revolution in psychology not only has infiltrated developmental psychology in general but has influenced how we think about children's socialization too.

Awareness of the increased importance of cognitive processes in socialization represents a radical departure from the views of behaviorism and classical psychoanalytic theory that dominated thinking about socialization for many years. Socialization clearly is much more than the overt behavior of children being determined by environmental experiences in a focused, narrow dimension of time. Socialization is also much more than unconscious thought, experiences with parents in the first five years of the child's life, and psychosexual stages. Our study of the important cognitive perspective on socialization focuses first on the applications of cognitive developmental theory to understanding socialization and then turns to the role of information processing in providing insight about socialization.

Cognitive Developmental Theory

In chapter 7 we spent considerable time describing Jean Piaget's cognitive developmental theory. Here we emphasize its implications for understanding children's socialization and then discuss Lawrence Kohlberg's cognitive developmental perspective.

At this time it would be helpful for you to review some of the main points in Piaget's theory. Return to chapter 7 and read the discussion of Piaget's approach to children's development. In doing so, think about how Piaget's ideas can be applied to our understanding of children's social development as well as more pure dimensions of cognitive development such as understanding of numbers and geometric shapes. Recall that Piaget stressed the importance of maturation in explaining development. However, Piaget preferred to emphasize the adaptiveness and organization that occur in any biological system rather than the instincts Freud believed were at the heart of biological maturation. From the cognitive developmental perspective, socialization occurs as the child adapts to the experiences of a particular moment and reorganizes past ways of thinking. To help you remember Piaget's main stages of cognitive development and see how they compare with the stages proposed by Freud and Erikson, turn to figure 11.6.

An example of socialization research that has been inspired by Piaget's theory is role taking (Flavell, 1974, 1985; Shantz, 1983). In many investigations the intent is not only to understand cognitive changes in role-taking ability but also to link these changes with empathy and moral judgment. Role-taking skills are important dimensions of both young children's social development and adolescents' social development. One of the most thorough accounts of how role-taking skills develop has been proposed by Robert Selman (1976). From Selman's perspective, as children approach adolescence, they learn to reason in a complex manner, so that they are increasingly able to put together such complicated thoughts as "I think that you think that I

Social and Personality Development

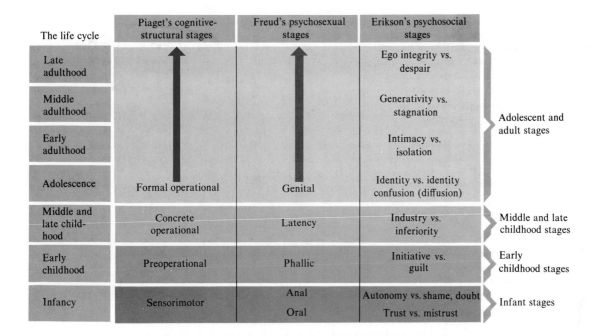

The life cycle	Piaget's cognitive-structural stages	Freud's psychosexual stages	Erikson's psychosocial stages	
Late adulthood			Ego integrity vs. despair	Adolescent and adult stages
Middle adulthood			Generativity vs. stagnation	
Early adulthood			Intimacy vs. isolation	
Adolescence	Formal operational	Genital	Identity vs. identity confusion (diffusion)	
Middle and late childhood	Concrete operational	Latency	Industry vs. inferiority	Middle and late childhood stages
Early childhood	Preoperational	Phallic	Initiative vs. guilt	Early childhood stages
Infancy	Sensorimotor	Anal / Oral	Autonomy vs. shame, doubt / Trust vs. mistrust	Infant stages

Figure 11.6
A comparison of Piaget's, Freud's, and Erikson's stages of development.

think. . . ." Further, adolescents discriminate more readily among alternative views of others than they did as children. Upon reaching early adolescence, they begin to coordinate their various thoughts about others into a more cohesive perspective on people. More information about Selman's view appears in chapter 14.

The application of cognitive developmental theory to socialization is quite recent. Lawrence Kohlberg (1969) believes that the American emphasis on behaviorism and social learning theory is a major reason our studies of socialization have not taken more of a developmental stance.

In addition to his contributions to understanding the development of moral thinking, Kohlberg (1969, 1976) has expanded Piaget's ideas on cognitive development to account for many social phenomena. For example, Kohlberg has applied the cognitive developmental perspective to gender role development, role-taking abilities, peer relations, attachment, and the development of identity.

Like Piaget, Kohlberg believes that biological maturation and environmental experiences interact to produce the individual's state of thought, which in turn influences how the child interprets his or her social world. Kohlberg says that children attempt to attain a balance, or *equilibrium,* as they process incoming social information. Hence, adolescents who have achieved a stable sense of identity ("I know who I am and where I am going") can handle threats to their identity ("You aren't working hard enough—you play around too much") without being overwhelmed. Gradually, over a long time, the balance that has been achieved in a particular stage of thought is disrupted because maturing children gain cognitive abilities that enable them to perceive inconsistencies and inadequacies in their thinking about the social world. Just as a scientist who is confronted with unexplained events and outcomes must reformulate a theory to explain them, so too children must shift their former way of thinking to account for new discrepancies. When children are able to balance the new information with past impressions, they have reached a new stage of thinking about social phenomena.

Kohlberg's ideas can be applied to many different areas of children's social lives, including the peer relations of the children shown here.

Lawrence Kohlberg, one of the most influential thinkers in the promotion of a social-cognitive approach to understanding children's socialization.

Hence, children in elementary school may categorize the identities of themselves and others along a limited number of dimensions, even just one or two, such as "He is a boy, and I am a girl." But as they grow into adolescence, they begin to realize that different people are categorized by traits other than just gender. They recognize, for example, that individuals' style of interaction may shape their personal identity just as much as or more than their "maleness" or "femaleness."

Much of Kohlberg's focus is on children's interactions with other individuals, while Piaget's writings are mainly concerned with the individual's understanding of the physical world. Kohlberg, however, believes that these two parts of the environment, sometimes labeled respectively the "hot" and "cold" sides of cognition, are not independent. In his perspective, physical and social worlds show parallel development.

> All the basic processes involved in physical conditions, and in stimulating developmental changes in these conditions, are also basic to social development. . . .
> Affective development and functioning and cognitive development and functioning are not distinct realms. "Affect" and "cognitive" development are *parallel;* they represent different perspectives and contexts in defining structural change. (Kohlberg, 1969, p. 349)

Kohlberg (1976) believes that personality develops within the framework of Piaget's stages of cognitive development. The concept of personality structure, then, is a part of rational thinking and the development of cognitive structures. The various strands of personality development (such as gender role development, moral development, identity, and so on) are wired together by the child's developing sense of self and perceptions of the self in relation to other individuals (especially in role-taking relationships). Kohlberg's model of the importance of cognition in children's social and personality development is shown in figure 11.7.

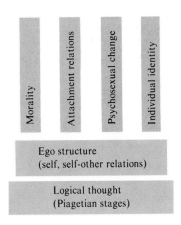

Figure 11.7
Kohlberg's model of personality development.

Information Processing

The cognitive approach to socialization is influenced by the information-processing perspective as well as cognitive developmental theory. Recall our extensive discussion of information processing in chapter 8, where we observed how children attend to information, store information, retrieve information, reason about information, and so forth. What is important for our interest here is that children process information about their social world just as they process information about a math problem or a sentence. We all remember information about our relationships with our parents and our peers just as we remember information about numbers and words. Children's attention to what a peer is doing in a social situation can be as important to understanding peer relations as attention to a teacher's demonstration of solving a math problem is to learning about math. For example, in our discussion of peer relations in chapter 13, we will see how children's processing of information in a social situation can influence how aggressive their actions will be and whether they are popular or are rejected by their peers (Dodge, Murphy, & Buchsbaum, 1984; Dodge & others, 1986; Pettit, Dodge, & Brown, 1988).

An impoverished area of knowledge about children's socialization involves the process of memory. There are two main reasons children's memory of social relationships has not been a primary interest in socialization research. First, the behavioral perspective dominated empirical research on socialization for many years. This led to a focused effort to uncover the immediate or more recent determinants of children's behavior rather than on what children had carried forward from past experiences in relationships. While psychoanalytic theory had emphasized the importance of the past (especially the distant, early years of development) in determining current social relationships, the disenchantment with psychoanalytic's clinical rather than empirical approach produced no research on children's social memory. Second, several studies of children's socialization demonstrated that mothers do a poor job of remembering the precise details of how their children were reared (e.g., Becker & Krug, 1964; Yarrow, Campbell, & Burton, 1968). Consequently,

Figure 11.8
Neisser's ecological model of perception.

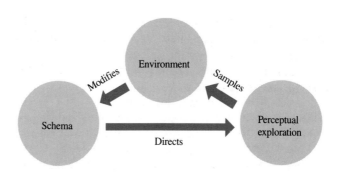

researchers assumed that such memories were so fraught with inaccuracies that they should be abandoned altogether in the search for empirical data about children's socialization.

By the time children are twelve years of age, they have spent more than 70,000 hours in life. If we were to investigate the social relationships of twelve-year-old children without in some way accounting for their past experiences in relationships, would we not be likely to ignore some important aspects of their development? While longitudinal studies that do not include retrospective information are clearly needed, cross-sectional studies that include memory of past social relationships and how they are carried forward in time are also clearly needed in our study of children's socialization.

Many questions about children's social memories need to be explored. Why do we remember some aspects of relationships and not others? When are memories trustworthy and when are they false? Why do we have so few memories from our early childhood? Do some individuals have more memories of childhood social relationships than others, and if so, why? What purpose do memories serve? How does the nature of social memory vary with age, culture, sex, and situation? And what happens when major sections of the past become inaccessible?

Ulric Neisser (1982) has been one of the major proponents of an increase in the study of memory in ecologically valid circumstances. One of the most important aspects of Neisser's commentary about ecologically valid memory study is his belief that in most cases of remembering, it is meanings and not surface details that are the most important aspect of social memory. Children recall the substance of what went on in relationships rather than verbatim details about relationships. Neisser believes that it is not a single clear memory children carry forward but something like "screen memories." Often the basis of such screen memories is a series of repeated experiences, as in hundreds of encounters with a friend. Neisser calls such memories *repisodic* to capture the multiple encounters on which they are based. Thus, children's memories of social relationships are not like a tape recorder, but they may well get the general message or gist of what was going on.

Let's explore Neisser's (1967) description of a schema to see how it may prove to be an important concept in understanding social memory. Recall from chapter 8 that a schema is an organized structure of knowledge. The schema is an important component in Neisser's ecological model of perception (figure 11.8). He emphasizes the role of schemata in directing and exploring the social environment. For Neisser, social perception is a never-ending cycle in which schemata direct exploration of the environment and in which schemata themselves are being continually modified by information picked up in the course of exploring one's social world.

Let's consider the developing child's schemata for friendship. A child's first friendship develops as the child socially interacts with peers. As the child develops a closer relationship with one or more children, a schema of what friendship is about develops. This schema is an organized set of knowledge about what a friend is like. As the child continues the friendship, he or she picks up more information about what a friend is like and the schema becomes modified. The child may initially have a schema of friendship indicating that a friend is someone who always is nice. However, as the friendship develops, negative interchanges may lead to a change in the schema suggesting that the friend is nice most of the time but in some circumstances is not. Exploratory activities with other peers may continue to modify the child's schema for friendship. The schema will also be influenced by the child's own maturational development. In infancy no schema for friendship even exists. Then as the child's cognitive abilities mature, the schema becomes more detailed, organized, and abstract. While Neisser's cyclic model of perception and schemata has been applied primarily in the realm of cognitive development, as you can see, it also has important implications for understanding the nature of children's social development.

Examples of a willingness of some researchers to include memories of past social relationships in their attempts to understand current social relationships are beginning to appear. One area of social relationships in which social memories have begun to reveal some valuable data focuses on intergenerational relationships. In one investigation (Frommer & O'Shea, 1973) researchers discovered that mothers who have difficult relationships with their one-year-old infants were more likely to have had poor relationships with their own mothers than did mothers not reporting problems with their infants. In another study (Ricks, 1983) the mothers of securely attached infants had more positive recollections of their own childhood relationships with their mother, father, and peers than did the mothers of insecurely attached infants.

Evaluating the Cognitive Perspective

Both the cognitive developmental views of Piaget and Kohlberg and the information-processing view contribute in important ways to our understanding of how children's socialization takes place. They have sensitized us to the importance of children's thoughts in the socialization process, challenged and at times modified the approach of other perspectives (such as stimulating social learning theory to be more cognitive and psychoanalytic theory to place more emphasis on conscious thoughts), and opened up new research corridors. The cognitive theories provide an optimistic view of children's social development, ascribing to children the ability and motivation to know their world and to cope with it in constructive ways.

Like all theories, the cognitive theories have their weaknesses. We learned in chapter 8 of the skepticism attached to Piaget's stages and how some of his concepts are somewhat loosely defined. The information-processing perspective has not yet produced an overall perspective on children's social development and has been insensitive to age-related changes in development. Both the Piagetian and information-processing views may have underestimated the importance of the unconscious mind and environmental experiences, especially those involving families, in determining children's development.

The Biological Perspective

Not only are cognitive processes becoming more prominent in the study of children's socialization, but there also has been increased recognition of children's biological heritage in understanding the socialization process. We no longer believe that children are simply socially molded in an infinite number of ways by environmental experiences. Rather, the trend in the study of children's socialization is to recognize the maturation of children and their biological underpinnings and how biological forces interact with environmental experiences (Bronson, 1987). You might want to review some of the basic ideas about biological processes and physical development we discussed in section 2, in this instance thinking about how they might influence children's socialization.

Genes and Socialization

Think once again about the nature-nurture controversy that has existed for so long in psychology. It involves the extent to which the child's mind and behavior are influenced by innate (genetically determined) factors and by learned (environmental) factors. As you know from our discussion in chapter 2, nearly every aspect of the child's mind and behavior, including social thoughts and social behavior, is influenced by the interaction of nature and nurture rather than either factor operating alone. The expression of a given social behavior requires a proper environment and the existence of social objects, that is, people. Similarly, no social behavior can be attributed to environmental factors alone. At the very least, the child must have sensory receptors, motor nerve cells, and a brain that detects and processes relevant social information, as well as muscles that perform the social behaviors. In this sense, the statement, "No genes, no organism; no environment, no organism" bears repeating.

Consider the personality characteristic of introversion-extraversion, an often-studied aspect of both child and adult development. Introverted children have an inward orientation; extraverted children have an outward, more gregarious orientation. The results of twin studies on the dimension of introversion-extraversion suggest that identical twins show much more similar patterns than do fraternal twins. Indications are that heredity plays a moderate to strong role in determining children's introversion-extraversion. However, remember our discussion of children's shyness in which experts emphasize that the proper environmental context can modify to some degree the tendency to be shy (Kagan, 1987 a & b). Parents help children overcome their inherited tendency to be shy by bringing other children into the home and by encouraging children to cope with stressful social circumstances. Also keep in mind that temperament seems to be more strongly influenced by biological factors in early infancy but becomes more malleable with experience. And another important consideration is the fit between the infant's temperament and the parent's temperament. More about infant temperament and maternal-infant interaction appears in Perspective on Child Development 11.2.

Infant Temperament and Socialization

Human beings are born into the world with different temperaments. They have different levels of activity, diverse reactions to novel events, varying degrees to which the rhythm of their daily lives is predictable, and different levels of intensity in their emotional peaks and valleys. One natural question to ask is: How does temperament influence the way infants are treated by their caregivers? If temperament lays the foundation for the style of interaction infants will have with their environment, how does the environment reciprocate? Caregivers, of course, are an important part of the environment, and it would be instructive to know how they treat infants with different perceived temperaments. A study by Pnina Klein (1984) suggests some intriguing answers.

Dr. Klein interviewed the mothers of forty infants and observed them interacting with their infants. The infants were all born in 1980 in the primarily middle-class community of Pietach Tikva, Israel. Twenty-one of the infants were boys and nineteen were girls. The observations were made when the infants were six months of age and again when they were twelve months old. Klein used a time-sampling technique in which some sixty-two different behavioral categories were rated. These included (1) various kinds of stimulation directed toward the infant—touch, movement (kinesthesia), visual experience, and sounds; (2) responsiveness of the mother to infant vocalizing or signals of distress; (3) positive emotions displayed by the mother as in smiles and manipulation of the infant's body; and (4) a variety of objects displayed around the infant. The objects varied in complexity and in how much they could change when the infant acted upon them (note that this last category is not behavioral; rather, it describes stimuli).

After the first observation period (six months), each mother was also requested to complete a questionnaire designed to measure the infant's temperament, as perceived by the mother. The scale is named the Infant Temperament Questionnaire. The items on it are designed to assess the nine original dimensions in the Thomas and Chess (1977) research (see chapter 2, table 2.1), which include activity level, approach-withdrawal, intensity, and distractibility.

The major results were as follows: (1) infants with one profile of temperament received more stimulation from their mothers than did other infants. The infants in this profile were rated as more adaptable, approaching, intense in response, and positive in mood than other babies in the sample. (2) The stimulation difference held for both the six-month and the twelve-month observation periods. (3) Although the infants' profile included several elements, one element was more critical to the observed relation than others. Intensity of response was the most powerful link in the findings. In investigator Klein's own words:

> Of all temperament variables, intensity was found to relate to more observed variables of mothers' behavior than any of the other ITQ scales. Both at six and twelve months of age, infants rated by their mothers as more intense were found to receive more of almost all observed variables of sensory and social stimulation. Furthermore, it is interesting to note that even characteristics of the object environment, that is, its complexity, responsivity, and variety, related significantly to intensity. In other words, what mothers think of infants' temperament, especially what they perceive as level of intensity of an infant's response, predicts not only the mother's direct contact with the infant, but it also related to the choice of the type and number of objects mothers provide for their infants to play with. (p. 1216)

Of course, the findings from this study are correlational. We cannot speak very confidently in causal terms. Specifically, we cannot claim that the more responsive, joyous infants made their mothers, in turn, more responsive to them. Just the reverse may have been true. Or some other mechanism may have been operating to produce the correlation. Nevertheless, the findings are provocative and suggest a potentially important dimension for examining future patterns of mother-child interactions.

Figure 11.9
Goslings following "mother" Lorenz. Konrad
Lorenz revealed that in the first thirty-six
hours of their life goslings would attach
themselves to the first moving object they
saw. Lorenz called this process imprinting.

Ethology

Sensitivity to different kinds of experiences varies over the course of children's development. The presence or absence of certain experiences at particular times in development influences the child well beyond the time they first occur. Ethologists believe that most psychologists underestimate the importance of these special time frames in development and the contribution biology makes to development.

Ethology emerged as an important view because of the work of European zoologists, especially Konrad Lorenz. **Ethology** stresses that behavior is biologically determined. Ethologists believe that we can only fully appreciate a person's behavior if we recognize that the behavior is tied to evolution. Ethologists also remind us that early experience plays an important part in development and potentially is irreversible.

Working mostly with graylag geese, Lorenz (1965) studied a behavior pattern that was considered to be programmed within the genes of the animals. A newly hatched gosling seemed to be born with the instinct for following its mother. Observations showed that the gosling was capable of such behavior as soon as it was hatched from the egg. Lorenz proved that it was incorrect to assume that such behavior was programmed in the animal.

In a remarkable set of experiments, Lorenz separated the eggs laid by one female goose into two groups. One group he returned to the female goose to be hatched by her; the other group was hatched in an incubator. The goslings in the first group performed as predicted; they followed their mother as soon as they were hatched. But those in the second group, who saw Lorenz when they were first hatched, followed him everywhere, just as though he were their mother. Lorenz marked the goslings and then placed both groups under a box. Mother goose and "mother" Lorenz stood aside as the box was lifted. Each group of goslings went directly to its "mother" (figure 11.9). Lorenz called this process **imprinting**—rapid, innate learning within a limited critical period of time that involves attachment to the first moving object seen.

The ethological view of Lorenz and the European zoologists forced American developmental psychologists to recognize the importance of the biological basis of behavior. But the research and theorizing of ethology still

seemed to lack the ingredients that would elevate it to the ranks of the other theories discussed so far in this chapter. In particular, there was little or nothing in the classical ethological view about the nature of social relationships across the human life cycle, something that any major theory of development must explain. And the concept of **critical period**—a fixed time period very early in development during which certain behaviors optimally emerge—seemed to be overdrawn. Classical ethological theory had been weak in stimulating studies with humans. Recent expansion of the ethological view has improved its status as a viable developmental perspective.

Ethologist Robert Hinde (1983) developed a view that goes beyond classical ethological theory by emphasizing the importance of social relationships, describing sensitive periods of development rather than critical periods, and presenting a framework that is beginning to stimulate research with human children and adults. Insight into Hinde's neo-ethological theory appears in the form of his discussion of selected issues of interest to ethologists.

Like behaviorists, ethologists are careful observers of behavior. Unlike behaviorists, ethologists believe that laboratories are not good settings for observing behavior; rather they observe behavior in its natural surroundings. Ethologists believe behavior should be meticulously observed in homes, playgrounds, neighborhoods, schools, hospitals, and so on.

Ethologists also point out that children's development is studied by adults, who see the end point of development as mature adulthood. However, ethologists believe that an infant's or child's behavior should not always be considered in terms of its importance for mature adulthood. Rather, a behavior may be adaptive at an early stage of development only. For example, caterpillars are excellent leaf eaters, but they do not pretend to be butterflies. Ethologists believe the word *development* too often diverts attention away from viewing each stage of development in its own right.

Perspectives on Socialization

Ethologists emphasize sensitive periods. Hinde distinguishes between critical and sensitive periods. Classical ethologists, such as Lorenz, argued for the importance of critical periods in development. The more recently developed concept of **sensitive period** emphasizes a more flexible band of time for a behavior to optimally emerge. Sensitive periods occur on the order of months and even years rather than days or weeks. With human children, there seem to be some flexible sensitive periods for processes such as language, vision, and attachment (Bornstein, 1987).

Ethologists also are becoming interested in social relationships and personality. Hinde argues that certain properties of relationships, such as synchrony and competitiveness, do not describe individuals in isolation. Relationships have properties that emerge from the frequency and patterning of interactions over time. For example, if the mother-infant relationship is studied at one point in development, researchers may not be able to describe it as rejecting, controlling, or permissive. But through detailed observations over a period of time, such categorization may be possible.

Evaluating the Biological Perspective

The biological perspective has contributed to a more complete understanding of children's socialization. For too long, we ignored the biological contributions to children's socialization. Heredity, physical development, sensitive periods, and hormones provide us with better information about the nature of children's social development. The ethologist's emphasis on careful observations in natural contexts has contributed to an increased study of children's social behavior in natural surroundings.

However, like other perspectives we have discussed, the biological perspective has its weaknesses. The emphasis still slants more toward biological-evolutionary explanations of social behavior rather than toward a more balanced biological-environment mix. Little emphasis is placed on the role of cognition in children's social development. At times, the ethologist's emphasis on sensitive periods seems too inflexible. The ethological view also has been better at explaining what happened to cause a child's behavior after it happens than at predicting its occurrence in the future.

The Ecological Perspective

In Brazil, almost every middle-class family can afford a nanny, and there is no such thing as a baby-sitting problem. However, because many of the nannies believe in black magic, it is not beyond the realm of possibility for Brazilian parents to return home from a movie and find their infant screaming, presumably, according to the nanny, from a voodoo curse. Contrast the world of the middle-class Brazilian family with the world of a typical family in Thailand, where farm families are large and can only afford to educate their most promising child—determined by which child is most capable of learning English. Such sociocultural and family experiences play important roles in the child's social development and they are among the key ingredients in the ecological approach to development.

Sociocultural influences range from the broad-based, global inputs of culture to a mother's or a father's affectionate touch. A view that captures the complexity of this sociocultural world was developed by Urie Bronfenbrenner (1979, 1987). Figure 11.10 portrays Bronfenbrenner's ecological model for understanding children's socialization. Notice that the child is placed at

(a)

(b)

(c)

(d)

Urie Bronfenbrenner's ecological model describes four different systems:
(a) Microsystem, the setting in which the child lives. Focus is on the direct interaction of the child with social agents, such as parents, teachers, and peers. (b) Mesosystem, relations between microsystems or connections between contexts, such as family experiences and peer experiences.
(c) Exosystem, when experiences in another setting influence what the child experiences in an immediate context. For example, the city government is an exosystem—it is responsible for the quality of parks and recreation facilities available to children.
(d) Macrosystem, the attitudes and ideologies of the culture.

Macrosystem
Attitudes and ideologies of the culture

Exosystem
Extended family

Mesosystem

Microsystem

Friends of family

Family   School

Neighbors

Health services

Child
Sex
Age
Health
etc.

Peers

Mass media

Church group

Neighborhood play area

Legal services

Social welfare services

Figure 11.10
Bronfenbrenner's model is one of the few comprehensive frameworks for understanding the environment's role in the child's development. Notice that the child is placed at the center and that four environmental systems are involved: microsystem, mesosystem, exosystem, and macrosystem.

Figure 11.11
(a) The peaceful !Kung of Southern Africa discourage any kind of aggression and are called the "harmless people." (b) The violent Yanomamo are called the "fierce people." Youth are told that manhood cannot be achieved unless they are capable of killing, fighting, and pummeling others.

(a) (b)

the center of the model and that the child's most direct interactions are with the **microsystem**—the setting in which the child lives. These contexts include the child's family, school, peers, and neighborhood. The child is not viewed as a passive recipient of experiences in these settings, but as someone who helps to construct the environment. Most research on sociocultural influences focuses on the microsystem, emphasizing the infant's attachment to parents, parenting strategies, sibling relationships, peer relations and friendships, and school experiences.

The **mesosystem** involves relations between microsystems or connections between contexts. Examples include the relation of family experiences to school experiences, school experiences to church experiences, or family experiences to peer experiences. For example, a child whose parents have rejected him may have difficulty developing a positive relationship with his teachers. Increasingly, developmentalists believe it is important to observe the child's behavior in multiple settings—such as family, peer, and school contexts—to provide a more complete picture of the child's social development.

Children also experience their environment in a more indirect way. The **exosystem** is involved when experiences in another social setting—in which the child does not have an active role—influence what the child experiences in an immediate context. For example, work experiences may affect a woman's relationship with her husband and children. She may receive a promotion that requires more travel. This might increase marital conflict and change caregiving—increased father care, increased day care, for example. Another example of an exosystem is the city government, which is responsible for the quality of parks and recreation facilities available to children.

The most abstract level in Bronfenbrenner's analysis of sociocultural influences is the **macrosystem**—the attitudes and ideologies of the culture. People in a particular culture share some broad-based beliefs. The people of Russia have certain beliefs; the people of China have certain beliefs; so do the people of a South Sea island culture. Consider the !Kung of southern Africa and the Yanomamo Indians of South America. The !Kung are peaceful people. They discourage any kind of aggression on the part of their children and resolve disputes calmly. The !Kung are described as "harmless people." By contrast, the Yanomamo Indians are called the "fierce people." They teach their sons that manhood cannot be attained unless they are capable of killing, fighting, and pummeling others. As they grow up, Yanomamo boys are instructed at great length in how to carry out these violent tasks (figure 11.11 shows the !Kung and Yanomamo). More information about cross-cultural influences on

Social and Personality Development

Swedish Fathers, Chinese Fathers, and Pygmy Fathers

Sweden has been a forerunner in promoting the father's involvement with infants. Prominently displayed public posters developed by the Swedish government portray a large, muscular man holding a tiny baby, an effort to communicate that "real men" can be actively involved in infant care. This message is important because many men still feel that active, nurturant parenting and masculinity are incompatible (Lamb, 1987). In Sweden, fathers, like mothers, can take parental leave during the first twelve months of the infant's life, and the first nine are fully paid leave. He can stay home and take care of the child and has the right to reduce his working time up to two hours per day until the child is eight years old (Hwang, 1987).

The father's role in China has been slower to change than in Sweden, but it is changing. Traditionally, in China, the father has been expected to be strict, the mother kind. The father is characterized as a stern disciplinarian, concerned very little with the child's feelings; the child is expected to fear the father. The notion of the strict father has ancient roots. The Chinese character for father (fu) evolved from a primitive character representing the hand holding a cane, which symbolizes authority. However, the twentieth century has witnessed a decline in the father's absolute authority. Younger fathers are becoming more inclined to emphasize the child's expression of opinions and independence, and they also are becoming more involved in child care, influenced to some degree by the increased employment of mothers. Intergenerational tension has resulted between fathers and sons, as younger generations behave in less traditional ways (Ho, 1987) (figure 11.A).

A culture markedly different from Sweden and China is the Aka pygmy culture of the south central region of Africa. Over the course of a year, the Aka spend about 56 percent

The father's role is changing at varying rates in different cultures. In China, the father's role has been slow to change, but it is changing. Today's fathers in China are becoming more involved in child care, for example.

of their time hunting, 27 percent of their time gathering, and 17 percent of their time in village work. What is the Aka pygmy father's role in the infant's development? Aka fathers are intimate and affectionate with their infants. They are not the infant's vigorous playmate like the American father is, but Aka fathers hold their infants extensively, possibly because the infant mortality rate is very high (Hewlitt, 1987).

North America harbors some rather unique cultures. We can better understand the father's role in our own culture when we compare it with the father's role in other cultures, such as Swedish, Chinese, and Aka pygmy.

children's social development appears in Perspective on Child Development 11.3, where you will read about the nature of Swedish fathers, Chinese fathers, and Pygmy fathers.

Within countries, subcultures have shared beliefs. The values and attitudes of children growing up in an urban ghetto may differ considerably from those of children growing up in a wealthy suburb. For example, middle-class mothers verbally interact with their infants more than do lower-class mothers (Tulkin & Kagan, 1971). They respond more when the infant frets, they entertain the infant more, they are more likely to give the infant objects and they talk more to the infant.

Of special concern to developmentalists is the lower-class subculture of the poor. Although the most noticeable aspect of the poor is their economic poverty, other psychological and social characteristics are present. First, the poor are often powerless. In occupations, they rarely are the decision makers;

rules are handed down to them in an authoritarian way. Second, the poor are vulnerable to disaster. They are not likely to be given advance notice if they are to be laid off from work, and usually they do not have financial resources to fall back on when problems arise. Third, their range of alternatives is restricted. A limited range of jobs is open to them. Even when alternatives are available, they may not know about them or are not prepared to make a wise decision because of an inadequate education and an inability to read well. Fourth, there is less prestige in being poor. This lack of prestige is transmitted to the child early in life; the poor child observes other children who wear nicer clothes and live in more attractive houses. Whether a child grows up in poverty or in a comfortable middle-class setting, experiences in the family constitute the most important sociocultural setting in the child's life.

Evaluating the Ecological Perspective

The ecological perspective expands our understanding of how environmental experiences are involved in children's socialization. The perspective not only captures the microinterchanges involved in children's everyday interactions with their social world but also captures the molar influences of social class and culture. The interconnectedness of social settings also is a highlight of this perspective—linkages between family and peer influences, for example.

What are some drawbacks of the ecological perspective? Too little concern for the child's biological heritage is present. And too little concern for the role of cognition in children's socialization is present. At times, the impact of culture and social class are described in a manner that is too abstract and too global.

Since our last review we have discussed three additional important perspectives on children's socialization—cognitive, biological, and ecological. A summary of these ideas is presented in Concept Table 11.2.

An Eclectic Theoretical Orientation

No single indomitable theory or perspective is capable of explaining the rich complexity of children's social development. Each of the theories and perspectives described in this chapter has made important contributions to our understanding of children's social development, but none provides a complete description and explanation. The psychoanalytic perspective best explains the child's unconscious mind. The behavioral and social learning and the ecological perspectives best explain the environment's role in children's social development. The cognitive perspective and cognitive social learning theory best explain the role of cognition in children's social development. And the biological perspective best explains the roles of heredity and biology in children's social development.

An effort was made in this chapter to present five theoretical perspectives on children's social development objectively. The same eclectic orientation will be maintained through the remainder of our discussion of children's social development.

Concept Table 11.2
Cognitive, Biological, and Ecological Perspectives

Concept	Processes/Related Ideas	Characteristics/Description
The cognitive perspective	Cognitive developmental theory	Both Piaget's theory and Kohlberg's theory have important implications for understanding children's socialization. An example of Piagetian-inspired research is role taking. Kohlberg's views have been applied to many areas of social development, especially moral development.
	Information processing	Children process information about their social world just as they process information about a math problem. Social memory and schemata are two important aspects of social information processing.
	Evaluating the cognitive perspective	The cognitive perspective has sensitized us to the role of cognition in social development, challenged other perspectives, and opened up new research corridors. Skepticism about Piaget's stages, lack of a developmental perspective in information processing, and inadequate attention to family processes and unconscious thoughts are criticisms.
The biological perspective	Genes and socialization	No longer do we view children's socialization only in terms of environmental experiences—heredity is important too.
	Ethology	The biological and evolutionary basis of social development is underscored. Lorenz stressed the importance of critical periods; Hinde and contemporary ethologists are more likely to describe sensitive periods of development. Emphasis is given to naturalistic observation. The biological perspective has corrected the overemphasis on environmental factors but at times goes too far in a biological direction. Inadequate attention to cognition also characterizes the perspective.
The ecological perspective	Bronfenbrenner's model	This model stresses both micro- and macrodimensions of the social environment; four systems are emphasized—microsystem, mesosystem, exosystem, and macrosystem.
	Evaluating the ecological perspective	This perspective expands our understanding by emphasizing both micro- and macrodimensions of socialization, as well as the interconnectedness of social settings. Some descriptions, however, may be too abstract and molar, and inadequate attention is given to biological and cognitive factors.

Summary

I. The Psychoanalytic Perspective

Freud said that our personality has three structures—id, ego, and superego—which conflict with each other. Most of our thoughts are unconscious in Freud's view and the id is completely unconscious. The conflicting demands of personality structures produce anxiety; defense mechanisms, especially repression, protect the ego and reduce anxiety. Freud was convinced that problems develop because of early childhood experiences. He said we go through five psychosexual stages—oral, anal, phallic, latency, and genital. During the phallic stage, the Oedipus complex is a main source of conflict. Erikson developed a theory that emphasizes eight psychosocial stages of development: trust versus mistrust, autonomy versus shame, initiative versus guilt, industry versus inferiority, identity versus identity confusion, intimacy versus isolation, generativity versus stagnation, and integrity versus despair. Strengths of the psychoanalytic perspective are an emphasis on the past, the developmental course of personality, mental representation of the environment, unconscious mind, and emphasis on conflict. Weaknesses are the difficulty of testing the main concepts, lack of an empirical data base and overreliance on reports of the past, too much emphasis on sexuality and the unconscious mind, and a negative view of human nature.

II. The Behavioral and Social Learning Perspective

Skinner argues that cognition is unimportant in understanding development; development is learned behavior. Learned behavior is determined by the environmental experiences of reinforcement and punishment. The environment is an important determinant of development, but so are cognitive processes. We have the capability of controlling our behavior through thoughts, beliefs, and values. Bandura's emphasis on observational learning exemplifies the social learning approach, as does his model of the reciprocal influences of behavior, person (cognition), and environment and also self-efficacy. The contemporary version of social learning theory is called cognitive social learning theory, first described by Walter Mischel. The strengths of both theories include emphases on environmental determinants and a scientific climate for investigating development, as well as a focus on cognitive processes and self-control in social learning theory. The behavioral view has been criticized for taking the person out of development and for ignoring cognition. These approaches have not given adequate attention to biological factors and to development as a whole.

III. The Cognitive Perspective

Both Piaget's theory and Kohlberg's theory have important implications for understanding children's socialization. An example of Piagetian-inspired research is role taking. Kohlberg's ideas have been applied to many areas of social development, especially moral development. The information-processing view suggests that children process information about their social world. Social memory and schemata are two important aspects of social information processing. The cognitive perspective has sensitized us to the role of cognition in social development, challenged other perspectives, and opened up new research corridors. Skepticisms about Piaget's stages, lack of a developmental perspective in information processing, and inadequate attention to family processes and unconscious thought are criticisms.

IV. The Biological Perspective

No longer do we view children's socialization only in terms of environmental experiences—heredity is important too. Ethological theory stresses the biological and evolutionary basis of development. Lorenz emphasized critical periods of development; Hinde and other contemporary ethologists emphasize sensitive periods. Ethologists believe data should be collected through naturalistic observation. The biological perspective has corrected the overemphasis on environmental factors but at times goes too far in a biological direction. Inadequate attention to cognition also characterizes the approach.

V. The Ecological Perspective

Bronfenbrenner's model stresses both micro- and macrodimensions of the social environment; four systems are emphasized—microsystem, mesosystem, exosystem, and macrosystem. The ecological perspective expands our understanding of socialization by emphasizing both micro- and macrodimensions, as well as the interconnectedness of settings. Some descriptions, however, are too abstract and molar, and inadequate attention is given to biological and cognitive factors.

VI. An Eclectic Theoretical Orientation

No single perspective or theory is indomitable. Each of the views contributes to our understanding of children's social development.

Key Terms

Suggested Readings

Bronfenbrenner, U., & Crouter, A. C. (1983). The evolution of environmental models in developmental research. In P. H. Mussen (Ed.), *Handbook of child psychology* (4th ed., Vol. 1). New York: John Wiley & Sons.

In this chapter, Bronfenbrenner's ecological model is described in considerable detail.

Erikson, E. H. (1968). *Identity: Youth and crisis.* New York: Norton.

Required reading for anyone interested in developmental psychology. Erikson outlines his eight stages of the life cycle and talks extensively about identity.

Hinde, R. (1983). Ethology and child development. In P. H. Mussen (Ed.), *Handbook of child psychology* (4th ed., Vol. 2). New York: John Wiley & Sons.

Hinde's views strongly influence thinking about child development. Here he outlines the questions ethologists ask and the issues they research.

Kohlberg, L. (1969). Stage and sequence: The cognitive-developmental approach to socialization. In D. A. Goslin (Ed.), *Handbook of socialization theory and research.* Chicago: Rand McNally.

In this paper, Kohlberg articulated his view about the important role of cognition in understanding children's socialization.

Mischel, W. (1973). Toward a cognitive social learning reconceptualization of personality. *Psychological Review, 80,* 252–283.

In this article, Mischel developed the concept of cognitive social learning theory, the current popular version of social learning theory.

Families

There's no vocabulary
for love within a family,
love that's lived in
but not looked at,
love within the light of which
all else is seen,
the love within which
all other love finds speech.
This love is silent.

T. S. Eliot *The Elder Statesman*

he newborns of some species function independently in the world. Other species are not so independent. At birth, the opossum is still considered fetal and is capable of finding its way around only in its mother's pouch, where it attaches itself to her nipple and continues to develop. This protective environment is similar to the uterus. By contrast, the wildebeest must run with the herd moments after birth. The newborn wildebeest's behavior is far more adultlike than the opossum's, although the wildebeest does have to obtain food through suckling. The maturation of the human infant lies somewhere between these two extremes. Much learning and development must take place before the infant can sustain itself (figure 12.1) (Maccoby, 1980).

Because it cannot sustain itself, the human infant requires extensive care. What kind of care is needed and how does the infant begin the road to social maturity? As part of our discussion of family processes, we will discuss the transition to parenthood and the importance of attachment in the child's development. Researchers are intensely exploring the nature of the infant's attachment, raising and evaluating a number of exciting questions, such as, Is a secure attachment to a caregiver necessary for the child's competent social development? What role does the infant's temperament play in the attachment process? What is the father's role in infant attachment? How does day care influence the infant's attachment?

Beyond the attachment process we explore different types of parenting styles and the nature of sibling relations. In keeping with the developmental theme of this text, we then turn our attention, first, to family processes in middle and late childhood and, second, to family processes in adolescence. As we move toward the end of the twentieth century, more children are experiencing socialization in a greater variety of family structures than at any point in history. To conclude the chapter, we consider children's development in the changing American family, giving special attention to children's lives in latchkey, divorced, and stepparent families.

Family Processes

Most of us began our lives in families and spent thousands of hours during our childhood interacting with our parents. Some of you already are parents, others of you will become parents. What is the transition to parenthood like? What is the nature of family processes?

(a)

(b)

(c)

Transition to Parenthood

When individuals become parents through pregnancy, adoption, or stepparenting, they face a disequilibrium that requires adaptation. Parents want to develop a strong attachment with their infant, but they still want to maintain a strong attachment to their spouse and friends and possibly continue their careers. Parents ask themselves how this new being will change their lives. A baby places new restrictions on partners—no longer are they able to rush off to a movie on a moment's notice, and money is not as readily available for trips. The mother with a career asks, "Will it harm my baby to place her in day care? Will I be able to find responsible baby-sitters?"

The excitement and joy that accompany the birth of a healthy baby are often followed by "postpartum blues" in mothers—a depressed state that lasts as long as nine months into the infant's first year (Culp & Osofsky, 1987; Fleming & others, 1988; Osofsky & others, 1985). The early months of the

cathy®   by Cathy Guisewite

baby's physical demands may bring not only the joy of intimacy but also the sorrow of exhaustion. Pregnancy and childbirth are demanding physical events that require recovery time for the mother. As one mother told it:

> When I was pregnant, I felt more tired than ever before in my life. Since my baby was born, I am 100 percent more tired. It's not just physical exhaustion from the stress of childbirth and subsequent days of interrupted sleep, but I'm slowed down emotionally and intellectually as well. I'm too tired to make calls to find a baby-sitter. I see a scrap of paper on the floor, and I'm too tired to pick it up. I want to be taken care of and have no demands made of me other than the baby's. (*Boston Women's Health Book Collective,* 1978, pp. 42–43)

Many fathers are not sensitive to these extreme demands placed on mothers. Busy trying to make enough money to pay the bills, the father may not be at home much of the time. His ability to sense and adapt to the stress placed on his wife during the first year of the infant's life has important implications for the success of the marriage and the family. Becoming a parent is both wonderful *and* stressful. For example, in a longitudinal investigation of couples from late pregnancy to three and one-half years after the baby was born, Carolyn and Phillip Cowan (Cowan, 1988; Cowan & Cowan, 1987) found that the couples enjoyed more positive marital relations before the baby was born than after. Still, almost one-third showed an increase in marital satisfaction. Some couples said that the baby had both brought them closer together *and* moved them farther apart. They commented that being parents enhanced their sense of themselves and gave them a new, more stable identity as a couple. Babies opened up men to a concern with intimate relationships, and the demands of juggling work and family roles stimulated women to manage family tasks more efficiently and pay attention to their personal growth.

At some point during the early years of a child's life, parents do face the difficult task of juggling their roles as parents and self-actualizing adults. Until recently in our culture, nurturing our children and having a career were thought to be incompatible. Fortunately, we have come to recognize that the balance between caring and achieving, nurturing and working—although difficult to manage—can be accomplished.

Reciprocal Socialization

For many years, the socialization process between parents and children was viewed as a one-way affair. Children were considered to be the products of their parents' socialization techniques. By contrast, the socialization process between parents and their children is now viewed as reciprocal—children socialize their parents just as parents socialize children. This process is called **reciprocal socialization.** For example, the interaction of mothers and their infants is symbolized as a dance or a dialogue in which successive actions of the partners are closely coordinated. This coordinated dance or dialogue can assume the form of mutual synchrony (each person's behavior depends on the partner's previous behavior), or it can be reciprocal in a more precise sense— the actions of the partners can be matched, as when one partner imitates the other or there is mutual smiling (Cohn & Tronick, 1987, 1988; Rutter & Durkin, 1987).

When reciprocal socialization has been investigated in infancy, mutual gaze or eye contact has been found to play an important role in early social interaction (Fogel, Toda & Kawa, 1988; Rutter & Durkin, 1987). In one investigation (Stern & others, 1977), the mother and infant engaged in a variety of behaviors while they looked at each other; by contrast, when they look away from each other, the rate of such behaviors dropped considerably. Quite clearly, the behaviors of mothers and infants are interconnected and synchronized.

The term **scaffolding** has been used to describe the mother's role in early parent-child interactions (Bruner & Sherwood, 1976; Ratner & Bruner, 1978). Through their attention and choice of behaviors, mothers are described as providing a framework around which they and their infants interact. For example, in the game of peekaboo, mothers initially cover their babies, then remove the covering, and finally register "surprise" at the reappearance. As infants become more skilled at peekaboo, the infants do the covering and uncovering. Recent research documents the importance of scaffolding in infant development (Hodapp, Goldfield, & Boyatzis, 1984; Vandell & Wilson, 1987). In the investigation by Deborah Vandell and Kathy Wilson, infants who had more extensive scaffolding experience with their parents, especially in the form of turn taking, were more likely to engage in turn taking in interactions with peers.

The question arises as to which partner is driving the relationship—is the mother doing most of the work in the partnership, being sensitive to the infant's states and changing her behavior according to her perception of the infant's needs? When the infant is very young, the mother is performing more work in facilitating interaction than the infant. Through all of the first year and into the second year, the mother is more likely to join the infant's nonsocial behavior than vice versa. Over time, as the child becomes capable of regulating his behavior, the mother and child interact on more equal terms; that is, both "drive" or initiate the relationship (Maccoby & Martin, 1983).

The Family As a System

As a social system, the family can be thought of as a constellation of subsystems defined in terms of generation, gender, and role. Divisions of labor among family members define particular subunits, and attachments define others.

Peek-a-boo is one of an infant's most enjoyable games, but peek-a-boo and other games such as pat-a-cake are more than just games. These games introduce some important rules of social behavior to infants. They are highly repetitive with simple roles for both the parents and the infant. These games help infants learn the rules of give and take in social interaction, and, even when infants are too young to play an active role in the games, the repetitive structure of the games may help infants sense the turn-taking aspects of social interaction.

The family is a system of interacting individuals.

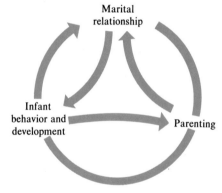

Figure 12.2
Family interaction patterns can have both direct and indirect effects. For example, the parent's behavior can have a direct effect on the infant's development, or the marital relationship can have indirect effects on the infant's development by influencing parenting behavior.

Each family member is a participant in several subsystems—some dyadic (involving two people), some polyadic (involving more than two people). The father and child represent one dyadic subsystem, the mother and father another; the mother-father-child represent one polyadic subsystem, the mother and two siblings another (Vuchinich, Emery, & Cassidy, in press).

An organizational scheme that highlights the reciprocal influences of family members and family subsystems is shown in figure 12.2 (Belsky, 1981). By following the arrows in the figure, you can see that marital relations, parenting, and infant behavior can have both direct and indirect effects on each other. An example of a direct effect is the influence of the parent's behavior on the child. An example of an indirect effect is how the relationship between the spouses mediates the way a parent acts toward the child. For example, marital conflict might reduce the efficiency of parenting, in which case marital conflict would have an indirect effect on the child's behavior. In the family system, a number of developmentalists believe the most important experiences involve the process of attachment.

Attachment

A small curly haired girl named Danielle, age eleven months, is beginning to whimper. After a few seconds, she begins to wail. The psychologist observing Danielle is conducting a research study on the nature of attachment between infants and their mothers. The psychologist is watching Danielle's behavior in a university laboratory filled with dolls, teddy bears, and other toys. In Danielle's case, the observation session begins with Danielle seated on her mother's lap for several minutes. Then the mother places Danielle down and leaves the room. At this point, the whimpering described earlier begins, followed by a loud cry. Subsequently, the mother reenters the room, and Danielle's crying ceases. Quickly, Danielle crawls over to where her mother is seated and reaches out to be held. This scenario is one of the main ways that psychologists study the nature of attachment during infancy.

Social and Personality Development

What Is Attachment?

In everyday language, attachment refers to a relationship between two individuals in which each individual feels strongly about the other and does a number of things to continue the relationship. Many pairs of people are attached: relatives, lovers, a teacher and a student. In the language of developmental psychology, though, **attachment** is often restricted to a relationship between particular social figures and to a particular phenomenon thought to reflect unique characteristics of the relationship. The developmental period is infancy, the social figures are the infant and one or more adult caregivers, and the phenomenon in question is a bond.

One of attachment's dimensions is separation anxiety—how much the infant protests the caregiver's departure by whining, crying, thrashing about. The infant shown here shows displeasure at his mother's attempt to leave him. What are some other important dimensions of attachment?

When researchers investigate attachment, what dimensions do they study? The most frequently used indicators of attachment are maintaining contact and proximity, protest at separation, and stranger anxiety. Infants often try to maintain physical contact with their caregiver in any way possible. If the caregiver moves across the room, the infant follows. If the caregiver puts the infant down, the infant may cling tenaciously. If the caregiver looks away, the infant may try to regain the caregiver's attention by calling, pulling on the caregiver, or shifting locations. Consider two-year-old David, whose father turned away to read the newspaper. Young David grabbed his father's face and forcibly turned it to reestablish visual contact.

Sometimes the infant cannot maintain physical contact, or may not actively try to do so, when the caregiver leaves. Instead, the infant may protest the departure by whining, crying, thrashing about, or otherwise indicating displeasure. This type of behavior has been referred to as **separation anxiety.** Closely associated with separation anxiety is a set of behaviors that occur when the caregiver returns after such a separation episode. The infant may smile, giggle, quickly approach, and cling to the caregiver. The corollary is not always simple though. Consider young David again. He and his seven-year-old sister spent a week with a baby-sitter while their parents vacationed. When his parents returned, David's reaction was more one of shock than glee. He held his distance, resisted efforts to be held or kissed, and produced a nasty facial expression.

Infants also may behave in ways that reflect distress and fear—when an unfamiliar individual approaches, for example. Crying, clinging to the caregiver, and moving away from or averting the gaze of the stranger are all illustrative behaviors. **Stranger anxiety,** or fear of strangers, is the term developmentalists use to describe this type of behavior. In many but not all infants, stranger anxiety appears later than attachment to a specific caregiver. For example, in one investigation specific attachment to the mother occurred at about six months, followed by stranger anxiety at about eight months (Schaffer & Emerson, 1964). However, stranger anxiety is influenced by the nature of the situation. Infants are less afraid of a nice stranger than a nasty stranger and are less afraid of a stranger when they are sitting on their mother's lap (Clarke-Stewart, 1978; Morgan & Ricciuti, 1969).

There is no shortage of theories about infant attachment. Freud believed that the infant becomes attached to the person or object that provides oral satisfaction; for most infants, this is the mother, since she is most likely to feed the infant.

But is feeding as important as Freud thought? A classic study by Harry Harlow and Robert Zimmerman (1959) suggests the answer is no. They evaluated whether feeding or contact comfort was more important to infant attachment. Infant monkeys were removed from their mothers at birth and reared

Figure 12.3
The classic Harlow and Zimmerman study
demonstrated that feeding is not the critical
factor in attachment but that contact comfort
is an important factor.

for six months by surrogate (substitute) "mothers." As shown in figure 12.3, one of the mothers was made of wire, the other of cloth. Half of the infant monkeys were fed by the wire mother, half by the cloth mother. Periodically the amount of time the infant monkeys spent with either the wire or the cloth monkey was computed. Figure 12.4 indicates that regardless of whether they were fed by the wire or the cloth mother, the infant monkeys spent far more time with the cloth mother. This study clearly demonstrates that feeding is not the crucial element in the attachment process and that contact comfort is important.

Might familiarity breed attachment? The famous study by Konrad Lorenz (1965) suggests that the answer is yes. Remember from our description of this study in chapter 11 that newborn goslings became attached to "father" Lorenz rather than their mother because he was the first moving object seen. The time period during which familiarity is important for goslings is the first thirty-six hours after birth; for humans, it is more on the order of the first year of life.

Erik Erikson (1968) believes the first year of life is the key time frame for the development of attachment. Recall his proposal—also discussed in chapter 11—that the first year of life represents the stage of trust versus mistrust. A sense of trust requires a feeling of physical comfort and a minimal amount of fear and apprehension about the future. Trust in infancy sets the

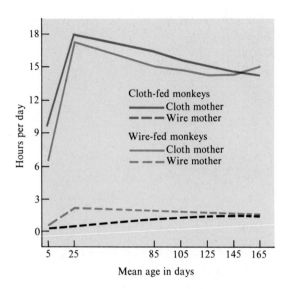

Figure 12.4
The average amount of time infant monkeys spent in contact with their cloth and wire mothers in the Harlow and Zimmerman study. The infant monkeys spent most of their time with the cloth monkey regardless of which mother fed them.

stage for a lifelong expectation that the world will be a good and pleasant place to be. Erikson also believes that responsive, sensitive parenting contributes to the infant's sense of trust.

The ethological perspective of British psychiatrist John Bowlby (1969, 1973, 1980, 1988) also stresses the importance of attachment in the first year of life and the responsiveness of the caregiver. Bowlby believes that the infant and the mother instinctively form an attachment. He argues that the newborn is biologically equipped to elicit the mother's attachment behavior. The baby cries, clings, coos, and smiles. Later the infant crawls, walks, and follows the mother. The goal for the infant is to keep the mother nearby. Research on attachment supports Bowlby's view that about six to seven months of age attachment of the infant to the caregiver intensifies (Ainsworth, 1967; Schaffer & Emerson 1964; Sroufe, in press).

Individual Differences

Although attachment to the caregiver intensifies midway through the first year, isn't it likely that some babies have a more positive attachment experience than others? Mary Ainsworth (1979, 1988) thinks so and says this variation can be categorized as secure or insecure attachment. In **secure attachment,** the infant uses the caregiver, usually the mother, as a secure base from which to explore the environment. The securely attached infant moves freely away from the mother but processes her location through periodic glances. The securely attached infant also responds positively to being picked up by others, and when put back down, moves freely to play. An insecurely attached infant, by contrast, avoids the mother or is ambivalent toward her. The insecurely attached infant fears strangers and is upset by minor, everyday separations.

Ainsworth and her colleagues (1978) believe the insecurely attached infant can be classified as either anxious-avoidant or anxious-resistant, forming three main attachment categories: secure (called **type B babies**), anxious-avoidant (called type A), and anxious-resistant (called type C). **Type A babies** exhibit insecurity by avoiding the mother, for example, ignoring her, averting her gaze, and failing to seek proximity. **Type C babies** exhibit insecurity by resisting the mother, for example, clinging to her but at the same time fighting against the closeness perhaps by kicking and pushing away.

Figure 12.5
Research by Alan Sroufe and his colleagues demonstrates that secure attachment in infancy is related to the child's social competence. Infants who were securely attached to their mothers at eighteen months of age showed less frustration behavior (top figure) and more positive affect (bottom figure) at two years of age.

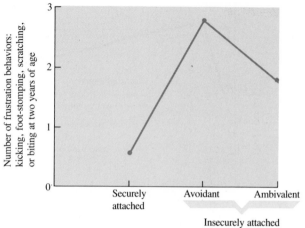

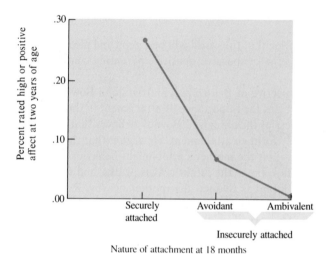

Why are some infants securely attached and others insecurely attached? Following Bowlby's lead, Ainsworth believes attachment security depends on how sensitive and responsive the caregiver is to the infant's signals. For example, infants who are securely attached are more likely to have mothers who are more sensitive, accepting, and expressive of affection toward them than those who are insecurely attached (Smith & Pederson, 1987).

If early attachment to the caregiver is important, it should relate to the child's social behavior later in development. Research by Alan Sroufe (1985, 1987) documents this connection. In one investigation, infants who were securely attached to their mothers early in infancy were less frustrated and happier at two years of age than their insecurely attached counterparts (figure 12.5) (Matas, Arend, & Sroufe, 1978).

Attachment, Temperament, and the Wider Social World

Not all developmentalists believe that a secure attachment in infancy is the only path to competence in life. Indeed, some developmentalists believe that too much emphasis is placed on the importance of the attachment bond in infancy. Jerome Kagan (1987), for example, believes that the infant is highly resilient and adaptive. He argues that the infant is evolutionarily equipped to

Social and Personality Development

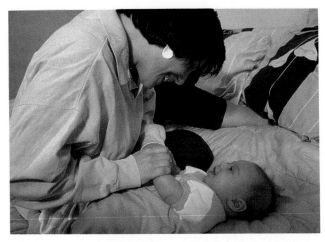

(a)

(b)

stay on a positive developmental course even in the face of wide variations in parenting. Kagan and others stress that genetic and temperament characteristics play more important roles in the child's social competence than the attachment theorists like Bowlby, Ainsworth, and Sroufe are willing to acknowledge (Goldsmith, 1988; Goldsmith & others, 1987; Trudel & Jacques, 1987). For example, an infant may have inherited a low tolerance for stress; this, rather than an insecure attachment bond, may be responsible for his inability to get along with peers.

Another criticism of attachment theory is that it ignores the diversity of social agents and social contexts that exist in the infant's world. Experiences with both the mother *and* the father, changing gender roles, day care, the mother's employment, peer experiences, socioeconomic status, and cultural values are not considered adequately in the attachment concept (Lamb & others, 1984). In all of these perspectives, the importance of social relationships with parents is recognized—their differences lie in the criticalness of the attachment bond. Keep in mind that there currently is a great deal of controversy surrounding the concept of secure attachment—some experts argue for its primacy in influencing the child's competent development, others argue that it is given too much weight.

At this point we have discussed a number of important ideas about sociocultural, family, and attachment processes. Now we turn our attention to other caregivers and settings in the infant's development, evaluating, first, the father's role, and second, day care.

The Father's Role

A father gently cuddles his infant son, softly stroking his forehead. Another father dresses his infant daughter as he readies her for her daily trip to a day-care center. How common are these circumstances in the life of fathers and their infants? Has the father's role changed dramatically?

The father's role has undergone major changes (Bronstein, 1988; Lamb, 1986, 1987; Pleck, 1984). During the colonial period of the Puritans, fathers were mainly responsible for moral teaching. Fathers provided moral guidance and values, especially through religion. As the Industrial Revolution progressed, the father's role changed—now he had the responsibility as the breadwinner, a role that continued through the Great Depression. By the end of World War II, another role for fathers emerged, that of a gender role model.

The attachment theorists argue that early experience plays an important role in the child's social behavior later in development. Secure attachment to the mother in infancy (a) was related to the preschool child's social competence as reflected in more happy feelings and less frustration (b) in one investigation (Matas, Arend, & Sroufe, 1978).

The father's role has undergone major changes in America's history. Puritan fathers were supposed to be moral teachers, Industrial Revolution fathers were supposed to be responsible breadwinners, 1950s fathers were supposed to be gender role models, and today's fathers are supposed to be active, nurturant caregivers. What do you think tomorrow's roles for fathers are likely to be?

While being a breadwinner and moral guardian continued to be important father roles, attention shifted to his role as a male, especially for sons. Then, in the 1970s, the current interest in the father as an active, nurturant, caregiving parent emerged. Rather than only being responsible for the discipline and control of older children and with providing the family's economic base, the father now is being evaluated in terms of his active, nurturant involvement with his children, even infants.

Are fathers more actively involved with their children than they were ten to twenty years ago? Few data document changes in the father's involvement from one point in history to another. One recent study (Juster, in press), however, compared the father's involvement in 1975 and 1981. In 1981, fathers spent about one-fourth more time in direct interaction with the child than in 1975. Mothers increased their direct interaction about 7 percent over this time period, but fathers—while increasing their direct interaction—still were far below mothers in this regard. In this study, the father's involvement was about one-third of the mother's, both in 1975 and 1981. If the mother is employed, does the father increase his involvement with his children? Only slightly. In sum, the father's active involvement with the child has increased somewhat, although this involvement does not approach the mother's, even when she is employed. Although fathers are spending more time with their infants and children, the evidence so far indicates that increased time does not necessarily mean quality time. In one investigation, there was no relation between the amount of time fathers spent with their five-year-old children and the quality of fathering (Grossman, Pollack, & Golding, 1988).

Can fathers do what mothers do? Observations of fathers and their infants suggest that fathers have the ability to act sensitively and responsively with their infants (Parke & Sawin, 1980). Probably the strongest evidence of the plasticity of male caregiving abilities is derived from information about male primates who are notoriously low in their interest in offspring but are forced to live with infants whose female caregivers are absent. Under these

Social and Personality Development

circumstances, the adult male competently rears the infants (Parke & Suomi, 1981). But remember, while fathers can be active, nurturant, involved caregivers with their infants, it is apparent that most of the time they choose not to follow this pattern.

Do fathers behave differently toward infants than do mothers? While maternal interactions usually center around child-care activities—feeding, changing diapers, bathing—paternal interactions are more likely to include playful activities. Fathers engage in more rough and tumble play, bouncing the infant, throwing him up in the air, tickling him, and so on (Lamb, 1986). Mothers do play with infants but their play is less physical and arousing than that of fathers.

Do infants prefer their mothers or their fathers in stressful circumstances? In one investigation (Lamb, 1977), twenty twelve-month-olds were observed interacting with their parents. With both parents present, infants preferred neither their mothers nor their fathers. The same was true when the infant was alone with the mother or the father. But, the entrance of a stranger, combined with boredom and fatigue, produced a shift in the infant's social behavior toward the mother. In stressful circumstances, then, infants show a stronger attachment to the mother.

Might the nature of parent-infant interaction be different in families who adopt nontraditional gender roles? This question was investigated by Michael Lamb and his colleagues (1982). They studied Swedish families in which the fathers were the primary caregivers of their firstborn, eight-month-old infants. The mothers worked full time. In all observations, the mothers were more likely to discipline, vocalize to, hold, soothe, and kiss the infants than the fathers. These mothers and fathers dealt with their infants differently, along the lines of American fathers and mothers following traditional gender roles. Having fathers assume the primary caregiving role did not seem to substantially alter the way they interacted with their infants. These findings may be due to biological reasons or to deeply ingrained socialization patterns in cultures.

Day Care

Each weekday at 8:00 A.M., Ellen Smith takes her one-year-old daughter, Tanya, to the day-care center at Brookhaven College in Dallas. Then Mrs. Smith goes off to work and returns in the afternoon to take Tanya home. Now, after three years at the center, Mrs. Smith reports that her daughter is adventuresome and interacts confidently with peers and adults. Mrs. Smith believes that day care has been a wonderful way to raise Tanya.

In Los Angeles, however, day care has been a series of horror stories for Barbara Jones. After two years of unpleasant experiences with baby-sitters, day-care centers, and day-care homes, Mrs. Jones quit her job as a successful real-estate agent to stay home and take care of her two-and-a-half-year-old daughter, Gretchen. "I didn't want to sacrifice my baby for my job," said Mrs. Jones, who was unable to find good substitute care in day-care homes. And, when she put Gretchen in a day-care center, she said that she felt like her daughter was being treated like a piece of merchandise—dropped off and picked up.

Many parents worry whether day care will adversely affect their children. They fear that day care will lessen the infant's emotional attachment to them, retard the infant's cognitive development, fail to teach the child how to control anger, and allow the child to be unduly influenced by their peers. How extensive is day care? Are the worries of these mothers justified?

The children shown here are attending a day-care center. Day care has become not only a basic need of the American family, but also a worry for many parents, who face the dilemma of having to work to meet economic necessities but relinquishing the care of their children to other caregivers for a large portion of the day. Should America's parents be worried about the quality of America's day care?

In the 1980s, far more young children are in day care than at any time in history—about two million children currently receive formal, licensed day care, and more than five million children attend kindergartens. Also, uncounted millions of children are cared for by unlicensed baby-sitters. Day care clearly has become a basic need of the American family.

The type of day care that young children receive varies extensively. Many day-care centers house large groups of children and have elaborate facilities. Some are commercial operations, others nonprofit centers run by churches, civic groups, and employers. Home care frequently is provided in private homes, at times by child-care professionals, at others by mothers who want to earn extra money.

The quality of care children experience in day care also varies extensively. Some caregivers have no training, others extensive training; some day care has a low caregiver-child ratio, other day care has a high caregiver-child ratio. Some experts have argued that the quality of day care most children receive in the United States is of poor quality. Jay Belsky (1987, in press) not only believes the quality of day care children experience is generally poor, he also believes this translates into negative developmental outcomes for children. Belsky concludes that extensive day-care experience during the first twelve months of life—at least as typically experienced in the United States—is associated with insecure attachment, as well as increased aggression, noncompliance, and possibly social withdrawal during the preschool and early elementary school years.

A study by Deborah Vandell and Mary Anne Corasaniti (1988) supports Belsky's beliefs. They found that extensive day care in the first year of the infant's life was associated with long-term negative outcomes. In contrast to children who began full-time day care later, children who began full-time day care (defined as more than thirty hours per week) as infants were rated by parents and teachers as being less compliant and as having poorer peer relations. In the first grade, they received lower grades and had poorer work habits.

Belsky's conclusions about day care are controversial. Other respected researchers have arrived at a different conclusion—their review of the day-care research suggests no ill effects of day care (Clarke-Stewart, in press; Clarke-Stewart & Fein, 1983; Scarr, 1984).

What can we conclude? Does day care have aversive effects on children's development? Trying to combine the results into an overall conclusion about the effects of day care is a problem because of the different types of day care children experience and the different measures used to assess the outcome. Belsky's analysis does suggest that parents should be very careful about the quality of day care they select for their infants, especially those one year of age or less. Even Belsky agrees, though, that day care itself is not the culprit, rather it is the quality of day care that is problematic in this country. Belsky acknowledges that no evidence exists to show that children in high-quality day care are at risk in any way (Doll, 1988).

What constitutes a quality day-care program for infants? The demonstration program developed by Jerome Kagan and his colleagues at Harvard University (1978) is exemplary. The day-care center included a pediatrician, a nonteaching director, and an infant-teacher ratio of three to one. Teachers' aides assisted at the center. The teachers and aides were trained to smile frequently, to talk with the infants, and to provide them with a safe environment that included many stimulating toys. No adverse effects of day care were observed in this project. More information about what to look for in a quality day-care center is presented in Perspective on Child Development 12.1. Using

What Is Quality Day Care?

A major concern about quality day care is that the facilities should provide more than custodial care. While adequate food, warmth, and shelter are important, by themselves they do not constitute good day care. Experts recommend that parents seeking day care for their children concern themselves with the following:

1. *Nutrition, Health, and Safety.* A balanced, nutritionally sound diet should be provided; the child's health should be carefully monitored and provisions for a sick child should be available; the physical environment should be free of hazards and the child's safety should be of utmost concern.
2. *Child-Caregiver Ratio.* The number of children for each caregiver is an important consideration. For children under the age of two, no more than five children should be cared for by a single caregiver; an even lower ratio is better.
3. *Caregiver Training and Behavior.* A competent caregiver does not need a Ph.D. in child development, but the caregiver should have some training and extensive experience in working with children. The caregiver should smile at the child, talk with the child, ask the child questions, and provide many stimulating toys.

4. *Peers, Play, and Exploration.* Infants and children spend considerable time with peers in day care. Caregivers need to supervise peer relations carefully, providing a good balance of structured and unstructured play, handling aggression and a lack of self-control judiciously. Exploration should be encouraged; adequate, safe space in which to curiously and creatively investigate the world should be available.
5. *Language and Cognitive Development.* Language and cognitive development, as well as social development, should be emphasized. Conversation between the caregivers and children should be plentiful and attention should be given to stimulating the child's cognitive abilities; reading books should be readily available. Long hours should not be spent watching television.
6. *Coordination of Home and Day Care.* What goes on in the child's home should be coordinated with what goes on in day care. Caregivers in quality day care maintain open communication with parents and are receptive to parent questions.

such criteria as those listed in Perspective on Child Development 12.1, Carollee Howes (1988) discovered that children who entered low-quality child care as infants were least likely to be socially competent in early childhood (less compliant, less self-controlled, less task-oriented, more hostile, and more problems in peer interaction).

Edward Zigler (1987) proposed a solution to the day-care needs of families. Zigler says that we should not think of school as an institution but rather as a building, one that is owned by taxpaying parents who need day care for their children. Part of the school building would be for teaching and part would be for child care and supervision. This system could provide parents with competent developmental child-care services. Zigler believes it should be available to every child over the age of three. He does not think children should start formal schooling at age three—they would only be in the schools for day care. At the age of five, children would start kindergarten, but only for half days. If the child has a parent at home, the child would spend the remainder of the day at home. If the parents are working, the child would spend the second half of the day in the day-care part of the school. For children aged six to twelve after-school and vacation care would be available to those who need it.

Zigler does not believe that teachers should provide day care. They are trained as educators and are too expensive. What we need, he says, is a child development associate, someone who is trained to work with children, someone

Concept Table 12.1
Family Processes and Attachment

Concept	Processes/Related Ideas	Characteristics/Description
Family processes	Transition to parenthood	Parenthood produces a disequilibrium, requiring considerable adaptation. Becoming a parent is often both wonderful *and* stressful.
	Reciprocal socialization and mutual regulation	Children socialize parents just as parents socialize children. Scaffolding, synchronization, and mutual regulation are important dimensions of reciprocal socialization.
	The family as a system	The family is a system of interacting individuals with different subsystems, some dyadic, others polyadic. Belsky's model describes direct and indirect effects.
Attachment	What is it?	Attachment is a relationship between two people in which each person feels strongly about the other and does a number of things to ensure the relationship's continuation. In infancy, attachment refers to the bond between the caregiver and the infant. Attachment indices include maintaining contact and proximity, protest at separation, and stranger anxiety. Feeding is not critical in attachment although contact comfort, familiarity, and trust are important. Bowlby's ethological theory stresses that the mother and the infant instinctively trigger attachment. Attachment to the caregiver intensifies at about six to seven months.
	Individual differences	Ainsworth believes that individual differences in attachment can be classified into secure, avoidant, and resistant categories. Ainsworth believes that securely attached babies have sensitive and responsive caregivers. In some investigations, secure attachment is related to social competence in childhood.
	Temperament and the wider social world	Some developmentalists believe too much emphasis is placed on the role of attachment; they believe that heredity and temperament, on the one hand, and the diversity of social agents and contexts on the other, deserve more credit.
	The father's role	Through history the father's role has evolved from moral teacher to breadwinner to gender role model to active, nurturant caregiver. Fathers have increased their interaction with children, but they still lag behind mothers, even when the mother is employed. Fathers can act sensitively to the infant's signals, but most of the time they do not. The mother's role in the infant's development is primarily caregiving, the father's playful interaction. Infants generally prefer the mother under stressful circumstances.
	Day care	Day care has become a basic need of the American family. Of special importance is the quality of day care. Researchers have found that day care by itself does not produce adverse developmental outcomes, but that poor quality day care, especially in the first year of life, may place the child at developmental risk. Quality day care can be achieved and has no adverse effects on children's development.

we can afford to pay. This is a large vision, one that involves a structural change in society and a new face for our school system. Zigler believes that by the early 1990s, a bill legislating such experimental schools will be introduced in Congress. As Zigler remembers, between the fall of 1964 and the summer of 1965 we managed to put 560,000 children into Head Start programs, an educational program for impoverished children. He believes we can do the same thing with day care (Trotter, 1987).

We have discussed a number of important ideas about the nature of family processes and attachment. A summary of these ideas is presented in Concept Table 12.1.

Social and Personality Development

Parenting Styles

Parents want their children to grow into socially mature individuals, and they may feel frustrated in trying to discover the best way to accomplish this. Developmentalists have long searched for the ingredients of parenting that promote competent social development in children. For example, in the 1930s, John Watson argued that parents were too affectionate with their children. In the 1950s, a distinction was made between physical and psychological discipline, with psychological discipline, especially reasoning, emphasized as the best way to rear a child. In the 1970s and beyond, the dimensions of competent parenting have become more precise.

Especially widespread is the view of Diana Baumrind (1971), who believes parents should be neither punitive nor aloof from their children but rather should develop rules and be affectionate with their children. She emphasizes three types of parenting that are associated with different aspects of the child's social behavior: authoritarian, authoritative, and laissez-faire (permissive). More recently, developmentalists have argued that permissive parenting comes in two different forms—permissive indulgent and permissive indifferent. What are these forms of parenting like?

Authoritarian parents are restrictive, punitive, exhort the child to follow their directions, respect work and effort, place limits and controls on the child, and offer little verbal give-and-take between the child and themselves. **Authoritarian parenting** is associated with these child behaviors: anxiety about social comparison, failure to initiate activity, and ineffective social interaction.

Authoritative parenting encourages that child to be independent but still places limits, demands, and controls on the child's actions. Verbal give-and-take is extensive and parents are warm and nurturant toward the child. Authoritative parenting is associated with the child's social competence, especially self-reliance and social responsibility.

Figure 12.6
The four types of parenting—authoritarian,
authoritative, permissive indulgent, and
permissive indifferent—involve the
dimensions of acceptance, responsiveness,
demand, and control.

	Accepting Responsive Child-centered	Rejecting Unresponsive Parent-centered
Demanding, controlling	Authoritative-reciprocal High in bidirectional communication	Authoritarian Power assertive
Undemanding, low in control attempts	Indulgent	Neglecting, ignoring, indifferent, uninvolved

Permissive indulgent parenting is undemanding but accepting and responsive. These parents are involved in their child's life but allow them extensive freedom and do not control their negative behavior. Their children grow up learning that they can get by with just about anything; they disregard and flaunt rules. In one family with permissive indulgent parents, the fourteen-year-old son moved his parents out of their master bedroom suite and claimed it—along with their expensive stereo system and color television—for himself. The boy is an excellent tennis player but behaves in the fashion of John McEnroe, raving and ranting around the tennis court. He has few friends, is self-indulgent, and never has learned to abide by rules and regulations.

Permissive indifferent parenting refers to a style in which parents are highly uninvolved in their children's lives; these parents are neglecting and unresponsive. This type of parenting consistently is associated with a lack of self-control on the part of children. In our discussion of parenting styles we have talked about parents who vary on the dimensions of acceptance, responsiveness, demand, and control. The four parenting styles—authoritarian, authoritative, permissive indulgent, and permissive indifferent—can be described in terms of these dimensions (figure 12.6). Further advice for parents that dovetails with the concept of authoritative parenting is presented in Perspective on Child Development 12.2.

Parents also need to adapt their behavior toward their child based on the child's developmental maturity. Parents should not treat a five-year-old in the same way as a two-year-old. The two-year-old and the five-year-old have different needs and abilities. In the first year, parent-child interaction moves from a heavy focus on routine caretaking—feeding, changing diapers, bathing, and soothing—to later include more noncaretaking activities like play and visual-vocal exchanges. During the child's second and third years, parents often handle disciplinary matters by physical manipulation: they carry the child away from a mischievous activity to the place they want the child to go; they put fragile and dangerous objects out of reach; they sometimes spank. But as the child grows older, parents turn increasingly to reasoning, moral exhortation, and giving and withholding privileges. As children move toward the elementary school years, parents show them less physical affection, become less protective, and spend less time with them (Maccoby & Martin, 1983). More about developmental changes in parenting appears shortly in our discussion of family processes in middle and late childhood and adolescence.

Keep in mind also that throughout childhood socialization is reciprocal: children socialize their parents, just as parents socialize their children. As we see next, in most families, there also are siblings to be socialized and to be socialized by.

Social and Personality Development

Making the Grade As Parents

In the 1980s, the Missouri Department of Education hired Michael Meyerhoff and Burton White to design a model parent education program and help set it up in four school districts across the state: one urban, one suburban, one small town, and one rural town. The families cover a wide range of social and economic backgrounds. The services include get-togethers—at which ten to twenty parents meet with a parent educator at the resource center—and individual home visits by a parent educator. Services begin during the final three months of pregnancy and continue until the child's third birthday, with increasing emphasis on private visits after the child is six months of age. The average amount of contact with the families is once a month for an hour and a half.

During group and private sessions, parents are given basic information about what kinds of parenting practices are likely to help or hinder their children's progress. Table 12.A shows the dos and don'ts told to parents, advice that makes sense and is likely to promote the child's competence (Meyerhoff & White, 1986; White, 1988).

Table 12.A
A Primer in Competent Parenting

The following recommendations are based on the lessons Michael Meyerhoff and Burton White learned from the parents of competent preschool children.

Things to do:	Things not to do:
Provide children with the maximum opportunity for exploration and investigation.	Don't confine your children regularly for long periods of time.
Be available to act as your children's personal consultant as much as possible. You don't have to hover, just be around to provide attention and support as needed.	Don't allow them to concentrate their energies on you so much that independent exploration and investigation are excluded.
Respond to your children promptly and favorably as often as you can, providing appropriate enthusiasm and encouragement.	Don't ignore attention-getting to the point where children have to throw a tantrum to gain your interest.
Set limits—do not give in to unreasonable requests or permit unacceptable behavior to continue.	Don't worry that your children won't love you if you say "no" on occasion.
Talk to your children often. Make an effort to understand what they are trying to do and concentrate on what they see as important.	Don't try to win all the arguments, especially during the second half of the second year when most children are passing through a normal period of negativism.
Use words they understand but also add new words and related ideas.	Don't be overprotective.
Provide new learning opportunities. Having children accompany you to the supermarket or allowing them to bake cookies with you is more enriching than sitting them down and conducting a flashcard session.	Don't bore your child if you can avoid it.
Give your children a chance to direct some of your shared activities from time to time.	Don't worry about when children learn to count or say the alphabet. Don't worry if they are slow to talk, as long as they seem to understand more and more language as time goes by.
Try to help your children be as spontaneous emotionally as your own behavior patterns will allow.	Don't try to force toilet training; it will be easier when they are two.
Encourage your child's pretend activities, especially those in which they act out adult roles.	Don't spoil your children, giving them the notion that the world was made just for them.

Siblings

Sandra describes to her mother what happened in a conflict with her sister:

> We had just come home from the ball game. I sat down on the sofa next to the light so I could read. Sally [the sister] said, "Get up. I was sitting there first. I just got up for a second to get a drink." I told her I was not going to get up and that I didn't see her name on the chair. I got mad and started pushing her—her drink spilled all over her. Then she got really mad; she shoved me against the wall, hitting and clawing at me. I managed to grab a handful of hair.

At this point, Sally comes into the room and begins to tell her side of the story. Sandra interrupts, "Mother, you always take her side." Sound familiar? Any of you who have grown up with siblings probably have a rich memory of aggressive, hostile interchanges; but sibling relationships have many pleasant, caring moments as well. Children's sibling relations include helping, sharing, teaching, fighting, and playing. Children can act as emotional supports, rivals, and communication partners (Vandell, 1987).

More than 80 percent of American children have one or more siblings—that is, brothers or sisters. Because there are so many possible sibling combinations, it is difficult to generalize about sibling influences. Among the factors to be considered are the number of siblings, age of siblings, birth order, age spacing, sex of siblings, and whether sibling relationships are different than parent-child relationships.

Is sibling interaction different than parent-child interaction? There is some evidence that it is. Observations indicate that children interact more positively and in more varied ways with their parents than with their siblings (Baskett & Johnson, 1982). Children also follow their parents' dictates more than those of their siblings, and they behave more negatively and punitively with their siblings than with their parents.

In some instances, siblings may be stronger socializing influences on the child than are parents (Cicirelli, 1977). Someone close in age to the child—such as a sibling—may be able to understand the child's problems and be able to communicate more effectively than parents can. In dealing with peers, coping with difficult teachers, and discussing taboo subjects—such as sex—siblings may be more influential in the socialization process than parents.

Birth order is of special interest both to sibling researchers and to each of us. We want to know the characteristics associated with being born into a particular slot in a family. When differences are found in relation to birth order, they usually are explained by variations in interactions with parents and siblings associated with the unique experiences of being in a particular position in a family. This is especially true of the firstborn child. The oldest child is the only one who does not have to share his parents' love and affection with other siblings—until another sibling comes along. An infant requires more attention than an older child. This means that the firstborn sibling now gets less attention than before the newborn arrived. Does this result in conflict between parents and the firstborn? In one research study, mothers became more negative, coercive, restraining, and played less with the firstborn following the birth of a second child (Dunn & Kendrick, 1982). Even though a new infant requires more attention from parents than does an older child, an especially intense relationship seems to be maintained between parents and firstborns throughout the life cycle. Parents have higher expectations for, put more presssure for achievement and responsibility on, and interfere more with the activities of firstborn than later-born children (Rothbart, 1971).

Given the differences in family dynamics involved in birth order, it is not surprising that firstborns and later-borns have different characteristics. First-born children are more adult oriented, helpful, conforming, anxious, self-controlled, and less aggressive than their siblings. Parental demands and high standards established for firstborns result in these children excelling in academic and professional endeavors. Firstborns are overrepresented in *Who's Who* and Rhodes scholars, for example. However, some of the same pressures placed on firstborns for high achievement may be the reason they also have more guilt, anxiety, difficulty in coping with stressful situations, and higher admission to child guidance clinics.

What are later-borns like? Characterizing later-borns is difficult because they can occupy so many different sibling positions. For example, a later-born might be the second-born male in a family of two siblings or a third-born female in a family of four siblings. In two-child families, the profile of the later-born child is related to the sex of his or her sibling. For example, a boy with an older sister is more likely to develop "feminine" interests than a boy with an older brother (Sutton-Smith & Rosenberg, 1970). Overall, later-borns also usually enjoy better relations with peers than firstborns (Miller & Maruyama, 1976). Last-borns, who are often described as the "baby" in the family even after they have outgrown infancy, run the risk of becoming overly dependent. Middle-borns tend to be more diplomatic, often performing the role of negotiator in times of dispute (Sutton-Smith & Rosenberg, 1970).

The popular conception of the only child is a "spoiled brat" with such undesirable characteristics as dependency, lack of self-control, and self-centered behavior. But research presents a more positive portrayal of the only child, who often is achievement oriented and displays a desirable personality, especially in comparison to later-borns and children from large families (Falbo & Polit, 1986).

Birth order also is associated with variations in sibling relationships. The oldest sibling is expected to exercise self-control and show responsibility in interacting with younger siblings. When the oldest sibling is jealous or hostile, parents restrain her and protect the younger sibling. The oldest sibling is more dominant, competent, and powerful than the younger siblings; the oldest sibling also is expected to assist and teach younger siblings. Indeed, researchers have shown that older siblings are both more antagonistic—hitting, kicking, and biting—and more nurturant toward their younger siblings than vice versa (Abramovitch, & others, 1986). There also is something unique about same-sex sibling relationships. Aggression, dominance, and cheating occur more in same-sex than opposite-sex sibling relationships (Minnett, Vandell, & Santrock, 1983).

Middle and Late Childhood and Adolescence

As children grow older the ability of parents to understand and adapt to their children's developmental changes continues to be an important factor in whether children become socially competent. And, just as developmental changes take place in children that require adaptation and understanding, so are there developmental changes that take place in parents.

Middle and Late Childhood

As children move into the middle and late childhood years, parents spend considerably less time with them. In one investigation, parents spent less than half as much time with their children aged five to twelve in caregiving, instruction, reading, talking, and playing than when the children were younger (Hill & Stafford, 1980). This drop in parent-child interaction may be even more extensive in families with little parental education. While parents spend less time with their children in middle and late childhood than in early childhood, parents continue to be extremely important socializing agents in their children's lives. What are some of the most important parent-child issues in middle and late childhood?

The focus of parent-child interaction during early childhood is on such matters as modesty, bedtime regularities, control of temper, fighting with siblings and peers, eating behavior and manners, autonomy in dressing, and attention seeking. While some of these issues—fighting and reaction to discipline, for example—are carried forward to the elementary school years, many new issues appear by the age of seven (Maccoby, 1984). These include whether children should be made to perform chores, and, if so, whether they should be paid for them; how to help children learn to entertain themselves rather than relying on parents for everything; and how to monitor children's lives outside the family in school and peer settings.

School-related matters are especially important for families during middle and late childhood. Children must learn to relate to adults outside the family on a regular basis—adults who interact with the child much differently than parents. During middle and late childhood, interactions with adults outside the family involve more formal control and achievement orientation.

Discipline during middle and late childhood is often easier for parents than was the case during early childhood and may also be easier than during adolescence. In middle and late childhood, children's cognitive development has matured to the point where it is possible for parents to reason with them about resisting deviation and controlling their behavior. By adolescence, children's reasoning has become more sophisticated and they may be less likely to accept parental discipline. Adolescents also push more strongly for independence, which contributes to parenting difficulties. Parents of elementary school children use less physical discipline than the parents of preschool children. By contrast, parents of elementary school children are more likely to use deprivation of privileges, appeals directed at the child's esteem, comments designed to increase the child's sense of guilt, and statements indicating to the child that she is responsible for her actions.

During middle and late childhood, there is some transfer of control from parent to child, although the process is gradual and involves **coregulation** rather than control by the child or the parent alone (Maccoby, 1984). The major shift to autonomy does not occur until about the age of twelve or later. During middle and late childhood, parents continue to exert general supervision and control while children are allowed to engage in moment-to-moment self-regulation. This coregulation process is a transition period between the strong parental control of early childhood and the increased relinquishment of general supervision of adolescence.

During this coregulation, parents should—

1. monitor, guide, and support children at a distance;
2. effectively use the times when they have direct contact with the child;
3. strengthen in their children the ability to monitor their own behavior, to adopt appropriate standards of conduct, to avoid hazardous risks, and to sense when parental support and contact are appropriate.

In the middle and late childhood years, parents and children increasingly label each other and make attributions about each others' motives. Parents and children do not react to each other only on the basis of each others' past behavior; rather, their reactions to each other are based on how they interpret behavior and their expectations for behavior. Parents and children label each other broadly. Parents label their children "smart" or "dumb," "introverted" or "extraverted," "mannerly" or "unruly," and "lazy" or "hard worker." Children label their parents as "cold" or "warm," "understanding" or "not understanding," and so on. Even though there probably are specific circumstances when children and parents do not conform to these labels, the labels represent a distillation of many hours, days, months, and years of learning what each other is like as a person.

Life changes in parents also influence the nature of parent-child interaction in middle and late childhood. Parents are more experienced in child rearing than they were when their children were infants or preschoolers. As child rearing demands are reduced in middle and late childhood, mothers are more likely to consider returning to a career or beginning a career. Marital relationships change as less time is spent in child rearing and more time is spent in career development, especially in the case of mothers.

Adolescence

Mark Twain once commented, "When I was a boy of fourteen my father was so ignorant I could hardly stand to have the man around. But when I got to be twenty-one, I was astonished at how much he learnt in seven years." What is the nature of autonomy and attachment in adolescence? How extensive is parent-adolescent conflict? Do maturation of the adolescent and maturation of the adolescents' parents contribute to our understanding of parent-adolescent relationships?

Autonomy and Attachment

It has been said that there are two lasting things parents can give to their youth, one is wings, the other roots. The adolescent's push for autonomy and a sense of responsibility puzzles and angers many parents. Parents see their teenager slipping away from their grasp. The urge may be to take stronger control as the adolescent seeks autonomy and responsibility. Heated emotional exchanges may ensue, with either side calling names, making threats, and doing whatever seems necessary to gain control. Parents may seem frustrated because they *expected* their teenager to heed their advice, to want to spend time with the family, and to grow up to do what is right. To be sure, they anticipated that their teenager would have some difficulty adjusting to the changes that adolescence brings, but few parents imagine and predict just how strong adolescents' desires will be to spend time with peers and how adolescents want to show that it is they— not their parents—who are responsible for their successes and failures.

The ability to attain autonomy and gain control over one's behavior in adolescence is acquired through appropriate adult reactions to the adolescent's desire for control. At the onset of adolescence, the average individual does not have the knowledge to make appropriate or mature decisions in all areas of life. As the adolescent pushes for autonomy, the wise adult relinquishes control in those areas in which the adolescent can make reasonable decisions and continues to guide the adolescent in areas in which the adolescent's knowledge is more limited. Gradually, adolescents acquire the ability to make mature decisions on their own.

But adolescents do not simply move away from parental influence into a decision-making process all their own. There is continued connectedness to parents as adolescents move toward and gain autonomy. Attachment to parents increases the probability the adolescent will be a competent adolescent and become a competent adult (Kobak & Sceery, 1988). Just as in childhood, parents provide an important support system that helps the adolescent to explore in a healthy way a wider, more complex social world full of uncertainties, challenges, and stresses (Cooper & Ayers-Lopez, 1985; Hill & Holmbeck, in press; Santrock, in press). Although adolescents show a strong desire to spend more time with peers, they do not move into a world isolated from parents. For example, in one investigation, adolescent girls who had the best relationships with their girlfriends showed a strong identification with their mothers, indicating that they would like to be like their mothers (Gold & Yanof, 1985). Of course, there are times when adolescents reject this closeness as they try to assert their own ability to make decisions and develop an identity. But, for the most part, the worlds of parent-adolescent and adolescent-peer relationships are coordinated and connected, not uncoordinated and disconnected.

In a recent investigation, Diana Baumrind (in press) analyzed parenting styles and social competence in adolescence. The comprehensive assessment involved observations and interviews with 139 fourteen-year-old boys and girls and their parents. More than any other factor, the responsiveness of the parents (considerate and supportive, for example) was related to the adolescents' social competence. And when parents had problem behaviors themselves (alcohol problems and marital conflict, for example), adolescents were more likely to have problems and show decreased social competence.

Parent-Adolescent Conflict

While attachment to parents remains strong during adolescence, the attachment is not always smooth. Early adolescence is a time when conflict with parents escalates beyond childhood levels (Montemayor & Hanson, 1985; Steinberg, 1987). This increase may be due to a number of factors: the biological changes of puberty, cognitive changes involving increased idealism and logical reasoning, social changes focused on independence and identity, maturational changes in parents, and violated expectations on the part of parents and adolescents. The adolescent compares her parents to an ideal standard and then criticizes the flaws. A thirteen-year-old girl tells her mother, "That is the tackiest looking dress I have ever seen. Nobody would be caught dead wearing that." The adolescent demands logical explanations for comments and discipline. A fourteen-year-old boy tells his mother, "What do you mean I have to be home at 10 P.M. because it's the way we do things around here? Why do we do things around here that way? It doesn't make sense to me."

Many parents see their adolescent changing from a compliant child to someone who is noncompliant, oppositional, and resistant to parental standards. The tendency on the part of parents is to clamp down and put more pressure on the adolescent to conform to parental standards (Collins, 1985, 1987). Parents often expect their adolescents to become mature adults overnight instead of understanding that the journey takes ten to fifteen years. Parents who recognize that this transition takes time handle their youth more competently and calmly than those who demand immediate conformity to adult standards. The opposite tactic—letting adolescents do as they please without supervision—also is unwise.

While conflict with parents does increase in early adolescence, it does not reach the tumultuous proportions envisioned by G. Stanley Hall at the beginning of the twentieth century. Rather, much of the conflict involves the everyday events of family life such as keeping a bedroom clean, dressing neatly, getting home by a certain time, not talking forever on the phone, and so on. The conflicts rarely involve major dilemmas like drugs and delinquency.

It is not unusual to talk to parents of young adolescents and hear them say, "Is it ever going to get better?" Things usually do get better as adolescents move from the early part of adolescence toward the end. Conflict between parents usually escalates during early adolescence, remains somewhat stable during the high school years, and then lessens as the adolescent reaches seventeen to twenty years of age. Parent-adolescent relationships become more positive if adolescents go away to college than if they stay at home and go to college (Sullivan & Sullivan, 1980).

The everyday conflicts that characterize parent-adolescent relationships may serve a positive developmental function (Blos, 1982; Hill & Holmbeck, in press). These minor disputes and negotiations facilitate the adolescent's transition from being dependent on parents to becoming an autonomous individual. For example, in one investigation adolescents who expressed disagreement with parents more actively explored identity development than adolescents who did not express disagreement with their parents (Cooper & others, 1982).

As suggested earlier, one way for parents to cope with the adolescent's push for independence and identity is to recognize that adolescence is a ten to fifteen-year transition period rather than an overnight accomplishment. Recognizing that conflict and negotiation can serve a positive developmental function can tone down parental hostility too. Understanding parent-conflict, though, is not simple. As we observe next, both the maturation of the adolescent and the maturation of parents probably are wrapped up in this conflict.

Maturation of the Adolescent and Parents

Physical, cognitive, and social changes in the adolescent's development influence the nature of parent-adolescent relationships. Parental changes also influence the nature of parent-adolescent relationships. Among the changes in the adolescent are puberty, expanded logical reasoning and increased idealistic and egocentric thought, violated expectations, changes in schooling, peers, friendships, dating, and movement toward independence. Several investigations have shown that conflict between parents and adolescents, especially between mothers and sons, is the most stressful during the apex of pubertal growth (Hill & others, 1985; Steinberg, 1981).

Parental changes include those involving marital dissatisfaction, economic burdens, career reevaluation and time perspective, and health and body concerns. Marital dissatisfaction is greater when the offspring is an adolescent than when a child or an adult. A greater economic burden is placed on parents during the rearing of their adolescents. Parents may reevaluate their occupational achievement, deciding whether they have met their youthful aspirations for success. Parents may look to the future and think about how much time they have remaining to accomplish what they want. Adolescents, however, look to the future with unbounded optimism, sensing that they have an unlimited amount of time to accomplish what they desire. Health concerns and an interest in body integrity and sexual attractiveness become prominent themes of adolescents' parents. Even when their body and sexual attractiveness are not deteriorating, many parents of adolescents perceive that they are. By contrast, adolescents are at or are beginning to reach the peak of their physical attractiveness, strength, and health. While both adolescents and their parents show a heightened preoccupation with their bodies, the adolescent's outcome probably is more positive.

The changes in adolescents' parents are those that characterize our development in middle adulthood. The majority of adolescents' parents either are in middle adulthood or are rapidly approaching middle adulthood. And, if current trends continue, adolescents' parents will be even older in the future since adults are waiting longer to get married and once married waiting longer to have children as they pursue career goals.

At this point we have discussed a number of ideas about parenting styles, sibling relations and birth order, and family processes in middle and late childhood and adolescence. A summary of these ideas is presented in Concept Table 12.2.

The Changing Family in a Changing Society

Children are growing up in a greater variety of family structures than ever before in history. Many mothers spend the greatest part of their day away from their children, even their infants. More than one of every two mothers with a child under the age of five is in the labor force; more than two of every three with a child from six to seventeen years of age are as well. And the increasing number of children growing up in single-parent families is staggering. One estimate suggests that 25 percent of the children born between 1910 and 1960 lived in single-parent families sometime during their childhoods. However, 40 to 50 percent of the individuals born in the 1980s will spend part of their childhoods in single-parent families (Glick & Lin, 1986).

Concept Table 12.2 Parenting Styles, Siblings, and Development		
Concept	**Processes/Related Ideas**	**Characteristics/Descriptions**
Parenting styles	The four major categories	Authoritarian, authoritative, permissive indulgent, and permissive indifferent are four main categories of parenting. Authoritative parenting is associated with children's social competence more than the other styles. Parents need to adapt their interaction strategies as children grow older, using less physical manipulation and more reasoning.
Siblings	Their nature	More than 80 percent of American children have one or more siblings. Siblings interact in more negative and less varied ways than parents and children interact. Sibling relationships involve both negative and positive interchanges. In some cases siblings are stronger socializing forces than parents.
	Birth order	The relationship of the firstborn child and parents seems to be especially close and demanding, which may account for a stronger achievement orientation and greater anxiety in firstborn children. Variations also are associated with later-borns and only children.
Developmental considerations	Middle and late childhood	Parents spend less time with children, including less time in caregiving, instruction, reading, talking, and playing. Nonetheless, parents still are powerful and important socializing agents in this period. New parent issues emerge and discipline changes. Control is more coregulatory, children and parents label each other more, and parents mature just as children do.
	Adolescence	Many parents have a difficult time handling the adolescent's push for autonomy, even though this push is one of the hallmarks of adolescent development. Adolescents do not simply move into a world isolated from parents; attachment to parents increases the probability the adolescent will be socially competent and explore a widening social world in healthy ways. Conflict with parents does increase in early adolescence. Such conflict usually is moderate, an increase that actually can serve the positive developmental function of promoting autonomy and identity. Physical, cognitive, and social changes in the adolescent's development influence parent-adolescent relationships. Parental changes—marital dissatisfaction, economic burdens, career reevaluation and time perspective, and health and body concerns—also influence parent-adolescent relationships.

Further, about 11 percent of all American households now are made up of so-called blended families; that is, families with stepparents or cohabiting adults. What are the effects of working mothers on children's development? What are the effects of divorce on children? What are the effects of remarriage on children's development? We consider each of these in turn.

Working Mothers

Because household operations have become more efficient and family size has decreased in America, it is not certain that children with mothers working outside the home actually receive less attention than children in the past whose mothers were not employed outside the home. Outside employment—at least for mothers with school-aged children—may simply be filling time previously taken up by added household burdens and more children. It also cannot be assumed that, if the mother did not go to work, the child would benefit from the time freed by streamlined household operations and smaller families.

The scene here of a working mother dropping her child off at a kindergarten has become commonplace in our society. What are some possible positive benefits of maternal employment? Some possible negative benefits?

Mothering does not always have a positive effect on the child. The educated, nonworking mother may overinvest her energies in her children, fostering an excess of worry and discouraging the child's independence. In such situations, the mother may inject more parenting than the child can profitably handle.

As Lois Hoffman (1979) comments, maternal employment is a part of modern life. It is not an aberrant aspect of it, but a response to other social changes that meets the needs the previous family ideal of a full-time mother and homemaker cannot. Not only does it meet the parent's needs, but in many ways, it may be a pattern better suited to socializing children for the adult roles they will occupy. This is especially true for daughters, but for sons too. The broader range of emotions and skills that each parent presents is more consistent with this adult role. Just as his father shares the breadwinning role and the child-rearing role with the mother, so the son, too, will be more likely to share these roles. The rigid gender-role stereotyping perpetuated by the divisions of labor in the traditional family is not appropriate for the demands children of either sex will have made on them as adults. The needs of the growing child require the mother to loosen her hold on the child, and this task may be easier for the working woman whose job is an additional source of identity and self-esteem.

While a mother's employment is not associated with negative child outcomes, a certain set of children from working mother families bear further scrutiny—those called latchkey children. They typically do not see their parents from the time they leave for school in the morning until about 6:00 or 7:00 P.M. They are called latchkey children because they are given the key to their home, they take the key to school, and then they use it to let themselves into the home while their parents are still at work. Latchkey children are largely unsupervised for two to four hours a day during each school week. During the summer months, they may be unsupervised for entire days, five days a week.

Thomas and Lynette Long (1983) interviewed more than 1,500 latchkey children. They concluded that a slight majority of these children had negative latchkey experiences. Some latchkey children may grow up too fast, hurried by the responsibility placed on them (Elkind, 1981). How do latchkey children handle the lack of limits and structure during the latchkey hours? Without limits and parental supervision, it becomes easier for latchkey children to find their way into trouble—possibly abusing a sibling, stealing, or vandalizing. The Longs point out that 90 percent of the adjudicated juvenile delinquents in Montgomery County, Maryland, are latchkey children. Joan Lipsitz (1983), in testifying before the Select Committee on Children, Youth, and Families, called the lack of adult supervision of children in the after-school hours one of the nation's major problems today. Lipsitz calls it the "three to six o'clock problem" because it is during this time frame that the Center for Early Adolescence in North Carolina, where she is director, experiences a peak of referrals for clinical help.

But while latchkey children may be vulnerable to problems, keep in mind that the experiences of latchkey children vary enormously, just as do the experiences of all children with working mothers. Parents need to give special attention to the ways their latchkey children's lives can be monitored effectively. Variations in latchkey experiences suggest that parental monitoring and authoritative parenting help the child cope more effectively with latchkey experiences, especially resisting peer pressure (Steinberg, 1986). Other research supports the conclusion that overall, no negative effects of latchkey experiences occur; in this analysis, though, third-grade latchkey children who stayed at day-care centers after school were having more adjustment problems than their counterparts in other after-school settings (Vandell & Corasaniti, in press).

The Effects of Divorce on Children

Early studies of the effects of divorce on children followed a **father-absence tradition;** children from father-absent and father-present families were compared, and differences in their development were attributed to the absence of the father. But family structure (such as father-present, divorced, and widowed) is only one of many factors that influence the child's adjustment. The contemporary approach advocates evaluating the strengths and weaknesses of the child prior to divorce, the nature of events surrounding the divorce itself, and postdivorce family functioning. Investigators are finding that the availability and use of support systems (baby-sitters, relatives, day care); an ongoing, positive relationship between the custodial parent and the ex-spouse; authoritative parenting; financial stability; and the child's competencies at the time of the divorce are related to the child's adjustment (Block, Block, & Gjerde, 1986; Chase-Lansdale & Hetherington, in press; Hetherington, in press; Hetherington, Cox, & Cox, 1982; Hetherington, Hagan, & Anderson, 1988; Kelly, 1987; Santrock & Warshak, 1986; Wallerstein & Kelly, 1980).

Many separations and divorces are highly emotional affairs that immerse the child in conflict. Conflict is a critical aspect of family functioning that seems to outweigh the influence of family structure on the child's development. Children in divorced families low in conflict function better than children in intact, never divorced families high in conflict, for example (Rutter, 1983; Wallerstein, Corbin, & Lewis, in press). Although escape from conflict may be a positive benefit for children, in the year immediately following a divorce, conflict does not decline but rather increases. At this time, children—especially boys—in divorced families show more adjustment problems than children in homes with both parents present. During the first year after the divorce, the quality of parenting the child experiences is often poor; parents seem to be preoccupied with their own needs and adjustment—experiencing anger, depression, confusion, and emotional instability—which inhibits their ability to respond sensitively to a child's needs. During the second year after the divorce, parents are more effective in their child-rearing duties, especially with daughters (Hetherington, Cox, & Cox, 1982; Hetherington, Hagan, & Anderson, in press).

Recent evaluations of children six years after the divorce of their parents by Mavis Hetherington and her colleagues (Hetherington, in press; Hetherington, Hagan, & Anderson, in press) found that living in a home in which the mother had custody and had not remarried had long-term negative effects on boys, with deleterious outcomes appearing consistently from preschool to adolescence. No negative effects of divorce on preadolescent girls were found. However, at the onset of adolescence early maturing girls from divorced families engaged in frequent conflict with their mothers, behaved in noncompliant ways, had lower self-esteem, and experienced more problems in heterosexual relations.

The sex of the child and the sex of the custodial parent are important considerations in evaluating the effects of divorce on children. One research study directly compared children living in father-custody and mother-custody families (Santrock & Warshak, 1979, 1986). On a number of measures, including videotaped observations of parent-child interaction, children living with the same-sex parent were more socially competent—happier, more independent, higher self-esteem, and more mature—than children living with the opposite-sex parent. Other research recently has supported these findings (Camara & Resnick, 1987; Furstenberg, in press; Maccoby, Depner, & Mnookin, in press).

Support systems are especially important for low-income divorced families (Coletta, 1978; Hetherington, in press). The extended family and community services may play a critical role in the functioning of low-income divorced families. These support systems may be crucial for low-income divorced families with infants and young children because the majority of these parents must work full-time but still may not be able to make ends meet.

The age of the child at the time of the divorce also needs to be considered. Young children's responses to divorce are mediated by their limited cognitive and social competencies, their dependency on parents, and their restriction to the home or inferior day care (Hetherington, Hagan, & Anderson, in press). During the interval immediately following divorce, young children less accurately appraise the divorce situation. These young children may blame themselves for the divorce, may fear abandonment by both parents, and may misperceive and be confused by what is happening (Wallerstein, Corbin, & Lewis, in press).

The cognitive immaturity that creates extensive anxiety for children who are young at the time of their parents' divorce may benefit the children over time. Ten years after the divorce of their parents, adolescents have few memories of their own earlier fears and suffering or their parents' conflict (Wallerstein, Corbin, & Lewis, in press). Nonetheless, approximately one-third of these children continue to express anger about not being able to grow up in an intact, never-divorced family. Those who were adolescents at the time of their parents' divorce were more likely to remember the conflict and stress surrounding the divorce some ten years later in their early adult years. They too expressed disappointment at not being able to grow up in an intact family and wondered if their life wouldn't have been better if they had been able to do so.

In sum, large numbers of children are growing up in divorced families. Most children initially experience considerable stress when their parents divorce and they are placed at risk for developing problem behaviors. However, divorce also can remove children from conflicted marriages. Many children emerge from divorce as competent individuals. In recent years, researchers have moved away from the view that single-parent families are atypical or pathological, focusing more on the diversity of children's responses to divorce and the factors that facilitate or disrupt the development and adjustment of children in these family circumstances (Hetherington, Hagan, & Anderson, in press).

Stepfamilies

The number of remarriages involving children has steadily grown in recent years, although both the rate of increase in divorce and stepfamilies has slowed in the 1980s. Stepfather families, in which a woman has custody of children from a previous marriage, make up 70 percent of stepfamilies. Stepmother families make up almost 20 percent of stepfamilies, and a small minority are blended with both parents bringing children from a previous marriage. A substantial percentage of stepfamilies also produce children of their own.

Research on stepfamilies has lagged behind research on divorced families, but recently a number of investigators have turned their attention to this increasingly common family structure (e.g., Brand, Clingempeel, & Bowen-Woodward, in press; Bray, in press; Furstenberg, in press; Hetherington, Hagan, & Anderson, in press; Pasley & Ihinger-Tallman, 1987; Santrock & Sitterle, 1987; Zill, in press). Following remarriage, children of all ages show a resurgence of problem behaviors. Younger children seem to be able to eventually form an attachment to a stepparent and accept the stepparent in a parenting role. However, the developmental tasks facing adolescents make them especially vulnerable to the entrance of a stepparent. At the time they are searching for an identity and exploring sexual and close relationships outside the family, a nonbiological parent may increase the stress associated with the accomplishment of these important tasks.

Following the remarriage of the custodial parent, a reemergence of emotional upheaval in girls and intensification of problems in boys often take place. Over time, preadolescent boys seem to improve more than girls in stepfather families. Sons who frequently are involved in conflicted, coercive relations with their custodial mothers likely have much to gain from the introduction of a warm, supportive stepfather. In contrast, daughters who frequently have a close relationship with their custodial mothers and considerable independence may find a stepfather disruptive and constraining.

Children's relationships with biological parents are more positive than with stepparents regardless of whether a stepmother or a stepfather family is involved. Stepfathers often have a distant, disengaged relationship with their stepchildren. And as a rule, the more complex the stepfamily the more difficult the children's adjustment. Families in which both parents bring children from a previous marriage are associated with the highest level of behavioral problems, for example.

In sum, as with divorce, entrance into a stepfamily involves a disequilibrium in children's lives. Most children initially experience their parents' remarriages as stressful. Remarriage, though, can remove children from stressful single-parent circumstances and provide additional resources for children. Many children emerge from their remarried family as competent individuals. As with divorced families, it is important to consider the complexity of stepfamilies, the diversity of child outcomes possible, and the factors that facilitate children's adjustment in stepfamilies (Hetherington, Hagan, & Anderson, in press; Santrock, Sitterle, & Warshak, 1988).

Summary

I. Family Processes

The transition to parenthood produces a disequilibrium, requiring considerable adaptation. Becoming a parent is often both wonderful *and* stressful. Children socialize their parents just as their parents socialize them—the process of reciprocal socialization. Scaffolding, synchrony, and mutual regulation are important dimensions of reciprocal socialization. The family is a system of interacting individuals with different subsystems, some dyadic, others polyadic. Belsky's model describes direct and indirect effects.

II. Attachment

Attachment is a relationship between two people in which each person feels strongly about the other and does a number of things to ensure the relationship's continuation. In infancy, attachment refers to the bond between the caregiver and the infant. Attachment indices include maintaining contact and proximity, protest at separation, and stranger anxiety. Feeding is not critical in attachment although contact comfort, familiarity, and trust are important. Bowlby's ethological theory stresses that the mother and the infant instinctively trigger attachment. Attachment to the caregiver intensifies at about six to seven months. Ainsworth believes that individual differences in attachment can be classified into secure, avoidant, and resistant categories. Ainsworth believes that securely attached babies have sensitive and responsive caregivers. In some investigations, secure attachment is related to social competence in childhood. Some developmentalists believe too much emphasis is placed on the role of attachment; they believe that heredity and temperament, on the one hand, and the diversity of social agents and contexts on the other, deserve more credit.

III. The Father's Role

Through history the father's role has evolved from moral teacher to breadwinner to gender role model to active, nurturant caregiver. Fathers have increased their interaction with children, but they still lag behind mothers, even when the mother is employed. Fathers can act sensitively to the infant's signals, but most of the time they do not. The mother's role in the infant's development is primarily caregiving, the father's playful interaction. Infants generally prefer their mother under stressful circumstances.

IV. Day Care

Day care has become a basic need of the American family. Of special importance is the quality of day care. Researchers have found that day care by itself does not produce adverse developmental outcomes, but that poor quality day care, especially in the first year of life, may place the child at developmental risk. Quality day care can be achieved and has no adverse effects on children's development.

V. Parenting Styles

Authoritarian, authoritative, permissive indulgent, and permissive indifferent are four main categories of parenting. Authoritative parenting is associated with children's social competence more than the other styles. Parents need to adapt their interaction strategies as children grow older, using less physical manipulation and more reasoning.

VI. Siblings

More than 80 percent of American children have one or more siblings. Siblings interact in more negative and in less varied ways than parents and children interact. However, sibling interaction involves positive as well as negative interchanges. In some cases, siblings can be stronger socializing influences than parents. The relationship of the firstborn child and parents seems to be especially close and demanding, which may account for a stronger achievement orientation and greater anxiety among firstborn children. Variations also are associated with later-borns and only children.

VII. Middle and Late Childhood and Adolescence

Parents spend less time with children, including less time in caregiving, instruction, reading, talking, and playing. Nonetheless, parents still are powerful and important socializing agents in this period. New parent issues emerge and discipline changes. Many parents have a difficult time handling the adolescent's push for autonomy, even though this push is one of the hallmarks of adolescent development. Adolescents do not simply move into a world isolated from parents; attachment to parents increases the probability the adolescent will be socially competent and explore a widening social world in healthy ways. Conflict with parents does increase in early adolescence. Such conflict usually is moderate, an increase that actually can serve the positive developmental function of promoting autonomy and identity. Physical, cognitive, and social changes in the adolescent's development influence parent-adolescent relationships. Parental changes also influence parent-adolescent relationships.

VIII. Working Mothers

Overall, whether or not the mother works full time outside the home does not seem to have an adverse effect on children's development. Neither do latchkey experiences, although parental monitoring of children's lives and participation in structured activities with competent supervision are important influences on latchkey children's adjustment.

IX. The Effects of Divorce on Children

The early father-absence tradition has been supplanted by an emphasis on the complexity of the divorced family, pre- and postdivorce family functioning, and varied responses to divorce. Among the factors that influence the child's adjustment in divorced families are conflict, time since divorce, sex of the child and sex of the custodial parent, support systems, and age of the child.

X. Stepfamilies

Just as divorce produces disequilibrium and stress for children, so does the entrance of a stepparent. Over time, preadolescent boys seem to improve more than girls in stepfather families. Adolescence appears to be an especially difficult time for adjustment to the entrance of a stepparent. Children's relationships with biological parents are consistently better than with stepparents and children's adjustment is adversely affected the more complex the stepfamily becomes.

Key Terms

reciprocal socialization   317

scaffolding   317

attachment   319

separation anxiety   319

stranger anxiety   319

secure attachment   321

type B babies   321

type A babies   321

type C babies   321

authoritarian parenting   329

authoritative parenting   329

permissive indulgent parenting   330

permissive indifferent parenting   330

coregulation   334

father-absence tradition   341

Suggested Readings

Birns, B., & Daye, D. (Eds.) (1988). *Motherhood and child care*. Boston: Auburn House.

A number of articles that describe the mother's role in the infant's development are provided; included is an excellent chapter on day care.

Bronstein, P., & Cowan, C. P. (1988). *Fatherhood today: Men's changing role in the family*. New York: John Wiley & Sons.

A very contemporary look at the father's role in families, including chapters on primary caregiving fathers, stepfathers, grandfathers, and fathers with custody, as well as prevention and intervention programs for fathers.

Hartup, W. W., & Zubin, R. (1986). *Relationships and development*. Hillsdale, NJ: Erlbaum.

This compendium of articles by leading experts gives insight into the new look in carrying forward relationships in families. It pays special attention to the role of development in family relationships.

Hetherington, E. M., Hagan, M. S., & Anderson, E. R. (in press). Family transitions: a child's perspective. *American Psychologist*.

Hetherington is a leading researcher in the investigation of the effects of divorce on children's development. In this article she and her colleagues review the recent literature on divorce, giving special attention to transitions in divorced and stepparent families.

Maccoby, E. E., & Martin, J. A. (1983). Socialization in the context of the family: Parent-child interaction. In P. H. Mussen (Ed.), *Handbook of child psychology* (3rd ed., Vol. 4). New York: John Wiley & Sons.

An extensive overview of the nature of parent-child relationships.

Peers, Schools, and the Media

A man's growth is seen in the successive choirs of his friends.

Ralph Waldo Emerson, 1841

ou jerk, what are you trying to do to me," Jess yelled at his teacher. "I got no use for this school and people like you. Leave me alone and quit hassling me."

Jess is ten years old and has already had more than his share of confrontations with society. He has been arrested three times for stealing, been suspended from school twice, and has a great deal of difficulty getting along with people in social circumstances. He especially has difficulty with authority figures. No longer able to cope with his outbursts in class, his teacher recommended that he be suspended from school once again. The principal was aware of a different kind of school she thought might help Jess.

Jess began attending the Manville School, a clinic in the Judge Baker Guidance Center in Boston for learning-disabled and emotionally disturbed children seven to fifteen years of age. Jess, like many other students at the Manville School, has shown considerable difficulty in interpersonal relationships. Since peer relationships become a crucial aspect of development during the elementary school years, Robert Selman (Selman, Newberger, & Jacquette, 1977) has designed a peer therapy program at the Manville School to help students like Jess improve their peer relations in classroom settings, group activities, and sports. The staff at the Manville School has been trained to help peers provide support and encouragement to one another in such group settings.

Structured programs at the Manville School are designed to help the children assist each other in such areas as cooperation, trust, leadership, and conformity. Four school activities were developed to improve the student's social reasoning skills in these areas.

First, there is a weekly peer problem-solving session in the classroom in which the peers work cooperatively to plan activities and relate problems. At the end of each week the peers evaluate their effectiveness in making improvements in areas like cooperation, conflict resolution, and so forth.

Second, the members of a class, numbering from six to eight students, plan a series of weekly field trips, for example, going to the movies or visiting historical sites. While the counselor provides some assistance, peer decision making dominates. When each activity is completed, the students discuss how things went and what might have been done to improve social relations with each other on the outings.

Third, Selman recognizes that there are times when the student has to get away from a setting where intense frustration occurs. When students find themselves in a highly frustrating situation (e.g., angry enough to strike out at a classmate), they are allowed to leave the room and go to a private "time-out" area of the school to regain composure. In time-out, students also are given the opportunity to discuss the problems with a counselor who has been trained to help children or adolescents improve social reasoning skills.

Fourth, during social studies and current events discussion sessions, the students evaluate a number of moral and societal issues that incorporate the thinking of theorists such as Lawrence Kohlberg.

In this chapter we turn our attention to children's socialization that takes place outside the family, describing the nature of children's peer relations, play, social experiences at school, and the influence of the media, especially television.

Peers

As children grow older, peer relations consume an increasing amount of time. What is the function of a child's peer group? What is the nature of children's peer relations at different points in their development? What makes children popular, rejected, or neglected? What is the role of cognition in peer relations? What is the nature of children's friendships? How do children function in groups? How distinct are the worlds of peers and families? We consider each of these in turn.

Peer Group Functions

Peers are children of about the same age or maturity level. Same-age peer interaction serves a unique role in our culture (Hartup, 1976). Age grading would occur even if schools were not age graded and children were left alone to determine the composition of their own societies. After all, one can only learn to be a good fighter among age-mates: The bigger guys will kill you, and the little ones are no challenge. One of the most important functions of the peer group is to provide a source of information and comparison about the world outside the family. From the peer group, children receive feedback about their abilities. Children evaluate what they do in terms of whether it is better than, as good as, or worse than what other children do. It is hard to do this at home because siblings are usually older or younger (Berndt & Ladd, 1989).

Are peers necessary for development? When peer monkeys who have been reared together are separated, they become depressed and less advanced socially (Suomi, Harlow, & Domek, 1970). The human development literature contains a classic example of the importance of peers in social development. Anna Freud (Freud & Dann, 1951) studied six children from different families who banded together after their parents were killed in World War II. Intensive peer attachment was observed; the children were a tightly knit group, dependent on one another and aloof with outsiders. Even though deprived of parental care, they became neither delinquent nor psychotic.

The Developmental Course of Peer Relations

We generally do not think of infants and toddlers when considering peer relations, but now more than ever infants are being placed in day-care centers as more mothers work outside the home. What is the peer interaction of babies like?

Peers as young as six months of age do interact when placed together (Vandell, Wilson, & Buchanan, 1980). They interact by smiling, touching, and vocalizing. In the second year of life, toys become more prominent in peer interaction and affect is more likely to accompany peer exchanges (Eckerman, Whatley, & Kutz, 1975; Mueller, 1979). For example, when an eighteen-month-old child touches another age-mate, he may smile. Not only are positive interactions and affective displays more common in the second year but so are negative interactions—more fights over toys, hitting, biting, and hair pulling, for example.

Early peer relations are more than a curious phenomena; they can be of enduring significance in the child's social and cognitive growth (Brownell & Brown, 1985; Hay, 1985; Mueller, 1985; Ross & Lollis, 1987; Vandell, 1985). For example, in one investigation (Howes, 1985) positive affect in infant peer relations was related to a child's easy access to peer play groups and peer popularity in early childhood.

The frequency of peer interaction, both positive and negative, picks up considerably during early childhood (Hartup, 1983). Although aggressive interaction and rough-and-tumble play increase, the *proportion* of aggressive

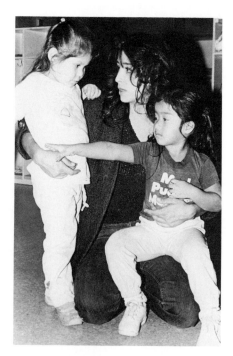

Peer relations make for some powerful moments in children's lives. They include some of our most positive and some of our most negative experiences as children. As reflected in the behavior of the four-year-old girls shown here, the frequency of aggressive peer bouts increases during the preschool years.

exchanges to friendly exchanges decreases. Children tend to abandon their immature and inefficient social exchanges with age and acquire more mature ways of relating to peers.

Children spend an increasing amount of time in peer interaction during middle and late childhood and adolescence. In one investigation, children interacted with peers 10 percent of their day at age two, 20 percent at age four, and more than 40 percent between the ages of seven and eleven. In a typical school day, episodes with peers totaled 299 times per day (Barker & Wright, 1951).

What do children do when they are with their peers? In one study, sixth graders were asked what they do when they are with their friends (Medrich & others, 1982). Team sports accounted for 45 percent of boys' nominations but only 26 percent of girls'. General play, going places, and socializing were common listings for both sexes. Most peer interactions occur outside the home (although close to home), they occur more often in private than public places, and they occur more between children of the same sex than the opposite sex.

By adolescence, peer relations occupy large chunks of an individual's life. In one investigation (Condry, Simon, & Bronfrenbrenner, 1968), over the course of one weekend boys and girls spent more than twice as much time with peers as with parents. Imagine you are back in junior or senior high school, especially during one of your good times. Peers, friends, cliques, dates, parties, and clubs probably come to mind. During early adolescence, we conformed more to peer standards than in childhood. Investigators have found that around the eighth and ninth grades, conformity to peers—especially their antisocial standards—peaks (Berndt, 1979; Douvan & Adelson, 1966). For example, at this point in adolescence, an individual is more likely to go along with a peer to steal hubcaps off a car, draw graffiti on a wall, or steal cosmetics from a store counter. Cross-sex peer interaction and dating also increase during adolescence.

Peer Popularity, Rejection, and Neglect

Children often think, "What can I do to get all of the kids at school to like me?" or "What's wrong with me? Something must be wrong or I would be more popular." What makes a child popular with peers? Children who give out the most reinforcements are often popular. So is a child who listens carefully to other children and maintains open lines of communication with peers. Being themselves, being happy, showing enthusiasm and concern for others, and being self-confident but not conceited are characteristics that serve children well in their quest for peer popularity (Hartup, 1983).

Recently developmentalists have distinguished between two types of children who are not popular with their peers—those who are neglected and those who are rejected (Asher & Dodge, 1986; French, in press). **Neglected children,** while they may not have friends, are not especially disliked by their peers. However, **rejected children** are overtly disliked by their peers. Rejected children are more likely to be disruptive and aggressive than are neglected children. And rejected children are more likely to continue to be unaccepted by peers even when they move into a new setting; neglected children seem to get a new social life in new groups. Rejected children say they are lonelier and less happy as well. Rejected children also have more serious adjustment problems, while the risk status of neglected children is less certain (Coie & Kupersmidt, 1983; Dodge & others, 1986; East, Hess, & Lerner, 1987).

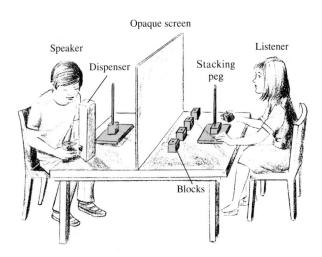

Figure 13.1
Experimental arrangement of speaker and
listener to study the development of
communication skills.

Opaque screen

Speaker

Listener

Dispenser

Stacking
peg

Blocks

Cognition and Peer Relations

How might children's thoughts contribute to their peer relations? Three possibilities are perspective-taking ability, social information-processing skills, and
social knowledge.

Perspective taking involves the ability to take another's point of view. As
children enter the elementary school years both their peer interaction and perspective-taking ability increase. Reciprocity is especially important in peer interchanges at this point in development—playing games, functioning in groups,
and cultivating friendships, for example. One of the important skills that helps
elementary school children to improve their peer relations is communication
effectiveness. In one investigation (Krauss & Glucksberg, 1969), the communication exchanges among peers at kindergarten, first-, third-, and fifth-
grade levels were evaluated. Children were asked to tell a peer about a new
set of block designs. The peer sat behind a screen with similar blocks as the
subject communicated to her (figure 13.1). The kindergarten children made
numerous errors in telling the peer how to duplicate the novel block stack. The
older children were much more efficient in communicating to a peer how to
construct the novel block stack, especially the fifth graders. They were sensitive to the communication demands of the task and were far superior at perspective taking and figuring out how they had to talk for the peer to understand
them (figure 13.2). During elementary school children also become more efficient at understanding complex messages, so the listening skills of the peer
in this experiment probably helped the communicating peer as well. Other
researchers have documented the link between perspective-taking skills and
the quality of peer relations, especially in the elementary school years (LeMare
& Rubin, 1987).

A peer accidentally trips and knocks a boy's soft drink out of his hand.
The boy misinterprets the encounter as hostile, which leads him to retaliate
aggressively against the peer. Through repeated encounters of this kind, peers
come to perceive the boy as having a habit of acting inappropriately. Kenneth
Dodge (1983) argues that children go through five steps in processing information about their social world: decoding of social cues, interpretation, response search, selecting an optimal response, and enactment. Dodge has found
that aggressive boys are more likely to perceive another child's actions as hostile when the peer's intention is ambiguous. And when aggressive boys search

Figure 13.2
The development of communication skills for kindergarten, first-, third-, and fifth-grade children: Number of errors in communicating information about a novel arrangement of blocks.

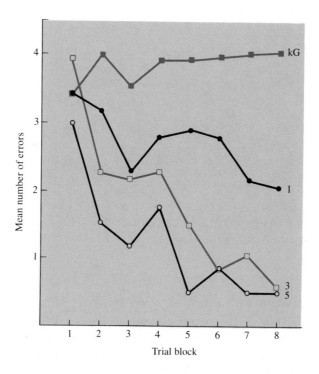

for cues to determine a peer's intention, they respond more rapidly, less efficiently, and less reflectively than nonaggressive children. These are among the social cognitive factors believed to be involved in children's conflicts with each other (Shantz, 1988).

Other recent efforts to teach social skills have been evaluated. In one investigation, middle school adolescents were instructed in ways to improve their self-control, stress management, and social problem solving (Weissberg, 1988). The 240 adolescents who participated in the program improved their ability to devise cooperative solutions to problem situations, and their teachers reported that the students showed improved social relations in the classroom following the program. In another investigation, boys and girls in a low-income area of New Jersey were given instruction in social decision making, self-control, and group awareness (Clabby & Elias, 1988). When compared with boys and girls who did not receive the training, the program participants were more sensitive to the feelings of others, more mindful of the consequences of their actions, and better able to analyze problem situations and act appropriately.

Social knowledge also is important in a child's ability to get along with peers. One dimension of a child's social life focuses on what goals to pursue in poorly defined or ambiguous social situations. Social relationship goals are also important, such as how to initiate and maintain a social bond. And children need to know what scripts to follow to get other children to be their friends. For example, as part of the script for getting friends, it helps to know that saying nice things, regardless of what the peer does or says, will make the peer like the child more.

One investigation explored the possibility that children who are maladjusted do not have the social cognitive skills necessary for positive social interaction (Asarnow & Callan, 1985). Boys with and without peer adjustment difficulties were identified and their social cognitive skills were assessed. Boys without peer adjustment problems generated more alternative solutions to problems, proposed more assertive and mature solutions, gave less intense aggressive solutions, showed more adaptive planning, and evaluated physically aggressive responses less positively than boys with peer adjustment problems.

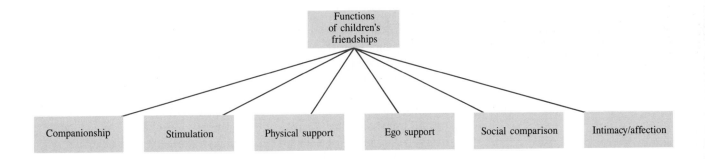

```
                          Functions
                         of children's
                          friendships
```

Companionship	Stimulation	Physical support	Ego support	Social comparison	Intimacy/affection

The world of peers is one of varying acquaintances—children interact with some children they barely know and with others for hours every day. It is to the latter type—friends—that we now turn.

Figure 13.3
The functions of children's friendships.

Friends

The following is a description of a friendship by a ten-year-old girl. My best friend is nice. She is honest, and I can trust her. I can tell her my innermost secrets and know that nobody else will find out about them. I have other friends, but she is my best friend. We consider each other's feelings and don't want to hurt each other. We help each other out when we have problems. We make up funny names for people and laugh ourselves silly. We make lists of which boys we think are the ugliest, which are the biggest jerks, and so on. Some of these things we share with other friends, some we don't. This description reflects the belief that children are interested in specific peers—in Barbara and Tommy—not just any peers. They want to share concerns, interests, information, and secrets with them.

Why are children's friendships important? They serve six functions: companionship, stimulation, physical support, ego support, social comparison, and intimacy/affection (Gottman & Parker, 1987; Parker & Gottman, 1989). Concerning companionship, friendship provides children with a familiar partner and playmate, someone who is willing to spend time with them and join in collaborative activities. Concerning stimulation, friendship provides children with interesting information, excitement, and amusement. Concerning physical support, friendship provides time, resources, and assistance. Concerning ego support, friendship provides the expectation of support, encouragement, and feedback that helps the child maintain an impression of herself as a competent, attractive, and worthwhile individual. Concerning social comparison, friendship provides information about where the child stands vis-à-vis others and whether the child is doing okay. Concerning intimacy/affection, friendship provides children with a warm, close, trusting relationship with another individual in which self-disclosure takes place (figure 13.3).

While friendships exist in early childhood, they become more predominant in middle and late childhood. Robert Selman (1980) proposed a developmental model that highlights friendship's changing faces. Friendship begins at three to seven years of age with momentary friendship—friends are valued because they are nearby and have nice toys. At four to nine years, friendship involves one-way assistance—a friend is a friend because he does what you want him to do. At six to twelve years of age, friendship consists of two-way fair-weather cooperation, followed at nine to fifteen years of age by intimate, mutually shared relationships. Finally, at twelve years of age and older, children gain enough perspective for autonomous interdependent friendships to become possible.

The secret shared by these two girls reflects the intimacy that is so important to many friendships. Might girls be more likely to engage in secret sharing and intimacy than boys? If so, are the friendships of tomorrow's male children likely to include more intimacy because of changing gender roles?

Peers, Schools, and the Media   353

Two of friendship's most common characteristics are intimacy and similarity. **Intimacy in friendship** is defined as self-disclosure and the sharing of private thoughts. Research reveals that intimate friendships may not appear until early adolescence (Berndt, 1982), and that intimacy characterizes girls' friendships more than boys' (Bukowski, Newcomb, & Hoza, 1987). Also, throughout childhood, friends are more similar than dissimilar—in terms of age, sex, race, and many other factors. Friends often have similar attitudes toward school, similar educational aspirations, and closely aligned achievement orientations. Friends like the same music, the same kinds of clothes, and the same kinds of leisure activities.

Children's Groups

An assemblage of children is not necessarily a group or a clique. A group exists when several children interact on an ongoing basis, sharing values and goals. Norms and status positions also are important in group functioning. **Norms** are the standards, rules, and guidelines by which the group abides. Status positions are those of greater or lesser power and control within the group.

Years ago social psychologist Muzafer Sherif brought together a group of eleven-year-old boys at a summer camp called Robbers Cave in Oklahoma (Sherif & others, 1961). The boys were divided into two groups. Competition between the boys was created by promoting in-groupness. In the first week one group hardly knew the other group existed. One group became known as the Rattlers (a tough and cussing group whose shirts were emblazoned with a snake insignia) and the other as the Eagles.

Near the end of the first week each group learned of the other's existence. It took little time for "we-they" talk to surface ("They had better not be on our ball field." "Did you see the way one of them was sneaking around?"). Sherif, who disguised himself as a janitor so he could unobtrusively observe the Rattlers and Eagles, then set up competition between the groups. Baseball, touch football, and tug-of-war were played. Counselors juggled and judged events so the teams were close. Each team perceived the other to be unfair. Raids, burning the other group's flag, and fights resulted. Ethnocentric out-group derogation was observed when the Rattlers and Eagles held their noses in the air as they passed each other. Rattlers described all Rattlers as brave, tough, and friendly and called all Eagles sneaky and smart alecks. The Eagles reciprocated by labeling the Rattlers crybabies.

After in-groupness and competition transformed the Rattlers and Eagles into opposing "armies," Sherif devised ways to reduce hatred between the groups. He tried noncompetitive contact but that did not work. Positive relations between the Rattlers and Eagles were attained only when both groups were required to work cooperatively to solve a problem. Three superordinate goals that required the efforts of both groups were: working together to repair the only water supply to the camp, pooling their money to rent a movie, and cooperating to pull the camp truck out of a ditch. All of these dilemmas were created by Sherif.

Might Sherif's idea—that of creating cooperation between groups rather than competition—be applied to racial groups? To learn about this possibility, turn to Perspective on Child Development 13.1.

Do children's groups differ from adolescents' groups? Children's groups do differ from adolescents' groups in several important ways. The members of children groups often are friends or neighborhood acquaintances. Their groups usually are not as formalized as many adolescent groups. During the

Social and Personality Development

The Jigsaw Classroom

When the schools of Austin, Texas, were desegregated through extensive busing, the outcome was increased racial tension among blacks, Mexican Americans, and Anglos, producing violence in the schools. The superintendent consulted with Eliot Aronson, a prominent social psychologist, who was at the University of Texas in Austin at the time. Aronson thought it was more important to prevent racial hostility than to control it. This led him to observe a number of elementary school classrooms in Austin. What he saw was fierce competition between individuals of unequal status.

Aronson stressed that the reward structure of the elementary school classrooms needed to be changed from a setting of unequal competition to one of cooperation among equals, without making any curriculum changes. To accomplish this, he put together the **jigsaw classroom.** How might this work? Consider a class of thirty students, some Anglo, some black, some Hispanic. The lesson to be learned focuses on the life of Joseph Pulitzer. The class might be broken up into five groups of six students each, with the groups being as equal as possible in terms of ethnic composition and academic achievement level. The lesson about Pulitzer's life could be divided into six parts, with one part given to each member of the six-person group. The parts might be paragraphs from Pulitzer's biography, such as how the Pulitzer family came to the United States, his childhood, his early work, and so on. The components are like parts of a jigsaw puzzle. They have to be put together to form the complete puzzle.

Each student in the group is given an allotted time to study her part. Then the group meets and each member tries to teach a part to the group. After an hour or so each member is tested on the entire life of Pulitzer with each member receiving an individual rather than a group score. Each student, therefore, must learn the entire lesson; learning depends on the cooperation and effort of other members. Aronson (1986) believes this type of learning increases the students' interdependence through cooperatively reaching a common goal.

The strategy of emphasizing cooperation rather than competition and the jigsaw classroom have been widely used in classrooms in the United States. A number of research studies reveal that this type of cooperative learning is associated with increased self-esteem, better academic

Cooperative learning has become a prominent feature of many American classrooms. In the cooperative learning situation here, the teacher and the students are working cooperatively to enhance the students' learning.

performance, friendships among classmates, and improved interethnic perceptions (Aronson, 1986; Slavin, 1987).

While the cooperative classroom strategy has many merits, it may have a built-in restriction to its effectiveness. Academic achievement is as much or more an individual as a team "sport" (Brown, 1986). It is individuals who enter college, take jobs, and follow a career, not groups. A parent with an advantaged child in the jigsaw classroom may react with increased ethnic hostility when the child brings home a lower grade than he typically got before the jigsaw classroom was introduced. The child tells his father, "The teacher is getting us to teach each other. In my group we have a kid named Carlos who can barely speak English." While the jigsaw classroom is an important strategy for reducing interracial hostility, caution needs to be exercised in its use because of the unequal status of the participants and the individual nature of achievement orientation.

It is not easy to get groups who do not like each other to cooperate. The air of distrust and hostility is difficult to overcome. Creating superordinate goals that require both the cooperation of both groups is one viable strategy, as evidenced by Sherif's and Aronson's work.

adolescent years, groups tend to include a broader array of members—in other words, adolescents other than friends or neighborhood acquaintances often are members of adolescent groups. Try to recall the student council, honor society, or football team at your junior high school. If you were a member of any of these organizations, you probably remember that they were made up of many individuals you had not met before and that they were a more heterogeneous

Figure 13.4
Dunphy's stages of group development in adolescence.

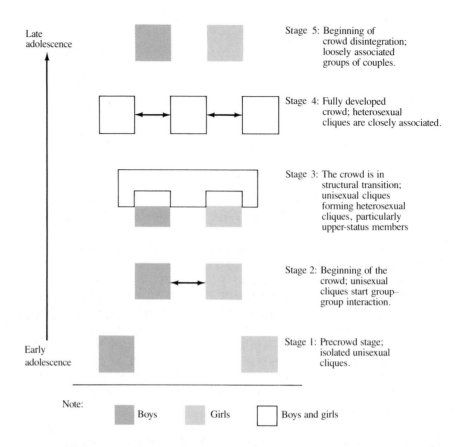

Late adolescence

Stage 5: Beginning of crowd disintegration; loosely associated groups of couples.

Stage 4: Fully developed crowd; heterosexual cliques are closely associated.

Stage 3: The crowd is in structural transition; unisexual cliques forming heterosexual cliques, particularly upper-status members

Stage 2: Beginning of the crowd; unisexual cliques start group–group interaction.

Stage 1: Precrowd stage; isolated unisexual cliques.

Early adolescence

Note: ▨ Boys ▨ Girls ☐ Boys and girls

group than your childhood peer groups. Rules and regulations were probably well defined, and captains or leaders were formally elected or appointed in the adolescent groups.

A well-known observational study by Dexter Dunphy (1963) supports the notion that opposite-sex participation in groups increases during adolescence. In late childhood, boys and girls participate in small, same-sex cliques. As they move into the early adolescent years, the same-sex cliques begin to interact. Gradually, the leaders and high-status members form further cliques based on heterosexual relationships. Eventually, the newly created heterosexual cliques replace the same-sex cliques. The heterosexual cliques interact in large crowd activities too—at dances and athletic events, for example. In late adolescence, the crowd begins to dissolve as couples develop more serious relationships and make long-range plans that may include engagement and marriage. A summary of Dunphy's ideas is presented in figure 13.4.

Family and Peer Worlds

What are some similarities and differences in peer and parent-child relationships? Children touch, smile, frown, and vocalize when they interact with both parents and other children. However, rough-and-tumble play occurs mainly with other children, not with adults. In times of stress, children usually move toward their parents rather than their peers.

The worlds of parent-child and peer relations are distinct but they are coordinated too. Some developmentalists believe that secure attachment to parents promotes healthy peer relations (e.g., Ainsworth, 1979; Sroufe, in press). But as we discussed in chapter 12, others believe the route to competency, including positive peer relations, is not always through secure attachment (e.g., Kagan, 1987). Nonetheless the data are consistent with the theory

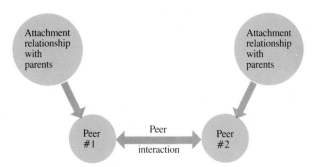

that children's relationships with their parents serve as emotional bases for exploring and enjoying peer relations (Hartup, 1983; Pettit, Dodge, & Brown, 1988).

One investigation (Olweus, 1980) reveals how the relationship history of each peer helps to predict the nature of peer interaction (figure 13.5). Some boys were typically aggressive and other boys were the recipients of aggression throughout the preschool years. The "bullies" as well as the "whipping boys" had distinctive relationship histories. The bullies' parents treated them with rejection and discord, power assertion, and permissiveness for aggression. By contrast, the whipping boys' mothers were anxious and overinvolved with their children and eschewed aggression. The well-adjusted boys were not as involved in aggressive interchanges. Their parents did not sanction aggression; their responsive involvement with their children promoted the development of self-assertion as an adaptive pattern.

Play

An extensive amount of peer interaction during childhood involves play. American children's freewheeling play once took place in rural fields and city streets, using equipment largely of their own making. Today, play is increasingly confined to backyards, basements, playrooms, and bedrooms and derives much of its content from video games, television dramas, and Saturday morning cartoons (Sutton-Smith, 1985). Modern children spend an increasingly large part of their lives alone with their toys, which was inconceivable several centuries earlier. Childhood was once a part of collective village life. Children did not play separately but joined youth and adults in seasonal festivals that intruded upon the work world with regularity and boisterousness (figure 13.6).

Play's Functions

Play increases affiliation with peers, releases tension, advances cognitive development, increases exploration, and provides a safe haven in which to engage in potentially dangerous behavior. Regarding affiliation, play increases the probability that children will converse and interact. During this interaction, children practice the roles they will assume later in life (Isenberg & Quisenberry, 1988).

For Freud and Erikson, play was an especially useful form of human adjustment, bringing the child mastery over anxieties and conflicts. Because these tensions are relieved in play, the child can cope with life's problems. Play permits the child to work off excess physical energy and to release pent up tensions.

Play therapy allows the child to work off frustrations and is a medium through which the therapist can analyze the child's conflicts and methods of coping with them. The child may feel less threatened and be more likely to express his true feelings in the context of play.

Figure 13.6
Children's Games by Pieter Breughel, 1560. Is the play of today's children different than the play of children in collective village life? (The Kunthistorisches Museum, Vienna.)

357

Piaget (1962) saw play as a medium that advances the child's cognitive development. At the same time, he said that the child's cognitive development constrains the way she plays. Play permits children to practice their competencies and acquired skills in a relaxed, pleasurable way. Piaget believed that cognitive structures need to be exercised—play provides the perfect setting for this exercise. For example, a child who has just learned to add or multiply begins to play with numbers in different ways as she perfects these operations, laughing as she does so. The interface of play and cognition and play and language represents an active dimension of contemporary play research (Fein, 1987; Rubin, Fein, & Vanderberg, 1983).

Daniel Berlyne (1960) sees play as exciting and pleasurable in itself because it satisfies the exploratory drive each of us possesses. This drive involves curiosity and a desire for information about something new or unusual. Play is a means whereby children can safely explore and seek out new information—something they might not otherwise do. Play encourages this exploratory behavior by offering children the possibilities of novelty, complexity, uncertainty, surprise, and incongruity (Görlitz & Wohlwill, 1987).

Play is an elusive concept. It ranges from an infant's simple exercise of a newfound sensorimotor talent to a preschool child's riding a tricycle to an older child's participation in organized games. One expert on play and games observed that there is no universally accepted definition of play because it encompasses so many different kinds of activities (Sutton-Smith, 1973).

Types of Play

Many years ago Mildred Parten (1932) developed one of the most elaborate attempts to categorize children's play. Based on observations of children in free play at nursery school, Parten arrived at these play categories:

Unoccupied The child is not engaging in play as it is commonly understood. He may stand in one spot, look around the room, or perform random movements that do not seem to have a goal. In most nursery schools, **unoccupied play** is less frequent than other forms.

Solitary The child plays alone and independently of those around him. The child seems engrossed in what he is doing and does not care much about anything else that is happening. Two- and three-year-olds engage more frequently in **solitary play** than do older preschoolers.

Onlooker The child watches other children playing. He may talk with them and ask them questions but does not enter into their play behavior. The child's active interest in other children's play distinguishes **onlooker play** from unoccupied play.

Parallel The child plays alone but with toys like those that other children are using or in a manner that mimics the behavior of other children who are playing. The older the child, the less frequently he engages in this type of play; even older preschool children, though, engage in **parallel play** quite often.

Associative Social interaction with little or no organization involved is called **associative play.** In this type of play, children seem to be more interested in associating with each other than in the tasks they are performing. Borrowing or lending toys and following or leading one another in line are examples of associative play.

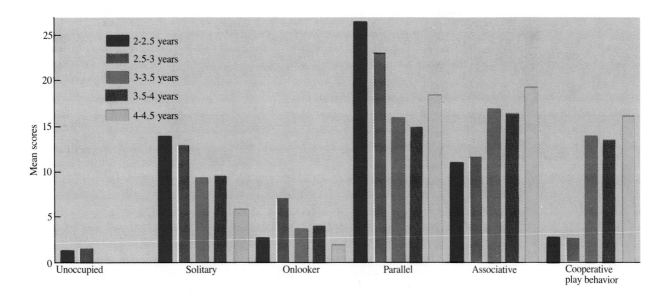

Cooperative Social interaction in a group with a sense of group identity and organized activity characterizes **cooperative play.** Children's formal games, competition aimed at winning something, and groups formed by the teacher for doing things together are examples of cooperative play. Cooperative play is the prototype for the games of middle childhood; little of it is seen in the preschool years.

Figure 13.7
Mean scores in five categories of social play for two-, three-, and four-year olds.

Parten's research on play was conducted more than half a century ago. To determine whether her findings were out of date, Keith Barnes (1971) observed a group of preschoolers using Parten's categories of play. He found that children in the 1970s did not engage in as much associative and cooperative play as they did in the 1930s. These changes in play probably occurred because children have become more passive as a consequence of heavy television viewing and because toys are more abundant and attractive than they were forty years ago. Today solitary play may be more natural and parents may encourage children to play by themselves more than parents did years ago. The developmental changes that were observed by Parten also were observed by Barnes. That is, three-year-old children engaged in solitary and parallel play more than five-year-old children, and five-year-old children engaged in cooperative and associative play more than other kinds of play (figure 13.7).

Another form of play that is pervasive in early childhood is **pretend play.** When children engage in pretend play, they transform the physical environment into a symbol. Make-believe play appears rather abruptly in the toddler's development—at about eighteen months of age, continues to develop between three and four years of age, peaks between five and six years of age, and then declines. In the early elementary school years, children's interests shift to games (Fein, 1987).

Piaget attached special significance to the onset of pretend play, believing it signaled the beginning of representational thinking and the appearance of the **semiotic function,** which overlays meaning on sound patterns, gestures, or images. For both Piaget and other cognitive developmental experts (e.g., Vygotsky, 1978; Werner & Kaplan, 1963), the main developmental occurrence is the child's awareness that one thing can signify something else, even when the something else is not present.

Pretend play—the type of play shown by these two children—has a special place in Piaget's theory. It signals the onset of representational thinking and the appearance of the semiotic function, which overlays meaning on sound patterns, gestures, or images.

As pretend play develops in the preschool years, children try out many different roles—they may be the mother, the father, the teacher, the next-door neighbor, and so on. Sometimes their pretend play reflects an adult role; at other times they make fun of it. Here is one example of pretend play:

> Harvey was playing with Karen, his twin sister. Karen began to push the carriage. Harvey said, "Let me be the baby, Karen," and started to talk like a baby. He got into the carriage. Karen pushed him around the room as he squinted his eyes and cried. She stopped the carriage, patted his shoulder, saying, "Don't cry, baby." He squirmed around, put his thumb in his mouth, and swayed his body.
>
> Josie came to the carriage and wanted to push Harvey. He jumped out and hit her in the face. She walked away almost crying. He went to her, put his arm around her, and said, in a sympathetic manner, "Come, you be the baby. I'll push you in the carriage." She climbed in. He ran and got the dog and gave it to her saying, "Here, baby." She smiled and began to play with the dog. He went to the housekeeping corner, got a cup, and held it to her mouth. He smacked his lips, looking at her, smiling. He pushed her around in the carriage. Karen ran to him and said, "Harvey, let me push the carriage. I'll be the mamma, you be the daddy." Harvey said, "O.K.," and reached his hand in his pocket and gave her money. He said, "Bye, baby," waving his hand. (Hartley, Frank, & Goldenson, 1952, pp. 70–72)

You probably can remember many episodes of pretend play from your own childhood—playing doctor, teacher, and so on. As you think about your early childhood years, play probably is one of the predominant themes.

The language development of preschool children undoubtedly contributes to their increase in pretend play. As they become more proficient at using language, preschool children use words in creative ways as they generate a world of fantasy. It also is in the preschool time frame that children may construct imaginary companions or playmates. From Piaget's perspective, the symbolic play of children allows them to practice their cognitive skills in a relaxed, nonthreatening atmosphere. Pretend play might be either a prerequisite for language and cognitive development, a concurrent achievement, or a consequence of having developed such abilities (Rubin, Fein, & Vanderberg, 1983).

| | **Concept Table 13.1** | |
| | Peers and Play | |
Concept	Processes/Related Ideas	Characteristics/Description
Peers	Peer group functions	Peers provide social comparison and a source of information outside the family.
	Developmental course	Peers as young as six months interact, but peer interaction increases substantially through childhood. Conformity to antisocial peer standards peaks around eighth to ninth grade.
	Peer popularity, rejection, and neglect	Listening skills and effective communication, being yourself, being happy, showing enthusiasm and concern for others, and having self-confidence but not being conceited are predictors of peer popularity. Rejected children are at risk for social problems; the risk status of neglected children is less clear.
	Cognition and peer relations	Perspective-taking ability, social information-processing skills, and social knowledge are associated with improved peer relations.
	Friends	Children's friendships serve six functions: companionship, stimulation, physical support, ego support, social comparison, and intimacy/affection. Intimacy and similarity are two common characteristics of friendships.
	Children's groups	Groups exist when several children interact on an ongoing basis, sharing values and goals. Norms and status positions develop in groups. Superordinate tasks may reduce intergroup conflict. Children's groups are not as formal, are less heterogeneous, and are less cross-sexed than adolescents' groups.
	Family and peer worlds	The worlds of peers and the family are distinct but coordinated. In some ways peer relations are similar to parent-child relations, in others ways they are different.
Play	Functions	The functions of play include affiliation with peers, tension release, advances in cognitive development, exploration, and provision of a safe haven in which to engage in potentially dangerous activities.
	Types	Unoccupied, solitary, onlooker, parallel, associative, and cooperative play are among the most characteristic play styles. One of the most enjoyable forms of play is pretend play, in which the child transforms the environment into a symbol. The ability to distinguish fantasy play from reality increases through the preschool and elementary school years.

From early in the preschool years through the elementary school years, children develop clearer boundaries between fantasy play and reality. For example, at age three, one child pretended to be a monster to scare other people. As he walked around the playroom making growling sounds, a look of fear came over his face. He broke into tears that required considerable comforting from the adult present. A five-year-old girl also was observed playing monster but showed much greater control of her fantasy production, simply transforming the monster into someone who was kind and who ate breakfast with her family (DiLalla & Watson, 1988). Researchers have demonstrated that the ability to distinguish appearance from reality continues to improve in the elementary school years (Flavell, Green, & Flavell, 1987).

At this point we have considered a number of ideas about children's peer relations and play. A summary of these ideas is presented in Concept Table 13.1.

Schools

It is justifiable to be concerned about the impact of schools on children's development. By the time individuals graduate from high school they have spent 10,000 hours in the classroom. Children spend many years in schools as members of a small society in which there are tasks to be accomplished, people who socialize them, and rules that define and limit behavior, feelings, and attitudes.

The children shown here playing with hula hoops are attending a kindergarten. What are some of the positive and negative benefits of early childhood education?

The experiences of children in this society influence their identities, competencies, images of life and career possibilities, social relationships, standards of right and wrong, and conceptions of how a social system beyond the family functions. Our developmental journey through schools takes us through early childhood, middle and late childhood, and adolescence as we explore early childhood education, elementary schools, and secondary schools.

Early Childhood Education

Early childhood education has become a pervasive experience of children in our society—even children from lower socioeconomic backgrounds have been widely exposed to education at the preschool level. The term **child-centered** is used to describe the most popular form of education before the first grade. Child-centered means an emphasis on the individual child, wide-ranging experiences, exploration, and enjoyment. But in reality there are a diversity of goals and curricula in preschool education. Some nursery schools emphasize social development, others cognitive development. Some stress daily structured activities, others more flexible activities. Given the diversity of preschool education, can we reach an overall conclusion about its effect on children's development? Children who attend preschool (Clarke-Stewart & Fein, 1983)—

1. interact more with peers, both positively and negatively;
2. are less cooperative with and responsive to adults than home-reared children;
3. are more socially competent and mature in that they are more confident, extraverted, assertive, self-sufficient, independent, verbally expressive, knowledgeable about the social world, comfortable in social and stressful circumstances, and better adjusted when they go to school—exhibiting more task persistence, leadership, and goal direction, for example;
4. are less socially competent in that they are less polite, less compliant to teacher demands, louder, and more aggressive and bossy, especially if the school or family supports such behavior.

In sum, early childhood education generally has a positive effect on children's development, since the behaviors just mentioned—while at times negative—seem to be in the direction of developmental maturity in the sense that they increase as the child progresses through the preschool years.

For many years, children from low-income families did not receive any education before they entered the first grade. In the 1960s, an effort was made to try to break the poverty and poor education cycle for young children in the United States through compensatory education. As part of this effort, **Project Head Start** began in the summer of 1965, funded by the Economic Opportunity Act. The program was designed to provide children from low-income families with an opportunity to experience an enriched environment. It was hoped that early intervention might counteract the disadvantages these children had experienced and place them on an equal level with other children when they entered the first grade.

Project Head Start consisted of many different types of preschool programs in different parts of the country. Initially, little effort was made to find out whether some programs worked better than others, although it became apparent that this was the case. Consequently, **Project Follow-Through** was established in 1967. A significant aspect of this program was planned variation, in which different kinds of educational programs were devised to see whether specific programs were effective. In the Follow-Through programs, the enriched planned variation was carried through the first few years of elementary school.

Were some Follow-Through programs more effective than others? Many of the variations were able to obtain their desired effects on children. For example, children in academically oriented, direct instruction approaches did better on achievement tests and were more persistent on tasks than children in the other approaches. Children in affective education approaches were absent from school less and showed more independence than children in other approaches. Thus, Project Follow-Through was important in demonstrating that variation in early childhood education does have significant effects in a wide range of social and cognitive areas (Stallings, 1975).

The effects of compensatory education in early childhood continue to be studied, and recent evaluations demonstrate its positive influence on both the social and cognitive development of disadvantaged young children (Lee, Brooks-Gunn, & Schnur, 1988). Of special interest is the long-term effect such intervention might have. Differences favor children who attended Head Start compared to those who did not by the time they reach early adulthood; the advantages also favor males more than females. These are the findings of an ongoing large study of improverished black children who participated in Head Start in Harlem during the 1960s (Deutch & others, 1981). More than 150 adults currently are involved in this study, half of whom entered Head Start when they were four years old. The others did not get this training and serve as the comparison group. All have been interviewed by psychologists every two to three years since the Head Start experience.

For the most part, the Head Start males have been successful in the school and job markets: 32 percent are attending college, only 20 percent of the non–Head Start group are; 57 percent are employed full time or part-time, compared with only 44 percent of the non–Head Start group. These positive benefits did not appear for the females, who seem to be no better off than those who started school at the usual age. The researchers are not sure why the young adult females are not doing as well as their male counterparts. The school system may absorb some of the blame. The preschool program stressed verbal skills, inquisitiveness, and self-confidence. In elementary school, boys were rewarded for these characteristics, but in many instances girls were punished for them. Some teachers even complained that the girls were too assertive and asked too many questions. But there are some indications that Head Start may indeed have left a positive impression on the females too. Many females had to leave school because they became pregnant, but preliminary indications suggest that those who were in the Head Start program are more likely to return to school and continue their education.

Other studies also suggest that competent education programs with preschool children can have a lasting effect. Irving Lazar, Richard Darlington, and their colleagues (1982) established a number of different model programs for educating low-income preschool children in the 1960s and 1970s. They pooled their resources into what they called a consortium for longitudinal studies, developed to share information about the long-term effects of preschool programs so that better designs and methods could be created. At the time the data from the eleven different early education studies were analyzed, the children ranged in age from nine to nineteen years. The early education models varied substantially, but all were carefully planned and carried out by experts in the field of early childhood education. Outcome measures included indicators of school competence (such as special education and grade retention), abilities (as measured by standardized intelligence and achievement tests), attitudes and values, and impact on the family. The results indicated substantial benefits of competent preschool education with low-income children on all four dimensions investigated. In sum, there is ample evidence that well-designed and implemented preschool education programs with low-income children are successful.

Elementary Schools

What is the transition to full-time schooling in the first grade like for children? What roles do teachers and peers play in the child's school? What makes a good teacher? Do some teaching styles work better with some children than others? Do schools heavily favor white, middle-class students? We consider each of these questions in turn.

For most children, entering the first grade signals a change from being a "home child" to being a "school child" in which new roles and obligations are experienced. Children take up a new role (being a student), interact and develop relationships with new significant others, adopt new reference groups, and develop new standards by which to judge themselves. School provides children with a rich source of new ideas to shape their sense of self.

A special concern about children's early school experiences is emerging. While we know little about the transitional nature of teaching in the early grades, what research is available suggests that early schooling proceeds mainly on the basis of negative feedback. For example, children's self-esteem in the latter part of elementary school is lower than it is in the earlier part and older children rate themselves as less smart, less good, and less hardworking than do younger ones (Blumenfeld & others, 1981; Eschel & Klein, 1981; Morse, 1964). In one investigation (Entwisle & others, 1987), the emergence of children's academic self-images was different for boys and girls. The academic self-images of first-grade girls strongly reflected stereotypic gender role notions. These first-grade girls did not consider their abilities in mathematics relevant to their academic self-images, even though they did as well in math as boys and were exposed to the same kind of math instruction as boys. By contrast, first-grade boys were more concerned with the achievement aspects of their student roles.

Teachers and peers have a prominent influence on children in middle and late childhood. Teachers symbolize authority and establish the classroom's climate, conditions of interaction among students, and the nature of group functioning. The peer group is an important source of status, friendship, and belonging in the school setting; the peer group also is a learning community in which social roles and standards related to work and achievement are formed.

Virtually everyone's life is affected in one way or another by teachers: You were probably influenced by teachers as you grew up; you may become a teacher yourself or work with teachers through counseling or psychological services; and you may one day have children whose education will be guided by many different teachers through the years. You can probably remember several of your teachers vividly: Perhaps one never smiled, another required you to memorize everything in sight, and yet another always appeared happy and vibrant and encouraged verbal interaction. Psychologists and educators have tried to create a profile of a good teacher's personality traits, but the complexity of personality, education, learning, and individual differences makes the task difficult. Nonetheless, some teacher traits are associated with positive student outcomes more than others—enthusiasm, ability to plan, poise, adaptability, warmth, flexibility, and awareness of individual differences, for example (Gage, 1965).

Erik Erikson (1968) believes that good teachers should be able to produce a sense of industry, rather than inferiority, in their students. Good teachers are trusted and respected by the community and know how to alternate work and play, study and games, says Erikson. They know how to recognize special efforts and to encourage special abilities. They also know how to create a setting in which children feel good about themselves and how to handle those children to whom school is not important. In Erikson's own words, children should be "mildly but firmly coerced into the adventure of finding out that one can learn to accomplish things which one would never have thought of by oneself." (p. 127)

Teacher characteristics and styles are important, but they need to be considered in concert with what children bring to the school situation. Some children may benefit more from structure than others, and some teachers may be able to handle a flexible curriculum better than others. The importance of both children's characteristics and the treatments or experiences they are given in classrooms is known as **aptitude-treatment interaction (ATI).** Aptitude refers to academic potential and personality dimensions on which students differ; treatment refers to educational techniques—structured versus flexible classrooms, for example (Cronbach & Snow, 1977). Research has shown that children's achievement levels (aptitudes) interact with classroom structure (treatment) to produce the best learning and most enjoyable learning environment (Peterson, 1977). That is, high achievement-oriented students usually do well in a flexible classroom and enjoy it; low achievement-oriented students usually fare worse and dislike the flexibility. The reverse often appears in structured classrooms.

Sometimes it seems as though the major function of schools in this country is to train children to contribute to a middle-class society. Politicians who vote on school funding are usually middle class, school board members are usually middle class, and principals and teachers usually are middle class. Critics argue that schools have not done a good job in educating lower-class children to overcome the barriers blocking the enhancement of their positions.

Teachers have lower expectations for children from low-income families than for children from middle-income families. A teacher who knows that a child comes from a lower-class background may spend less time trying to help the child solve a problem and may anticipate that the child will get into trouble. The teacher may perceive that the parents in low-income families are not interested in helping the child so she may make fewer efforts to communicate with them. There is evidence that teachers with lower-class origins may have different attitudes toward lower-class students than teachers from middle-class origins (Gottlieb, 1966). Perhaps because they have experienced many inequities themselves, teachers with lower-class origins may be more empathetic to problems these children encounter. When asked to rate the most outstanding characteristics of their lower-class students, middle-class teachers checked lazy, rebellious, and fun-loving; lower-class teachers checked happy, cooperative, energetic, and ambitious. The teachers with lower-class backgrounds perceived the lower-class children's behaviors as adaptive; the middle-class teachers viewed the same behaviors as falling short of middle-class standards.

Martin Luther King once said, "I have a dream that my four little children will one day live in a nation where they will not be judged by the color of their skin but by the content of their character." Not only have children from lower-class backgrounds had difficulties in school, so have children from different ethnic backgrounds. In most American schools, blacks, Mexican

Describing what a good teacher is has been a difficult assignment. The teacher shown here has the ability to stimulate enthusiasm in her students. Think for a moment about your own experiences with teachers. What attributes of your good teachers come to mind? What attributes of your bad teachers come to mind?

Americans, Puerto Ricans, Native Americans, Japanese, and Asian Indians are minorities. The social and academic development of children from minority groups depends on teacher expectations, the teacher's experience in working with children from different backgrounds, the curriculum, the presence of role models in the schools for minority students, the quality of relations between school personnel and parents from different ethnic, economic, and educational backgrounds, and the relations between the school and the community (Minuchin & Shapiro, 1983; Scott-Jones & Clark, 1986). Remember from our discussion of group behavior earlier in the chapter that cooperative learning experiences, such as those involving the jigsaw classroom, show promise in reducing interracial tension among children (Aronson, 1986; Slavin, 1987).

Secondary Schools

What should be the function of secondary schools? What are effective schools for young adolescents like? What is the nature of the transition from elementary to middle or junior high school? We consider each of these questions.

Secondary schools seem to have always been wrapped in controversy. One of the controversies revolves around whether adolescents should be treated more like children or more like adults. In the United States, adolescents have been kept in school for as long as possible. This policy has practical implications because it has delayed the entry of youth into the labor force. Further, high schools have been perceived as the most competent environment for adolescents to gain the maturity and skills they need to function in the adult world. For more than 150 years, compulsory school attendance has been mandated.

However, in the 1960s, the distress over alienated and rebellious youth brought up the issue of whether secondary schools were actually beneficial to adolescents. During the 1970s, three independent panels agreed that high school contributes to adolescent alienation and actually restricts the transition to adulthood (Brown, 1973; Coleman & others, 1974; Martin 1976). These prestigious panels argued that adolescents should be given educational alternatives to the comprehensive high school—in the form of on-the-job community work, for example—to increase their exposure to adult roles and to decrease their sense of isolation from the adult world. In response to these reports, a number of states lowered the age at which adolescents could leave school from sixteen to fourteen.

In the 1980s, the back-to-basics movement gained momentum, arguing that the main function of schools should be rigorous training of intellectual skills through subjects like English, math, and science. Proponents of the back-to-basics movement emphasize that there is too much fluff in the secondary school curricula, with students being allowed to select from too many alternatives that will not give them a basic education in intellectual subjects. Critics of the fluff in secondary schools also argue that the school day should be longer and that the school year should be extended into the summer months. Some critics believe that too much emphasis is placed on extracurricular activities. They argue that schools should be in the business of imparting knowledge to adolescents and should show little or no concern for their social and emotional development. Related to the issue of the function of secondary schools is the proverbial dilemma of whether schools should include a vocational curriculum in addition to training in such basic subjects as English, math, science, and history.

Should the main and perhaps only goal of schooling for adolescents be the development of an intellectually mature individual? Or should schools also show a strong concern for emotional and social maturity? Should schools be comprehensive and provide a multifaceted curriculum that includes many elective and alternative subjects in addition to a basic set of core subjects? These provocative questions continue to be debated in educational and community circles (Cross, 1984; Cuban, 1988; Goodlad, 1983; Kearns, 1988; Sizer, 1984).

What makes an effective school for young adolescents? Joan Lipsitz and her colleagues (1984) searched the nation for the best middle schools. Extensive contacts and observations were conducted. Eventually, based on the recommendations of education experts and observations in schools in different parts of the United States, four middle schools were chosen for their outstanding ability to educate young adolescents. What were these middle schools like? The most striking feature of the four best middle schools was their willingness and ability to adapt all school practices to the individual differences in physical, cognitive, and social development of their students. The schools took information about early adolescent development seriously. This seriousness was reflected in decisions about different aspects of school life. For example, one middle school fought to keep its schedule of minicourses on Friday so that every student could be with friends and pursue personal interests. Two other middle schools expended considerable energy on a complex school organization so that small groups of students worked with small groups of teachers who could vary the tone and pace of the school day, depending on the students' needs. Another middle school developed an advisory scheme so that each student had daily contact with an adult who was willing to listen, explain, comfort, and prod the adolescent. Such school policies reflect thoughtfulness and personal concern about individuals whose developmental needs are compelling.

Another aspect of the effective middle schools observed was that, early in their existence—the first year in three of the schools and the second year in the fourth school—they emphasized the importance of creating an environment that was positive for the adolescent's social and emotional development. This goal was established not only because such environments contribute to academic excellence but also because social and emotional development are intrinsically valued as important in themselves in the schooling of adolescents. Perspective on Child Development 13.2 presents more information about effective middle schools, as well as information about some that are not so effective.

What is the nature of the transition to middle or junior high school? The organization of junior high schools—and more recently middle schools—has been justified on the basis of early adolescents' physical, cognitive, and social changes. The growth spurt and the onset of puberty were the basis for removing seventh- and eighth-grade students from elementary schools (Hill, 1980). Because puberty has been coming earlier, the same kind of thinking has been applied to the formation of middle schools that house sixth- and sometimes fifth-graders in separate buildings along with seventh- and eighth-graders.

The transition to middle or junior high school from an elementary school is of interest to developmentalists because, even though it is a normative experience for virtually all children in our society, this transition can be stressful

The adolescents shown here are students in an effective middle school, one that emphasizes the importance of creating an environment that is positive for their social and emotional development.

Beyond the Zoo

When teachers complain about young adolescents, animal imagery is pervasive: "This school is a zoo," "Those students are like animals," "It is a jungle in the classroom." In schools that seem like "zoos," students usually do not learn effectively and often are not very happy. Consider these vignettes from four ineffective middle schools (Lipsitz, 1984).

A teacher sits in the back of the room, her legs up on her desk, asking students questions from a textbook. The students, bored and listless, sit in straight rows facing no one in the front of the room, answering laconically to a blank blackboard. When the principal enters the room, the teacher lowers her legs to the floor. Nothing else changes.

A teacher drills students for a seemingly endless amount of time on prime numbers. After the lesson, not one of them can say why it is important to learn prime numbers.

A visitor asks a teacher if hers is an eighth-grade class. "It's called eighth grade," she answers archly, "but we know it's really kindergarten—right, class?" In a predominantly Hispanic school, only the one adult hired as a bilingual teacher speaks Spanish.

In a biracial school, the principal and the guidance counselor cite test scores with pride. They are asked if the difference between the test scores of black and white students is narrowing. "Oh, that's an interesting question!" the guidance counselor says in surprise. The principal agrees. It has never been asked by or of them before.

A teacher in a social studies class squelches several imaginative questions, exclaiming, "You're always asking 'what if' questions. Stop asking 'what if!'" When a visitor asks who will become president if the president-elect dies before the electoral college meets, the teacher explodes: "You're as bad as they are! That's another 'what if' question!" (pp. 169–170)

By contrast, consider the following circumstances in effective middle schools (Lipsitz, 1984).

Everything is peaceful. There are open cubbies instead of locked lockers. There is no theft. Students walk quietly in the corridors. "Why?" they are asked. "So as not to disturb the media center," they answer, which is self-evident to them but not the visitor who is left wondering. . . . When asked, "Do you like this school?" (They) answer: "No, we don't like it. We love it!" (p. 27)

When asked how the school feels, one student answered, "It feels smart. We're smart. Look at our test scores." Comments from one of the parents of a student at the school are revealing: "My child would have been a dropout. In elementary school, his teacher said to me: 'That child isn't going to give you anything but heartaches.' He had perfect attendance here. He didn't want to miss a day. Summer vacation was too long and boring. Now he's majoring in communications at the University of Texas. He got here and all of a sudden someone cared for him. I had been getting notes about Roger every other day, with threats about expulsion. Here, the first note said: "It's just a joy to have him in the classroom.' " (p. 84)

The humane environment that encourages teachers' growth . . . is translated by the teachers . . . into a humane environment that encourages students' growth. The school feels cold when one first enters. It has the institutional feeling of any large school building with metal lockers and impersonal halls. Then one opens the door to a team area, and it is filled with energy, movement, productivity, doing. There is a lot of informal relating among students and between students and teachers. Visible from one vantage point are students working on written projects, putting the last touches on posters, watching a film, and working independently from reading kits. . . . Most know what they are doing, can say why it is important, and go back to work immediately after being interrupted. (p. 109)

Authors' Week is yet another special activity built into the school's curriculum that entices students to consider themselves in relation to the rich variety of making and doing in people's lives. Based on student interest, availability, and diversity, authors are invited . . . to discuss their craft. Students sign up to meet with individual authors. They must have read one individual book by the author. . . . Students prepare questions for their sessions with the authors. . . . Sometimes, an author stays several days to work with a group of students on his or her manuscript. (p. 141)

These exerpts about a variety of schools in different areas of the United States reveal the great diversity among schools for adolescents. They also tell us that—despite the inefficiency of many schools for adolescents—others are very effective. Secondary schools can be breeding grounds for competent academic *and* social development.

because of the point in development at which the transition takes place (Hawkins & Berndt, 1985; Simmons & others, 1987). Transition to middle or junior high school occurs at a time in development when a number of simultaneous changes are occurring:

—puberty and related concerns about body image
—emergence of at least some aspects of formal operational thought and social cognition
—increased responsibility and independence and decreased dependency on parents
—change from a small, contained classroom structure to a larger, more impersonal school structure
—change from one teacher to many teachers and from a small, homogeneous set of peers to a larger, more heterogeneous set of peers
—increased focus on achievement and performance and their assessment

Moving from the top position (in elementary school, as the oldest, biggest, and most powerful students in the school) to the bottom position (in middle or junior high school, as the youngest, smallest, and least powerful group of students) may create a number of problems for students. This has been referred to as the **top-dog phenomenon.**

The transition to middle or junior high school does have some positive possibilities too. Students are more likely to feel grown up, to have more subjects from which to select, to have more opportunities to spend time with peers and more chances to locate compatible friends, to enjoy increased independence from direct parental and teacher monitoring, and to be more challenged intellectually by academic work. Researchers have found that schools providing more supportiveness, less anonymity, more stability, and less complexity have a salutary effect on student adjustment in the transition to middle and junior high school (Hawkins & Berndt, 1985; Simmons & others, 1987).

Television

Few developments in society over the last twenty-five years have had a greater impact on children than has television. Many children spend more time in front of a television set than they do with their parents. Although only one of mass media's vehicles that affects children's behavior—books, comics, movies, and newspapers are others—television is the most influential. The persuasion capabilities of television are staggering; the 20,000 hours of television watched by the time the average American adolescent graduates from high school is far more than the number of hours spent in the classroom.

Television's Functions

Television has been called a lot of things, not all of them good. Depending on one's point of view, it may be a "window on the world," "the one-eyed monster," or the "boob tube." Television has been attacked as one of the reasons that scores on national achievement tests in reading and mathematics are lower now than in the past. Television, it is claimed, attracts children away from books and schoolwork. In one study (Huston, Seigle, & Bremer, 1983), children who read books and the printed media watched television less than those who did not. Further, it is argued that television trains the child to become a passive learner. Rarely, if ever, does television require active responses from

From *It's a Mom's Life* by David Sipress. Copyright © 1988 by David Sipress. Reprinted by arrangement with NAL Penguin Inc., New York, NY.

the observer. Heavy television viewing may not only produce passive learners it may also produce passive life styles. In one recent investigation of 406 adolescent males, light television viewers were more physically fit and physically active than heavy television viewers (Tucker, 1987).

Television also is said to deceive; that is, it teaches children that problems are easily resolved and that everything always comes out right in the end. For example, it usually takes only thirty to sixty minutes for detectives to sort through a complex array of clues and discover the killer—and they always find the killer. Violence is pictured as a way of life in many shows. It is all right for police to use violence and break moral codes in their fight against evildoers. And the lasting results of violence are rarely brought home to the viewer. An individual who is injured suffers only for a few seconds; in real life the individual might take months or years to recover or perhaps does not recover at all. Yet, one out of every two first-grade children says that the adults on television are like adults in real life (Lyle & Hoffman, 1972).

But there are some positive aspects to television's influence on children. For one, television presents children with a world that is different than the one in which they live. This means that, through television, children are exposed to a wider variety of views and knowledge than may be the case when children are informed only by their parents, teachers, and peers.

Just how much television do young children watch? They watch a lot and they seem to be watching more all the time. In the 1950s, three-year-old children watched television for less than 1 hour a day; five-year-olds watched just over 2 hours a day. But in the 1970s, preschool children watched television for an average of 4 hours a day; elementary school children watched for as long as 6 hours a day (Friedrich & Stein, 1973). In 1980–81, children aged two to five years viewed 27.8 hours per week (Nielson Television Index, 1981). Of special concern is the extent children are exposed to violence and aggression on television. Up to 80 percent of the prime-time shows include violent acts—beatings, shootings, and stabbings, for example. The frequency of violence even increases on the Saturday morning cartoon shows—they average more than twenty-five violent episodes per hour.

Children's Attention to Television

How strong is the child's increase in attention to television during the preschool years? In one investigation (Anderson, Choi, & Lorch, 1987), two video cameras and a time-lapse recorder were used to observe the young child's attention to television in the natural setting of the home. Ninety-nine families that included 460 individuals were observed; the time samples included 4,672 hours of recordings. The results: Visual attention to television dramatically increased during the preschool years (figure 13.8).

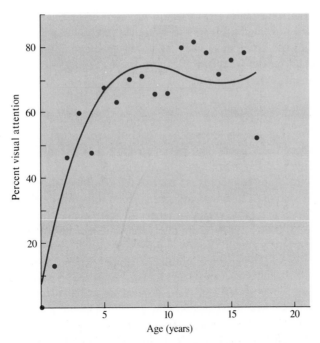

Figure 13.8 at top right.

Figure 13.8
Increase in visual attention to television during the preschool years.

The formal features of television programming influence the child's attention. Formal features that signal child-oriented content not only enhance children's attention, but they increase the probability that children will process the content more actively and, it is hoped, learn the content more thoroughly. One investigation clearly revealed this process (Campbell, Wright, & Huston, 1983). Two parallel sets of public service announcements containing nutritional information were developed. The content of the two announcements was virtually identical, but the forms were different. One set was produced with child-oriented forms—animation, character voices, and lively music. The second set was made with adult-oriented forms—live photography, adult male narration, and soft music. Five- and six-year-old children attended more to the child-oriented than to the adult-oriented version. And children recalled more of the content of the child-oriented version, regardless of how difficult the message was. The implication: The form of a television show can lure children into doing some cognitive work when the form signals that the content is age appropriate, interesting, comprehensible, or in some other way worth some mental effort (Wright & Huston, 1985). The current innovation of interaction being developed by such television shows as "Sesame Street," in which the child can actually engage in a conversation with a television character, promises to further promote the child's mental effort.

The Social Context of Viewing

To what degree do parents take an active role in discussing television with their children? For the most part, parents do not discuss the content of television shows with their children (Leiffer, Gordon, & Graves, 1974). Parents need to be especially sensitive to young children's viewing habits because the age period of two and one-half to six is when long-term television-viewing habits begin to be established. Children from lower socioeconomic status families watch television more than children from higher socioeconomic status families (Huston, Seigle, & Bremer, 1983). And children who live in families involved in high conflict watch more television than children who live in families low in conflict (Price & Feshbach, 1982). In one recent investigation (Tangney, in

371

Television pours massive doses of violent aggression into the minds of children. Does television violence—as shown here—merely stimulate the child observer to go out and buy a Darth Vader ray gun, or does it trigger an attack on a playmate?

press), the children of parents who showed more empathy and were more sensitive to them preferred less fantasy fare on television. In dysfunctional families, children may use the lower developmental level of fantasy-oriented children's programs to escape from the taxing, stressful circumstances of the home environment.

Children's Behavior

How extensively does television influence children's behavior? Three areas where researchers have discovered a link between television viewing and children's behavior are aggression, prosocial behavior, and eating behavior.

Some psychologists believe television violence has a profound influence on shaping children's aggressive thoughts and behaviors; others believe the effects are exaggerated (Liebert & Spratkin, 1988; McQuire, 1986; Roberts & Maccoby, 1985). Does television violence merely stimulate a child to go out and buy a Darth Vader ray gun? Or does it trigger an attack on a playmate and even increase the number of violent attacks and murders?

Violence on television is associated with aggression in individuals who watch it. For example, in one investigation the amount of television violence watched by children when they were in elementary school was associated with how aggressive they were at age nineteen and at age thirty (Eron, 1987; Huesmann & others, in press; Lefkowitz & others, 1972). In another investigation, long-term exposure to television violence increased the likelihood of aggression in 1,565 boys aged twelve to seventeen (Belson, 1978). Boys who watched the most aggression on television were the most likely to commit some violent action, swear, be aggressive in sports, threaten violence toward another boy, write slogans on walls, or break windows. The types of television violence most often associated with aggression were realistic, took place between individuals in close relationships rather than between strangers, and were committed by the "good guys" rather than the "bad guys."

But it is another step to conclude that television violence in itself causes aggressive behavior. Children who watch the most violence may be more aggressive in the first place; other factors such as poverty and unpleasant life experiences may be culprits too. So far we have not been able to establish a causal link from television violence to aggression (Freedman, 1984). Like other behaviors, aggression is multiply determined.

Television can also teach children that it is better to behave in positive, prosocial ways rather than in negative, antisocial ways. Aimee Leiffer (1973) demonstrated how television is associated with prosocial behavior in young children. She selected a number of episodes from the television show "Sesame Street" that reflected positive social interchanges. She was especially interested in situations that taught children how to use their social skills. For example, in one interchange, two men were fighting over the amount of space available to them. They gradually began to cooperate and to share the space. Children who watched these episodes copied these behaviors and in later social situations applied the prosocial lessons they had learned.

When we watch television, we are exposed to commercials as well as regular programming. For example, the average television-viewing child sees more than 20,000 commercials per year! A significant portion of the commercials shown during children's television shows involve food products that are high in sugar (Barcus, 1978). In one investigation, three- to six-year-old children were exposed to television cartoons over a four-week period. The advertising content of the shows consisted of either commercials for food products with added sugar, food products with no added sugar, or pronutritional

Social and Personality Development

Table 13.1
Average Proportion of Snacks with Added Sugar Selected during Four
Weeks of Experimental Intervention

	Condition				
Intervention week	S-NC	NS-NC	S-C	NS-C	CT
3	.86	.88	.80	.71	.90
4	.74	.80	.73	.58	.84
5	.77	.86	.76	.68	.87
6	.83	.81	.83	.71	.88

Note: S-NC Commercials for food products with added sugar viewed without adult commentary.

NS-NC No sugar added and public service announcement without adult commentary.

S-C Sugar added and adult commentary.

NS-C No sugar added and pronutritional public service announcement with adult commentary.

CT The control condition, in which children had no television exposure.

From J. P. Galst, ''Television Food Commercials and Pro-Nutritional Public Service Announcements as Determinants of Young Children's Snack Choices'' in *Child Development 51:* 935–938. Copyright © 1980 The Society for Research in Child Development, Chicago, IL. Reprinted by permission.

public service announcements, with or without adult comments about the portrayed product (Galst, 1980). The most effective treatment in reducing the child's selection of sugar snacks was exposure to commercials with food products without added sugar combined with pronutritional public service announcements with accompanying positive comments by an adult (see table 13.1—the NS-C condition with the lower proportions, .71 in week three, .58 in week four, .68 in week five, and .71 in week six).

Some Practical Suggestions

Parents can make television a more positive influence in children's lives. The following guidelines developed by Dorothy and Jerome Singer (1987) can go a long way in reducing television's negative effects and improving its role as a positive influence in children's development.

1. Develop good viewing habits early in the child's life.
2. Encourage planned viewing of specific programs rather than random viewing. Be active with young children between planned programs.
3. Look for children's programs that feature children in the child's age group.
4. Make sure that television is not used as a substitute for participating in other activities.
5. Develop discussion about sensitive television themes with children. Give them the opportunity to ask questions about the programs.
6. Balance reading and television activities. Children can "follow up" interesting television programs by checking out the library book from which some programs are adapted and by pursuing additional stories by the authors of those books.
7. Help children to develop a balanced viewing schedule of education, action, comedy, fine arts, fantasy, sports, and so on.
8. Point out positive examples that show how various ethnic and cultural groups all contribute to making a better society.
9. Point out positive examples of females performing competently both in professions and at home.

Since our last review, we have discussed a number of ideas about the influence of schools and television on children's lives. A summary of these ideas is presented in Concept Table 13.2.

Concept Table 13.2 Schools and Television

Concept	Processes/Related Ideas	Characteristics/Description
Schools	Early childhood education	The predominant approach is child-centered. Children who attend preschool are usually more competent than those who do not attend, although they show more negative behaviors too. Compensatory education has tried to break through the poverty cycle with programs such as Head Start and Project Follow-Through. Longitudinal studies indicate that Head Start's effect on development is positive.
	Elementary schools	A special concern is that early schooling proceeds mainly on the basis of negative feedback to children. A profile of a good teacher's personality traits is difficult to construct, although some traits are clearly superior to others. Aptitude-treatment interaction is an important consideration. Schools have a stronger middle-class than lower-class orientation. Not only do many lower-class children have problems in schools, so do children from ethnic minorities.
	Secondary schools	The function of secondary schools has been wrapped in controversy. Some maintain that the function should be intellectual development, others argue for a more comprehensive function. Effective schools for young adolescents take individual differences in development seriously, show a deep concern for what is known about early adolescence, and emphasize social and emotional development as much as intellectual development. The organization of junior high schools—and more recently middle schools—has been justified on the basis of physical, cognitive, and social changes in adolescents. The earlier onset of puberty has led to the formation of middle schools. The transition to middle or junior high schools coincides with a number of individual, familial, and social changes; one problem involves going from a top-dog position to a bottom position.
Television	Functions	Functions of television include provision of information and entertainment. Television portrays a world beyond the family, peers, and school. However, television may train children to become passive learners, it is deceiving, and it often takes children away from reading and studying. Children watch a lot of television; preschool children watch an average of four hours a day. Up to 80 percent of prime-time shows have violent episodes.
	Attention	Children's attention to television increases dramatically during the preschool years. The formal features of television programming influence children's attention.
	Social context	Parents rarely discuss television's contents with their children. The early childhood years are a formative period for viewing habits. Children from lower socioeconomic status backgrounds watch more than their higher socioeconomic status counterparts. Family conflict is associated with increased viewing, especially fantasy fare.
	Impact on children's behavior	Television violence is associated with children's aggression, but no causal link has been established. Prosocial behavior on television is associated with increased positive behavior on the part of young children. The average television-viewing child sees 20,000 commercials per year! Commercials influence children's food preferences.
	Some practical suggestions	Parents can be effective mediators of television's influence on children through discussion and monitoring.

Summary

I. Peers

Peers provide social comparison and a source of information outside the family. Peers as young as six months of age interact, but peer interaction increases dramatically during childhood. Conformity to antisocial peer standards peaks around the eighth and ninth grades. Listening skills and effective communication, being yourself, being happy, showing enthusiasm and concern for others, and having self-confidence but not being conceited are predictors of peer popularity.

Rejected children are at risk for social problems but the risk status of neglected children is less clear. Perspective-taking ability, social information-processing skills, and social knowledge are associated with improved peer relations. Children's friendships serve six functions: companionship, stimulation, physical support, ego support, social comparison, and intimacy/affection. Intimacy and similarity are two common characteristics of friendship. Groups exist when several children interact on an ongoing basis, sharing values and goals.

Norms and status positions develop in groups. Superordinate tasks may reduce intergroup conflict. Children's groups are not as formal, are less heterogeneous, and are less cross-sexed than adolescents' groups. The worlds of peers and the family are distinct but coordinated. In some ways peer relations are similar to parent-child relations, in other ways they are different.

II. Play

The functions of play include affiliation with peers, tension release, advances in cognitive development, exploration, and provision of a safe haven in which to engage in potentially dangerous activities. Types of play include unoccupied, solitary, onlooker, parallel, associative, and cooperative. One of the most enjoyable forms of play is pretend play, in which the child transforms the environment into a symbol. The ability to distinguish fantasy play from reality increases through the preschool and elementary school years.

III. Schools

The predominant approach in early childhood education is child-centered. Children who attend preschool are usually more competent than those who do not attend, although they show more negative behaviors too. Compensatory education has tried to break through the poverty cycle with programs such as Head Start and Project Follow-Through. Longitudinal studies indicate that Head Start's effect on development is positive. A special concern is that early schooling proceeds mainly on the basis of negative feedback to children. A profile of a good teacher's personality traits has been difficult to construct, although some traits are clearly superior to others. Aptitude-treatment interaction is an important consideration. Schools have a stronger middle-class than lower-class orientation. Not only do many lower-class children have problems in schools, so do many children from ethnic minorities. The function of secondary schools has been wrapped in controversy. Some maintain that the function should be intellectual development, others argue for a more comprehensive function. Effective schools for young adolescents take individual differences in development seriously, show a deep concern for what is known about early adolescence, and emphasize social and emotional development as much as intellectual development. The organization of junior high schools—and more recently middle schools—has been justified on the basis of physical, cognitive, and social changes in adolescents. The earlier onset of puberty has led to the formation of middle schools. The transition to middle or junior high schools coincides with a number of individual, familial, and social changes; one problem involves going from a top-dog position to a bottom position.

IV. Television

The functions of television include provision of information and entertainment. Television portrays a world beyond the family, peers, and school. However, television may train children to become passive learners, it is deceiving, and it often takes children away from reading and studying. Children watch a lot of television; preschool children watch an average of four hours per day. Up to 80 percent of prime-time shows have violent episodes. Children's attention to television increases dramatically during the preschool years. The formal features of television programming influence children's attention. Parents rarely discuss television's contents with their children. The early childhood years are a formative period for viewing habits. Children from lower socioeconomic status backgrounds watch more than their higher socioeconomic status counterparts. Family conflict is associated with increased viewing, especially fantasy fare. Television violence is associated with children's aggression, but no causal link has been established. Prosocial behavior on television is associated with increased positive behavior on the part of children. The average television-viewing child sees 20,000 commercials per year! Commercials influence children's food preferences. Parents can effectively mediate television's influence on children through discussion and monitoring.

Key Terms

peers 349
neglected children 350
rejected children 350
intimacy in friendship 354
norms 354
jigsaw classroom 355
play therapy 357
unoccupied play 358
solitary play 358
onlooker play 358
parallel play 358
associative play 358
cooperative play 359
pretend play 359
semiotic function 359
child-centered 362
Project Head Start 362
Project Follow-Through 362
aptitude-treatment interaction (ATI) 365
top-dog phenomenon 369

Suggested Readings

Görlitz, D., & Wohlwill, J. F. (Eds.). (1987). *Curiosity, imagination, and play.* Hillsdale, NJ: Erlbaum.
A volume with a number of articles by leading experts on the nature of children's play.

Hartup, W. W. (1983). The peer system. In P. H. Mussen (Ed.), *Handbook of child psychology* (4th ed., Vol. 4). New York: John Wiley & Sons.
A detailed look at the development of peer relations by one of the leading experts in the field.

Liebert, R. M., & Spratkin, J. N. (1988). *The early window: Effects of television on children and youth* (3rd ed.). Elmsford, NY: Pergamon.
An updated account of theory and research that addresses the effects of television on children's development.

Lipsitz, J. (1984). *Successful schools for young adolescents.* New Brunswick. NJ: Transaction Books.
Required reading for anyone interested in better schools for young adolescents. Filled with rich examples of successful schools and the factors that contribute to the effective education of young adolescents.

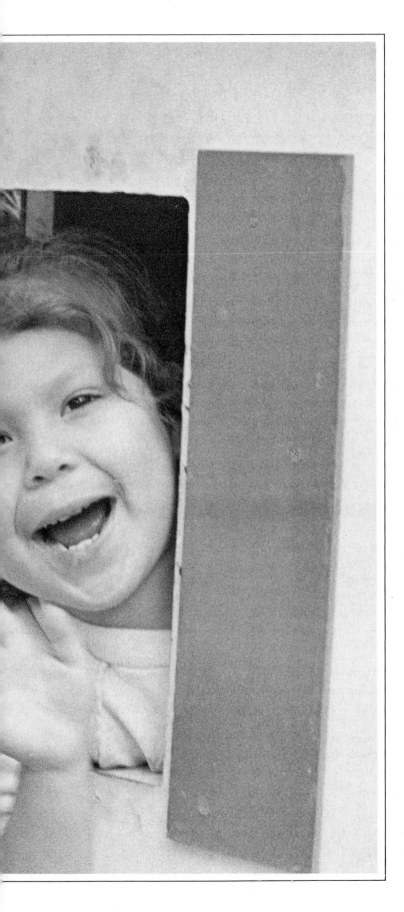

The Self,
Social Competence,
and Identity

Who are you when you say "I"? Who are your best friends when they say "I"? If you look in the mirror, you see a face, one that always looks back at you. When your best friends look in the mirror, they see faces that are very different from yours. When each of us looks in the mirror, we see someone "absolutely unique not to be confused with any other," as Ugo Betti's words so vividly describe. "I" does mean a unique individual as each of us is, was, and will be. And "I" means a physical person, the someone whose skin, stature, and shape you see in the mirror.

Beyond the self's uniqueness and physical nature lie other important dimensions—those that are psychological and social in nature. As you look in the mirror, you see the color of your skin. Each of us has a racial identity, a psychological part of our self that goes beyond the mere white, red, brown, or black tone of our skin. You might also see a learned individual in the mirror, one who possibly has become more educated than prior generations in your family. And you might see someone who is at ease in social situations and has developed positive close relationships with others. These are some of the most important characteristics of the self—its unique nature, its physical nature, its cognitive nature, and its social nature.

But in thinking about what "I" means, would you have described yourself differently when you were a child or an adolescent than you do at this point in your life cycle? Probably so. Wasn't there a point early in your existence as a human being when you didn't even distinguish between yourself and others? When did you begin to recognize this self-identity? Didn't you become much more acutely conscious of who you are, what you are all about as a person, and where you are headed in life during your adolescent years?

This chapter is about the self and its development and about what it takes to be socially competent—as an infant, as a child, and as an adolescent. Among the important concepts to be evaluated are the self, self-concept, social competence, and identity. Why are these concepts together in the same chapter? Each of these concepts attempts to look at children and adolescents in a global way. They strive to portray children as whole children, not merely as pieces of children. Children have only one mind and one body, only one set of behaviors, thoughts, and feelings. The concepts we discuss in this chapter are integrative—they attempt to synthesize the many dimensions of children. The synthesis is not an easy task. As you will see there is not always agreement on what the integration and synthesis should be. Some critics, especially those of a behavioral persuasion, believe it does not make sense to study children in such a broad, global manner. Their strategy is to focus on the pieces of the child, the fine-grained aspects of a child's makeup. However, in recent years there has been increased acceptance of conceptualizing and measuring both molar and molecular, broad and fine-grained, dimensions of children's development (Maccoby, 1983). We begin our evaluation of the self by making a distinction that has been a part of psychology for many years.

I and Me

Early in psychology's history, William James (1890) distinguished between the "I" and the "me" of the self. "I" is the knower, "me" is the object of what is known. "I" is the active observer, "me" is the observed (the product of the observing process). "I" conveys the sense of independent existence, agency, and volition (that is, when my eyes close it gets dark; when I cry, my mother comes; when I bump my hand, it hurts; and so on). This part of the self, "I," emerges first in development. Later, the child learns that not only do "I" exist, but "I" also know the categories that go into making "me." "I" know, for example, that I am a boy and not a girl. Some researchers refer to "I" as the **existential self** and to "me" as the **categorical self.** Development proceeds in a sequence from the existential to the categorical self—from a conception that I am, that I exist, to what or who I am (Lapsley, 1988; Lewis & Brooks-Gunn, 1979; Wylie, 1979). Most of our discussion of the self focuses on the categorical self, especially self-concept.

The Self and Children's Development

Erik Erikson (1968) defined the self in the first year of life as, "I am what hope I have and give," and in the second year of life as, "I am what I can will freely." Erikson's life-cycle theory, which initially was described in chapter 11, will be discussed in greater detail in this chapter with special attention to his view that the major issues for the self to negotiate vary with the individual's developmental status.

Infancy

Among the most important characteristics of the self to emerge during infancy are a sense of trust, self-identification, and independence. We consider each of these in turn.

Trust

According to Erik Erikson (1968), approximately the first year of life is characterized by the stage of development known as **trust versus mistrust.** Following a life of regularity, warmth, and protection in the mother's womb, the infant faces a world that is less secure. Erikson believes that infants learn trust when they are cared for in a consistent, warm manner. If the infant is not well fed and kept warm on a consistent basis, a sense of mistrust is likely to develop.

We briefly described Erikson's ideas about the role of trust in attachment earlier. His thoughts have much in common with Mary Ainsworth's concept of secure attachment. The infant who has a sense of trust is likely to be securely attached and have the confidence to explore new circumstances; the infant who has a sense of mistrust is likely to be insecurely attached and not have such confidence and positive expectations.

Trust versus mistrust is not resolved once and for all in the first year of life; it arises again at each successive stage of development. There is both hope and danger in this. The child who enters school with a sense of mistrust may trust a particular teacher who takes the time to make herself trustworthy—with this second chance he overcomes his early mistrust. By contrast, a child who leaves infancy with a sense of trust can still have his sense of mistrust activated at a later stage if, perhaps, his parents separate and divorce under conflicting circumstances. An example is instructive (Elkind, 1970). A four-year-old boy was seen by a clinical psychologist at a court clinic because his adoptive parents, who had had him for six months, now wanted to give him back to the agency. They said that he was cold and unloving, took things, and could not be trusted. He was indeed a cold and apathetic boy, but with good reason. About a year after his illegitimate birth, he was taken from his mother, who had a drinking problem, and shuttled back and forth among several foster homes. At first he tried to relate to people in the foster homes, but the relationships never had an opportunity to develop because he was moved so frequently. In the end he gave up trying to reach out to others because the inevitable separations hurt too much. Like the burned child who dreads the flame, this emotionally burned child shunned the pain of close relationships. He had trusted his mother, but now he trusted no one. Only years of devoted care and patience could undo the damage to this child's sense of trust.

The Developing Sense of Self and Independence

Individuals carry with them a sense of who they are and what makes them different from everyone else. They cling to this identity and begin to feel secure in the knowledge that this identity is becoming more stable. Real or imagined, this sense of self is a strong motivating force in life. When does the individual begin to sense an existence separate from others?

Children begin to develop a sense of self by learning to distinguish themselves from others (Lewis, 1987). To determine whether infants can recognize themselves, psychologists have used mirrors. In the animal kingdom, only the great apes learn to recognize their reflection in the mirror, but human infants accomplish this feat by about eighteen months of age. How does the mirror technique work? The mother puts a dot of rouge on her infant's nose. The observer watches to see how often the infant touches his nose. Next, the infant is placed in front of a mirror and observers detect whether nose touching increases. In two separate investigations in the second half of the second year of life infants recognized their own images and coordinated the images they saw with the actions of touching their own bodies (figure 14.1) (Amsterdam, 1968; Lewis & Brooks-Gunn, 1979).

The infant's development of a sense of self, then, is based both on the infant's relationship with caregivers (Bretherton, 1987; Mahler, 1979; Pines, 1987) and the infant's developing cognitive skills, especially the ability to represent an image (Harter, 1983; Piaget, 1952; Pipp, Fischer, & Jennings, 1987). Language may also be wrapped up in the self's representation early in life. In

The infant shown here touching his nose and mouth against the mirror reveals the development of a sense of self, which most infants accomplish by about eighteen months of age.

Social and Personality Development

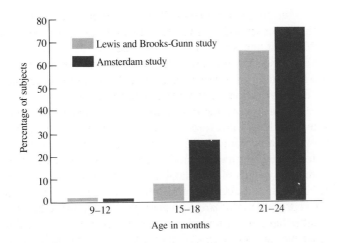

Figure 14.1
The development of self-recognition in infancy. Percentage of subjects showing recognition of the rouge by touching, wiping, or verbally referring to it in two different studies at different ages.

one investigation (Pipp, Fischer, & Jennings, 1987), at eighteen to twenty-three months of age, girls detected more features of themselves than did boys. This is the age at which one type of representational ability, use of sophisticated language, is first emerging, and girls seem to be more advanced in this ability than boys (McCall, Eichorn, & Hogarty, 1977).

Not only does the infant develop a sense of self in the second year of life, but independence becomes a more central theme of the infant's life as well. The theories of Margaret Mahler and Erik Erikson have important implications for both self-development and independence. Mahler (1979) believes that the child goes through a separation and then an individuation process—separation involves the infant's movement away from the mother and individuation involves the development of self.

Mother-child interaction can interfere with the development of individuation. For example, Anna's mother was emotionally unavailable. Never certain of her mother's availability, Anna was preoccupied with it; she found it difficult to explore her surroundings. After a brief spurt of practicing, she would return to her mother and try to interact with her in an intense way. Sometimes she would spill cookies on the floor, always with an eye to gaining her mother's attention. Anna's mother was absorbed with her own interests. During the preschool years, Anna threw temper tantrums and clung to her teacher. Then the clinging would turn to hitting and yelling. In Mahler's view, Anna wanted only one thing to happen—her mother to return through the door. As can be seen in Anna's case, an unsatisfactory mother-infant relationship led to problems in her development of independence.

Erikson (1968), like Mahler, believes that independence is an important issue in the second year of life. Erikson describes the second stage of development as **autonomy versus shame and doubt.** Autonomy builds on the infant's developing mental and motor abilities. At this point in development the infant not only can walk but also can climb, open and close, drop, push and pull, hold and let go. The infant feels pride in these new accomplishments and wants to do everything himself, whether it is flushing the toilet, pulling the wrapping off of a package, or deciding what to eat. It is important for parents to recognize the toddler's need to do what he is capable of doing at his own pace and in his own time. Then, he can learn to control his muscles, his impulses, himself, and his environment. But when caregivers are impatient and do for him what he is capable of doing himself, shame and doubt are developed. Every parent has rushed a child from time to time. It is only when parents are consistently overprotective and critical of accidents (wetting, soiling, spilling, or

The Self, Social Competence, and Identity

breaking, for example) that the child develops an excessive sense of shame with respect to others and an excessive sense of doubt about his ability to control himself and his world.

Erikson also believes that the autonomy versus shame and doubt stage has important implications for the development of independence and identity during adolescence. The development of autonomy during the toddler years gives the adolescent the courage to be an independent individual who can choose and guide her own future.

Too much autonomy, though, can be as harmful as too little. A seven-year-old boy who had a heart condition learned quickly how afraid his parents were of any signs of him having cardiac problems. It was not long before he ruled the household. The family could not go shopping or for a drive if he did not approve. On the rare occasions his parents defied him, he would get angry and his purple hue and gagging would frighten them into submission. This boy actually was afraid of his power and eager to relinquish it. When the parents and the boy realized this, and recognized that a little shame and doubt were a healthy opponent of an inflated sense of autonomy, the family began to function much more smoothly (Elkind, 1970).

Childhood

During early childhood and middle and late childhood, a child's sense of self continues to develop and change. Erikson's view focuses on the psychosocial dimensions of self-development in childhood while cognitive developmental theory focuses on social cognitive changes of self-development, each of which we now consider.

Erikson's Childhood Stages

Early childhood is a time when Erikson believes children come to grips with the issue of **initiative versus guilt;** middle and late childhood is a time when he believes children negotiate the issue of **industry versus inferiority.** By early childhood, the child has become convinced that she is a person on her own. During early childhood she must discover what kind of person she will become. She is deeply identified with her parents, who most of the time appear to her to be powerful and beautiful, although often unreasonable, disagreeable, and sometimes even dangerous. During early childhood, children use their perceptual, motor, cognitive, and language skills to make things happen. They have a surplus of energy that permits them to forget failures quickly and to approach new areas that seem desirable—even if they seem dangerous—with undiminished zest and an increased sense of direction. On their own *initiative,* then, children at this stage exhuberantly move out into a wider social world.

The great governor of initiative is *conscience.* Children now not only feel afraid of being found out, but they also begin to hear the inner voices of self-observation, self-guidance, and self-punishment. Their initiative and enthusiasm not only may bring them rewards but also punishments. Widespread disappointment at this stage leads to an unleashing of guilt that drastically lowers the child's self-concept.

Whether a child leaves this stage with a sense of initiative outbalancing the sense of guilt depends to a considerable degree on how parents respond to the child's self-initiated activities. A child who is given freedom and opportunities to initiate motor play such as running, bike riding, sliding, skating, tussling, and wrestling has her sense of initiative supported. Initiative also is supported when parents answer their children's questions and do not deride or inhibit fantasy or play activity. In contrast, if a child is made to feel that her motor activity is bad, that her questions are a nuisance, and that her play is silly and stupid, then she may develop a sense of guilt over self-initiated activities that will persist through life's later stages (Elkind, 1970).

Erikson's fourth stage of the human life cycle is industry versus inferiority and it appears during middle and late childhood. The term *industry* captures a dominant theme of this period: children become interested in how things are made and how they work. It is the Robinson Crusoe age in the sense that the enthusiasm and minute detail Crusoe used to describe his activities appeals to the child's own budding sense of industry. When children are encouraged in their efforts to make and build and work—whether building a model airplane, constructing a treehouse, fixing a bicycle, solving an addition problem, or cooking—their sense of industry is increased. However, parents who see their child's efforts at making things as "mischief" or "making a mess" encourage the child's sense of inferiority.

A child's social world beyond the family also contributes to a sense of industry. School becomes especially important in this regard. Consider a child who is slightly below average in intelligence. He is too bright to be in special classes but not bright enough to be in gifted classes. He experiences frequent failures in his academic efforts, developing a sense of inferiority. By contrast, consider a child who has his sense of industry derogated at home. A series of sensitive and committed teachers may revitalize his sense of industry (Elkind, 1970).

Cognitive Developmental Changes

Remember that by the age of two children have a sense of self. Among the cognitive changes related to self-development in childhood are those involving inner and outer dimensions and the dimensions of differentiation, individuation, stability, and perspective taking, each of which we consider in turn.

Children as young as three years of age have a basic idea that they have private selves to which others do not have access (Flavell, Shipstead, & Croft, 1978). For example, consider this exchange between an experimenter and a three-year-old:

(Can I see you thinking?) "No." (Even if I look in your eyes, do I see you thinking?) "No." (Why not?) "Cause I don't have any big holes." (You mean there would have to be a hole there for me to see you thinking?) Child nods. (p. 16)

Another child said that the experimenter could not see his thinking processes because he had a skin over his head.

Once a child has developed an awareness of an inner self, between the ages of three and four, the child distinguishes between this inner self and the outer or bodily self. Indeed, when asked to describe themselves, preschool children present self-portraits of external characteristics. They describe themselves in terms of how they look ("I'm big"), where they live ("I live in Chicago"), and the activities in which they participate ("I play with dolls"). It is not until about six to seven years of age that children begin to describe themselves more in terms of psychological traits—how they feel, their personality characteristics, and their relationships with others, for example.

Perspective taking is thought by Robert Selman to be an important dimension of children's social development. What level of perspective taking are these two nine-year-old boys likely to be showing, according to Selman's model?

Children also develop more differentiated views of themselves as they grow older (McCandless & Evans, 1973). As young children, they may simply have perceived themselves as "good" or "bad." By late childhood and adolescence, they perceive themselves in more detailed ways, such as, "I am a good person most of the time, except when my older sister bugs me, or when my father won't let me have the car, or when I have to study for an exam."

Older children also develop more individuated views of themselves than they had as young children. Older children view themselves as more unique and more readily differentiate themselves from others. As young children they may have labeled themselves in terms of how similar they were to their peers, but as they approach adolescence, they tend to describe themselves more in terms of how they are different from their peers.

Older children also are more likely to have stable self-concepts than are younger children. But in an extreme form stability can lead to rigidity and unrealistic self-appraisal. Even though we know that children's self-conceptions become more stable, this does not imply that self-conceptions do not change. Self-conceptions clearly do change, but as children and adolescents mature cognitively, they become more capable of integrating incoming information into stable senses of who they are (Hart, Maloney, & Damon, 1987).

The question of how we know that we continue to be ourselves despite the transformations we undergo in appearance, thoughts, values, and behaviors has intrigued both philosophers and psychologists for centuries (Aboud & Ruble, 1987; Chandler & others, 1987). Perceptions of continuity and consistency of different dimensions of the self are thought to be important ingredients of mental health. Children are adaptive beings. They are resilient throughout the course of their development, but they do not form entirely new selves. In a sense children change but they remain the same—amidst the change is an underlying coherence and stability.

Yet another important dimension of the self is children's increasing abilities to understand how they are viewed by others. Young children have difficulty in understanding others' perspective of them, and they often are unaware of the impressions their behaviors make on others. But gradually, children come to understand that their behaviors trigger reactions from others, and they begin to monitor their actions, acting differently depending on whom they are with and which aspect of their social selves they wish to be seen. This represents a time when children are more cautious about revealing themselves to others (Maccoby, 1980).

Robert Selman (1976, 1980) has expanded our knowledge of the child's perception of self-other relations by describing a developmental sequence of perspective taking. Selman believes that perspective taking moves through a series of five stages, ranging from three years of age through adolescence. These stages span the egocentric viewpoint of the preschool child to the in-depth perspective taking of the adolescent (table 14.1). To assess the child's level of perspective taking, Selman individually interviews the child, focusing on such dilemmas as the following:

Eight-year-old Tom is trying to decide what to buy his best friend, Mike, for his birthday party. By chance, he meets Mike on the street and learns that Mike is extremely upset because his dog, Pepper, has been lost for two weeks. In fact, Mike is so upset he tells Tom, "I miss Pepper so much I never want to look at another dog again." Tom goes off, only to pass a store with a sale on puppies; only two are left and these soon will be gone. (Selman, 1980, p. 94)

Social and Personality Development

Table 14.1
Selman's Stages of Perspective Taking

Social role-taking stage	Description
Stage 0—egocentric viewpoint (age range 3 to 6)	Child has a sense of differentiation of self and other but fails to distinguish between the social perspective (thoughts, feelings) of other and self. Child can label other's overt feelings but does not see the cause-and-effect relation of reasons to social actions.
Stage 1—social-informational role taking (age range 6 to 8)	Child is aware that other has a social perspective based on other's own reasoning, which may or may not be similar to child's. However, child tends to focus on one perspective rather than coordinating viewpoints.
Stage 2—self-reflective role taking (age range 8 to 10)	Child is conscious that each individual is aware of the other's perspective and that this awareness influences self and other's view of each other. Putting self in other's place is a way of judging other's intentions, purposes, and actions. Child can form a coordinated chain of perspectives but cannot yet abstract from this process to the level of simultaneous mutuality.
Stage 3—mutual role taking (age, range 10 to 12)	Child realizes that both self and other can view each other mutually and simultaneously as subjects. Child can step outside the two-person dyad and view the interaction from a third-person perspective.
Stage 4—social and conventional system role taking (age range 12 to 15)	Person realizes mutual perspective taking does not always lead to complete understanding. Social conventions are seen as necessary because they are understood by all members of the group (the generalized other), regardless of their position, role, or experience.

From R. L. Selman, "Social-Cognitive Understanding" in T. Lickona (Ed.), *Moral Development and Behavior*, 1976; reprinted by permission of the editor.

The dilemma is whether to buy the puppy and how this will influence Mike psychologically. To explore the issue of self-awareness, the interviewer now begins with a general question, such as, "Mike said he never wants to see another puppy again. Why did he say that?" Depending in part on the child's response, the interviewer subsequently chooses from a range of questions related to the stages.

Together Erikson's view and the cognitive developmental view give us a more complete picture of children's self-development, Erikson's focusing more on the social affective domain of the self and the cognitive developmental view more on the social cognitive domain. Next, we look in greater detail at children's self-concept, including another theoretical view of the self—that of Carl Rogers.

Self-Concept

An increasing number of clinicians and developmentalists believe that the core of the self—its basic inner organization—is derived from regularities in experience (Kohut, 1977; Sroufe, 1988). The child carries forward into early childhood a history of experiences with caregivers that provides the child with expectations about whether the world is pleasant or unpleasant. And in early childhood, the child continues to experience the positive or negative affect of caregivers. Despite developmental changes and context changes (increased peer contact, a wider social world), an important feature of the self's healthy development is continuity in caregiving and support, especially in the face of environmental challenges and stresses. As the child moves through the early

Carl Rogers.

childhood years, this continuity and support in caregiving gives the child confidence to show initiative and to increasingly be the author of her own experiences, something that enhances self-pride and self-esteem. Many clinicians stress that difficulties in interpersonal relationships derive from low self-esteem, which in turn derives from a lack of nurturance and support (Bowlby, 1988; Erikson, 1968; Kohut, 1977; Rogers, 1980; Sullivan, 1953). The view of Carl Rogers has been instrumental in promoting the importance of self-concept in children's development and the role of nurturance and support in achieving a healthy self-concept.

Carl Rogers's View of Children's Self-Conceptions

Like Sigmund Freud, Carl Rogers (1961) began his inquiry about human nature with troubled personalities. Rogers explored the human potential for change. In the knotted, anxious, defensive verbal stream of his clients, Rogers concluded that individuals are prevented from becoming who they are.

Rogers believed that most individuals have considerable difficulty accepting their own true feelings, which are innately positive. As children grow, significant others condition them to move away from these positive feelings. Parents, siblings, teachers, and peers place constraints and contingencies on children's behavior. Too often children hear, "Don't do that," "You didn't do that right," "How could you be so stupid?" "You naughty boy," "You didn't try hard enough." When children don't do something right, they often get punished. Parents even may threaten to take their love away. Thus, Rogers believed that children are the victims of conditional personal regard, meaning that love and praise are not given unless the children conform to parental or social standards. The result, says Rogers, is that children's self-esteem is lowered.

Through the child's experiences with the world a self emerges. Rogers did not believe that all aspects of the child's self are conscious, but he did believe they are accessible to consciousness. The self is construed as whole. It consists of self-perceptions (how attractive I am, how well I get along with others, how good an athlete I am) and the values children attach to these perceptions (good-bad, worthy-unworthy, for example).

Rogers also considered the congruence between the real self, that is, the self as it really is as a result of a child's experiences, and the ideal self, which is the self a child would like to be. The greater the discrepancy between the real self and the ideal self the more maladjusted the child will be, said Rogers. To improve adjustment, a child can develop more positive perceptions of her real self, not worry so much about what others want, and increase her positive experiences in the world. In such ways, a child's real self and ideal self will be closer.

Rogers thought that each child should be valued regardless of the child's behavior. Even when the child's behavior is obnoxious, below acceptable standards, or inappropriate, the child needs the respect, comfort, and love of others. When these positive behaviors are given without contingency this is known as **unconditional positive regard.** Rogers believed strongly that unconditional positive regard elevates a child's self-worth and positive self-regard. Unconditional positive regard is directed at the child as a human being of worth and dignity, not to the child's behavior, which might not deserve positive regard (Rogers, 1974).

Rogers also believed that each child has a self-actualizing potential that is hard to keep down. Rogers's positive view of the child's development can be seen in his comparison of a child with a plant he once observed on the coastline of northern California. Rogers was looking at the waves beating furiously against the jagged rocks, shooting mountains of spray into the air. He noticed a tiny palm tree on the rocks, no more than two or three feet high, taking the pounding of the breakers. The plant was fragile and top-heavy. It seemed clear that the waves would crush the tiny specimen. A wave would crunch the plant, bending its slender trunk almost flat and whipping its leaves in a torrent of spray. Yet the moment the wave passed, the plant was erect, tough, and resilient once again. It was incredible the plant could take this incessant pounding hour after hour, week after week, year after year, all the time nourishing itself, maintaining its position, and growing. In this tiny plant, Rogers saw the child's tenacity for life, the forward thrust of development, and the ability of a living thing to push into a hostile environment and not only hold its own, but adapt, develop, and become itself. So it is with each child Rogers (1963) thought. As we develop, Rogers said, each of us has the ability to break through and understand ourselves and our world. We can burst the cocoon and become a butterfly.

Rogers's approach has both strengths and weaknesses. His view sensitized psychologists to the importance of children's perceptions of themselves, to considering the whole child and the child's positive nature, and to the power of self-understanding in improving human relations and communication with others. Some critics point out that while it is well and good to have a positive view of children's development, at times Rogers's view is almost too optimistic, possibly overestimating the freedom and rationality of individuals. Some critics also argue that the approach encourages self-love and narcissism. And a major weakness of Rogers's approach is that it is extremely difficult to test scientifically. Verification has come primarily from clinical experiences rather than controlled scientific study. For example, self-concept is described in a very global way. Indeed, as we see next, while self-concept has been an elusive concept to study empirically, recent efforts have made some progress.

Measuring Self-Concept

While it is recognized that every child has a self-concept and that self-evaluation is an important part of personality and development, psychologists have had a difficult time trying to measure self-concept (Wylie, 1979; Yardley, 1987). One method that frequently has been used is the Piers-Harris Scale (Piers & Harris, 1964), which consists of eighty items designed to measure the child's overall self-concept. School psychologists often use the scale with boys and girls who have been referred to them for evaluation. By responding yes or no to such items as "I have good ideas," children reveal how they view themselves. The Piers-Harris Scale requires fifteen to twenty minutes for completion and can be administered to groups as well as to individuals.

Children's self-perceptions often change according to the situation, although self-concept measures like the Piers-Harris Scale are designed to measure a stable, consistent aspect of personality. Also, with self-reporting, it is difficult to determine whether children are telling about the way they really are or the way they want someone else to think they are. Even though the

Figure 14.2
The Harter Perceived Competence Scale for
Children.

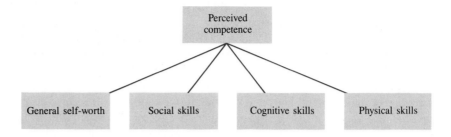

instructions on the Piers-Harris Scale and other measures of self-concept direct children to respond as they really are, there is no assurance that they will do so (Wylie, 1979).

A promising measure of self-concept has been developed by Susan Harter (1982). Her scale is called the **Perceived Competence Scale for Children.** Emphasis is placed on assessing the child's sense of competence across different domains rather than viewing perceived competence as a unitary concept. Three types of skills are assessed on separate subscales: cognitive (good at schoolwork; remember things easily); social (have a lot of friends; most kids like me); and physical (do well at sports; first chosen for games). A fourth subscale measures general self-worth (sure of myself; happy the way I am) independent of any particular skill domain (figure 14.2). The importance of Harter's measure is that prior measures of self-concept, such as the Piers-Harris, lump together the child's perceptions of his or her competencies in a variety of domains in an effort to come up with an overall measure of the child's self-concept. Harter's scale does an excellent job of separating children's self-perceptions of their abilities in different skill areas; and when general self-worth is assessed, questions that focus on overall perceptions of the self are used rather than questions that are directed at specific skill domains.

Recently, Susan Harter and Robin Pike (1984) developed the Pictorial Scale of Perceived Competence and Social Acceptance for Young Children, a downward extension of the Perceived Competence Scale for Children. There are two versions of the measure, one for preschool children and the other for first- and second-grade children. Each version taps four domains: cognitive competence, physical competence, peer acceptance, and maternal acceptance (table 14.2). Analysis of preschool and early elementary school children's responses suggest that two factors are present: first, a general competence factor (physical and cognitive) and second, a general social acceptance factor (peer and maternal). The measure should not be viewed as a general self-concept measure but rather as a measure that evaluates perceived competence and social acceptance.

It is important to develop self-concept and perceived competence scales that are appropriate for the child's or adolescent's level of development. For example, notice that Harter has developed a different scale for use with young children and even this scale has two versions, one for preschool children the other for first- and second-grade children. The Harter Perceived Competence Scale for Children was designed for use with children in the third to sixth grades. If we are interested in studying the self-concept or perceived competence of adolescents might there be issues involved in adolescents' lives that require different types of questions and items than those on scales for children or scales for adults?

Social and Personality Development

Table 14.2
Pictorial Scale of Perceived Competence and Social Acceptance for Young Children—Items Grouped According to Subscale for Each Form

Subscale and item no.	Preschool–kindergarten	First–second grades
Cognitive competence		
1	Good at puzzles	Good at numbers
5	Gets stars on paper	Knows a lot in school
9	Knows names of colors	Can read alone
13	Good at counting	Can write words
17	Knows alphabet	Good at spelling
21	Knows first letter of name	Good at adding
Physical competence		
3	Good at swinging	Good at swinging
7*	Good at climbing	Good at climbing
11	Can tie shoes	Good at bouncing ball
15*	Good at skipping	Good at skipping
19*	Good at running	Good at running
23	Good at hopping	Good at jump-roping
Peer acceptance		
2*	Has lots of friends	Has lots of friends
6	Stays overnight at friends'	Others share their toys
10*	Has friends to play with	Has friends to play with
14*	Has friends on playground	Has friends on playground
18*	Gets asked to play with others	Gets asked to play with others
22	Eats dinner at friends' house	Others sit next to you
Maternal acceptance		
4	Mom smiles	Mom lets you eat at friends
8*	Mom takes you places you like	Mom takes you places you like
12*	Mom cooks favorite foods	Mom cooks favorite foods
16*	Mom reads to you	Mom reads to you
20	Mom plays with you	Mom plays with you
24*	Mom talks to you	Mom talks to you

Note: Item number refers to position of the item in the order administered to the child. Asterisk designates items common to both forms.

Anne Petersen and her colleagues (1984) think so. They developed a self-concept measure for young adolescents called the Self-Image Questionnaire for Young Adolescents (SIQYA). It is a downward extension of the Offer Self-Image Questionnaire and uses nine scales: emotional tone, impulse control, body image, peer relationships, family relationships, mastery and coping, vocational-educational goals, psychopathology, and superior adjustment (table 14.3). The adolescent chooses the extent to which each of the ninety-eight items describes him or her—from "very well" to "not me at all."

Some assessment experts believe that a combination of several methods should be used in measuring self-concept. In addition to self-reporting, rating of a child's self-concept by others and observations of the child's behavior in various settings could give a more complete and more accurate picture of the child's self-concept. Peers, teachers, parents, and even others who do not know the child can be asked to rate the child's self-concept. Children's facial expressions and the extent to which they congratulate or condemn themselves are also good indicators of how children view themselves. For example, a child who rarely smiles or acts happy is revealing something about his self-concept. One investigation that used behavioral observations in the assessment of self-concept provides insight into some of the positive as well as some of the negative behaviors that may provide clues to the child's self-concept (table 14.4)

Table 14.3
Scales and Sample Items from SIQYA

Scale (item example)

1. Impulse control
   (I keep an even temper most of the time)
2. Emotional tone
   (I feel nervous most of the time)
3. Body image
   (I feel proud of my body)
4. Peer relationships
   (I think that other people just do not like me)
5. Family relationships
   (My parents are usually patient with me)
6. Mastery and coping
   (I am fearful of growing up)
7. Vocational-educational goals
   (I enjoy learning new things)
8. Psychopathology
   (I fear something constantly)
9. Superior adjustment
   (I am a leader in school)

From A. C. Petersen, J. E. Schulenberg, R. H. Abramowitz, D. Offer, and H. D. Jarcho, "A Self-Image Questionnaire for Young Adolescents. (SIQYA): Reliability and Validity Studies" in *Journal of Youth and Adolescence, 13,* 1984. Copyright © 1984 Plenum Publishing Corporation, New York, NY. Reprinted by permission.

Table 14.4
Positive and Negative Indicators of a Child's Self-Concept

Positive indicators

1. Gives others directives or commands
2. Voice quality is appropriate for situation
3. Expresses opinions
4. Sits with others during social activities
5. Works cooperatively in a group
6. Faces others when speaking or being spoken to
7. Maintains eye contact during conversation
8. Initiates friendly contact with others
9. Maintains comfortable space between self and others
10. Little hesitation in speech, speaks fluently

Negative indicators

1. Puts down others by teasing, name calling or gossiping
2. Gestures are dramatic or out of context
3. Inappropriate touching or avoids physical contact
4. Gives excuses for failures
5. Glances around to monitor others
6. Brags excessively about achievements, skills, appearance
7. Verbally puts self down; self depreciation
8. Speaks too loudly, abruptly or in a dogmatic tone
9. Does not express views or opinions, especially when asked
10. Assumes a submissive stance

Reprinted from the *Journal of Early Adolescence, 3,* 121–140, 1983. By permission of the Publisher, H.E.L.P. Books, Inc., Tucson, AZ.

<table>
<tr><td colspan="3" align="center">**Concept Table 14.1**
The Self</td></tr>
<tr><td>**Concept**</td><td>**Processes/Related Ideas**</td><td>**Characteristics/Description**</td></tr>
<tr><td>I and me</td><td>Their nature</td><td>"I" is the knower, "me" is the object of what is known. "I" is also known as the existential self, "me" as the categorical self. Most of our discussion focuses on the categorical self, especially self-concept.</td></tr>
<tr><td>The self and children's development</td><td>Infancy</td><td>Erikson argues that the first year is characterized by the issue of trust versus mistrust. At some point in the second half of the second year, the infant develops a sense of self. Independence becomes a central theme in the second year. Mahler argues that infants separate themselves from their mothers and then develop individuation. Erikson stresses that the second year is characterized by the issue of autonomy versus shame and doubt.</td></tr>
<tr><td></td><td>Childhood</td><td>Both Erikson's view and the cognitive developmental view have proposed changes in the self during childhood, Erikson focusing more on social affective changes, cognitive developmentalists more on social cognitive changes. Early childhood is a period when Erikson believes the most important issue is initiative versus guilt; in middle and late childhood, he believes the most important issue is industry versus inferiority. Cognitive developmental changes focus on developing a sense of inner and outer dimensions and increased differentiation, individuation, stability, and perspective taking.</td></tr>
<tr><td>Self-concept</td><td>Rogers's view</td><td>Children are the victims of conditional personal regard. The result is that their selves are not valued. The self is the core of a child's development; it includes a real self and an ideal self. Rogers advocates unconditional positive regard to enhance children's self-conceptions. Roger's approach sensitized us to the importance of children's self-conceptions in development, but critics stress that the view is too optimistic, too global, and too unscientific.</td></tr>
<tr><td></td><td>Measuring self-concept</td><td>Measuring self-concept is a difficult task. Harter's Perceived Competence Scale for Children is a promising measure because it recognizes the importance of assessing children's general self-concepts and their perceived competencies in different skill domains. Separate tests of self-concept, as well as perceived competence, are being developed for children and adolescents of different ages.</td></tr>
</table>

(Savin-Williams & Demo, 1983). By using a variety of measures (such as self-report and behavioral observations) and obtaining information from different sources (such as the child, parents, friends, and teachers), a more accurate construction of the child's self-concept probably will be achieved.

At this point we have discussed a number of ideas about the self and children's self-concepts. A summary of these ideas is presented in Concept Table 14.1.

Notice that rather than calling her scale a measure of self-concept or merely the self, Harter refers to her scale as an assessment of perceived competence. Also notice that one important domain of perceived competence is social competence. As we see next, in recent years increased interest has been generated in defining social competence.

Children's Social Competence

What is social competence? Does social competence vary with the child's developmental level? How can we assess children's social competence? These are among the questions we attempt to answer here.

Table 14.5
The Ingredients of Social Competence: Martin Ford's Model

Defining issue	Type of goal	
	Self-assertive goals	*Integrative goals*
Identity	Individuality	Belongingness
Control	Self-determination	Social responsibility
Social comparison	Superiority	Equity
Resource distribution	Resource acquisition	Resource provision

From M. Ford, ''A Living Systems Conceptualization of Social Intelligence: Outcomes, Processes, and Developmental Change'' in *Advances in the Psychology of Human Intelligence, 3,* 1986, edited by R. J. Sternberg. Copyright © 1986 Lawrence Erlbaum Associates, Inc., Hillsdale, NJ. Reprinted by permission.

What Is Social Competence?

It is the goal of virtually all parents to rear their children to become socially competent. What does this mean? The term **social competence** has been defined in a variety of ways reflecting the varying perspectives of social theorists (Dodge & others, 1986). Among the definitions are "effective response of the individual to life situations" (Goldried & d'Zurilla, 1969), "capacity to interact effectively with the environment" (White, 1959), "one who is able to make use of environmental and personal resources to achieve a developmental outcome" (Waters & Sroufe, 1983). Socrates even had a definition for social competence, "those who manage well the circumstances they encounter daily."

Let's consider further the thinking of Everett Waters and Alan Sroufe (1983). Resources in the environment are those things that can support or develop the child's ability to coordinate affect, cognition, and behavior both in the service of short-term adaptation and in long-term developmental progress. In infancy, adult social agents clearly are important environmental resources. In early childhood and beyond, play and peer relations become more important. From early childhood on, the range of potential resources expands.

Resources within the child are an important part of social competence too. The possibilities range from specific skills and abilities to general constructs, such as self-esteem. Delay of gratification, ego resiliency (adaptation, flexibility), and self-control are important strengths of the socially competent child. Need for achievement (the motivation to do something well) also is an important aspect of being socially competent especially in the achievement-oriented American society. The entire class of constructs labeled self, self-esteem, self-concept, and the like, denote important resources in the child. Keep in mind that both environmental resources and resources within the child have to be referenced to a particular level of development. For example, dependency is a positive characteristic early in infancy but is more likely to be associated with social incompetence in adolescence.

The ideas of Martin Ford (1986, 1987) emphasize that a portrayal of the socially competent child or adolescent involves both individual and social goals. Thus, social competence is not solely a property of the individual or of the social world. Rather the most socially competent children accomplish both self-assertive (individual) and integrative (social) goals. Ford believes social competence consists of four defining issues, each of which has a self-assertive and an integrative goal (table 14.5). The four defining issues are identity, control, social comparison, and resource distribution.

Regarding identity, the self-assertive task is to develop and express one's individuality. Examples of this type of social competence might be a unique behavioral style or an unusual pattern of interests. The self-assertive child or adolescent also may reveal a strongly endorsed set of social values and a clear, stable set of self-conceptions. The self-assertive nature of the child or adolescent would not depend on other individuals or social groups for self-definition. The integrative aspect of identity development is belongingness. It involves efforts to create, maintain, or enhance the identity of the social units of which the child or adolescent is a part. The units might be small and intimate, as in one's family or close friendships, or large, abstract units such as ethnic groups. Ford believes the emphasis should be on active engagement of the social environment to create situations that enhance the self-assertive and belongingness aspects of identity.

Regarding the second issue, control, self-determination is the self-assertive goal, social responsibility the integrative goal. Children and adolescents who are making progress in self-determination are beginning to establish and maintain personal control over their life circumstances and regain control when it is lost. Social responsibility is attained by accepting legitimate and necessary types of social control. The control is exercised to some degree through the broad rules of society, such as the prohibition of certain immoral or illegal actions (e.g., violence and theft) and through the regulation of conduct in social contexts, such as the classroom and the neighborhood. Social control also is developed through formal obligations to personal roles such as being a student and later being an employee. Social control also is established by informal obligations involving social contracts with friends, relatives, and others. Thus, social responsibility occurs in situations when duties are upheld, commitments are kept, and roles are fulfilled. Social responsibility also is reflected in such characteristics as dependability, trustworthiness, and integrity.

The third issue in Ford's model of social competence is social comparison. When children or adolescents compare themselves to others, the self-assertive consequence is the sense that they are better or higher on some relevant dimension than the other person or reference group. Since superiority is relative rather than absolute, self-assertiveness occurs most often in competitive situations. In these situations, a high social status is achieved through active engagement of the social world than through social assignment or social accident. Superiority also is revealed through commerce with peers, since individuals who are dissimilar, such as adults, usually do not provide the best basis for meaningful comparison. The integrative aspect involved in this part of social competence is equity, an important interest of group leaders such as teachers, parents, and employers, who need to be concerned about demands for fair, unbiased treatment. Equity can occur in relationships with siblings, peers, and friends, where powerful norms about sharing and fairness are important in maintaining the positive quality of the relationships. Equity also may be demonstrated in relationships with dissimilar others, such as children who are disadvantaged (those who have less money, lower intelligence, and so on).

The final issue in Ford's model of social competence is resource allocation. Children and adolescents need to be competent at resource allocation. And, alternatively, resource provision may be needed to improve the functioning of other individuals and social groups. Such resources might involve goods and possessions, such as food, clothing, or money. The resources might also pertain to assistance, advice, or cognitive validation. Since social resources usually are distributed in friendships and social support networks developed through mutual give-and-take, resource acquisition and provision often can be attained in the same contexts. Indeed, the child's or adolescent's unwillingness to provide resources reciprocally to others may make it difficult for the child or adolescent to acquire resources.

In sum, Ford argues that children and adolescents who maintain and promote the functioning of themselves and others are more socially competent than those who do not. Again, we underscore the importance of viewing social competence in terms of both internal, self, self-assertive dimensions and external, social, environmental dimensions. Both Ford's and Waters and Sroufe's models capture this dual nature of social competence.

Measuring Social Competence

In describing the important features of assessing social competence, Waters and Sroufe (1983) point out four considerations: (1) broadband versus narrow assessments; (2) real behavior versus laboratory tasks; (3) assessments emphasizing the coordination of affect, cognition, and behavior; and (4) taxing behavioral and integrative/adaptive capacity.

It is important to assess both the global and more fine-grained aspects of the child's social behavior. Waters and Sroufe (1983) argue that, at least initially, it would be wise to understand broadly what the child's social competence is like. For example, in studying toddler problem solving, the focus might be on enthusiasm, persistence, flexibility, and enjoyment in dealing with the problem rather than the part of the problem first addressed, the tool used first, or even the time required to solve the problem. In the attachment literature, researchers have often assessed the infant's tendency to stay close to its mother in terms of specific discrete behaviors. Often, counts of touching the mother, looking at her, and the like are selected for measurement. However, such measures tend to be more situation-specific than broad-based measures. An alternative approach is to select more broadly defined measures of proximity-seeking or contact-maintaining behaviors. Assessments of this nature usually do not involve frequency counts of behaviors but rather rating scales. Thus, in assessing attachment, Ainsworth, Sroufe, Waters, Main, and others have begun to use ratings of secure and insecure attachment rather than frequency counts of proximity seeking in their attempt to accurately capture the nature of social competence in infants. Keep in mind, however, that in our assessment of the child's development it is wise to consider both fine-grained, behavioral measures of the child and the more broadly based measures Waters and Sroufe recommend (e.g., Maccoby & Martin, 1983).

A second issue in assessment focuses on whether we should be assessing social competence through specific tasks in controlled laboratory contexts or designing more naturalistic and ecologically valid measures. Advantages and disadvantages are associated with either choice. Developmental psychologists interested in assessing social competence are likely to find themselves going into and out of laboratory situations. However, Waters and Sroufe (1983) argue that, early in the development of assessment devices for measuring social competence, it is especially important to conduct ecologically valid assessment in real-life circumstances. They reason that laboratory measures often evaluate a narrow dimension of social competence, whereas real-life, naturalistic assessments typically are more broadly based, which fits with their first assessment recommendation.

A third assessment issue in social competence focuses on the evaluation of how the child coordinates affect, cognition, and behavior. Waters and Sroufe believe that information about early social behavior (social attachment, problem solving, peer interaction, and self/behavior relationships) suggests that psychologists should be studying how affect, cognition, and behavior are coordinated. Assessing the coordination of these three dimensions rather than each dimension alone fits nicely with the belief that broad-based measures of social competence are needed. This also meshes with the belief that the affective world of children is important, just as their cognitive and behavioral worlds are. Cognition and behavior are obviously important dimensions of the child's development, but in isolation, they may not effectively reflect social competence. Social competence clearly is linked to motivation and control, and in circumstances where these are relevant, affect often is involved and frequently arises from either success or failure. As we see next, inclusion of affect in the assessment of social competence is important when critical events or transactions occur in the child's world.

Waters and Sroufe also believe that assessment of social competence needs to include measures that plug into the child's integrative/adaptive capacity in dealing with critical events or transactions in his or her world. Even within the range of typical behaviors, there are circumstances that challenge or tax the child's integrative capacity: for example, temperature change, sustained face-to-face interaction, response to separation and union, exploration of new environments, responses to success and failure, and sustained social play.

In Martin Ford's model of social competence, identity is one of the four key ingredients. Next, we consider the nature of identity in much greater detail, focusing heavily on Erik Erikson's view that identity becomes an issue of special importance in the adolescent years.

Measuring social competence has not been an easy task for developmentalists. How would Waters and Sroufe tackle the task of assessing this young girl's social competence?

Identity

It is not unusual for adolescents to try on one face after another in an attempt to find a face of their own. "Who am I?" asks every adolescent. Recall from our discussion of perspectives in chapter 11 that Erik Erikson (1968) believes the major issue to be negotiated in adolescence is **identity versus identity confusion.** Our discussion of identity focuses on further details about Erikson's view of identity versus identity confusion, James Marcia's four statuses of identity, family influences, and assessment of identity.

Identity versus Identity Confusion

During adolescence, world views become important to the individual, who enters what Erikson (1968) calls a *psychological moratorium*—a gap between childhood security and adult autonomy. Numerous identities can be drawn from the surrounding culture. As adolescents explore who they are and search the culture's identity files, they experiment with different roles. The youth who successfully copes with these conflicting identities emerges with a new sense of self that is both refreshing and acceptable. Adolescents who do not successfully resolve this identity crisis are confused, suffering what Erikson calls identity confusion. This confusion can take one of two courses: Individuals withdraw, isolating themselves from peers and family, or they may lose their identity in the crowd.

Because Erikson's ideas about identity represent one of the most important statements about adolescent development and because they reveal rich insight into the thoughts and feelings of adolescents, try to read one or more of his original writings. A good starting point is *Identity: Youth and Crisis*

Hitler, Luther, and Gandhi—the Development of their Identities

rik Erikson is a master at analyzing famous individual's lives and discovering historical clues about their identity formation. Erikson also developed ideas for his view of identity development by analyzing the developmental history of clients in his clinical practice. Erikson (1968) believes that an individual's developmental history must be carefully scrutinized and analyzed to obtain clues about identity. He also believes that to understand the world's history the best clues appear in the composite of individual life cycles. In the excerpts that follow, Erikson analyzes the lives of Adolf Hitler, Martin Luther, and Mahatma Gandhi.

About Hitler, Erikson (1962) commented:

I will not go into the symbolism of Hitler's urge to build except to say that his shiftless and brutal father had consistently denied the mother a steady residence: one must read how Adolf took care of his mother when she wasted away from breast cancer to get an inkling of this young man's desperate urge to cure. But it would take a very extensive analysis, indeed, to indicate in what way a single boy can daydream his way into history and emerge a sinister genius, and how a whole nation becomes ready to accept the emotive power of that genius as a hope of fulfillment for its national aspirations and as a warrant for national criminality. . . .

The memoirs of young Hitler's friend indicate an almost pitiful fear on the part of the future dictator that he might be nothing. He had to challenge this possibility by being deliberately and totally anonymous; and only out of this self-chosen nothingness could he become everything. (pp. 108–109)

But while the identity crisis of Adolf Hitler led him to turn toward politics in a pathological effort to create a world order, the identity crisis of Martin Luther in a different era led him to turn toward theology in an attempt to deal systematically with human nothingness or lack of identity:

In confession, for example, he was so meticulous in the attempt to be truthful that he spelled out every intention as well as every deed; he splintered relatively acceptable purities into smaller and smaller impurities; he reported temptations in historical sequence, starting back in childhood; and after having confessed for hours, would ask for special appointments in order to correct previous statements. In doing this, he was obviously both exceedingly compulsive and, at least unconsciously, rebellious. . . .

At this point, we must note a characteristic of great young rebels: their inner split between the temptation to surrender and the need to dominate. A great young rebel is torn between, on the other hand, tendencies to give in and fantasies of defeat (Luther used to resign himself to an early death at times of impending success), and the absolute need, on the other hand, to take the lead, not only over himself but over all the forces and people who impinge on him. (Erikson, 1968, pp. 155–157)

And in his Pulitzer Prize–winning novel on Mahatma Gandhi's life, Erikson (1969) describes the personality formation of Gandhi during his youth:

Straight and yet not stiff; shy and yet not withdrawn; intelligent and yet not bookish; willful and yet not stubborn; sensual and yet not

(1968). Other works that portray identity development are *Young Man Luther* (1962) and *Gandhi's Truth* (1969)—the latter won a Pulitzer Prize. A sampling of Erikson's writings from these books is presented in Perspective on Child Development 14.1.

Contemporary views of identity development suggest several important considerations. First, identity development is a lengthy process, in many instances a more gradual, less cataclysmic transition than Erikson's term *crisis* implies. Second, identity development is extraordinarily complex (Marcia, 1980, 1987). Identity formation neither begins nor ends with adolescence. It begins with the appearance of attachment, the development of a sense of self, and the emergence of independence in infancy and reaches its final phase with a life review and integration in old age. What is important about identity in adolescence, especially late adolescence, is that for the first time physical development, cognitive development, and social development advance to the point

Hitler in elementary school. He is in the center of the top row.

What did Erikson believe were some of the key ingredients in Mahatma Gandhi's development of identity?

soft. . . . We must try to reflect on the relation of such a youth to his father, because the Mahatma places service to the father and the crushing guilt of failing in such service in the center of his adolescent turbulence. Some historians and political scientists seem to find it easy to interpret this account in psychoanalytic terms; I do not. For the question is not how a particular version of the oedipal complex "causes" a man to be both great and neurotic in a particular way, but rather how such a young person . . . manages the complexes which constrict other men. (p. 113)

In these passages, the workings of an insightful, sensitive mind is shown looking for a historical perspective on personality development. Through analysis of the lives of such famous individuals as Hitler, Luther, and Gandhi, and through the thousands of youth he has talked with in person, Erikson has pieced together a descriptive picture of identity development.

at which the individual can sort through and synthesize childhood identities and identifications to construct a viable pathway toward adult maturity. Resolution of the identity issue during adolescence does not mean identity will be stable through the remainder of one's life. An individual who develops a healthy identity is flexible and adaptive, open to changes in society, in relationships, and in careers. This openness assures numerous reorganizations of identity content throughout the individual's life.

Identity formation does not happen neatly and it usually does not happen cataclysmically. At the bare minimum, it involves commitment to a vocational direction, an ideological stance, and a sexual orientation. Synthesizing identity components can be a long and drawn out process with many negations and affirmations of various roles and faces. Identity development gets done in bits and pieces. Decisions are not made once and for all, but have to be made again and again. The decisions may seem trivial at the time: whom to date, whether

Reprinted with special permission by King Features Syndicate, Inc.

or not to break up, whether or not to have intercourse, whether or not to take drugs, whether to go to college or finish high school and get a job, what to major in, whether to study or whether to play, whether or not to be politically active, and so on. Over the years of adolescence, these decisions form a core of what the individual is all about as a person—what is called identity.

The Four Statuses of Identity

James Marcia (1966, 1980, 1987) analyzed Erikson's theory of identity development and concluded that four identity statuses, or modes of resolution, appear in the theory—identity diffusion, identity foreclosure, identity moratorium, and identity achievement. The extent of an adolescent's commitment and crisis is used to classify the individual according to one of the four identity statuses. *Crisis* is defined as a period during which the adolescent is choosing among meaningful alternatives. Most researchers now use the term *exploration* rather than *crisis,* although in the spirit of Marcia's original formulation, we will refer to crisis. *Commitment* is defined as the extent to which the adolescent shows a personal investment in what she is going to do.

In **identity diffusion,** adolescents have not yet experienced a crisis (that is, they have not explored meaningful alternatives) or made any commitments. Not only are they undecided about occupational or ideological choices, they also are likely to show little interest in such matters. In **identity foreclosure,** adolescents have made a commitment but have not experienced a crisis. This occurs most often when parents simply hand down commitments to their adolescents, more often than not in an authoritarian way. In these circumstances, adolescents have not had adequate opportunities to explore different approaches, ideologies, and vocations on their own. In **identity moratorium,** adolescents are in the midst of a crisis but their commitments either are absent or are only vaguely defined. These adolescents are searching for commitments by actively questioning alternatives. In **identity achievement,** adolescents have undergone a crisis and have made a commitment. A summary of Marcia's four statuses of identity is presented in table 14.6.

The majority of research on identity development focuses on high school and college students with few investigators studying young adolescents (Adams & Montemayor, 1983). Early adolescents are primarily in identity diffusion or identity moratorium. Marcia (1987) described three aspects of the young adolescent's life that are important in identity formation. A young adolescent must establish confidence in parental support, develop a sense of industry, and gain a self-reflective perspective about the future.

Social and Personality Development

Table 14.6
The Four Statuses of Identity

	Identity status			
Position on occupation and ideology	Identity moratorium	Identity foreclosure	Identity diffusion	Identity achievement
Crisis	Present	Absent	Absent	Present
commitment	Absent	Present	Absent	Present

Some researchers believe the most important identity changes take place in late adolescence. For example, in one investigation (Meilman, 1979) the most significant changes in identity status occurred between the ages of eighteen and twenty-one. The college years may be especially important in identity development. Over time, during the college years, individuals move in the direction of identity achievement (Marcia, 1987; Waterman & Waterman, 1972).

The identity status approach has come under sharp criticism by some researchers and theoreticians (Blasi, 1988; Lapsley & Power, 1988). They believe the identity status approach distorts and trivializes Erikson's notions of crisis and commitment. For example, concerning crisis, Erikson emphasized the youth's questioning of the perceptions and expectations of one's culture and the development of an autonomous position with regard to one's society. In the identity status approach these complex questions and development are dealt with by simply evaluating whether a youth has thought about certain issues and considered alternatives. Erikson's idea of commitment loses the meaning of investing one's own self in certain lifelong projects in the identity status approach, simply being interpreted as having made a firm decision or not.

Family Influences on Identity

Parents are important figures in the adolescent's development of identity. Harold Grotevant and Catherine Cooper (Grotevant, 1984; Grotevant & Cooper, 1985) highlight the power of both connectedness to parents and the

Carol and Janet, Individuated and Nonindividuated Family Experiences

Family experiences play an important role in the adolescent's development of identity. In excerpts from the lives of two adolescent girls, we will see the importance of family interaction in the development of identity. When involved in a family planning activity, Carol's father said, "I think probably what we all ought to do is decide the things that we want to do, each one of us individually. And, then maybe we'll be able to reconcile from that point. . . . Let's go ahead and take a few minutes to decide where we'd like to go and what we would like to do. And, maybe we'll be able to work in everything everybody wants to do in these fourteen days. Okay?" In this planning of a two-week vacation, Carol, her mother, and her father all were active and involved, displaying humor, candor, spontaneity, and vulnerability. For example, Carol's mother commented, "I think we all have good imaginations," while the father said, "I think that's kind of nice. I think we ought to be a rich gang."

Carol seemed to be aware of her role in the family and of the boundary between the adolescent and parent generations. During her identity interview, she said, "I have a say, but not a deciding vote in family decisions." Carol's identity exploration rating was very high. A distinctive quality of her identity exploration was that she experienced her parents as providing room for her to explore beyond their own experiences or needs. For example, she reported that both parents felt that religion had been forced on them as children, so they decided not to force it on her.

Family planning activities are the focus of some researchers' efforts to assess family processes during adolescent development. In a typical example, the adolescent(s) and parents will be seated at a table—either at home or in the laboratory—and asked to plan one or more activities, such as a trip, a weekend, and so on. The researcher audiotapes and/or videotapes the discussion, subsequently coding the behavior of the participants according to various categories of social interaction, such as individuation and connectedness.

Consequently, she had been able to explore several religions as possible alternatives with her friends. In the domain of friendship, Carol had maintained a relationship with a girl who had been a close friend but who later became involved with drugs and turned against her parents. Carol had been able to maintain this relationship and see how it differed from her other close friendships without

presence of a family atmosphere that promotes individuation in the adolescent's identity development. **Connectedness** is reflected in mutuality and permeability. Mutuality refers to the adolescent's sensitivity to and respect for others' views. Permeability refers to openness and responsiveness to others' views. Mutuality provides adolescents with support, acknowledgement, and respect for their own beliefs; permeability lets the adolescent sense how to manage the boundaries between the self and others. **Individuation** has two main components—separateness and self-assertion. Separateness is seen in the expressions of how distinctive the self is from others. Self-assertion is involved in the adolescent's expression of her personal point of view and in taking responsibility for communicating this clearly. Parents who have both a connectedness with their adolescents and who promote individuation encourage the adolescent's development of identity. As with social competence, with identity we see the importance of thinking about both an individual orientation and a social or relationship orientation. More about Grotevant and Cooper's ideas on family processes involved in identity development appears in Perspective on Child Development 14.2.

compromising her own standards. Her parents were concerned about this friendship, but they trusted Carol and permitted her to work through this situation. In a comparable pattern, Carol's score of fifteen on the Role-Taking Task was also very high. She achieved the highest reciprocal level score by clearly coordinating the perspective of two characters in her story and by elaborating both their external and psychological states.

In contrast, the family of Janet, the firstborn of two, reflected nonindividuated spousal and parent-child relationships with few disagreements, self-assertions that largely coincided with the family's point of view, and frequent expressions of connectedness. The ratio of agreements to disagreements between mother and father (sixteen) was unusually high, suggesting a marked imbalance between expression of individuality and connectedness. In addition, Janet disagreed with her father only once, and he never disagreed with her, whereas she was responsive to him twenty-nine times, and he was responsive to her ten times. Enmeshment in this family's interaction was illustrated in the first five utterances on the Family Interaction Task:

Mother: Where shall we go?
Father: Back to Spain.
Mother: Back to Spain.
Janet: Back to Spain.
Sister: Back to Spain.

When Janet's father later asked for more suggestions, she said, "And then, I don't . . . I mean, you go on, Dad, 'cause I don't know . . . what else."

Janet's low identity exploration rating of thirteen may reflect a lack of exploration of issues outside consensual family beliefs. In this family, in which signs of individuated spousal and parent-child relationships were less evident, the necessity for agreement and connectedness among family members and the family members' excessive involvement in each other's identity appeared to hinder the adolescent's development of individual ideas regarding career, dating, and other issues. With regard to career choice, Janet commented, "I'm having a hard time deciding what to do. It would be easier if they would tell me what to do, but of course I don't want that."

Janet's low role-taking score of nine suggests a lack of ability to express both separate and reciprocal points of view. While telling her story, Janet commented, "I don't know what the others are thinking, because I'm thinking of it only as if I'm the girl." Perhaps the nonindividuated communication patterns that Janet observed in her parents' relationship and that she participated in with her father inhibited her ability both to engage in identity exploration and to coordinate different perspectives. (Cooper, Grotevant, & Condon, 1983, pp. 54–55)

Measuring Identity

Identity is as difficult, if not more difficult, to measure than self-concept. Until recently, even though experts recognized the importance of identity as an integrative concept in adolescence, there was little empirical research about identity. Much of what we knew was based on clinical case studies and psychobiographies (such as Erikson's analysis of Hitler's identity development). Some experts question whether the process of identity formation is spelled out in sufficient detail to permit empirical studies to be derived from Erikson's formulation (Hill, 1983). While empirical documentation of the developmental course of identity development is still sketchy, a number of recent efforts have been directed at improving the assessment of identity (Grotevant & Adams, 1984; Hart, Maloney, & Damon, 1987; Marcia, 1987). Even with its measurement being elusive, the concept of identity—especially the search for self—seems to capture an extremely important theme of the adolescent's development.

Since our last review we have discussed a number of ideas about social competence and identity. A summary of these ideas is presented in Concept Table 14.2.

Concept	Processes/Related Ideas	Characteristics/Description
Children's social competence	What is it?	Social competence has been defined in various ways. Both the definitions of Waters and Sroufe and of Ford emphasize its internal, self, self-assertive dimensions and its external, social, environmental dimensions. Waters and Sroufe emphasize the use of personal and environmental resources. Ford emphasizes four issues—identity, control, social comparison, and resource distribution—and their self-assertive and integrative components.
	Measurement	Measurement should include broadband and narrow assessments; real-world behavior and laboratory tasks; coordination of affect, cognition, and behavior; and taxing behavioral and integrative/adaptive capacity.
Identity	Identity versus identity confusion	Erikson's fifth stage of the human life cycle, focusing on the search for self in adolescence. Contemporary views of identity development emphasize its lengthy process (in many instances being gradual) and its complexity.
	Four statuses of identity	Developed by Marcia, they involve both crisis and commitment. The four statuses are diffusion, foreclosure, moratorium, and achievement. Identity change may be most prominent in late adolescence. Recently, the identity status approach has been criticized for distorting and trivializing Erikson's ideas.
	Family influences	An important aspect of identity development. Grotevant and Cooper believe both individuation and connectedness in parent-adolescent relationships promote identity development.
	Measurement	Identity is a global construct, and like many such broad concepts, it is difficult to measure. Nonetheless, researchers are developing improved methods of assessing identity.

Summary

I. I and Me
"I" is the knower, "me" is the object of what is known. "I" is also known as the existential self, "me" as the categorical self. Most of our discussion focuses on the categorical self, especially self-concept.

II. The Self in Children's Development
Erikson argues that the first year is characterized by the issue of trust versus mistrust. At some point in the second half of the second year, the infant develops a sense of self. Mahler argues that infants separate themselves from their mothers and then develop individuation. Erikson stresses that the second year is characterized by the issue of autonomy versus shame and doubt. Both Erikson's view and the cognitive developmental view have proposed changes in the self during childhood, Erikson focusing more on social affective changes, cognitive developmentalists more on social cognitive changes. Early childhood is a period when Erikson believes the most important issue is initiative versus guilt; in middle and late childhood, he believes the most important issue is industry versus inferiority. Cognitive developmental changes focus on developing a sense of inner and outer dimensions and increased differentiation, individuation, stability, and perspective taking.

III. Self-Concept
Children are the victims of conditional personal regard. The result is that their selves are not valued. The self is the core of the child's development; it includes a real self and an ideal self. Rogers advocates unconditional positive regard to enhance children's self-conceptions. Rogers's approach sensitized us to the importance of self-conceptions in development, but critics stress that the view is too optimistic, too global, and too unscientific. Measuring self-concept is difficult. Harter's Perceived Competence Scale for Children is a promising measure because it recognizes the importance of assessing both children's general self-concepts and their perceived competencies in different skill domains. Separate tests of self-concept, as well as perceived competence, are being developed for children and adolescents of different ages.

IV. Children's Social Competence
Social competence has been defined in various ways. Both the definitions of Waters and Sroufe and of Ford emphasize its internal, self, self-assertive dimensions and its external, social, environmental dimensions. Waters and Sroufe emphasize the use of personal and environmental resources. Ford emphasizes four issues—identity, control, social comparison, and resource

distribution—and their self-assertive and integrative components. Measurement should include broadband and narrow assessment; real-world assessment and laboratory assessment; coordination of affect, cognition, and behavior; and taxing behavioral and integrative/adaptive capacity.

V. Identity

Erikson's fifth stage of the human life cycle is called identity versus identity confusion, focusing on the adolescent's search for self. Contemporary views of identity development emphasize its lengthy process (in many instances being gradual) and its complexity. Developed by Marcia, the four identity statuses are diffusion, foreclosure, moratorium, and achievement. The statuses involve the dimensions of crisis and commitment. Identity change may be most prominent in late adolescence. Recently, the identity status approach has been criticized for distorting and trivializing Erikson's conceptions. Parent-adolescent relationships are an important aspects of the adolescent's development of identity. Grotevant and Cooper believe both individuation and connectedness promote identity development. Identity is a global construct, and like many such broad concepts, it is difficult to measure. Nonetheless, researchers are developing improved methods of assessing identity.

Key Terms

existential self 379

categorical self 379

trust versus mistrust 379

autonomy versus shame and doubt 381

initiative versus guilt 382

industry versus inferiority 382

unconditional positive regard 386

Perceived Competence Scale for Children 388

social competence 392

identity versus identity confusion 395

identity diffusion 398

identity foreclosure 398

identity moratorium 398

identity achievement 398

connectedness 400

individuation 400

Suggested Readings

Erikson, E. H. (1969). *Gandhi's truth*. New York: Norton.
In this Pulitzer Prize–winning novel, Erikson weaves an insightful picture of Gandhi's development of identity.

Ford, M., & Ford, D. (Eds.). (1987). *Humans as self-constructing living systems*. Hillsdale, NJ: Erlbaum.
This book provides an extensive interpretation of social competence, including Martin Ford's model of social competence in terms of self-assertive and integrative criteria.

Harter, S. (1983). Developmental perspectives on the self-system. In P. H. Mussen (Ed.), *Handbook of child psychology* (4th ed., Vol. 4). New York: John Wiley & Sons.
A thorough overview of the development of the self, particularly in terms of its development during childhood. Provides extensive information about self-concept and self-esteem.

Honess, T., & Yardley, K. (1987). *Self and identity: Perspectives across the lifespan*. London: Routledge & Kegan Paul.
This excellent volume includes articles by leading theorists and researchers who study the development of the self and identity.

Lapsley, D., & Power, F. C. (1988). *Self, ego, and identity*. New York: Springer.
An up-to-date, authoritative treatment of issues involved in the nature of the self and identity by leading scholars.

Selman, R. L. (1980). *The growth of interpersonal understanding*. New York: Academic Press.
Presents considerable detail about Selman's developmental theory of perspective taking and self-development. Includes information about clinical implications for helping children with problems.

CHAPTER

15

Gender Roles

We are born twice over:
the first time for existence,
the second time for life;
once as human beings and
later as men and women.

Jean Jacques Rousseau

magine . . . two four-year-olds are playing and one says to the other, "You stay here with the baby while I go fishing." Don't you immediately assume that one of the preschool children is a boy and the other is a girl? And don't you also infer that the sex of the child speaking is male? If you made these inferences, you are correct. These two preschool children—Shane and Barbara—were playing at their nursery school. As Shane walked away, Barbara called to him: "I want to go fishing, too." Shane replied, "No. Girls don't go fishing. But I will take you to a French restaurant when I get back."

Barbara returned to playing with her dolls after Shane left. The director of the nursery school talked to Shane's mother about his behavior. She wanted to know whether Shane was merely mimicking his father's behavior. Shane's mother said that he was not, because the entire family went fishing together. The gender roles children display, then, are not merely replications of parental actions.

Another play scene observed by the nursery school director focused on three boys sitting around a table in a play kitchen. The boys began issuing orders: "I want a cup of coffee." "Some more jelly for the toast over here." Girls were running back and forth between the stove and the table as they cooked and served breakfast. In one situation, the boys got out of hand, demanding cups of coffee one after another as a four-year-old girl, Ann, raced around in a dizzy state. Finally, Ann gained some control over the situation by announcing that the coffee was all gone. It didn't seem to occur to Ann to sit down at the table and demand coffee from the boys.

Sexist behavior from young children is nothing new, but viewing it as a problem is. Such behavior has become somewhat of an obsession with preschool teachers and directors, and it bothers many parents who are trying to rear their offspring free of sexist bias (Carper, 1978). Each of us is curious about our gender, young children especially so. This chapter is about gender, about our world as males and females. Among the questions to be evaluated are: What are the components of gender roles? What are the biological, cognitive, and social influences on gender roles? Are there many gender differences or is most of what we think are differences actually stereotypes? What is the course of gender role development through the infant, childhood, and adolescent years?

Gender Role Components

Nowhere in children's social and personality development have more sweeping changes occurred in recent years than in the area of gender roles. **Gender roles** are social expectations of how we should act, think, and feel as males and females. How can we classify gender roles?

Table 15.1
Are You Androgynous?

The following items are from the Bem Sex-Role Inventory. To find out whether you score as androgynous on it, first rate yourself on each item, on a scale from 1 (never or almost never true) to 7 (always or almost always true).

1. self-reliant	16. strong personality	31. makes decisions easily	46. aggressive
2. yielding	17. loyal	32. compassionate	47. gullible
3. helpful	18. unpredictable	33. sincere	48. inefficient
4. defends own beliefs	19. forceful	34. self-sufficient	49. acts as a leader
5. cheerful	20. feminine	35. eager to soothe hurt feelings	50. childlike
6. moody	21. reliable	36. conceited	51. adaptable
7. independent	22. analytical	37. dominant	52. individualistic
8. shy	23. sympathetic	38. soft-spoken	53. does not use harsh language
9. conscientious	24. jealous	39. likable	54. unsystematic
10. athletic	25. has leadership abilities	40. masculine	55. competitive
11. affectionate	26. sensitive to the needs of others	41. warm	56. loves children
12. theatrical	27. truthful	42. solemn	57. tactful
13. assertive	28. willing to take risks	43. willing to take a stand	58. ambitious
14. flatterable	29. understanding	44. tender	59. gentle
15. happy	30. secretive	45. friendly	60. conventional

SCORING

(a) Add up your ratings for items 1, 4, 7, 10, 13, 16, 19, 22, 25, 28, 31, 34, 37, 40, 43, 46, 49, 55, and 58. Divide the total by 20. That is your masculinity score.

(b) Add up your ratings for items 2, 5, 8, 11, 14, 17, 20, 23, 26, 29, 32, 35, 38, 41, 44, 47, 50, 53, 56, and 59. Divide the total by 20. That is your femininity score.

(c) If your masculinity score is above 4.9 (the approximate median for the masculinity scale) and your femininity score is above 4.9 (the approximate femininity median) then you would be classified as androgynous on Bem's scale.

From Janet S. Hyde, *Half the Human Experience: The Psychology of Women*, 3d ed. Copyright © 1985 D.C. Heath and Company, Lexington, MA. Reprinted by permission.

Masculinity, Femininity, and Androgyny

At a point not too long ago, it was accepted that boys should grow up to be masculine and that girls should grow up to be feminine, that boys are made of frogs and snails and puppy dogs' tails and that girls are made of sugar and spice and everything nice. Today, diversity characterizes children's gender roles and the feedback they receive from their environment. A young girl's mother might promote femininity, the girl might be close friends with a tomboy in the neighborhood, and the girl's teacher at school might encourage her assertiveness.

In the past, the well-adjusted male was expected to be independent, aggressive, and power oriented; the well-adjusted female was expected to be dependent, nurturant, and uninterested in power and dominance. By the mid-1970s, though, the landscape of gender roles was changing. Many females were unhappy with the label "feminine" and felt stigmatized by its association with characteristics such as passiveness and unassertiveness. Many males were uncomfortable with being called "masculine" because of its association with such characteristics as insensitivity and aggressiveness.

Many lay people as well as developmentalists believed that something more than "masculinity" and "femininity" was needed to describe the change in gender roles that was taking place. The byword became **androgyny,** meaning the combination of masculine and feminine characteristics in the same individual (Bem, 1977; Spence & Helmreich, 1978). The androgynous child might be a male who is assertive (masculine) and nurturant (feminine) or a female who is dominant (masculine) and sensitive to others' feelings (feminine).

Table 15.1 provides examples of items from a widely used measure of gender roles—the Bem Sex-Role Inventory. To see whether you are androgynous or not rate yourself on the items in the table. The androgynous individual is simply a male or a female who has a high degree of both feminine and masculine characteristics. No new characteristics are used to describe the androgynous individual. An individual can be classified as masculine, feminine, or androgynous. A fourth category, **undifferentiated,** also is used in gender

(a)

(b)

The gender times are changing. Androgyny has become a prevalent theme of contemporary gender roles. The helpful, sensitive male (a) and the independent, freedom-oriented female (b) are but two of the many ways children are becoming more androgynous.

Figure 15.1
The four classifications of gender roles.

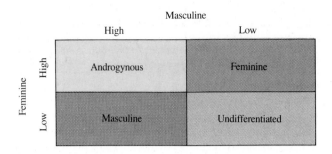

role classification. This category describes an individual who has neither masculine nor feminine characteristics. The four classifications of gender roles are shown in figure 15.1.

Debate still flourishes on what components should go into making up the masculine and feminine categories. Because these are combined to make up the androgyny category, the composition of masculinity and femininity is crucial to what it means to be androgynous. This raises an important issue in psychology. When a concept or construct is developed and evaluated, it is critical to pin down the dimensions of the concept. Specifying the dimensions of a concept in a logical, organized, and empirical way is one of psychology's great lessons. Unfortunately, in the case of androgyny, this lesson has sometimes been lost. In many cases, the concept of androgyny has been based on a hodgepodge of stereotypical ideas, especially those of college students, about personality differences between males and females (Downs & Langlois, 1988; Ford, 1986; Gill & others, 1987).

Adding to the complexity of determining whether a child is masculine, feminine, or androgynous is the child's developmental level (Maccoby, 1987a). A four-year-old boy would be labeled masculine if he enjoyed and frequently engaged in rough-and-tumble play, if he preferred to play with blocks and trucks, and if he tended to play outdoors in the company of other boys during free play periods at his preschool. A four-year-old girl would be labeled feminine if she liked to wear dresses, played with dolls and art materials, and did not get into fights. At age ten, a masculine boy would be one who engaged in active sports, avoided girls, and was not especially diligent about his schoolwork. At age ten, a feminine girl would be one who had one or two close girlfriends, did not try to join boys' sports play groups, paid attention to the teacher in class, liked to baby-sit, and preferred romantic television fare. At age fifteen, a masculine boy would be one who excelled in spatial-visual tasks, liked and did well in math, was interested in cars and machinery, and knew how to repair mechanical gadgets. At age fifteen, a feminine girl would be more interested in English and history than math or science and would wear lipstick and makeup. These examples are not exhaustive but they give the flavor of how the characteristics of masculinity and femininity depend to some degree on the child's developmental status.

In a recent longitudinal investigation, both the developmental and multifaceted nature of gender roles was evident (Maccoby & Jacklin, in press). When the children were almost four years old, parents were asked whether their daughters were flirtatious, liked frilly clothes, cared how their hair looked, and liked to wear jewelry. These items formed a feminine scale. A second scale inquired about how rough and noisy their daughter was in playing with her age-mates, whether she preferred to play with boys, girls, or both equally,

Social and Personality Development

whether she ever got into fights, and what her favorite pretend roles were. On the basis of these items, a "tomboy" scale was constructed, indicating the girl's motivation to play with boys, engage in rough and noisy play, fight occasionally, and engage in masculine fantasy roles. Somewhat surprisingly, the girls who were the most feminine on the first scale also were somewhat more likely to be tomboys. This finding raises several important points. Clearly, individuals may show some dimensions but not others among the set of stereotyped masculine or feminine attributes. Also, different aspects of the clusters may take on more or less importance at different ages. For example, two attributes—sexual attractiveness and gentle-kind-considerate-nurturant—are probably involved in the concept of femininity at all ages, but the sexual aspect probably is dominant in adolescence, while the second component may emerge most strongly in adulthood when many women are involved in the care of their children.

According to Martin Ford (1986), greater specification of gender roles is accomplished by describing masculinity in terms of self-assertion and femininity in terms of integration. **Self-assertion** includes such components as leadership, dominance, independence, competitiveness, and individualism. **Integration** includes such components as sympathy, affection, and understanding. An androgynous individual would be high on both self-assertion and integration. Sandra Gill and her colleagues (1987) believe greater specification in gender roles is accomplished by describing masculinity in terms of an instrumental orientation and femininity in terms of an expressive orientation. An **instrumental orientation** is concerned with the attainment of goals and an emphasis on the individual's accomplishments. An **expressive orientation** is concerned with facilitating social interaction, interdependence, and relationships. In both the descriptions by Ford and by Gill and her colleagues we find the same dual emphasis on the individual and social relations that also is proposed as the best way to describe social competence. Recall that in chapter 14 we described the most socially competent children as those who are both individually and socially oriented, who have both internal and external resources. So it is too with androgynous children. They are both self-assertive and integrative, instrumental and expressive.

If you were constructing a scale for evaluating a tomboy orientation in girls, what would its components be?

Are Androgynous Children the Most Competent?

Which children are the most competent? Children who are undifferentiated are the least competent; they are the least socially responsible, they have the least self-control, and they receive the poorest grades in school (Ford, 1986). This category is not well understood by psychologists and few children are classified in this way. But what about the majority of children, those who are either masculine, feminine, or androgynous—which group is the most competent?

This is not an easy question to answer because the dimensions of androgyny and the dimensions of competence are not clearly spelled out in research on the issue. In many instances androgynous children are the most competent, but a key point involves the criteria for competence. If the criteria for competence involve self-assertion and integration or an instrumental and an expressive orientation, then androgynous children usually are more competent. However, if the criteria for competence primarily involve self-assertion or an instrumental orientation, then a masculine gender role is favored; if they primarily involve integration or an expressive orientation, then a feminine gender role is preferred. For example, masculine individuals might be more competent in school achievement and work while feminine individuals might be more competent in relationships and helping.

The self-assertive and instrumental dimensions of gender roles have been valued in our culture more than the integrative or expressive dimensions. When psychologists have assessed the relation of gender roles to competence, their criteria for competence have included twice as many self-assertive and instrumental as integrative and expressive items. A disturbing outcome of such cultural standards and research bias is that masculine dimensions are perceived to mean competence. We need to place a higher value on the integrative and expressive dimensions of our own and our children's lives and give these dimensions adequate weight in our assessment of competence.

Biological and Cognitive Influences

How much does our biological heritage determine our gender role? What cognitive factors are involved in gender roles? We consider each of these questions in turn.

Biological Influences

One of Freud's basic assumptions is that human behavior and history are directly related to reproductive processes. From this assumption arises the belief that sexuality is essentially unlearned and instinctual. Erikson (1968) extended this argument, claiming that the psychological differences between males and females stem from anatomical differences. Erikson argued that—because of genital structure—males are more intrusive and aggressive, females are more inclusive and passive. Erikson's belief has become known as "anatomy is destiny." Critics of the anatomy is destiny view believe that Erikson has not given experience an adequate audience. They argue that males and females are more free to choose their gender role than Erikson allows. In response to the critics, Erikson has modified his view, saying that females in today's world are transcending their biological heritage and correcting society's overemphasis on male intrusiveness.

Biology's influence on gender roles also involves sex hormones, among the most powerful and subtle chemicals in nature. These hormones are controlled by the master gland in the brain, the pituitary. In females, hormones from the pituitary carry messages to the ovaries to produce the hormone **estrogen.** In males, the pituitary messages travel to the testes where the sex hormone **androgen** is manufactured.

The secretion of androgen from the testes of the young male fetus (or the absence of androgen in the female) completely controls sexual development in the womb. If enough androgen is produced, as happens with a normal developing boy, male organs and genitals develop. In instances where the hormone level is imbalanced (as in a developing male with insufficient androgen, or a female exposed to excess androgen), the genitals are intermediate between male and female. Such individuals are referred to as **hermaphrodites** (Money, 1987; Money & Ehrhardt, 1972).

Although estrogen is the dominant sex hormone in females and androgen fills this role in males, each individual's body contains both hormones. The amount of each hormone varies from one individual to the next. For example, a boy's bass voice is the result of more androgen than another boy with a tenor voice (Durden-Smith & Desimone, 1983). As we move from animals to humans, hormonal control over sexual behavior is less dominant. For example, when the testes of the male rat are removed (castration), sexual behavior declines and eventually ceases. In humans, castration produces much greater variation in sexual response.

No one argues about the presence of genetic, biochemical, and anatomical differences between the sexes. Even psychologists with a strong environmental orientation acknowledge that boys and girls are treated differently because of their physical differences and their different roles in reproduction. The importance of biological factors is not at issue. What is at issue is the directness or indirectness of their effects on social behavior (Huston, 1983). For example, if a high androgen level directly influences the central nervous system, which in turn produces a higher activity level, then the effect is more direct. By contrast, if a high level of androgen produces strong muscle development, which in turn causes others to expect the child to be a good athlete and in turn leads her to participate in sports, then the biological effect is more direct.

While virtually everyone is an interactionist in thinking that children's behavior as males and females is due to an interaction of biological and environmental factors, an interactionist position means different things to different people (Maccoby, 1987a, 1988; Money, 1987). For some it suggests that certain environmental conditions are required to make preprogrammed dispositions appear. For others it suggests that the same environment will have different effects depending on the predispositions of the child. Yet for others it means that children shape their environments, including their interpersonal environments, as well as vice versa. Circular processes of influence and counterinfluence unfold over time. Throughout childhood, boys and girls are involved in active construction of their own version of acceptable masculine and feminine behavior patterns. As we see next, cognitive factors play an important role in this active construction.

Cognitive Influences

Cognitive factors influence gender roles during early childhood through self-categorization and language. Lawrence Kohlberg (1966) argued that to have an idea of what is masculine or feminine, a child must be able to categorize objects into these two groups—masculine and feminine. According to Kohlberg, the categories become relatively stable by the age of six. That is, by the age of six, children have a fairly definite idea of which category is theirs. Further, they understand what is entailed in belonging to one category or the other and seldom fluctuate in their category judgments. From Kohlberg's perspective, this self-categorization is the impetus for gender role development. Kohlberg reasons that gender role development proceeds in the following sequence: "I am a boy, I want to do boy things; therefore, the opportunity to do boy things is rewarding." Having acquired the ability to categorize, children strive toward consistency in the use of the categories and their actual behavior. The striving for consistency forms the basis for gender role development (Ruble, 1987).

Others have expanded on Kohlberg's cognitive theme. One proposal suggests that initially there is a period of undifferentiated gender role concepts among infants, then comes a period of adopting very rigid, conventional gender roles at some point in the preschool and elementary school years (Pleck, 1975). This rigidity is thought to peak in the early adolescent years as males strive

How Good Are Girls at Wudgemaking
if the Wudgemaker Is a "He"?

n one investigation, the following description of a fictitious, gender-neutral occupation, wudge-maker, was read to third- and fifth-grade children, with repeated reference either to *he, they, he or she,* or *she* (Hyde, 1984):

> Few people have heard of a job in factories, being a wudgemaker. Wudges are made of oddly shaped plastic, and are an important part of video games. The wudgemaker works from a plan or pattern posted at eye level as *he or she* puts together the pieces at a table while *he or she* is sitting down. Eleven plastic pieces must be snapped together. Some of the pieces are tiny, so that *he or she* must have good coordination in *his or her* fingers. Once all eleven pieces are put together, *he or she* must test out the wudge to make sure that all of the moving pieces move properly. The wudgemaker is well paid, and must be a high school graduate, but *he or she* does not have to have gone to college to get the job. (p. 702)

One-fourth of the children were read the story with *he* as the pronoun, one-fourth with *they,* one-fourth with *he or she* (as shown), and one-fourth with *she.* The children were asked to rate how well women could do the job of wudgemaking and also how well they thought men could perform the job. As shown in figure 15.A, ratings of how

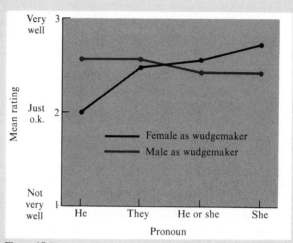

Figure 15.A
Mean ratings of how well women and men would do as wudgemakers, according to pronoun used in the description.

well women could make wudges were influenced by the pronoun used; ratings were lowest for *he,* intermediate for *they* and *he or she,* and highest for *she.* This suggests that the use of the gender-neutral *he,* compared to other pronouns, influences children's conceptions of how competent males and females are in our society.

to be the very best male possible and girls strive to be the very best female possible. Then at some point later in development, often not until the adult years, a stronger androgyny orientation emerges (Block, 1973; Pleck, 1975).

An important theme in the cognitive approach to children's gender role development is that the child's mind is set up to perceive and organize information according to a network of associations called a schema (remember our discussion of this concept in chapter 8). A **gender schema** organizes the world in terms of female and male (Bem, 1985). Gender is a powerful organizing category to which children connect many experiences and attitudes. The gender schema approach emphasizes children's active construction of their gender roles but also accepts that societies determine which schemata are important and the associations that are involved.

Gender roles also are present in the language children use and are exposed to. The nature of the language children hear most of the time is sexist. That is, the English language contains sex bias, especially in the use of "he" and "man" to refer to everyone. For example, in one investigation, mothers and their one- to three-year-old children looked at popular children's books, such as *The Three Bears,* together (DeLoache, Cassidy, & Carpenter, 1987). The Three Bears almost always were boys: 95 percent of all characters of indeterminate gender were referred to by the mothers as males. To learn more about children's experiences with sexism in language, turn to Perspective on Child Development 15.1.

Concept Table 15.1
Gender Role Components and Biological and Cognitive Influences

Concept	Processes/Related Ideas	Characteristics/Description
Gender role components	Masculinity, femininity, and androgyny	Gender roles focus on society's expectations for males and for females. Recent interest has emphasized the concept of androgyny, the belief that competent individuals have both masculine and feminine characteristics. The four gender role classifications are masculine, feminine, androgynous, and undifferentiated. Specification of the dimensions of masculinity, femininity, and androgyny has not always been consistent. Conceptualizing masculine dimensions as self-assertive and instrumental and feminine dimensions as integrative and expressive provides greater specification of gender roles. Developmental considerations also are important.
	Are androgynous children more competent?	Controversy surrounds this question. In answering this question it is important to specify not only the criteria for androgyny but also the criteria for competence. Masculine dimensions have been more valued in our culture and the criteria for competence also have followed this pattern. In contexts in which both self-assertive or instrumental and integrative or expressive characteristics are required for competence, androgynous individuals are more competent.
Biological and cognitive influences	Biological	Freud's and Erikson's theories promote the idea that anatomy is destiny. Hormones influence sexual development, although not as pervasively in humans as in animals. Today's psychologists are all interactionists when biological and environmental influences on gender roles are considered. However, interaction means different things to different people.
	Cognitive	Cognitive factors are involved in children's active construction of their gender roles; two such cognitive factors are self-categorization and language development. An important theme in the cognitive approach is that children develop a gender schema.

Cognitive factors contribute to our understanding of children's active construction of their gender roles, but gender role development has already started before children reach a stable sense of gender identity. For example, two-year-old boys choose masculine toys even before they are aware such toys are more appropriate for them than for girls (Blakemore, LaRue, & Olejnik, 1979). And three-year-old children have already acquired many gender role stereotypes (Maccoby, 1980). Children's social exchanges probably are at work in contributing to these aspects of gender role development, a topic we turn to next. At this point we have discussed a number of ideas about gender role components and biological and cognitive influences. A summary of these ideas is presented in Concept Table 15.1.

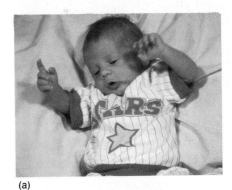
(a)

Social Influences

In our culture, adults discriminate between the sexes shortly after the infant's birth. The "pink and blue" treatment may be applied to girls and boys before they leave the hospital. Soon afterward, differences in hairstyles, clothes, and toys become obvious. Adults and other children reward these differences throughout childhood, but girls and boys also learn appropriate gender role behavior by watching what other people say and do. For example, a seven-year-old boy who knows he is a boy and readily labels objects appropriately as male or female may have parents who support equality between the sexes; his behavior probably will be less stereotyped along masculine lines than boys reared in traditional homes.

In recent years, the idea that parents are the critical social agents in gender role development has come under fire. Parents are only one of many sources—culture, schools, peers, the media, and other family members are

(b)

The "pink and blue" treatment is often applied to girls and boys, respectively, soon after they are born. Look at the infants in (a) and (b). It is not too difficult to tell which is a boy and which is a girl.

(a)

(b)

Psychological theorizing has emphasized the role of the same-sex parent. In reality, both fathers and mothers are psychologically important for children of both sexes. Developmentalists have found that fathers are more likely to engage in rough-and-tumble play with their children (a) and that mothers are more likely to be given responsibility for nurturing children and caring for them (b).

others—through which the child learns about gender roles. Yet it is important to guard against swinging too far in this direction, because—especially in the early years of development—parents are important influences on children's gender roles.

Parent-Child Relationships

Parents, by action and by example, influence their children's gender role development. In the psychoanalytic view, this influence stems principally from the child's identification with the parent of the same sex. The child is motivated to be like and emulate the parent of the same sex. In the social learning view, children are motivated to imitate the behavior patterns of nurturant, powerful models. In reality, both fathers and mothers are psychologically important for children. Mothers are consistently given responsibility for children's nurturance and physical care. Fathers are more likely to engage in playful interaction with children and be given responsibility for seeing that children conform to existing cultural norms. Fathers are more exacting and demanding with children than are mothers. And whether or not they have more influence on them, fathers are more involved in socializing their sons than their daughters (Lamb, 1986). Fathers seem to play an especially important part in gender role development—they are more likely to act differently toward sons and daughters than are mothers (Huston, 1983).

Many parents encourage boys and girls to engage in different types of play and activities even during infancy (Lewis, 1987). Girls are more likely to be given dolls to play with, and when old enough, they are more likely to be assigned baby-sitting duties. Girls are encouraged to be more nurturant and emotional than boys, and fathers are more likely to engage in rough-and-tumble play with sons than with daughters. With increasing age, boys are permitted more freedom by parents, who allow them to be away from home without supervision, than are girls.

Without much doubt, parents do treat boys and girls differently in many instances. However, when parents treat boys and girls differently it is not always easy to sort through the direction of the effects (Maccoby, 1987a). Do young boys like rough-and-tumble play because their fathers trained them to enjoy it, or because they, as well as their fathers, have a low threshold for initiation of this male-male pattern? The same types of questions crop up with regard to higher rates of punishment and other coercive treatment directed to boys by their parents. Is this a form of differential pressure initiated by parents that produces distinctively male behavior in boys, or is it a consequence of something boys are doing in interacting with their parents that elicits this kind of parent behavior? Probably reciprocal and circular processes are at work as parents differentially socialize their sons and daughters and their sons and daughters socialize them.

Peers

Parents provide the earliest discrimination of gender roles in children's development, but before long peers and teachers join the societal process of responding to and providing feedback about masculine and feminine behavior. Most children have already acquired a preference for masculine or feminine toys and activities before they are exposed to school. During the preschool and elementary school years, teachers and peers maintain these preferences through feedback to the child. Children who play in sex-appropriate activities tend to

be rewarded for doing so by their peers. Those who play in cross-sexed activities tend to be criticized by their peers or left to play alone. Children show a clear preference for being with and liking same-sex peers (Maccoby & Jacklin, in press), and this tendency often becomes stronger as children move from the preschool years through the middle elementary school years (Hayden-Thomson, Rubin, & Hymel, 1987). This increase probably reflects children's growing awareness of culturally prescribed expectations for males and females. Even when a deliberately engineered program of reinforcing children for cross-sex play reduces segregation temporarily, playmate choices return quickly toward a segregated pattern once the behavior modification program is discontinued (Serbin, Tonick, & Sternglanz, 1977).

After extensive observations of school playgrounds, two researchers characterized the play settings as "gender school," pointing out that boys teach each other the required masculine behavior and enforce it strictly (Luria & Herzog, 1985). Girls also pass on the female culture (distinctively female games such as jump rope or jacks) and congregate mostly with each other. Individual "tomboy" girls can join boys' activities without losing their status in the girls' groups, but the reverse is not true for boys, reflecting our society's greater sex-typing pressure for boys.

Gender segregation is important because it provides the conditions under which two different childhood cultures are formed and maintained (Maccoby, 1987a, 1988). Children's bias toward same-sex play suggests that any society, or any set of parents, would have to exert extensive pressure if they wanted to get children to select playmates without regard to gender. Yet adults clearly do affect the extent that play is segregated by establishing the conditions under which play normally occurs.

Teachers and Schools

In a recent Gallup poll, 80 percent of the respondents agreed that the federal government should promote educational programs intended to reduce such social problems as poverty and unequal educational opportunities for minorities and females (Gallup & Clark, 1987). Discriminatory treatment involving gender involves all ability groups, but in many cases the stereotypically lower valued group (by sex, by race, and so on) is treated similarly to the lower valued ability group. For example, girls with strong math abilities often receive fewer quality instructional interactions from teachers than their male counterparts (Eccles, MacIver, & Lange, 1986). And minority females are given fewer teacher interactions than females, who are given fewer than black males, who are given fewer than white males (Sadker, Sadker, & Klein, 1986).

In a recent study, researchers were trained in an observation system to collect data in more than one hundred fourth-, sixth-, and eighth-grade classrooms (Sadker & Sadker, 1986). At all three grade levels, male students were involved in more interactions than female students, and male students were given more attention from teachers. Male students also were given more remediation, more criticism, and more praise than female students.

Historically, education in the United States has been male-defined rather than gender-balanced. In many instances, traditional male activities, especially white male activities, have been the educational norm. Although females mature earlier, are ready for verbal and math training at a younger age, and have control of small-motor skills earlier than males, educational curricula has been constructed mainly to mirror the development of males. Decisions

(a)

(b)

Gender segregation in children's groups is prominent, especially during middle and late childhood. Boys play with boys (a) and girls play with girls (b) during this developmental time frame. Children's bias toward same-sex play is so strong that in any society parents would have to exert extensive pressure to get children to select playmates without regard to gender.

about the grade in which students should learn Huckleberry Finn, do long division, or begin to write essays are based primarily on male developmental patterns. Some experts believe that this state of educational affairs means that some girls may become bored or give up, with most learning simply to hold back, be quiet, and smile (Shakeshaft, 1986).

Three trends in sex equity education research have been identified (Klein, 1988). First, there is a trend toward greater investigation of subtle discrimination and stereotyping. Much of the sex equity research and initial sex equity policies in the 1970s focused on identifying and putting an end to overt discrimination and stereotyping. By 1981, it was noted that while some progress had been made toward equity in areas of overt sex discrimination, such as athletics and college admissions, many subtle types of sex discrimination and stereotyping, such as sex bias in classroom interactions, still remained. Sex equity researchers are now calling attention to sex discrimination and stereotyping in less visible problem areas such as home economics, foreign language, visual arts, and sex education (Klein, in press; Sandell, Collins, & Sherman, 1985; Spencer, 1986; Thompson, 1986).

A second trend in sex equity education research is a shift toward male and female valued educational outcome goals. In addition to helping females to achieve parity with males, researchers and policymakers are focusing more on the development of skills associated with females (Belendy & others, 1986; Tetreault, 1986). For example, placing more value on skills such as writing and human relations, areas in which females excel, can change the content covered in many standardized academic achievement tests. This type of change could improve females' achievement test scores, self-esteem, and job prospects.

A third trend in sex equity education research is an increased emphasis on sex equity outcomes. Much of the early sex equity education research focused simply on identifying the inequities or problems. Once researchers understand the problems in terms of distance from attaining sex equity goals, they can emphasize the effectiveness of various solutions in reaching these goals. For example, researchers have found that girls' participation and achievement in mathematics becomes more equal to boys' through the use of multiple strategies that include anxiety reduction, "hands-on" math instructional experiences, career awareness activities, "girl friendly" classrooms, and role models (Eccles & others, 1986; Stage & others, 1985).

The Media

Children watch an average of three to five hours of television every day of their lives. The programs they watch portray distinct male and female roles. The messages carried by television about behavior considered appropriate for males and for females may well be an important influence on children's gender role development.

A special concern is the way females are pictured on television. In the 1970s it became evident that television was portraying females in less competent ways than males. For example, about 70 percent of the prime-time characters were males, men were more likely to be shown in the work force, women were more likely to be shown as a housewife or in a romantic role, men were more likely to appear in higher-status jobs and in a greater diversity of occupations, and men were presented as more aggressive and constructive (Sternglanz & Serbin, 1974).

In the 1980s television networks have become more sensitive to how males and females are portrayed in television shows. Many programs now focus on divorced families, cohabitation, and women in high-status roles. But even with the onset of this type of programming, researchers continue to find that television pictures males as more competent than females (Durkin, 1985; Wroblewski & Huston, 1987).

Gender role stereotypes also appear in the print media. In magazine advertising, females are more likely to appear in advertisements for beauty products, cleaning products, and home appliances, while males are more likely to appear in advertisements for cars, liquor, and travel. As with television programs, females are portrayed more competently in advertisements than in the past, but advertisers have not yet given them equal status with males.

Changing Gender Role Behavior

Efforts to change children's gender role behavior have moved in two directions (Huston, 1983). "Gender deviant" children are trained to show more appropriate behavior for their gender or attempts are made to free normal children from rigid gender role patterns. Both types of interventions create ethical concerns, yet both provide valuable information about gender roles.

Most studies of gender deviance have focused on boys, who are diagnosed as gender deviant when they play mostly with feminine toys, dress up in female clothes, choose girls rather than boys as playmates, fantasize about being a girl, and express themselves with feminine gestures (Green, 1974). It has been found that girls use very different gestural patterns than boys, such as hanging their wrists and limply holding books with their arms folded toward their body (Rekers, 1979). Gender deviant boys not only prefer feminine activities but also purposely avoid masculine activities, especially rough-and-tumble play (Zucker, 1988). In a recently completed longitudinal investigation, Richard Green (1987) initially identified a group of sixty-six feminine boys and a group of fifty-six masculine boys with a mean age of seven years. At a follow-up mean age of nineteen years of age, approximately seventy-five percent of the feminine boys at age seven were either homosexual or bisexual in fantasy and/or behavior. All but one of the masculine boys at age seven were heterosexual at follow-up.

Gender deviance among girls has received less attention possibly because our society allows girls more flexibility in their dress, play activities, and gender role interests than it does boys. For example, in one investigation a majority of the junior high school girls described themselves as "sort of tomboyish," and a majority of women indicated that they were tomboys during childhood (Hyde, Rosenberg, & Behrman, 1977).

Both behavioral and psychoanalytic therapies have been used in attempts to alter children's gender deviant behavior. These treatments have produced changes in children's play patterns but usually only in the situation where the treatment took place. Consequently, clinical treatment is augmented by direct interventions at home and at school. Parents and teachers have been taught behavior modification techniques and young male adults have visited the boys at home or at school, attempting to teach the gender deviant boys athletic skills because feminine boys tend to perform poorly in athletics. Indications are that such programs led to more normal gender behavior in boys, lasting as long as one to three years after the intervention (Rekers, 1979).

Table 15.2
Adjectives that Describe Possible Gender Differences

What are the differences in the behavior and thoughts of boys and girls? For each of the adjectives below, indicate whether you think it *best* describes boys or girls—or neither—in our society. Be honest and follow your first impulse.

	Girls	Boys
Verbal skills	☐	☐
Sensitive	☐	☐
Active	☐	☐
Competitive	☐	☐
Compliant	☐	☐
Dominant	☐	☐
Math skills	☐	☐
Suggestible	☐	☐
Social	☐	☐
Aggressive	☐	☐
Visual spatial skills	☐	☐

We still do not have a good sense about the origins of such gender deviant patterns. One possibility is that many parents are indifferent to young children's gender deviant behavior. Some parents think it is cute when little boys dress up as females and play with dolls. These children are often referred for treatment only after someone outside the family points out the boy's effeminate behavior. Other factors that show up in the developmental history of some gender deviant boys are maternal overprotection, restrictions on rough-and-tumble play, absence of an adult male, weak father-son relationship, physical beauty of the small boy that leads him to be treated as a girl, absence of male playmates, and maternal dominance.

In addition to changing the behavior of gender deviant boys, another effort to change gender role behavior focuses on teaching children about androgyny. Believing that rigid gender roles may be detrimental to both males and females, a number of educators and psychologists have developed materials and created courses to teach androgyny to children (Gaskell & Knapp, 1976; Guttentag & Bray, 1976; Kahn & Richardson, 1983; National Education Association, 1974). Details about two efforts to teach children and adolescents at different developmental levels to be more androgynous and the ethical issues involved are presented in Perspective on Child Development 15.2.

Gender Stereotyping and Differences

How pervasive is gender role stereotyping? What are the real differences in gender role behavior? What is the nature of gender roles in achievement-related matters? Each of these questions we consider in turn.

Gender Role Stereotyping

Gender role stereotypes are broad categories that reflect our impressions and beliefs about males and females. All stereotypes, whether based on gender, race, or other groupings, refer to an image of what the typical member of a particular social category is like. The world is extremely complex. Every day we are confronted with thousands of different stimuli. The use of stereotypes is one way we simplify this complexity. If we simply assign a label (such as the quality of softness) to someone, we then have much less to consider when we think about the individual. However, once labels are assigned they are remarkably difficult to abandon, even in the face of contradictory evidence. Do you think you have a set of gender role stereotypes? Table 15.2 provides a brief exercise in understanding gender role behavior. Record your answers on a separate sheet so you can check them later when they are discussed.

Can and Should Androgyny Be Taught to Children in School?

In one investigation (Kahn & Richardson, 1983), tenth-through twelfth-grade students from three high schools in British Columbia were given a twenty-unit course in gender roles. Students analyzed the history and modern development of male and female gender roles and evaluated the function of traditionally accepted stereotypes of males and females. The course centered on student discussion supplemented by films, videotapes, and guest speakers. The materials included exercises to heighten awareness of one's own attitudes and beliefs, role reversal of typical gender role behavior, role play of difficult work and family conflict circumstances, and assertiveness training for direct, honest communication.

A total of sixty-nine students participated in the gender role course. To determine whether the course changed the adolescents' gender role orientation, these students were compared to fifty-nine students from the same schools who did not take the gender role course. Prior to the start of the course, all students were given the Bem Sex-Role Inventory. No differences between the two groups were found at that time. After the students completed the course, they and the control group were given the Attitudes toward Women Scale (Spence & Helmreich, 1972). Scores on this measure can range from 25 (highly traditional) to 100 (highly liberal). In schools 1 and 2, the students who took the gender role course had more liberal attitudes about the female's role in society than students who did not take the course (table 15.A). In these schools, the students were primarily girls who chose to take the course as an elective. In school 3, students who took the gender role course actually had more conservative attitudes toward the female's role in society than those who did not. The gender role class in school 3 was required and it was made up almost equally of males and females.

Another attempt to produce a more androgynous gender role orientation in students also met with mixed results (Guttentag & Bray, 1976). The curriculum lasted for one year and was implemented in the kindergarten, fifth,

Table 15.A
Gender Role Attitudes Related to the Woman's Role in Society Following a High School Course on Gender Roles Emphasizing Androgyny

School	Groups	
	Experimental (took gender role course)	Control (did not take course)
1	83.3	75.6
2	85.3	73.9
3	68.8	76.2

From S. E. Kahn and A. Richardson, "Evaluation of a Course in Sex Roles for Secondary School Students" in *Sex Roles, 9*:431–440. Copyright © 1975 Plenum Publishing Corporation, New York, NY. Reprinted by permission.

and ninth grades. It involved books, discussion materials, and classroom exercises. The program was most successful with the fifth graders and least successful with the ninth graders, who actually displayed a boomerang effect of more rigid gender role orientation. The program's success varied from class to class, seeming to be most effective when the teacher produced sympathetic reaction in the peer group. However, some classes ridiculed and rejected the curriculum.

Ethical concerns are aroused when the issue is one of teaching children to depart from socially approved behavior patterns, especially when there is no evidence of extreme sex typing in the groups of children to whom the interventions are applied. The advocates of androgyny programs believe that traditional sex typing is psychologically harmful for all children and that it has prevented many girls and women from experiencing equal opportunity. While some people believe androgyny is more adaptive than either a traditional masculine or feminine pattern, it is not possible to ignore the imbalance within our culture that values masculinity more than femininity. (Huston, 1983; Hyde, 1988)

Many stereotypes are so general that they are ambiguous. Consider the stereotypes "masculine" and "feminine." Diverse behaviors can be called on to support each stereotype, such as scoring a touchdown or growing facial hair for "masculine" and playing with dolls or wearing lipstick for "feminine." And the stereotype may be modified in the face of cultural change. At one point in history, muscular development may be thought of as masculine, whereas at another point a more lithe, slender physique may represent "masculine." The behaviors popularly agreed upon as reflecting a stereotype also may fluctuate according to socioeconomic and ethnic groups. A masculine stereotype might be more likely to include "rough and tough" in lower socioeconomic than higher socioeconomic groups, for example.

Reprinted by permission of UFS, Inc.

Even though the behaviors that are supposed to fit the stereotype often do not, the label itself can have significant consequences for the individual. Labeling an individual "homosexual," "queer," or "sissy" can produce dire social consequences in terms of status and acceptance in groups, even if the individual so labeled is not homosexual, queer, or sissy. Regardless of their accuracy, stereotypes can produce tremendous emotional upheaval in individuals and undermine their own opinions about themselves and their status (Mischel, 1970).

Gender Differences

How well did you do with adjectives in table 15.2? According to a classic review of gender differences in 1974, Eleanor Maccoby and Carol Jacklin concluded that boys have better math skills, have superior visual-spatial ability (the kind of skills an architect would need to design a building's angles and dimensions), and are more aggressive, while girls are better at verbal abilities. Recently, Eleanor Maccoby (1987b) revised her conclusion about several gender role dimensions. She commented that accumulation of research evidence suggests that boys now are more active than girls and she is less certain that girls have greater verbal ability than boys, mainly because boys score as high as girls on the verbal part of the Scholastic Aptitude Test (SAT).

Evidence is accumulating that some gender differences are vanishing, especially in the area of verbal abilities (Feingold, 1988; Hyde & Linn, 1986). In a recent analysis, Alan Feingold (1988) evaluated gender differences in cognitive abilities on two widely used tests—the Differential Aptitude Test

A special concern in gender roles today is whether the computer world is extensively sex-typed. How extensively is computer use a male-typed activity? In what areas are females having the greatest access to computers? What do you forecast the future gender use of computers to be?

and the SAT—from 1947 to 1983. Girls scored higher than boys on scales of grammar, spelling, and perceptual speed; boys scored higher on measures of spatial visualization, high school mathematics, and mechanical aptitude. No gender differences were found on verbal reasoning, arithmetic, and reasoning about figures. Gender differences declined precipitously over the years. One important exception to the rule of vanishing gender differences is the well-documented gender gap at the upper levels of performance on high school mathematics, which has remained constant over three decades.

As can be seen, few data about gender differences seem to be cast in stone. As our culture has changed, so have some of our findings about gender differences and similarities. As our expectations and attitudes about gender roles have become more similar for boys and girls, in many areas gender differences are vanishing.

But gender differences are not vanishing in all areas, as indicated by the differences that still persist in the area of math. One area of special concern about gender roles in today's society related to math and science focuses on expectations and attitudes involving computer ability. In two recent novels, *Turing's Man* (Bolter, 1984) and *The Second Self* (Turkle, 1984), technology overwhelms humanity. In both stories, females are not portrayed as having integral roles in this technological, computer culture. One character notes, "There are few women hackers. This is a male world." (Turkle, 1984). Unfortunately, both boys and girls are socialized to associate computer programming with math skills and typically programming is taught in math departments by males. Male-female ratios in computer classes range from two to one to five to one, although computers in offices tend to be used equally by females and males. Males also have more positive attitudes toward computers. It is hoped that Turkle's male computer hacker will not serve as the model for computer users of the future (Lockheed, 1985; Miura, 1987).

Achievement in Females

For some areas of achievement, gender differences are so large they can best be described as nonoverlapping. For example, no major league baseball players are female, and 96 percent of all registered nurses are female. In contrast, many measures of achievement-related behaviors yield no gender differences. For example, girls show just as much persistence at tasks. The answer to the question of whether males and females differ in their expectations for success at various achievement tasks is not yet settled (Eccles, 1987).

Because females are often stereotyped as less competent than males, incorporation of gender role stereotypes into a child's self-concept could lead girls to have less confidence in their general intellectual abilities than boys. This could lead girls to have lower expectations for success at difficult academic and vocational activities. It also could lead girls to expect to have to work harder to achieve success at these activities than boys expect to have to work. Evidence supports these predictions (Eccles, 1987; Nicholls, 1975; Parsons & others, 1976). Either of these beliefs could keep girls from selecting demanding educational or vocational options, especially if these options are not perceived as important or interesting.

Gender roles also could produce different expectations of success depending on the gender stereotyping of the activity. Both educational programs and vocational options are gender stereotyped in our culture. Many high-level professions and both math-related and scientific technical courses and vocational fields are thought to be male activities. In contrast, teaching below the college level, working in clerical and related support jobs, and excelling in language-related courses are thought to be female activities by both children and adults (Eccles, 1987; Eccles & Hoffman, 1984; Huston, 1983). Incorporating these beliefs into self-concept could cause girls to have lower expectations for success in male-typed activities and higher expectations for success in female-typed activities. This pattern could lead girls to select female-typed activities over male-typed activities. Some support for this perspective has been found (Eccles, 1987). At times, though, researchers have found no gender differences in achievement expectations.

An intriguing view about gender roles involving achievement argues that on the basis of an instrumental-achievement (male) versus expressive-affiliation (female) dichotomy, we might expect male superiority in achievement patterns. This is not always the case. In an investigation by Lloyd Lueptow (1984), adolescent females had both higher levels of achievement value orientations and higher levels of academic achievement than did adolescent boys. It may be that achievement is a stronger component of the female gender role than the male gender role. Or, it may be that a distinction between achievement based on excellence and accomplishment (a stronger focus of females) and achievement based on assertion and aggressive competition (a stronger focus of males) is necessary. That is, females may be stronger achievers, males stronger competitors. Since researchers often have neglected this distinction, it may be that the achievement orientation of females has been underestimated.

A special concern is that some of the brightest and most gifted girls do not have achievement and career aspirations that match their talents. In one investigation, high-achieving girls had much lower expectations for success than high-achieving boys (Stipek & Hoffman, 1980). In the gifted research

program at Johns Hopkins University many mathematically precocious girls did select scientific and medical careers, although only 46 percent aspired to a full-time career compared to 98 percent of the boys (Fox, Brody, & Tobin, 1979).

To help talented female youth redirect their paths, some high schools are using programs developed by colleges and universities. Project CHOICE (Creating Her Options In Career Education) was designed by Case Western University to detect barriers in reaching one's potential. Gifted eleventh-grade females received individualized counseling that included interviews with female role models, referral to appropriate occupational groups, and information about career workshops. A program at the University of Nebraska (Kerr, 1983) was successful in encouraging talented female high school students to pursue more prestigious careers. This was accomplished by individualized counseling and participation in a "Perfect Future Day," in which girls shared career fantasies and discussed barriers that might impede their fantasies. Internal and external constraints were evaluated, gender-role stereotypes were discouraged, and high aspirations were applauded. While these programs have shown short-term success in redirecting the career paths of high-ability females, in some instances the benefits fade over time—six months or more, for example (Fox, 1976). It is important to be concerned about improving the awareness of career alternatives for all female youth, however, and not just those of high ability.

Gender Role Development

Most research focused on gender role development has been conducted with children from two to nine years of age (Huston, 1983). While some gender typing occurs in the first several years of life, it is difficult to assess. During the eighteen-month to three-year-old age period, children start expressing considerable interest in gender-type activities and classify themselves according to gender. From three to seven years of age, children begin to acquire an understanding of gender constancy and increasingly enjoy being with same-sex peers. During early childhood, young children also tend to make grand generalizations about gender roles. For example, three-year-old William accompanied his mother to the doctor's office. A man in a white coat walked by and William said, "Hi, Doc." Then a woman in a white coat walked by and William greeted her, "Hi, nurse." William's mother asked him how he knew which individual was a doctor and which was a nurse. William replied, "Because doctors are daddies and nurses are mommies." As Piaget warned, young children are so sure of their thoughts, yet so often they inaccurately understand the world. William's "nurse" turned out to be his doctor and vice versa (Carper, 1978).

In the middle childhood years, two divergent trends in gender roles take place. Children increase their understanding of culturally defined expectations for males and females, and simultaneously the behavior and attitudes of boys increasingly reflect masculine gender typing. However, during the middle childhood years, girls do not show an increased interest in feminine activities. Many girls even begin to show a stronger preference for masculine activities, a finding that has appeared in research studies conducted from the 1920s to the present. In one research investigation (Richardson & Simpson, 1982), the toy preferences of children five to nine years old were assessed by evaluating

Table 15.3
Proportions of Males and Females Requesting Items in Each Category

	Male (%)	Female (%)
Classes of items requested by significantly more males:		
Vehicles	43.5	8.2
Sport	25.1	15.1
Spatial-temporal	24.5	15.6
Military toys	23.4	.8
Race cars	23.4	5.1
Doll (humanoid)	22.8	6.6
Real vehicles	15.3	9.7
Doll (male)	10.0	2.8
Outer space toys	7.5	.3
Depots	6.4	.5
Machines	4.5	.8
Classes of items requested by significantly more females:		
Doll (female)	.6	27.4
Doll (baby)	.6	23.0
Domestic	1.7	21.7
Educational-art	11.4	21.4
Clothes	11.1	18.9
Doll houses	1.9	16.1
Clothing accessories	2.2	15.3
Doll accessories	1.1	12.5
Stuffed animals	5.0	9.7
Furnishings	1.9	5.4

From J. G. Richardson and C. H. Simpson, "Children, Gender, and Social Structure: An Analysis of the Contents of Letters to Santa Claus" in *Child Development* 53:429–436. Copyright © 1982 The Society for Research in Child Development, Inc., Chicago, IL. Reprinted by permission.

their letters to Santa Claus. While such requests for toys were gender typed, more girls than boys asked for cross-gender items (table 15.3). Boys and girls, though, do begin to show more flexibility in their understanding of gender role stereotypes in the elementary school years, seeing that stereotypes are not absolute and that alternatives are possible.

During adolescence the individual's gender role development becomes more wrapped up in sexuality than was true during childhood. As puberty proceeds, young adolescents increasingly think of themselves and other adolescents as sexual beings. Many of these thoughts are uncertain and idealistic. Adolescents also give more abstract definitions of gender roles. The abstractness and idealism of their thoughts lead adolescents to think about what an ideal male and what an ideal female are like. Inevitably, adolescents compare themselves and others to these ideal standards. Individuals the adolescent does not know personally, such as media stars, are more likely to approach the ideal standard. As their bodies are flooded with sex hormones and they think about what the ideal male and female are like, adolescent males strive to be the very best male possible and adolescent females strive to be the very best female possible. Adolescence also is a time when males and females focus more attention on integrating vocational and life-style choices (Aneshensel & Rosen, 1980). A special concern for older adolescents is whether to combine career and family interests.

At this point we have discussed a number of ideas about social influences on gender roles, gender stereotyping and differences, and the development of gender roles. A summary of these ideas is presented in Concept Table 15.2.

Social and Personality Development

Concept	Processes/Related Ideas	Characteristics/Description
Social influences	Parent-child relationships	Parents by action and example, influence their children's gender role development. Mothers and fathers often play different roles—mothers are more nurturant and responsible for physical care, fathers are more playful and demanding. Fathers are more likely to act differently toward sons and daughters than are mothers. Parent-child interaction is reciprocal and it is not easy to sort through the direction of effects.
	Peers and teachers	Children's peer groups are heavily gender segregated and children show clear preferences for being with same-sex peers. Historically, in the United States, education has been male-defined rather than gender balanced. Males receive more attention and teacher interaction in schools. Current trends focus on subtle sex discrimination and stereotyping, male and female valued educational goals, and sex equity outcomes.
	The media	Despite improvements, television still portrays males in more competent ways than females. Males also are portrayed in more competent ways in advertisements.
	Changing gender role behavior	Boys who are feminine in childhood are more likely to have a homosexual or bisexual orientation in late adolescence than boys who are masculine in childhood. Clinical treatment has been somewhat successful in getting feminine boys to behave in more masculine ways. Little interest has been shown in changing girls' gender deviant behavior. Efforts also have been made to teach androgyny to children in school. This has met with mixed success. Girls seem to be more receptive than boys, with adolescent boys especially resistant to the instruction.
Gender stereotyping and differences	Gender role stereotypes	These are broad categories that reflect our impressions and beliefs about males and females. Because stereotypes are broad categories, diverse behaviors can be called on to support the stereotypes.
	Gender differences	In the 1970s it was concluded that boys have better math skills, have superior visual-spatial ability, and are more aggressive, while girls are better at verbal abilities. Today's conclusions suggest that boys are more active and the differences in verbal abilities have virtually vanished. The other differences—math, visual-spatial ability, and aggression—persist, although continued cultural change may chip away at these differences.
	Achievement in females	While the answer to the question of whether males and females differ in their expectations for success is not yet settled, special concern is evidenced that some of the brightest and most gifted girls do not have achievement and career aspirations that match their talents. An often neglected distinction by researchers is that females may be more achievement oriented, males more competitive and assertive.
Gender role development	Its nature	From eighteen months to three years, children begin to express considerable interest in gender role activities and classify themselves according to gender. From three to seven years, children begin to acquire an understanding of gender constancy and increasingly enjoy being with same-sex peers. During middle childhood, children understand more about culturally defined expectations about males and females, and the behavior of boys becomes increasingly masculine. During adolescence, sexuality becomes a more prominent part of gender roles, interpretations of gender roles are more abstract and idealistic, males and females are motivated to be the very best representative of their respective sex, and there are greater career and life-style considerations.

Summary

I. Gender Role Components

Gender roles focus on society's expectations for males and for females. Recent interest has emphasized the concept of androgyny, the belief that competent individuals have both masculine and feminine characteristics. The four gender role classifications are masculine, feminine, androgynous, and undifferentiated. Specification of the dimensions of masculinity, femininity, and androgyny has not always been consistent. Conceptualizing masculine dimensions as self-assertive and instrumental and feminine dimensions as integrative and expressive provides greater specification. Developmental considerations also are important. Controversy surrounds the question of whether androgynous children are more competent. In answering this question it is important to specify not only the criteria for androgyny but also the criteria for competence. Masculine dimensions have been more valued in our culture and the criteria for competence also have followed this pattern. In contexts in which both self-assertive or instrumental and integrative or expressive characterstics are required for competence, androgynous individuals are more competent.

II. Biological and Cognitive Influences

Freud's and Erikson's theories promote the idea that anatomy is destiny. Hormones influence sexual development, although not as pervasively in humans as in animals. Today's psychologists are all interactionists when biological and environmental influences on gender roles are considered. However, interaction means different things to different people. Cognitive factors are involved in the child's active construction of gender roles; two such cognitive factors are self-categorization and language development. An important theme in the cognitive approach is that children develop a gender schema.

III. Social Influences

Parents, by action and by example, influence their children's gender role development. Mothers and fathers often play different roles—mothers are more nurturant and responsible for physical care, fathers are more playful and demanding. Fathers are more likely to act differently towards sons and daughters than are mothers. Parent-child interaction is reciprocal and it is not easy to sort through the direction of effects. Children's peer groups are heavily gender segregated and children show clear preferences for being with same-sex peers. Historically, in the United States, education has been male-defined rather than gender balanced. Males receive more attention and teacher interaction than females in schools. Current trends focus on subtle sex discrimination and stereotyping, male and female valued educational goals, and sex equity outcomes. Despite improvements, television still portrays males in more competent ways than females, as do advertisements. Boys who are feminine in childhood are more likely to have a homosexual or bisexual orientation in late adolescence than boys who were masculine in childhood. Clinical treatment has been somewhat successful in getting feminine boys to behave in more masculine ways. Little interest has been shown in changing girls' gender deviant behavior. Efforts also have been made to teach androgyny to children in school. This has met with mixed success. Girls seem to be more receptive than boys, with adolescent boys especially resistant to the instruction.

IV. Gender Stereotyping and Differences

These are broad categories that reflect our impressions and beliefs about males and females. Because stereotypes are broad categories, diverse behaviors can be called on to support the stereotypes. In the 1970s it was concluded that boys have better math skills, have superior visual-spatial ability, and are more aggressive, while girls are better at verbal abilities. Today's conclusions suggest that boys are more active and the difference in verbal abilities has virtually vanished. The other differences—math, visual-spatial ability, and aggression—still persist, although continued cultural change may chip away at these differences. While the answer to the question of whether males and females differ in their achievement expectations has not been settled, special concern is evidenced that some of the brightest and most gifted girls do not have achievement and career aspirations that match their talents. An often neglected distinction by researchers is that females may be more achievement oriented, males more competitive and assertive.

V. Gender Role Development

From eighteen months to three years, children begin to express considerable interest in gender role activities and classify themselves according to gender. From three to seven years, children begin to acquire an understanding of gender constancy and increasingly enjoy being with same-sex peers. During middle childhood, children understand more about culturally defined expectations for males and females, and the behavior of boys becomes increasingly masculine. During adolescence, sexuality becomes a more prominent part of gender roles, interpretation of gender roles is more abstract and idealistic, males and females are motivated to be the very best representative of their respective sex, and there are greater career and life-style considerations.

Key Terms

gender roles   406

androgyny   407

undifferentiated   407

self-assertion   409

integration   409

instrumental
orientation   409

expressive orientation   409

estrogen   410

androgen   410

hermaphrodites   410

gender schema   412

Suggested Readings

Bem, S. L. (1985). Androgyny and gender schema theory:
Conceptual and empirical integration. In T. B.
Sonderegger (Ed.), *Nebraska symposium on motivation*.
Lincoln, NE: University of Nebraska Press.
Bem, a leading androgyny expert, describes her views on
androgyny and gender schema.

Feingold, A. (1988). Cognitive gender differences are
disappearing. *American Psychologist, 43,* 95–103.
Recent information about cognitive gender differences is
presented, suggesting that many of the differences are
vanishing.

Huston, A. C. (1983). Sex-typing. In P. H. Mussen (Ed.),
Handbook of child psychology (4th ed., Vol. 4). New
York: John Wiley & Sons.
A lengthy, comprehensive review of what is known about
children's gender role development.

Hyde, J. S. (1988). *Half the human experience* (4th ed.).
Lexington, MA: D. C. Heath.
An excellent overview of female gender role development.

Reinisch, J. M., Rosenblum, L. A., & Sanders, S. A. (Eds.).
(1987). *Masculinity/femininity*. New York: Oxford
University Press.
An outstanding collection of articles by leading experts
such as Eleanor Maccoby, John Money, and Jacqueline
Eccles. Includes a special section of papers on the
development of gender roles.

Moral Development

an children understand concepts like discrimination, economic inequality, affirmative action, and comparable worth? Probably not if we used these terms, but might we be able to construct circumstances involving these terms that they might be able to understand? Phyllis Katz (1987) asked elementary school-aged children to pretend that they had taken a long ride on a spaceship to a make-believe planet called Pax and to give opinions about different situations in which they found themselves. The situations involved conflict, socioeconomic inequality, and civil-political rights. For example, conflict items included asking what a teacher should do when two students were tied for a prize or when they have been fighting. The economic equality dilemmas included a proposed field trip that not all students could afford, a comparable worth situation where janitors were paid more than teachers, and an employment situation that discriminated against those with dots on their noses instead of stripes. The rights items dealt with minority rights and freedom of the press.

The elementary school children did indeed recognize injustice and often came up with interesting solutions to problems. For example, all but two children believed that teachers should earn as much as janitors—the holdouts said teachers should make less because they stay in one room or because cleaning toilets is more disgusting and therefore deserves higher wages. Children were especially responsive to the economic inequality items. All but one thought that not giving a job to a qualified applicant who had different physical characteristics (a striped rather than a dotted nose) was unfair. The majority recommended an affirmative action solution—giving the job to the one from the discriminated minority. None of the children verbalized the concept of freedom of the press or seemed to understand that a newspaper could have the right to criticize a mayor in print without being punished. What are our schools teaching children about democracy? Some of the courses of action suggested were intriguing. Several argued that the reporters should be jailed. One child said that if she were mayor she would worry, make speeches, and say I didn't do anything wrong, not unlike what American presidents have done in recent years. Another said that the mayor should not put the newspaper people out of work because that might make them print more bad things. "Make them write comics instead," he said.

Children believed that poverty existed on Earth but mainly in Africa, big cities, or Vietnam. War was mentioned as the biggest problem on Earth, although children were not certain where it is presently occurring. Other problems mentioned were crime, hatred, school, smog, meanness, and Delta Airlines (the questions were asked in the summer of 1986 just after a Delta Airlines crash killed hundreds of passengers). Overall, the types of rules the children believed a society should abide by were quite sensible—almost all included the need for equitable sharing of resources and work and prohibitions against aggression.

This chapter is about such matters as equitable sharing, helping, rules and regulations, and moral dilemmas. Developmentalists want to know how children behave, think, and feel regarding standards of right and wrong. It is this area of children's lives we call moral development.

What Is Moral Development?

The study of moral development is one of the oldest topics of interest to those who are curious about human nature. In prescientific periods philosophers and theologians heatedly debated the child's moral status at birth, which they felt had important implications for how the child was to be reared. Today people are hardly neutral about moral development; most have very strong opinions about acceptable and unacceptable behavior, ethical and unethical conduct, and the ways in which acceptable and ethical behaviors are to be fostered in children.

Moral development concerns rules and conventions about what people *should* do in their interactions with other people. In studying these rules, developmentalists examine three different domains. First, how do children *reason* or *think* about rules for ethical conduct? For example, consider cheating. The child can be presented with a story in which someone has a conflict about whether or not to cheat in a particular situation, such as when taking a test in school. The child is asked to decide what is appropriate for the character to do and why. The focus is placed on the *reasoning* children use to justify their moral decisions.

Second, how do children actually *behave* in moral circumstances? In our example of cheating, emphasis is on observing the child's cheating and the environmental circumstances that produced and maintain the cheating. Children might be presented with some toys and asked to select which one they believe is the most attractive. Then, the experimenter tells the young child that the particular toy selected is someone else's and is not to be played with. Observations of different conditions under which the child deviates from the prohibition or resists temptation are conducted.

Third, how does the child *feel* about the moral matters? In the example of cheating, does the child feel enough guilt to resist temptation? If children do cheat, do feelings of guilt after the transgression keep them from cheating the next time they face temptation? In the remainder of this chapter, we focus on these three facets of moral development—thought, action, and feeling. Then, we evaluate the positive side of children's moral development—altruism. Finally, we discuss the nature of children's moral education.

Moral Thoughts

How do children think about standards of right and wrong? Piaget had some thoughts about this question and so did Lawrence Kohlberg. We consider each of their approaches to children's moral thoughts then turn to a recent interest in distinguishing moral reasoning from social conventional reasoning.

Piaget's Ideas about Moral Development

Interest in how the child thinks about moral issues was stimulated by Piaget (1932), who extensively observed and interviewed children from the ages of four to twelve. Piaget watched children play marbles to learn how they used and thought about the game's rules. He also asked children questions about ethical rules—theft, lies, punishment, and justice, for example. Piaget concluded that children think in two distinctly different ways about morality depending on their developmental maturity. The more primitive way of thinking—**heteronomous morality**—is displayed by younger children (from four to seven years of age). The more advanced way of thinking—**autonomous morality**—is displayed by older children (ten years of age and older). Children seven to ten years of age are in a transition between the two stages, evidencing some features of both.

By observing children play various games, Piaget learned how they used and thought about the rules of games. What kind of questions would you want to ask these second and third graders about their chess play to discover their judgments about rules?

What are some of the characteristics of heteronomous morality and autonomous morality? The heteronomous thinker judges the rightness or goodness of behavior by considering the consequences of the behavior, not the intentions of the actor. For example, the heteronomous thinker says that breaking twelve cups accidentally is worse than breaking one cup intentionally while trying to steal a cookie. For the moral autonomist, the reverse is true. The actor's intention assumes paramount importance. The heteronomous thinker also believes that rules are unchangeable and are handed down by all-powerful authorities. When Piaget suggested that new rules be introduced to the game of marbles, the young children resisted. They insisted that the rules had always been the same and could not be changed. By contrast, older children—who were moral autonomists—accept change and recognize that rules are merely convenient, socially agreed upon conventions, subject to change by consensus.

The heteronomous thinker also believes in **immanent justice**—if a rule is broken, punishment will be meted out immediately. He believes that the violation is connected in some automatic or mechanical way to the punishment. Thus, young children often look around worriedly after committing a transgression, expecting inevitable punishment. Research continues to verify that the belief in immanent justice declines toward the end of the elementary school years (e.g., Jose, 1985). Older children—who are moral autonomists—recognize that punishment is socially mediated and occurs only if a relevant person witnesses the wrongdoing and that, even then, punishment is not inevitable.

Piaget argued that as children develop they become more sophisticated in their thinking about social matters, especially about the possibilities and conditions of cooperation. Piaget believed that this social understanding comes about through the mutual give-and-take of peer relations. In the peer group—where others have power and status similar to the individual—plans are negotiated and coordinated, disagreements are reasoned about and eventually settled. Parent-child relations—where parents have the power and the child does not—are less likely to advance moral reasoning because rules are often handed down in an authoritarian way, thought Piaget.

Remember that Piaget believed adolescents usually become formal operational thinkers. Thus, they are no longer tied to immediate and concrete phenomena but are more logical, abstract, and deductive reasoners. Formal operational thinkers frequently compare the real to the ideal; create contrary-to-fact propositions; are cognitively capable of relating the distant past to the present; understand their roles in society, in history, and in the universe; and can conceptualize their own thoughts and think about their mental constructs as objects. For example, it usually is not until about the age of eleven or twelve that boys and girls spontaneously introduce concepts of belief, intelligence, and faith into their definitions of their religious identities. Thus, many of Piaget's tenets of cognitive developmental theory have significant implications for the moral development of the adolescent.

When children move from the relatively homogeneous grade school neighborhood to more heterogeneous high school and college environments, they are faced with contradictions between the moral concepts they have accepted and events in the world outside their families and neighborhoods. Adolescents are ripe for recognizing that their beliefs are but one of many and that there often is a great deal of debate about right and wrong in ethical matters. Consequently, many adolescents may start to question and sometimes reject their former beliefs, and in the process they may develop their own moral system. Martin Hoffman (1980) refers to this Piagetian-related view of moral development as **cognitive disequilibrium theory.**

Kohlberg's Ideas about Moral Development

The most provocative view of moral development in recent years was crafted by Lawrence Kohlberg (Colby & Kohlberg, 1987; Kohlberg, 1958, 1976, 1986; Kohlberg & Higgins, 1987). Kohlberg believes that moral development is based primarily on moral reasoning and unfolds in a series of stages. He arrived at his view after some twenty years of using a unique interview with children. In the interview, children are presented with a series of stories in which characters face moral dilemmas. The following is the most popular of the Kohlberg dilemmas:

> In Europe a woman was near death from a special kind of cancer. There was one drug that the doctors thought might save her. It was a form of radium that a druggist in the same town had recently discovered. The drug was expensive to make, but the druggist was charging ten times what the drug cost him to make. He paid $200 for the radium and charged $2,000 for a small dose of the drug. The sick woman's husband, Heinz, went to everyone he knew to borrow the money, but he could only get together $1,000 which is half of what it cost. He told the druggist that his wife was dying and asked him to sell it cheaper or let him pay later. But the druggist said, "No, I discovered the drug, and I am going to make money from it," So Heinz got desperate and broke into the man's store to steal the drug for his wife. (Kohlberg, 1969, p. 379)

This story is one of eleven devised by Kohlberg to investigate the nature of moral thought. After reading the story, the interviewee answers a series of questions about the moral dilemma. Should Heinz have stolen the drug? Was it right or wrong? Why? Is it a husband's duty to steal a drug for his wife if he cannot get it any other way? Would a good husband do this? Did the druggist have the right to charge that much when there was no law actually setting a limit on the price? Why?

Based on the reasons individuals gave to this and other moral dilemmas, Kohlberg believes three levels of moral development exist, each of which is characterized by two stages. Each stage also is described in terms of a general structural principle, called the level of sociomoral reflection or perspective. This refers to the point of view taken by the individual in both defining social reality and in choosing moral values.

At level 1, **preconventional moral reasoning,** the individual shows no internalization of moral values. Morality is truly external to the individual. Children conform to rules imposed by authority figures to avoid punishment or to obtain rewards. During stage 1, **punishment and obedience orientation** (egocentric point of view), moral thinking is based on punishments. Children obey because adults tell them to obey. In the Heinz and the druggist story, the child might respond that Heinz should not let his wife die because he would be in big trouble. Or he might say that Heinz should not steal the drug because he might get caught and sent to jail.

During stage 2, **naive hedonism or instrumental orientation** (concrete individualistic perspective), moral thinking is based on rewards and self-interest. Children obey when they want to obey and when it is in their best interests to obey. What is right is what feels good and what is rewarding. Why should Heinz steal the drug? If Heinz gets caught he could give the drug back and they might not give him a long jail sentence. Why shouldn't Heinz steal the drug? The druggist is a businessman and needs to make money.

At level 2, **conventional moral reasoning,** internalization is intermediate. The individual abides by certain standards (internal), but they are the standards of others (external). The individual is motivated to obey the rules of others, such as parents, peers, and social groups, to obtain praise recognition for moral behavior, or to maintain the social order. During stage 3, **good boy** or **good girl orientation** (social relational perspective), the individual values trust, caring, and loyalty to others as the basis of moral judgments. At this stage, children often adopt their parents' moral standards, seeking to be thought of by their parents as a "good boy" or a "good girl." Why should Heinz steal the drug? He was only doing something that a good husband would do. It shows how much he loves his wife. Why shouldn't Heinz steal the drug? If his wife dies, he can't be blamed for it. It is the druggist's fault. He is the selfish one.

During stage 4, **authority and social-order maintaining morality** (member of society perspective), moral judgments are based on understanding social order, law, justice, and duty. Why should Heinz steal the drug? If you did nothing, you would be letting your wife die. It is your responsibility if she dies. You have to steal it with the idea of paying the druggist later. Why shouldn't Heinz steal the drug? It is always wrong to steal. Heinz will always feel guilty if he steals the drug.

At level 3, **postconventional moral reasoning,** morality is completely internalized and not based on others' standards. The individual recognizes alternative moral courses, explores the options, and then decides on a personal moral code. During stage 5, **community rights versus individual rights** (prior to society perspective), the individual understands that values and laws are relative and that standards may vary from one individual to another. The individual recognizes that laws are important for society but also believes that laws can be changed. The individual believes that some values, such as liberty, are more important than the law. Why should Heinz steal the drug? The law was not set up to take into account these circumstances. Taking the drug may not be completely right, but Heinz should do it. Why shouldn't Heinz steal the drug? At stage 5, the individual invariably argues that Heinz *should* steal the drug because life takes priority over property rights.

During stage 6, **individual conscience** (rational-moral perspective), individuals have, in rare instances, developed moral standards based on universal human rights. When faced with a conflict between a law and conscience, the individual will always follow his conscience, even if the decision entails personal risk. At stage 6, the moral reasoner values abstract moral principles that are considered universal and binding. The stage 6 reasoner self-consciously uses certain checks on the validity of moral reasoning. For example, "Would you judge this action to be fair if you were in the other person's shoes?" "Would it be right if everyone did X?" Also, at stage 6, trust and community are the preconditions to agreements necessary to protect human rights. At stage 5, the reverse is true: agreements lead to trust and community. And, in stage 6, the intrinsic moral worth and respect of persons is recognized and upheld in the course of resolving a moral dilemma. Again, in stage 6 as in stage 5, Heinz would invariably steal the drug, because by not stealing the drug he would not be recognizing the intrinsic moral worth of a human life.

Kohlberg believes these levels and stages occur in a sequence and are age-related: Before age nine, most children reason about moral dilemmas in a preconventional way; by early adolescence, they reason in more conventional ways; and by early adulthood, a small number of individuals reason in postconventional ways. In a twenty-year longitudinal investigation, the uses of stages 1 and 2 decreased. Stage 4, which did not appear at all in the moral reasoning of the ten-year-olds, was reflected in 62 percent of the moral thinking of the thirty-six-year-olds. Stage 5 did not appear until the ages of twenty to twenty-two and never characterized more than 10 percent of the individuals.

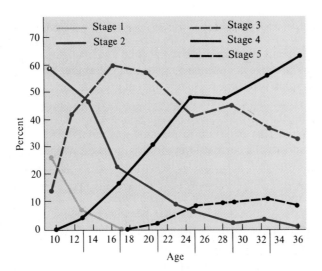

Figure 16.1
Age and Kohlberg's moral judgment stages.

Thus, the moral stages appeared somewhat later than Kohlberg initially envisioned, and the higher stages, especially stage 6, was extremely elusive (see figure 16.1) (Colby & others, 1983). Recently, stage 6 was removed from the Kohlberg moral judgment scoring manual but it still is considered to have a great deal of theoretical importance in the Kohlberg scheme of moral development. A recent review of data from forty-five studies in twenty-seven diverse world cultures provided striking support for the universality of Kohlberg's first four stages, although there was more cultural diversity at stages 5 and 6 (Snarey, 1987).

Influences on the Kohlberg Stages

Kohlberg believes that children's moral orientation unfolds as a consequence of cognitive development. Children construct their moral thoughts as they pass from one stage to the next rather than passively accepting a cultural norm of morality. Investigators have sought to understand factors that influence children's movement through the moral stages, among them modeling, cognitive conflict, peer relations, and perspective-taking opportunities.

Several investigators have attempted to advance an individual's level of moral development by providing arguments that reflect moral thinking one stage above the individual's established level. These studies are based on the cognitive developmental concepts of equilibrium and conflict. By finding the correct environmental match slightly beyond the individual's cognitive level, a disequilibrium is created that motivates her to restructure her moral thought. The resolution of the disequilibrium and conflict should be toward increased competence, but the data are mixed on this question. In one of the pioneer studies on this topic, Eliot Turiel (1966) discovered that children preferred a response one stage above their current level over a response two stages above it. However, they actually chose a response one stage below their level more often than a response one stage above it. Apparently the children were motivated more by security needs than by the need to reorganize thought to a higher level. Other studies indicate that children do prefer a more advanced stage over a less advanced stage (e.g., Rest, Turiel, & Kohlberg, 1969).

Since the early studies of stage modeling, a number of investigations have attempted to more precisely determine the effectiveness of various forms of stage modeling and argument (Lapsley & Quintana, 1985). The upshot of these studies is that virtually any plus-stage discussion format, for any length

of time, seems to promote more advanced moral reasoning. For example, in one investigation (Walker, 1982), exposure to plus-two stage reasoning (arguments two stages above the child's current stage of moral thought) was just as effective in advancing moral thought as plus-one stage reasoning. Exposure to plus-two stage reasoning did not produce more plus-two stage reasoning but rather, like exposure to plus-one stage reasoning, increased the likelihood that the child would reason one stage above her current stage. Other research has found that exposure to reasoning only one-third of a stage higher than the individual's current level of moral thought will advance moral thought (Berkowitz & Gibbs, 1983). In sum, current research on modeling and cognitive conflict reveals that moral thought can be moved to a higher level through exposure to models or discussion that is more advanced than the child's.

Kohlberg believes that peer interaction is a critical part of the social stimulation that challenges individuals to change their moral orientations. Whereas adults characteristically impose rules and regulations on children, the mutual give-and-take in peer interaction provides the child with an opportunity to take the role of another person and to generate rules democratically. Kohlberg stresses that role-taking opportunities can, in principle, be engendered by any peer group encounter. While Kohlberg believes that such role-taking opportunities are ideal for moral development, he also believes that certain types of parent-child experiences can induce the child to think at more advanced levels of moral thinking. In particular, parents who allow or encourage conversation about value-laden issues promote more advanced moral thought in their children. Unfortunately, many parents do not systematically provide their children with such role-taking opportunities.

Kohlberg's Critics

Kohlberg's provocative theory of moral development has not gone unchallenged. Among the criticisms are those involving the link between moral thought and moral behavior, the quality of the research, the care perspective, and societal contributions.

Moral reasons can often be a shelter for immoral behavior. Bank embezzlers and presidents address the loftiest of moral virtues when analyzing moral dilemmas but their own moral behavior may be immoral. No one wants a nation of cheaters and thieves who can reason at the postconventional level. The cheaters and the thieves may know what is right and what is wrong but still do what is wrong.

Some developmentalists believe more attention should be paid to the way moral development is assessed. For example, James Rest (1976, 1983, 1986, 1988) points out that alternative methods should be used to collect information about moral thinking instead of relying on a single method that requires individuals to reason about hypothetical moral dilemmas. Rest further indicates that Kohlberg's stories are extremely difficult to score. To help remedy this problem, Rest developed his own measure of moral development, called the Defining Issues Test (DIT).

In the DIT, an effort is made to determine which moral issues individuals feel are most crucial in a given situation. They are presented with a series of dilemmas and a list of definitions of the major issues involved (Kohlberg's procedure does not make use of such a list). In the dilemma of Heinz and the druggist, individuals might be asked whether a community's laws should be upheld or whether Heinz should risk being injured or caught as a burglar. They might also be asked to list the most important values that govern human interaction. They are given six stories and asked to rate the importance of each issue involved in deciding what ought to be done. Then they are asked to list

Table 16.1
Actual Moral Dilemmas Generated by Adolescents

Story subject	Grade		
	7	9	12
	Percentage		
Alcohol	2	0	5
Civil rights	0	6	7
Drugs	7	10	5
Interpersonal relations	38	24	35
Physical safety	22	8	3
Sexual relations	2	20	10
Smoking	7	2	0
Stealing	9	2	0
Working	2	2	15
Other	11	26	20

From S. R. Yussen, "Characteristics of Moral Dilemmas Written by Adolescents" in *Developmental Psychology 13*:162–63. Copyright © 1977 by the American Psychological Association. Reprinted by permission of the author.

Kohlberg's theory has been criticized by Carol Gilligan, because she believes he has underplayed the care perspective. Gilligan would argue that the connectedness orientation of these girls and their camaraderie in close relationships is missed in the Kohlberg scheme.

what they believe are the four most important issues. Rest argues that this method provides a more valid and reliable way to assess moral thinking than Kohlberg's method.

Researchers also have found that the hypothetical moral dilemmas posed in Kohlberg's stories do not match up with the moral dilemmas many children and adults face in their everyday lives (Walker, de Vries, & Trevethan, 1987; Yussen, 1977). Most of Kohlberg's stories focus on the family and authority. However, when one of your authors (Yussen, 1977) invited adolescents to write stories about their own moral dilemmas, adolescents generated dilemmas that were broader in scope, focusing on friends, acquaintances, and other issues, as well as family and authority. The moral dilemmas also were analyzed in terms of their content. As shown in table 16.1, the moral issue that concerned adolescents more than any other was interpersonal relationships.

Another criticism of Kohlberg's ideas, one that has been given considerable publicity, is that his view does not adequately reflect connectedness with and concern for others. Carol Gilligan (1982, 1985) argues that Kohlberg's theory emphasizes a **justice perspective,** that is, a focus on the rights of the individual. People are differentiated and seen as standing alone in making moral decisions. By contrast, the **care perspective** sees people in terms of their connectedness with others and the focus is on interpersonal communication. According to Gilligan, Kohlberg has vastly underplayed the care perspective in moral development. She believes this may be because most of his research was with males rather than females. More insight into Gilligan's belief in the importance of the care perspective in understanding children's moral development appears in Perspective on Child Development 16.1. Other experts on moral development also believe that caring attachments and judgments of fairness are key ingredients of children's moral growth (Damon, 1988).

Gilligan also thinks that moral development has three basic levels. She calls level I preconventional morality, which reflects a concern for self and survival. Level II, conventional morality, shows a concern for being responsible and caring for others. Level III, postconventional morality, shows a concern for self and others as interdependent. Gilligan believes that Kohlberg has underemphasized the care perspective in the moral development of *both* males and females and that morality's highest level for both sexes involves a search for moral equality between one's self and others (Muuss, 1988).

Many critics also argue that moral development is more culture-specific than Kohlberg believes. As Urie Bronfenbrenner and James Garbarino (1976) have observed, moral standards in other cultures are not always consistent

Amy Says They Should Just Talk It Out and Find Some Other Way to Make Money

The main character in Kohlberg's most widely used dilemma is a male—Heinz. Possibly females have a difficult time identifying with him. Some of the Kohlberg dilemmas are gender neutral, but one is about the captain of a company of marines. The subjects in Kohlberg's original research were all males. Going beyond her critique of Kohlberg's failure to consider females, Gilligan (1982) argues that an important voice is not present in his view. Following are two excerpts from children's responses to the story of Heinz and the druggist, one from eleven-year-old Jake, the other from eleven-year-old Amy. First, Jake's comments:

> For one thing, human life is worth more than money, and if the druggist only makes $1,000, he is still going to live, but if Heinz doesn't steal the drug, his wife is going to die. (*Why is life worth more than money?*) Because the druggist can get $1,000 later from rich people with cancer, but Heinz can't get his wife again. (p. 26)

And Amy's comments:

> Well, I don't think so. I think there might be other ways besides stealing it, like if he could borrow the money or make a loan or something, but he really

shouldn't steal the drug—but his wife shouldn't die either. (*Why shouldn't he steal the drug?*) If he stole the drug, he might save his wife then, but if he did, he might have to go to jail, and then his wife might get sicker again, and he couldn't get more of the drug, and it might not be good. So, they should really just talk it out and find some other way to make the money. (p. 28)

Jake's comments would be scored as a mixture of Kohlberg's stages 3 and 4, but they also include some of the components of a mature level III moral thinker. Amy, by contrast, does not fit into Kohlberg's scoring system so well. Jake sees the problem as one of rules and balancing the rights of people. However, Amy views the problem as involving relationships—the druggist fails to live up to his relationship to the needy woman, the need to maintain the relationship between Heinz and his wife, and the hope that a bad relationship between Heinz and the druggist can be avoided. Amy concludes that the characters should talk it out and try to repair their relationships.

with the standards that children abide by in the United States. They believe that the more a child is exposed to different social agents with different sociopolitical views, the more advanced will be the child's moral development. Their research suggests that children who grow up in a culture that is more sociopolitically plural (United States, West Germany) are less likely to be authority oriented and will have more plural ideas about moral dilemmas than their counterparts who grow up in less sociopolitically plural cultures (Poland, Hungary). Bronfenbrenner and Garbarino also argue that more diverse family styles and more individual freedom within families occur in sociopolitically plural countries such as the United States. By being exposed to greater diversity and freedom in the culture and in the family, children's moral development should be advanced.

Moral Reasoning and Social Conventional Reasoning

In recent years considerable interest has been generated in whether reasoning about social matters is distinct from reasoning about moral matters (Nucci, 1982; Smetana, 1983, 1985; Turiel, 1977, 1978). Adherents of the belief that social reasoning is distinct from moral reasoning cast their thoughts within a cognitive developmental framework (Enright, Lapsley, & Olson, 1984).

The architects of the social reasoning approach argue that conventional rules focus on behavioral irregularities. To control such behavioral improprieties, conventional rules are created. In this manner the actions of individuals can be controlled and the existing social system maintained. Such conventional rules are thought to be arbitrary, with no prescription necessary. For example, not eating food with our fingers is a social conventional rule, as is not talking before raising one's hand in class.

By contrast, it is argued that moral rules are not arbitrary and certainly do involve prescription. Furthermore, moral rules are not created through any social consensus but rather are obligatory, virtually universally applicable, and somewhat impersonal (Turiel, 1978). Thus, rules pertaining to lying, stealing, cheating, and physically harming another person are moral rules because violation of these rules confronts ethical standards that exist apart from social consensus and convention. In sum, moral judgments are constructed as concepts of justice, whereas social conventional judgments are structured as concepts of social organization (Lapsley, Enright, & Serlin, 1986).

A review of research on **social conventional reasoning** suggests that the major thrust has been to demonstrate the independence of this form of reasoning apart from moral reasoning and to reveal how even young children make this distinction (Lapsley, Enright, & Serlin, 1986). For example, in two studies children were queried about spontaneously occurring moral and social conventional transgressions (Nucci & Nucci, 1982; Nucci & Turiel, 1978). Children were asked, "If there was no rule in the school about (the observed event), would it be all right to do it?" Approximately 80 percent of the children at each grade level believed the social conventional act would be appropriate if no rule existed to prohibit it. By contrast, more than 85 percent of the children at each grade level said that moral transgressions would not be appropriate even if there were no rules related to the transgressions. Other research suggests that children are more likely to evaluate actions in the moral domain on the basis of their intrinsic features (such as justice or harm), while social conventional actions are more likely to be interpreted in terms of their regulatory status in a social context (Nucci, 1982). Thus, it seems that actions in the social conventional area are judged wrong only if a social rule exists prohibiting them. By contrast, moral transgressions appear to be judged as universally wrong even in the absence of social consensus.

At this point we have discussed a number of ideas about the nature of moral development with special attention given to cognitive approaches. A summary of these ideas is presented in Concept Table 16.1.

Moral Behavior

The study of moral behavior has been influenced primarily by social learning theory. The familiar processes of reinforcement, punishment, and imitation have been invoked to explain how and why children learn certain responses and why their responses differ from one another; the general conclusions to be drawn are the same as elsewhere. When children are reinforced for behavior that is consistent with laws and social conventions, they are likely to repeat that behavior. When models who behave "morally" are provided, children are likely to adopt their actions. Finally, when children are punished for "immoral" or unacceptable behaviors, those behaviors can be eliminated, but at the expense of sanctioning punishment by its very use and of causing emotional side effects for the child.

The Nature of Moral Development and Moral Thoughts

Concept	Processes/Related Ideas	Characteristics/Description
What is moral development?	Rules and regulations	Moral development concerns rules and regulations about what people should do in their interactions with other people.
	Components	The three main domains of moral development are thought, behavior, and feeling.
Moral thoughts	Piaget's ideas	Piaget argued that children from four to seven years of age are in the stage of heteronomous morality and from about the age of ten years move into the stage of autonomous morality. Formal operational thought may undergird changes in the moral reasoning of adolescents.
	Kohlberg's ideas	Kohlberg proposed a provocative theory of moral development with three levels—preconventional, conventional, and postconventional—and six stages. Increased internalization characterizes movement to levels 2 and 3. Kohlberg's longitudinal data show a relation of the stages to age although the higher two stages, especially stage 6, rarely appear.
	Influences on the stages	Influences include cognitive development, imitation and cognitive conflict, peer relations, and perspective taking.
	Critics	Criticisms involve an overemphasis on cognition and an underemphasis on behavior, the quality of the research, inadequate consideration of the care perspective, and underestimation of the role of culture.
	Social conventional reasoning	Moral reasoning pertains to ethical matters; social conventional reasoning pertains to thoughts about social convention and consensus. Moral reasoning is prescriptive; conventional reasoning is more arbitrary. Moral reasoning emphasizes justice; social conventional reasoning emphasizes social regulation.

To these general conclusions we add the usual qualifiers. The effectiveness of reward and punishment depends on the consistency with which they are administered and the schedule (e.g., continuous, partial) that is adopted. The effectiveness of modeling depends on the characteristics of the model (e.g., esteem, power) and the presence of symbolic codes to enhance retention of the modeled behavior.

What kind of adult moral models are children being exposed to in our society? Do such models usually do what they say? There is evidence that the adult models children are exposed to often display a double standard, with their moral thinking not always corresponding to their actions. A poll of 24,000 Americans sampled American views on a wide variety of moral issues. Eight detailed scenarios of everyday moral problems were developed to test moral decision making. A summary of the responses to these moral dilemmas is shown in table 16.2. Consider the example of whether the person queried would knowingly buy a stolen color television set. More than 20 percent of the respondents said they would, even though 87 percent said that such an act is probably morally wrong. Further, approximately 31 percent of the adults said that if they knew they would not get caught, they would be more likely to buy the stolen television. While moral thought is a very important dimension of moral development, these data glaringly point out that what people believe about right and wrong does not always predict how they will act in moral situations.

In addition to emphasizing the role of reinforcement, punishment, and imitation in determining moral behavior, behaviorists make a strong claim that moral behavior is situationally dependent. That is, from the behavioral perspective, children do not consistently display moral behavior in different situations. In a classic investigation of moral behavior, one of the most extensive

Table 16.2
Adults as Moral Models for Children

Would you:	Percent who said yes, or probably:	Percent who said it is, or probably is, unethical:	Percent who would, or probably would, be more likely to if sure they wouldn't get caught:
Drive away after scratching a car without telling the owner?	44	89	52
Cover for a friend's secret affair?	41	66	33
Cheat on your spouse?	37	68	42
Keep $10 extra change at a local supermarket?	26	85	33
Knowingly buy a stolen color television set?	22	87	31
Try to keep your neighborhood segregated?	13	81	8
Drive while drunk?	11	90	24
Accept praise for another's work?	4	96	8

ever conducted, Hugh Hartshorne and Mark May (1928–30) observed the moral responses of 11,000 children who were given the opportunity to lie, cheat, and steal in a variety of circumstances—at home, at school, at social events, and in athletics. A completely honest or a completely dishonest child was difficult to find. Situation-specific behavior was the rule. Children were more likely to cheat when their friends put pressure on them to do so and when the

The young girl shown here is being disciplined for her lack of self-control and inability to resist temptation. How did your parents discipline you when you were not very good at controlling your behavior or when you did something wrong? How did it influence your behavior? Was their discipline effective in promoting your self-control over long time frames?

chance of being caught was slim. Other analyses of the consistency of moral behavior suggest that while moral behavior is influenced by situational determinants, some children are more likely to cheat, lie, and steal than others (Burton, 1984).

Resistance to Temptation and Self-Control

A key ingredient of moral development from the social learning perspective is the child's ability to resist temptation and to develop self-control (Bandura, 1986; Mischel, 1987). When pressures mount for children to cheat, lie, or steal, it is important to ask whether they have developed the ability to control themselves and to resist such temptations.

Developmentalists have invented a number of ways to investigate such temptations. In one procedure, children are shown attractive toys and told that the toys belong to someone else, who has requested that they not be touched. Children then experience some social influence, perhaps in the form of a discussion of virtues about respecting other people's property or a model shown resisting or giving in to the temptation to play with prohibited objects. Children are left alone in the room to amuse themselves when the experimenter departs (under some pretext), announcing that he or she will return in ten to fifteen minutes. The experimenter then observes through a one-way mirror to see whether children resist or give in to the temptation to play with the toys.

There has been considerable interest in examining the effects of punishment on children's ability to resist temptation (Parke, 1972, 1977). For the most part, cognitive rationales enhance almost any form of punishment. These rationales include reasons as to why the child should not play with the forbidden toy. Cognitive rationales have been more effective in getting children to resist temptation over a period of time than strategies that do not use reasoning, such as when parents place children in their rooms without explaining the consequences of the children's deviant behavior for others.

The ability to resist temptation is closely tied to delay of gratification. Self-control is involved in both the ability to resist temptation and the ability to delay gratification. In the case of resistance to temptation, children must overcome their impulses to get something that is desired but is known to be prohibitive. Similarly, children must show a sense of patience and self-control in delaying gratification for a desirable future reward rather than succumbing to the immediate pressure of pursuing a smaller reward.

Considerable research has been conducted on children's self-control. Walter Mischel (1974, 1987) believes that self-control is strongly influenced by cognitive factors. Researchers have shown that children can instruct themselves to be more patient and in the process show more self-control. In one investigation (Mischel & Patterson, 1976), preschool children were asked to perform a very dull task. Close by was a very enticing talking mechanical clown who tried to persuade the children to come play with him. The children who had been trained to say to themselves, "I'm not going to look at Mr. Clown when Mr. Clown says to look at him" were more likely to control their behavior and continue working on the dull task than children who were not given the self-instructional strategy.

Interest in cognitive factors in resistance to temptation, delay of gratification, and self-control reflect the increasing interest among social learning theorists in the manner in which such cognitions mediate the link between environmental experiences and moral behavior. Next, we present a view that captures this cognitive trend.

Cognitive Social Learning Theory

Combining elements of cognitive development and social learning highlights the cognitive social learning view of Walter and Harriet Mischel (1975; Mischel, 1987). The Mischels distinguish between children's **moral competence,** or ability to produce moral behaviors, and children's **moral performance** of those behaviors in specific situations. Competence or acquisition depends primarily on cognitive-sensory processes; it is an outgrowth of these processes. Competencies include what children are able to do, what they know, their skills, their awareness of moral rules and regulations, and their cognitive ability to construct behaviors. Children's moral performance, or behavior, however, is determined by their motivation and the rewards and incentives to act in a specific moral way.

In general, social learning theorists have been critical of Kohlberg's view. Among other reasons, they believe he places too little emphasis on moral behavior and the situational determinants of morality. However, while Kohlberg argues that moral judgment is an important determinant of moral behavior, he, like the Mischels, stresses that the individual's interpretation of both the moral and factual aspects of a situation leads her to a moral decision (Kohlberg & Candee, 1979). For example, Kohlberg mentions that "extra-moral" factors, like the desire to avoid embarrassment, may cause the child to avoid doing what she believes to be morally right. In sum, both the Mischels and Kohlberg believe that moral action is influenced by a complex of factors. Overall, the findings are mixed with regard to the association of moral thought and behavior, although one recent investigation with college students found that individuals with both high principled moral reasoning and high ego strength were less likely to cheat in a resistance to temptation situation than their low-principled and low-ego strength counterparts (Hess, Lonky, & Roodin, 1985).

So far we have seen that both the moral thought and the moral behavior of an individual are important components of moral development. Although psychoanalytic theory has always placed strong faith in the role of feelings in personality development, the emotional aspects of moral development were virtually ignored for many years. Now there seems to be a reemergence of interest in the affective aspects of moral development (Eisenberg, 1987; Hoffman, 1979).

This young girl is showing empathy toward her friend. How can parents encourage empathy in their children?

Moral Feelings and Altruism

In the psychoanalytic account of guilt, children avoid transgressing to avoid anxiety; by contrast, a child with little guilt has little reason to resist temptation. Guilt is responsible for harnessing the id's evil drives and for maintaining the world as a safe place to be. Early childhood is a special time for the development of guilt. It is during this time period—thought Freud—that through identification with parents and parents' use of love withdrawal for discipline, children turn their hostility inward and experience guilt. The guilt is primarily unconscious and reflects the structure of the personality known as the superego. Remember also that Erikson believes early childhood has special importance in the development of guilt; he even called the major conflict to be resolved in early childhood, initiative versus **guilt.**

Moral feelings or affect have traditionally been thought of in terms of guilt, but recently there has been considerable interest in the role of empathy in the child's moral development. **Empathy** is the ability to understand the feelings of another individual, and it is believed to be an important aspect of the child's altruism.

In studying guilt, cheating, lying, stealing, and resistance to temptation, we are investigating the antisocial, negative side of moral development. Today, we recognize that it is important not to dwell too much on the dark side of morality; perhaps we should spend more time evaluating and promoting the positive side of morality—prosocial behavior, altruism, and empathy, for example.

Altruism is an unselfish interest in helping someone. Human acts of altruism are plentiful—the hardworking laborer who places a $5 bill in a Salvation Army kettle, rock concerts organized by Bob Geldof and Willie Nelson to feed the hungry and help farmers, and a child who takes in a wounded cat and cares for it. How do psychologists account for such frequent accounts of altruism?

Reciprocity and exchange are important aspects of altruism (Brown, 1986). Reciprocity is found throughout the human world. It not only is the highest moral principle in Christianity but also is present in every widely practiced religion in the world—Judaism, Hinduism, Buddhism, and Islam. Reciprocity encourages us to do unto others as we would have them do unto us. Certain human sentiments are wrapped up in this reciprocity: trust probably is the most important principle over the long run; guilt emerges if we do not reciprocate; and anger results if someone else does not reciprocate. Not all human altruism is motivated by reciprocity and social exchange, but this view alerts us to the importance of considering self-other interactions and relationships in understanding altruism. The circumstances most likely to involve altruism are empathetic or sympathetic emotion for an individual in need or a close relationship between the benefactor and the recipient (Batson, in press; Clark & others, 1987; Lerner, 1982).

Although altruism seems to increase as children become older, examples of caring for others and comforting someone in distress are abundant during the preschool years (Eisenberg, 1987). The following vivid episode suggests its presence even as early as the second year of life:

> Today, Jerry was kind of cranky; he just started completely bawling and he wouldn't stop. John kept coming over and handing Jerry toys, trying to cheer him up, so to speak. He'd say things like, "Here, Jerry," and I said to John: "Jerry's sad; he doesn't feel good; he had a shot today." John would look at me with his eyebrows kind of wrinkled together like he really understood that Jerry was crying because he was unhappy, not that he was just being a crybaby. He went over and rubbed Jerry's arm and said, "Nice Jerry" and continued to give him toys. (Zahn-Waxler, Radke-Yarrow, & King, 1979, pp. 321–322)

One way to explain the presence of altruism in young children is their motivation to understand the feelings of others and to experience those feelings themselves (Denham, 1986; Fogel & Melson, 1987). If we see people cry or become sad and we share their distress, we may become motivated to help them relieve the distress. The empathy we feel and share with others, then, may be altruism's engine. The early preschool years may have a special importance in understanding empathy and altruism because it is at this point in development when children begin to recognize that other people have their own feelings and needs. Are there ways parents can develop these positive feelings in their young children? Several suggestions include the following: Expose children to a wide range of feelings; it is hard for them to empathize with someone who is experiencing an emotion they have never felt. Direct the child's attention to others' feelings—say to the child something like, "How do you think Sam felt when you socked him?" Ensure that children have models around them in their daily lives who not only show altruistic behavior but who verbalize the empathetic feelings that underlie it. Emerson once said, "The meaning of good and bad, better and worse, is simply helping or hurting." By developing young children's capacity for empathy and altruism, we can become a nation of *good* people who *help* rather than hurt.

Moral education has been a hotbed of controversy. How might the teacher in this classroom be providing a moral atmosphere for the students? What was the moral atmosphere of your schools like? What could have been done to improve the moral atmosphere of the schools you attended while you were growing up?

Moral Education

More than half a century ago, John Dewey (1933) recognized that whether or not they offer specific programs, schools provide moral education. This moral education includes school and classroom rules, attitudes toward academics and extracurricular activities, the moral orientation of administrators and teachers, and text materials. The pervasive moral atmosphere that characterizes schools is called the **hidden curriculum** by educators. Dewey was right—every school has a moral atmosphere, whether there is a specific moral education program or not. Schools, like families, are settings for moral development. Teachers serve as models of ethical or unethical behavior. Classroom rules and peer relations transmit attitudes about cheating, lying, stealing, and consideration for others. And the school administration, through its rules and regulations, represents a value system to adolescents.

Approaches to moral education can be classified as direct or indirect (Benninga, 1988). **Direct moral education** involves either emphasizing values or character traits during specified time slots or integrating those values or traits throughout the curriculum. **Indirect moral education** involves encouraging students to define their own and others' values and to help them define the moral perspectives that support those values.

In the direct moral education approach, instruction in specified moral concepts can assume the form of example and definition, class discussions and role playing, or rewarding students for proper behavior (Jensen & Knight, 1981). The use of McGuffey Readers during the early part of the twentieth century exemplifies the direct approach. The stories and poems in the readers taught moral behavior and character in addition to academics. A number of contemporary educators advocate a direct approach to moral education. Former U.S. Secretary of Education William Bennett (1986) wrote:

> If a college is really interested in teaching its students a clear lesson in moral responsibility, it should tell the truth about drugs in a straightforward way. This summer our college presidents should send every student a letter saying they will not tolerate drugs on campus—period. The letter should then spell out precisely what the college's policy will be toward students who use drugs. Being simple and straightforward about moral responsibility is not the same as being simplistic and unsophisticated.

Bennett also believes that every elementary and secondary school should have a discipline code, making clear to adolescents and parents what the school expects of them. Then the school should enforce the code.

The most widely adopted indirect approaches to moral education involve values clarification and cognitive moral education. **Values clarification** focuses on helping students to clarify what their lives are for and what is worth working for. In values clarification, students are asked questions or presented with dilemmas and expected to respond, either individually or in small groups. The intent is to help students define their own values and to become aware of others' values.

In the following example of values clarification, students are asked to select from among ten people the six who will be admitted to a fallout shelter during World War III:

> Suppose you are a government decision maker in Washington, DC, when World War III breaks out.
>
> A fallout shelter under your administration in a remote Montana highland contains only enough space, air, food, and water for six people for three months, but ten people wish to be admitted.
>
> The ten have agreed by radio contact that for the survival of the human race you must decide which six of them shall be saved. You have exactly thirty minutes to make up your mind before Washington goes up in smoke. These are your choices:
>
> 1. A 16-year-old girl of questionable IQ, a high school dropout, pregnant.
> 2. A policeman with a gun (which cannot be taken from him), thrown off the force recently for brutality.
> 3. A clergyman, 75.
> 4. A woman physician, 36, known to be a confirmed racist.
> 5. A male violinist, 46, who served seven years for pushing narcotics.
> 6. A 20-year-old black militant, no special skills.
> 7. A former prostitute, female, 39.
> 8. An architect, a male homosexual.
> 9. A 26-year-old law student.
> 10. The law student's 25-year-old wife who spent the last nine months in a mental hospital, still heavily sedated. They refuse to be separated. (Volkmor, Pasanella, & Raths, 1977, p. 1)

In this exercise, no answers are considered right or wrong. The clarification of values is left up to the individual student. Advocates of the values clarification approach argue that it is value-free. Critics argue that because of its controversial content, it offends community standards (Eger, 1981). Critics also say that because of its relativistic nature, values clarification undermines accepted values and fails to stress truth and what is right behavior (Oser, 1986).

Like values clarification, cognitive moral education also challenges direct moral instruction. However, advocates of **cognitive moral education** do not believe that moral education can be value free. Rather, they argue that through more indirect development of students' moral reasoning, values such as democracy and justice will be adopted. The cognitive moral education enthusiasts believe that moral standards should be allowed to develop within students through environmental settings and exercises that encourage more advanced moral thinking. If standards are imposed, they stress, children can never completely integrate and fully understand moral principles. Only through participation and discussion can children learn to apply the rules and principles of cooperation, trust, community, and self-reliance.

The Just Community and Schools' Moral Atmosphere

In 1974 Kohlberg established the "Just Community," a small school for black and white students from different socioeconomic backgrounds. In the Just Community emphasis was placed on considering realistic issues that arise in school, the nature of moral behavior as well as moral thought, and an active role for teachers as moral advocates.

The Just Community shared with other alternative schools a belief in self-governance, mutual caring, and group solidarity. The goal for moral development was geared toward increasing students' responsibility to the community (stage 4 in Kohlberg's theory) rather than self-principled reasoning. In an investigation of the effectiveness of the Just Community—actually named the Cluster School—(Power, 1984), it was found that a more positive orientation toward the community did develop and that students were likely to adhere to the rules they had established. However, although the moral reasoning of the students at the Cluster School did advance, students who simply participated in moral discussion programs advanced their moral reasoning just as much as the students in the Cluster School.

The manner in which Kohlberg set up the Cluster School brings him closer to educators who are concerned with the moral "givens" in life. However, as indicated before, most programs that have included Kohlberg's ideas emphasize the process of moral reasoning rather than a specific moral content. The effectiveness of the programs often varies from school to school and from student to student. Success is usually better at the lower stages (2, 3, and 4) than at postconventional levels (5, 6) (Minuchin & Shapiro, 1983) and in open schools rather than traditional schools (Sullivan, 1975). There is also some question about the persistence of the effects—how long lasting are the effects of such moral education programs? Usually, assessment takes place immediately after the semester in which moral education is taught, and rarely are there long-term followups.

With the development of the Cluster School in the middle 1970s Kohlberg himself seemed to change his ideas about moral education. Kohlberg (1981) reported that he was not satisfied with the discussion approach to moral education. He realized that attempts to instill principled reasoning about morality in adolescents may be unrealistic because most people do not reach this level of cognitive maturity even in adulthood. And he began to believe that the moral climate of the country was shifting to an emphasis on the self and away from a concern for others in the 1970s. As a consequence, Kohlberg began to show a stronger interest in the school as a social system and in creating moral school communities (Minuchin & Shapiro, 1983).

As a further indication of Kohlberg's belief in the importance of the moral atmosphere of the school, he has developed the Moral Atmosphere Interview. This interview poses dilemmas that deal with typically occurring problems in high schools, problems that are likely to involve social responsibility. In a recent investigation (Higgins, Power, & Kohlberg, 1983), the Moral Atmosphere Interview was administered to samples of approximately twenty students from three democratic alternative high schools and three more traditional, authoritarian high schools. Students in the democratic schools perceived the rules of their schools to be more collective and described themselves and their peers as more willing to act responsibly than did students from the traditional schools.

Lawrence Kohlberg's theory of moral development has extensively influenced the cognitive moral education approach. Contrary to what some critics say, Kohlberg's theory is not completely relativistic, and it is not completely morally neutral. It clearly treats higher-level moral thinking as better than lower-level moral thinking. And it stresses that higher-level thinking can be stimulated through focused discussion of moral dilemmas. Also, in the 1980s, Kohlberg (1981, 1986) revised his views on moral education by placing more emphasis on the school's moral atmosphere, not unlike John Dewey did many years ago. A summary of Kohlberg's revisionist thinking about moral education can be found in Perspective on Child Development 16.2.

Concept	Processes/Related Ideas	Characteristics/Discussion
Moral behavior	Social learning theory	The focus is on learned moral behavior, learned through interaction with people, especially through the familiar processes of reinforcement, punishment, and imitation. Situational variation in moral behavior is emphasized.
	Resistance to temptation and self-control	These are two dimensions often studied by social learning theorists. These aspects of moral behavior are closely tied to a third aspect, delay of gratification. Cognitive factors are important determinants of these aspects of moral behavior.
	Cognitive social learning theory	This theory argues that cognitive processes mediate the influence of the environment on children's moral behavior. Also stressed is the distinction between moral competence and moral performance, suggesting that what children morally know does not always predict what they will morally do.
Moral feelings and altruism	Moral feelings	The study of moral feelings focuses on guilt and psychoanalytic theory, as well as the more recent emphasis on empathy.
	Altruism	Altruism refers to an unselfish interest in helping someone. Circumstances most likely to involve altruism are empathetic or sympathetic emotion for an individual in need or a close relationship between the benefactor and the recipient. Altruism increases as children get older, but examples are abundant in the preschool years as well. One way to understand altruism in young children is their motivation to understand the feelings of others and to experience those feelings themselves.
Moral education	Its nature	The hidden curriculum involves the pervasive moral atmosphere that characterizes schools. Direct moral education focuses on either an emphasis on character traits or values during specified time slots or integration of those traits or values throughout the curriculum. Indirect moral education involves encouraging students to define their own values and others' values and to help in defining their own moral perspectives to support those values. The two main indirect approaches are values clarification and cognitive moral education (influenced heavily by Kohlberg).

Summary

I. What Is Moral Development?

Moral development concerns rules and regulations about what people should do in their interactions with other people. The three main domains of moral development are thought, behavior, and feeling.

II. Moral Thoughts

Piaget argued that children from four to seven years of age are in the stage of heteronomous morality and from about the age of ten years move into the stage of autonomous morality. Formal operational thought may undergird changes in the moral reasoning of adolescents. Kohlberg proposed a provocative theory of moral development with three levels—preconventional, conventional, and postconventional—and six stages. Increased internalization characterizes movement to levels 2 and 3. Kohlberg's longitudinal data show a relation of the stages to age although the higher two stages, especially stage 6, rarely appear. Kohlberg's stages are influenced by cognitive development, imitation and cognitive conflict, peer relations, and

perspective taking. Criticisms involve an overemphasis on cognition and an underemphasis on behavior, the quality of the research, inadequate consideration of the care perspective, and underestimation of the role of culture. Moral reasoning pertains to ethical matters; social conventional reasoning pertains to convention and consensus. Moral reasoning is prescriptive; conventional reasoning is more arbitrary. Moral reasoning emphasizes justice; social conventional reasoning emphasizes social regulation.

III. Moral Behavior

The focus is on learned moral behavior, learned through interaction with people, especially through the familiar processes of reinforcement, punishment, and imitation. Situational variation in moral behavior is emphasized. Two dimensions often studied by social learning theorists are resistance to temptation and self-control. These aspects of moral behavior are closely tied to a third aspect, delay of gratification. Cognitive factors are important determinants of these aspects of moral behavior. Cognitive social learning theory argues that cognitive processes mediate the influence of the environment on children's moral behavior. Also stressed is the distinction between moral competence and moral performance, suggesting that what children morally know does not always predict what they will morally do.

IV. Moral Feelings and Altruism

Moral feelings focus on guilt and psychoanalytic theory, as well as the more recent emphasis on empathy. Altruism refers to an unselfish interest in helping someone. Circumstances most likely to involve altruism are empathetic or sympathetic emotion for an individual in need or a close relationship between the benefactor and the recipient. Altruism increases as children grow older, but examples are abundant in the preschool years as well. One way to understand altruism in young children is their motivation to understand the feelings of others and to experience those feelings themselves.

V. Moral Education

The hidden curriculum involves the pervasive moral atmosphere that characterizes schools. Direct moral education focuses either on an emphasis on character traits or values during specified time slots or integration of those traits or values throughout the curriculum. Indirect moral education focuses on encouraging students to define their own values and others' values and to help in defining their own moral perspectives to support those values. The two main indirect approaches are values clarification and cognitive moral education (influenced heavily by Kohlberg).

Key Terms

moral development 431
heteronomous morality 431
autonomous morality 431
immanent justice 432
cognitive disequilibrium theory 432
preconventional moral reasoning 433
punishment and obedience orientation 433
naive hedonism or instrumental orientation 433
conventional moral reasoning 433
good boy or good girl orientation 433–434
authority and social-order maintaining morality 434
postconventional moral reasoning 434

community rights versus individual rights 434
individual conscience 434
justice perspective 437
care perspective 437
social conventional reasoning 439
moral competence 443
moral performance 443
guilt 443
empathy 444
altruism 444
hidden curriculum 445
direct moral education 445
indirect moral education 445
values clarification 446
cognitive moral education 446

Suggested Readings

Gilligan, C. (1982). *In a different voice.* Cambridge, MA: Harvard University Press.
This book advances Gilligan's provocative view that a care perspective is underrepresented in Kohlberg's theory and research.

Lapsley, D. K., Enright, R. D., & Serlin, R. C. (1986). Moral and social education. In J. Worrell and F. Danner (Eds.), *Adolescent development: Issues for education.* New York: Academic Press.
A thorough overview of what is known about moral education and the more recently developed field of social education. Includes thoughtful, detailed comments about the nature of moral and social conventional reasoning.

Lickona, T. (Ed.). (1976). *Moral development and behavior.* New York: Holt, Rinehart & Winston.
Contemporary essays outlining the major theories, research findings, and educational implications of moral development. Included are essays by Kohlberg, Hoffman, Mischel, Aronfreed, Bronfenbrenner, and Rest.

Modgil, S., & Modgil, C. (Eds.). (1986). *Lawrence Kohlberg.* Philadelphia: The Falmer Press.
A number of experts evaluate Kohlberg's theory of moral development. Includes a concluding chapter by Kohlberg.

Radke-Yarrow, M., Zahn-Waxler, C., & Chapman, M. (1983). Children's prosocial dispositions and behaviors. In P. H. Mussen (Ed.), *Handbook of child psychology* (4th ed., Vol. 4). New York: John Wiley & Sons.
These prominent researchers in the field of children's prosocial development review what is known about children's altruism.

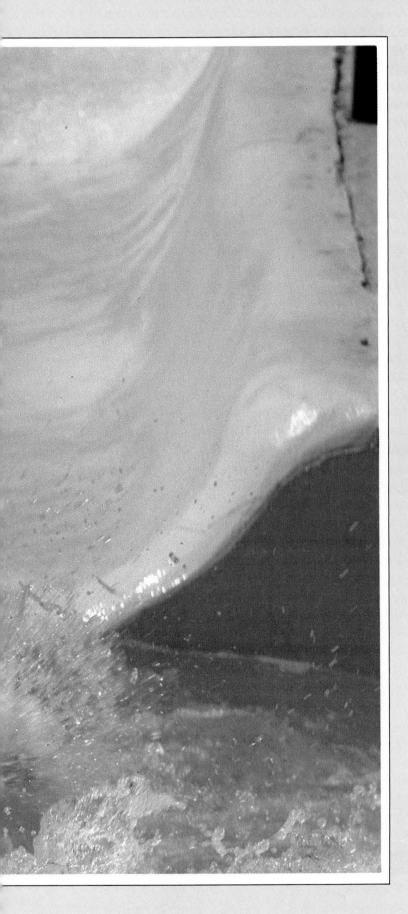

Abnormal Behavior, Stress, and Health

There is no easy path leading out of life, and few are the easy ones that lie within it.

Walter Savage Landor *Imaginary Conversations*, 1824

Problems and Disturbances

Disappointment tears the bearable film of life.

Elizabeth Bowen
The House in Paris, 1935

Cindy's parents consulted a clinical psychologist because of their concern that she might be emotionally disturbed. Their concerns stemmed from their observations of her change from a happy child who liked almost everything to a sad child who seemed to be constantly down. Her parents first became concerned when Cindy's third-grade teacher reported that she was unable to concentrate at school and seemed to be poorly motivated. Soon afterward they observed that she was more irritable, was eating less, and lost interest in many of the activities she had always enjoyed. Her parents indicated how Cindy always looked sad, was prone to periodic outbursts of crying, and just wanted to sit around the house rather than engage in any activities. Cindy's mother was especially concerned because she herself had had a serious problem with depression and did not want her daughter to experience this.

Edward's parents reported that their difficulties with him began when he was three years old. He just wouldn't listen to them. Initially he simply failed to respond when asked to do things like leave the television and come to dinner or to come inside after playing outdoors. Both parents noted that this problem had become worse in the past three years and that Edward had become increasingly argumentive and aggressive with his younger brother and older sister. Edward's mother reported that he often verbally abused her, responding to requests with statements such as, "I don't have to if I don't want to," "You can't make me," and "I hate you." In addition to these problems at home, Edward's third-grade teacher recommended that he be referred to the school psychologist because his behavior in the classroom had become so out of control he was learning very little and he was interfering with the learning of other children. Edward's teacher reported that he not only was disruptive in class but also was aggressive on the playground and on several occasions had stolen items from other children's desks (Johnson, Rasbury, & Siegel, 1986).

Cindy's depression and Edward's conduct disorder are but two of the many problems and disturbances that can emerge in the child's journey to maturity. Throughout this text we have focused on normal children's development, although many examples of children with problems and disturbances have been discussed. This chapter lends a closer eye to some of the major problems and disturbances infants, children, and adolescents can develop.

The Nature of Abnormality

At various points in history, malevolent gods, demons, witches, vampires, and even the moon and planets were labeled the culprits in children's abnormal behavior. We no longer believe these supernatural forces are responsible for children's disturbances. What do we believe is responsible?

Models of Children's Abnormalities

Defining what is normal and what is abnormal is not a simple task; the line between the two can be precariously thin. Attempts to define abnormality and search for its causes include statistics, biological factors, psychological factors, culture, and experiences.

The Statistical Approach

When Ludwig von Beethoven was six years old he played concertos and trios at a concert. When Steffi Graf was seventeen she became the number-one women's tennis player in the world. Are these individuals abnormal or deviant? The **statistical approach** defines abnormal behavior as that which deviates substantially from the average. We don't usually think of Beethoven as abnormal because he was a musical genius or Graf as deviant because she is such a masterful tennis player.

We all are deviant from one another on certain dimensions. Because one child likes classical music and her friends do not does not make her abnormal. It is in the areas of social behavior and thought where we look for statistical differences that might underscore abnormality. If a child sits on the floor day after day rocking back and forth uttering bizarre, confused statements while staring blankly at the wall, his behavior deviates dramatically from what commonly is displayed by children in our culture.

Sometimes, though, statistical incidences vary from one culture to another and from one point in history to another within the same culture. Women of the Mangaian culture in the South Sea Islands train young adolescent males in sexual techniques; the young males are then encouraged to practice their skills with young adolescent females. In the United States, we would consider such behavior abnormal, but in the Mangaian culture it is the norm. Early in this century, masturbation was thought to cause everything from warts to insanity; today less than 15 percent of adolescents think masturbation is wrong (Hyde, 1988).

The Biological Approach

Proponents of the biological approach believe that children's abnormal behavior is due to some malfunctioning of their bodies. If children behave in some uncontrollable way, are out of touch with reality, or are severely depressed, biological factors are thought to be the culprits. Today special interest focuses on the role of brain processes and drug therapy in understanding and treating children's abnormal behaviors. Interest also focuses on genetic factors.

The forerunner of the biological approach was the **medical model** (also called the disease model). The medical model emphasizes that children's abnormalities are diseases or illnesses precipitated by internal body causes. From this perspective, children's abnormalities are called mental *illnesses* and the children afflicted are *patients* in *hospitals* who are treated by *doctors*.

Psychological and Sociocultural Approaches

While the biological approach is an important perspective in understanding children's abnormal behavior, many developmentalists believe it underplays the importance of psychological and sociocultural factors. Emotional turmoil, inappropriate learning, disordered thoughts, and inadequate relationships are of interest in the psychological and sociocultural approaches rather than brain processes or genes. The theories of socialization discussed in chapter 11 provide insight about abnormal as well as normal behavior. The psychoanalytic perspective and the behavioral and social learning perspective contain valuable insights about the psychological and sociocultural determinants of children's abnormalities. Advocates of the psychological and sociocultural approaches criticize the medical model because they believe it encourages labeling of mental disturbances. A label such as "anxiety disorder" may persist even though the child's behavior is temporary. Also the child may accept the label and then display the abnormal behavior more frequently (Scheff, 1966; Szasz, 1977).

An Interactionist Approach

When considering children's behavior, whether abnormal or normal, it is important to remember the complexity of children and the multiple influences on their behavior. Neither the biological nor the psychological and sociocultural approaches can independently capture this complexity and multiple influence.

Children's abnormal behavior is influenced by an interplay of biological, cognitive, and environmental factors. Current areas of interest in studying biological factors are computer imaging techniques to discover abnormalities in children's brain structures and functioning; the role of neurotransmitters in different mental disturbances; the use of drugs to treat abnormal behavior; and the degree to which the disorders are inherited (Pardes, 1986). Among the current areas of interest in studying cognitive factors are the roles of symbolic thought, decision making, planning, imagery, reasoning, memory, and problem-focused coping in disturbances that involve depression, phobias, personality problems, drug abuse, and schizophrenia (Millon & Klerman, 1986). And among the current areas of interest in studying environmental factors are the importance of close relationships, especially family processes; support systems; reward and punishment; and the incidence of mental disturbances in different cultures and subcultures (Bowlby, 1988; Kazdin, 1988; Schwartz & Wiggins, 1986).

Types of Children's Disturbances

The spectrum of children's disturbances is wide. The disturbances vary in their severity, developmental level, sex, and social class. Some of children's disturbances are short-lived, others may persist over many years. One six-year-old may show a pattern of behavior that is disruptive to his classroom and when we look at his behavior as a seven-year-old he is assertive and aggressive, but the disruptive behavior has virtually disappeared. Another six-year-old may show a similar pattern of disruptive behavior and when we look at his behavior at age fifteen he has been arrested for numerous juvenile offenses and is still a disruptive influence in the classroom. We will have more to say about the nature of continuity and discontinuity in disturbances toward the end of the chapter.

Some disturbances are more likely to appear at one developmental level than another. Infantile autism, a severe disorder we will discuss shortly, has its onset in infancy, school-related disturbances come into play later, and drug problems are more likely to appear in adolescence. In one investigation, fears (of animals, situations, or places) were more common in early childhood than in middle and late childhood or adolescence. Nonetheless, these fears did not distinguish between children who were referred for psychological services and those who were not (Achenbach & Edelbrock, 1981). In this large-scale investigation, it was found that children from lower-class backgrounds were more likely to have disturbances than children from middle-class backgrounds. Most of the problems reported for children from lower-class backgrounds were undercontrolled, externalizing behaviors—destroys others' things or fighting, for

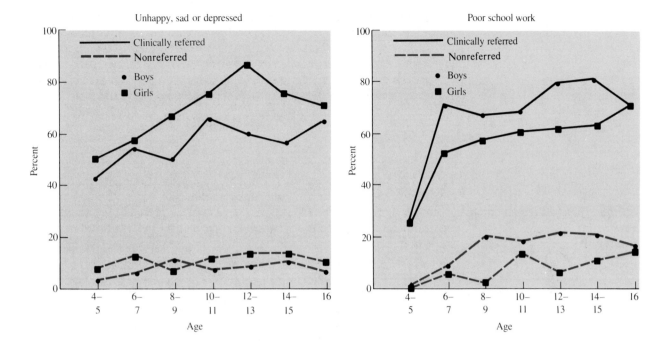

example; these behaviors also were more characteristic of boys than girls. The problems and disturbances of middle-class children and girls were more likely to be overcontrolled and internalizing—anxiety or depression, for example.

The behavioral problems that most likely caused children to be referred to a clinic for mental health treatment were those in which the children felt unhappy, sad, or depressed and were not doing well in school (figure 17.1). Difficulties in school achievement, whether secondary to other kinds of disturbances or primary problems in themselves, seem to account for the most clinical referrals of children (Weiner, 1980).

At this point we have discussed a number of ideas about the nature of children's abnormalities and types of disturbances. A summary of these ideas is presented in Concept Table 17.1. As we indicated earlier, the spectrum of children's disturbances is broad. From that broad range of disturbances we have selected a series of problems to discuss in greater detail. We now turn our attention to these more specific disorders, beginning with infantile autism and childhood schizophrenia.

Figure 17.1
The two items most likely to differentiate between clinically referred children and nonreferred children.

Infantile Autism and Childhood Schizophrenia

Two of the most severe disturbances in childhood are infantile autism and childhood schizophrenia. What are these disturbances like?

Infantile Autism

As its name suggests, **infantile autism** has its onset in infancy. It is a very severe developmental disturbance that includes deficiencies in social relationships, abnormalities in communication, and restricted, repetitive, and stereotyped patterns of behavior (Dawson, 1989; Rutter & Schopler, 1987). Social deficiencies include a failure to use eye-to-eye gaze to regulate social interaction, rarely seeking others for comfort or affection, rarely initiating play with others, and no peer relations involving mutual sharing of interests and emotions. As babies, these children require very little from their parents: they do not demand much attention and they do not reach out (literally or figuratively) for their parents. They rarely smile. When someone tries to hold

Concept Table 17.1
The Nature of Abnormality

Concept	Processes/Related Ideas	Characteristics/Description
Models of children's abnormalities	Statistical approach	Children are abnormal if they deviate substantially from the average; refers to social behavior.
	Biological approach	Disturbances have biological causes. Today's interest focuses on the brain, drugs, and genetics. The forerunner of the biological model is the medical model.
	Psychological and sociocultural approaches	Disturbances have psychological and sociocultural causes. Today's interest focuses on emotional turmoil, inappropriate learning, disordered thoughts, and inadequate relationships.
	Interactionist approach	Children's abnormal behavior is complex; a more complete understanding can be achieved by considering the interplay of biological, cognitive, and environmental factors.
Types of children's disturbances	Their nature	The spectrum of disturbances is large. Disturbances vary in severity and developmental level. One common classification is in terms of internalizing and externalizing disorders. Boys and lower-class children are more likely to have externalizing problems, girls and middle-class children internalizing problems.

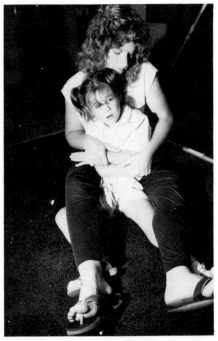

A mother with her autistic daughter. Describe the behaviors shown by an autistic child. Why has autism been so frustrating for parents?

them, they usually withdraw by arching their back and pushing away. In their cribs or playpens, they appear oblivious to what is going on around them, often sitting and staring into space for long periods of time.

In addition to these social deficiencies, these children also show communication abnormalities that focus on the problems of using language for social communication—poor synchrony and lack of reciprocity in conversation and stereotyped, repetitive use of language. As many as one of every two autistic children never even learns to speak. Those who do learn to speak sometimes display **echolalia,** a condition in which the child echoes what they hear. If you ask, "How are you Chuck?" Chuck responds with, "How are you Chuck?" Autistic children also confuse pronouns, inappropriately substituting *you* for *I,* for example (Durand & Crimmins, 1987; Koegel, O'Dell, & Koegel, 1987).

Stereotyped patterns of behavior by autistic children include compulsive rituals, repetitive motor mannerisms, and distress over changes in small details of the environment. Rearrangement of a sequence of events or even furniture in the course of a day may cause autistic children to become extremely upset, suggesting that they are not flexible in adapting to new routines and changes in their daily lives.

What causes autism? Autism seems to involve some form of organic brain dysfunction and may also have a hereditary basis. There has been no satisfactory evidence developed to document that family socialization causes autism (Rutter & Schopler, 1987). To learn more about the everyday life of an autistic child and his family, read Perspective on Child Development 17.1.

Childhood Schizophrenia

Some children and adolescents show an assortment of bizarre behaviors but without as much deviance in language and unresponsiveness to social overtures as in autism. The bizarreness of these children's behaviors begins in childhood or adolescence rather than infancy. **Childhood schizophrenia** includes disordered thinking, disturbed perceptions, and a lack of control over ideas, affect, and behavior (Weiner, 1982). Consider Jason, age thirteen, who was referred to a therapist because his parents had noticed that his behavior changed considerably over an eight- to ten-month period (Johnson, Rasbury,

A Child Called Noah

The impact an autistic child can have on parents is described in the following excerpts from the popular book *A Child Called Noah*, written in 1972 by Josh Greenfield about his autistic son Noah.

4-16-67: We've decided to stop worrying about Noah. He isn't retarded, he's just pushing the clock hands about at his own slow speed. Yet . . .

8-16-67: We took Noah to a pediatrician in the next town, who specializes in neurology. He said that, since Noah is talking now, there was little cause to worry; that Noah seemed "hypertonic," a floppy baby, a slow developer, but that time would be the maturing agent. We came away relieved. But I also have to admit that lately I haven't worried that much.

6-6-69: Noah is two. He still doesn't walk, but I do think he's trying to teach himself how to stand up. We're still concerned. And I guess we'll remain concerned until he stands up and walks like a boy.

7-14-69: Our fears about Noah continue to undergo dramatic ups and downs. Because of his increased opacity, the fact that he doesn't respond when we call his name and fails to relate completely to his immediate environment—pattern of retardation or autism—we took him to a nearby hospital. . . . I guess we both fear that what we dread is so, that Noah is not a normal child, that he is a freak, and his condition is getting worse.

2-19-70: I'm a lousy father. I anger too easily. I get hot with Karl and take on a four-year-old kid. I shout at Noah and further upset an already disturbed one. Perhaps I am responsible for Noah's problems.

8-70: I also must note how very few people can actually understand our situation as a family, how they assume we are aloof when we tend not to accept or extend the usual social invitations. Nor have I mentioned the extra expenses a child like Noah entails—those expenses I keep in another book.

8-71: Even more heartbreaking has been the three-year period it has taken us to pierce the organized-medicine, institutionalized-mental-health gauze curtain. Most doctors, if they were unable to prescribe any form of curative aid, did their best to deter us from seeking it. Freudian-oriented psychiatrists and psychologists, if ill-equipped to deal with the problems of those not verbal, tried to inflict great feelings of guilt upon us as all-too-vulnerable parents. Neurologists and pediatricians, if not having the foggiest notions about the effects of diet and nutrition, vitamins and enzymes, and their biochemical workings, would always suggest such forms of therapy as practiced only by quacks. And county mental-health boards, we discovered, who have charge of the moneys that might be spent helping children like Noah, usually tossed their skimpy fundings away through existing channels that do not offer proper treatment for children like Noah. (pp. 91–92)

& Siegel, 1986). He frequently giggled for no apparent reason and tended to talk without making any sense. His answers to questions often had little to do with what was asked. His parents also noticed that he now avoided ever touching the television set. When his parents asked him why, Jason responded that his body was full of electric charges that would cause the television set to explode if he came into contact with it. Occasionally he made comments that he feared others would hurt him with their electrical impulses.

Fortunately, childhood schizophrenia is a somewhat rare disorder, occuring in about 3 to 4 of every 10,000 children. As with autism, the causes of childhood schizophrenia are not well understood. Among the causes that have been proposed are heredity, biochemical abnormalities, and deviant family communication patterns, especially disturbed mother-child relationships. The role of heredity in schizophrenia has received some support. For example, as genetic similarity increases, so does an individual's chance of becoming schizophrenic (figure 17.2) (Gottesman & Shields, 1982). An identical twin of a schizophrenic has a 46 percent chance of developing the disorder while a fraternal twin has only a 14 percent chance. But genetic factors are not the entire

Figure 17.2
Lifetime risk of becoming schizophrenic according to genetic relatedness.

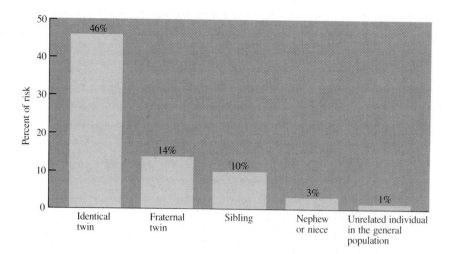

Chart showing Percent of risk by genetic relatedness:
- Identical twin: 46%
- Fraternal twin: 14%
- Sibling: 10%
- Nephew or niece: 3%
- Unrelated individual in the general population: 1%

story. The most widely accepted view today is that genetic and possibly other biological factors may predispose an individual to become schizophrenic but the disorder's development depends on an interaction between genetic predisposition and environmental experiences (Goldstein & Tuma, 1987).

Child Abuse

A much more frequently occurring problem in childhood than autism or schizophrenia is child abuse. Unfortunately, parental hostility toward children in some families reaches the point where one or both parents abuse the child. Child abuse is an increasing problem in the United States. Estimates of its incidence vary, but in 1987 nearly one million cases of child abuse and neglect were reported to child protection agencies in the United States. Laws in many states now require doctors and teachers to report suspected cases of child abuse. Yet, many cases go unreported, especially those of "battered" infants (Fontana, 1988; Hutchings, 1988).

For some years, it was believed that parents who committed child abuse were severely disturbed, "sick" individuals. However, researchers find that parents who abuse children rarely can be classified as having a severe mental illness (Blumberg, 1974). To better understand child abuse, it is helpful to shift the focus from parents' personality traits to three aspects of the social environment—culture, family, and community (Kazdin, 1988; Parke, 1976).

The extensive violence in the American culture is reflected in the occurrence of violence in the family. A regular diet of violence appears on television screens and parents frequently resort to power assertion as a disciplinary tactic. American television contains more violence than Japanese television. And, in China, where physical punishment rarely is used to discipline children, the incidence of child abuse is very low (Geis & Monahan, 1976; Stevenson, 1974).

To understand child abuse in the family, the interaction of all family members needs to be considered, regardless of who actually performs the violent acts against the child (Daro, 1988). For example, even though the father may be the individual who physically abuses the child, contributions of the mother, siblings, and even the abused child need to be evaluated too. Many parents who abuse their children come from families in which physical punishment was used. These parents may view physical punishment as a legitimate way of controlling the child's behavior, and physical punishment may be part of this sanctioning. Children themselves may unwittingly contribute to

Our nation's child abuse rate has been a matter of great concern in recent years. What factors might be involved in this case of abuse?

Abnormal Behavior, Stress, and Health

Shattered Innocence—the Sexual Abuse of Children

Headlines about day-care center scandals and feminist protests against sexist exploitation have increased public awareness of what we now know is a widespread problem—the sexual abuse of children. It has been estimated that as many as forty million American children are sexually abused—about one in six. A 1984 Gallup poll of 2,000 men and women in 210 Canadian communities found that 22 percent of the respondents were sexually abused as children. Clearly, children's sexual abuse is more widespread than was thought in the past. One reason the problem of children's sexual abuse was a dark secret for so long is that people understandably kept this painful experience to themselves.

The sexual abuse of children occurs most often between the ages of nine and twelve, although the abuse of two- and three-year-olds is not unusual. The abuser is almost always a man and he typically is known to the child, often being a relative. In many instances, the abuse is not limited to a single episode. No race, ethnic group, or economic class is immune.

While children do not react uniformly to sexual abuse, certain behaviors and feelings occur with some regularity. The immediate effects include sleeping and eating disturbances, anger, withdrawal, and guilt. The children often appear to be afraid or anxious. Two additional signs occur so often that professionals rely on them as indicators of abuse when they are present together. The first is sexual preoccupation—excessive or public masturbation and an unusually strong interest in sexual organs, play, and nudity. The second sign consists of a host of physical complaints or problems, such as rashes, headaches, and vomiting, all without medical explanation. When it is discovered that these children have been sexually abused, a check of their medical records usually produces years of such mysterious ailments. While there are patterns in the immediate effects of sexual abuse of children, it is far more difficult to connect such abuse with later psychological problems. It is impossible to say that every child who has been abused will develop this or that problem, and we still have not developed a profile of the child abuse victim that everyone can agree on (Walker, Bonner, & Kaufman, 1988).

One of the most disturbing findings about childhood sexual abuse is its strong intergenerational pattern. Boys who are sexually abused are far more likely to turn into offenders, molesting the next generation of children; girls who are sexually abused are more likely to produce children who are abused. And victimization can lead to re-victimization. Individuals who have been sexually abused as children may become later victims of rape or attempted rape. Women, of course, are not to blame for being victims.

How can the intergenerational transmission of abuse be broken? In one investigation, the group of adults most likely to break the abuse cycle was more likely to receive emotional support from a nonabusive adult during childhood, participate in therapy, and have a less abusive and more stable, emotionally supportive and satisfying relationship with a mate (Egeland, Jacobvitz, & Papatola, in press; Egeland, Jacobvitz, & Sroufe, 1987). The prognosis also is better if an individual has not been abused by more than one person, when force is not used during the abuse, and when the abuser is not a close relative (Kohn, 1987).

child abuse—an unattractive child receives more physical punishment than an attractive child, and a child from an unwanted pregnancy may be especially vulnerable to child abuse. The interaction of parents with each other may produce child abuse, too (Harter, Alexander, & Neimeyer, 1988). Husband-wife violence and financial problems may result in displaced aggression toward a defenseless child. Displaced aggression is commonly involved in child abuse.

Community support systems are especially important in alleviating stressful family circumstances and thereby preventing or reducing child abuse. An investigation of the support systems in fifty-eight counties in New York state revealed a relation between the incidence of child abuse and the absence of support systems available to the family (Garbarino, 1976). Both family resources—relatives and friends, for example—and formal community resources—crisis centers and child abuse counseling, for example—were associated with a reduction in child abuse. In another recent investigation, both parent group discussion and a behavioral training program were successful in reducing child abuse (Wolfe & others, 1988). One form of child abuse can be especially devastating for a child—sexual abuse, which is described in Perspective on Child Development 17.2.

What might be the causes of this boy's impulsive behavior?

Learning Disabilities

Paula doesn't like kindergarten and can't seem to remember the name of her teacher or her classmates. Bobby's first-grade teacher complains that he never sits still to listen to a story. Eleven-year-old Tim hates to read—he says it is too hard for him and the words just don't seem to make any sense half of the time. Each of these children is learning disabled. Children with **learning disabilities** (1) are of normal intelligence or above, (2) have difficulties in several academic areas but usually do not show deficits in others, and (3) are not suffering from some other condition or disorder that could explain their learning problems (Reid, 1988). The breadth of definitions of learning disabilities has generated controversy about just what learning disabilities are (Ceci, 1986; Farnham-Diggory, 1986). Within the global concept of learning disabilities fall problems in listening, thinking, memory, reading, writing, spelling, and math. Attention deficits involving an inability to sit still, pay attention, and concentrate also are classified under learning disabilities. Table 17.1 reveals the heterogeneity of characteristics that lead teachers to classify children as learning disabled. Estimates of the number of learning disabled students are as broad as the definition, ranging from 1 to 30 percent (Lerner, 1988). The United States Department of Education puts the number of identified learning disabled children between the ages of three and twenty-one at approximately two million.

Improving the lives of learning disabled children will come from (1) recognizing the complex, multifaceted nature of learning disabilities—biological, cognitive, and social aspects of learning disabilities need to be considered—and (2) becoming more precise in our analysis of the learning environments in which learning disabled children participate. The following discussion of one subtype of learning disability, attention deficit disorder, exemplifies consideration of this complexity and preciseness.

Children are described as having **attention deficit disorder,** sometimes called hyperactivity, if they are extremely active, impulsive, distractible, and excitable. In short they do not pay attention and have great difficulty concentrating on what they are doing. Estimates of the number of children with attention deficit disorder vary from less than 1 percent to 5 percent. While young children or even infants may show this disorder's characteristics, the vast majority of hyperactive children is identified in the first three grades of elementary school when teachers quickly recognize that they have great difficulty paying attention, sitting still, and concentrating on their schoolwork.

What causes Jimmy to be so impulsive, Sandy to be so distractible, and Harvey to be so excitable? The complexity of understanding attention deficit disorder is revealed when we consider the causes of these children's hyperactive behavior. Possible causes include heredity, prenatal hazards, diet, family dynamics, and the physical environment. As we saw in chapter 2, the influence of heredity on temperament is increasingly considered, with activity level as one aspect of temperament that very early in development differentiates one child from another. Approximately four times as many boys as girls are hyperactive. This sex difference may be due to differences in the brains of boys and girls determined by genes on the Y chromosome. The prenatal hazards we discussed in chapter 3 also may produce hyperactive behavior. Excessive drinking by women during pregnancy is associated with poor attention and concentration on the part of their offspring at four years of age, for example (Streissguth & others, 1984). With regard to diet, severe vitamin deficiencies can lead to attentional problems. Vitamin B deficiencies are a special concern. Caffeine and sugar also may be contributors to attentional problems.

Abnormal Behavior, Stress, and Health

Table 17.1
Descriptions of Behavior Most Frequently Checked by Teachers for Second-Grade Children Meeting Diagnostic Guidelines for Learning Disabilities

Description of behavior	Percentage of children for whom description was checked	Description of behavior	Percentage of children for whom description was checked
1. Substitutes words which distort meaning ("when" for "where")	70	19. Reverses and/or rotates letters and numbers (reads *b* for *d, u* for *n,* and *6* for *9*) far more than most peers	47
2. Reads silently or aloud far more slowly than peers (word by word while reading aloud)	68	20. Difficulty with arithmetic (e.g., can't determine what number follows 8 or 16, may begin to add in the middle of a subtraction problem)	46
3. Unusually short attention span for daily work	67	21. Poor drawing of crossing, wavy lines compared with peers' drawing	46
4. Easily distracted from schoolwork (can't concentrate with even the slightest disturbances from other students' moving around or talking quietly)	66	22. Omits words while reading grade-level material aloud (omits more than one of every 10)	44
5. Can't follow written directions, which most peers can follow, when read orally or silently	65	23. Poor drawing of a person compared with peers' drawings	43
6. Does very poorly in written spelling tests compared with peers	64	24. Can read orally but does not comprehend the meaning of written grade-level words (word-caller)	43
7. Can't sound out or "unlock" words	64	25. Excessive inconsistency in quality of performance from day to day and even hour to hour	43
8. Reading ability at least three-fourths of a year below most peers	63		
9. Has trouble telling time	62	26. Seems quite immature (doesn't act his or her age)	43
10. Doesn't seem to listen to daily classroom instructions or directions (often asks to have them repeated whereas rest of class goes ahead)	61	27. Unable to learn the sounds of letters (can't associate appropriate phoneme with its grapheme)	41
11. Is slow to finish work (doesn't apply self, daydreams a lot, falls asleep in school)	56	28. Avoids work calling for concentrated visual attention	39
12. Repeats the same behavior over and over again	56	29. Mistakes own left from right (confuses left-hand side of paper)	39
13. Has trouble organizing written work (seems scatterbrained, confused)	56	30. Demands unusual amount of attention during regular classroom activities	39
14. Can't correctly recall oral directions (e.g., item 10 above) when asked to repeat them	54	31. Loses place more than once while reading aloud for more than one minute	38
15. Poor handwriting compared with peers' writing	52	32. Cannot apply the classroom or school regulations to own behavior whereas peers can	37
16. Reverses and/or rotates letters, numbers, or words (writes *p* for *q, saw* for *was, 2* for *7*) far more frequently than peers	52	33. Tense or disturbed (bites lip, needs to go to the bathroom often, twists hair, high-strung)	36
17. Seems very bright in many ways but does poorly in school	50	34. Poor drawing of diamond compared with peers' drawings	36
18. Points at words while reading silently or aloud	49	35. Overactive (can't sit still in class—shakes or swings legs, fidgety)	34

Depression has been called the "common cold" of mental problems because it has become so prevalent in our society. Why is the depression of this young adolescent girl so difficult to diagnose?

The social and physical environments in which children live also can contribute to attentional problems. Children with attention deficit disorder are more likely to come from families who frequently move and who are more concerned about controlling the child's behavior than the child's academic work (Lambert & Hartsough, 1984). Hyperactive children are more likely to misbehave when they are in exciting but unstructured circumstances (the typical birthday party) or in circumstances with many behavioral demands (the typical school classroom). And, lead poisoning also can produce attention problems and hyperactive behavior.

Children with attention deficit disorder may continue to have problems in adolescence, although the attentional problem is usually less severe. By adulthood, approximately one-third to one-half continue to be troubled by their attentional difficulties (Weiss & Hechtman, 1986). A wide range of psychotherapies and drug therapy has been used to improve the lives of hyperactive children. For unknown reasons, some drugs that stimulate the brains and behaviors of adults have a quieting effect on the brains and behaviors of children. The drugs most widely prescribed for hyperactive children are amphetamines, especially Ritalin. Amphetamines are widely prescribed for hyperactive children and work effectively in some but not all instances. As many as 20 percent of hyperactive children treated with Ritalin do not respond to it. Even when Ritalin works it is also important to consider the social worlds of the hyperactive child. The teacher is especially important in this social world, helping to monitor the child's academic and social behavior to determine if the drug works and whether the prescribed dosage is correct.

Depression and Suicide

Earlier in the chapter we found that the most frequent characteristics of children referred for psychological treatment involve sadness or depression. What is children's depression like? What is the nature of suicide?

Children's Depression

In childhood the features of depression are mixed with a broader array of behaviors than in adult depression. For example, during childhood, aggression, school failure, anxiety, antisocial behavior, and poor peer relations are often related to depression, which makes its diagnosis more difficult (Weiner, 1980). In the following example of an eleven-year-old girl, depression is mixed with anxiety and school-related matters.

Elizabeth is a pretty eleven-year-old black girl, who was brought to the hospital because she had thrown a book at the school principal. The principal had been trying to find out the reason Elizabeth was crying in the classroom. Elizabeth was restless and confused and could not concentrate for more than a few minutes. She said that people didn't like her, that everybody thought she was ugly. She believed that she had been justified in throwing the book at the principal: "He was bugging me; I was nervous." While Elizabeth's mother was interviewed in another room at the hospital, Elizabeth began to pace up and down, saying that she was feeling hot. She showed someone her clammy, perspiring hands, and began to cry, saying, "I'm dying. Something in my throat doesn't let me breathe. My stomach isn't pumping. People are trying to kill me. I'll die if I stay here. I was normal before I came. Now I am dying."

During the next three days, Elizabeth had one or two severe anxiety attacks a day. Between the attacks, she was anxious, restless, and depressed. She did not show any signs of psychosis in clinical or psychological testings.

The background history obtained on Elizabeth revealed that she had been an insecure, timid, and friendless child since entering school. When Elizabeth was seven years old, her father had been charged with attempting to seduce a thirteen-year-old female neighbor; and though the charges had been dismissed, the family was alienated and ostracized from the neighborhood. Elizabeth's father had then deserted the family, leaving Elizabeth, her thirteen-year-old brother, and her mother with no source of income. Elizabeth's mother was a tense, depressed woman, who felt harassed by the responsibilities of finding a job and caring for her children. Six months before Elizabeth's admission to the hospital, her mother had found a job that kept her away from home from 8:00 A.M. to 6:00 P.M. She had not had time to go over to school when Elizabeth brought a letter from her teacher reporting that Elizabeth seemed very unhappy, that her schoolwork had deteriorated, and that she was frequently absent. Elizabeth's mother was now extremely angry at Elizabeth. She explained, "I knew she was sad and hypersensitive, but it was not causing anybody else any problem. Now she has become violent and I can't take that" (Chess & Hassibi, 1978).

Why does depression occur in childhood? As with other disturbances, biogenetic and social environmental causes have been offered. As researchers explore the nature of children's depression, they have discovered that depression is more likely to emerge in adolescence than in childhood and to involve girls more than boys (Johnson, Rasbury, & Siegel, 1986).

John Bowlby (1980, 1988) believes that insecure mother-infant attachment, a lack of love and affection in child rearing, or the actual loss of a parent in childhood leads to a negative cognitive set. This schema that is built up during early experiences causes children to interpret later losses as yet other failures to create enduring and close positive relationships. From Bowlby's view, early experiences, especially those involving loss, produce cognitive schemata that are carried forward to influence the way later experiences are interpreted. When these new experiences involve further loss, the loss serves as the immediate precipitant of depression. Another cognitive view stresses that individuals become depressed because early in their development they acquire cognitive schemata that are characterized by self-devaluation and lack of confidence about the future (Beck, 1973). These habitual negative thoughts magnify and expand a depressed individual's negative experiences. Depressed children may blame themselves far more than is warranted.

One of the environmental factors thought to be important in understanding children's depression is **learned helplessness** (Seligman, 1975). When individuals are exposed to stress or prolonged pain over which they have no control, they learn helplessness. In other words, depressed children may be apathetic because they cannot reinstate the rewards that they previously experienced. For example, an adolescent girl may not be able to make her boyfriend come back to her.

Suicide

Suicide is a common problem in our society. Its rate has quadrupled during the last thirty years in the United States; each year about 25,000 individuals take their own lives. Beginning at about the age of fifteen, the rate of suicide

Figure 17.3
Suicide rates by sex, age, and race in the United States.

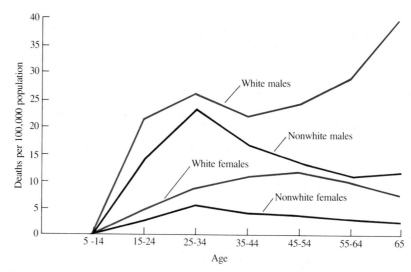

Source: After data presented by the U.S. Bureau of the Census, 1980, U.S. Government Printing Office.

begins to rise rapidly (figure 17.3). Males are about three times as likely to commit suicide as females; this may be due to their more active methods for attempting suicide—shooting, for example. By contrast, females are more likely to use passive methods such as sleeping pills, which are less likely to produce death. While males commit suicide more frequently, females attempt it more frequently (Maltsberger, 1988).

Estimates indicate that six to ten suicide attempts occur for every suicide in the general population; for adolescents the figure is as high as fifty attempts for every life taken. As many as two in every three college students has thought about suicide on at least one occasion; their methods range from drugs to crashing into the White House in an airplane.

Why do adolescents attempt suicide? There is no simple answer to this important question. It is helpful to think of suicide in terms of proximal and distal factors. Proximal, or immediate, factors can trigger a suicide attempt. Highly stressful circumstances such as loss of a boyfriend or girlfriend, failing a class at school, or an unwanted pregnancy can produce suicide attempts (Blumenthal & Kupfer, 1988). Drugs also have been involved in suicide attempts in recent years more than in the past (Rich, Young, & Fowler, 1986).

But distal, or earlier, experiences often are involved in suicide attempts as well. A long-standing history of family instability and unhappiness may be present. A lack of affection and emotional support, high control, and a strong push for achievement by parents during early childhood are related to depression among adolescents, especially adolescent girls; a combination of these early childhood experiences can set the stage for poor coping when further stresses are encountered during adolescence (Gjerde, 1985). In a recent investigation of suicide among gifted women, previous suicide attempts, anxiety, conspicuous instability in work and relationships, depression, or alcoholism were present in the women's lives (Tomlinson-Keasey, Warren, & Elliott, 1986). These factors are similar to those found to predict suicide among gifted women (Schneidman, 1971).

Just as genetic factors are an issue in depression, they appear in suicide too; the closer the genetic relation to someone who has committed suicide the more likely the individual will commit suicide (Wender & others, 1986). We

Abnormal Behavior, Stress, and Health

Table 17.2
What to Do and What Not to Do When You Suspect Someone Is Likely to Commit Suicide

What to do

1. Ask direct, straightforward questions in a calm manner. "Are you thinking about hurting yourself?"
2. Assess the seriousness of the suicidal intent by asking questions about feelings, important relationships, who else the person has talked with, and the amount of thought given to the means to be used. If a gun, pills, rope, or other means has been obtained and a precise plan developed, clearly the situation is dangerous. Stay with the person until some type of help arrives.
3. Be a good listener and be very supportive without being falsely reassuring.
4. Try to persuade the person to obtain professional help and assist him or her in getting this help.

What not to do

1. Do not ignore the warning signs.
2. Don't refuse to talk about suicide if a person approaches you about the topic.
3. Do not react with horror, disapproval, or repulsion.
4. Don't give false reassurances by saying things like, "Everything is going to be o.k." Also don't give out simple answers or platitudes like "You have everything to be thankful for."
5. Do not abandon the adolescent after the crisis has gone by or after professional help has commenced.

From Center for Early Adolescence, University of North Carolina at Chapel Hill, Carrboro, NC. Reprinted by permission.

do not have the complete answers for detecting when an individual is considering suicide or how to prevent it (Pfeffer, 1989; Pfeffer & others, 1988), but table 17.2 provides some valuable suggestions about effective ways to communicate with someone you think may be contemplating suicide.

Delinquency

The label **juvenile delinquent** is applied to an adolescent who breaks the law or engages in behavior that is considered illegal. Like other categories of disturbance, juvenile deliquency is a broad concept; legal infractions range from littering to murder. Because the adolescent technically becomes a juvenile delinquent only after being judged guilty of a crime by a court of law, official records do not accurately reflect the number of illegal acts committed. Nevertheless, there is every indication that in the last ten to fifteen years, juvenile delinquency has increased in relation to the number of crimes committed by adults. Estimates regarding the number of juvenile delinquents in the United States are sketchy, although FBI statistics indicate that at least 2 percent of all youths are involved in juvenile court cases. The number of girls found guilty of juvenile delinquency has increased substantially in recent years. Delinquency rates among blacks, other minority groups, and the lower class are especially high in comparison to the overall population of these groups. However, such groups have less influence over the judicial decision-making process in the United States and therefore may be judged delinquent more readily than their white, middle-class counterparts (Binder, 1987; Gold, 1987).

What causes delinquency? Many causes have been proposed, including heredity, identity problems, community influences, and family experiences. Erik Erikson (1968), for example, believes that adolescents whose development has restricted them from acceptable social roles or made them feel that they cannot

What are the attractions of gang membership in today's ghettos?

Cocaine use has become a dangerous problem in adolescence. This stimulant is far more deadly than the drug of an earlier generation, marijuana.

measure up to the demands placed on them may choose a negative identity. The adolescent with a negative identity may find support for his delinquent image among peers, reinforcing the negative identity. For Erikson, delinquency is an attempt to establish an identity, although it is a negative identity.

Although delinquency is less exclusively a lower-class phenomenon than it was in the past, some characteristics of the lower-class culture may promote delinquency. The norms of many lower-class peer groups and gangs are antisocial, or counterproductive, to the goals and norms of society at large. Getting into and staying out of trouble become prominent features of some adolescents in low-income neighborhoods. Adolescents from low-income backgrounds may sense that they can gain attention and status by performing antisocial actions. Being "tough" and "masculine" are high-status traits for lower-class boys, and these traits often are measured by the adolescent's success in performing delinquent acts and getting away with them. A community with a high crime rate also lets the adolescent observe many models who engage in criminal activities. These communities may be characterized by poverty, unemployment, and feelings of alienation toward the middle class. Quality schooling, educational funding, and organized neighborhood activities may be lacking in these communities.

Family support systems also are associated with delinquency (Snyder & Patterson, 1987). The parents of delinquents are less skilled in discouraging antisocial behavior and in encouraging skilled behavior than the parents of nondelinquents. Parental monitoring of adolescents is especially important in whether an adolescent becomes a delinquent. In one investigation, parental monitoring of the adolescent's whereabouts was the most important family factor in predicting delinquency (Patterson & Stouthamer-Loeber, 1984). "It's 10 P.M., do you know where your children are?" seems to be an important question for parents to answer affirmatively. Family discord and inconsistent and inappropriate discipline also are associated with delinquency.

A special concern in delinquency has surfaced in recent years—escalating gang violence. Gang violence is being waged on a level more lethal than ever before. Knives and clubs have been replaced by grenades and automatic weapons, frequently purchased with money made from selling drugs. More about drugs and gangs appears in Perspective on Child Development 17.3. The lure of gang membership is powerful, especially for children who are disconnected from family, school, work, and the community. Children as young as nine to ten years of age cling to the fringes of neighborhood gangs, eager to prove themselves worthy of membership by age twelve. Once children are members of a gang it is difficult to get them to leave. Recommendations for prevention of gang violence involve attempts to identify disconnected children in elementary schools and initiate counseling of the children and their families (Calhoun, 1988).

Drugs and Alcohol

How pervasive is drug use in adolescence? How extensive is alcohol abuse? What factors contribute to drug and alcohol abuse? These are among the questions we now evaluate.

Drugs

Extensive monitoring of drug use by adolescents has been conducted by Lloyd Johnston, Patrick O'Malley, and Gerald Bachman (1987, 1988) for a number of years. Each year since 1975, they have surveyed the drug use of high school

Abnormal Behavior, Stress, and Health

Frog and Dolores

He goes by the name of Frog. He is the cocky prince of the barrio in East Los Angeles. He has street smarts. Frog happily smiles as he talks about raking in $200 a week selling crack cocaine. He proudly details his newly acquired membership in a violent street gang—the Crips. Frog brags about using his drug money to rent a convertible on weekends, even though at less than five feet in height he can barely see over the dashboard. Frog is thirteen years old.

With the advent of crack, juvenile arrests in New York City tripled from 1983 to 1987 and almost quadrupled in the same time frame in Washington, D.C. Adults who founded the crack trade recognized early on that young adolescents do not run the risk of mandatory jail sentences that courts hand out to adults. Being a lookout is the entry level position for nine- and ten-year-olds. They can make as much as $100 a day warning dealers that police are in the area. The next step up the ladder is runner, a job that can pay as much as $300 a day. A runner transports drugs to the dealers on the street from makeshift factories where cocaine powder is cooked into rock-hard crack. And, at the next level, an older adolescent can reach the status of dealer—in a hot market like New York City, he can make over $1,000 a day.

The escalating drug-related gang violence is difficult to contain or reduce. Police crackdowns across the country seem to have had a minimal impact. In a recent weekend-long raid of drug-dealing gangs in Los Angeles, police arrested 1,453 individuals, including 315 adolescents. Half had to be released for lack of evidence. The Los Angeles County juvenile facilities are designed to house 1,317. Today more than 2,000 adolescents are overflowing their facilities.

Counselors, school officials, and community workers report that it is extremely difficult to turn around the lives of children and adolescents involved in drug-related gang violence. When impoverished children can make $100 a day, it is hard to wean them away from gangs. Federal

Dolores Bennett, volunteer in a low-income area of Detroit, Michigan, shown here talking with and listening to two of her "children."

budgets for training and employment programs, which provide crucial assistance to disadvantaged youth, have been reduced dramatically.

In Detroit, Michigan, Dolores Bennett, though, has made a difference. For twenty-five years, she has worked long hours trying to keep children from low-income families busy. Her activities have led to the creation of neighborhood sports teams, regular fairs and picnics, and an informal job-referral service for the children and youth in her neighborhood. She also holds many casual get-togethers for the youth in her small, tidy yellow frame house. The youth talk openly and freely about their problems and their hopes, knowing that Dolores will listen. Dolores says that she has found being a volunteer to be priceless. On the mantel in her living room are hundreds of pictures of children and adolescents she has worked with. She points out that most of them did not have someone in their homes who would listen to them and give them love. Our nation needs more Dolores Bennetts.

seniors in a wide range of public and private high schools across the United States. From time to time, they also sample the drug use of younger adolescents and young adults.

An encouraging finding from the most recent survey (conducted in 1987) of 16,300 high school seniors is the continued gradual downturn in the overall use of illicit drugs. Only 3.3 percent of the high school seniors used marijuana on a daily basis, down from the levels of the mid-1980s, and substantially down from the peak level of 10.7 percent in 1978. Also encouraging is that in 1987, for the first time in eight years, cocaine use showed a significant drop. Slightly more than 10 percent of high school seniors used cocaine at least once a year, down from a 12.7-percent annual prevalence in 1986. Cocaine use by college students also declined from a 17.1-percent annual prevalence in 1986 to 13.7

Figure 17.4
Trends in lifetime, annual, and thirty-day
prevalence of cocaine (all seniors).

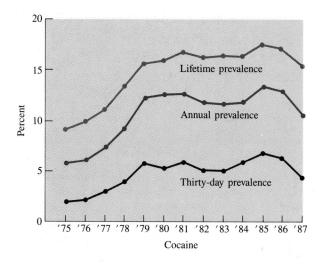

percent in 1987. A growing proportion of high school seniors and college students are reaching the conclusion that cocaine use entails considerable, unpredictable risk for the user. Still, the percentage of adolescents and young
adults using cocaine is precariously high. About one of every six high school
seniors has tried cocaine at least once and one in eighteen has tried crack cocaine specifically, for example. The trends in lifetime, annual, and thirty-day
prevalence of cocaine use by high school seniors from 1975 to 1987 is shown
in figure 17.4. As can be seen, while a significant drop in cocaine use occurred
in 1987 prevalence is still very high in comparison to use in the 1970s. And,
for students who drop out of high school, cocaine use is estimated to be higher.

A troublesome part of the cocaine story appears in the dangerous shift
in the mode of administration used, due in large part to the advent of crack
cocaine—an inexpensive, purified, smokeable form of the drug. The proportion of high school seniors who said they smoked cocaine more than doubled
between 1983 and 1986, from 2.5 percent to 6 percent. For the first time, in
1986, seniors were asked specifically about crack use. In 1986 and 1987,
4 percent of the seniors said they had used crack in the prior twelve months.
Crack use was especially heavy in noncollege-bound youth and in urban settings.

Another widely used class of illicit drugs showed an important shift in
1986 and 1987—stimulants, more specifically, amphetamines. There were
sizeable declines in use among high school seniors, college students, and young
adults. Since 1982, annual use of amphetamines fell from 20 percent to 13
percent among seniors and from 21 percent to 10 percent among college students. However, there has been a sharp increase in the use of over-the-counter
stay-awake pills, which usually contain caffeine as their active ingredient. Their
annual prevalence has risen from 12 percent in 1982 to more than 20 percent
in 1986 and 1987. Two other classes of stimulants—"look alikes" and over-
the-counter diet pills—actually declined in use in recent years. Still, 40 percent of females had tried diet pills by the end of their senior years, and 10
percent had used them within the last month.

A number of important findings have emerged from the study of adolescent patterns of cigarette smoking, in which the active drug is nicotine, a
stimulant. By late adolescence sizeable portions of youth are still establishing
regular cigarette smoking habits, despite the demonstrated health risks associated with smoking. Since the national surveys by Johnston, O'Malley, and

Bachman began in 1975, cigarettes have been the substance most frequently used by high school students on a daily basis. While their daily smoking rate did drop considerably between 1977 and 1981 (from 29 percent to 20 percent), it has dropped little in the last five years (by another 1.6 percent). A full one-third of high school seniors still do not feel that there is a great risk associated with smoking. Initiation of daily smoking is most likely to occur in grades seven through nine.

What factors are associated with drug abuse by adolescents? In one recent longitudinal investigation (Block & Block, in press), undercontrol by boys at age four was related to their drug use in adolescence and permissive parenting in the families of girls at age four was related to their drug use in adolescence. And in another study (Newcomb & Bentler, 1988), social support during adolescence substantially reduced drug use. In this investigation social support included good relationships with parents, family, adults, and peers. Multiple drug use in adolescence was related to drug and alcohol, health, and family problems in early adulthood. While a gradual downturn in drug use by adolescents has occurred, America's adolescents still have the highest drug use rate of all industrialized nations in the world (Alford, 1989). In 1987, 57 percent of the nation's high school seniors had tried an illicit drug other than marijuana (Johnston, O'Malley, & Bachman, 1988). Next, we turn our attention to the widespread problem of alcohol abuse.

Drinking is a major problem for today's adolescents. Heavy drinking—when adolescents have five or more drinks in a row—is a special concern. What recommendations can you make to reduce heavy drinking by adolescents?

Alcohol

Some mornings, Annie, a fifteen-year-old cheerleader, was too drunk to go to school. Other days, she'd stop for a couple of beers or a screwdriver on the way to school. She was tall, blonde, and good looking, and no one who sold her liquor, even at 8:00 in the morning, questioned her age. Where did she get her money? From baby-sitting and what her mother gave her to buy lunch. Annie is no longer a cheerleader—she was kicked off the squad for missing practice so often. Soon, she and several of her peers were drinking almost every morning. Sometimes, they skipped school and went to the woods to drink. Annie's whole life began to revolve around her drinking. It went on for two years, and during the last summer, anytime she saw anybody she was drunk. After awhile, her parents began to detect Annie's problem. But even when they punished her, it did not stop her drinking. Finally, this year, Annie started dating a boy she really likes and who would not put up with her drinking. She agreed to go to Alcoholics Anonymous and has just successfully completed treatment. She has stopped drinking for four consecutive months now, and it is hoped that her abstinence continues.

During the recent period of decline in the use of marijuana and other drugs there appears not to have been a displacement effect in terms of an increase in alcohol use by high school seniors. The opposite actually seems to have occurred. Since 1980, the monthly prevalence of alcohol use by seniors has gradually declined, from 72 percent in 1980 to 66 percent in 1987. Daily use declined from a peak of 6.9 percent in 1979 to 4.8 percent in 1984, with no further decline through 1987. And the prevalence of drinking five or more drinks in a row during the prior two-week interval fell from 41 percent in 1983 to 37 percent in 1987. There remains a substantial sex difference among high school seniors in the prevalence of heavy drinking (28 percent for females versus 46 percent for males in 1986), but this difference has been diminishing gradually over the last decade. However, data from college students show little drop in alcohol use, and an increase in the prevalence of heavy drinking actually has occurred—45 percent in 1986, up 2 percent from the previous year. Heavy party drinking among college males is common and becoming more so.

Unfortunately, there are hundreds of thousands of adolescents just like the fifteen-year-old cheerleader named Annie with a serious drinking problem. They live in both wealthy suburbs and inner-city housing projects. Annie grew up in a Chicago suburb and said she started drinking when she was ten because her older brothers always looked like they were having fun when they were doing it. Researchers have found that young adolescents who take drugs are more likely to have older friends than their counterparts who do not take drugs (e.g., Blyth, Durant, & Moosbrugger, 1985). Adolescents also have strong expectancies that alcohol will produce personal effects, such as tension reduction, even more so than adults expect (McLaughlin & Chassin, 1985). The use of alcohol to reduce stress and tension in their lives seems to be very common among adolescents. For adolescent males, a strong motive for power also is evident. Adolescent alcohol use also is related to parent and peer relations. Adolescents who drink heavily often come from unhappy homes in which there is a great deal of tension and also from homes in which parents sanction alcohol use (Barnes, 1984). And the peer group provides the social context for drinking and reinforces adolescent behavior that is learned as part of the family socialization process. The ability of the family to function as a support system for the adolescent seems to be an especially important factor in preventing heavy drinking by adolescents.

A strong family support system is clearly an important preventive strategy in reducing alcohol abuse by adolescents. Are there others? Would raising the minimum drinking age have an effect? In one investigation, raising the minimum drinking age did lower the frequency of automobile crashes involving adolescents, but raising the drinking age alone did not seem to reduce alcohol abuse (Wagennar, 1983). Another effort to reduce alcohol abuse involved a school-based program in which adolescents discussed alcohol-related issues with peers (Wodarski & Hoffman, 1984). At a one-year follow-up, students in the intervention schools reported less alcohol abuse and had discouraged each other's drinking more often than had students in schools who had not been involved in the peer discussion of alcohol-related issues.

Efforts to help the adolescent with a drinking problem vary enormously. Therapy may include working with other family members, peer-group discussion sessions, and specific behavioral techniques. Unfortunately, there has been little in the way of interest in identifying different types of adolescent alcohol abusers and then attempting to match treatment programs to particular problems. Most efforts simply assume that adolescents with drinking problems are a homogeneous group and do not take into account the varying developmental patterns and social histories of different adolescents. Some adolescents with drinking problems may be helped more through family therapy, others through peer counseling, and yet others through intensive behavioral strategies, depending on the type of drinking problem and the social agents who have the most influence on the adolescent (Finney & Moos, 1979).

At this point we have discussed a number of ideas about different types of disturbances. A summary of these ideas is presented in Concept Table 17.2.

Concept Table 17.2
Types of Disturbances

Concept	Processes/Related Ideas	Characteristics/Description
Infantile autism and childhood schizophrenia	Infantile autism	Infantile autism is a severe disorder with an onset in infancy; it includes deficiencies in social relationships, abnormalities in communication, and restricted, repetitive, and stereotyped behavior.
	Childhood schizophrenia	This involves an assortment of bizarre behaviors but not as much disturbance in language or lack of responsiveness as autism. Its onset is from early childhood through adolescence and includes distorted thinking, disturbed perceptions, and lack of control over ideas, affect, and behavior. Both hereditary and environmental experiences are involved.
Child abuse	Its nature	Child abuse has become a major problem in children's families. It is important to consider its cultural, familial, and community determinants.
Learning disabilities	Its nature	Children with learning disabilities are of normal intelligence or above, they have difficulties in several areas but not others, and they are not suffering from some other disorder that could explain their learning problems. Learning disabilities are complex and multifaceted and require precise analysis.
	Attention deficit disorder	Sometimes called hyperactivity, this describes children who are extremely active, impulsive, distractible, and excitable. Possible causes include heredity, prenatal hazards, diet, family dynamics, and the physical environment. Amphetamines have been used with some success for treatment but do not work with all hyperactive children.
Depression and suicide	Depression	Childhood depression has more mixed characteristics than in adulthood. It is more likely to emerge in adolescence than earlier and is more frequent in girls. Loss of attachment, cognitive distortion, and learned helplessness are possible explanations along with biogenetic factors.
	Suicide	Its rate has quadrupled in the last thirty years in the United States. Its causes involve both distal and proximal factors.
Delinquency	Its nature	A juvenile delinquent is an adolescent who breaks the law or engages in conduct that is considered illegal. Heredity, identity problems, community influences, and family experiences have been proposed as causes. Parents' failure to discourage antisocial behavior and encourage skilled behavior, as well as lack of parental monitoring, are related to delinquency.
Drugs and alcohol	Drugs	A downward trend in overall illicit drug use by adolescents has recently been detected, although the United States still has the highest adolescent drug use rate of any industrialized nation. Cocaine use by high school seniors declined in 1987, the first significant drop in eight years, but still remains precariously high. Cigarette smoking has decreased, but in light of demonstrated health risks it remains alarmingly high. Undercontrol by boys and permissive parenting in the families of girls during early childhood are related to drug use in adolescence. Social support in adolescence is related to reduced drug use.
	Alcohol	One of the most pervasive drug problems in adolescence is alcohol abuse—use of alcohol by high school seniors has decreased slightly but is still very high. The family's ability to function as a support system seems to be an important factor in decreased drinking by adolescents.

Continuity and Discontinuity in Disturbances

In chapter 1 and at various points in other chapters, we have emphasized the importance of heredity and environment, continuity and discontinuity in children's development. So far in our discussion of disturbances we have underscored that disturbances involve both biogenetic and social environmental causes. How are continuity and discontinuity also involved in understanding the nature of children's disturbances?

Continuity

Three reasons why children's disturbances may be linked to earlier disturbances or circumstances are biological processes, the continuing influence of early experiences, and early experience plus consistent later experience. We consider each of these in turn.

First, with regard to biological processes, children may inherit certain disorders or tendencies that increase the likelihood of developing a disturbance. Similarly, during prenatal development, a number of environmental experiences may lead to the development of an abnormality. For example, a number of forms of mental retardation involve a major gene defect or damage to a chromosome, leading to a biochemical error in the brain's development. Also recall from our discussion of prenatal development in chapter 3 that considerable interest has been generated in discovering the teratogens that underlie the development of disturbances. These teratogens range from the mother's diet, to the possible use of drugs and chemicals, to the mother's emotional state. Developmental psychopathologists, in their effort to identify as early as possible children who have or will have psychological or learning disturbances, have coined the term **at risk** to describe those infants and children most likely to develop disturbances.

In a comprehensive study of children at risk, a variety of biological, social, and developmental characteristics were identified as predictors of problems and disturbances at age eighteen. They included moderate to severe perinatal (at or near birth) stress and birth defects; low socioeconomic status at two and ten years of age; level of maternal education below eight years; low family stability between two and eight years; very low or very high infant responsiveness at one year; a Cattell score below eighty at age two (the Cattell is one of the early measures of infant intelligence); and the need for long-term mental health services or placement in a learning disability class at age ten. When four or more of these factors were present, the stage was set for serious coping problems in the second decade of life (Werner & Smith, 1982).

In summarizing what we know about children at risk, Claire Kopp (1983, 1987) pointed out that a variety of biological risk conditions can impinge on the organism at the time of conception or during prenatal, perinatal, and postnatal life. The outcome of this assault varies and depends on the particular type and timing of the influence, but in general the earlier the assault, the greater the effects. The range of outcome for all perinatal and postnatal assaults is from severe impairment to normal development, although the processes accounting for variability are not fully documented. Factors in the environment act upon biological risk by heightening or attenuating effects. In some instances, as in perinatal stress, environmental influences may outweigh biological risk. Biological risk and adverse rearing conditions combine to have a more negative impact than either factor would alone.

Table 17.3
Salient Developmental Issues

Age (years)	Issues
0–1	Biological regulation; harmonious dyadic interaction; formation of an effective attachment relationship
1–2½	Exploration, experimentation, and mastery of the object world (caregiver as secure base); individuation and autonomy; responding to external control of impulses
3–5	Flexible self-control; self-reliance; initiative; identification and gender concept; establishing effective peer contacts (empathy)
6–12	Social understanding (equity, fairness); gender constancy; same-sex chumships; sense of "industry" (competence); school adjustment
13+	"Formal operations" (flexible perspective taking; "as if" thinking); loyal friendships (same sex); beginning heterosexual relationships; emancipation; identity

From L. A. Sroufe and M. Rutter, "The Domain of Developmental Psychopathology" in *Child Development* 55:17–29. Copyright © 1984 The Society for Research in Child Development, Chicago, IL. Reprinted by permission.

What are some of the ways early experience might be connected to later disturbances? According to Michael Rutter (1980), the following are possibilities: (1) experience produces the disorder at the time, and the disorder persists; (2) experience creates bodily changes that affect later functioning; (3) experience alters patterns of behavior at the time, which later take the form of a disorder; (4) early experiences can change family relationships and circumstances that over time lead to a disorder, (5) sensitivities to stress or coping strategies are changed and later predispose the person to disorder or buffer the person from stress; (6) experiences change the child's self-concept or attitudes, which in turn influence behavior in later circumstances; and (7) experience influences behavior by affecting the selection of environments or the opening or closing of opportunities.

Alan Sroufe (1979) has described a number of salient developmental issues that need to be considered when the study of developmental psychopathology is being planned (table 17.3). As you can see from table 17.3, during the first year of life biological regulation, harmonious dyadic relationships, and the formation of an attachment relationship are central developmental tasks. As the infant progresses through the second year of life, exploration, experimentation, and mastery of the object world, as well as individuation and the development of self-control, become prominent developmental tasks. It is Sroufe's as well as Rutter's belief (Sroufe & Rutter, 1984) that issues at one developmental period lay the groundwork for subsequent issues, in much the same way as the life cycle framework proposed by Erik Erikson (1968).

An extensive longitudinal study conducted with a group of boys and girls in New York City provided some answers to the question of how various dimensions of personality change or remain stable (Thomas, Chess, & Birch, 1970). This New York Longitudinal Study began with individuals in infancy and continued through their college years. We will draw from the vivid descriptions of the lives of several individuals to illustrate how early experiences and consistent later experiences can predict disorders. When we discuss discontinuity in disorders we will present information about another individual in this study.

In early childhood, David was one of the most active boys studied. He was always in motion and came across with a friendly and cheerful manner. Unfortunately, however, a considerable number of parental problems surfaced during David's childhood, including a growing sense of competitiveness in his parents. They continually bragged to others about what a superior child David was, although he did not have a superior IQ; any problems David had in school they attributed to poor teaching. As he developed in his elementary and secondary school years, his school performance and interest in other activities went downhill. The parents totally blamed the school and its teachers.

Picking up on his parents' cues that his failures were not his fault, David never developed a critical, evaluative approach to himself: when problems surfaced, he always put the blame—just as his parents did—on someone else. As David moved into the college years, apathy began to dominate his daily life, and, unfortunately, the attitudes of his parents as well as his own self-insulation and reluctance to take responsibility for his actions led to complete resistance to counseling that might have helped him out of his dilemma.

Discontinuity

Possible reasons for discontinuity involve changes in specific life experiences, regular changes in developmental tasks at different points in development that produce unique demands, and changes in society at different points in the individual's development. We consider each of these in turn.

Changes in specific life circumstances can diminish earlier disorders or they can produce disorders that were not present earlier in development. Consider first the example of Carl, one of Chess and Thomas's subjects.

He requested a discussion with Dr. Chess at the end of his first year in college because he felt depressed and was not coping very well with academic or social matters. He had few friends and said that he had difficulty studying, that he was unable to remember what he had read. By contrast, Carl had been a good student in high school, where he had had a number of friends and many interests. During his interview he did not appear depressed but expressed bewilderment at his situation, saying that it just wasn't like him to be doing so poorly socially and academically.

The background data indicated that during childhood Carl had been one of the most extreme "difficult child" types: he was intense, had negative reactions to new situations, and was slow to adapt to situations even after many exposures to them. This was true whether it was his first bath, his first day at elementary school, or his first shopping trip. Each of these experiences prompted Carl to stormy behavior, such as temper tantrums and shouting. The parents realized that Carl's reactions to his world were not due to their "bad parenting" but instead were part of his temperament. They were patient with him and often gave him considerable time and many opportunities to adapt to new situations that were frustrating to him. As a result, he did not become a behavior "problem," even though the "difficult group" has a higher risk for disturbed development.

Later on in his elementary and secondary school years, Carl met up with few new situations and in the process was able to develop a positive view of himself. College, however, meant a lot of changes in his life. He now was away from home in unfamiliar situations, with new teachers who placed more complex demands on him, with new peers who were harder to get to know, and with a girl with whom he started living. According to Chess and Thomas, the radically different college experiences reawakened the "difficult child" behavioral reactions and brought Carl in for help.

Abnormal Behavior, Stress, and Health

After only one session, Carl began to get back on a more positive track. He discussed his temperamental pattern with Dr. Chess, including coping mechanisms that he might employ to help him out in social and academic situations. By the end of the academic year, his grades had improved, he broke off the living arrangement with the girl, and he started forcing himself to get more involved in peer-group activities.

How might regular changes in developmental tasks be involved in disturbances? While adolescence sometimes has been incorrectly stereotyped as a period of stress for all adolescents, the developmental changes that characterize adolescence can trigger problems and disturbances in some individuals. We have seen that independence and identity are important themes of adolescent development. As the adolescent pushes for autonomy and searches for an identity, parents may adopt more stringent controls or become highly permissive in response to the changes going on with their adolescent. Such changes during adolescent development may precipitate problems and disturbances during adolescence that did not appear earlier in development.

How might changes in society at different points in an individual's development be involved in disturbances? A child may have developed a serious obesity problem, but when we look at the individual in adolescence we see no evidence of the earlier problem. One reason this positive development may have occurred is changes in society over the years as he moved from childhood through adulthood. For example, a child with a serious obesity problem has been strongly influenced by the wave of media attention given to health and nutrition in recent years. Always made to clean his plate as a child, never involved in exercise, and filling his arteries full of sugar for a number of years, he looked in the mirror in adolescence and made the decision to do something about his life. For two years now he has eaten well-balanced but reduced-calorie meals, exercised regularly, and removed processed sugar from his diet. His psychological well-being has improved along with his physical fitness.

Conclusions about Continuity-Discontinuity

For decades, we assumed considerable individual consistency in the development of disorders. More recently, this view has been questioned by the adult contextualists. The results of major studies, such as the New York Longitudinal Study and the California Longitudinal Study, that trace the lives of individuals across the childhood years and into the adult years suggest that either extreme in the continuity-discontinuity controversy is unsupported, although they give comfort to both. We reach the same conclusion, then, about the development of disorders as we did about the development of personality in chapter 14. The infant and early childhood years are far from meaningless in predicting later disorders, but later experiences are important as well. Thus, in trying to understand the development of disorders it would be a mistake to look only at the child's or adolescent's life in the present tense, ignoring the unfolding of development. So too would it be an error if we only searched through the first two years of life in trying to predict why an individual has a disorder. The truth about disorders lies somewhere between the infant determinism of Freud and a contextual approach that ignores the developmental unfolding of disorders completely.

Summary

I. Models of Children's Abnormalities

Four views are the statistical approach, biological approach, psychological and sociocultural approaches, and the interactionist approach. In the statistical approach, children are abnormal if they deviate substantially from the average; it refers to social behavior. In the biological approach, disturbances have biological causes; today's interest focuses on the brain, drugs, and genetics. The forerunner of the biological model is the medical model. In the psychological and sociocultural approaches, disturbances are believed to involve emotional turmoil, inappropriate learning, disordered thoughts, and inadequate relationships. In the interactionist approach, it is recognized that children's abnormal behavior is complex; a more complete understanding can be achieved by considering the interplay of biological, cognitive, and environmental factors.

II. Types of Children's Disturbances

The spectrum of disturbances is large. Disturbances vary in severity and developmental level. One common classification is in terms of internalizing and externalizing disorders. Boys and lower-class children are more likely to have externalizing problems, girls and middle-class children internalizing problems.

III. Infantile Autism and Childhood Schizophrenia

Infantile autism is a severe disorder with an onset in infancy. It includes deficiencies in social relationships, abnormalities in communication, and restricted, repetitive, and stereotyped behavior. Childhood schizophrenia involves an assortment of bizarre behaviors but not as much disturbance in language or lack of social responsiveness as autism. The onset of the disorder is from early childhood through adolescence and it includes distorted thinking, disturbed perceptions, and lack of control over ideas, affect, and behavior. Both hereditary and environmental factors are involved.

IV. Child Abuse

This disturbance has become a major problem in many children's families. It is important to consider its cultural, familial, and community determinants.

V. Learning Disabilities

Learning disabled children are children with normal intelligence or above, they have difficulties in some areas but not others, and they are not suffering from some other disorder that could explain their learning problems. Learning disabilities are complex and multifaceted and require precise analysis. A disorder classified under learning disabilities is attention deficit disorder. Sometimes called hyperactivity, it describes children who are extremely active, impulsive, distractible, and excitable. Possible causes include heredity, prenatal hazards, diet, family dynamics, and the physical environment. Amphetamines have been used with some success in the disorder's treatment but do not work with all hyperactive children.

VI. Depression and Suicide

Depression has more mixed characteristics in children than in adults. It is more likely to have its onset in adolescence than childhood and it occurs more in girls than in boys. Loss of attachment, cognitive distortion, and learned helplessness are possible explanations along with biogenetic factors. The rate of suicide has quadrupled in the last thirty years in the United States. Its causes involve both proximal and distal factors.

VII. Delinquency

A juvenile delinquent is an adolescent who breaks the law or engages in conduct that is considered illegal. Heredity, identity problems, community influences, and family experiences have been proposed as causes. Parents' failure to discourage antisocial behavior and encourage skilled behavior, as well as lack of parental monitoring, are related to delinquency.

VIII. Drugs and Alcohol

A downward trend in overall illicit drug use by adolescents has recently been detected, although the United States still has the highest adolescent drug use rate of any industrialized nation. Cocaine use by high school seniors declined in 1987, the first significant downturn in eight years, but still remains precariously high. Cigarette smoking has decreased, but in light of demonstrated health risks, it remains alarmingly high. Undercontrol by boys and permissive parenting in the families of girls during early childhood are related to drug use in adolescence. Social support in adolescence is related to reduced drug use. Alcohol abuse is one of the most pervasive drug problems in adolescence. Use of alcohol by high school seniors has decreased slightly but is still very high. The family's ability to function as a support system seems to be an important factor in decreased drinking by adolescents.

IX. Continuity-Discontinuity

Reasons for continuity involve biological processes, the continuing influence of early experiences, and early experience plus consistent later experience. Possible reasons for discontinuity involve changes in specific life experiences, regular changes in developmental tasks at different points in development that produce unique demands, and changes in society at different points in the individual's development. Children's disturbances involve both continuity and discontinuity.

Key Terms

statistical approach   455
medical model   455
infantile autism   457
echolalia   458
childhood
schizophrenia   458

learning disabilities   462
attention deficit
disorder   462
learned helplessness   465
juvenile delinquent   467
at risk   474

Suggested Readings

Belsky, J., & Nezworski, T. (Eds.). (1988). *Clinical implications of attachment*. Hillsdale, NJ: Erlbaum.
A volume focused on the role of attachment in the development of children's disturbances. Includes information about interventions with infants who are insecurely attached.

Child Development, February 1984.
This special issue is devoted to developmental psychopathology. Includes articles on stress, intervention, social skills, autism, child abuse, and many other topics.

Coleman, J. (Ed.). (1987). *Working with troubled adolescents*. Orlando, FL: Academic Press.
Includes chapters on adolescent individuation and family therapy, social skills training for adolescents, helping adolescents improve their identity, eating disorders, and suicide.

Johnson, J. H., Rasbury, W. C., & Siegel, L. J. (1986). *Approaches to child treatment*. New York: Pergamon.
A comprehensive description of various treatments for children's disturbances. Includes chapters on family therapy and on group therapy with children.

Rutter, M., & Garmezy, N. (1983). Developmental psychopathology. In P. H. Mussen (Ed.), *Handbook of child psychology* (4th ed., Vol. 4). New York: John Wiley & Sons.
This lengthy, highly detailed chapter spells out many important dimensions of the field of developmental psychopathology. Includes considerable discussion of Rutter's and Garmezy's important research.

Stress and Health

*Look to your health and if you have it value it next to a good
conscience; for health is a blessing that we mortals are capable
of.*

Izaak Walton
The Compleat Angler, 1653

Around 2600 B.C. Oriental physicians, and later around 500 B.C. Greek
physicians, recognized that good habits were essential for good health.
Instead of blaming magical thinking or the gods for illness, they realized that human beings have the capability of exercising some control over
their health. The physician was viewed as a guide, assisting the patient in
restoring a natural physical and emotional balance. In more recent times,
medical professionals have tended to be specialists. While this tendency continues, as we move toward the twenty-first century an interest in integrated
health care has developed. Once again, family medicine is viewed as an important approach in caring for children's health problems. The belief has
emerged that a child's illness and health are multidimensional and complex,
often requiring knowledge about different medical and psychological disciplines.

The new approach to preventing illness and promoting health is a **holistic orientation.** Instead of linking a child's illness to a specific cause such as
genes or germs, this approach recognizes the complex, multidimensional nature
of illness and health. Genes and germs might be involved, say the holistic health
advocates, but a better understanding of the child's problem will transpire if
we know something about psychological factors, the family's life-style, and
the nature of the health-care delivery system, for example. Interest in the psychological factors involved in illness and the promotion of health led to the
development of a new division in 1978 in the American Psychological Association called health psychology (Matarazzo, 1979). Every indication points
toward health psychology playing an increasingly important role in understanding children's illnesses and promoting children's health (Feist & Brannon,
1989; Rodin & Solovey, in press).

A theme of children's health is woven through this chapter. You will read
about many different aspects of children's nutrition, health, illness, and exercise. But first we focus on something that sometimes impairs our health—
stress—with special attention directed at effective strategies for coping with
stress.

Stress

Stress is a sign of the times. No one really knows whether we or children experience more stress than our predecessors, but it seems that child and adult
stressors have increased dramatically. What is the nature of children's stress?
How do children cope with stress?

The Nature of Children's Stress

Stress is a part of all children's lives. All kinds of experiences—from the eu-
phoria of finding a lost kitten to the pain of a cut finger—produce similar
biological responses that have been called stress. The longer stress persists the

more damage it causes to the child's body (Selye, 1974, 1983). But while stress can be described as the wear and tear on children's bodies, we also need to consider the nature of children's stressful experiences.

Most research on children's stress has been limited to negative experiences. As yet we know little about the nature of stress that occurs when children are chosen captain of the best team, visit affectionate grandparents, or open gifts and find coveted toys. Researchers found that adults rank such positive experiences as an outstanding personal achievement or a decrease in the number of arguments between parents as involving low levels of stress for children (Chandler, 1982). Hans Selye (1983), the Austrian-born founding father of stress research, recognized that all stress is not bad for children. Selye called stress's positive features **eustress.**

Children can experience a spectrum of negative stresses that range from ordinary to severe (Brenner, 1984). At the ordinary end are experiences that occur in most children's lives and for which there are reasonably well-defined coping patterns. For example, most parents are aware that older children probably will be jealous of a newborn sibling. They know how children's jealousy works and how they can help children to cope with it. More severe stress is involved when children become separated from their parents. Healthy coping strategies for this stressful experience are not spelled out well. Some children are well cared for while others are ignored when there is a separation caused by divorce, death, illness, or foster placement. Even more severe are the experiences of children who live for years in situations of neglect or abuse. Victims of incest also experience severe stress with little coping guidelines.

In many instances, more than one stress occurs at a time in children's lives. Researchers have found that when several stresses are combined, the effects may be compounded (Brenner, 1984; Capaldi & Patterson, 1989; Rutter & Garmezy, 1983; Rutter & Schopler, 1987). For example, in one investigation, Michael Rutter (1979) found that ten-year-old children under two chronic life stresses were four times as likely to eventually need psychological services as children who had to cope with only one chronic stress. A similar multiplier effect also was found for children who experienced more than one short-term strain at a time.

Recently, psychologists have emphasized that it may be life's daily experiences as well as life's major events that are the culprits in stress. Enduring a tense family and living in poverty do not show up on scales of major life events in children's development, yet the everyday pounding children take from these living conditions can add up to a highly stressful life and eventually psychological disturbance or illness (Folkman & others, 1986; Lazarus & Folkman, 1984). In one recent investigation, adolescents who experienced the most daily hassles had the most negative self-images (Tolan, Miller, & Thomas, 1988). More about daily hassles and uplifts in the lives of sixth-grade boys and girls is presented in Perspective on Child Development 18.1.

Coping with Stress

How can children cope with stress? In some instances, certain coping techniques may be used more at one developmental level than another (Brenner, 1984). For example, three-year-old children are more likely to cope with loneliness by inventing imaginary companions than are eleven-year-olds. Yet most coping mechanisms can be used effectively from infancy through adolescence. As part of coping with stress, children usually call on more than one strategy at a time. For example, in the course of the day when Brian's kitten died, he constructed a shoe-box coffin and ceremonially buried it in the backyard, a

(a)

(b)

It may be life's daily experiences that mount up to become the causes of stress for children and their parents. Enduring a life in poverty (a) and pleasant interactions between a father and son (b) would not show up on life events surveys, but they represent daily hassles and daily uplifts, respectively, that contribute to the degree of stress children experience.

(a)

(b)

By becoming absorbed in games, sports, or hobbies, such as ice skating (a) and toy trains (b), children may be able to sublimate their problems.

thus reducing stress. **Withdrawal** takes place when children remove themselves either physically or mentally from the stress. They might run away from the stressful environment or become very quiet and almost invisible. They might focus on their pet or lose themselves in their daydreams to escape mentally. These efforts afford them temporary refuge from the stress. **Impulsive acting out** occurs when children act impulsively and sometimes flamboyantly to avoid thinking either of the past or the consequences of their current actions. They conceal their pain by making others angry at them, seeking easy and quick solutions to reduce their misery. By doing so they draw attention to themselves and momentarily ease their tension. However, in the long run, this coping strategy is almost guaranteed to be self-destructive.

In contrast to these evasive strategies, there are ways children accept and face stress. These include altruism, humor, suppression, anticipation, and sublimation (Brenner, 1984; Vaillant, 1977). As with the evasive strategies, each of these strategies has both positive and negative aspects. When children use **altruism,** they forget their own troubles by helping others, especially their parents and siblings. They feel good about their helper role and from knowing that they are useful. The negative side of this picture is that sometimes children who use altruism as a coping strategy do not let themselves be carefree—their seriousness may push them into adultlike behavior too early in their development. Children also sometimes joke about their difficulties, using humor to express anger and tension. However, taken to its extreme, children may lose the ability to cry and to reach out to others for help. **Suppression** allows children to set aside their tensions temporarily. For hours they may forget their cares, yet they are not afraid to go back to them when their free time is over. When a family death occurs, preschool children may unconsciously suppress it. They may cry for awhile, then go and play as if nothing happened. The negative side is that children may suppress feelings to the point of denial. Children who use **anticipation** are able to foresee and plan for their next stressful episode. When the stress appears they are better prepared to protect themselves and to accept what cannot be avoided. Anticipation can be a strong coping mechanism. It becomes negative when children become too fearful and develop compulsive needs to know and plan in rigid, overly compulsive ways. With **sublimation,** children discover ways to vent their anger, overcome their fears, or express their sadness by becoming absorbed in games, sports, or hobbies. These activities become their satisfactions and compensate for their stress. Sublimation becomes negative when children become so engrossed in these activities that other pleasures or family needs are ignored.

How can parents, teachers, and helping professionals most effectively work with children in stressful circumstances? Avis Brenner (1984) proposes three intelligent strategies: removing at least one stressor; teaching new coping strategies; and showing children ways they can transfer existing coping strategies to other, more appropriate life circumstances.

Based on Michael Rutter's (1979) research indicating the multiple effects of stress, it makes sense that removing one stress or hassle can help children feel stronger and more competent. For example, consider Lisa, who had been coming to school hungry each morning. Her teacher arranged for Lisa to have a hot breakfast at school each morning, which improved her concentration in school. This in turn helped Lisa to suppress for a time her anxieties about her parents' impending divorce.

Children who have a number of coping techniques seem to have the best chance of adapting and functioning competently in the face of stress. By learning new coping techniques, children may no longer feel as incompetent

Abnormal Behavior, Stress, and Health

	Concept Table 18.1	
	Stress	

Concept	Processes/Related Ideas	Characteristics/Description
The nature of stress	Bodily wear and tear	Selye described stress as the wear and tear on the body. The longer stress persists the more damage it causes to the child's body.
	Eustress	Selye also argued that all stress is not bad for children. The positive features of stress are referred to as eustress.
	Range and multiplier effects	The range of stress is from ordinary to severe. In many instances more than one stress occurs. Two or more stresses can have a multiplier effect on children's disturbances.
	Daily hassles and uplifts	Some approaches to stress focus on major life events. Recently, it has been argued that life's daily hassles and uplifts also are important to consider when evaluating the nature of children's stress.
Coping with stress	Avoiding stress	Avoiding stress is considered to be a wiser short-term than long-term strategy. Avoiding stress can be accomplished by denial, regression, withdrawal, and impulsive acting out.
	Accepting and facing stress	Strategies include altruism, humor, suppression, anticipation, and sublimation. Adults can help children deal with stress by removing at least one stressor, teaching new coping strategies, and showing transfer to other circumstances.

and their self-confidence may improve. For example, Kim was relieved when a clinical psychologist helped her to anticipate what it would be like to visit her seriously ill sister. She had been frightened by the hospital and used withdrawal as part of her coping, saying she did not want to see her sister, even though she missed her a great deal. Children tend to apply their coping strategies only in the situations in which they are developed. Adults can show children how to use these coping skills to their best advantage in many other situations as well. For example, Jennifer used altruism to cope with her mother's hospitalization for cancer. She coped with separation by mothering her father, her little brother, and her classmates. Her classmates quickly became annoyed at her and began to tease her. Jennifer's teacher at school recognized this problem and helped her to transfer her altruism to taking care of the class's pet animals and being responsible for some daily cleanup chores. Her mothering of the children stopped and so did the teasing. By following such guidelines, both helping professionals and lay people can help children cope more effectively with stress.

At this point we have discussed a number of ideas about the nature of stress and coping with stress. A summary of these ideas is presented in Concept Table 18.1. Now we turn our attention to information about children's health.

Health

While we have become a health-conscious nation, aware of the importance of nutrition and exercise in our lives, many of us still eat junk food, have extra flab hanging around our middles, and spend too much of our lives as couch potatoes. In too many instances, this description fits children as well as adults. Let's explore further the nature of these dimensions of children's health.

Nutrition

Has our increased health consciousness influenced the way infants are fed? The foods children eat? How does malnourishment affect children's development? What kinds of eating disorders do children and adolescents face? We consider each of these questions in turn.

Eating Behavior in Infancy

Because infants grow so rapidly, they must consume approximately fifty calories per day for each pound they weigh—more than twice an adult's requirement per pound. In the 1980s, we became more nutrition conscious as adults. Does the same type of nutrition that makes us healthy as adults also make young infants healthy?

Some parents do not know the recipe for a healthy baby: whole milk and an occasional cookie, along with fruits, vegetables, and other foods. Some affluent, well-educated parents starve their babies by feeding them the low-fat, low-calorie diet they eat themselves. Diets designed for adult weight loss and prevention of heart disease can retard growth and development in babies. Fat is very important. Nature's food—the mother's breast milk—is not low in fat or calories. No child below age two should be given skim milk.

In a recent investigation (Lifshitz & others, 1987), seven cases were documented in which babies aged seven to twenty-two months were unwittingly undernourished by their health-conscious parents. In some cases the parents had been fat themselves and were determined that their child would not be. The well-meaning parents substituted vegetables, skim milk, and other low-fat foods for what they called junk food. Growing infants need high-calorie, high-energy food for a well-balanced diet—in such cases, broccoli is not necessarily a good substitute for a cookie.

Most experts agree that young infants should be fed several times a day, but controversy surrounds just how this should be accomplished. For years, developmentalists have debated whether breast-feeding an infant has substantial benefits over bottle-feeding. The growing consensus is that it generally is better to breast-feed (Auerback, 1987; Corboy, 1987). Breast-feeding provides milk that is clean and digestible and helps to immunize the newborn from disease. Breast-fed babies also gain weight more rapidly than bottle-fed babies. However, only about one-half of mothers nurse newborns and even fewer continue to nurse their infants after several months. Mothers who work outside the home may find it impossible to breast-feed their young infant for many months, but even though breast-feeding provides more ideal nutrition for the infant, bottle-fed infants are not psychologically harmed.

Some years ago, controversy also surrounded the issue of whether a baby should be fed on demand or on a regular schedule. For example, John Watson (1930) argued that scheduled feeding was superior because it increased the child's orderliness. An example of a recommended schedule for newborns was four ounces of formula every six hours. In recent years, demand feeding—in which the timing and amount of feeding are determined by the infant—has become more popular.

Children's Nutrition

Feeding and eating habits are important aspects of development during early childhood. It is widely recognized that what we eat affects our skeletal growth, body shape, and susceptibility to disease. Recognizing that nutrition is important for the child's growth and development, the federal government provides money for school lunch programs. On the average, the preschool child

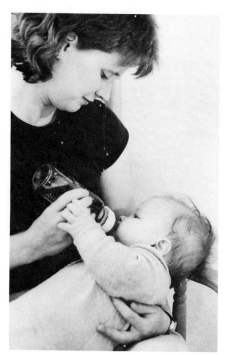

Bottle-feeding, as shown here, is more widely practiced than breast-feeding, yet the consensus is that breast-feeding is better for the infant's health.

Abnormal Behavior, Stress, and Health

Table 18.1
Recommended Energy Intakes for Children of Various Ages

	Age	Weight (kg)	Height (cm)	Energy needs (calories)	Ranges
Children	1–3	13	90	1,300	900–1,800
	4–6	20	112	1,700	1,300–2,300
	7–10	28	132	2,400	1,650–3,300

Source: Food and Nutrition Board, National Research Council: Recommended Dietary Allowances, Revised Ed. 9, Washington, D.C., 1980, National Academy of Sciences.

Table 18.2
Fat and Calorie Intake of Selected Fast-Food Meals

Selected meal	Calories	Percent of calories from fat
Burger King Whopper, fries, vanilla shake	1,250	43
Big Mac, fries, chocolate shake	1,100	41
McDonald's Quarter-Pounder with cheese	418	52
Pizza Hut ten-inch pizza with sausage, mushrooms, pepperoni, and green pepper	1,035	35
Arby's roast beef plate (roast beef sandwich, two potato patties, and coleslaw), chocolate shake	1,200	30
Kentucky Fried Chicken dinner (three pieces chicken, mashed potatoes and gravy, coleslaw, roll)	830	50
Arthur Treacher's fish and chips (two pieces breaded fried fish, french fries, cola drink)	900	42
Typical restaurant "diet plate" (hamburger patty, cottage cheese, etc.)	638	63

From Virginia Demoss, "Good, the Bad and the Edible" in *Runner's World*, June 1980. Copyright Virginia Demoss. Reprinted with permission.

requires 1,700 calories per day. Table 18.1 shows the increasing energy requirements of children as they move from infancy through the middle and late childhood years. Energy requirements for individual children are determined by **basal metabolism rate (BMR),** which is the minimum amount of energy an individual uses in a resting state, rate of growth, and activity. Energy needs of individual children of the same age, sex, and size vary. Reasons for these differences are unexplained. Differences in physical activity, basal metabolism rate, and the efficiency with which individuals use energy are among the candidates for explanation (Pipes, 1988).

A special concern in our culture is the amount of fat in our diets. While some Yuppie mothers may be providing too little fat in their infant's and children's diets, other parents are raising their children on diets in which the percentage of fat is far too high. Our changing life-styles, in which we often eat on the run and pick up fast-food meals, probably contribute to the increased fat levels in children's diets. Table 18.2 lists the number of calories and the percentage of fat in the offerings of a number of fast-food restaurants. Most fast-food meals are high in protein, especially meat and dairy products. But the average American child does not need to be concerned about getting enough protein. What must be of concern is the vast number of young children who are being weaned on fast foods that not only are high in protein but also high in fat. It is during the preschool years that many individuals get their first taste of fast foods, and unfortunately, eating habits become ingrained very early in life. The American Heart Association recommends that the daily limit for calories from fat should be approximately 35 percent. Compare this figure with the figures in table 18.2. Clearly, many fast-food meals contribute to excess fat intake by children.

Not only is there concern about excessive fat in children's diets, but there also is concern about excessive sugar. To learn more about sugar's effect on young children's behavior, turn to Perspective on Child Development 18.2. The jury is still out on how extensively sugar affects children's behavior. Some

Young Children's Sugar Consumption and Inappropriate Behavior

Robert, age three, already loves chocolate. His mother lets him have a daily dose of a chocolate candy bar, a bag of M&Ms candy, and chocolate milk. Robert also drinks three to four cans of Pepsi a day and eats sugar-coated cereal each morning for breakfast. How does sugar consumption influence young children's health and behavior?

The association of sugar consumption and children's health problems—dental cavities and obesity, for example—has been widely documented (e.g., Warren, 1975). In recent years, a growing interest in the influence of sugar on children's behavior has surfaced. In one investigation (Goldman & others, 1986), eight preschool children on separate mornings each received six ounces of juice, sweetened one morning with sucrose and on the other with an artificial sweetener. They were observed for ninety minutes following the drinks. After the sucrose drink, the children exhibited more inappropriate play—they were less

Might the everyday eating patterns of children be related to their behavior, such as the aggressive behavior of these two boys?

attentive and overly active, for example. Other findings support the belief that sugar consumption by young children increases their aggression, especially in unstructured circumstances and when the child is bored (Goldman & others, 1987).

reviews conclude that we do not have good evidence for sugar's role in promoting aggressive or hyperactive behavior (e.g., Pipes, 1988). However, investigations such as the one described in Perspective on Child Development 18.2 argue for a closer look at the contribution of sugar to children's behavior.

In sum, while there is individual variation in appropriate nutrition for children, children's diets should include well-balanced proportions of fats, carbohydrates, protein, vitamins, and minerals. An occasional candy bar does not hurt and can even benefit a growing body, but a steady diet of hamburgers, french fries, milkshakes, and candy bars should be avoided.

Malnutrition

Imagine that you are five years old and live in the Bayambang area of the Philippines. Your parents are very poor. They do not get enough food to eat, and what they are able to afford does not constitute a well-balanced diet. There is a limited amount of protein in the Philippines; only the wealthy people get enough. Even if protein were plentiful, the price would probably be too high for your parents.

The most direct evidence of malnutrition on development comes from studies of animals. In one investigation (Zamenhof, van Marthens, & Margolis, 1968), one month before impregnation, one group of female rats was placed on a high protein diet while a second group was placed on a low protein diet. The brains and body weights of the offspring born to the high protein diet mothers were greater than those born to the low protein diet mothers. Also, the brains of the mothers on the high protein diet had more cells than the brains of the mothers on the low protein diet. Malnutrition in the form of inadequate protein intake not only had an adverse affect on the pregnant rat's brain but on her offspring's as well.

In another investigation, two groups of black South African infants, all one year old, were extremely malnourished. The children in one group were given adequate nutrition during the next six years; there was no intervention in the poor nutrition of the other group. After the seventh year, the poorly nourished group of children had significantly lower IQs than did the adequately nourished group (Bayley, 1970).

Malnutrition adversely influences children's intelligence. Might undernourishment also adversely influence their emotional well-being? David Barrett, Marian Radke-Yarrow, and Robert Klein (1982) discovered that undernourishment during infancy is associated with undesirable socioemotional patterns at the time children enter elementary school. In San Diego, children whose mothers were undernourished during pregnancy and whose weight was low at birth were compared with children whose mothers had better diets. The undernourished group interacted less with their school-age peers, was more dependent on adults, and appeared sadder and less friendly. The researchers concluded that the undernourished child experiences a cycle in which subtle alterations in the central nervous system and lack of energy combine with a poor home environment to stunt the child's emotional growth. The result may be withdrawal on the part of the child and neglect or rejection on the part of the caregiver. It seems that children attempt to adapt to the physiological stress of nutritional deficit by developing behaviors that remove them from the environment and inhibit the later development of appropriate social interaction patterns.

Eating Disorders

A tall, slender sixteen-year-old girl goes into the locker room of a fitness center, throws her towel across the bench, and looks squarely in the mirror. She yells, "You fat pig. You are nothing but a fat pig." We are a nation obsessed with food, spending extraordinary amounts of time thinking about, eating, and avoiding food. Understanding eating disorders is complex; it involves genetic inheritance, physiological factors, cognitive factors, and environmental experiences. The three most prominent eating disorders are obesity, anorexia nervosa, and bulimia. We consider each of these in turn.

Obesity   Children and adolescents may have inherited a tendency to be overweight. Only 10 percent of children who do not have obese parents become obese themselves; about 40 percent of children with one obese parent become obese; about 70 percent of children who have two obese parents become obese themselves. The extent to which this is due to experiences with parents or genes cannot be determined in studies with humans, but research with animals indicates they can be bred to have a propensity for fatness (Blundell, 1984).

Every child has a set point for body weight. **Set point** is the weight maintained when no effort is made to gain or lose weight. The amount of stored fat in your body is an important factor in the set point of your body weight. It seems that when we gain weight the number of fat cells increases, and we may not be able to get rid of them. Interestingly, though, adults who were not obese as children but who become overweight as adults have larger fat cells than their normal weight counterparts, but they do not have more fat cells (VanItallie, 1984). Another biological factor involved is the basal metabolism factor mentioned earlier. Slow metabolism is an important dimension of understanding obesity because individuals with slow metabolisms are most likely to gain weight. A slow metabolism has been detected as early as three months of age. And, as indicated in figure 18.1, BMR sharply declines from the beginning to the end of adolescence. During the adult years, BMR drops off

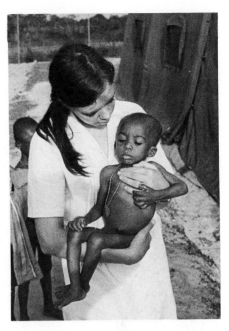

Malnutrition is still common among infants in many parts of the world. In the infant's first year of life, severe protein-calorie deficiency can lead to a wasting away of the infant's body tissues. One of the main causes of this wasting away is early weaning from breast milk to inadequate nutrients, such as unsuitable and unsanitary cow's milk formula. In many of the third world countries, mothers used to breast-feed their infants for at least two years. To become more modern, they began to stop breast-feeding much earlier and to replace it with bottle-feeding. In impoverished countries, such as Afghanistan, Haiti, Ghana, and Chili, comparisons of bottle-fed and breast-fed infants reveal a death rate that is at times 500 percent higher for bottle-fed infants.

Figure 18.1
Basal metabolism rates (BMR) for adolescent females and males.

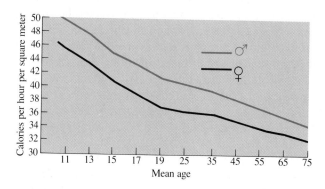

much more slowly. To some extent a declining BMR contributes to an understanding of why there are more fat older adolescents than fat younger adolescents. Scientists are working on drugs they hope will be able to raise the basal metabolism rate of overweight children and adolescents, although as we will see shortly exercise can also raise metabolic rate and burn calories.

A child's insulin level also is an important factor in eating behavior and obesity. Judy Rodin (1984, 1987) argues that what children eat influences their insulin levels. When children eat complex carbohydrates such as cereals, bread, and pasta, insulin levels go up but fall off gradually. When children consume simple sugars such as candy bars and soda, insulin levels rise and then fall off sharply—the sugar low with which many of us are all too familiar.

Glucose levels in the blood also are affected by these complex carbohydrates and simple sugars in similar ways. The consequence is that children are more likely to eat within the next several hours after eating simple sugars than complex carbohydrates. And the food children eat at one meal influences how much they will eat at the next meal. So consuming doughnuts and candy bars, in addition to providing minimal nutritional value, sets up an ongoing sequence of what and how much children will crave the next time they eat.

Rodin also believes that exercise is an important part of weight loss and weight maintenance for children and adolescents. She points out that no matter what the child's genetic background, aerobic exercise increases metabolic rate, which helps to burn calories. Exercise not only burns up calories but it continues to raise metabolic rate for several hours *after* the exercise. Exercise actually lowers the body's set point for weight, making it much easier to maintain a lower weight (Bennett & Gurin, 1982).

Many obese adolescents feel that if they could only lose weight everything would be great in their lives. As one adolescent commented, "Losing weight would make my parents happy, my peers at school would like me, and I could concentrate on other things." A typical example is Debby, age seventeen, who has been obese since she was twelve. She comes from a middle-class family in which her parents have pressured her to lose weight, repeatedly sending her to reducing centers and to physicians. One summer, Debby was sent to a diet camp, where she went from 200 to 150 pounds. On returning home, she was terribly disappointed when her parents pressured her to lose more. With increased tension and parental preoccupation with her weight, she gave up all efforts at dieting and her weight rose rapidly. Debby isolated herself and continued her preoccupation with food. Later, clinical help was sought and fortunately Debby was able to work through her hostility toward her parents and understand her self-destructive behavior. Eventually, she gained a sense of self-control and became willing to reduce for herself and not for her parents or her peers.

Anorexia Nervosa and Bulimia   Fifteen-year-old Jane gradually eliminated foods from her diet to the point where she subsisted by eating *only* applesauce and eggnog. She spent hours observing her own body, wrapping her fingers around her waist to see if it was getting any thinner. She fantasized about becoming a beautiful fashion model and wearing designer bathing suits. But even when she reached eighty-five pounds, Jane still felt fat. She continued to lose weight, eventually emaciating herself. She was hospitalized and treated for **anorexia nervosa,** an eating disorder that involves the relentless pursuit of thinness through starvation. Eventually anorexia nervosa can lead to death, as it did for popular singer Karen Carpenter.

Anorexia nervosa has become an increasingly frequent problem among adolescent females.

Anorexia nervosa affects primarily females during adolescence and the early adulthood years (only about 5 percent of anorexics are male). Most adolescents with this disorder are white and from well-educated, middle- and upper-income families. Although anorexics avoid eating, they have an intense interest in food, they cook for others, they talk about food, and they insist on watching others eat. Anorexics have a distorted body image, perceiving themselves as beautiful even when they become skeletal in appearance. As self-starvation continues and the fat content of the body drops to a bare minimum, menstruation usually stops. Behavior is often hyperactive (Polivy & Thomsen, 1987).

Numerous causes of anorexia have been proposed; they include societal, psychological, and physiological factors (Brumberg, 1988). The societal factor most often held responsible is the current fashion image of thinness. Psychological factors include motivation for attention, desire for individuality, denial of sexuality, and a way of coping with overcontrolling parents. Anorexics sometimes have families that place high demands for achievement on them. Unable to meet their parents' high standards, they feel an inability to control their own lives. By limiting their food intake, anorexics gain some sense of self-control. Physiological causes focus on the hypothalamus, which becomes abnormal in a number of ways when an adolescent becomes anorexic (Garfinkel & Garner, 1982). But the bottom line is that, at this time, we are uncertain of exactly what causes anorexia nervosa.

An eating disorder related to anorexia nervosa is **bulimia.** Anorexics occasionally follow a binge-and-purge pattern, but bulimics do this on a regular basis. The bulimic binges on large amounts of food and then purges by self-induced vomiting or using laxatives. The binges sometimes alternate with fasting or at other times with normal eating behavior. Like anorexia nervosa, bulimia is primarily a female disorder. Bulimia has become prevalent among college women. Some estimates suggest that one in two college women binge and purge at least some of the time. However, recent estimates suggest that true bulimics—those who binge and purge on a regular basis—make up less than 2 percent of the female college population (Stunkard, in press). While anorexics can control their eating, bulimics cannot. Depression is a common

Stress and Health

characteristic of bulimics. Bulimia can lead to gastric irritation and chemical imbalance in the body. Many of the same causes proposed for anorexia nervosa are offered for bulimia.

Health, Illness, and Exercise

While there has been great national interest in the psychological aspects of health among adults, only recently has a developmental perspective on psychological aspects of health among children been proposed. Special concern focuses on exercise and cardiovascular disease.

Health and Illness

The uniqueness of children's health-care needs is evident when we consider their motor, cognitive, and social development (Maddux & others, 1986). For example, think about infant's and preschool children's motor development—inadequate to ensure personal safety while riding in an automobile. Adults must take preventive measures to restrain infants and young children in car seats. Young children may lack the intellectual skills—including reading ability—to discriminate between safe and unsafe household substances. And they may lack the impulse control to keep them from running out in a busy street while going after a ball or a toy.

Health education programs for preschool children need to be cognitively simple. Three simple but important goals for health education programs for preschool children are to be able to (Parcel & others, 1979): (1) identify feelings of wellness and illness and be able to express them to adults; (2) identify appropriate sources of assistance for health-related problems; and (3) independently initiate the use of sources of assistance for health problems.

The first recommendation deserves further consideration. Arthur Parmalee (1986) worries about how young children may confuse "feel bad" with bad behavior and "feel good" with good behavior. For example, a young child might say, "I feel bad. I want aspirin," "I bad girl, I wet my pants," and "Me can do it, me good girl." Young children do often attribute their illnesses to what they view as a transgression, such as having eaten the wrong food or played outdoors in the cold when told not to (e.g., Brewster, 1982).

Caregivers play an important health role for children. For example, by controlling the speed of the vehicles they drive, by decreasing their drinking—especially before driving—and by not smoking around children, caregivers enhance children's health. Caregivers can actively affect young children's health and safety by training the child in appropriate dental hygiene, proper nutrition, recreational safety, and self-protection skills.

Illnesses, especially those that are not life threatening, provide an excellent opportunity for children to expand their development. The preschool period is a time when illnesses such as respiratory infections (colds, flu) and gastrointestinal upsets (nausea, diarrhea) peak. These illnesses usually are of short duration and are often handled outside of the medical community through the family, day care, or school. Such minor illnesses can increase the young child's knowledge of health and illness, sense of empathy, and realistic understanding of the sick role (Parmalee, 1986).

When elementary school children are asked about their health, they seem to understand that it is not just something that will stay positive but rather that good health is something they have to work at on a regular basis (O'Connor-Francoeur, 1983). But while elementary school children and adolescents may recognize the contributions of nutrition and exercise to health, their behaviors do not always follow suit. Adolescents seem to have an especially difficult time applying health information and knowledge to their own personal lives. For example, in one investigation (Weinstein, 1984), adolescents reported that they probably would never have a heart attack or a drinking problem but that other adolescents would. The adolescents also said that no relation existed between their risk of heart attack and how much they exercised, smoked, or ate red meat or high cholesterol food such as eggs, even though they correctly recognized that factors such as family history influenced risk. Many adolescents, it appears, have unrealistic, overly optimistic beliefs about their future health risks.

Adolescents often reach a level of health, strength, and energy they will never match during the remainder of their lives. Adolescents also have a sense of uniqueness and invulnerability, leading them to think that illness and disorder will not enter their lives. And they possess a time perspective that looks toward a future with no boundaries, thinking they can live forever and recoup any lost health or modify any bad habits they might develop. Given this combination of physical and cognitive factors, is it any wonder that so many adolescents practice such poor health habits?

Exercise

Many of our patterns of health and illness are long-standing. Our experiences as children and adolescents contribute to our current health practices as adults. Did your parents seek medical help at your first sniffle, or did they wait until your temperature was 104 degrees? Did they feed you heavy doses of red meat and sugar or a more rounded diet with vegetables and fruits? Did they get you involved in exercise programs or did you lie around watching television all the time? Did you grow up in a tense family atmosphere or one in which stress was handled calmly and life was low key.

Are children getting enough exercise? The 1985 School Fitness Survey tested 18,857 children aged six to seventeen on nine fitness tasks. Compared to a similar survey in 1975 there was virtually no improvement on the tasks. For example, 40 percent of the boys six to twelve years of age could not do more than one pull-up and a full 25 percent could not do any! Fifty percent of the girls aged six to seventeen and 30 percent of the boys aged six to twelve could not run a mile in less than ten minutes. In the fifty-yard dash, the adolescent girls in 1975 were faster than the adolescent girls in 1985.

Some experts suggest that television is at least partially to blame for the poor physical shape of our nation's children. In one investigation, light television-viewing children were significantly more physically fit than their heavy television-viewing counterparts (Tucker, 1987). The more children watch television, the more they are likely to be overweight. No one is quite sure whether this is because children spend their leisure time in front of the television set instead of chasing each other around the neighborhood or whether they tend to eat a lot of junk food they see advertised on television.

Some of the blame also falls on the nation's schools, many of which fail to provide physical education classes on a daily basis. In the 1985 School Fitness Survey, 37 percent of the children in the first through the fourth grades take gym classes only once or twice a week. The investigation also revealed that parents are poor role models when it comes to physical fitness. Less than 30 percent of the parents of children in grades one through four exercised three days a week. Roughly half said they never get any vigorous exercise. In one recent extensive investigation of children's behavior in physical education classes at four different elementary schools, how little vigorous exercise takes place in these classes was revealed (Parcel & others, 1987). Children moved through space only 50 percent of the time they were in the class and they moved continuously an average of only 2.2 minutes. In summary, not only do

We have become a more health-conscious nation. Everywhere we turn, we hear about the importance of exercise and good nutrition. Yet our nation's schoolchildren are not in good physical shape. What recommendations do you have for improving the physical fitness of our nation's schoolchildren?

children's school weeks not include adequate physical education classes, but the majority of children do not exercise vigorously even when they are in physical education classes. Further, most children's parents are poor role models when it comes to vigorous physical exercise.

Does it make a difference if we push children to exercise more vigorously in elementary school? One recent investigation gives an affirmative answer to this question (Tuckman & Hinkle, 1988). One hundred fifty-four elementary school children were randomly assigned to either three thirty-minute running programs per week or to regular attendance in physical education classes. Although the results sometimes varied for the sex of the children, for the most part the cardiovascular health as well as the creativity of children in the running program were enhanced. For example, the boys in this program had less body fat and the girls had more creative involvement in their classrooms.

Earlier in the chapter we discussed ways children cope with stress. An exciting possibility is that physical exercise might provide a buffer to children's stress. In one recent investigation of 364 females in grades 7 to 11 in Los Angeles, the negative impact of stressful events on health declined as exercise levels increased, suggesting that exercise can be a valuable resource for combating children's life stresses (Brown & Siegel, 1988).

In addition to the school's role, the family plays an important part in the child's exercise program. A wise strategy is for the family to take up activities involving vigorous physical exercise that parents and children can enjoy together. Running, swimming, cycling, and hiking are especially recommended. It is important that in encouraging children to exercise more, parents do not push them beyond their physical limits or expose them to competitive pressures that remove the enjoyment from sports and exercise. For example, long-distance running may be too strenuous for young children and could result in bone injuries.

Type-A Behavior

The role of exercise in preventing cardiovascular disease has become a prominent concern, along with the roles of obesity and **type-A behavioral pattern**—a cluster of characteristics that includes being excessively competitive, an accelerated pace of ordinary activities, impatience, doing several things at the same time, and an inability to hide that time is a struggle in life (Friedman & Rosenman, 1974). Most of the research on type-A behavior has been conducted with adults. Currently, the type-A cluster is controversial, with some researchers arguing that only specific components of the cluster, especially hostility, are linked with coronary disease (Dimsdale, 1988; Williams, Barefoot, & Haney, 1986), while others still believe the type-A cluster as a whole is related to cardiovascular disease (Fischman, 1987).

Recent research with children does reveal that children with a type-A behavioral pattern have more illnesses, cardiovascular symptoms, muscle tension, and sleep disturbances (Eagleston & others, in press; Murray & others, 1988; Thoresen & others, 1985). The type-A children also were more likely than other children to have type-A parents. When these type-A parents were observed interacting with their type-A children they often criticized their children's failures and compared them to other children when evaluating their performances. Such stressful family experiences may set the tone for ineffective ways of coping with stress and a tendency to develop cardiovascular problems.

Abnormal Behavior, Stress, and Health

Heart Smart

he school is the focus of the Heart Smart intervention. Since 95 percent of children ages five to eighteen are in school, schools are an efficient context in which to educate children about health. Intervention includes training school personnel, curriculum, physical education, a school lunch program, and parent education. Special attention is given to teachers who serve as role models. Teachers who value the role of health in life and who engage in health-enhancing behaviors present children with positive role models for health. Teacher in-service education is conducted by an interdisciplinary team of specialists including physicians, psychologists, nutritionists, physical educators, and exercise physiologists. The school's staff is introduced to heart health education, the nature of cardiovascular disease, and risk factors for heart disease. Coping behavior, exercise behavior, and eating behavior are discussed with the staff. And a heart smart curricula is explained. For example, the heart smart curricula for grade 5 includes the content areas of cardiovascular health (e.g., risk factors associated with heart disease), behavior skills (e.g., self-assessment and monitoring), eating behavior (e.g., the effects of food on health), and exercise behavior (e.g., the effects of exercise on the heart).

The physical education component of heart smart involves two to four class periods each week to incorporate a "Superkids-Superfit" exercise program. The physical education instructor teaches skills required by the school system plus aerobic activities aimed at cardiovascular conditioning including jogging, race walking, interval workouts, rope skipping, circuit training, aerobic dance, and games. Classes begin and end with five minutes of walking and stretching.

The school lunch program serves as an intervention site where sodium, fat, and sugar levels are decreased. Children are given reasons why they should choose to eat healthy foods such as a tuna sandwich rather than unhealthy foods such as a hot dog with chili. The school lunch program includes a salad bar where children can serve themselves. The amount and type of snack foods sold on school premises also is monitored.

The Heart Smart program also uses family modeling and support to augment the school's intervention efforts. A monthly newsletter, Heart Smart Gazette, is sent home with children in grades K–6. The newsletter focuses on cardiovascular health topics that coincide with curriculum content for that month, with suggestions for "heart healthy" family activities. The newsletter also informs parents of community activities relevant to cardiovascular education.

High-risk children—those with elevated blood pressure, cholesterol, and weight—are identified as part of the Heart Smart intervention. A multidisciplinary team of physicians, nutritionists, nurses, and behavioral counselors work with the high-risk children and their parents through group-oriented activities and individual-based family counseling. High-risk children and their parents receive diet, exercise, and relaxation prescriptions in an intensive twelve-session program, followed by long-term monthly interventions.

Extensive evaluation is a part of this ongoing program. Short-term and long-term changes in children's knowledge about cardiovascular disease and changes in their behavior are being assessed.

One large-scale investigation, the Bogalusa Heart Study, involves an ongoing evaluation of 8,000 children in Bogalusa, Louisiana (Berenson & others, 1980; Downey & others, 1987; Rosenbaum & others, 1987). Observations show the precursors of heart disease begin at a young age with many children already possessing one or more clinical risk factors—hypertension, obesity, and adverse lipoprotein changes. Based on the Bogalusa Heart Study, a cardiovascular health intervention model for elementary school children has been developed. The model is called Heart Smart and an overview of its components is described in Perspective on Child Development 18.3.

An exciting prospect of health psychology is that psychological principles can be used to prevent illness and promote health in children or to reduce illness and restore health even when children have learned bad health habits. At this point we have discussed many different aspects of children's nutrition, health, illness, and exercise. A summary of the main points of this discussion is presented in Concept Table 18.2.

Concept	Processes/Related Ideas	Characteristics/Description
Holistic orientation	Its nature	An approach that recognizes the complex, multidimensional nature of children's illness and health. Special emphasis is given to psychological factors and life-styles.
Nutrition	Eating behavior in infancy	There are many healthy advantages to breast-feeding, but a large percentage of American mothers choose to bottle-feed their infants, mainly for convenience. Debate also focuses on scheduled versus demand feeding; more recently parents have been likely to adopt a demand feeding schedule. Parents need to be aware that infants need high-calorie, high-energy food for a well-balanced diet.
	Children's nutrition	As children move through the early and middle childhood years their total energy needs increase as their bodies become larger. However, a special concern in our culture is the amount of fat and sugar in children's diets—the consensus is that there is too much.
	Malnutrition	In the United States most children receive adequate protein, but in some locations such as the Bayambang area of the Philippines, children's protein intake is inadequate. Malnutrition not only is related to impaired physical development but also to impoverished socioemotional behavior.
	Eating disorders in adolescence	Obesity, anorexia nervosa, and bulimia are prevalent among adolescents, especially adolescent females. Physiological and psychological explanations of these disorders have been proposed.
Health, illness, and exercise	Health and illness	Children's health-care needs involve their motor, cognitive, and social development. Caregivers play an important role in children's health care. Adolescents seem to have an especially difficult time applying health knowledge to their personal circumstances.
	Exercise and cardiovascular disease	Every indication suggests that our nation's children are not getting enough exercise. Exercise's role in preventing cardiovascular disease has become a prominent concern, along with the roles of obesity and type-A behavioral pattern.

Summary

I. The Nature of Stress

Selye described stress as the wear and tear on the body. The longer stress persists the more damage it causes to the child's body. Selye also argued that all stress is not bad for children. The positive features of stress are referred to as eustress. The range of stress is from ordinary to severe. In many instances more than one stress occurs. Two or more stresses may have a multiplier effect on children's disturbances. Some approaches to stress focus on major life events. Recently, it has been argued that life's daily hassles and uplifts also are important to consider when evaluating the nature of children's stress.

II. Coping with Stress

Avoiding stress is viewed as a wiser short-term than long-term strategy. Avoiding stress can be accomplished by denial, regression, withdrawal, and impulsive acting out. Accepting and facing stress include altruism, humor, suppression, anticipation, and sublimation. Adults can help children deal with stress by removing at least one stressor, teaching new coping strategies, and showing transfer to other circumstances.

III. Holistic Health Orientation

This approach recognizes the complex, multidimensional nature of children's illness and health. Special emphasis is given to psychological factors and life-styles.

IV. Nutrition

There are many health advantages to breast-feeding, but a large percentage of American mothers choose to bottle-feed their infants, mainly for convenience. Debate also focuses on scheduled versus demand feeding; more recently parents have been likely to adopt a demand feeding schedule. Parents need to be aware that infants require high-calorie, high-energy food for a well-balanced diet. As children move through the early and middle childhood years their total energy needs increase as their bodies become larger. However, a special concern in our culture is the amount of fat and sugar in children's diets—the consensus is that there is too much. In the United States, most children receive adequate protein, but in some locations such as the Bayambang area of the Philippines, children's protein intake is inadequate. Malnutrition not only is related to impaired physical development but also to impoverished socioemotional behavior. Obesity, anorexia nervosa, and bulimia are prevalent among adolescents, especially among adolescent females. Physiological and psychological explanations of these disorders have been proposed.

V. Health, Illness, and Exercise

Children's health-care needs involve their motor, cognitive, and social development. Caregivers play an important role in children's health care. Adolescents seem to have an especially difficult time applying health knowledge to their personal circumstances. Every indication suggests that our nation's children are not getting enough exercise. Exercise's role in preventing cardiovascular disease has become a prominent concern, along with the roles of obesity and type-A behavioral pattern.

Key Terms

holistic orientation   482
eustress   483
denial   485
regression   485
withdrawal   486
impulsive acting out   486
altruism   486
suppression   486
anticipation   486
sublimation   486
basal metabolism rate (BMR)   489
set point   491
anorexia nervosa   493
bulimia   493
type-A behavioral pattern   496

Suggested Readings

Brenner, A. (1984). *Helping children cope with stress.* Lexington, MA: D. C. Heath.

An excellent, insightful portrayal of children's stress and effective ways of coping with the stress. Includes many case examples.

Journal of School Health

This journal includes a number of articles about children's nutrition, health, illness, and exercise. Leaf through the issues of the last several years to get a feel for the type of interventions being used in school settings to improve children's health.

Melamed, B. G., Matthews, K., Routh, D. K., Stabler, B., & Schniederman, N. (Eds.). (1988). *Child health psychology.* Hillsdale, NJ: Erlbaum.

Includes chapters by a number of experts on child health psychology. Ideas about prevention and life-style, personality and emotional behavior, developmental aspects of illness, and chronic health problems in children are covered.

Williams, S. R., & Worthington, B. S. (1988). *Nutrition through the life cycle.* St. Louis, MO: Times Mirror/ Mosby.

This book brings together information about nutrition and eating behavior at different periods in the human life cycle. Separate chapters focus on nutrition in infancy, in childhood, and in adolescence.

The Odyssey of Childhood

I am the heir of all the ages,
In the foremost files of time.

Alfred Lord Tennyson

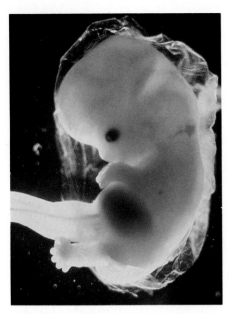

What web is this of will be, is, and was?
—Jorge Luis Borges

As the twenty-first century approaches, the well-being of children is one of America's foremost concerns. We all cherish our children's futures. Today's world is both the best of times and the worst of times for children, a world that possesses powers and perspectives inconceivable fifty years ago: computers, longer life expectancies, the entire planet accessible through television, satellites, air travel. So much knowledge, though, can be chaotic, and even dangerous. School curricula have been adapted to teach new topics: AIDS, suicide, drug and alcohol abuse, incest. The hazards of the adult world—its sometimes fatal temptations—descend upon children so early that their ideals may be demolished. It is not that children have changed so much. What has changed is the world in which they live and develop.

As developmentalists observe, evaluate, and probe children's lives, they seek not only the answers to science's questions but also the answers that will enrich children's lives. The problems of today's children are not with the children themselves. What children need is access to a range of legitimate opportunities and to long-term support from adults who deeply care about them.

The history of interest in children is long and varied, but the modern era of studying children spans only little more than a century, an era in which the investigation of children's development has matured into a sophisticated science. Development is a pattern of movement or change that occurs throughout life's human cycle. The rhythm and meaning of children's development is determined by an interplay of biological, cognitive, and social processes. Some developmentalists subscribe to the view that development is continuous (gradual, cumulative). Others subscribe to the view that development is discontinuous (abrupt, sequence of stages). Most developmentalists, though, view the pattern weaved by children's development as both continuous and discontinuous. The odyssey of children's lives involves beginnings, infancy, early childhood, middle and late childhood, and adolescence.

Beginnings

The beginning of children's development raises questions of whence and whither, when and how; of how from so simple a beginning endless forms develop and grow and mature; of heredity's and environment's contributions; of what this organism is, was, and will be.

No matter what the species, there must be some mechanism for transmitting characteristics from one generation to the next. Each of us carries a genetic code we inherited from our parents. Physically, this code is located in every cell of our bodies. Genetic transmission is complex. Most of our characteristics are due to multiple gene combinations. All aspects of our development are influenced by heredity, from the color of our eyes to our temperament to our intelligence. But genes do not operate alone. The path of children's development always involves an environment. Remember the statement: No genes, no organism; no environment, no organism.

Children begin life as a single cell weighing about one twenty-millionth of an ounce. Their prenatal development is divided into three periods—germinal (from conception to about fourteen days), embryonic (from two weeks to eight weeks after conception), and fetal (from two months after conception until the infant is born). Most offspring develop through the prenatal period without complications, but many teratogens—among them maternal diseases and drugs—can cause birth defects.

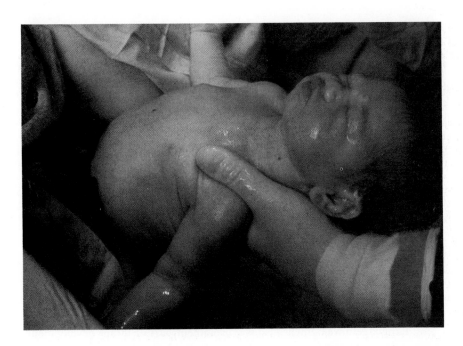

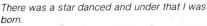

A controversy exists over how childbirth should proceed. Standard childbirth has been criticized and the Leboyer and Lamaze methods have been developed as alternatives. Special concerns involve preterm and low-birth-weight infants. As intensive-care technology has improved, these infants have benefited enormously, although infants born with a developmental problem and those from low-income families have a poorer developmental future. For many years the Apgar Scale has been used to assess the newborn's health. A more recently developed test—the Brazelton Neonatal Behavioral Assessment Scale—is used for long-term neurological assessment. If the newborn is sluggish, Brazelton training is recommended. There is no evidence that bonding is required for optimal child development, although it may stimulate interaction for some mother-infant pairs.

Infancy

As newborns, children are not empty-headed organisms. They have some basic reflexes, among them crying, coughing, kicking, and sucking. They sleep a lot and occasionally smile, although the meaning of their first smiles is not entirely clear. They eat and they grow. As infants, they crawl and then they walk. Sometimes they conform to others, sometimes others conform to them. As Piaget observed, their development is a continuous creation of increasingly complex forms.

Infant development follows cephalocaudal (from the top down) and proximodistal (from the center out) patterns. Both gross and fine motor skills undergo extensive change in the first two years of life. The infant's brain grows dramatically as it did in prenatal development. The newborn's perception is more advanced than previously thought. Newborns can see, hear, smell, touch, taste, and sense pain. Infants as young as four months of age have bimodal perception, the ability to coordinate and integrate perceptual information across two modalities such as hearing and seeing.

Development is a continuous creation of increasingly complex forms.

—Jean Piaget

Infant's cognitions also develop dramatically. Piaget described the stage of sensorimotor development as spanning the first two years of life. It involves a progression in the infant's ability to organize and coordinate sensations with physical movements. Object permanence is a special accomplishment in the infant's cognitive development because it enables the infant to understand that objects and events continue to exist even though the infant no longer is in contact with them. Newborn infants can habituate although this becomes more acute over the first three months of infancy. In the first six months, infants learn adaptive skills but conscious memory does not develop until later in the first year. Infants only one day old imitate facial expressions of emotion by adults, although it is open to interpretation whether this is learned or innate.

Developmental scales for infants grew out of the tradition of IQ testing with older children. The Bayley scales are the most widely used developmental scales, consisting of a motor scale, a mental scale, and an infant behavior profile. Infant intelligence tests have been better at assessing the influence of environmental events than at predicting later intelligence. However, recently it has been found that habituation is related to IQ in childhood, suggesting greater continuity in intelligence between infancy and childhood than was previously believed.

Language development also is a prominent part of infant development. Language is a sequence of words that involves infinite generativity, displacement, and rule systems. The rule systems include phonology, morphology, syntax, semantics, and pragmatics. Evidence for biology's role in language is strong. Chompsky argued that children are biologically prewired to learn language. McNeil said that children have a language acquisition device that includes wiring for deep and surface structures. Evolution shaped humans into linguistic creatures. Reinforcement and imitation probably play a facilitative rather than a necessary role in language development. Most children are bathed in language from early in their development. Among the ways adults teach language to infants are the baby-talk register, recasting, echoing, expanding, and labeling. Vocalization begins with babbling at about three to six months of age. A baby's earliest communications are pragmatic. One-word utterances occur at about ten to thirteen months; the holophrase hypothesis has been applied to this. By eighteen to twenty-four months, most infants use two-word utterances. Language at this point is called telegraphic. Roger Brown developed the concept of mean length of utterance (MLU). Five stages have been identified, providing a valuable indicator of language maturity.

Infants not only live in physical and cognitive worlds but also in social worlds. The transition to parenthood produces a disequilibrium, which requires considerable adaptation. Infants socialize parents just as parents socialize infants—the process of reciprocal socialization. Parent-infant relationships are mutually regulated by the parent and the infant. In infancy, much of the relationship is driven by the parent, but as the infant gains self-control, the relationship is initiated more on an equal basis.

Many developmentalists believe the attachment of the infant to a caregiver is a key factor in promoting optimal development. In infancy, attachment is described as a bond between the caregiver and the infant. Feeding is not the critical factor in attachment, although contact comfort, familiarity, and trust are important. John Bowlby's ethological theory stresses that the infant and mother instinctively trigger attachment. Attachment to the caregiver intensifies at about six to seven months. Mary Ainsworth believes that securely attached babies have sensitive and responsive caregivers. In some investigations, secure attachment is related to social competence later in childhood.

Some developmentalists, though, believe too much emphasis is placed on the role of attachment. They believe genetics and temperament on the one hand, and the diversity of social agents and contexts on the other, deserve more credit.

It also is important to consider the father's role in the infant's development. Over time, the father's role has evolved from moral teacher to breadwinner to gender role model to active, nurturant caregiver. Fathers have increased their interaction with children, but they still lag far behind mothers, even when the mother is employed. Fathers can act sensitively to the infant's signals, but in many instances they do not seem motivated to do so. The mother's role in the infant's development is primarily caregiving, the father's primarily playful interaction. Infants usually prefer their mothers under stressful circumstances.

Day care has become a basic need of the American family. Of special importance is the quality of day care. Researchers have found that day care by itself does not produce adverse developmental outcomes, but that poor quality day care, especially in the first year of life, may place a child at developmental risk. Quality day care can be achieved and has no adverse effects on children's development.

Another important aspect of infant's lives involves their emotions, which are adaptive and promote survival, serve as a form of communication, and provide regulation. Interest and disgust are present in the newborn, a social smile, anger, surprise, sadness, fear, and shame develop in the first year, and guilt and contempt develop in the second year.

Erik Erikson argues that the first year of life is characterized by the stage of trust versus mistrust. His ideas about trust have much in common with Mary Ainsworth's ideas about secure attachment. At some point in the second half of the second year of life, the infant develops a sense of self. Independence also becomes a central theme in the second year of life. Margaret Mahler believes that infants separate themselves from their mothers and then develop individuation. Erikson thinks the second year of life is characterized by the stage of autonomy versus shame and doubt.

Early Childhood

In early childhood, children skip and play and run all the sun long, never in their lives so busy, busy becoming something they have not quite grasped yet. Their thoughts and images and drawings take wings. Their small world widens as they discover new refuges and new people. They become more aware of being boys and being girls.

Growth is slower in early childhood than in infancy. Considerable progress, though, is made in gross motor skills, especially in the arms and legs. The average preschool child requires 1,400 to 1,800 calories per day. Poor nutrition influences not only physical development but behavior as well. More attention needs to be given to children's nutrition and exercise because by the age of six many already are in poor physical shape.

For Piaget, the ages of approximately two to seven are when preoperational thought develops—the beginning of the ability to reconstruct at the level of thought what has been established in behavior and a transition from primitive to more sophisticated use of symbols. The child does not yet think in an operational way. Operations are internalized sets of actions that allow the child to do mentally what was done before physically. Between four and seven years of age children are so sure about their knowledge yet they are so

Children are on a different plane, they belong to a generation and a way of feeling properly their own.

—George Santayana

unaware of how they know what they know. Preoperational children also ask a barrage of questions and begin to show interest in reasoning and finding out why things are the way they are.

Children's abilities to process information also advance during early childhood. For example, children's attention dramatically improves during this time frame. Significant improvement in short-term memory also takes place with advances being influenced by increased rehearsal and speed of processing. By analyzing task components and making tasks more simple and relevant, developmentalists have shown that some cognitive abilities appear earlier than once was thought. Language development continues to advance with improvements in phonology, morphology, syntax, semantics, and pragmatics. Early childhood education also becomes a concern of parents, the predominant approach being child-centered. Children who attend preschool are usually more competent than those who do not, although they show more negative behaviors too. Special concern has been given to the children of poverty by developing compensatory education programs such as Project Head Start and Project Follow-Through, both of which have shown positive impacts on children's lives.

As with infancy, life in early childhood involves a social world. By early childhood, parenting styles have become well established. Four major categories of parenting styles are authoritarian, authoritative, permissive indulgent, and permissive indifferent. Authoritative parenting is associated with children's social competence more than the other styles. Parents need to adapt their interaction strategies as children grow older, using less physical manipulation and more reasoning in the process. Life for many children also involves siblings, who can be strong socializing influences on children. The relationship of the firstborn child and parents seems to be especially close and demanding, which may account for the greater achievement and anxiety of firstborn children.

Children live in a changing world and a changing set of family circumstances with more children living in divorced and working mother families than at any time in history. A mother's working fulltime outside the home can have positive or negative effects on children. There are no indications of long-term negative effects overall. Family conflict seems to outweigh family structure in its impact on children. Conflict is the greatest, however, in the first year after divorce. A continuing ongoing positive relationship with the ex-spouse is important for children's adjustment, support systems enhance children's adaptation to divorce, and boys fare better in father-custody families, girls in mother-custody families.

Peers also are powerful social agents. They provide a source of information outside the family. The frequency of peer interaction, both positive and negative, increases during the preschool years. Young children also spend long hours in play, which promotes affiliation with peers, releases tension, advances cognitive development, stimulates exploration, and provides a safe haven in which to engage in potentially dangerous activities. The types of play engaged in by children are unoccupied, solitary, onlooker, parallel, associative and cooperative, as well as pretend play.

Television also is a powerful influence in children's lives, providing both entertainment and information. Strange fragments of violence and sex come flashing out of the television set and lodge in children's minds. The messages are powerful and contradictory. Oprah Winfrey and Phil Donahue conduct seminars on lesbian nuns, exotic drugs, transsexual surgery, and serial murders. Television pours a bizarre version of reality into children's imaginations. Television may train children to become passive learners; it is deceiving, and it often takes children away from study and reading. The huge amounts of television children watch is associated with both their aggressive and their altruistic behavior.

Early childhood is a time when Erikson believes the stage of initiative versus guilt unfolds and when children begin to understand that their selves have both inner and outer dimensions. Early childhood also is a time when children become more aware of their gender roles, the social expectations of how they should act as males or as females. Gender roles are influenced by biological, cognitive, and social factors. And early childhood also is a time when children begin to develop a stronger sense of right and wrong. Piaget believed that children from four to seven years of age are in the stage of heteronomous morality, then from about the age of ten move into the stage of autonomous morality. Developmentalists study how children think, feel, and behave regarding standards of right and wrong. Empathy plays a key role in young children's development of altruism. By developing young children's capacity for empathy and altruism, we can become a nation of people who help rather than hurt.

Middle and Late Childhood

Such is the wisdom of the human life cycle that at no time are children more ready to learn than at the end of early childhood's expansive imagination. During middle and late childhood, children develop a sense of wanting to make things, and not just make them, but make them perfectly, according to Erikson. They thirst to know and to understand. They are remarkable for their intelligence and their curiosity. Parents continue to be important influences but growth is also shaped by successive choirs of friends. At this point in their lives, children don't think much about the future, or about the past, but enjoy the present time.

Physical growth is slow and consistent in middle and late childhood—the calm before the rapid growth spurt of adolescence. In Piaget's view, between approximately the ages of seven and eleven children's thought is concrete operational in nature, meaning that thoughts are now made up of operations, mental actions that are reversible. Concrete operational children have conservation and classification skills but they still need clearly available perceptual supports to reason. Piaget was a genius at observing children. He showed us some important changes and mapped out some general cognitive changes. However, some critics believe his stages are not as unitary as he proposed and that children's cognitive development does not always follow the timetable he envisioned. A child's long-term memory also improves during middle and late childhood. Control processes or strategies such as rehearsal, organization, and imagery are among the processes responsible for memory improvement. A child's knowledge also influences memory. A special kind of knowledge—metamemory—concerns control processes. Schemata and scripts become prominent in the elementary school child's cognitive world.

A child's world also involves intelligence and achievement. Extensive effort has been expended to assess individual differences in children's intelligence. The Binet and Wechsler scales are the most widely used individual tests of children's intelligence. Psychologists debate whether intelligence is a general ability or a number of specific abilities. Early tests favored white, middle-class, urban children. Current tests try to reduce this bias. The mechanisms of intelligence and its development are both those of changing information-processing abilities and changing expertise and knowledge. Sternberg's triarchic

Life's aspirations come in the guise of children.

—Rabindranath Tagore, *Fireflies, 1928*

model of intelligence emphasizes both information processing and knowledge. Despite limitations, when used by a judicious examiner, intelligence tests can be valuable tools for determining individual differences in children. Developmentalists also are interested in the extremes of intelligence—mental retardation and giftedness, as well as creativity. Early interest in children's achievement, stimulated by David McClelland's ideas, focused on the need for achievement. Contemporary ideas include an emphasis on internal and external dimensions, as well as a concern about achievement motivation in ethnic minority children and females.

What are the social worlds of children like in middle and late childhood? Parents spend less time with children than earlier in their development, including less time in caregiving, instruction, reading, talking, and playing. Nonetheless, parents still are powerful and important socializing agents in this period. New parent-child issues emerge and discipline changes. Control is more coregulatory, children and parents label each other more, and parents mature just as children do. During middle and late childhood, two major changes in many children's lives are becoming latchkey children and moving into a stepfamily.

Children spend considerably more time with peers in middle and late childhood. Listening skills and effective communication, being yourself, being happy, showing enthusiasm and concern for others, and indicating self-confidence but not conceit are predictors of peer popularity. Rejected children are at risk for developmental problems. The risk status of neglected children is less clear. Social information-processing skills and social knowledge are two important dimensions of social cognition in peer relations. Children's friendships serve many functions, ranging from intimacy to ego support. Friends are similar on many dimensions.

Children spend more than 10,000 hours in the classroom as members of a small society in which there are tasks to be accomplished, people to be socialized and socialized by, and rules that limit and define behavior, feelings, and attitudes. A special concern is that early schooling proceeds mainly on the basis of negative feedback to children. A profile of a good teacher's personality traits is difficult to establish, although some traits are clearly superior to others. Aptitude-treatment also is an important consideration. Schools have a stronger middle-class than lower-class orientation. Not only do many lower-class children have problems in schools, so do children from ethnic minorities. Efforts to reduce these biases are being made, among them the cooperative learning orientation of the jigsaw classroom.

In Erikson's view, the middle and late childhood years are when the stage of industry versus inferiority appears. During these years, children's self-conceptions continue to be an important part of their makeup. In this period, their self-concepts are influenced by their increasing abilities to understand how they are perceived by others. In considering children's self-conceptions, it is important to distinguish between their general self-worth and their self-perceptions of social skills, cognitive skills, and physical skills. Developmentalists have increasingly become interested in pinning down the nature of children's social competence. A current theme is that children's social competence involves both internal, self, self-assertive dimensions and external, social, integrative dimensions.

Children's gender role development continues in middle and late childhood. Recent emphasis focuses on the concept of androgyny, the belief that competent individuals possess both masculine and feminine characteristics.

The most widely used criteria for masculinity are self-assertion and instrumental orientation, for femininity integration and expressive orientation. Controversy surrounds whether androgynous children are more competent. The criteria for competence need to be considered in this evaluation. In the 1970s, it was concluded that boys have better math skills, have superior visual-spatial abilities, and are more aggressive, while girls are better at verbal abilities. Today's conclusions suggest that boys are more active and the difference in verbal abilities has virtually vanished. The other differences—math, visual-spatial ability, and aggression—still persist, although continued cultural change may chip away at these differences.

Changes in moral development also characterize middle and late childhood. The most provocative theory of moral development was proposed by Lawrence Kohlberg. He argued that children's moral development follows an age-related sequence of three levels (each with two stages) that vary according to the degree moral development is internalized—preconventional, conventional, and postconventional. Few individuals, even adults, are classified according to the postconventional level. Kohlberg's theory has not gone unchallenged. For one, moral reasons can always be a shelter for immoral behavior. For another, Carol Gilligan believes that Kohlberg vastly underplayed the care perspective's role in moral development. As with social competence and gender role, the highest level of moral development involves a combined individual and social orientation, in Gilligan's view.

Adolescence

In no order of things is adolescence a time of simple life. Adolescents feel like they can last forever. At times they think they know everything and are quite sure about it. In many ways, today's adolescents are privileged, wielding unprecedented economic power, but at the same time they move through a seemingly endless preparation for life. They try on one face after another, seeking to find faces of their own. They want their parents to understand them and hope that their parents give them the privilege of understanding them. They want to fly but discover that they first have to stand and walk and dance. In their most awkward and pimply moments they become acquainted with sex. They play furiously at "adult games" but are confined to a society of their peers. Their generation of young people is the fragile cable by which the best and worst of their parents' generation is transmitted to the present. In the end, there are only two lasting bequests parents can leave youth—one is roots, the other wings.

Growing up has never been easy. In many ways, the developmental tasks of today's adolescents are no different than those of the adolescents in Ozzie and Harriet's world thirty years ago. Adolescence is not a time of rebellion, crisis, pathology, deviance. A far more accurate vision of adolescence is that it is a time of evaluation, a time of decision making, a time of commitment, a time of carving out a place in the world.

Puberty is a rapid change to maturation that does not involve a single event but rather is part of a lengthy developmental process. Menarche is the girl's first menstruation, and this has occurred earlier in recent decades, probably because of improved health and nutrition. As adolescents undergo a growth spurt in early adolescence, they make rapid gains in height. The spurt occurs approximately two years earlier for girls (ten and a half) than boys (twelve and a half). Adolescents are extremely curious about their body images. Young

Youth is the time to go flashing from one end of the world to the other, both in mind and body.

—Robert Louis Stevenson,
Virginia Puerisque, *1881*

adolescents are more preoccupied and dissatisfied with their bodies than late adolescents. Early maturation favors boys at least during adolescence, although late maturing boys may achieve more successful identities. The results for girls are more mixed than for boys. Being on-time or off-time in pubertal development is a complex affair. Adolescents may be at risk when the demands of a particular context and the adolescent's physical and behavioral characteristics are mismatched. As part of their many changes, the sexual interests of adolescents heighten. Surveys indicate that at age sixteen, slightly over 40 percent of males and between 30 to 40 percent of females have had intercourse. In some inner-city areas, the percentages are higher. Adolescents in the United States have an extremely high pregnancy rate.

The changes of adolescents also involve cognitions. Piaget believed that formal operational thought comes into play between eleven and fifteen years of age. Formal operational thought is more abstract, idealistic, and logical than concrete operational thought. Piaget believed that adolescents become capable of using hypothetical deductive reasoning. Language changes that accompany formal operational thought involve an increased understanding of satire and metaphor, improved writing ability, and superior conversational skills. There is more individual variation in formal operational thought than Piaget imagined. Many adolescents do not think in full-fledged formal operational ways. Impressive changes in social cognition also characterize an adolescent's development. Adolescents develop a special type of egocentrism that involves an imaginary audience and a personal fable about being unique and indestructible, they begin to think about personality not unlike the way personality theorists do, and they monitor their social worlds in more sophisticated ways.

Family influences continue to play powerful roles in development during the adolescent years. Many parents have a difficult time handling the adolescent's push for autonomy, even though this push is one of the hallmark's of normal adolescent development. Adolescents do not simply move into a world isolated from parents. Attachment to parents increases the probability that the adolescent will explore a widening social world in healthy ways. Conflict with parents does often increase in early adolescence, but such conflict is usually of the moderate variety. The moderate increase in conflict may serve a positive developmental function of promoting autonomy and identity. Physical, cognitive, and social changes in the adolescent's development influence parent-adolescent relationships. Parental changes—marital dissatisfaction, economic burdens, career reevaluation and time perspective, and health and body concerns—also influence parent-adolescent relationships.

The pressure to conform to peers is strong during adolescence, especially during the eighth to ninth grades. There usually are three to six well-defined cliques in every secondary school. Membership in certain cliques—especially jocks and populars—is associated with increased self-esteem. Independents also have high self-esteem. Children's groups are less formal, less heterogeneous, and less heterosexual than adolescent's groups. Interest in dating expands considerably in adolescence with dating serving as a form of recreation, a source of status, a setting for learning about close relationships, and mate selection.

Schools continue to be important as the path of development moves through adolescence. The function of secondary schools has been wrapped in controversy. Some maintain that the function should be the intellectual development of the adolescent. Others argue that secondary schools should have more comprehensive functions—in addition to intellectual development, they should foster social and emotional development, and they should prepare the adolescent for adult work and existence as a life-long learner. Effective schools for young adolescents take individual differences in development seriously and show a deep concern for what is known about adolescent development. These successful schools emphasize social and emotional development as much as intellectual development. The organization of junior high schools—and more recently middle schools—has been justified on the basis of physical, cognitive, and social changes in adolescents. The earlier onset of puberty has led to the formation of middle schools. The transition to middle or junior high school coincides with a number of individual, familial, and social changes. One special problem involves going from a top-dog position to a bottom position.

According to Erikson, adolescence is characterized by the stage of identity versus identity confusion, focusing on the adolescent's search for self. Contemporary views of identity development emphasize its lengthy, often gradual process as well as its complexity. James Marcia believes adolescents and young adults can be classified in terms of one of four identity statuses—diffusion, foreclosure, moratorium, and achievement. The statuses involve the dimensions of crisis (exploration) and commitment. Identity change may be more prominent in late adolescence than early adolescence. For Erikson, in industrialized countries the development of a vocational identity, especially through exploration of alternative careers, is a key ingredient of identity. Parent-adolescent relationships in the form of both individuation and connectedness enhance the adolescent's identity development.

Generations will depend on the ability of every procreating individual to face his children.

—*Erik Erikson,*
Identity: Youth in Crisis, *1968*

The Transition to Adulthood and the Human Life Cycle

In the words of singer Bob Dylan, "How many roads must a man walk down before you call him a man?" For some of us, finding our place in adult society and committing ourselves to a more stable life take longer than we imagine. Kenneth Kenniston proposed that the transition from adolescence to adulthood be called youth, a period of economic and personal temporariness. This period averages two to eight years but can be longer. Two criteria that have been proposed for adult status are economic independence and independent decision making, although clear-cut criteria are yet to be established.

Both Sigmund Freud and the Russian Count Leo Tolstoy described an adult's main tasks as love and work, sometimes leaving little time for anything else. As adults we continue to ask ourselves who we are and wonder whether it isn't enough to just be. Our dreams continue and our thoughts may be bold, but at some point we become more pragmatic and more realistic. We may marry or we may remain single, as increasing waves of young adults have. We may have children, possibly never knowing the love of our parents until we become parents. Every stable society transmits values from one generation to the next. That is civilization's work. In Erikson's life-cycle perspective, it is not until middle age that we come to understand that future generations depend on the ability of procreating individuals to face their children. Twenty-one centuries ago, the Roman poet and philosopher Lucretius described another of adult life's tasks: Grasping that the generations of living things pass in a short while, and like runners, pass on the torch of life. More than twenty centuries later, the American writer James Agee captured yet another of life's richest meanings: In every child who is born the potentiality of the human race is born again.

Glossary

n achievement Need for achievement; McClelland's description of the general motivation for achievement. The individual's motivation to overcome obstacles, achieve success, and seek out tasks and do them well and as quickly as possible. *155*

ABC method A technique for learning to read that emphasizes memorization of the names of the letters of the alphabet. *241*

A-B error A Piagetian concept in which the infant selects the familiar hiding place (A) of an object instead of the new location (B). *172*

accommodation Occurs when we have to adjust to new information; Piagetian concept. *165*

adaptation The effective interaction of the child and environment. *165*

adolescence The period of transition from childhood to early adulthood, entered at approximately eleven to thirteen years of age and ending at age eighteen to twenty-two. This period is characterized by the onset of physical, cognitive, and social changes. *14*

adolescent egocentrism A cognitive change in adolescence that consists of two main parts—the imaginary audience and the personal fable. *185*

adoption study A strategy of research used to assess the role of heredity in behavior by comparing an adopted child's similarity to his or her biological parents and to his or her adopted parents. *46*

afterbirth The third birth stage; involves the detachment and expelling of the placenta, fetal membranes, and umbilical cord after delivery. *71*

AIDS (Acquired Immune Deficiency Syndrome) A failure of the body's immune system that leaves afflicted individuals vulnerable to a variety of diseases. *125*

altruism An unselfish interest in helping someone. *444*

amniocentesis A procedure by which cells of the fetus are removed from the amniotic sac to test for the presence of certain chromosomal and metabolic disorders. *43*

amnion A sort of bag or envelope that contains clear fluid in which the developing embryo floats. *59*

anal stage Freud's second stage of development, lasting from about one and a half to three years of life; pleasure involves the anus. *283*

androgen Sex hormones that are primarily involved in the development of male sex characteristics. *410*

androgyny A term that describes the existence of masculine and feminine characteristics in both males and females. *407*

animism The belief that inanimate objects have "life-like" qualities and are capable of action. *176*

anorexia nervosa An eating disorder characterized by the relentless pursuit of thinness through starvation. *493*

anoxia Lack of sufficient oxygen to the brain, causing neurological damage or death. *71*

anticipation The ability to foresee and plan for the next stressful episode. *486*

Apgar Scale Method used to assess the health of newborns one and five minutes after birth; evaluates heart rate, respiratory effort, muscle tone, body color, and reflex irritability. *74*

aptitude-treatment interaction (ATI) A field of educational research that determines the best learning conditions for a particular student's abilities and various teaching methods. *365*

artificial intelligence The branch of computer science devoted to creating computers capable of handling complicated tasks that require some "thinking." *195*

assimilation Incorporation of new information into our existing knowledge; Piagetian concept. *165*

associative play Social interaction with little or no organization. In this type of play, children seem to be more interested in associating with each other than in the tasks they are performing. *358*

at risk Term used to describe those infants and children most likely to develop disturbances. *474*

attachment A relationship between two individuals in which they feel strongly about each other and try to ensure the continuation of the relationship. *319*

attention The focusing of perception to produce an increased awareness of a stimulus. The point at which a stimulus is noticed. *149*

attention deficit disorder Sometimes called hyperactivity; children are characterized as being extremely active, impulsive, distractible, and excitable and have great difficulty concentrating on what they are doing. *462*

authoritarian parenting A restrictive, punitive style of parenting. *329*

authoritative parenting A style of parenting that encourages a child to be independent but still places limits and controls on the child's actions; extensive verbal give-and-take occurs between parent and child. This style of parenting is associated with social competence among the children. *329*

authority and social-order maintaining morality Moral judgments are based on understanding the social order, law, justice, and duty. *434*

autonomous morality Level of moral development in which children accept change and recognize that rules are merely convenient, socially agreed upon conventions, subject to change by consensus. *431*

autonomy versus shame and doubt Erikson's second stage of development, corresponding approximately to the second year of life; the bipolar conflict is between developing a sense of autonomy and a sense of doubt. *287*

baby-talk register A characteristic way of talking to young language learners. *233*

basal metabolism rate (BMR) The minimum amount of energy an individual uses in a resting state. *489*

baseline A measure of how often a behavior occurs before attempts are made to change the behavior. *140*

behavior genetics The discipline concerned with the degree and nature of the hereditary basis of behavior. *46*

behavior modification The use of learning principles to reduce or eliminate maladaptive behavior or to teach new responses. *144*

bimodal perception The ability to relate and integrate information about two sensory modalities, such as vision and hearing. *101*

biological processes The influences of evolution, genetics, neurological development, and physical growth on development. *13*

blastocyst The inner layer of blastula that later develops into the embryo. *59*

blastula An early embryo form typically having the form of a hollow, fluid-filled, rounded cavity bounded by a single layer of cells. *58*

bonding The forming of a close personal relationship (as between a mother and child) especially through frequent or constant association. *76*

Brazelton Neonatal Behavioral Assessment Scale A test that detects an infant's neurological integrity; includes an evaluation of the infant's reaction to people along with assessment of twenty reflexes and the infant's reaction to various circumstances. *74*

Brazelton training Involves using the Brazelton scale to show parents how their newborn responds to people. Parents are shown how the neonate can respond positively to people and how such responses can be stimulated. Brazelton training has been shown to improve infants' social skills. *76*

breech position The baby's position in the uterus that would cause the buttock to be the first part to emerge from the vagina. *71*

Broca's area An area in the left hemisphere of the brain that is important for speech production. *229*

bulimia An eating disorder that consistently follows a binge-and-purge pattern. *493*

care perspective Gilligan's view that moral development should include more emphasis on a person's connectedness to others. *437*

case study An in-depth look at an individual that provides information that helps the psychologist understand the individual. *22*

categorical self Refers to the "me" part of the self. *379*

centration The focusing of attention on one characteristic to the exclusion of all others. *178*

cephalocaudal pattern A general pattern of physical growth that suggests that the greatest growth in anatomical differentiation occurs first in the region of the head and later in the lower regions. *90*

child-centered Term used to describe the most popular form of preschool education. *362*

childhood schizophrenia Involves an assortment of bizarre behaviors but not as much disturbance in language and lack of responsiveness as autism. Its onset is from early childhood through adolescence and it includes distorted thinking, disturbed perceptions, and lack of control over ideas, affect, and behavior. Both hereditary and environmental experiences are involved. *458*

chlamydia A sexually transmitted disease that affects as many as 10 percent of all college students. *125*

chorionic villus test A procedure by which a small sample of the placenta is removed during the first trimester, between the ninth and tenth week; diagnosis usually takes two to three weeks. *43*

chromosomes Threadlike structures in each human cell that come in structurally similar pairs (twenty-three pairs in humans). *37*

classical conditioning The process—initially discovered by Pavlov—in which a previously neutral stimulus acquires the ability to elicit a response by being associated with a stimulus that naturally produces a similar response. *137*

cognitive disequilibrium theory When children move from the relatively homogeneous grade school neighborhood to more heterogeneous high school and college environments, they are faced with contradictions between the moral concepts they have accepted and events in the world outside their family and neighborhood. Many adolescents may start to question and sometimes reject their former beliefs, and in the process they may develop their own moral system. *432*

cognitive monitoring The process of taking stock of what one is currently doing, what will be done next, and how effectively the mental activity is unfolding. *203*

cognitive processes Mental activities, such as thought, perception, attention, problem solving, and language, that influence development. *13*

cognitive social learning theory The theory developed by Bandura and Mischel that behavior can be explained through a combination of environmental and cognitive factors. *290*

cohort effects Effects that are due to a subject's time of birth or generation but not actually to his or her age. *26*

community rights versus individual rights Kohlberg's fifth stage. The individual understands that values and laws are relative and that standards may vary from one individual to another. *434*

competence motivation Also called mastery motivation; the motivation to deal effectively with the environment, to be competent and do well what is attempted, to process information efficiently, and to change the world in hope of making it better. *153*

concept A category used to group objects, events, and characteristics on the basis of common properties. *210*

concrete operational stage Piaget's stage that roughly corresponds to the seven to eleven age period; the child can think operationally, reasoning about virtually anything he or she can perceive. The ability to classify objects improves dramatically during this period. *167*

concurrent validity Assesses the relation of a test's scores to a criterion that is presently available. *250*

conditioned response (CR) A response that is produced by a conditioned stimulus; a classical conditioning term. *138*

conditioned stimulus (CS) An initially neutral stimulus that produces a conditioned response after being associated with an unconditioned stimulus; a classical conditioning term. *138*

conditioning The institution of a program to change an individual's undesirable behavior. *141*

connectedness Reflected in mutuality and permeability. Mutuality refers to the adolescent's sensitivity to and respect for others' views. Permeability refers to openness and responsiveness to others' views. *400*

conservation The idea that amount stays the same or is conserved regardless of how shape changes. *178*

constructivist view The belief that what one experiences is a construction based on sensory input plus information retrieved from memory—a kind of representation of the world one builds up in one's mind. *96*

content validity A test's ability to give a broad picture of what is to be measured. *250*

continuity of development A gradual, cumulative change from conception to death. *17*

control group The group in psychological experiments that is exposed to all experimental conditions except the independent variable; the comparison or baseline group. *24*

control processes Learning and memory strategies that draw heavily on information-processing capacities and are under the learner's conscious control. *201*

conventional moral reasoning At this level of morality, internalization is intermediate. The individual abides by certain standards but they are the standards of others (external). *433*

convergent thinking Thinking that goes toward one correct answer, characteristic of the thinking that most intelligence tests elicit. *270*

cooperative play Social interaction in a group with a sense of group identity and organized activity. *359*

coordination of secondary reactions Develops between eight and twelve months of age; the infant readily combines and recombines previously learned schemes in a coordinated way. *170*

coregulation A gradual transfer of control from parent to child; a transition period between the strong parental control of the preschool years and the increased relinquishment of general supervision that occurs during adolescence. *334*

correlation coefficient A measure of the degree of the relationship between two distributions (samples) that ranges from + 1.00 to − 1.00. A positive coefficient means that the distribution increases together; a negative coefficient means that as one increases the other decreases; and a zero coefficient means no correlation exists. *23*

correlational strategy A research strategy in which the investigator observes if and how two factors are associated but does not systematically change characteristics in the child's environment. From research using a correlational strategy one cannot infer causal relationships. *23*

counterconditioning A procedure for weakening the conditioned response by associating the stimuli with a new response incompatible with the CR. *139*

creativity The ability to think about something in a novel way and to come up with unique solutions to problems. *271*

criterion validity A test's ability to predict other measures, or criteria, of the attribute. *250*

critical period A fixed time period very early in development during which certain behaviors optimally emerge. *303*

cross-sectional approach A method used to study a large number of representative persons or variables at a given period in time; frequently employed in the establishment of normative data. *25*

cultural-familial retardation Individuals who make up the majority of the mentally retarded population; they have no evidence of organic damage or brain dysfunction. *269*

culture-fair tests Tests designed to reduce cultural bias in intelligence tests. *265*

deep structure The syntactic relation of the words in a sentence. *225*

defense mechanisms Means by which the ego resolves conflicts between its demands for reality and the id's wishes; defense mechanisms protect the ego and reduce conflict. *281*

denial When children act as if stress does not exist. *485*

Denver Developmental Screening Test Test devised to diagnose developmental delay in children from birth through six years of age. The test includes an evaluation of language and personal-social ability in addition to separate assessments of gross and fine motor skills. *105*

dependent variable The variable that is measured or recorded by the experimenter for changes that are presumed to be under the control of the independent or manipulated variable. *24*

development A pattern of change or movement that begins at conception and continues throughout the entire life span. *13*

developmental scales Intelligence tests created for infants. *258*

discontinuity of development Stresses distinct stages in the life span; emphasizes change. *17*

dishabituation Renewed interest shown by an infant when a new stimulus is presented and distinguished from the old stimulus after habituation has occurred. *145*

displacement The characteristic of language that enables us to communicate information about another place and time. *223*

divergent thinking Thinking that produces many different answers to the same question; Guilford believes this form of thinking is closely related to creativity. *270*

divided attention The problem of handling two or more information "channels" at once. *199*

dizygotic A term that refers to fraternal twins who come from two different eggs and are therefore genetically more different than identical twins. *46*

DNA (deoxyribonucleic acid) A complex molecule running along the length of each chromosome; forms the bases for genetic structure in humans. *37*

dominant-recessive genes In the process of genetic transmission, a dominant gene is one that exerts its full characteristic effect regardless of its gene partner; a recessive gene is one whose code is masked by a dominant gene and is only expressed when paired with another recessive gene. *42*

Down's syndrome A disorder characterized by physical and mental retardation and a rather typical appearance. In the most common cases, individuals have forty-seven instead of forty-six chromosomes, with three rather than two chromosomes in the twenty-first set. *41*

drive An aroused state that occurs because of a physiological need; motivates the organism to reduce the tension involved. *153*

drive-reduction theory The view that as a drive becomes stronger, it creates tension, which organisms are motivated to reduce. *153*

early childhood Also called the preschool years. This period extends from the end of infancy to about five or six years of age, roughly corresponding to the period when the child prepares for formal schooling. *14*

echoing Repeating what the child says to you, especially if it is an incomplete phrase or sentence. *234*

echolalia Speech disorder associated with autistic children in which the children echo what they hear. *458*

ecological view A view that sees complex information being perceived "directly" by picking up the invariants rather than engaging in any complex constructive mental activity. *96*

ectoderm The outer layer of the blastocyst; eventually becomes the child's hair, skin, nails, and nervous system. *59*

ectomorphic Characterized by a thin body shape. *106*

ego The executive branch of personality, according to Freud; the structure of personality that operates according to the demands and constraints of society; it includes our higher cognitive processes, such as reasoning and problem solving. *280*

egocentrism Piaget's term for the preoperational child's inability to distinguish between his or her own and another's perspectives. *176*

embryonic period A period lasting from about two to eight weeks after conception during which the ectoderm, mesoderm, and endoderm develop and primitive human form takes shape. *59*

empathy The ability to understand the feelings of another individual; it is believed to be an important aspect of a child's altruism. *444*

endoderm The inner layer of the blastocyst; develops into the digestive system, lungs, pancreas, and liver. *59*

endomorphic A rounded somewhat "chubby" body build. *106*

epigenetic principle Erikson's concept that anything that grows has a ground plan, out of which the parts arise, each having a special time of ascendency, until all of the parts have arisen to form a functioning whole. *286*

equilibration In Piaget's theory, the mechanism by which the child resolves cognitive conflict and reaches a balance of thought. *166*

erogenous zones Freud's concept that at each stage of development, pleasure is experienced in one part of the body more than others. *282*

estradiol One of the hormones in a complex hormonal system associated with the physical changes of puberty in females. *114*

estrogen Sex hormones that are primarily involved in the development of female sex characteristics. *410*

ethology The view that stresses that behavior is biologically determined. Special emphasis is given to the evolutionary basis of behavior and critical or sensitive periods. *302*

eustress Selye's term for the positive features of stress. *483*

existential self Refers to the "I" part of the self. *379*

exosystem Settings in which the adolescent does not participate although important decisions that affect the adolescent's life are made in these settings. *306*

expanding Restating what the child has said in a linguistically sophisticated form. *234*

experimental group The group of subjects in an experiment that is exposed to the independent variable. *24*

experimental strategy A research strategy in which the experimenter introduces a change into the child's environment and then measures the effects of that change on the child's subsequent behavior. The experimental strategy allows for the inference of causal relationships. *24*

expert Someone who has a great deal of knowledge about a domain of human interest and a great deal of experience performing tasks typical of that domain. *214*

expressive orientation Describes the feminine dimension of gender roles; concerned with facilitating social interaction, interdependence, and relationships. *409*

extinction The removal of the consequences of an individual's on-task behavior, so that the individual is treated as they were in the baseline period. *141*

extrinsic motivation Motivation due to external factors in the environment, especially rewards. *156*

father-absence tradition Children from father-absent and father-present families compared, and differences in their development are attributed to the absence of the father. *341*

fetal alcohol syndrome (FAS) A cluster of characteristics identified in children born to mothers who are heavy drinkers. Children may show abnormal behavior, such as hyperactivity or seizures, and the majority of FAS children score below average on intelligence, with a number of them in the mentally retarded range. *66*

fetal period The period of prenatal development that begins eight weeks after conception and lasts, on the average, for seven months. *60*

fine motor skills Skills involving more fine-grained movements, such as finger dexterity. *91*

first habits and primary circular reactions Develops between one and four months of age; the infant learns to coordinate sensation and types of schemes or structures. *170*

fixation This occurs when an individual becomes stuck at a particular stage of development because his or her needs are under- or overgratified. *282*

fixed-action patterns A series of responses chained together in a stereotyped fashion. *152*

formal operational stage The stage that Piaget believed individuals enter between the ages of eleven and fifteen; thought becomes more abstract, more logical, and more idealistic. *167*

gametes The sex cells; the means by which genes are transmitted from parents to offspring. *37*

gender roles Social expectations of how we should act, think, and feel as males and females. *406*

gender schema A cognitive structure that organizes the world in terms of female and male. *412*

generativity versus stagnation Erikson's seventh stage, corresponding approximately to middle adulthood. Generativity refers to helping the younger generation in developing and leading useful lives. Stagnation refers to the feeling of not having helped the younger generation. *288*

genes Segments of chromosomes; comprised of DNA. *37*

genetic epistemology Refers to how knowledge changes over the course of the child's development. *12*

genital stage Freud's fifth stage of development, lasting from the onset of puberty throughout adulthood; a time of sexual reawakening; the source of pleasure now becomes someone outside the family. *284*

genotype The unique combination of genes that forms the genetic structure of each individual. *45*

germinal period The period from conception until about twelve to fourteen days later. *58*

gifted An individual with well-above-average intelligence and/or a superior talent for something. *269*

good boy or good girl orientation The individual values trust, caring, and loyalty to others as the basis of moral judgments. Children often adopt their parents' moral standards, seeking to be thought of by their parents as a "good boy" or a "good girl." *433*

grammar Closely related to syntax, this refers to the formal description of syntactical rules. *225*

gross motor skills Skills involving large muscle activities, like moving one's arms or walking. *91*

guilt In the psychoanalytic account of guilt, children avoid transgressing to avoid anxiety; by contrast, a child with little guilt has little reason to resist temptation. *443*

habituation Technique used to study an infant's perceptual world. Repeated presentation of the same stimulus causes a drop in the infant's interest. *145*

heritability A mathematical estimate of the degree to which a particular characteristic is genetically determined. *46*

hermaphrodites Individuals with genitals that are intermediate between male and female. *410*

heteronomous morality The first stage of moral development in Piaget's theory. Justice and rules are conceived of as unchangeable properties of the world, removed from the control of people. *431*

heuristics Strategies, or rules of thumb, that suggest a solution to a problem but do not ensure that it will work. *216*

hierarchy of motives Maslow's view of motivation that states that some motives (such as physiological) have to be satisfied before others (such as safety). *154*

holistic orientation An approach that recognizes the multidimensional nature of illness and health; includes an emphasis on life-style, psychological factors, and the nature of the health-care delivery system. *482*

holophrase hypothesis A single word used to imply a complete sentence. *237*

homeostasis The tendency to maintain a balanced equilibrium, or steady state. *153*

hormones The secretions of endocrine glands, which are powerful chemical substances that regulate bodily organs. *114*

hypotheses Assumptions that can be tested to determine their accuracy. *18*

hypothetical deductive reasoning Reasoning that occurs for the first time during adolescence; the person develops hypotheses about ways to solve a problem and then deduces or concludes which is the best path to follow. *184*

id A structure of personality in Freud's theory; the reservoir of psychic energy and instincts that perpetually presses us to satisfy our basic needs. *280*

identity achievement Period in which adolescents have undergone a crisis and have made a commitment. *398*

identity diffusion Period in which adolescents have not yet experienced a crisis or made any commitments. *398*

identity foreclosure Period in which adolescents have made a commitment but have not experienced a crisis. *398*

identity moratorium Period in which adolescents are in the midst of a crisis but their commitments either are absent or are only vaguely defined. *398*

identity versus identity confusion Erikson's fifth stage, which corresponds approximately to adolescence; adolescents seek to know who they are, what they are all about, and where they are headed in life. *287, 395*

imagery Refers to sensations without the presence of an external stimulus. *202*

imaginary audience The belief of adolescents that others are as preoccupied with their behavior as they are. *185*

imitation (modeling) A form of learning in which new behaviors are acquired by observing others performing the behaviors. *134*

immanent justice If a rule is broken punishment will be meted out immediately; a Piagetian concept. *432*

implantation The firm attachment of the zygote to the uterine wall, which occurs about ten days after conception. *59*

imprinting Lorenz's term for the rapid, innate learning within a critical period of time that involves attachment to the first moving object seen. *302*

impulsive acting out Occurs when children act impulsively and sometimes flamboyantly to avoid thinking either of the past or the consequences of their current actions. *486*

independent variable The factor in an experiment that is manipulated or controlled by the experimenter to determine its impact on the subject's behavior. *24*

individual conscience In rare instances, individuals have developed moral standards based on universal human rights. When faced with a conflict between a law and conscience, the individual will always follow his conscience, even if the decision might entail personal risk. Kohlberg's sixth stage. *434*

individual differences The consistent, stable ways we are different from each other. *249*

individuation Comprised of two components—separateness and self-assertion. Separateness is seen in the expressions of how distinctive the self is from others. Self-assertion is involved in the adolescent's expression of her personal point of view and in taking responsibility for communicating this clearly. *400*

industry versus inferiority Erikson's fourth stage, corresponding approximately to the elementary school years; children develop either a sense of industry and work or a feeling of inferiority. *287*

infancy This period begins at birth and extends through the eighteenth to twenty-fourth month; a time of extensive dependency on adults and development of abilities such as thought and language. *14*

infantile autism A very severe developmental disturbance that includes deficiencies in social relationships, abnormalities in communication, and restricted, repetitive, and stereotyped patterns of behavior. *457*

infinite generativity An individual's ability to generate an infinite number of meaningful sentences from a finite set of words and rules. *223*

information-processing approach Theory of cognition that is concerned with the processing of information; involves such processes as attention, perception, memory, thinking, and problem solving. *193*

initiative versus guilt Erikson's third stage, corresponding approximately to early childhood; children develop either a sense of initiative or a sense of guilt in this period. *287*

innate goodness Eighteenth-century belief that children are basically and inherently good and should be permitted to grow naturally with little parental monitoring or constraint. *9*

instrumental orientation Describes the masculine dimension of gender roles. It is concerned with the attainment of goals and an emphasis on the individual's accomplishments. *409*

integration The term used to describe the feminine dimension of gender roles. It describes femininity and includes such components as sympathy, affection, and understanding. *409*

integrity versus despair Erikson's final stage of development, corresponding approximately to late adulthood; involves looking back and evaluating what we have accomplished in our lives. *288*

intelligence Verbal ability, problem-solving skills, and the ability to learn from and adapt to the experiences of everyday life. *251*

intelligence quotient (IQ) A term devised in 1912 by William Stern. IQ consists of a child's mental age divided by chronological age multiplied by 100. *252*

internalization of schemes In Piaget's theory, this develops between eighteen and twenty-four months; the infant's mental functioning shifts from a purely sensorimotor plane to a symbolic plane and the infant develops the ability to use primitive symbols. *171*

interviews A method of study in which the researcher asks questions of a person and records that person's responses. *21*

intimacy in friendship Intimate self-disclosure and the sharing of private thoughts; private and personal knowledge. *354*

intimacy versus isolation Erikson's sixth stage, corresponding approximately to early adulthood; the individual either develops a sense of intimacy or a sense of isolation. *288*

intrinsic motivation An underlying need for competence and self-determination; internal motivation. *156*

intuitive thought substage In Piaget's theory, stretches from approximately four to seven years of age; the child begins to reason primitively and wants to know the answers to all sorts of questions. *177*

in vitro fertilization A procedure in which the mother's ovum is removed surgically and fertilized in a laboratory medium with live sperm cells obtained from the father or male donor. Then the fertilized egg is stored in a laboratory solution that substitutes for the uterine environment and is finally implanted in the mother's uterus. *40*

jigsaw classroom Aronson's technique emphasizing cooperation to reduce ethnic hatred and to improve interpersonal relations and learning in racially mixed classrooms. *355*

justice perspective A moral development perspective that emphasizes the rights of the individual. Gilligan said that Kohlberg's theory is in error because it places too much emphasis on this approach. *437*

juvenile delinquent An adolescent who breaks the law or engages in conduct that is considered illegal. Heredity, identity problems, community influences, and family experiences have been proposed as causes. *467*

keyword method A powerful imagery strategy that has been used to teach children how to rapidly master new information. *202*

Klinefelter's syndrome Males have an extra X chromosome making them XXY instead of XYY. *42*

labeling Identifying the names of objects. *234*

laboratory A controlled setting in which many of the complex factors of the "real world" are removed. *20*

Lamaze method A form of prepared or natural childbirth that allows the pregnant mother to cope with the pain of childbirth in an active way to avoid or reduce medication. *69*

language A set of sequences of words that convey information. *224*

language acquisition device (LAD) The natural ability to detect certain categories of language (phonological, syntactic, and semantic); emphasizes the biological basis of language. *227*

latency stage Freud's fourth stage of development, corresponding approximately to the elementary school years; the child represses sexual urges and focuses on intellectual and social skills. *284*

learned helplessness Seligman's concept describing individuals who have been exposed to prolonged pain or stress, over which they have no control, and who thus learn to be helpless. The concept has been applied to depression. *465*

learning A relatively permanent change in behavior that occurs through some form of experience. *135*

learning disabilities Within the global concept of learning disabilities fall problems in listening, thinking, memory, reading, writing, spelling, and math. Children with learning disabilities are of normal intelligence or above, they have difficulties in several academic areas but usually do not show deficits in others, and they are not suffering from some other condition or disorder that could explain their learning problems. *462*

Leboyer method A birth procedure developed to make the birth experience less stressful for the infant; "birth without violence." *69*

longitudinal approach A method of study in which the same subject or group of subjects is repeatedly tested over a significant period of time. *26*

long-term memory The retention of information for an indefinite period of time. *200*

low-birth-weight infants Infants born after a regular gestation period of thirty-eight to forty-two weeks, but who weigh less than five and one-half pounds. *72*

macrosystem The attitudes and ideologies of the culture. *306*

maturation The orderly sequence of changes dictated by the genetic blueprint we each have. *16*

medical model Also called the disease model; the view that abnormal behavior is a disease or illness precipitated by internal body causes. *455*

meiosis The process by which gametes reproduce, which allows for the mixing of genetic material. *37*

memory The retention of information over time. *199*

menarche The first menstruation in pubertal females. *112*

mental age (MA) An individual's level of mental development relative to others. *252*

mental retardation Refers to an individual who has a low IQ, usually below seventy on a traditional intelligence test, and who has difficulty adapting to everyday life. *268*

mesoderm The middle layer of cells in the embryo; becomes the circulatory system, bones, muscle, excretory system, and reproductive system. *59*

mesomorphic An athletic, muscular body build. *106*

mesosystem Linkages between microsystems or connectiveness between contexts; for example, relation of family experiences to school experiences. *306*

metaphor An implied comparison between two ideas that is conveyed by the abstract meaning contained in the words used. *185*

microsystem Contexts in which the adolescent has face-to-face interactions with others who are influential in his or her life. *306*

middle and late childhood This period extends from about six to eleven years of age and is sometimes called the elementary school years; a time when a sense of industry is developed. *14*

monozygotic A term that refers to identical twins, meaning that they come from the same egg. *46*

moral competence The ability to produce moral behaviors. *443*

moral development The acquisition of rules and conventions about what people should do in their interactions with others. *431*

moral performance Those behaviors in specific moral situations; children's moral performance is determined by their motivation and the rewards and incentives to act in a specific moral way. *443*

Moro reflex An infantile startle response that is common to all neonates but disappears by about three to four months of age. When startled, the neonate arches its back and throws its head back, flinging out its arms and legs. The neonate then rapidly closes its arms and legs to the center of the body. *83*

morpheme The string of sounds. *224*

morphology The rules for combining morphemes. *224*

motherese A characteristic way of talking to young language learners. It includes shorter sentence use, exaggerated intonation contours, long pauses between sentences, and great stress placed on important words. *233*

motivation Focuses on the question of "why" individuals think, feel, and behave the way they do with special consideration of the activation and the direction of their behaviors. *136*

motor reproduction Another process in imitation. A child may attend to a model and code in memory what he or she has seen, but because of limitations in motor development the child may not be able to reproduce the model's action. *150*

multiple-factor theory of intelligence Thurstone's view that we have seven primary mental abilities: verbal comprehension, number ability, word fluency, spatial visualization, associative memory, reasoning, and perceptual speed. *256*

naive hedonism or instrumental orientation Moral thinking is based on rewards and self-interest. Children obey when they want to obey and when it is in their best interest to obey. *433*

naturalistic observation Research conducted in real-world or natural settings; for example, observing a child at home, in school, on the playground, etc. *20*

nature-nurture controversy The "nature" proponents claim that biological and genetic factors are the most important determinants of development; the "nurture" proponents claim that environment and experience are more important. *16*

need Involves a physiological state; a physical deprivation. *153*

neglected children Children who are not necessarily disliked by their peers even though they often do not have many friends. *350*

nonnutritive sucking Sucking behavior by the child that is unrelated to the child's feeding. *85*

normal distribution Also called the normal curve; a symmetrical distribution of scores on a graph, in which a majority of the cases fall in the middle range of possible scores and fewer scores appear toward the ends of this range. *252*

norms Rules that apply to all members of a group. *251, 354*

object permanence Piaget's concept for the infant's ability to understand that objects and events still exist even though the infant is not in direct contact with them. *171*

Oedipus complex A condition that exists when a young child develops an intense desire to replace the parent of the same sex and enjoy the affections of the opposite-sex parent. *283*

onlooker play The child watches other children playing. He or she may talk with them and ask questions but does not enter into their play behavior. *358*

operant conditioning A form of learning in which the consequences of behavior lead to changes in the probability of that behavior's occurrence; the form of learning stressed by Skinner. *140, 290*

operations Mental representations that are reversible; a Piagetian concept. *167*

oral stage Freud's first stage of development, corresponding approximately to the first year of life; pleasure focuses on the mouth. *283*

organic retardation Individuals who are retarded because of a genetic disorder or brain damage. *269*

organization The tendency of isolated behaviors or thoughts to be grouped into a higher-order, more smoothly functioning system. *166, 201*

organogenesis The first two months of prenatal development when the organ systems are formed; may be adversely influenced by environmental events. *59*

original sin Middle Ages, Catholic, and Puritan concept of children, reflecting the philosophical perspective that children are basically evil. *9*

overextensions The tendency of children to misuse words by extending one word's meaning to include a whole set of objects that are not related to or are inappropriate for the word's meaning. *237*

oxytocin A hormone that stimulates uterine contractions and is widely used to speed up delivery. *71*

parallel play The child plays alone but with toys like those that other children are using or in a manner that mimics the behavior of other children who are playing. *358*

partial reinforcement Also called intermittent reinforcement; the organism's responses are only reinforced occasionally, not each time they occur. *142*

peers Refers to children who are about the same age or the same behavioral level. *349*

Perceived Competence Scale for Children Measure of self-concept emphasizing the assessment of the child's sense of competence across different domains rather than viewing perceived competence only as a unitary concept. Developed by Susan Harter. *388*

perception The interpretation of what is sensed. *95*

permissive indifferent parenting A parenting style in which the parent is very uninvolved with the child; associated with social incompetence on the part of the child, especially a lack of self-control. *330*

permissive indulgent parenting A parenting style in which parents are involved with their children but place few demands or limits on them; associated with a lack of self-control on the part of children. *330*

personal fable A story or fable that the adolescent may make up to protect his or her sense of uniqueness and indestructibility. Part of adolescent egocentrism. *186*

phallic stage Freud's third stage, corresponding to the preschool years; pleasure focuses on the genitals. *283*

phenotypes The observed and measurable characteristics of individuals, including physical characteristics, such as height, weight, eye color, and skin pigmentation, and psychological characteristics, such as intelligence, creativity, personality, and social tendencies. *45*

phobias Irrational fears. *138*

phonemes The basic sounds that comprise language. *224*

phonics method A technique for learning to read that stresses the sounds that letters make when in words—such sounds can differ from the names of these letters. *241*

phonology The study of the sound system of language. *224*

pituitary gland A small endocrine gland located at the base of the skull, which is responsible for the secretion of hormones that directly affect the activity of glands elsewhere in the body. *115*

PKU syndrome (phenylketonuria) A disorder, caused by a recessive gene, that leads to the absence of an enzyme necessary to convert phenylalanine into tyrosine. This leads to an accumulation of phenylpyruvic acid, which has a damaging effect on the developing nervous system of a child. *40*

placenta A disk-shaped group of tissues in which small blood vessels from the mother and the offspring intertwine but do not join. *59*

play therapy Therapy that allows the child to work off frustrations through play and is a medium through which the therapist can analyze the child's conflicts and ways of coping with them. *357*

pleasure principle Always seeking pleasure and avoiding pain; the way the id works. *280*

polygenic inheritance A complex form of genetic transmission involving the interaction of many different genes to produce certain traits. *44*

postconventional moral reasoning This is the highest level of moral reasoning in Kohlberg's theory. Morality is completely internalized and not based on others' standards. *434*

pragmatics The ability to engage in appropriate conversation. *226*

precipitate A delivery that takes the baby less than ten minutes to be squeezed through the birth canal. The rapidity of this delivery may disturb the normal flow of blood in the infant, and the pressure on the head may lead to hemorrhaging. *71*

preconventional moral reasoning The level at which the individual shows no internalization of moral values. Morality is truly external to the individual. *433*

predictive validity Assesses the relation of a test's scores to an individual's performance at some point in the future. *250*

prenatal period The period from conception to birth. *14*

preoperational stage In Piaget's theory, the stage at which a child develops stronger symbolic representations of the world but still cannot perform operations; corresponds approximately to the two to seven age period. *167*

pretend play When children engage in pretend play, they transform the physical environment into a symbol. *359*

preterm infant Refers to babies born before thirty-eight weeks in the womb. *72*

primary and secondary reinforcement Inborn, unlearned aspects of behavior involve primary reinforcement; learned aspects of behavior involve secondary reinforcement. Food is a primary reinforcer, and a pat on the back is a secondary reinforcer. *143*

primary circular reaction A scheme based on the infant's attempt to reproduce an interesting or pleasurable event that initially occurred by chance. *170*

problem solving An attempt to find an appropriate way of attaining a goal when the goal is not readily available. *206*

Project Follow-Through A program instituted in 1967 as an adjunct to Project Head Start. Under this program, different kinds of educational programs were devised to see whether specific programs were effective. *362*

Project Head Start Compensatory education program designed to provide the children from low-income families with an opportunity to experience an enriched early environment and to acquire the skills and experiences considered prerequisite for success in school. *362*

proximodistal pattern A general pattern of physical growth and development that suggests that growth starts at the center of the body and moves toward the extremities. *90*

psychometrics The field that involves the assessment of individual differences; involves the use of paper-and-pencil tests. *249*

puberty The point in development at which the individual becomes capable of reproduction; usually linked with the onset of adolescence; a period of rapid change to maturation. *112*

punishment A consequence that decreases the probability a behavior will occur. *140, 290*

punishment and obedience orientation Kohlberg's first stage of moral reasoning. Moral thinking is based on punishments; children obey because parents tell them to obey. *433*

questionnaires Similar to a highly structured interview except that the respondent reads the question and marks his or her answer on paper rather than verbally responding to the interviewer. *21*

reaction formation A defense mechanism by which we express an unacceptable impulse by transforming it into its opposite. *281*

reaction range A range of one's potential phenotypical outcomes, given one's genotype and the influences of environmental conditions. The reaction range limits how much environmental change can modify an individual's behavioral characteristics. *45*

reality principle The way the ego operates, taking into account the constraints and demands of reality. *280*

recasting Phrasing the same or a similar meaning of a sentence in a different way. *234*

reciprocal socialization The view that socialization is a bidirectional process; children socialize parents just as parents socialize children. *317*

reciprocal teaching A method of teaching that involves a small group of students, often working with an adult leader, actively discussing a short text, with the goal of summarizing it, asking questions to promote understanding, offering clarifying statements for difficult or confusing words and ideas, and predicting what will come next. *204*

reflexive smile A smile that does not occur in response to external stimuli. *85*

regression A defense mechanism by which we behave in a way that characterized a previous developmental level. *281, 485*

rehearsal The extended processing of to-be-remembered material after it has been presented; a control process used to facilitate long-term memory. *201*

reinforcement (reward) Stimulation following a response that increases the probability that the same response will occur again in the same situation. *134, 290*

reinforcement or incentive conditions Process in which children attend to what a model says or does, retains the information in memory, and possesses the motor capabilities to perform the action yet fails to repeat the behavior because adequate reinforcement is not present. *150*

rejected children Children who are overtly disliked by their peers and who often have more long-term maladjustment than neglected children. *350*

reliability An attribute of a test that is based on how consistently an individual performs on the test. *249*

REM sleep Rapid eye movement sleep. *89*

repression The most powerful and pervasive defense mechanism, according to Freud; it works to push unacceptable id impulses out of awareness and back into our unconscious mind. *281*

reproduction A process that involves the fertilization of a female gamete (ovum) by a male gamete (sperm) to create a single-celled zygote. *37*

retention Processes involved in accessing previously stored information. *150*

rhythmic motor behavior Rapid, repetitive movement of the limbs, torso, and head during the first year of life. These motor behaviors occur frequently and appear to be a source of pleasure for the infant. *92*

satire Refers to irony, wit, or derision used to expose folly or wickedness. *185*

scaffolding Term used to describe the mother's role in early parent-child interactions. Through their attention and choice of behaviors, mothers are described as providing a framework around which they and their infants interact. *317*

schedules of reinforcement Rules governing partial reinforcement that determine the occasion when a response will be reinforced. *142*

schema (schemata) The existing set of information we have about various concepts, events, and knowledge. *210*

scientific method A series of steps used to obtain accurate information: identify and analyze the problem, collect data, draw conclusions, and revise theories. *19*

secondary circular reactions In Piaget's theory, develops between four and eight months of age; the infant becomes more object oriented or focused on the world, moving beyond preoccupation with the self in sensorimotor interactions. *170*

secure attachment The infant uses the caregiver, usually the mother, as a secure base from which to explore the environment. *321*

selective attention The ability to focus and concentrate on a narrow band of information. *198*

self-assertion The term used to achieve greater specificity of gender role. It describes masculinity and includes such components as leadership, dominance, independence, competitiveness, and individualism. *409*

self-efficacy The belief that one can master a situation and produce positive outcomes. *292*

semantic elaboration The process of making something more meaningful by associating it with other ideas. *202*

semantic networks The idea that simple concepts are organized into rich patterns that gradually grow in size and complexity. *210*

semantics Refers to the meaning of words and sentences. *225*

semiotic function Piagetian term in which the main developmental occurrence is the child's awareness that one thing can signify something else, even when the something else is not present. *359*

sensation The detection of the environment through stimulation of receptors in the sense organs. *95*

sensitive period Concept that emphasizes a more flexible band of time for a behavior to emerge optimally; sensitive periods occur on the order of months and even years rather than days or weeks. *304*

sensorimotor stage The Piagetian stage lasting from birth to about two years of age; the infant constructs an understanding of the world by coordinating sensory experiences with physical, motoric actions. *167*

separation anxiety Behavior in which an infant may protest the departure of a caregiver by whining, crying, thrashing about, or otherwise indicating displeasure. *319*

sequential approach A research approach that combines the features of cross-sectional and longitudinal designs in a search for more effective ways to study development. This approach allows researchers to see whether the same pattern of development is produced by each of the research strategies. *28*

set point The weight maintained when no effort is made to gain or lose weight. *491*

short-term memory The retention of recently encountered information or information retrieved from long-term memory for a brief period of time, usually about fifteen to thirty seconds. *200*

sickle-cell anemia A genetic disease of the red blood cells. This is a common disorder among blacks. A red blood cell is usually

shaped like a disk but a change in a recessive gene modifies its shape to a hook-shaped "sickle." *41*

simple reflexes The basic means of coordinating sensation and action is through reflexive behaviors—such as rooting and sucking—which the infant has at birth. *169*

social competence The capacity to interact effectively with the environment. *392*

social conventional reasoning Moral reasoning pertains to ethical matters, and social conventional reasoning pertains to thoughts about social convention and consensus. Moral reasoning is prescriptive, conventional reasoning more arbitrary. Social conventional reasoning emphasizes social regulation. *439*

social learning theory A theory with behavioral ties that emphasizes the environment's role in behavior. The most recent version, cognitive social learning theory, stresses the role of cognition and environment in determining behavior. *290*

social processes A person's interaction with other individuals in the environment and the effect of these interactions on development. *13*

social smile A smile that occurs in response to a face. *85*

solitary play The child plays alone and independently of others. The child seems engrossed in what he or she is doing and does not care much about anything else that is happening. Usually seen in two- to three-year-olds. *358*

split-half reliability Reliability that is assessed by comparing an individual's performance on two halves of the same test. *250*

stability-change issue How consistent individual differences are over time. Addresses the degree we become older renditions of our early existence or whether we can develop into someone different from who we were at an earlier point in development. *17*

standardization Development of uniform procedures for giving and scoring a test; giving test items to a large group representative of the population for whom the test is intended; allowing the test constructor to determine the distribution of test scores. *251*

standardized tests Questionnaires, structured interviews, or behavioral tests that are developed to identify an individual's characteristics or abilities, relative to those of a large group of similar individuals. *22*

statistical approach A theory of abnormality that defines abnormal behavior as that which deviates substantially from the average. *455*

stranger anxiety An infant's fear of strangers. *319*

structure-process dilemma The basic issue of what the mechanisms of intelligence are and how they develop: whether by expanding information-processing abilities (process), growing knowledge and expertise (structure), or both. *266*

sublimation A defense mechanism by which a socially useful course of action replaces a distasteful one. *281, 486*

superego The moral branch of personality, according to Freud; much like our "conscience." *280*

suppression Strategy that allows children to set aside their tensions temporarily. *486*

surface structure The actual order of words in a sentence. *225*

symbolic function substage In Piaget's theory, occurs roughly between the ages of two and four years; the child has the ability to mentally represent an object. *173*

syntax The way words are combined to form acceptable phrases and sentences. *225*

tabula rasa Locke's view that children are not innately evil but instead are like a blank tablet, becoming a particular kind of child or adult because of particular life experiences. *9*

telegraphic speech Speech that includes content words, such as nouns and verbs, but omits the extra words that only serve a grammatical function, such as prepositions and articles. *238*

teratology The field of study that investigates the causes of congenital (birth) defects. *63*

tertiary circular reactions, novelty, and curiosity Develops between twelve and eighteen months of age; the infant becomes intrigued by the variety of properties that objects possess and by the multiplicity of things he or she can make happen to objects. Piagetian concept. *170*

testis determining factor (TDF) Genes carried on the twenty-third chromosome pair, believed to determine an individual's sex. *44*

testosterone A male sex hormone important in the development of sexual characteristics and behavior. *114*

test-retest reliability Reliability that is assessed by giving an individual the same test on two different occasions. *249*

theories General beliefs that help us to explain the data or facts we have observed and make predictions. *18*

top-dog phenomenon Moving from the top position (in elementary school, as the oldest, biggest, and most powerful students in the school) to the lowest position (in middle or junior high school, the youngest, smallest, and least powerful group of students). *369*

triarchic theory of intelligence R. J. Sternberg's belief that every child has three types of intelligence: componential, experiential, and contextual. *267*

trophoblast The outer layer of the blastula that provides nutrition and support for the embryo. *59*

trust versus mistrust Erikson's first stage of development, corresponding approximately to the first year of life; in this bipolar conflict, infants develop either a trust in themselves and the world or a sense of mistrust. *287*

Turner's syndrome Women are minus an X chromosome, making them XO instead of XX. *42*

twin study A strategy of research that focuses on the genetic relationship between identical twins (monozygotic) and fraternal twins (dizygotic). *46*

two-factor theory Spearman's view that we have both general intelligence and a number of specific intelligences. *255*

type A babies These babies exhibit insecurity by avoiding the mother, for example, ignoring her, averting her gaze, and failing to seek proximity. *321*

type-A behavioral pattern A cluster of characteristics—excessively competitive, an accelerated pace of ordinary activities, impatience, thinking about doing several things at once, hostility, and an inability to hide the fact that life is a struggle—thought to be related to the incidence of heart disease. *496*

type B babies A positive bond develops between the infant and the caregiver; this promotes the healthy exploration of the world because the caregiver provides a secure base to which the infant can return if stressors are encountered. *321*

type C babies These babies exhibit insecurity by resisting the mother, for example, clinging to her but at the same time fighting against the closeness, perhaps by kicking and pushing away. *321*

ultrasound sonography A test in which high-frequency sound waves are directed into the pregnant woman's abdomen. The echo from the sounds is transformed into a visual representation of the fetus's inner structures. *43*

umbilical cord Contains two arteries and one vein and connects the baby to the placenta. *59*

unconditional positive regard Positive behaviors given without contingency. Rogers's concept. *386*

unconditioned response (UCR) A reflexive response produced by a stimulus in the absence of learning; a classical conditioning term. *137*

unconditioned stimulus (UCS) A stimulus that causes reflexive or unlearned behavior; a term used in classical conditioning. *137*

underextension The tendency of children to misuse words by not extending one word's meaning to other appropriate contexts for the word. *237*

undifferentiated The category that describes an individual who has neither masculine nor feminine characteristics. *407*

unoccupied play The child is not engaging in play as it is commonly understood and may stand in one spot, look around the room, or perform random movements that do not seem to have a goal. *358*

validity The extent to which a test measures what it is intended to measure. *250*

Wechsler scales Widely used individual intelligence tests developed by David Wechsler. *253*

Wernicke's area An area in the left hemisphere that is important in speech comprehension. *229*

whole-word method A technique for learning to read that focuses on learning direct associations between whole words and their meanings. *241*

withdrawal Takes place when children remove themselves either physically or mentally from stress. *486*

XYY syndrome An extra Y chromosome in the male. *42*

zygote A single-celled fertilized ovum (egg) created in the reproductive process. *37*

References

Aboud, F. E., & Ruble, D. N. (1987). Identity constancy in children: Developmental processes and implications. In T. Honess & K. Yardley (Eds.), *Self and identity: Perspectives across the lifespan.* London: Routledge & Kegan Paul.

Abramovitch, R., Corter, C., Pepler, D. J., & Stanhope, L. (1986). Sibling and peer interaction: A final follow-up and comparison. *Child Development, 57,* 217–229.

Achenbach, T. M., & Edelbrock, C. S. (1981). Behavioral problems and competencies reported by parents of normal and clinic-referred children 4 to 16. *Monographs of the Society for Research in Child Development, 46*(1, Serial No. 188).

Ackerman, B. P. (in press). Thematic influences on children's judgments about story accuracy. *Child Development.*

Acredelo, L. P., & Hake, J. L. (1982). Infant perception. In B. B. Wolman (Ed.), *Handbook of developmental psychology.* Englewood Cliffs, NJ: Prentice-Hall.

Adams, G. R., & Montemayor, R. (1983). Identity formation during early adolescence. *Journal of Early Adolescence, 3,* 193–202.

Adelson, J., & Doehrman, M. J. (1980). The psychodynamic approach to adolescence. In J. Adelson (Ed.), *Handbook of adolescent psychology.* New York: Wiley.

Agnew, N., McK., & Pyke, S. W. (1987). *The science game* (4th ed.). Englewood Cliffs, NJ: Prentice-Hall.

Ainsworth, M. D. S. (1967). *Infancy in Uganda: Infant care and the growth of love.* Baltimore, MD: Johns Hopkins University Press.

Ainsworth, M. D. S. (1979). Infant-mother attachment. *American Psychologist, 34,* 932–937.

Ainsworth, M. D. S. (1988, August). *Attachments beyond infancy.* Paper presented at the annual meeting of the American Psychological Association, Atlanta, GA.

Ainsworth, M. D. S., Blehar, M. C., Waters, E., & Wall, S. (1978). *Patterns of attachment: A psychological study of the strange situation.* Hillsdale, NJ: Erlbaum.

Alan Guttmacher Institute. (1981). *Teenage pregnancy: The problem that has not gone away.* New York: Author.

Alexander, D. (1987, April). *High interest areas in child development for the NICHD in the NIH centennial year.* Paper presented at the biennial meeting of the Society for Research in Child Development, Baltimore, MD.

Alford, G. S. (1989). Substance use disorders. In L. K. G. Hsu & M. Herson (Eds.), *Recent developments in adolescent psychiatry.* New York: Wiley.

Als, H. (1988, November). *Intensive care unit stress for the high-risk preterm infant: Neurofunctional and emotional sequelae.* Paper presented at the Developmental Interventions in Neonatal Care Conference, San Diego, CA.

Amsterdam, B. K. (1968). *Mirror behavior in children under two years of age.* Unpublished doctoral dissertation, University of North Carolina, Chapel Hill, NC.

Anastasi, A. (1988). *Psychological testing* (6th ed.). New York: Macmillan.

Anders, T. F., & Chalemian, R. J. (1974). The effect of circumcision on sleep-wake states in human neonates. *Psychosomatic Medicine, 36,* 174–179.

Anderson, D. R., Choi, H. P., & Lorch, E. P. (1987). Attentional inertia reduces distractibility during young children's TV viewing. *Child Development, 58,* 798–806.

Anderson, J. R. (1988). Cognitive principles in the design of computer tutors. In P. E. Morris (Ed.), *Modelling cognition.* New York: Wiley.

Anderson, L. D. (1939). The predictive value of infant tests in relation to intelligence at 5 years. *Child Development, 10,* 202–212.

Anderson, R. C., & Pearson, P. D. (1984). A schema theoretic view of basic processes in reading comprehension. In P. D. Pearson (Ed.), *Handbook of reading research.* New York: Longman.

Aneshensel, C., & Rosen, B. (1980). Domestic roles and sex differences in occupational expectations. *Journal of Marriage and the Family, 42,* 121–131.

Aries, P. (1962). *Centuries of childhood* (R. Baldrick, Trans.). New York: Knopf.

Aronson, E. (1986, August). *Teaching students what they think they already know about: The case of prejudice and desegregation.* Paper presented at the meeting of the American Psychological Association, Washington, DC.

Asarnow, J. R., & Callan, J. W. (1985). Boys with peer adjustment problems: Social cognitive processes. *Journal of Consulting and Clinical Psychology, 53,* 80–87.

Asher, J. (1987, April). Born to be shy? *Psychology Today,* pp. 56–64.

Asher, J., & Garcia, R. (1969). The optimal age to learn a foreign language. *Modern Language Journal, 53,* 334–341.

Asher, S. R., & Dodge, K. A. (1986). Identifying children who are rejected by their peers. *Developmental Psychology, 22,* 444–449.

Aslin, R. N. (1987). Visual and auditory development in infancy. In J. D. Osofsky (Ed.), *Handbook of infant development* (2nd ed.). New York: Wiley.

Astin, A. W., Green, K. C., & Korn, W. S. (1987). *The American freshman: Twenty-year trends.* Los Angeles: UCLA Higher Education Research Institute.

Atkinson, J. W., & Raynor, I. O. (1974). *Motivation and achievement.* New York: Wiley.

Auerback, K. (1987, April). *Breastfeeding and attachment in employed mothers.* Paper presented at the biennial meeting of the Society for Research in Child Development, Baltimore, MD.

Bachman, J. G., Johnston, L. D., & O'Malley, P. M. (1987). *Monitoring the future.* Ann Arbor: University of Michigan, Institute of Social Research.

Bahrick, L. E. (1988). Intermodal learning in infancy: Learning on the basis of two kinds of invariant relations in audible and visible events. *Child Development, 59,* 197–209.

Bakeman, R., & Brown, J. V. (1980). Early interaction: Consequences for social and mental development at three years. *Child Development, 51,* 437–447.

Baker, L. (1984). Children's effective use of multiple standards for evaluating their comprehension. *Journal of Educational Psychology, 76,* 588–597.

Baker, L., & Brown, A. L. (1984). Metacognitive skills and reading. In P. D. Pearson (Ed.), *Handbook of reading research, Part 2.* New York: Longman.

Baltes, P. B. (1973). Prototypical paradigms and questions in life-span research on development and aging. *The Gerontologist, 113,* 458–467.

Bandura, A. (1965). Influence of models' reinforcement contingencies on the acquisition of imitative responses. *Journal of Personality and Social Psychology, 1,* 589–595.

Bandura, A. (1971). *Social learning theory.* New York: General Learning Press.

Bandura, A. (1977). *Social learning theory.* Englewood Cliffs, NJ: Prentice-Hall.

Bandura, A. (1986). *Social foundations of thought and action: A social cognitive theory.* Englewood Cliffs, NJ: Prentice-Hall.

Banks, M. S., & Salapatek, P. (1983). Infant visual perception. In P. H. Mussen (Ed.), *Handbook of child psychology* (4th ed., Vol. 2). New York: Wiley.

Barcus, F. E. (1978). *Commercial children's television on weekends and weekday afternoons.* Newtonville, MA: Action for Children's Television.

Barker, R., & Wright, H. F. (1951). *One boy's day.* New York: Harper & Row.

Barnes, G. M. (1984). Adolescent alcohol abuse and other problem behaviors: Their relationships and common parental influences. *Journal of Youth and Adolescence, 13,* 329–348.

Barnes, K. E. (1971). Preschool play norms: A replication. *Developmental Psychology, 5,* 99–103.

Baron, J. B., & Sternberg, R. J. (Eds.). (1987). *Teaching thinking skills.* New York: W. H. Freeman.

Barrett, D. E., Radke-Yarrow, M., & Klein, R. E. (1982). Chronic malnutrition and child behavior: Effects of caloric supplementation on social and emotional functioning at school age. *Developmental Psychology, 18,* 541–556.

Barrett, K. C., & Campos, J. J. (1987). A functionalist approach to emotions. In J. D. Osofsky (Ed.), *Handbook of infant development* (2nd ed.). New York: Wiley.

Baskett, L. M., & Johnson, S. M. (1982). The young child's interaction with parents versus siblings. *Child Development, 53,* 643–650.

Bates, E., O'Connell, B., & Shore, C. (1987). Language and communication in infancy. In J. D. Osofsky (Ed.), *Handbook of infant development.* New York: Wiley.

Batson, C. D. (in press). Prosocial motivation: Is it ever truly altruistic? In L. D. Berkowitz (Ed.), *Advances in experimental social psychology.* New York: Academic Press.

Baumeiser, A. A. (1987). Mental retardation: Some conceptions and dilemmas. *American Psychologist, 42,* 796–800.

Baumrind, D. (1971). Current patterns of parental authority. *Developmental Psychology Monographs, 4*(1, Pt. 2).

Baumrind, D. (in press). Effective parenting during the early adolescent transition. In P. A. Cowan & E. M. Hetherington (Eds.), *Advances in family research* (Vol. 2). Hillsdale, NJ: Erlbaum.

Bayley, N. (1943). Mental growth during the first three years. In R. G. Barker, J. S. Kounin, & H. F. Wright (Eds.), *Child behavior and development.* New York: McGraw-Hill.

Bayley, N. (1970). Development of mental abilities. In P. H. Mussen (Ed.), *Manual of child psychology* (3rd ed., Vol. 1). New York: Wiley.

Beck, A. T. (1973). *The diagnosis and management of depression.* Philadelphia, PA: University of Pennsylvania Press.

Becker, W. C., & Krug, R. S. (1964). *A comparison of the ability of the PAS, PARI, parent self-ratings and empirically keyed questionnaire scales to predict ratings of child behavior.* Mimeographed report, University of Illinois, Champaign, IL.

Belenky, M. F., Clinchy, B. M., Goldberger, N. R., & Tarule, J. M. (1986). *Women's ways of knowing: The development of self, voice and mind.* New York: Basic Books.

Belfer, M. L., Krener, P. K., & Miller, F. B. (1988). AIDS in children and adolescents. *Journal of the American Academy of Child and Adolescent Psychiatry, 27,* 147–151.

Bell, A. P., Weinberg, M. S., & Mammersmith, S. K. (1981). *Sexual preference: Its development in men and women.* New York: Simon & Schuster.

Bell, S. M., & Ainsworth, M. D. S. (1972). Infant crying and maternal responsiveness. *Child Development, 43,* 1171–1190.

Belsky, J. (1981). Early human experience: A family perspective. *Developmental Psychology, 17,* 3–23.

Belsky, J. (1987, April). *Science, social policy, and day care: A personal odyssey.* Paper presented at the Society for Research in Child Development, Baltimore, MD.

Belsky, J. (in press). Nonmaternal care in the first year of life and infant-parent attachment security. *Child Development.*

Belson, W. (1978). *Television violence and the adolescent boy.* London: Saxon House.

Bem, S. L. (1977). On the utility of alternative procedures for assessing psychological androgyny. *Journal of Consulting and Clinical Psychology, 45,* 196–205.

Bem, S. L. (1985). Androgyny and gender schema theory: Conceptual and empirical integration. In T. B. Sonderegger (Ed.), *Nebraska Symposium on Motivation.* Lincoln, NE: University of Nebraska Press.

Bennett, W. I., & Gurin, J. (1982). *The dieter's dilemma: Eating less and weighing more.* New York: Basic Books.

Bennett, W. J. (1986). *First lessons: A report on elementary education in America.* Washington, DC: U.S. Government Printing Office.

Bennigna, J. S. (1988, February). An emerging synthesis in moral education. *Phi Delta Kappan,* pp. 415–418.

Bereiter, C., & Scardamilia, M. (1982). From conversation to composition: The role of instruction in a developmental process. In R. Glaser (Ed.), *Advances in instructional psychology.* Hillsdale, NJ: Erlbaum.

Berenson, G. S., McMahan, C. A., Voors, A. W., & others. (1980). *Cardiovascular risk factors in children: The early natural history of atherosclerosis and essential hypertension.* New York: Oxford University Press.

Berg, C. A., & Sternberg, R. J. (1985, April). *Novelty as a component of intelligence throughout development.* Paper presented at the biennial meeting of the Society for Research in Child Development, Toronto.

Berg, W. K., & Berg, K. M. (1987). Psychophysiological development in infancy: State, startle, & attention. In J. D. Osofsky (Ed.), *Handbook of infant development* (2nd ed.). New York: Wiley.

Berko, J. (1958). The child's learning of English morphology. *Word, 14,* 150–177.

Berkowitz, M., & Gibbs, J. (1983). Measuring the developmental features of moral discussion. *Merrill-Palmer Quarterly, 29*, 399–410.

Berlyne, D. (1960). *Conflict, arousal, and curiosity.* New York: McGraw-Hill.

Berlyne, D. E. (1960). *Conflict, arousal, and curiosity.* New York: McGraw-Hill.

Berndt, T. J. (1979). Developmental changes in conformity to peers and parents. *Developmental Psychology, 15*, 608–616.

Berndt, T. J. (1982). The features and effects of friendships in early adolescence. *Child Development, 53*, 1447–1460.

Berndt, T. J., & Ladd, G. W. (Eds.). (1989). *Peer relationships in child development.* New York: Wiley.

Bernstein, A. (1988). Cultural literacy: Process and content. *Change, 20*, 4.

Binder, A. (1987). An historical and theoretical introduction. In H. C. Quay (Ed.), *Handbook of juvenile delinquency.* New York: Wiley.

Bjorklund, D. F. (1989). *Children's thinking: Developmental function and individual differences.* Pacific Grove, CA: Brooks/Cole.

Blakemore, J. E. O., LaRue, A. A., & Olejnik, A. B. (1979). Sex-appropriate toy preference and the ability to conceptualize toys as sex-role related. *Developmental Psychology, 15*, 339–340.

Blasi, A. (1988). Identity and the development of the self. In D. Lapsley & F. C. Power (Eds.), *Self, ego, and identity: Integrative approaches.* New York: Springer.

Block, J., & Block, J. H. (in press). Longitudinally foretelling drug usage in adolescence: Early childhood personality and environmental precursors. *Child Development.*

Block, J. H. (1973). Conception of sex roles: Some cross-cultural and longitudinal perspectives. *American Psychologist, 28*, 512–516.

Block, J. H., Block, J., & Gjerde, P. F. (1986). The personality of children prior to divorce. *Child Development, 57*, 827–840.

Bloom, B. S. (1983, April). *The development of exceptional talent.* Paper presented at the biennial meeting of the Society for Research in Child Development, Detroit, MI.

Blos, P. (1962). *On adolescence.* New York: Free Press.

Blos, P. (1985). *Son and father.* New York: Free Press.

Blum, R. W., & Goldhagen, J. (1981). Teenage pregnancy in perspective. *Clinical Pediatrics, 20*, 335–340.

Blumberg, M. L. (1974). Psychopathology of the abusing parent. *American Journal of Psychotherapy, 28*, 1121–1129.

Blumenfeld, P. C., Pintrich, P. R., Wessels, K., & Meece, J. (1981, April). *Age and sex differences in the impact of classroom experiences on self-perceptions.* Paper presented at the biennial meeting of the Society for Research in Child Development, Boston, MA.

Blumenthal, S. J., & Kupfer, D. J. (1988). Overview of early detection and treatment strategies for suicidal behavior in young people. *Journal of Youth and Adolescence, 17*, 1–14.

Blumstein, P., & Schwartz, P. (1983). *American couples: Money, work, sex.* New York: Morrow.

Blundell, J. E. (1984). Systems and interactions: An approach to the pharmacology of feeding. In A. J. Stunkard & E. Stellar (Eds.), *Eating and its disorders.* New York: Raven Press.

Blyth, D. A., Bulcroft, R., & Simmons, R. G. (1981, August). *The impact of puberty on adolescents: A longitudinal study.* Paper presented at the meeting of the American Psychological Association, Los Angeles, CA.

Blyth, D. A., Durant, D., & Moosbrugger, L. (1985, April). *Perceived intimacy in the social relationships of drug- and nondrug-using adolescents.* Paper presented at the biennial meeting of the Society for Research in Child Development, Toronto.

Bohannon, J. N. III, & Marquis, A. L. (1977). Children's control of adult speech. *Child Development, 48*, 1002–1008.

Bohannon, J. N. III, & Stanowicz, L. (1988). The issue of negative evidence: Adult responses to children's language errors. *Developmental Psychology, 24*, 684–689.

Bolter, J. D. (1984). *Turing's man.* Chapel Hill, NC: University of North Carolina Press.

Boring, E. G. (1950). *A history of experimental psychology.* New York: Appleton-Century-Crofts.

Bornstein, M. (Ed.). (1987). *Sensitive periods in development.* Hillsdale, NJ: Erlbaum.

Bornstein, M. H. (1988). Perceptual development across the life cycle. In M. H. Bornstein & M. E. Lamb (Eds.), *Developmental psychology* (2nd ed.). Hillsdale, NJ: Erlbaum.

Bornstein, M. H., & Sigman, M. D. (1986). Continuity in mental development from infancy. *Child Development, 57*, 251–274.

Borstelmann, L. J. (1983). Children before psychology: Ideas about children from antiquity to the late 1800s. In P. H. Mussen (Ed.), *Handbook of child psychology* (4th ed., Vol. 1). New York: Wiley.

Boston Women's Health Book Collective. (1978). *Ourselves and our children: A book by and for parents.* New York: Random House.

Bouchard, T. J., Heston, L., Eckert, E., Keyes, M., & Resnick, S. (1981). The Minnesota study of twins reared apart: Project description and sample results in the developmental domain. *Twin Research, 3*, 227–233.

Bower, G. H., Black, J. B., & Turner, T. J. (1979). Scripts in memory for text. *Cognitive Psychology, 11*, 177–220.

Bower, T. G. R. (1982). *Development in infancy* (2nd ed.). San Francisco, CA: W. H. Freeman.

Bowlby, J. (1969). *Attachment and loss* (Vol. 1). London: Hogarth.

Bowlby, J. (1973). *Attachment and loss* (Vol. 2). New York: Basic Books.

Bowlby, J. (1980). *Attachment and loss* (Vols. 2 & 3). London: Hogarth.

Bowlby, J. (1988). Developmental psychiatry comes of age. *American Journal of Psychiatry, 145*, 1–10.

Boxer, A. M. (1988, August). *Developmental continuities of gay and lesbian youth.* Paper presented at the annual meeting of the American Psychological Association, Atlanta, GA.

Brackbill, Y. (1962). *Research and clinical work with children.* Washington, DC: American Psychological Association.

Brackbill, Y. (1979). Obstetric medication and infant behavior. In J. D. Osofsky (Ed.), *Handbook of infant development.* New York: Wiley.

Brand, E., Clingempeel, W. E., & Bowen-Woodward, K. (in press). Family relationships and children's psychological adjustment in stepmother and stepfather families: Findings and conclusions from the Philadelphia Stepfamily Research Project. In E. M. Hetherington & J. D. Arasteh (Eds.), *Impact of divorce, single-parenting, and stepparenting on children.* Hillsdale, NJ: Erlbaum.

Bray, J. H. (in press). The effects of early remarriage on children's development: Preliminary analyses of the developmental issues in stepfamily research project. In E. M. Hetherington & J. D. Arasteh (Eds.), *Impact of divorce, single-parenting, and stepparenting on children.* Hillsdale, NJ: Erlbaum.

Brazelton, T. B. (1956). Sucking in infancy. *Pediatrics, 17*, 400–404.

Brazelton, T. B. (1973). *Neonatal behavioral assessment scale.* London: Heinemann Medical Books.

Brazelton, T. B. (1979). Behavioral competence in the newborn infant. *Seminars in Perinatology, 3*, 35–44.

Brazelton, T. B. (1984). *Neonatal Behavioral Assessment Scale* (2nd ed.). Philadelphia, PA: Lippincott.

Brazelton, T. B. (1987, August). *Opportunities for intervention with infants at risk*. Paper presented at the meeting of the American Psychological Association, New York, NY.

Brazelton, T. B. (1988, November). *Family stresses and emotional issues of parents during NICU hospitalization*. Paper presented at the Developmental Interventions in Neonatal Care Conference, San Diego, CA.

Brazelton, T. B., Nugent, J. K., & Lester, B. M. (1987). Neonatal Behavioral Assessment Scale. In J. D. Osofsky (Ed.), *Handbook of infant development* (2nd ed.). New York: Wiley.

Brenner, A. (1984). *Helping children cope with stress*. Lexington, MA: D.C. Heath.

Bretherton, I. (1987). New perspectives on attachment relations: Security, communication, and internal working models. In J. D. Osofsky (Ed.), *Handbook of infant development* (2nd ed.). New York: Wiley.

Bretherton, I., Fritz, J., Zahan-Waxler, C., & Riedgeway, D. (1986). Learning to talk about emotions. *Child Development, 57,* 529–548.

Brewster, A. B. (1982). Chronically ill hospitalized children's concepts of illness. *Pediatrics, 69,* 355–362.

Brinker, R. P., & Lewis, M. (1982). Discovering the competent handicapped infant: A process approach to assessment and intervention. *Topics in Early Childhood Special Education, 2,* 121–151.

Bronfenbrenner, U. (1970). *Two worlds of childhood: U.S. and U.S.S.R.* New York: Russell Sage Foundation.

Bronfenbrenner, U. (1979). Contexts of child rearing. *American Psychologist, 34,* 844–850.

Bronfenbrenner, U. (1987, August). *Recent advances in theory and design*. Paper presented at the meeting of the American Psychological Association, New York, NY.

Bronfenbrenner, U., & Garbarino, J. (1976). The socialization of moral judgment and behavior in cross-cultural perspective. In T. Lickona (Ed.), *Moral development and behavior*. New York: Holt, Rinehart, & Winston.

Bronson, G. W. (1987). Blurring the behavioral-biological distinction: A commentary. *Child Development, 58,* 1474–1475.

Bronstein, P. (1988). Marital and parenting roles in transition. In P. Bronstein & C. P. Cowan (Eds.), *Fatherhood today*. New York: Wiley.

Brookman, R. R. (1988). Sexually transmitted diseases. In M. D. Levine & E. R. McAnarney (Eds.), *Early adolescent transitions*. Lexington, MA: Lexington Books.

Brooks-Gunn, J. (1988). Antecedents and consequences of variations in girls' maturational timing. In M. D. Levine & E. R. McAnarney (Eds.), *Early adolescent transitions*. Lexington, MA: Lexington Books.

Brooks-Gunn, J., & Warren, M. P. (in press). The psychological significance of secondary sexual characteristics in 9- to 11-year-old girls. *Child Development*.

Brown, A. L., Bransford, J. D., Ferrara, R. A., & Campione, J. C. (1983). Learning, remembering, and understanding. In P. H. Mussen (Ed.), *Handbook of child psychology* (4th ed., Vol. 3). New York: Wiley.

Brown, A. L., & Palincsar, A. S. (1987). Reciprocal teaching of comprehension strategies: A natural history of one program for enhancing learning. In J. Borkowski and J. D. Day (Eds.), *Intelligence and cognition in special children: Comparative studies of giftedness, mental retardation and learning disabilities*. New York: Ablex Publishing.

Brown, A. L., & Smiley, S. S. (1977). Rating the importance of structural units of prose passages: A problem of metacognitive development. *Child Development, 48,* 1–8.

Brown, A. L., Smiley, S. S., Day, J. D., Townsend, M. A. R., & Lawton, S. C. (1977). Intrusion of a thematic idea in children's comprehension and retention of stories. *Child Development, 48,* 1454–1466.

Brown, F. (1973). *The reform of secondary education: Report of the national commission on the reform of secondary education*. New York: McGraw-Hill.

Brown, J. D., & Siegel, J. D. (1988). Exercise as a buffer of life stress: A prospective study of adolescent health. *Health Psychology, 7,* 341–353.

Brown, J. L. (1964). States in newborn infants. *Merrill-Palmer Quarterly, 10,* 313–327.

Brown, J. S., & Burton, R. B. (1978). Diagnostic models for procedural bugs in basic mathematical skills. *Cognitive Science, 2,* 155–192.

Brown, R. (1973). *A first language: The early stages*. Cambridge, MA: Harvard University Press.

Brown, R. (1986). *Social psychology* (2nd ed.). New York: Free Press.

Brown, R., Cazden, C. B., & Bellugi-Klima, U. (1969). The child's grammar from I to III. In J. P. Hill (Ed.), *Minnesota Symposia on Child Psychology*, Vol. 2. Minneapolis: University of Minnesota Press.

Brownell, C. A., & Brown, E. (1985, April). *Toddler peer interactions in relation to cognitive development*. Paper presented at the meeting of the Society for Research in Child Development, Toronto.

Brumberg, J. J. (1988). *Fasting girls*. Cambridge, MA: Harvard University Press.

Bruner, J. (1983). *Child talk*. New York: Norton.

Bruner, J., & Sherwood, V. (1976). Peek-a-boo and the learning of rule structures. In J. Bruner, A. Jolly, & K. Silva (Eds.), *Play: Its role in evolution and development*. Harmondsworth, Middlesex (England): Penguin.

Bryant, B. K. (1985). The neighborhood walk: Sources of support in middle childhood. *Monographs of the Society for Research in Child Development, 50*(3, Serial No. 210).

Bukowski, W. M., Newcomb, A. F., & Hoza, B. (1987). Friendship conceptions among early adolescents: A longitudinal study of stability and change. *Journal of Early Adolescence, 7,* 143–152.

Bullock, M. (1985). Animism in childhood thinking: A new look at an old question. *Developmental Psychology, 21,* 217–225.

Burtchaell, J. (in press). University policy on experimental use of aborted fetal tissue. *IRB, A Review of Human Subjects*.

Burton, R. V. (1984). A paradox in theories and research in moral development. In W. W. Kurtines & J. L. Gewirtz (Eds.), *Morality, moral behavior, and moral development*. New York: Wiley.

Buss, A. H., & Plomin, R. (1984). *A temperament theory of personality development*. New York: Wiley-Interscience.

Buss, A. H., & Plomin, R. (1987). Commentary. In H. H. Goldsmith, A. H. Buss, R. Plomin, M. K. Rothbart, A. Thomas, A. Chess, R. R. Hinde, & R. B. McCall (Eds.), Roundtable: What is temperament? Four approaches. *Child Development, 58,* 505–529.

Buss, R. R., Yussen, S. R., Mathews, S. R., Miller, G. E., & Rembold, K. L. (1983). Development of children's use of a story schema to retrieve information. *Developmental Psychology, 19,* 22–28.

Butler, R. A. (1953). Discrimination learning by rhesus monkeys to visual-exploration motivation. *Journal of Comparative and Physiological Psychology, 46,* 95–98.

References

Cairns, R. B. (1983). The emergence of developmental psychology. In P. H. Mussen (Ed.), *Handbook of child psychology* (4th ed., Vol. 1). New York: Wiley.

Calhoun, J. A. (1988, March). *Gang violence.* Testimony to the House Select Committee on Children, Youth, and Families, Washington, DC.

Camara, K. A., & Resnick, G. (in press). Interparental conflict and cooperation: Factors moderating children's post-divorce adjustment. In E. M. Hetherington & J. D. Arasteh (Eds.), *Impact of divorce, single-parenting, and stepparenting on children.* Hillsdale, NJ: Erlbaum.

Campbell, T. A., Wright, J. C., & Huston, A. C. (1983, August). *Format cues and content difficulty as determinants of children's cognitive processing of televised educational messages.* Paper presented at the annual meeting of the American Psychological Association, Anaheim, CA.

Campos, J. J., Barrett, K. C., Lamb, M. E., Goldsmith, H. H., & Stenberg, C. (1983). Socioemotional development. In P. H. Mussen (Ed.), *Handbook of child psychology* (4th ed., Vol 2). New York: Wiley.

Campos, J. J., Langer, A., & Krowitz, A. (1970). Cardiac responses on the visual cliff in prelocomotor human infants. *Science, 170,* 196–197.

Capaldi, D. M., & Patterson, G. R. (1989). *The relation of transition problems to boys' adjustment problems.* Unpublished manuscript, Oregon Social Learning Center, Eugene, OR.

Carey, S. (1977). The child as word learner. In M. Halle, J. Bresman, & G. A. Miller (Eds.), *Linguistic theory and psychological reality.* Cambridge, MA: MIT Press.

Carpenter, T. P., Moser, J. M., & Romberg, T. A. (Eds.). (1982). *Addition and subtraction: A cognitive perspective.* Hillsdale, NJ: Erlbaum.

Carper, L. (1978, April). Sex roles in the nursery. *Harper's.*

Case, R. (1985). *Intellectual development: A systematic reinterpretation.* New York: Academic Press.

Case, R., Kurland, D. M., & Goldberg, J. (1982). Operational efficiency and the growth of short-term memory span. *Journal of Experimental Child Psychology, 33,* 386–404.

Cassell, C. (1984). *Swept away: Why women fear their own sexuality.* New York: Simon & Schuster.

Ceci, S. J. (Ed.). (1986). *Handbook of cognitive, social, and neuropsychological aspects of learning disabilities* (Vol. 1). Hillsdale, NJ: Erlbaum.

Center for Early Adolescence. (1982). *Living with 10–15 year olds. A planning guide for a one-day conference.* Carrboro, NC.

Chandler, L. A. (1982). *Children under stress.* Springfield, IL: Charles C. Thomas.

Chandler, M., Boyes, M., Ball, L., & Hala, S. (1987). The conservation of selfhood: A developmental analysis of children's changing conceptions self-continuity. In T. Honess & K. Yardley (Eds.), *Self and identity: Perspectives across the lifespan.* London: Routledge & Kegan Paul.

Chase-Lansdale, P. L., & Hetherington, E. M. (in press). The impact of divorce on life-span development: Short- and long-term effects. In P. B. Baltes, D. L. Featherman, & R. M. Lerner (Eds.), *Life-span development and behavior.* Hillsdale, NJ: Erlbaum.

Chasnoff, I. J., Burns, K. A., & Burns, W. J. (1987, April). *Cocaine and pregnancy.* Paper presented at the Society for Research in Child Development, Baltimore, MD.

Cherry-Wilkinson, L., Clevenger, M., & Dolloghan, C. (1981). Communication in small instructional groups: A sociolinguistic approach. In W. P. Dickson (Ed.), *Children's oral communication skills.* New York: Academic Press.

Chess, S., & Hassibi, M. (1978). *Principles and practice of child psychiatry.* New York: Plenum.

Chess, S., & Thomas, A. (1977). Temperamental individuality from childhood to adolescence. *Journal of Child Psychiatry, 16,* 218–226.

Chess, S., & Thomas, A. (1986). *Temperament in clinical practice.* New York: Guilford.

Chi, M. T. H., & Koeske, R. D. (1983). Network representation of a child's dinosaur knowledge. *Developmental Psychology, 19,* 29–39.

Chilman, C. (1979). *Adolescent sexuality in a changing American society: Social and psychological perspectives.* Washington, DC: Public Health Service, National Institute of Mental Health.

Chomsky, N. (1957). *Syntactic structures.* The Hague: Mouton.

Cicirelli, V. (1977). Family structure and interaction: Sibling effects on socialization. In M. McMillan & M. Sergio (Eds.), *Child psychiatry: Treatment and research.* New York: Brunner/Mazel.

Clabby, J. G., & Elias, M. J. (1988). Improving social problem-solving and awareness. *William T. Grant Foundation Annual Report,* p. 18.

Clark, E. V. (1983). Meanings and concepts. In P. H. Mussen (Ed.), *Handbook of child psychology* (4th ed., Vol. 4). New York: Wiley.

Clark, H. H., & Clark, E. V. (1977). *Psychology and language.* New York: Harcourt Brace Jovanovich.

Clark, M. S., Powell, M. C., Ovellette, R., & Milberg, S. (1987). Recipient's mood, relationship type, and helping. *Journal of Personality and Social Psychology, 43,* 94–103.

Clark, S. D., Zabin, L. S., & Hardy, J. B. (1984). Sex, contraception, and parenthood: Experience and attitudes among urban black young men. *Family Planning Perspectives, 16,* 77–82.

Clarke-Stewart, K. A. (in press). Infant day care: Maligned or malignant? *American Psychologist.*

Clarke-Stewart, K. A. (1978). Recasting the lone stranger. In J. Glick & K. A. Clarke-Stewart (Eds.), *The development of social understanding.* New York: Gardner Press.

Clarke-Stewart, K. A., & Fein, G. (1983). Early childhood programs. In P. H. Mussen (Ed.), *Handbook of child psychology* (4th ed., Vol. 2). New York: Wiley.

Cohn, J. F., & Tronick, E. Z. (1987). Mother-infant face-to-face interaction: The sequence of dyadic states at 3, 6, and 9 months. *Developmental Psychology, 23,* 68–77.

Cohn, J. F., & Tronick, E. Z. (1988). Mother-infant face-to-face interaction: Influence is bidirectional and unrelated to periodic cycles in either partner's behavior. *Developmental Psychology, 24,* 396–397.

Coie, J. D., & Kupersmidt, J. (1983). A behavioral analysis of emerging social status in boys' groups. *Child Development, 54,* 1400–1416.

Colby, A., & Kohlberg, L. (1987). *The measurement of moral judgment: Volumes I and II.* Cambridge, England: Cambridge University Press.

Colby, A., Kohlberg, L., Gibbs, J., & Lieberman, M. (1983). A longitudinal study of moral judgment. *Monographs of the Society for Research in Child Development* (Serial No. 201).

Coleman, J., Bremner, R., Clark, B., Davis, J., Eichorn, D., Grilliches, Z., Kett, J., Ryder, N., Doering, Z., & Mays, J. (1974). *Youth: Transition to adulthood.* Chicago, IL: University of Chicago Press.

Coletta, N. D. (1979). *Divorced mothers at two income levels: Stress, support, and child-rearing practices.* Unpublished manuscript, Cornell University.

Collins, W. A. (1985, April). *Cognition, affect, and development in parent-child relationships.* Paper presented at the biennial meeting of the Society for Research in Child Development, Toronto.

Collins, W. A. (1987). *Research on the transition to adolescence.* Unpublished manuscript, University of Minnesota.

Condry, J. C., Simon, M. L., & Bronfenbrenner, U. (1968). *Characteristics of peer- and adult-oriented children.* Unpublished manuscript, Cornell University, Ithaca, NY.

Conger, J. J. (1981). Freedom and commitment: Families, youth, and social change. *American Psychologist, 36,* 1475–1484.

Conger, J. J. (1988). Hostages to the future: Youth, values, and the public interest. *American Psychologist, 43,* 291–300.

Coons, S., & Guilleminault, C. (1982). Development of sleep-wake patterns and non-rapid eye movement sleep stages during the first six months of life in normal infants. *Pediatrics, 69,* 793–798.

Coons, S., & Guilleminault, C. (1984). Development of consolidated sleep and wakeful periods in relation to the day/night cycle in infancy. *Developmental Medicine and Child Neurology, 26,* 169–176.

Cooper, C. R., & Ayers-Lopez, S. (1985). Family and peer systems in early adolescence: New models of the role of relationships in development. *Journal of Early Adolescence, 5,* 9–22.

Cooper, C. R., Grotevant, H. D., & Condon, S. M. (1983). Individuality and connectedness in the family as a context for adolescent identity formation and role-taking skill. In H. D. Grotevant & C. R. Cooper (Eds.), *Adolescent development in the family.* San Francisco, CA: Jossey-Bass.

Cooper, C. R., Grotevant, H. D., Moore, M. S., & Condon, S. M. (1982, August). *Family support and conflict: Both foster adolescent identity and role taking.* Paper presented at the meeting of the American Psychological Association, Washington, DC.

Corboy, L. (1987, April). *Interventions for increasing breastfeeding rates among low-income women.* Paper presented at the biennial meeting of the Society for Research on Child Development, Baltimore, MD.

Corrigan, R. (1981). The effects of task and practice on search for invisibly displaced objects. *Developmental Review, 1,* 1–17.

Corsini, D. A., Wisendale, S., & Caruso, G. A. (1988, September). Family day care. *Young Children,* pp. 17–23.

Cowan, C. P., & Cowan, P. A. (1987). Men's involvement in parenthood. In P. Berman & F. Pedersen (Eds.), *Men's transitions to parenthood.* Hillsdale, NJ: Erlbaum.

Cowan, P. A. (1988). Becoming a father: A time of change, an opportunity for development. In P. Bronstein & C. P. Cowan (Eds.), *Fatherhood today.* New York: Wiley.

Cronbach, L. J., & Snow, R. E. (1977). *Aptitudes and instructional methods.* New York: Irvington Books.

Cross, K. P. (1984, November). The rising tide of school reform reports. *Phi Delta Kappan,* pp. 167–172.

Crowder, R. (1982). *The psychology of reading.* New York: Oxford University Press.

Cuban, L. (1988, April). You're on the right track, David. *Phi Delta Kappan,* 571–572.

Culp, R. E., & Osofsky, J. D. (1987, April). *Transition to parenthood in the early postpartum period.* Paper presented at the biennial meeting of the Society for Research in Child Development, Baltimore, MD.

Curtiss, S. (1977). *Genie.* New York: Academic Press.

D

Dachman, R. S., Alessi, G. J., Vrazo, G. J., Fugua, R. W., & Kerr, R. H. (1986). Development and evaluation of an infant-care training program with first-time fathers. *Journal of Applied Behavior Analysis, 19,* 221–230.

Damon, W. (1988). *The moral child.* New York: The Free Press.

Darling, C. A., Kallen, D. J., & VanDusen, J. E. (1984). Sex in transition, 1900–1984. *Journal of Youth and Adolescence, 13,* 385–399.

Daro, D. (1988). *Confronting child abuse.* New York: The Free Press.

Dawson, G. (Ed.). (1989). *Autism: Nature, diagnosis and treatment.* New York: Guilford.

de Villiers, J. G., & de Villiers, P. A. (1978). *Language acquisition.* Cambridge, MA: Harvard University Press.

Deci, E. L. (1975). *Intrinsic motivation.* New York: Plenum.

DeFries, J. C., Plomin, R., Vandenberg, S. G., & Kuse, A. R. (1981). Parent-offspring resemblance in cognitive abilities in the Colorado adoption project: Biological, adoption, and control parents and one-year-old children. *Intelligence, 5,* 245–277.

DeLoache, J. S., Cassidy, D. J., & Brown, A. L. (1985). Precursors of mnemonic strategies in very young children's memory. *Child Development, 56,* 125–137.

DeLoache, J. S., Cassidy, D. J., & Carpenter, C. J. (1987). The Three Bears are all boys: Mother's gender labeling of neutral picture book characters. *Sex Roles, 17,* 163–178.

Demorest, A., Meyer, C., Phelps, E., Gardner, H., & Winner, E. (1984). Words speak louder than actions: Understanding deliberately false remarks. *Child Development, 55,* 1527–1534.

Dempster, F. N. (1981). Memory span: Sources of individual and developmental differences. *Psychological Bulletin, 89,* 63–100.

Denham, S. A. (1986). Social cognition, prosocial behavior, and emotion in preschoolers: Contextual validation. *Child Development, 52,* 194–201.

Deutsch, C., Deutsch, M., Jordan, T., & Grallo, R. (1981, August). *Long-term effects of Project Head Start.* Paper presented at the meeting of the American Psychological Association, Los Angeles, CA.

Dewey, J. (1933). *How we think: A restatement of the relation of reflective thinking to the educative process.* Lexington, MA: D.C. Heath.

Diamond, A. (1985). Development of the ability to use recall to guide action, as indicated by infants' performance on AB. *Child Development, 56,* 868–883.

DiLalla, L. F., & Watson, M. W. (1988). Differentiation of fantasy and reality: Preschoolers' reactions to interruptions in their play. *Developmental Psychology, 24,* 286–291.

Dillon, R. F., & Sternberg, R. J. (Eds.). (1988). *Cognition and instruction.* San Diego, CA: Academic Press.

Dillon, R. S. (1980). *Diagnosis and management of endocrine and metabolic disorders* (2nd ed.). Philadelphia, PA: Lea & Febiger.

Dimsdale, J. E. (1988). A perspective on Type A behavior and coronary heart disease. *The New England Journal of Medicine, 318,* 110–112.

Dodge, K. A. (1983). Behavioral antecedents of peer social status. *Child Development, 54,* 1386–1399.

Dodge, K. A., Murphy, R. R., & Buchsbaum, K. (1984). The assessment of intention-cue detection skills: Implications for developmental psychopathology. *Child Development, 55,* 163–173.

Dodge, K. A., Pettit, G. S., McClaskey, C. L., & Brown, M. M. (1986). Social competence in children. *Monographs of the Society for Research in Child Development, 51*(2, Serial No. 213).

Dolgin, K. G., & Behrend, D. A. (1984). Children's knowledge about animates and inanimates. *Child Development, 55,* 1646–1650.

Doll, G. (1988, Spring). Day care. *Vanderbilt Magazine,* p. 29.

Douvan, E., & Adelson, J. (1966). *The adolescent experience.* New York: Wiley.

Downey, A. M., Frank, G. C., Webber, L. S., Harsha, D. W., Virgilio, S. J., Franklin, F. A., & Berenson, G. S. (1987). Implementation of "Heart Smart": A cardiovascular school health promotion program. *Journal of School Health, 57,* 98–104.

Downs, A. C., & Langlois, J. H. (1988). Sex typing: Construct and measurement issues. *Sex Roles, 18,* 87–100.

Dreyer, P. H. (1982). Sexuality during adolescence. In B. B. Wolman (Ed.), *Handbook of developmental psychology.* Englewood Cliffs, NJ: Prentice-Hall.

Dreyfus, H. L., & Dreyfus, S. E. (1986). *Mind over machine.* New York: Free Press.

Dugdale, S., & Kibbey, D. (1980). *Fractions curriculum of the PLATO elementary mathematical project.* Urbana-Champaign, IL: Computer-based Education Research Laboratory.

Duncker, K. (1945). On problem solving. *Psychological Monographs, 58*(Whole No. 270).

Dunn, J., & Kendrick, C. (1982). *Siblings.* Cambridge, MA: Harvard University Press.

Dunphy, D. C. (1963). The social structure of urban adolescent peer groups. *Society, 26,* 230–246.

Durand, V. M., & Crimmins, D. B. (1987). Assessment and treatment of psychotic speech in an autistic child. *Journal of Autism and Developmental Disorders, 17,* 17–28.

Durden-Smith, J., & Desimone, D. (1983). *Sex and the brain.* New York: Arbor House.

Dwyer, C. A. (1987). Across the great divide: Research and practice in test development. *Contemporary Psychology, 32,* 520–522.

Eagleston, J. R., Kirmil-Gray, K., Thoresen, C. E., Wiedenfield, S. A., Bracke, P., Heft, L., & Arnow, B. (in press). Physical health correlates of Type A behavior in children and adolescents. *Journal of Behavioral Medicine.*

East, P. L., Hess, L. E., & Lerner, R. M. (1987). Peer social support and adjustment of early adolescent peer groups. *Journal of Early Adolescence, 7,* 153–163.

Eccles, J., & Hoffman, L. W. (1984). Sex roles, socialization, and occupational behavior. In H. W. Stevenson & A. E. Siegel (Eds.), *Research in child development and public policy* (Vol. 1). Chicago, IL: University of Chicago Press.

Eccles, J., MacIver, D., & Lange, L. (1986). *Classroom practices and motivation to study math.* Paper presented at the annual meeting of the American Educational Research Association, San Francisco.

Eccles, J. S. (1987). Gender roles and achievement patterns: An expectancy value perspective. In J. M. Reinisch, L. A. Rosenblum, & S. A. Sanders. (Eds.), *Masculinity/Femininity.* New York: Oxford University Press.

Eckerman, C. O., Whatley, J. L., & Kutz, S. L. (1975). The growth of social play with peers during the second year of life. *Developmental Psychology, 11,* 42–49.

Edleman, M. W. (1987). *Families in peril: An agenda for social change.* New York: Alan Guttmacher Institute.

Egeland, B., Jacobvitz, D., & Papatola, K. (1987). Intergenerational continuity of parental abuse. In R. Gelles & J. Lancaster (Eds.), *Child abuse and neglect: Biosocial influences.* New York: Aldine de Gruyter.

Egeland, B., Jacobvitz, D., & Sroufe, L. A. (in press). Breaking the cycle of abuse. *Child Development.*

Eger, M. (1981). The conflict in moral education: An informal case study. *Public Interest, 63,* 62–80.

Eisenberg, N. (1987). The relation of altruism and other moral behaviors to moral cognition: Methological and conceptual issues. In N. Eisenberg (Ed.), *Contemporary topics in developmental psychology.* New York: Wiley.

Elkind, D. (1970, April 5). Erik Erikson's eight ages of man. *New York Times Magazine.*

Elkind, D. (1976). *Child development and education.* New York: Oxford University Press.

Elkind, D. (1978). Understanding the young adolescent. *Adolescence, 13,* 127–134.

Elkind, D. (1981). *The hurried child.* Reading, MA: Addison-Wesley.

Elkind, D. (1985). Egocentrism redux. *Developmental Review, 5,* 218–226.

Emde, R. N., Gaensbauer, T. G., & Harmon, R. J. (1976). Emotional expression in infancy: A biobehavioral study. *Psychological Issues, 10* (Monograph Series, No. 37).

Enright, R., Lapsley, D., & Olson, L. (1984). Moral judgment and the social cognitive developmental research program. In S. Modgil & C. Modgil (Ed.), *Lawrence Kohlberg: Consensus and controversy.* Slough: NFER Press.

Entus, A. K. (1975, April). *Hemispheric asymmetry in processing of dichotically presented speech and nonspeech stimuli by infants.* Paper presented at the biennial meeting of the Society for Research in Child Development, Denver.

Entwisle, D. R., Alexander, K. L., Pallas, A. M., & Cadigan, D. (1987). The emergent academic self-image of first graders: Its response to social structures. *Child Development, 58,* 1190–1206.

Ericsson, K. A., Chase, W. G., & Faloon, S. (1980). Acquisition of a memory skill. *Science, 208,* 1181–1182.

Erikson, E. H. (1950). *Childhood and society.* New York: Norton.

Erikson, E. H. (1962). *Young man Luther.* New York: Norton.

Erikson, E. H. (1968). *Identity: Youth and crisis.* New York: Norton.

Erikson, E. H. (1969). *Gandhi's truth.* New York: Norton.

Eron, L. D. (1987). The development of aggression from the perspective of a developing behaviorism. *American Psychologist, 42,* 435–442.

Escalona, S. (1988). Cognition in its relationship to total development in the first year. In B. Inhelder, D. DeCaprona, & A. Cornu-Wells (Eds.), *Piaget today.* Hillsdale, NJ: Erlbaum.

Eschel, Y., & Klein, Z. (1981). Development of academic self-concept of lower-class and middle-class primary school children. *Journal of Educational Psychology, 73,* 287–293.

Fagan, J. F., III. (1985, April). *Early novelty preferences and later intelligence.* Paper presented at the biennial meeting of the Society for Research in Child Development, Toronto.

Fagot, B. I. (1975, April). *Teacher reinforcement of feminine-preferred behavior revisited.* Paper presented at the biennial meeting of the Society for Research in Child Development, Denver, CO.

Fagot, B. I. (1977). Consequences of moderate cross-gender behavior in preschool children. *Child Development, 48,* 902–907.

Falbo, T., & Polit, D. F. (1986). A quantitative review of the only-child literature: Research evidence and theory development. *Psychological Bulletin, 100,* 176–189.

Fantz, R. L. (1958). Pattern vision in young infants. *Psychological Record, 8,* 43–49.

Fantz, R. L. (1961). The origin of form perception. *Scientific American, 204,* 66–72.

Farnham-Diggory, S. (1986). Time, now, for a little serious complexity. In S. J. Ceci (Ed.), *Handbook of cognitive, social, and neuropsychological aspects of learning disabilities* (Vol. 1). Hillsdale, NJ: Erlbaum.

Faust, M. S. (1977). Somatic development of adolescent girls. *Monographs of the Society for Research in Child Development, 42*(1, Serial No. 169).

Fein, G. G. (1987). Pretend play. In D. Görlitz & J. F. Wohlwill (Eds.), *Curiosity, imagination, and play.* Hillsdale, NJ: Erlbaum.

Feingold, A. (1988). Cognitive gender differences are disappearing. *American Psychologist, 43,* 95–103.

Feist, J., & Brannon, L. (1989). *An introduction to health.* Belmont, CA: Wadsworth.

Field, T., Woodson, R., Greenberg, R., & Cohen, D. (1982). Discrimination and imitation of facial expressions in neonates. *Science, 218,* 179–181.

Field, T. M. (1979). Visual and cardiac responses to animate and inanimate faces by young term and preterm infants. *Child Development, 50,* 188–194.

Fincher, J. (1982). Before their time. *Science 82.*

Finney, J. W., & Moos, R. H. (1979). Treatment and outcome for empirical subtypes of alcoholic patients. *Journal of Consulting and Clinical Psychology, 47,* 25–38.

Fischer, K. W., & Lazerson, A. (1984). *Human development.* San Francisco, CA: W. H. Freeman.

Fischman, S. H. (1987, February). Type A on trial. *Psychology Today,* pp. 42–50.

Fisher, T. D. (1987). Family communication and the sexual behavior and attitudes of college students. *Journal of Youth and Adolescence, 16,* 481–495.

Fishman, D. B., Rotgers, R., & Franks, C. M. (1988). *Paradigms in behavior therapy.* New York: Springer.

Flavell, J. H. (1974). The development of inferences about others. In T. Mischel (Ed.), *Understanding other persons.* Oxford: Blackwell, Basil, Mott.

Flavell, J. H. (1980, Fall). A tribute to Piaget. *Society for Research in Child Development Newsletter.*

Flavell, J. H. (1985). *Cognitive development* (2d ed.). Englewood Cliffs, NJ: Prentice-Hall.

Flavell, J. H., Beach, D. R., & Chinsky, J. M. (1966). Spontaneous verbal rehearsal in a memory task as a function of age. *Child Development, 37,* 283–299.

Flavell, J. H., Green, F. L., & Flavell, E. R. (1987). Developmental knowledge about the appearance-reality distinction. *Monographs of the Society for Research in Child Development, 41*(1, Serial No. 212).

Flavell, J. H., Shipstead, S. G., & Croft, K. (1978). *What young children think you see when their eyes are closed.* Unpublished manuscript, Stanford University, Palo Alto, CA.

Fleming, A. S., Ruble, D. N., Flett, G. L., & Shaul, D. L. (1988). Postpartum adjustment in first-time mothers: Relations between mood, maternal attitudes, and mother-infant interactions. *Developmental Psychology, 24,* 71–81.

Fogel, A., Toda, S., & Kawai, M. (1988). Mother-infant face-to-face interaction in Japan and the United States: A laboratory comparison using 3-month-old infants. *Developmental Psychology, 24,* 398–406.

Folkman, S., Lazarus, R. S., Dunkel-Schetter, C., Delongis, A., & Gruen, R. J. (1986). Dynamics of a stressful encounter: Cognitive appraisal, coping, and encounter outcomes. *Journal of Personality and Social Psychology, 50,* 992–1003.

Fontana, V. J. (1988, February). Detection and management of child sexual abuse. *Medical Aspects of Human Sexuality,* pp. 126–142.

Food and Nutrition Board, National Research Council. (1980). *Recommended dietary allowances* (rev. ed. 9). Washington, DC: National Academy of Sciences.

Ford, M. (1986). *Androgyny as self-assertion and integration: Implications for psychological and social competence.* Unpublished manuscript, Stanford University, School of Education, Stanford, CA.

Ford, M. E. (1986). A living systems conceptualization of social intelligence: Outcomes, processes, and developmental change. In R. J. Sternberg (Ed.), *Advances in the psychology of human intelligence* (Vol. 3). Hillsdale, NJ: Erlbaum.

Ford, M. E., & Ford, D. (Eds.). (1987). *Humans as self-constructing living systems.* Hillsdale, NJ: Erlbaum.

Fowler, J. W. (1976). Stages in faith: The structural-developmental approach. In T. Hennessy (Ed.), *Values and moral development.* New York: Paulist Press.

Fox, L. H. (1976). *Changing behaviors and attitudes of gifted girls.* Paper presented at the meeting of the American Psychological Association, Washington, DC.

Fox, L. H., Brody, L., & Tobin, D. (1979). *Women and mathematics.* Baltimore, MD: Intellectually Gifted Study Group, Johns Hopkins University.

Fraiberg, S. (1977). *Insights from the blind: Comparative studies of blind and sighted infants.* New York: Basic Books.

Freedman, J. L. (1984). Effects of television violence on aggressiveness. *Psychological Bulletin, 96,* 227–246.

French, D. (in press). Heterogeneity of peer-rejected boys: Aggressive and nonaggressive subtypes. *Child Development.*

Freud, A. (1958). Adolescence. In R. S. Eissler (Ed.), *Psychoanalytic study of the child* (Vol. 13). New York: International Universities Press.

Freud, A. (1966). *The ego and the mechanisms of defense.* New York: International Universities Press.

Freud, A., & Dann, S. (1951). An experiment in group upbringing. In R. S. Eissler, A. Freud, H. Hartmann, & E. Kris (Eds.), *The psychoanalytic study of the child* (Vol. 6). New York: International Universities Press.

Freud, S. (1917). *A general introduction to psychoanalysis.* New York: Washington Square Press.

Friedman, M., & Rosenman, R. (1974). *Type A behavior and your heart.* New York: Knopf.

Friedrich, L. K., & Stein, A. H. (1973). Aggressive and prosocial TV programs and the natural behavior of preschool children. *Monographs of the Society for Research in Child Development, 38*(4, Serial No. 151).

Frisch, R., & Revelle, R. (1970). Height and weight at menarche and a hypothesis of critical body weights and adolescent events. *Science, 169,* 397–399.

Frommer, E., & O'Shea, G. (1973). Antenatal identification of women liable to have problems managing their infants. *British Journal of Psychiatry, 123,* 149–156.

Furstenberg, F. F. (in press). Child care after divorce and remarriage. In E. M. Hetherington & J. Arasteh (Eds.), *Impact of divorce, single-parenting, and stepparenting on children.* Hillsdale, NJ: Erlbaum.

Furstenberg, J. J., Brooks-Gunn, J., & Morgan, S. P. (1987). *Adolescent mothers in later life.* New York: Cambridge University Press.

Furth, H. G. (1973). *Deafness and learning: A psychosocial approach.* Belmont, CA: Wadsworth.

Furth, H. G., & Wachs, H. (1975). *Thinking goes to school.* New York: Oxford University Press.

Gage, N. L. (1965). Desirable behaviors of teachers. *Urban Education, 1,* 85–96.

Gagne, E. D. (1985). *The cognitive psychology of school learning.* Boston, MA: Little, Brown.

Gagne, E. D., Weidemann, C., Bell, M. S., & Ander, T. D. (in press). Training thirteen-year-olds to elaborate while studying text. *Journal of Human Learning.*

Gagnon, J. H., & Simon, W. (1973). *Sexual conduct.* New York: Aldine.

Gallup, A. M., & Clark, D. L. (1987). The 19th annual Gallup poll of the public's attitude toward the public schools. *Phi Delta Kappan, 69,* 17–30.

Galst, J. P. (1980). Television food commercials and pronutritional public service announcements as determinants of young children's snack choices. *Child Development, 51,* 935–938.

Garbarino, J. (1976). The ecological correlates of child abuse: The impact of socioeconomic stress on mothers. *Child Development, 47,* 178–185.

Gardner, B. T., & Gardner, R. A. (1971). Two-way communication with an infant chimpanzee. In A. Schrier & F. Stollnitz (Eds.), *Behavior of nonhuman primates* (Vol. 4). New York: Academic Press.

Gardner, B. T., & Gardner, R. A. (1986). Discovering the meaning of primate signals. *British Journal for the Philosophy of Science, 37,* 477–495.

Gardner, H. (1983). *Frames of mind.* New York: Basic Books.

Garelik, G. (1985, October). Are the progeny prodigies? *Discover Magazine, 6,* 45–47, 78–84.

Garfinkel, P. E., & Garner, D. M. (1982). *Anorexia nervosa.* New York: Brunner/Mazel.

Garner, R. (1987). *Metacognition and reading comprehension.* Norwood, New Jersey: Ablex Publishing.

Garrison, K. C. (1968). Physiological changes in adolescence. In J. F. Adams (Ed.), *Understanding adolescence.* Boston, MA: Allyn & Bacon.

Gaskell, J., & Knapp, H. (1976). *Resource guide for women's studies for high school students.* Victoria, BC: Department of Education.

Gazzaniga, M. S. (1986). *The social brain.* New York: Plenum.

Geiger, K., & Turiel, E. (1983). Disruptive school behavior and concepts of social convention in early adolescence. *Journal of Educational Psychology, 75,* 677–685.

Geis, G., & Monahan, J. (1976). The social ecology of violence. In T. Lickona (Ed.), *Moral development and behavior.* New York: Holt, Rinehart, & Winston.

Gelman, R. (1969). Conservation acquisition: A problem of learning to attend to relevant attributes. *Journal of Experimental Child Psychology, 7,* 67–87.

Gelman, R. (1979). Preschool thought. *American Psychologist, 34,* 900–905.

Gelman, R., & Baillargeon, R. (1983). A review of some Piagetian concepts. In P. H. Mussen (Ed.), *Handbook of child psychology* (4th ed., Vol. 3). New York: Wiley.

Gesell, A. (1954). The ontogenesis of infant behavior. In L. Carmichael (Ed.), *Manual of child psychology.* New York: Wiley.

Gesell, A. L. (1928). *Infancy and human growth.* New York: Macmillan.

Gewirtz, J. (1977). Maternal responding and the conditioning of infant crying: Directions of influence within the attachment-acquisition process. In B. C. Etzel, J. M. LeBlanc, & D. M. Baer (Eds.), *New developments in behavioral research.* Hillsdale, NJ: Erlbaum.

Gibson, E. J. (1969). *The principles of perceptual learning and development.* New York: Appleton-Century-Crofts.

Gibson, E. J. (1986, October). *The concept of affordance in development.* Paper presented at the Symposium on Human Development and Communication Sciences, University of Texas at Dallas, Richardson, TX.

Gibson, E. J. (in press). Exploratory behavior in the development of perceiving, acting, and acquiring of knowledge. *Annual Review of Psychology.*

Gibson, E. J., & Spelke, E. S. (1983). The development of perception. In P. H. Mussen (Ed.), *Handbook of child psychology* (4th ed., Vol. 3). New York: Wiley.

Gibson, E. J., & Walk, R. D. (1960). The "visual cliff." *Scientific American, 202,* 64–71.

Gibson, J. J. (1979). *The ecological approach to visual perception.* Boston, MA: Houghton Mifflin.

Gill, S., Stockard, J., Johnson, M., & Williams, S. (1987). Measuring gender differences: The expressive dimension and critique of the androgyny scales. *Sex Roles, 17,* 375–400.

Gilligan, C. (1982). *In a different voice.* Cambridge, MA: Harvard University Press.

Gilligan, C. (1985, April). *Response to critics.* Paper presented at the biennial meeting of the Society for Research in Child Development, Toronto.

Ginsburg, H., & Opper, S. (1988). *Piaget's theory of intellectual development.* Englewood Cliffs, NJ: Prentice-Hall.

Gjerde, P. (1985, April). *Adolescent depression and parental socialization patterns: A prospective study.* Paper presented at the biennial meeting of the Society for Research in Child Development, Toronto.

Glaser, R., & Bassok, M. (in press). Learning theory and the study of instruction. *Annual Review of Psychology, 40.*

Gleason, J. B. (1988). Language and socialization. In F. Kessel (Ed.), *The development of language and language researchers.* Hillsdale, NJ: Erlbaum.

Glick, P. C., & Lin, S. (1986). Recent changes in divorce and remarriage. *Journal of Marriage and the Family, 48,* 737–747.

Globerson, T. (1983). Mental capacity and cognitive functioning: Developmental and social class differences. *Developmental Psychology, 19,* 225–230.

Gogel, A., & Melson, G. F. (Eds.). (1987). *Origins of nurturance.* Hillsdale, NJ: Erlbaum.

Gold, M. (1987). Social ecology. In H. C. Quay (Ed.), *Handbook of juvenile delinquency.* New York: Wiley.

Gold, M., & Yanof, D. S. (1985). Mothers, daughters, and girlfriends. *Journal of Personality and Social Psychology, 49,* 654–659.

Goldfried, M. R., & d'Zurilla, T. J. (1969). A behavioral-analytic model for assessing competence. In C. D. Speilberger (Ed.), *Current topics in clinical and community psychology* (Vol. 1). New York: Academic Press.

Goldman, J. A., Fujimura, J. B., Contois, J. H., & Lerman, R. H. (1987, April). *Interactions among preschool children following the ingestion of sucrose.* Paper presented at the biennial meeting of the Society for Research in Child Development, Baltimore, MD.

Goldman, J. A., Lerman, R. H., Contois, J. H., & Udall, J. N. (1986). Behavioral effects of sucrose on preschool children. *Journal of Abnormal Child Psychology, 14*, 565–577.

Goldsmith, H. H. (1988, August). *Does early temperament predict later development?* Paper presented at the annual meeting of the American Psychological Association, Atlanta, GA.

Goldsmith, H. H., & Gottesman, I. I. (1981). Origins of variation in behavioral style: A longitudinal study of temperament in young twins. *Child Development, 52*, 91–103.

Goldsmith, H. H., Buss, A. H., Plomin, R., Rothbart, M. K., Thomas, A., & Chess, S. (1987). Roundtable: What is temperament? Four approaches. *Child Development, 58*, 505–529.

Goldstein, M. J., & Tuma, A. H. (1987). High-risk research: Editor's introduction. *Schizophrenia Bulletin, 13*, 369–371.

Goldston, S. (1986). Primary prevention: Historical perspectives and a blueprint for action. *American Psychologist, 41*, 453–460.

Golman-Rakic, P. S., Isseroff, A., Schwartz, M. L., & Bugbee, N. M. (1983). The neurobiology of cognitive development. In P. H. Mussen (Ed.), *Handbook of child psychology* (4th ed., Vol. 2). New York: Wiley.

Goodchilds, J. D., & Zellman, G. L. (1984). Sexual signalling and sexual aggression in adolescent relationship. In N. M. Malamuth & E. D. Donnerstein (Eds.), *Pornography and sexual aggression.* New York: Academic Press.

Goodlad, J. I. (1983). *A place called school.* New York: McGraw-Hill.

Gordon, S., & Gilgun, J. F. (1987). Adolescent sexuality. In V. B. Van Hasselt & M. Hersen (Eds.), *Handbook of adolescent psychology.* New York: Pergamon.

Görlitz, D., & Wohlwill, J. F. (Eds.). (1987). *Curiosity, imagination, and play.* Hillsdale, NJ: Erlbaum.

Gorski, P. A. (1988, November). *Iatrogenic stressors: Progress, plight, and promise.* Paper presented at the Developmental Interventions in Neonatal Care Conference, San Diego, CA.

Gottesman, I. L., & Shields, J. (1982). *The schizophrenic puzzle.* New York: Cambridge University Press.

Gottlieb, D. (1966). Teaching and students: The views of Negro and white teachers. *Sociology of Education, 37*, 345–353.

Gottman, J. M., & Parker, J. G. (Eds.). (1987). *Conversations of friends.* New York: Cambridge University Press.

Gould, C. G. (1983, April). Out of the mouths of beasts. *Science '83.*

Graham, D. (1981). The obstetric and neonatal consequences of adolescent pregnancy. In E. R. McAnarney & G. Stickle (Eds.), *Pregnancy and childbearing during adolescence: Research priorities for the 1980s.* New York: Alan R. Liss.

Graham, S. (1984). Communicating sympathy and anger to black and white students: The cognitive (attributional) antecedents of affective cues. *Journal of Personality and Social Psychology, 47*, 40–54.

Graham, S. (1986, August). *Can attribution theory tell us something about motivation in blacks?* Paper presented at the meeting of the American Psychological Association, Washington, DC.

Graham, S. (1987, August). *Developing relations between attributions, affect, and intended social behavior.* Paper presented at the meeting of the American Psychological Association, New York, NY.

Green, R. (1974). One-hundred-ten feminine and masculine boys: Behavioral contrasts and demographic similarities. *Archives of Sexual Behavior, 5*, 425–446.

Green, R. (1987). *The "sissy boy syndrome" and the development of homosexuality.* New Haven, CT: Yale University Press.

Greenberg, M. T., & Crnic, K. A. (1988). Longitudinal predictors of developmental status and social interaction in premature and full-term infants at age two. *Child Development, 59*, 554–570.

Greenfield, J. (1972). *A child called Noah.* New York: Holt, Rinehart, & Winston.

Grieser, D. L., & Kuhl, P. K. (1988). Maternal speech to infants in tonal language: Support for universal prosodic features in motherese. *Developmental Psychology, 24*, 14–20.

Grossman, F. K., Pollack, W. S., & Golding, E. (1988). Fathers and children: Predicting the quality and quantity of fathering. *Developmental Psychology, 24*, 82–91.

Grotevant, H. D. (1984, February). *Exploration and negotiation of differences within families during adolescence.* Paper presented at the conference on adolescent development, Tucson, AZ.

Grotevant, H. D., & Adams, G. R. (1984). Development of an objective measure to assess ego identity in adolescence: Validation and application. *Journal of Youth and Adolescence, 13*, 419–438.

Grotevant, H. D., & Cooper, C. R. (1985). Patterns of interaction in family relationships and the development of identity exploration in adolescence. *Child Development, 56*, 415–428.

Guilford, J. P. (1967). *The structure of intellect.* New York: McGraw-Hill.

Gunnar, M. R., Malone, S., & Fisch, R. O. (1987). The psychobiology of stress and coping in the human neonate: Studies of the adrenocortical activity in response to stress in the first week of life. In T. Field, P. McCabe, & N. Schneiderman (Eds.), *Stress and coping.* Hillsdale, NJ: Erlbaum.

Guttentag, M., & Bray, H. (1976). *Undoing sex stereotypes: Research and resources for educators.* New York: McGraw-Hill.

Guttentag, R. E. (1984). The mental effort requirement of cumulative rehearsal: A developmental study. *Journal of Experimental Child Psychology, 37*, 92–106.

Haas, A. (1979). *Teenage sexuality: A survey of teenage sexual behavior.* New York: Macmillan.

Hall, G. S. (1904). *Adolescence* (Vols. I and II). Englewood Cliffs, NJ: Prentice-Hall.

Halpern, R. (1984). Home-based early intervention: Emerging purposes, intervention approaches, and evaluation strategies. *Infant Mental Health Journal, 5*, 206–220.

Hamburg, B. (1974). Early adolescence: A specific and stressful stage of the life cycle. In G. Coelho, D. A. Hamburg, & J. E. Adams (Eds.), *Coping and adaptation.* New York: Basic Books.

Hamburg, B. (1986). Subsets of adolescent mothers: Developmental, biomedical and psychosocial issues. In J. Lancaster & B. Hamburg (Eds.), *Schoolage pregnancy and parenthood: Biosocial dimensions.* New York: Aldine DeGruyter.

Hamm, C. M. (1977). The content of moral education, or in defense of the "bag of virtues." *School Review, 85*, 218–228.

Harlow, H. F., & Zimmerman, R. R. (1959). Affectional responses in the infant monkey. *Science, 130*, 421–432.

Harris, P. L. (1975). Development of search and object permanence during infancy. *Psychological Bulletin, 82*, 332–344.

Harris, R. F., Wolf, M. M., & Baer, D. M. (1964). Effects of adult social reinforcement on child behavior. *Young Children, 20*, 8–17.

Hart, D., Maloney, J., & Damon, W. (1987). The meaning and development of identity. In T. Honess & K. Yardley (Eds.), *Self and identity: Perspectives across the lifespan*. London: Routledge & Kegan Paul.

Harter, S. (1980). A model of intrinsic motivation in children: Individual differences and developmental change. In W. A. Collins (Ed.), *Minnesota Symposium on Child Psychology* (Vol. 14). Hillsdale, NJ: Erlbaum.

Harter, S. (1981). A new self-report scale of intrinsic versus extrinsic motivation in the classroom: Motivational and informational components. *Developmental Psychology, 17*, 300–312.

Harter, S. (1982). The perceived competence scale for children. *Child Development, 53*, 87–97.

Harter, S. (1983). Developmental perspectives on the self system. In P. H. Mussen (Ed.), *Handbook of child psychology* (4th ed., Vol. 4). New York: Wiley.

Harter, S., Alexander, P. C., & Neimeyer, R. A. (1988). Long-term effects of incestuous child abuse in college women: Social adjustment, social cognition, and family characteristics. *Journal of Consulting and Clinical Psychology, 56*, 5–8.

Harter, S., & Pike, R. (1984) The pictorial scale of perceived competence and social acceptance for young children. *Child Development, 55*, 1969–1982.

Hartley, R. E., Frank, L. K., & Goldenson, R. M. (1952). *Understanding children's play*. New York: Columbia University Press.

Hartshorne, H., & May, M. S. (1928–30). *Moral studies in the nature of character: Studies in deceit* (Vol. 1); *Studies in self-control* (Vol. 2); *Studies in the organization of character* (Vol. 3). New York: Macmillan.

Hartup, W. W. (1976). Peer interaction and the development of the individual child. In E. Schopler & R. J. Reichler (Eds.), *Psychopathology and child development*. New York: Plenum.

Hartup, W. W. (1983). The peer system. In P. H. Mussen (Ed.), *Handbook of child psychology* (4th ed., Vol. 4). New York: Wiley.

Hawkins, J. A., & Berndt, T. J. (1985, April). *Adjustment following the transition to junior high school*. Paper presented at the biennial meeting of the Society for Research in Child Development, Toronto.

Hay, A. (1987, April). *Learning to control a conversation*. Paper presented at biennial meeting of the Society for Research in Child Development, Baltimore, MD.

Hay, D. F. (1985, April). *The search for general principles in social life: Some lessons from young peers*. Paper presented at the meeting of the Society for Research in Child Development, Toronto.

Hayden-Thomson, L., Rubin, K. H., & Hymel, S. (1987). Sex preferences in sociometric choices. *Developmental Psychology, 23*, 558–562.

Hayes, D. (Ed.). (1987). *Risking the future: Adolescent sexuality, pregnancy, and childbearing* (Vol. 1). Washington, DC: National Academy Press.

Hayes, K. J., & Hayes, C. (1951). Picture perception in a home-raised chimpanzee. *Journal of Comparative and Physiological Psychology, 46*, 470–474.

Hazen, N. L., Lockman, J. J., & Pick, H. L. (1978). The development of children's representations of large-scale environments. *Child Development, 49*, 623–636.

Heinicke, C. M., Beckwith, L., & Thompson, A. (1988). Early intervention in the family system: A framework and review. *Infant Mental Health Journal, 9*, 2.

Henderson, N. (1982). Human behavior genetics. *Annual Review of Psychology, 33*, 403–440.

Herdt, G. H. (1988, August). *Coming out processes as an anthropological rite of passage*. Paper presented at the annual meeting of the American Psychological Association, Atlanta, GA.

Hess, L., Lonky, E., & Roodin, P. A. (1985, April). *The relationship of moral reasoning and ego strength to cheating behavior*. Paper presented at the meeting of the Society for Research in Child Development, Toronto.

Hetherington, E. M. (in press). Coping with family transitions: Winners, losers, and survivors. *Child Development*.

Hetherington, E. M., Cox, M., & Cox, R. (1982). Effects of divorce on children and parents. In M. E. Lamb (Ed.), *Nontraditional families*. Hillsdale, NJ: Erlbaum.

Hetherington, E. M., Hagan, M. S., & Anderson, E. R. (in press). Family transitions: A child's perspective. *American Psychologist*.

Hewlitt, B. S. (1987). Intimate fathers: Patterns of paternal holding among Aka pygmies. In M. E. Lamb (Ed.), *The father's role: Cross-cultural perspectives*. Hillsdale, NJ: Erlbaum.

Hiebert, J., & Wearne, D. (1988). Instruction and cognitive change in mathematics. *Educational Psychologist, 23*, 105–118.

Higgins, A., Power, C., & Kohlberg, L. (1983, April). *Moral atmosphere and moral judgment*. Paper presented at the biennial meeting of the Society for Research in Child Development, Detroit.

Higgins, A. T., & Turnure, J. E. (1984). Distractibility and concentration of attention in children's development. *Child Development, 55*, 1799–1810.

Hill, C. R., & Stafford, F. P. (1980). Parental care of children: Time diary estimate of quantity, predictability, and variety. *Journal of Human Resources, 15*, 219–239.

Hill, J. P. (1980). The early adolescent and the family. In *The seventy-ninth yearbook of the National Society for the Study of Education*. Chicago, IL: University of Chicago Press.

Hill, J. P. (1983, April). *Adolescent development*. Paper presented at the biennial meeting of the Society for Research in Child Development, Detroit, MI.

Hill, J. P., & Holmbeck, G. N. (in press). Attachment and autonomy during adolescence. *Annals of Child Development*.

Hill, J. P., Holmbeck, G. N., Marlow, L., Green, T. M., & Lynch, M. E. (1985). Pubertal status and parent-child relations in families of seventh-grade boys. *Journal of Early Adolescence, 5*, 31–44.

Hinde, R., & Stevenson-Hinde, J. (Eds.). (1987). *Towards understanding families*. London: Cambridge University Press.

Hinde, R. A. (1983). Ethology and child development. In P. H. Mussen (Ed.), *Handbook of child psychology* (4th ed., Vol. 2). New York: Wiley.

Hirsch, E. D. (1987). *Cultural literacy: What every American needs to know*. Boston, MA: Houghton Mifflin.

Ho, D. Y. F. (1987). Fatherhood in Chinese culture. In M. E. Lamb (Ed.), *The father's role: Cross-cultural perspectives*. Hillsdale, NJ: Erlbaum.

Hodapp, R. M., Goldfield, E. C., & Boyatzis, C. J. (1984). The use and effectiveness of maternal scaffolding in mother-infant games. *Child Development, 55*, 772–781.

Hoffman, L. W. (1979). Maternal employment: 1979. *American Psychologist, 34*, 859–865.

Hoffman, M. L. (1979). Development of moral thought, feeling, and behavior. *American Psychologist, 34*, 958–966.

Hoffman, M. L. (1980). Moral development in adolescence. In J. Adelson (Ed.), *Handbook of adolescent psychology*. New York: Wiley.

Honzik, M. P., MacFarlane, J. W., & Allen, L. (1948). The stability of mental test performance between two and eighteen years. *Journal of Experimental Education, 17,* 309–324.

Howard, J. (1988, November). *Developmental and behavioral concerns of drug dependent mothers.* Paper presented at the Developmental Interventions in Neonatal Care Conference, San Diego, CA.

Howes, C. (1985, April). *Predicting preschool sociometric status from toddler peer interaction.* Paper presented at the biennial meeting of the Society for Research in Child Development, Toronto.

Howes, C. (1988, April). *Can the age of entry and the quality of infant child care predict behaviors in kindergarten?* Paper presented at the International Conference on Infant Studies, Washington, DC.

Huesmann, L. R., Eron, L. D., Dubow, E. F., & Seebauer, E. (in press). Television viewing habits in childhood and adult aggression. *Child Development.*

Humphreys, L. G. (1985). A conceptualization of intellectual giftedness. In F. D. Horowitz & M. O'Brien (Eds.), *The gifted and the talented.* Washington, DC: American Psychological Association.

Hunt, M. (1974). *Sexual behavior in the 1970s.* Chicago: Playboy Press.

Hurley, L. S. (1980). *Developmental nutrition.* Englewood Cliffs, NJ: Prentice-Hall.

Huston, A. C. (1983). Sex-typing. In P. H. Mussen (Ed.), *Handbook of child psychology* (4th ed., Vol. 4). New York: Wiley.

Huston, A. C., Siegle, J., & Bremer, M. (1983, April). *Family environment television use by preschool children.* Paper presented at the biennial meeting of the Society for Research in Child Development, Detroit, MI.

Huston-Stein, A., & Higgens-Trenk, A. (1978). Development of females from childhood through adulthood: Career and feminine role orientations. In P. Baltes (Ed.), *Life-span development and behavior* (Vol. 1). New York: Academic Press.

Hutchings, D. E., & Fifer, W. P. (1986). Neurobehavioral effects in human and animal offspring following prenatal exposure to methadone. In E. P. Riley & C. V. Vorhees (Eds.), *Handbook of behavioral teratology.* New York: Plenum.

Hutchings, N. (Ed.). (1988). *The violent family.* New York: Human Sciences Press.

Hwang, P. (1987). The changing role of Swedish fathers. In M. E. Lamb (Ed.), *The father's role: Cross-cultural perspectives.* Hillsdale, NJ: Erlbaum.

Hyde, J. S. (1984). Children's understanding of sexist language. *Developmental Psychology, 20,* 697–706.

Hyde, J. S. (1988). *Half the human experience* (4th ed). Lexington, MA: D.C. Heath.

Hyde, J. S., & Linn, M. C. (Eds.). (1986). *The psychology of gender: Advances through meta-analysis.* Baltimore, MD: Johns Hopkins University Press.

Hyde, J. S., Rosenberg, B. G., & Behrman, J. A. (1977). Tomboyism. *Psychology of Women Quarterly, 2,* 73–75.

Inhelder, B., De Capron, D., & Cornu-Wells, A. (Eds.). (in press). *Piaget today.* Hillsdale, NJ: Erlbaum.

Inoff-Germain, G., Arnold, G. S., Nottelmann, E. D., Susman, E. J., Cutler, G. B., & Chrousos, G. P. (1988). Relations between hormone levels and observational measures of aggressive behavior of young adolescents in family interactions. *Developmental Psychology, 24,* 129–139.

Irvin, F. S. (1988, August). *Clinical perspectives on resilience among gay and lesbian youth.* Paper presented at the annual meeting of the American Psychological Association, Atlanta, GA.

Isenberg, J., & Quisenberry, N. L. (1988). Play: A necessity for all children. *Childhood Education, 64,* 138–145.

Izard, C. E. (1982). *Measuring emotions in infants and young children.* New York: Cambridge University Press.

Izard, C. E., & Malatesta, C. Z. (1987). Differential emotions theory of early emotional development. In J. D. Osofsky (Ed.), *Handbook of infant development* (2nd ed.). New York: Wiley.

James, W. (1890). *The principles of psychology.* New York: Dover.

Janos, P. M., & Robinson, N. M. (1985). Psychosocial development in intellectually gifted children. In F. D. Horowitz & M. O'Brien (Eds.), *The gifted and the talented.* Washington, DC: American Psychological Association.

Jeans, P. C., Smith, M. B., & Stearns, G. (1955). Incidence of prematurity in relation to maternal nutrition. *Journal of the American Dietary Association, 31,* 576–581.

Jensen, A. R. (1969). How much can we boost IQ and scholastic achievement? *Harvard Educational Review, 39,* 1–123.

Jensen, L. C., & Knight, R. S. (1981). *Moral education: Historical perspectives.* New York: University Press of America.

Johnson, J. H., Rasbury, W. C., & Siegel, L. J. (1986). *Approaches to child treatment.* New York: Pergamon.

Johnston, L. D., Bachman, J. G., & O'Malley, P. M. (1986). *Monitoring the future.* Ann Arbor: University of Michigan, Institute of Social Research.

Johnston, L. D., Bachman, J. G., & O'Malley, P. M. (1988, January). *Illicit drug use by American high school seniors, college students, and young adults.* Ann Arbor, MI: Institute for Social Research, University of Michigan.

Johnston, L. D., O'Malley, P. M., & Bachman, J. G. (1987). *National trends in drug use and related factors among American high school seniors and young adults, 1975–1986.* Ann Arbor, MI: Institute for Social Research, University of Michigan.

Jones, E. R., Forrest, J. D., Goldman, N., Henshaw, S. K., Lincoln, R., Rosoff, J. I., Westoff, C. G., & Wulf, D. (1985). Teenage pregnancy in developed countries: Determinants and policy implications. *Family Planning Perspectives, 17,* 53–63.

Jones, L. V. (1984). Black-white achievement differences: Narrowing the gap. *American Psychologist, 39,* 308–315.

Jones, M. C. (1924). A laboratory study of fear. *Journal of Genetic Psychology, 31,* 308–315.

Jones, M. C. (1965). Psychological correlates of somatic development. *Child Development, 36,* 899–911.

Jose, P. E. (1985, April). *Development of the immanent justice judgment in moral evaluation.* Paper presented at the biennial meeting of the Society for Research in Child Development, Toronto.

Juster, F. T. (in press). A note on recent changes in time use. In F. T. Juster & F. Stafford (Eds.), *Studies in the measurement of time allocation.* Ann Arbor, MI: Institute for Social Research.

Kagan, J. (1984). *The nature of the child.* New York: Basic Books.

Kagan, J. (1987a). Perspectives on infancy. In J. Osofsky (Ed.), *Handbook of infant development* (2nd ed.). New York: Wiley.

Kagan, J. (1987b, April). *Temperamental bases for reactions to uncertainty*. Paper presented at the biennial meeting of the Society for Research in Child Development, Baltimore, MD.

Kagan, J. (1988, August). *The idea of temperament categories*. Paper presented at the annual meeting of the American Psychological Association, Atlanta, GA.

Kagan, J., Kearsley, R. B., & Zelazo, P. R. (1978). *Infancy*. Cambridge, MA: Harvard University Press.

Kahn, S. E., & Richardson, A. (1983). Evaluation of a course in sex roles for secondary school students. *Sex Roles, 9,* 431–440.

Kail, R. (in press). Reply to Stigler, Nusbaum, & Chalip (1988). *Child Development*.

Kail, R., & Pellegrino, J. W. (1985). *Human intelligence*. New York: W. H. Freeman.

Kaitz, M., Meschulach-Sarfaty, O., Auerbach, J., & Eidelman, A. (1988). A reexamination of newborns' ability to imitate facial expressions. *Developmental Psychology, 24,* 3–7.

Kanfer, F. H., & Schefft, B. K. (1987). *Guiding the process of therapeutic change*. Champaign, IL: Research Press.

Kanner, A. D., Feldman, S. S., Weinberg, D. A., & Ford, M. E. (1987). Uplifts, hassles, and adaptational outcomes in early adolescents. *Journal of Early Adolescence, 7,* 371–394.

Katz, P. A. (1987, August). *Children and social issues*. Paper presented at the meeting of the American Psychological Association, New York, NY.

Kazdin, A. E. (1988). Introduction to special series. *Journal of Consulting and Clinical Psychology, 56,* 3–4.

Kearns, D. T. (1988, April). An education recovery plan for America. *Phi Delta Kappan*, pp. 565–570.

Keeney, T. J., Cannizzo, S. R., & Flavell, J. H. (1967). Spontaneous and induced verbal rehearsal in a recall task. *Child Development, 38,* 953–966.

Keil, F. C. (1984). Mechanisms in cognitive development and the structure of knowledge. In R. J. Sternberg (Ed.), *Mechanisms of cognitive development*. New York: W. H. Freeman.

Keith, T. Z., Cool, V. A., Novak, C. G., White, L. J., & Pottebaum, S. M. (1988). Confirmatory factor analysis of the Stanford-Binet fourth edition. *Journal of Educational Psychology, 26,* 253–274.

Kellogg, W. N., & Kellogg, C. A. (1933). *The ape and the child*. New York: McGraw-Hill.

Kelly, J. B. (1987, August). *Children of divorce: Long-term effects and clinical implications*. Paper presented at the meeting of the American Psychological Association, New York, NY.

Kerr, B. A. (1983). Raising the career aspirations of gifted girls. *Vocational Guidance Quarterly, 32,* 37–43.

Kessen, W., Haith, M. M., & Salapatek, P. (1970). Human infancy. In P. H. Mussen (Ed.), *Manual of child psychology* (3rd ed., Vol. 1). New York: Wiley.

Kinsey, A. C., Pomeroy, W. B., & Martin, E. E. (1948). *Sexual behavior in the human male*. Philadelphia: W. B. Saunders.

Klaus, M. H. (1988, November). *Recognizing and managing stress in the caregiver*. Paper presented at the Developmental Interventions in Neonatal Care Conference, San Diego, CA.

Klaus, M. H., & Kennell, H. H. (1976). *Maternal-infant bonding*. St. Louis, MO: Mosby.

Klein, P. (1984). Behavior of Israeli mothers toward infants in relation to infants' perceived temperament. *Child Development, 55,* 1212–1218.

Klein, S. S. (1988). Using sex equity research to improve education policies. *Theory into Practice, 27,* 152–160.

Klein, S. S. (in press). Sex equity and gender equity. *Educational Leadership*.

Kobak, R. R., & Sceery, A. (1988). Attachment in late adolescence: Working models, affect regulation, and representations of self and others. *Child Development, 59,* 135–146.

Koegel, R. L., Dyer, K., & Bell, L. K. (1987). The influence of child-preferred activities on autistic children's social behavior. *Journal of Applied Behavior Analysis, 20,* 243–252.

Koegel, R. L., O'Dell, M. C., & Koegel, L. K. (1987). A natural language teaching paradigm for nonverbal autistic children. *Journal of Autism and Developmental Disorders, 17,* 187–194.

Kohlberg, L. (1958). *The development of modes of moral thinking and choice in the years 10 to 16*. Unpublished doctoral dissertation, University of Chicago, Chicago, IL.

Kohlberg, L. (1966). A cognitive-developmental analysis of children's sex-role concepts and attitudes. In E. E. Maccoby (Ed.), *The development of sex differences*. Stanford, CA: Stanford University Press.

Kohlberg, L. (1969). Stage and sequence: The cognitive-developmental approach to socialization. In D. A. Goslin (Ed.), *Handbook of socialization theory and research*. Chicago, IL: Rand McNally.

Kohlberg, L. (1976). Moral stages and moralization: The cognitive-developmental approach. In T. Lickona (Ed.), *Moral development and behavior*. New York: Holt, Rinehart, & Winston.

Kohlberg, L. (1981). *The philosophy of moral development: Moral stages and the idea of justice*. New York: Harper & Row.

Kohlberg, L. (1986). A current statement on some theoretical issues. In S. Modgil & C. Modgil (Eds.), *Lawrence Kohlberg*. Philadelphia, PA: Falmer Press.

Kohlberg, L., & Candee, D. (1979). *Relationships between moral judgment and moral action*. Unpublished manuscript, Harvard University, Cambridge, MA.

Kohlberg, L., & Higgins, A. (1987). School democracy and social interaction. In W. M. Kurtines & J. L. Gewirtz (Eds.), *Moral development through social interaction*. New York: Wiley.

Kohn, A. (1987). *No contest: The case against competition*. Boston: Houghton Mifflin.

Kohut, H. (1977). *The restoration of the self*. New York: International Universities Press.

Kopp, C. B. (1983). Risk factors in development. In P. H. Mussen (Ed.), *Handbook of child psychology* (4th ed., Vol. 2). New York: Wiley.

Kopp, C. B. (1987). Developmental risk: Historical reflections. In J. D. Osofsky (Ed.), *Handbook of infant development* (2nd ed.). New York: Wiley.

Kopp, C. B., & Parmalee, A. H. (1979). Prenatal and perinatal influences on behavior. In J. D. Osofsky (Ed.), *Handbook of infant development*. New York: Wiley.

Korner, A. F., Hutchinson, C. A., Koperski, J. A., Kraemer, H. C., & Schneider, P. A. (1981). Stability of individual differences of neonatal motor and crying responses. *Child Development, 40,* 137–141.

Krauss, R. A., & Glucksberg, S. (1969). The development of communication: Competence as a function of age. *Child Development, 40,* 255–266.

Kreutzer, M. A., Leonard, C., & Flavell, J. H. (1975). An interview study of children's knowledge about memory. *Monographs of the Society for Research in Child Development, 40*(Whole No. 159).

Krogman, W. M. (1970). Growth of head, face, trunk, and limbs in Philadelphia white and Negro children of elementary and high school age. *Monographs of the Society for Research in Child Development, 35*(3, Serial No. 136).

Kuhn, D. (1984). Cognitive development. In M. H. Bornstein & M. E. Lamb (Eds.), *Developmental psychology: An advanced textbook*. Hillsdale, NJ: Erlbaum.

La Barbera, J. D., Izard, C. E., Vietze, P., & Parisi, S. A. (1976). Four- and six-month-old infants' visual responses to joy, anger, and neutral expressions. *Child Development, 47*, 535–538.

Lamb, M. E. (1977). The development of mother-infant and father-infant attachments in the second year of life. *Developmental Psychology, 13*, 637–648.

Lamb, M. E. (1986). *The father's role: Applied perspectives*. New York: Wiley.

Lamb, M. E. (Ed.). (1987). *The father's role: Cross-cultural perspectives*. Hillsdale, NJ: Erlbaum.

Lamb, M. E., Frodi, A. M., Hwang, C. P., Frodi, M., & Steinberg, J. (1982). Mother- and father-infant interaction involving play and holding in traditional and nontraditional Swedish families. *Developmental Psychology, 18*, 215–221.

Lamb, M. E., & Roopnarine, J. L. (1979). Peer influences on sex-role development in preschoolers. *Child Development, 50*, 1219–1222.

Lamb, M. E., Thompson, R. A., Gardner, W. P., Charnov, E. L., & Estes, D. (1984). Security of infantile attachment as assessed in the strange situation: Its study and biological interpretation. *The Behavioral and Brain Sciences, 7*, 121–171.

Lambert, N. M., & Hartsough, C. S. (1984). Contribution of predispositional factors to the diagnosis of hyperactivity. *American Journal of Orthopsychiatry, 54*, 97–109.

Landesman-Dwyer, S., & Sackett, G. P. (1983, April). *Prenatal nicotine exposure and sleep-wake patterns in infancy*. Paper presented at the biennial meeting of the Society for Research in Child Development, Detroit, MI.

Lane, H. (1976). *The wild boy of Aveyron*. Cambridge, MA: Harvard University Press.

Lapsley, D. K. (1988, May). Personal communication. Department of Psychology, Notre Dame University, South Bend, IN.

Lapsley, D. K., Enright, R. D., & Serlin, R. C. (1986). Moral and social education. In J. Worrell & F. Danner (Eds.), *Adolescent development: Issues in education*. New York: Academic Press.

Lapsley, D. K., Milstead, M., Quintana, S. M., Flannery, D., & Buss, R. R. (1986). Adolescent egocentrism and formal operations: Tests of a theoretical assumption. *Developmental Psychology, 22*, 800–807.

Lapsley, D. K., & Murphy, M. N. (1985). Another look at the theoretical assumptions of adolescent egocentrism. *Developmental Review, 5*, 201–217.

Lapsley, D. K., & Power, F. C. (Eds.). (1988). *Self, ego, and identity*. New York: Springer.

Lapsley, D. K., & Quintana, S. M. (1985). Recent approaches in children's elementary moral and social education. *Elementary School Guidance and Counseling Journal, 19*, 246–251.

Lazar, I., Darlington, R., & Collaborators. (1982). Lasting effects of early childhood education: A report from the consortium for longitudinal studies. *Monographs of the Society for Research in Child Development, 47*(2–3, Whole No. 195).

Lazarus, R. S., & Folkman, S. (1984). *Stress, appraisal, and coping*. New York: Springer.

Leboyer, F. (1975). *Birth without violence*. New York: Knopf.

Lee, V. E., Brooks-Gunn, J., & Schnur, E. (1988). Does Head Start work? A 1-year follow-up comparison of disadvantaged children attending Head Start, no preschool, and other preschool programs. *Developmental Psychology, 24*, 210–222.

Lefkowitz, M. M., Eron, L. D., Walder, L. O., & Huesmann, L. R. (1972). Television violence and children's aggression: A follow-up study. In G. A. Comstock & E. A. Rubenstein (Eds.), *Television and social behavior* (Vol. 3). Washington, DC: U.S. Government Printing Office.

Lehrer, R., & Yussen, S. R. (1988, April). *Conceptions of computer and human intelligence*. Paper presented at the annual meeting of the American Educational Research Association, New Orleans, LA.

Leiffer, A. D. (1973). *Television and the development of social behavior*. Paper presented at the meeting of the International Society for the Study of Behavioral Development, Ann Arbor, MI.

Leiffer, A. D., Gordon, N. J., & Graves, S. B. (1974). Children's television: More than entertainment. *Harvard Educational Review, 44*, 213–245.

LeMare, L. J., & Rubin, K. H. (1987). Perspective taking and peer interaction: Structural and developmental analyses. *Child Development, 58*, 306–315.

Lenneberg, E. H. (1962). *Biological foundations of language*. New York: Wiley.

Lenneberg, E. H., Rebelsky, F. G., & Nichols, I. A. (1965). The vocalization of infants born to deaf and hearing parents. *Human Development, 8*, 23–37.

Lepper, M. R. (1985). Microcomputers in education: Motivational and social issues. *American Psychologist, 40*, 1–19.

Lepper, M. R., Greene, D., & Nisbett, R. R. (1973). Undermining children's intrinsic interest with extrinsic rewards. *Journal of Personality and Social Psychology, 28*, 129–137.

Lerner, J. (1988). *Learning disabilities*. Boston, MA: Houghton-Mifflin.

Lerner, M. J. (1982). The justice motive in human relations and the economic model of man: A radical analysis of facts and fictions. In V. J. Derlega & J. Grzelak (Eds.), *Cooperation and helping behavior*. New York: Academic Press.

Lerner, R. M. (1987). A life-span perspective for early adolescence. In R. M. Lerner & T. T. Foch (Eds.), *Biological-psychosocial interactions in early adolescence*. Hillsdale, NJ: Erlbaum.

Lerner, R. M. (1988). Early adolescent transitions: The lore and the laws of adolescence. In M. D. Levine & E. R. McAnarney (Eds.), *Early adolescent transitions*. Lexington, MA: Lexington Books.

Lerner, R. M., & Karabenick, S. A. (1974). Physical attractiveness, body attitudes, and self-concept in late adolescence. *Journal of Youth and Adolescence, 3*, 307–316.

Lesser, G., Fifer, G., & Clark, D. (1965). Mental abilities of children from different social classes and cultural groups. *Monographs of the Society for Research in Child Development, 30*(4, Whole No. 102).

Levin, J. (1980). *The mnemonic '80s: Keywords in the classroom*. Theoretical paper No. 86. Wisconsin Research and Development Center for Individualized Schooling, Madison, WI.

Lewin, T. (1987, August 16). The new debate over life, death. *Dallas Morning News*, pp. 1A, 19A.

Lewis, M. (1987). Early sex role behavior and school age adjustment. In J. M. Reinisch, L. A. Rosenblum, & S. A. Sanders (Eds.), *Masculinity/Femininity*. New York: Oxford University Press.

Lewis, M. (1987). Social development in infancy and childhood. In J. D. Osofsky (Ed.), *Handbook of infant development* (2nd ed.). New York: Wiley.

Lewis, M., & Brooks-Gunn, J. (1979). *Social cognition and the acquisition of the self*. New York: Plenum.

Lewis, V. G., Money, J., & Bobrow, N. A. (1977). Idiopathic pubertal delay beyond the age of fifteen: Psychological study of twelve boys. *Adolescence, 12,* 1–11.

Lewkowicz, D. J. (1988). Sensory dominance in infants: 1. Six-month-old infants' response to auditory-visual compounds. *Developmental Psychology, 24,* 155–171.

Liberman, I. Y. (1987). Language literacy: The obligation of the schools of education. In W. Ellis (Ed.), *Intimacy with language: A forgotten basic in teacher education.* Baltimore, MD: The Orton Dyslexia Society.

Liebert, R. M., & Spratkin, J. N. (1988). *The early window: Effects of television on children and youth* (3rd ed.). Elmsford, NY: Pergamon.

Lifshitz, F., Pugliese, M. T., Moses, N., & Weyman-Daum, M. (1987). Parental health beliefs as a cause of non-organic failure to thrive. *Pediatrics, 80,* 175–182.

Lipsitt, L. P., Engen, T., & Kaye, H. (1963). Developmental changes in the olfactory threshold of the neonate. *Child Development, 34,* 371–376.

Lipsitt, L. P., Reilly, B. M., Butcher, M. J., & Greenwood, M. M. (1976). The stability and interrelationships of newborn sucking and heart rate. *Developmental Psychology, 9,* 305–310.

Lipsitz, J. (1983, October). *Making it the hard way: Adolescents in the 1980s.* Testimony prepared for the Crisis Intervention Task Force, House Select Committee on Children, Youth, and Families, Washington, DC.

Lipsitz, J. (1984). *Successful schools for young adolescents.* New Brunswick, NJ: Transaction Books.

Lockheed, M. (1985). Women, girls, and computers: A first look at the evidence. *Sex Roles, 13,* 115–122.

Long, T., & Long, L. (1983). *The handbook for latchkey children and their parents.* New York: Arbor House.

Lorden, R. B., & Falkenberg, S. D. (1988, August). *Applications of cognitive research to improvement of classroom teaching and learning.* Paper presented at the annual meeting of the American Psychological Association, Atlanta, GA.

Lorenz, K. Z. (1965). *Evolution and the modification of behavior.* Chicago, IL: University of Chicago Press.

Lovaas, O. I. (1977). *The autistic child: Language development through behavior modification.* New York: Halstead Press.

Lovaas, O. I., Koegel, R. L., & Schreibman, L. (1979). Stimulus overselectivity in autism: A review of research. *Psychological Bulletin, 86,* 1236–1254.

Lueptow, L. (1984). *Adolescent sex roles and social change.* New York: Columbia University Press.

Luria, A., & Herzog, E. (1985, April). *Gender segregation across and within settings.* Paper presented at the biennial meeting of the Society for Research in Child Development, Toronto.

Lykken, D. T. (1982). Research with twins: The concept of emergenesis. *Psychophysiology, 19,* 361–373.

Lyle, J., & Hoffman, H. R. (1972). Children's use of television and other media. In E. A. Rubenstein, G. A. Comstock, & J. P. Murray (Eds.), *Television and social behavior* (Vol. 4). Washington, DC: U.S. Government Printing Office.

Maccoby, E. E. (1980). *Social development.* San Diego, CA: Harcourt Brace Jovanovich.

Maccoby, E. E. (1984). Middle childhood in the context of the family. In *Development during middle childhood.* Washington, DC: National Academy Press.

Maccoby, E. E. (1987a). The varied meanings of "masculine" and "feminine." In J. M. Reinisch, L. A. Rosenblum, & S. A. Sanders (Eds.), *Masculinity/Femininity.* New York: Oxford University Press.

Maccoby, E. E. (1987b, November). Interview with Elizabeth Hall: All in the family. *Psychology Today,* pp. 54–60.

Maccoby, E. E. (1988). Gender as a social category. *Developmental Psychology, 24,* 755–765.

Maccoby, E. E., Depner, C. E., & Mnookin, R. H. (in press). Custody of children after divorce. In E. M. Hetherington & J. Arasteh (Eds.), *The impact of divorce, single-parenting, and stepparenting on children.* Hillsdale, NJ: Erlbaum.

Maccoby, E. E., & Jacklin, C. N. (1974). *The psychology of sex differences.* Stanford, CA: Stanford University Press.

Maccoby, E. E., & Jacklin, C. N. (in press). Gender segregation in childhood. In H. Reese (Ed.), *Advances in child development and behavior* (Vol. 20). New York: Academic Press.

Maccoby, E. E., & Martin, J. A. (1983). Socialization in the context of the family: Parent-child interaction. In P. H. Mussen (Ed.), *Handbook of child psychology* (4th ed., Vol. 4). New York: Wiley.

MacFarlane, J. A. (1975). Olfaction in the development of social preferences in the human neonate. In *Parent-infant interaction,* Ciba Foundation Symposium 33. Amsterdam: Elsevier.

MacTurk, R. H., McCarthy, M. E., Vietze, P. M., & Yarrow, L. J. (1987). Sequential analysis of mastery behavior in 6- and 12-month-old infants. *Developmental Psychology, 23,* 199–203.

Maddux, J. E., Roberts, M. C., Sledden, E. A., & Wright, L. (1986). Developmental issues in child health psychology. *American Psychologist, 41,* 24–34.

Mahler, M. (1979). *Separation-individuation* (Vol. 2). London: Jason Aronson.

Maltsberger, J. T. (1988). *Suicide risk.* New York: New York University Press.

Mandler, J. M. (1983). Representation. In P. H. Mussen (Ed.), *Handbook of child psychology* (4th ed., Vol. 3). New York: Wiley.

Maratsos, M. (1983). Some current issues in the study of the acquisition of grammar. In P. H. Mussen (Ed.), *Handbook of child psychology* (4th ed., Vol. 3). New York: Wiley.

Marcia, J. (1966). Development and validation of ego-identity status. *Journal of Personality and Social Psychology, 3,* 551–558.

Marcia, J. (1980). Ego identity development. In J. Adelson (Ed.), *Handbook of adolescent psychology.* New York: Wiley.

Marcia, J. (1987). The identity status approach to the study of ego identity development. In T. Honess & K. Yardley (Eds.), *Self and identity: Perspectives across the lifespan.* London: Routledge & Kegan Paul.

Markman, E. M. (1977). Realizing that you don't understand: A preliminary investigation. *Child Development, 48,* 986–992.

Markman, E. M. (1979). Realizing that you don't understand: Elementary school children's awareness of inconsistencies. *Child Development, 50,* 643–655.

Markman, E. M., & Callanan, M. (1983). An analysis of hierarchical classification. In R. Sternberg (Ed.), *Advances in the psychology of human intelligence.* Hillsdale, NJ: Erlbaum.

Marr, D. B., & Sternberg, R. J. (1985, April). *Effects of contextual relevance on attention to novel information.* Paper presented at the biennial meeting of the Society for Research in Child Development, Toronto.

Martin, J. (1976). *The education of adolescents.* Washington, DC: U.S. Office of Education.

Maslow, A. H. (1954). *Motivation and personality.* New York: Harper & Row.

Maslow, A. H. (1971). *The farther reaches of human nature.* New York: Viking.

Massey, C. M., & Gelman, R. (1988). Preschoolers' ability to decide whether a photographed unfamiliar object can move itself. *Developmental Psychology, 24,* 307–317.

Masters, J. C., Burish, T. G., Hollow, S. D., & Rimm, D. C. (1988). *Behavior therapy.* San Diego, CA: Harcourt Brace Jovanovich.

Matarazzo, J. D. (1979). Health psychology: APA's newest division. *The Health Psychologist, 1,* 1.

Matas, L., Arend, R. A., & Sroufe, L. A. (1978). Continuity in adaptation: Quality of attachment and later competence. *Child Development, 49,* 547–556.

Matheny, A. P., Dolan, R. S., & Wilson, R. S. (1976). Relation between twins' similarity: Testing an assumption. *Behavior Genetics, 6,* 343–351.

Mayer, R. (1987). *Educational psychology: A cognitive approach.* Boston, MA: Little, Brown & Co.

McAdoo, H. P., & McAdoo, J. L. (Eds.). (1985). *Black children: Social, educational, and parental environments.* Beverly Hills, CA: Sage.

McCall, R. B. (1985, April). *Discussion—Novelty as a source of developmental continuity in intelligence.* Paper presented at the biennial meeting of the Society for Research in Child Development, Toronto.

McCall, R. B., Applebaum, M. I., & Hogarty, P. S. (1973). Developmental changes in mental performance. *Monographs of the Society for Research in Child Development, 38*(Serial No. 150).

McCall, R. B., Eichorn, D. H., & Hogarty, P. S. (1977). Transitions in early mental development. *Monographs of the Society for Research in Child Development, 41*(3, Serial No. 171).

McCandless, B. R. (1973). *Male caregivers in day care: Demonstration Project.* Atlanta, GA: Emory University.

McCandless, B. R., & Evans, E. (1973). *Children and youth.* New York: Holt, Rinehart, & Winston.

McClelland, D. C. (1955). Some social consequences of achievement motivation. In M. R. Jones (Ed.), *The Nebraska Symposium on Motivation.* Lincoln, NE: University of Nebraska Press.

McClelland, D. C., Atkinson, J. W., Clark, R. W., & Lowell, E. L. (1953). *The achievement motive.* New York: Appleton-Century-Crofts.

McDaniel, M. A., & Pressley, M. (1987). *Imagery and related mnemonic process.* New York: Springer-Verlag.

McKnight, C. C., Crosswhite, F. J., Dossey, J. A., Kifer, E., Swafford, J. O., Travers, K. J., & Cooney, T. J. (1987). *The underachieving curriculum: Assessing U.S. school mathematics from an international perspective.* Champaign, IL: Stipes.

McLaughlin, B. (1978). *Second-language acquisition in childhood.* Hillsdale, NJ: Erlbaum.

McLaughlin, L., & Chassin, L. (1985, April). *Adolescents at risk for future alcohol abuse.* Paper presented at the biennial meeting of the Society for Research in Child Development, Toronto.

McNeil, D. (1970). *The acquisition of language.* New York: Harper & Row.

McQuire, W. J. (1986). The myth of mass media effectiveness. In G. Comstock (Ed.), *Public communication and behavior* (Vol. 1). New York: Academic Press.

McWhirter, D. P., Reinsch, J. M., & Sander, S. A. (in press). *Homosexuality/heterosexuality.* New York: Oxford University Press.

Medrich, E. A., Rosen, J., Rubin, V., & Buckley, S. (1982). *The serious business of growing up.* Berkeley, CA: University of California Press.

Meilman, P. W. (1979). Cross-sectional age changes in ego identity status during adolescence. *Developmental Psychology, 15,* 230–231.

Meltzoff, A. N. (1987, April). *Imitation by nine-month-olds in immediate and deferred tests.* Paper presented at the biennial meeting of the Society for Research in Child Development, Baltimore, MD.

Meltzoff, A. N. (1988). Infant imitation and memory: Nine-month-olds in immediate and deferred tests. *Child Development, 59,* 217–225.

Meltzoff, A. N., & Moore, M. K. (1977). Interpreting "imitative" responses in early infancy. *Science, 205,* 217–219.

Meredith, H. V. (1978). Research between 1960 and 1970 on the standing height of young children in different parts of the world. In H. W. Reese & L. P. Lipsitt (Eds.), *Advances in child development and behavior* (Vol. 12). New York: Academic Press.

Mervis, B. B., & Rosch, E. (1982). Categorization of natural objects. *Annual Review of Psychology, 32,* 89–115.

Messer, D. J., Rachford, D., McCarthy, M. E., & Yarrow, L. J. (1987). Assessment of mastery behavior at 30 months: Analysis of task-directed activities. *Developmental Psychology, 23,* 771–781.

Messer, D. J., Yarrow, L. J., & Vietze, P. M. (1982, August). *Mastery in infancy and competence in early childhood.* Paper presented at the meeting of the American Psychological Association, Washington, DC.

Meyerhoff, M. K., & White, B. L. (1986, September). Making the grade as parents. *Psychology Today,* pp. 38–45.

Milham, J., Widmayer, S., Bauer, C. R., & Peterson, L. (1983, April). *Predictory cognitive deficits for pre-term, low birthweight infants.* Paper presented at the biennial meeting of the Society for Research in Child Development, Detroit.

Miller, G. A. (1956). The magical number seven, plus or minus two: Some limits on our capacity for information processing. *Psychological Review, 63,* 81–97.

Miller, G. A. (1981). *Language and speech.* New York: W. H. Freeman.

Miller, N., & Maruyama, G. (1976). Ordinal position and peer popularity. *Journal of Personality and Social Psychology, 33,* 123–131.

Millon, T., & Klerman, G. L. (Eds.). (1986). *Contemporary directions in psychopathology.* New York: Guilford Press.

Minnett, A. M., Vandell, D. L., & Santrock, J. W. (1983). The effects of sibling status on sibling interaction: Influence of birth order, age spacing, sex of the child, and sex of the sibling. *Child Development, 54,* 1064–1072.

Minuchin, P. P., & Shapiro, E. K. (1983). The school as a context for social development. In P. H. Mussen (Ed.), *Handbook of child psychology* (4th ed., Vol. 4). New York: Wiley.

Mischel, W. (1970). Sex-typing and socialization. In P. H. Mussen (Ed.), *Manual of child psychology* (3rd ed., Vol. 2). New York: Wiley.

Mischel, W. (1973). Toward a cognitive social learning reconceptualization of personality. *Psychological Review, 80,* 252–283.

Mischel, W. (1974). Process in delay of gratification. In L. Berkowitz (Ed.), *Advances in experimental social psychology* (Vol. 7). New York: Academic Press.

Mischel, W. (1984). Convergences and challenges in the search for consistency. *American Psychologist, 39,* 351–364.

Mischel, W. (1987). *Personality* (4th ed.). New York: Holt, Rinehart, & Winston.

Mischel, W., & Mischel, H. (1975, April). *A cognitive social-learning analysis of moral development.* Paper presented at the meeting of the Society for Research in Child Development, Denver, CO.

Mischel, W., & Patterson, C. J. (1976). Substantive and structural elements of effective plans for self-control. *Journal of Social and Personality Psychology, 34,* 942–950.

Miura, I. T. (1987). Gender and socioeconomic status differences in middle-school computer interest and use. *Journal of Early Adolescence, 7,* 243–254.

Moely, B. E., Olson, F. A., Halwes, T. G., & Flavell, J. H. (1969). Production deficiency in young children's clustered recall. *Developmental Psychology, 1,* 26–34.

Money, J. (1987). Propaedeutics of Diecious G-I/R: Theoretical foundations for understanding dimorphic gender-identity role. In J. M. Reinisch, L. A. Rosenblum, & S. A. Sanders (Eds.), *Masculinity/Femininity.* New York: Oxford University Press.

Money, J. (1987). Sin, sickness, or status? Homosexual gender identity and psychoneuroendocrinology. *American Psychologist, 42,* 384–399.

Money, J., & Ehrhardt, A. A. (1972). *Man and woman, boy and girl.* Baltimore, MD: Johns Hopkins Press.

Monroe, R. (1988). *Creative brainstorms.* New York: Irvington.

Montemayor, R., & Hanson, E. (1985). A naturalistic view of conflict between adolescents and their parents and siblings. *Journal of Early Adolescence, 5,* 23–30.

Morgan, G. A., & Ricciuti, H. N. (1969). Infants' responses to strangers during the first year. In B. M. Foss (Ed.), *Determinants of infant behavior* (Vol. 4). London: Methuen.

Morgan, M. (1987). Television, sex-role attitudes, and sex-role behavior. *Journal of Early Adolescence, 7,* 269–282.

Morris, P. E. (Ed.). (1988). *Modelling cognition.* New York: Wiley.

Morrison, D. M. (1985). Adolescent contraceptive behavior: A review. *Psychological Bulletin, 98,* 538–568.

Morse, W. C. (1964). Self-concept in the school setting. *Childhood Education, 41,* 195–198.

Mueller, E. (1979). (Toddlers + Toys) = (An autonomous social system). In M. Lewis & L. A. Rosenblum (Eds.), *The child and its family.* New York: Plenum.

Mueller, E. (Discussant). (1985, April). *Early peer relations: Ten years of research.* Symposium presented at the meeting of the Society for Research in Child Development, Toronto.

Murray, D. M., Matthews, K. A., Blake, S. M., Prineas, R. J., & Gillum R. F. (1988). Type A behavior in children: Demographic, behavioral, and physiological correlates. In B. G. Melamed & others (Eds.), *Child health psychology.* Hillsdale, NJ: Erlbaum.

Murray, F. B. (1978, August). *Generation of educational practice from developmental theory.* Paper presented at the meeting of the American Psychological Association, Toronto.

Muuss, R. E. (1988). Carol Gilligan's theory of sex differences in the development of moral reasoning during adolescence. *Adolescence, 23,* 229–241.

National Education Association. (1974). *Today's changing roles: An approach to nonsexist teaching.* Minneapolis, MN: Author.

Neisser, U. (1967). *Cognitive psychology.* New York: Appleton-Century-Crofts.

Neisser, U. (1982). *Memory observed.* New York: W. H. Freeman.

Nelson, K. E. (1978). How children represent knowledge of their world in and out of language. In R. S. Siegler (Ed.), *Children's thinking: What develops?* Hillsdale, NJ: Erlbaum.

Newcomb, M. D., & Bentler, P. M. (1988). Impact of adolescent drug use and social support on problems of young adults: A longitudinal study. *Journal of Abnormal Psychology, 97,* 64–75.

Nicholls, J. G. (1975). Causal attributions and other achievement-related cognitions: Effects of task outcomes, attainment value, and sex. *Journal of Personality and Social Psychology, 31,* 379–389.

Nicholls, J. G. (1984). Conceptions of ability and achievement motivation. In R. E. Ames & C. Ames (Eds.), *Motivation in education.* New York: Academic Press.

Nielson, L. (1987). *Adolescent psychology.* New York: Holt, Rinehart, & Winston.

Nielson Television Index. (1981). *Child and teenage television viewing* (Special Release). New York: NTI.

Niemark, E. D. (1982). Adolescent thought: Transition to formal operations. In B. B. Wolman (Ed.), *Handbook of developmental psychology.* Englewood Cliffs, NJ: Prentice-Hall.

Ninio, A., & Bruner, J. (1978). The achievement and antecedent of labeling. *Journal of Child Language, 5,* 1–15.

Nottelmann, E. D., Susman, E. J., Blue, J. H., Inoff-Germain, G., Dorn, L. D., Loriaux, D. L., Cutler, G. B., & Chrousos, G. P. (1987). Gonadal and adrenal hormone correlates of adjustment in early adolescence. In R. M. Lerner & T. T. Foch (Eds.), *Biological-psychological interactions in early adolescence.* Hillsdale, NJ: Erlbaum.

Nucci, L. (1982). Conceptual development in the moral and conventional domains: Implications for values education. *Review of Educational Research, 52,* 93–122.

Nucci, L., & Nucci, M. (1982). Children's responses to moral and social conventional transgressions in free-play settings. *Child Development, 53,* 1337–1342.

Nucci, L., & Turiel, E. (1978). Social interactions and the development of social concepts in preschool children. *Child Development, 49,* 400–407.

O'Conner, M. J., Cohen, S., & Parmalee, A. H. (1984). Infant auditory discrimination in preterm and full-term infants as a predictor of 5-year intelligence. *Child Development, 20,* 159–165.

O'Connor-Francoeur, P. (1983, April). *Children's concepts of health and their health behavior.* Paper presented at the biennial meeting of the Society for Research in Child Development, Detroit, MI.

O'Leary, K. D., & Wilson, G. T. (1987). *Behavior therapy* (2nd ed.). Englewood Cliffs, NJ: Prentice-Hall.

Olweus, D. (1980). Bullying among schoolboys. In R. Barnen (Ed.), *Children and violence.* Stockholm: Adaemic Litteratur.

Oppenheimer, M. (1982, October). What you should know about herpes. *Seventeen Magazine,* pp. 154–155, 170.

Oser, F. K. (1986). Moral education and values education: The discourse perspective. In M. C. Wittrock (Ed.), *Handbook of research on teaching.* New York: Macmillan.

Osofsky, H. J., Osofsky, J. D., Culp, R., Krantz, K., & Tobiasen, J. (1985). Transition to parenthood: Risk factors for parents and infants. *Journal of Psychosomatic Obstetrics & Gynecology, 4,* 303–315.

Ottinger, D. R., & Simmons, J. E. (1964). Behavior of human neonates and prenatal maternal anxiety. *Psychological Reports, 14,* 391–394.

Oyama, S. (1973). *A sensitive period for the acquisition of a second language.* Unpublished doctoral dissertation, Harvard University, Cambridge, MA.

Page, D. C., Mosher, R., Simpson, E. M., Fisher, E. M. C., Mardon, G., Pollack, J., & Brown, L. G. (1987). The sex-determining region of the human Y chromosome encodes a finger protein. *Cell, 51,* 1091–1104.

Paivio, A. (1971). *Imagery and verbal processes.* New York: Holt.

Paivio, A. (1986). *Mental representation: A dual coding approach.* New York: Oxford University Press.

Palincsar, A. S., & Brown, A. L. (1984). Reciprocal teaching of comprehension-fostering and comprehension-monitoring activities. *Cognition and Instruction, 1,* 117–175.

Parcel, G. S., Simons-Morton, G. G., O'Hara, N. M., Baranowski, T., Kolbe, L. J., & Bee, D. E. (1987). School promotion of healthful diet and exercise behavior: An integration of organizational change and social learning theory interventions. *Journal of School Health, 57,* 150–156.

Parcel, G. S., Tiernan, K., Nadar, P. R., & Gottlob, D. (1979). Health education and kindergarten children. *Journal of School Health, 49,* 129–131.

Pardes, H. (1986). Neuroscience and psychiatry: Marriage or coexistence? *American Journal of Psychiatry, 143,* 1205–1212.

Paris, S. G., & Lindauer, B. K. (1976). The role of inferences in children's comprehension and memory for sentences. *Cognitive Psychology, 8,* 217–227.

Paris, S. G., & Lindauer, B. K. (1982). The development of cognitive skills during childhood. In B. B. Wolman (Ed.), *Handbook of developmental psychology.* Englewood Cliffs, NJ: Prentice-Hall.

Paris, S. G., Lindauer, B. K., & Cox, G. L. (1977). The development of inferential comprehension. *Child Development, 48,* 1728–1733.

Parke, R. D. (1972). Some effects of punishment on children's behavior. In W. W. Hartup (Ed.), *The young child* (Vol. 2). Washington, DC: National Association for the Education of Young Children.

Parke, R. D. (1976). *Child abuse: An overview of alternative models.* Paper presented at the meeting of the American Psychological Association, Washington, DC.

Parke, R. D. (1977). Some effects of punishment on children's behavior— revisited. In E. M. Hetherington & R. D. Parke (Eds.), *Readings in contemporary child psychology.* New York: McGraw-Hill.

Parke, R. D., & Sawin, D. B. (1980). The family in early infancy. In F. Pedersen (Ed.), *The father-infant relationship: Observational studies in a family context.* New York: Praeger.

Parke, R. D., & Suomi, S. (1981). Adult male-infant relationships: Human and non-human primate evidence. In K. Immelmann, G. W. Barlow, L. Petrinovitch, & M. Main (Eds.), *Behavioral development: The Bielefeld Interdisciplinary Project.* New York: Cambridge University Press.

Parker, J. G., & Gottman, J. M. (1989). Social and emotional development in a relational context: Friendship interaction from early childhood to adolescence. In T. J. Berndt & G. W. Ladd (Eds.), *Peer relationships in child development.* New York: Wiley.

Parmalee, A. H. (1986). Children's illnesses: Their beneficial effects on behavioral development. *Child Development, 57,* 1–10.

Parmalee, A. H., Wenner, W., & Schulz, H. (1964). Infant sleep patterns from birth to 16 weeks of age. *Journal of Pediatrics, 65,* 576–582.

Parsons, J. E., Ruble, D. N., Hodges, K. L., & Small, A. W. (1976). Cognitive-developmental factors in emerging sex differences in achievement-related expectancies. *Journal of Social Issues, 32,* 47–61.

Parten, M. (1932). Social play among preschool children. *Journal of Abnormal and Social Psychology, 27,* 243–269.

Pasley, K., & Ihinger-Tallman, M. (Eds.). (1987). *Remarriage and stepparenting.* New York: Guilford.

Patterson, G. R. (1982). *Coercive family processes.* Eugene, OR: Castalia Press.

Patterson, G. R. (1986). Performance models for antisocial boys. *American Psychologist, 41,* 432–444.

Patterson, G. R., Reid, J. B., & Dishion, T. D. (in press). *Antisocial boys.* Eugene, OR: Castalia Press.

Patterson, G. R., & Stouthamer-Loeber, M. (1984). The correlation of family management practices and delinquency. *Child Development, 55,* 1299–1307.

Pavlov, I. P. (1927). *Conditioned reflexes* (F. V. Anrep, Trans. and Ed.). New York: Dover.

Pawson, M., & Morris, N. (1972). The role of the father in pregnancy and labor. In N. Morris (Ed.), *Psychological medicine in obstetrics and gynecology.* Basel: Karger.

Penner, S. G. (1987). Parental responses to grammatical and ungrammatical child utterances. *Child Development, 58,* 376–384.

Peskin, H. (1967). Pubertal onset and ego functioning. *Journal of Abnormal Psychology, 72,* 1–15.

Petersen, A. C. (1979, January). Can puberty come any faster? *Psychology Today,* pp. 45–56.

Petersen, A. C. (1987a, September). Those gangly years. *Psychology Today,* pp. 28–34.

Petersen, A. C. (1987b). The nature of biological-psychosocial interactions: The sample case of early adolescence. In R. M. Lerner & T. T. Foch (Eds.), *Biological-psychosocial interactions in early adolescence.* Hillsdale, NJ: Erlbaum.

Petersen, A. C., Schulenberg, J. E., Abramowitz, R. H., Offer, D., & Jarcho, H. D. (1984). A self-image questionnaire for young adolescents (SIQYA): Reliability and validity studies. *Journal of Youth and Adolescence, 13,* 93–111.

Peterson, P. L. (1977). Interactive effects of student anxiety, achievement orientation, and teacher behavior on student achievement and attitude. *Journal of Educational Psychology, 69,* 779–792.

Pettit, G. S., Dodge, K. A., & Brown, M. M. (1988). Early family experience, social problem solving patterns, and children's social competence. *Child Development, 59,* 107–120.

Pfeffer, C. R. (1989). Suicide. In L. K. G. Hsu & M. Herson (Eds.), *Recent developments in adolescent psychiatry.* New York: Wiley.

Pfeffer, C. R., Lipkins, R., Plutchik, R., & Mizruchi, M. (1988). Normal children at risk for suicidal behavior: A two-year follow-up study. *Journal of the American Academy of Child and Adolescent Psychiatry, 27,* 34–41.

Phares, E. J. (1984). *Personality.* Columbus, OH: Charles E. Merrill.

Piaget, J. (1932). *The moral judgment of the child.* New York: Harcourt Brace Jovanovich.

Piaget, J. (1952a). Jean Piaget. In C. A. Murchison (Ed.), *A history of psychology in autobiography* (Vol. 4). Worchester, MA: Clark University Press.

Piaget, J. (1952b). *The origins of intelligence in children* (M. Cook, Trans.). New York: International Universities Press.

Piaget, J. (1962). *Play, dreams, and imitation in childhood.* New York: Norton.

Piaget, J. (1967). *The child's construction of the world.* Totowa, NJ: Littlefield, Adams & Co.

Piaget, J. (1970). Piaget's theory. In P. H. Mussen (Ed.), *Manual of child psychology* (3rd ed., Vol. 1). New York: Wiley.

Piaget, J., & Inhelder, B. (1969). *The child's conception of space* (F. J. Langdon & J. L. Lunzer, Trans.). New York: Norton (originally published 1948).

Pierce, C., & VanDeVeer, D. (1988). *AIDS.* Belmont, CA: Wadsworth.

Piers, E. V., & Harris, D. V. (1964). Age and other correlates of self-concept in children. *Journal of Educational Psychology, 55,* 91–95.

Pillow, B. H. (1988). Young children's understanding of attentional limits. *Child Development, 49,* 38–46.

Pines, M. (1987). Mirroring and child development. In T. Honess & K. Yardley (Eds.), *Self and identity: Perspectives across the lifespan.* London: Routledge & Kegan Paul.

Pinker, S. (1984). *Language learnability and language development.* Cambridge, MA: Harvard University Press.

Pipes, P. (1988a). Nutrition in infancy. In S. R. Williams & B. S. Worthington-Roberts (Eds.), *Nutrition throughout the life cycle.* St. Louis, MO: Times Mirror/ Mosby.

Pipes, P. (1988b). Nutrition in childhood. In S. R. Williams & B. S. Worthington-Roberts (Eds.), *Nutrition throughout the life cycle.* St. Louis, MO: Time Mirror/ Mosby.

Pipp, S., Fischer, K. W., & Jennings, S. (1987). Acquisition of self- and mother knowledge in infancy. *Developmental Psychology, 23,* 86–96.

Pittman, T. S., & Heller, J. S. (1987). Social motivation. *Annual Review of Psychology, 38,* 461–489.

Pleck, J. H. (1975). Masculinity-femininity: Current and alternative paradigms. *Sex Roles, 1,* 161–178.

Pleck, J. H. (1984). *Working wives and family well-being.* Beverly Hills, CA: Sage.

Plomin, R. (1987, April). *Adoption studies: Nurture as well as nature.* Paper presented at the biennial meeting of the Society for Research in Child Development, Baltimore, MD.

Plomin, R., DeFries, J. C., & Fulker, D. W. (1988). *Nature and nurture during infancy.* New York: Cambridge University Press.

Plomin, R., & Thompson, L. (1987). Life-span developmental behavior genetics. In P. B. Baltes, D. L. Featherman, & R. M. Lerner (Eds.), *Life-span development and behavior* (Vol. 7). Hillsdale, NJ: Erlbaum.

Polivy, J., & Thomsen, L. (1987). Eating, dieting, and body image. In E. A. Blechman & K. D. Brownell (Eds.), *Handbook of behavioral medicine for women.* Elmsford, NY: Pergamon.

Porter, F. L., Porges, S. W., & Marshall, R. E. (1988). Newborn pain cries and vagal tone: Parallel changes in response to circumcision. *Child Development, 59,* 495–515.

Posner, M. I. (1987, August). *Structure and function of selective attention.* Paper presented at the meeting of the American Psychological Association, New York, NY.

Power, C. (1984). *Moral atmosphere.* Paper presented at the meeting of the American Educational Research Association, New Orleans, LA.

Prechtl, H. F. R. (1965). Problems of behavioral studies in the newborn infant. In D. S. Lehrman, R. A. Hinde, & E. Shaw (Eds.), *Advances in the study of behavior.* New York: Academic Press.

Premack, A. J., & Premack, D. (1972). Teaching language to an ape. *Scientific American, 227,* 92–98.

Price, J., & Feshbach, S. (1982, August). *Emotional adjustment correlates of television viewing in children.* Paper presented at the meeting of the American Psychological Association, Washington, DC.

Quinn, T. C., Glasser, D., Cannon, R. O., & others. (1988). Human immunodeficiency virus infection among patients attending clinics for sexually transmitted diseases. *The New England Journal of Medicine, 318,* 197–202.

Rahman, T., & Bisanz, G. L. (1986). Reading ability and use of a story schema in recalling and reconstructing information. *Journal of Educational Psychology, 5,* 323–333.

Ramey, C., Bryant, D., & Suarez, T. (1985). Preschool compensatory education and the modifiability of intelligence: A critical review. In D. Detterman (Ed.), *Current topics in human intelligence.* Norwood, NJ: Ablex.

Ramey, C. T., & Haskins, R. (1981). The modification of intelligence through early experience. *Intelligence, 5,* 43–57.

Rapaport, J. L. (1986). Diet and hyperactivity. *Nutrition Review, 158* (Supplement).

Ratner, N., & Bruner, J. S. (1978). Games, social exchange, and the acquisition of language. *Journal of Child Language, 5,* 1–15.

Rauh, V. A., Achenbach, T. M., Nurcombe, B., Howell, C. T., & Teti, D. M. (1988). Minimizing adverse effects of low birthweight: Four-year results of an early intervention program. *Child Development, 49,* 544–553.

Reid, D. K. (1988). *Teaching the learning disabled.* Boston, MA: Allyn & Bacon.

Rekers, G. A. (1979). Psychosexual and gender problems. In E. J. Mash & L. G. Terdal (Eds.), *Behavioral assessment of childhood disorders.* New York: Guilford Press.

Rest, J. (1988, November). *With the benefits of hindsight.* Paper presented at the 13th Annual Conference of the Association for Moral Education, Pittsburgh, PA.

Rest, J. R. (1976). New approaches in the assessment of moral judgment. In T. Lickona (Ed.), *Moral development and behavior.* New York: Holt, Rinehart, & Winston.

Rest, J. R. (1983). Morality. In P. H. Mussen (Ed.), *Handbook of child psychology* (4th ed., Vol. 3). New York: Wiley.

Rest, J. R. (1986). *Moral development: Advances in theory and research.* New York: Praeger.

Rest, J. R., Turiel, E., & Kohlberg, L. (1969). Relations between level of moral judgment and preference and comprehension of the moral judgments of others. *Journal of Personality, 37,* 225–252.

Rice, F. P. (1989). *Human sexuality.* Dubuque, IA: Wm. C. Brown.

Rich, C. L., Young, D., & Fowler, R. C. (1986). San Diego suicide study. *Archives of General Psychiatry, 43,* 577–582.

Richardson, J. G., & Simpson, C. H. (1982). Children, gender, and social structure: An analysis of the contents of letters to Santa Claus. *Child Development, 53,* 429–436.

Rickel, A. V. (1989). *Teenage pregnancy and parenting.* New York: Hemisphere Pub.

Ricks, M. (1983). *The origins of individual differences in competence: Attachment history and environmental support.* Unpublished doctoral dissertation, University of Massachusetts, Amherst, MA.

Riddle, D. B., & Prinz, R. (1984, August). *Sugar consumption in young children.* Paper presented at the meeting of the American Psychological Association, Toronto.

Roberts, D. E., & Maccoby, N. (1985). Effects of mass media effectiveness. In G. Linzey & E. Aronson (Eds.), *Handbook of social psychology* (3rd ed., Vol. 2). New York: Random House.

Robinson, H. F. (1977). *Exploring teaching in early childhood education.* Boston, MA: Allyn & Bacon.

Robinson, N. M. (1987). Psychology and mental retardation. *American Psychologist, 42,* 791.

Rode, S. S., Chang, P., Fisch, R. O., & Sroufe, L. A. (1981). Attachment patterns of infants separated at birth. *Developmental Psychology, 17,* 188–191.

Rodin, J. (1984, December). Interview: A sense of control. *Psychology Today,* pp. 38–45.

Rodin, J. (1987, August). *Hunger, taste, and mother: Biobehavioral determinants of eating and its disorders.* Paper presented at the meeting of the American Psychological Association, New York, NY.

Rodin, J., & Salovey, P. (in press). Health psychology. *Annual Review of Psychology, 40.*

Rogers, C. R. (1961). *On becoming a person.* Boston, MA: Houghton-Mifflin.

Rogers, C. R. (1963). The actualizing tendency in relation to "motives" and consciousness. In M. R. Jones (Ed.), *Nebraska Symposium on Motivation.* Lincoln, NE: University of Nebraska Press.

Rogers, C. R. (1974). In retrospect: Forty-six years. *American Psychologist, 29,* 115–123.

Rogers, C. R. (1980). *A way of being.* Boston, MA: Houghton-Mifflin.

Rose, S. A., Feldman, J. F., McCarton, C. M., & Wolfson, J. (1988). Information processing in seven-month-old infants as a function of risk status. *Child Development, 59,* 489–603.

Rose, S. A., & Ruff, H. A. (1987). Cross-modal abilities in human infants. In J. D. Osofsky (Ed.), *Handbook of infant development* (2nd ed.). New York: Wiley.

Rose, S. A., & Wallace, I. F. (1985). Visual recognition memory: A predictor of late cognitive functioning in preterms. *Child Development, 56,* 843–852.

Rosenbaum, P. A., Elston, R. C., Srinivasan, S. R., Webber, L. S., & Berenson, G. S. (1987). Predictive value of parental measures in determining cardiovascular risk factor variables early in life. *Pediatrics,* Supplement, 807–815.

Rosenblith, J. F., & Sims-Knight, J. E. (1985). *In the beginning: Development in the first two years.* Monterey, CA: Brooks/Cole.

Rosenthal, R., & Jacobsen, L. (1968). *Pygmalian in the classroom.* New York: Holt, Rinehart, & Winston.

Ross, H. S., & Lollis, S. P. (1987). Communication within infant games. *Developmental Psychology, 23,* 241–248.

Rothbart, M. L. K. (1971). Birth order and mother-child interaction. *Dissertation Abstracts, 27,* 45–57.

Rothbart, M. L. K. (in press). Temperament and the development of inhibited approach. *Child Development.*

Rovee-Collier, C. (1987). Learning and memory in infancy. In J. D. Osofsky (Ed.), *Handbook of infant development* (2nd ed.). New York: Wiley.

Rubin, K. H. (1978). Role-taking in childhood: Some methodological considerations. *Child Development, 49,* 428–433.

Rubin, K. H., Fein, G. G., & Vanderber, B. (1983). Play. In P. H. Mussen (Ed.), *Handbook of child psychology* (4th ed., Vol. 4). New York: Wiley.

Ruble, D. N. (1987). The acquisition of self-knowledge: A self-socialization perspective. In N. Eisenberg (Ed.), *Contemporary topics in developmental psychology.* New York: Wiley.

Rumbaugh, D. M. (1988, August). *Comparative psychology and the great apes: Their competency in learning, language, and numbers.* Paper presented at the annual meeting of the American Psychological Association, Atlanta, GA.

Rutter, D. R., & Durkin, K. (1987). Turn-taking in mother-infant interaction: An examination of vocalization and gaze. *Developmental Psychology, 23,* 54–61.

Rutter, M. (1979). Protective factors in children's response to stress and disadvantage. In M. W. Kent & J. E. Rolf (Eds.), *Primary prevention in psychopathology* (Vol. 3). Hanover, NH: University Press of New England.

Rutter, M. (1983, April). *Influences from family and school.* Paper presented at the meeting of the Society for Research in Child Development, Detroit, MI.

Rutter, M. (Ed.). (1980). *Scientific foundations of developmental psychiatry.* London: Heinemann.

Rutter, M., & Garmezy, N. (1983). Developmental psychopathology. In P. H. Mussen (Ed.), *Handbook of child psychology* (4th ed., Vol. 4). New York: Wiley.

Rutter, M., & Schopher, E. (1987). Autism and pervasive developmental disorders: Concepts and diagnostic issues. *Journal of Autism and Developmental Disorders, 17,* 159–186.

Sadker, M., & Sadker, D. (1986, March). Sexism in the classroom: From grade school to graduate school. *Phi Delta Kappan,* pp. 512–515.

Sadker, M., Sadker, D., & Klein, S. S. (1986). Abolishing misperceptions about sex equity in education. *Theory into Practice, 25,* 219–226.

Sandell, R., Collings, G. C., & Sherman, A. (1985). Sex equity in visual arts education. In S. S. Klein (Ed.), *Handbook for achieving sex equity through education.* Baltimore, MD: Johns Hopkins University Press.

Santrock, J. W. (1972). The relations of onset and type of father absence to cognitive development. *Child Development, 43,* 455–469.

Santrock, J. W. (1987). *Adolescence* (3rd ed.). Dubuque, IA: Wm. C. Brown Publishers.

Santrock, J. W. (1988). *Psychology* (2nd ed.). Dubuque, IA: Wm. C. Brown Publishers.

Santrock, J. W. (in press). *Adolescence* (4th ed.). Dubuque, IA: Wm. C. Brown Publishers.

Santrock, J. W., & Sitterle, K. A. (1987). Parent-child relationships in stepmother families. In K. Pasley & M. Ihinger-Tallman (Eds.), *Remarriage and stepparenting.* New York: Guilford.

Santrock, J. W., Sitterle, K. A., & Warshak, R. A. (1988). Parent-child relationships in stepfather families. In P. Bronstein & C. P. Cowan (Eds.), *Fatherhood today.* New York: Wiley.

Santrock, J. W., & Warshak, R. A. (1979). Father custody and social development in boys and girls. *Journal of Social Issues, 35,* 112–125.

Santrock, J. W., & Warshak, R. A. (1986). Development, relationships, and legal/clinical considerations in father custody families. In M. E. Lamb (Ed.), *The father's role: Applied perspectives.* New York: Wiley.

Savin-Williams, R. C., & Demo, D. H. (1983). Conceiving or misconceiving the self: Issues in adolescent self-esteem. *Journal of Early Adolescence, 3,* 121–140.

Scardamalia, M., Bereiter, C., & Goelman, H. (1982). The role of production factors in writing ability. In M. Nystrand (Ed.), *What writers know: The language, process, and structure of written discourse.* New York: Academic Press.

Scarr, S. (1984, May). [Interview]. *Psychology Today,* pp. 59–63.

Scarr, S. (1984). *Mother care/Other care.* New York: Basic Books.

Scarr, S., & Kidd, K. K. (1983). Developmental behavior genetics. In P. H. Mussen (Ed.), *Handbook of child psychology* (4th ed., Vol. 2). New York: Wiley.

Scarr, S., & Weinberg, R. A. (1976). IQ test performance of black children adopted by white families. *American Psychologist, 31,* 726–739.

Scarr, S., & Weinberg, R. A. (1980). Calling all camps! The war is over. *American Sociological Review, 45,* 859–865.

Schaffer, H. R. (1977). *Mothering.* Cambridge, MA: Harvard University Press.

Schaffer, H. R., & Emerson, P. E. (1964). The development of social attachments in infancy. *Monographs of the Society for Research in Child Development, 29* (3, Serial No. 94).

Schaie, K. W. (1965). A general model for the study of developmental problems. *Psychological Bulletin, 64,* 92–107.

Schank, R., & Abelson, R. (1977). *Scripts, plans, goals, and understanding.* Hillsdale, NJ: Erlbaum.

Scheff, T. J. (1966). *Being mentally ill: A sociological theory.* Chicago, IL: Aldine.

Schiff, A. R., & Knopf, I. J. (1985). The effects of task demands on attention allocation in children of different ages. *Child Development, 56,* 621–630.

Schorr, L. B. (in press). *Within our reach: Breaking the cycle of disadvantage and despair.* New York: Doubleday/Anchor.

Schunk, D. H. (1983). Developing children's self-efficacy and skills: The roles of social comparative information and goal-setting. *Contemporary Educational Psychology, 8,* 76–86.

Schwartz, D., & Mayaux, M. J. (1982). Female fecundity as a function of age: Results of artificial insemination in nulliparous women with azoospermic husbands. *New England Journal of Medicine, 306,* 404–406.

Schwartz, M. A., & Wiggins, O. P. (1986). Systems and structuring of meaning: Contributions to a biosocial medicine. *American Journal of Psychiatry, 143,* 1213–1221.

Scott-Jones, D., & Clark, M. L. (1986, March). The school experiences of black girls. *Phi Delta Kappan,* pp. 520–526.

Seligman, M. E. P. (1975). *Learned helplessness.* San Francisco, CA: W. H. Freeman.

Selman, R. L. (1976). Social-cognitive understanding. In T. Lickona (Ed.), *Moral development and behavior.* New York: Holt, Rinehart, & Winston.

Selman, R. L. (1980). *The growth of interpersonal understanding.* New York: Academic Press.

Selman, R. L., Newberger, C. M., & Jacquette, D. (1977, March). *Observing interpersonal reasoning in a clinic/educational setting: Toward the integration of development and clinical-child psychology.* Paper presented at the biennial meeting of the Society for Research in Child Development, New Orleans, LA.

Selye, H. (1974). *Stress without distress.* Philadelphia, PA: W. B. Saunders.

Selye, H. (1983). The stress concept: Past, present, and future. In C. L. Cooper (Ed.), *Stress research.* New York: Wiley.

Senn, M. J. (1975). Insights on the child development movement in the United States. *Monographs of the Society for Research in Child Development, 40*(3–4, Serial No. 161).

Serbin, L. A., Tonick, I. J., & Sternglanz, S. (1977). Shaping cooperative cross-sex play. *Child Development, 48,* 924–929.

Sexton, M., & Hebel, J. R. (1984). A clinical trial of change in maternal smoking and its effects on birth weight. *Journal of the American Medical Association, 251,* 911–915.

Sexton, M. A., & Geffen, G. (1979). Development of three strategies of attention in dichotic listening. *Developmental Psychology, 15,* 299–310.

Shakeshaft, C. (1986, March). A gender at risk. *Phi Delta Kappan,* 499–503.

Shantz, C. O. (1988). Conflicts between children. *Child Development, 59,* 283–305.

Shantz, C. U. (1983). The development of social cognition. In P. H. Mussen (Ed.), *Handbook of child psychology* (4th ed., Vol. 3). New York: Wiley.

Shatz, M., & Gelman, R. (1973). The development of communication skills: Modifications in the speech of young children as a function of the listener. *Monographs of the Society for Research in Child Development, 38*(Serial No. 152).

Sherif, M., Harvey, O. J., White, B. J., Hood, W. R., & Sherif, C. W. (1961). *Intergroup conflict and cooperation: The Robber's Cave experiment.* Norman, OK: Institute of Group Relations, University of Oklahoma.

Shirley, M. M. (1933). *The first two years.* Minneapolis, MN: University of Minnesota Press.

Shneidman, E. S. (1971). Suicide among the gifted. *Suicide and Life-threatening Behavior, 1,* 23–45.

Shuey, A. (1966). *The testing of Negro intelligence.* New York: Social Science Press.

Siegel, L. S. (1984). Home environment influences on cognitive development in preterm and full-term infants during the first five years. In A. W. Gottfried (Ed.), *Home environment and early mental development.* New York: Academic Press.

Siegler, R. S. (1986). *Children's thinking.* Englewood Cliffs, NJ: Prentice-Hall.

Siegler, R. S. (1987, April). *How children acquire arithmetic skill.* Paper presented at the biennial meeting of the Society for Research in Child Development, Baltimore, MD.

Siegler, R. S. (in press). Individual differences in strategy choices: Good students, not-so-good students, perfectionists. *Child Development.*

Siegler, R. S. (in press). Mechanisms of cognitive development. *Annual Review of Psychology, 40.*

Simmons, R. G., & Blyth, D. A. (1987). *Moving into adolescence.* Hawthorne, NY: Aldine.

Simmons, R. G., Burgeson, R., Carton-Ford, S., & Blyth, D. A. (1987). The impact of cumulative change in early adolescence. *Child Development, 58,* 1235–1243.

Singer, D. (1972, June). Piglet, Pooh, & Piaget. *Psychology Today,* pp. 70–74, 96.

Singer, D. G., & Singer, J. L. (1987). Practical suggestions for controlling television. *Journal of Early Adolescence, 7,* 365–369.

Singer, J. L. (1984). *The human personality.* San Diego, CA: Harcourt Brace Jovanovich.

Sizer, T. R. (1984). *Horace's compromise: The dilemma of the American high school today.* Boston, MA: Houghton-Mifflin.

Skeels, H. (1966). Adult status of children with contrasting early life experiences. *Monographs of the Society for Research in Child Development, 31*(3, Serial No. 105).

Skinner, B. F. (1938). *The behavior of organisms: An experimental analysis.* New York: Appleton-Century-Crofts.

Skinner, B. F. (1953). *Science and human behavior.* New York: Macmillan.

Skinner, B. F. (1957). *Verbal behavior.* New York: Appleton-Century-Crofts.

Slavin, R. E. (1987). Developmental and motivational perspectives on cooperative learning: A reconciliation. *Child Development, 58,* 1161–1167.

Slavin, R. E. (1988). *Educational psychology.* New York: Macmillan.

Slobin, D. (1972, July). Children and language: They learn the same all around the world. *Psychology Today,* pp. 71–76.

Smetana, J. (1983). Social-cognitive development: Domain distinctions and coordinations. *Developmental Review, 3,* 131–147.

Smetana, J. (1985). Preschool children's conceptions of transgressions: Effects of varying moral and conventional domain-related attributes. *Developmental Psychology, 21,* 18–29.

Smith, P. B., & Pederson, D. R. (1987, April). *Maternal sensitivity and patterns of infant-mother attachment.* Paper presented at the biennial meeting of the Society for Research in Child Development, Baltimore, MD.

Snarey, J. (1987, June). A question of morality. *Psychology Today,* pp. 6–8.

Snow, C. E. (1977). The development of conversation between mothers and babies. *Journal of Child Language, 4,* 1–22.

Snyder, J., & Patterson, G. R. (1987). Family interaction and delinquent behavior. In H. C. Quay (Ed.), *Handbook of juvenile delinquency.* New York: Wiley.

Sophian, C. (1985). Perseveration and infants' search: A comparison of two- and three-location tasks. *Developmental Psychology, 21,* 187–194.

Sorenson, R. C. (1983). *Adolescent sexuality in contemporary America.* New York: World.

Sowers-Hoag, K. W., Thyer, B. A., & Bailey, J. S. (1987). Promoting automobile safety belt use by young children. *Journal of Applied Behavior Analysis, 20,* 133–138.

Spearman, C. (1927). *The abilities of man.* New York: Macmillan.

Spelke, E. S. (1979). Perceiving bimodally specified events in infancy. *Developmental Psychology, 15,* 626–636.

Spence, J. T., & Helmreich, R. (1972). The Attitudes Toward Women Scale. An objective instrument to measure the rights and roles of women in contemporary society. *JSAS Catalog of Selected Documents in Psychology, 2,* 66.

Spence, J. T., & Helmreich, R. L. (1978). *Masculinity and femininity: Their psychological dimensions.* Austin, TX: University of Texas Press.

Spence, M., & DeCasper, A. J. (1982). *Human fetuses perceive human speech.* Paper presented at the International Conference on Infant Studies, Austin, TX.

Spencer, M. L. (1986). Sex equity in bilingual education, English as a second language, and foreign language instruction. *Theory into Practice, 25,* 257–266.

Sperry, R. W. (1974). Lateral specialization in surgically separated hemispheres. In F. O. Schmitt & F. G. Worden (Eds.), *The neurosciences: Third study program.* Cambridge, MA: MIT Press.

Spitz, R. A. (1945). Hospitalism: An inquiry into the genesis of psychiatric conditions in early childhood. *Psychoanalytic Study of the Child, 1,* 53–74.

Sroufe, L. A. (1979). The coherence of individual development. *American Psychologist, 34,* 834–841.

Sroufe, L. A. (1985). Attachment classification from the perspective of infant-caregiver relationships and infant temperament. *Child Development, 56,* 1–14.

Sroufe, L. A. (1987). *The role of infant-caregiver attachment in development.* Unpublished manuscript, Institute of Child Development, University of Minnesota.

Sroufe, L. A. (in press). The role of infant-caregiver attachment in development. In J. Belsky & T. M. Nezworski (Eds.), *Clinical implications of attachment.* Hillsdale, NJ: Erlbaum.

Sroufe, L. A., & Rutter, M. (1984). The domain of developmental psychopathology. *Child Development, 55,* 17–29.

Sroufe, L. A., & Waters, E. (1976). The ontogenesis of smiling and laughter: A perspective on the organization of development in infancy. *Psychological Review, 83,* 173–189.

Stage, E. K., Kreinberg, N., Eccles, J., & Becker, J. R. (1985). Increasing the participation and achievement of girls and women in mathematics, science, and engineering. In S. S. Klein (Ed.), *Handbook for achieving sex equity through education.* Baltimore, MD: Johns Hopkins University Press.

Stallings, J. (1975). Implementation and child effects of teaching practices in Follow Through classrooms. *Monographs of the Society for Research in Child Psychology, 40*(Serial No. 163).

Stein, N. L., & Glenn, C. G. (1979). An analysis of story comprehension in elementary school children. In R. O. Freedle (Ed.), *Discourse processing: Multidisciplinary perspectives* (pp. 53–120). Norwood, NJ: Ablex.

Steinberg, L. D. (1981). Transformations in family relations at puberty. *Developmental Psychology, 17,* 833–840.

Steinberg, L. D. (1986). Latchkey children and susceptibility to peer pressure: An ecological analysis. *Developmental Psychology, 22,* 433–439.

Steinberg, L. D. (1987). Impact of puberty on family relations: Effects of pubertal status and pubertal timing. *Developmental Psychology, 23,* 451–460.

Steiner, J. E. (1979). Human facial expressions in response to taste and smell stimulation. In H. Reese & L. Lipsitt (Eds.), *Advances in child development and behavior* (Vol. 13). New York: Academic Press.

Stern, D. N., Beebe, B., Jaffe, J., & Bennett, S. L. (1977). The infant's stimulus world during social interaction: A study of caregiver behaviors with particular reference to repetition and timing. In H. R. Schaffer (Ed.), *Studies in mother-infant interaction.* London: Academic Press.

Sternberg, R. J. (1985). *Beyond IQ.* New York: Cambridge University Press.

Sternberg, R. J. (1986). *Intelligence applied.* San Diego, CA: Harcourt Brace Jovanovich.

Sternberg, R. J. (1987). Intelligence. In R. J. Sternberg & E. E. Smith (Eds.), *The psychology of human thought.* New York: Cambridge University Press.

Sternberg, R. J. (1987). Overview. In J. B. Baron and R. J. Sternberg (Eds.), *Teaching thinking skills.* New York: W. H. Freeman.

Sternberg, R. J. (1988). What theorists of intellectual development among children can learn from their counterparts studying adults. In E. M. Hetherington, R. M. Lerner, & M. Perlmutter (Eds.), *Child development in life-span perspective.* Hillsdale, NJ: Erlbaum.

Sternberg, R. J., Conway, B. E., Ketron, J. L., & Berstein, M. (1981). People's conceptions of intelligence. *Journal of Personality and Social Psychology, 41,* 37–55.

Stevenson, H. W. (1972). *Children's learning.* New York: Appleton-Century-Crofts.

Stevenson, H. W. (1974). Reflections on the China visit. *Society for Research in Child Development Newsletter, 3.*

Stevenson, H. W., Stigler, J. W., & Lee, S. (1986). Achievement in mathematics. In H. W. Stevenson, H. Azuma, & K. Hakuta (Eds.), *Child development and education in Japan.* San Francisco, CA: W. H. Freeman.

Stigler, J. W., Nusbaum, H.C., & Chalip, L. (1988). Developmental changes in speed of processing: Central limiting mechanism or skill transfer? *Child Development.*

Stine, E. L., & Bohannon, J. N. (1983). Imitations, interactions, and language acquisition. *Journal of Child Language, 10,* 589–603.

Stipek, D. J., & Hoffman, J. M. (1980). Children's achievement-related expectancies as a function of academic performance, histories and sex. *Journal of Educational Psychology, 72,* 861–865.

Streissguth, A. P., Martin, D. C., Sandman, B. M., Kirchner, G. L., & Darby, B. L. (1984). Intra-uterine alcohol and nicotine exposure: Attention and reaction time in four-year-old children. *Developmental Psychology, 20,* 533–541.

Stunkard, A. J. (in press). The regulation of body weight and the treatment of obesity. In H. Weiner & A. Baum (Eds.), *Eating regulation and discontrol.* Hillsdale, NJ: Erlbaum.

Styne, D. M. (1988). The physiology of normal and delayed puberty. In M. D. Levine & E. R. McAnarney (Eds.), *Early adolescent transitions.* Lexington, MA: Lexington Books.

Sullivan, E. V. (1985). *Moral learning: Findings, issues, and questions.* Paramus, NJ: Paulist/Newman Press.

Sullivan, H. S. (1953). The interpersonal theory of psychiatry. New York: Norton.

Sullivan, K., & Sullivan, A. (1980). Adolescent-parent separation. *Developmental Psychology, 16,* 93–99.

Suomi, S. (1987, April). *Individual differences in rhesus monkey behavioral and adrenocortical responses to social challenge: Correlations with measures of heart rate variability.* Paper presented at the biennial meeting of the Society for Research in Child Development, Baltimore, MD.

Suomi, S. J., Harlow, H. F., & Domek, C. J. (1970). Effect of repetitive infant-infant separations of young monkeys. *Journal of Abnormal Psychology, 76,* 161–172.

Susman, E. J., Inoff-Germain, G., Nottelmann, E. D., Loriaux, D. L., Cutler, G. B., & Chrousos, G. P. (1987). Hormones, emotional dispositions, and aggressive attributes in young adolescents. *Child Development, 58,* 1114–1134.

Sutton-Smith, B. (1973). *Child psychology.* New York: Appleton-Century-Crofts.

Sutton-Smith, B. (1982). Birth order and sibling status effects. In M. E. Lamb & B. Sutton-Smith (Eds.), *Sibling relationships: Their nature and significance across the lifespan.* Hillsdale, NJ: Erlbaum.

Sutton-Smith, B. (1985, October). The child at play. *Psychology Today,* pp. 64–65.

Sutton-Smith, B., & Rosenberg, B. G. (1970). *The sibling.* New York: Holt, Rinehart, & Winston.

Swadesh, M. (1971). *The origin and diversification of language.* Chicago, IL: Aldine-Atherton.

Szasz, T. (1977). *Psychiatric slavery: When confinement and coercion masquerade as care.* New York: Free Press.

Tangney, J. P. (in press). Aspects of the family and children's television viewing content preferences. *Child Development.*

Tanner, J. M. (1970). Physical growth. In P. H. Mussen (Ed.), *Manual of child psychology* (3rd ed., Vol. 1). New York: Wiley.

Tellegen, A., Lykken, D. T., Bouchard, T. J., Wilcox, K. J., Segal, N. L., & Rich, S. (in press). *Journal of Personality and Social Psychology.*

Terman, L. (1925). *Genetic studies of genius: Vol. 1. Mental and physical traits of a thousand gifted children.* Stanford, CA: Stanford University Press.

Terrace, H. (1979). *Nim.* New York: Knopf.

Tetreault, M. K. T. (1986). The journey from male-defined to gender balanced education. *Theory into Practice, 25,* 276–283.

Thelen, E. (1981). Rhythmical behavior in infancy: An ethological perspective. *Developmental Psychology, 17,* 237–257.

Thelen, E. (1987, October). *Order, adaptation, and change: A synergetic approach to development.* Paper presented at the 22nd Annual Minnesota Symposium on Child Psychology, Minneapolis, MN.

Thomas, A., & Chess, S. (1977). *Temperament and development.* New York: Brunner/Mazel.

Thomas, A., & Chess, S. (1987). Commentary. In H. H. Goldsmith, A. H. Buss, R. Plomin, M. K. Rothbart, A. Thomas, A. Chess, R. R. Hinde, & R. B. McCall (Eds.), Roundtable: What is temperament? Four approaches. *Child Development, 58,* 505–529.

Thomas, A., Chess, S., & Birch, H. G. (1970). The origin of personality. *Scientific American, 233,* 102–109.

Thompson, P. J. (1986). Beyond gender: Equity issues in home economics education. *Theory into Practice, 25,* 276–283.

Thoresen, C. E., Eagleston, J. R., Kirmil-Gray, K., & Bracke, P. E. (1985, August). *Exploring the Type A behavior pattern in children and adolescents.* Paper presented at the meeting of the American Psychological Association, Los Angeles, CA.

Thornburg, H. D. (1981). Sources of sex education among early adolescents. *Journal of Early Adolescence, 1,* 171–184.

Thorndike, R. L., Hagan, E. P., & Sattler, J. M. (1985). *Stanford-Binet* (4th ed.). Chicago, IL: Riverside Publishing.

Thurstone, L. L. (1938). *Primary mental abilities.* Chicago, IL: University of Chicago Press.

Timberlake, B., Fox, R. A., Baisch, M. J., & Goldberg, B. D. (1987). Prenatal education for pregnant adolescents. *Journal of School Health, 57,* 105–108.

Tolan, P., Miller, L., & Thomas, P. (1988). Perception and experience of types of social stress and self-image among adolescents. *Journal of Youth and Adolescence, 17,* 147–163.

Tomlinson-Keasey, C., Warren, L. W., & Elliott, J. E. (1986). Suicide among gifted women: A prospective study. *Journal of Abnormal Psychology, 95,* 123–130.

Trotter, R. J. (1987, December). Project Day-Care. *Psychology Today,* pp. 32–38.

Trudel, M., & Jacques, M. (1987, April). *A cross-lag analysis of associations between temperament and attachment in the first year.* Paper presented at the biennial meeting of the Society for Research in Child Development, Baltimore, MD.

Tucker, L. A. (1987). Television, teenagers, and health. *Journal of Youth and Adolescence, 16,* 415–425.

Tuckman, B. W., & Hinkle, J. S. (1988). An experimental study of the physical and psychological effects of aerobic exercise on schoolchildren. In B. G. Melamed & others (Eds.), *Child health psychology.* Hillsdale, NJ: Erlbaum.

Tulkin, S. R., & Kagan, J. (1971). Mother-child interaction in the first year of life. *Child Development, 43,* 31–41.

Turiel, E. (1966). An experimental test of the sequentiality of developmental stages in the child's moral judgments. *Journal of Personality and Social Psychology, 3,* 611–618.

Turiel, E. (1977). A critical analysis of Kohlberg's contributions to the study of moral thought. *Journal of Social Behavior, 7,* 41–63.

Turiel, E. (1978). Social regulations and domains of social concepts. In W. Damon (Ed.), *New directions for child development, Vol. 1: Social cognition.* San Francisco, CA: Jossey-Bass.

Turkle, S. (1984). *The second self.* Cambridge, MA: Harvard University Press.

United States Public Health Service. (1988). *Moratorium on certain fetal tissue research.* Washington, DC: U.S. Government Printing Office.

Uttal, D. Y., Lummis, M., & Stevenson, H. W. (1988). Low and high mathematics achievement in Japanese, Chinese, and American elementary-school children. *Developmental Psychology, 24,* 335–342.

Vaillant, G. E. (1977). *Adaptation to life.* Boston: Little, Brown.

Vandell, D. L. (1985, April). *Relationship between infant-peer and infant-mother interactions: What we have learned.* Paper presented at the meeting of the Society for Research in Child Development, Toronto.

Vandell, D. L. (1987). Baby sister/Baby brother: Reactions to the birth of a sibling and patterns of early sibling relations. New York: Haworth Press.

Vandell, D. L., & Corasaniti, M. A. (1988). Variations in early child care: Do they predict subsequent social, emotional, and cognitive differences? *Child Development, 59,* 868–875.

Vandell, D. L., & Wilson, K. S. (1987). Infants' interactions with mother, sibling, and peer: Contrasts and relations between interaction systems. *Child Development, 58,* 176–186.

Vandell, D. L., Wilson, K. S., & Buchanan, N. R. (1980). Peer interaction in the first year of life: An examination of its structure, content, and sensitivity of toys. *Child Development, 51,* 481–488.

VanItallie, T. B. (1984). The enduring storage capacity for fat: Implications for treatment of obesity. In A. J. Stunkard & E. Stellar (Eds.), *Eating and its disorders.* New York: Raven Press.

Volkmor, C. B., Pasanella, A. L., & Raths, L. E. (1977). *Values in the classroom.* Columbus, OH: C. E. Merrill.

Vorhees, C. V., & Mollnow, E. (1987). Behavioral teratogenesis: Long-term influences in behavior from early exposure to environmental agents. In J. D. Osofsky (Ed.), *Handbook of infant development* (2nd ed.). New York: Wiley.

Vuchinich, S., Emery, R. E., & Cassidy, J. (in press). Family members as third parties in dyadic family conflict: Strategies, alliances, and outcomes. *Child Development.*

Vurpillot, E. (1968). The development of scanning strategies and their relation to visual differentiation. *Journal of Experimental Child Psychology, 6,* 632–650.

Vygotsky, L. S. (1978). Play and its role in mental development. *Soviet Psychology, 12,* 62–76.

Wachs, T. D. (1987). Specificity of environmental action as manifest in environmental correlates of infant's mastery motivation. *Developmental Psychology, 23,* 782–790.

Waddington, C. H. (1957). *The strategy of the genes.* London: Allen & Son.

Wagennar, A. C. (1983). *Alcohol, young drivers, and traffic accidents.* Lexington, MA: D.C. Heath.

Walker, C. W., Bonner, B. L., & Kaufman, K. L. (1988). *The physically and sexually abused child.* Elmsford, NY: Pergamon Press.

Walker, L. (1982). The sequentiality of Kohlberg's stages of moral development. *Child Development, 53,* 1330–1336.

Walker, L. J., de Vries, B., & Trevethan, S. D. (1987). Moral stages and moral orientation in real-life and hypothetical dilemmas. *Child Development, 58,* 842–858.

Wallach, M. A. (1985). Creative testing and giftedness. In F. D. Horowitz & M. O'Brien (Eds.), *The gifted and the talented.* Washington, DC: American Psychological Association.

Wallach, M. A., & Kogan, N. (1965). *Modes of thinking in young children.* New York: Holt, Rinehart, & Winston.

Wallerstein, J., Corbin, S. B., & Lewis, J. M. (in press). Children of divorce: A ten-year study.

Wallerstein, J. S., & Kelly, J. B. (1980). *Surviving the breakup: How children actually cope with divorce.* New York: Basic Books.

Warren, J. V. (1975). Medical and toxicological issues. In *Sweeteners: Issues and Uncertainties,* National Academy of Science Forum, Fourth of a Series (pp. 36–40). Washington, DC: National Academy of Sciences.

Washburn, K. J., & Hakes, D. T. (1985, April). *Changes in children's semantic and syntactic acceptability judgments.* Paper presented at the biennial meeting of the Society for Research in Child Development, Toronto.

Waterman, A. S., & Waterman, C. K. (1972). Relationship between ego identity status and subsequent academic behavior: A test of the predictive validity of Marcia's categorization for identity status. *Developmental Psychology, 6,* 179.

Waters, E., & Sroufe, L. A. (1983). Social competence as a developmental construct. *Developmental Review, 3,* 79–97.

Watson, J. B. (1928). *Psychological care of infant and child.* New York: Norton.

Watson, J. B. (1930). *Behaviorism.* Chicago, IL: University of Chicago Press.

Watson, J. B., & Raynor, R. (1920). Emotional reactions. *Journal of Experimental Psychology, 3,* 1–14.

Weaver, S. J. (Ed.). (1988). *Testing children.* Kansas City, MO: Test Corporation of America.

Webb, W. B. (1975). *Sleep: The gentle tyrant.* Englewood Cliffs, NJ: Prentice-Hall.

Wechsler, D. (1949). *Wechsler Intelligence Scale for Children.* New York: Psychological Corporation.

Wechsler, D. (1955). *Wechsler Adult Intelligence Scale manual.* New York: Psychological Corporation.

Wechsler, D. (1967). *Wechsler Preschool and Primary Scale of Intelligence.* New York: Psychological Corporation.

Wechsler, D. (1974). *Wechsler Intelligence Scale for Children—Revised.* New York: Psychological Corporation.

Wechsler, D. (1981). *Wechsler Adult Intelligence Scale—Revised.* New York: Psychological Corporation.

Weiner, I. (1982). *Child and adolescent psychopathology.* New York: Wiley.

Weiner, I. B. (1980). Psychopathology in adolescence. In J. Adelson (Ed.), *Handbook of adolescent psychology.* New York: Wiley.

Weinstein, N. D. (1984). Reducing unrealistic optimism about illness susceptibility. *Health Psychology, 3,* 431–457.

Weisberg, R. P. (1988). Teaching of social skills. *William T. Grant Foundation Annual Report,* p. 18.

Weiss, G., & Hechtman, L. T. (1986). *Hyperactive children grow up.* New York: Guilford.

Wellman, H. M., Cross, D., & Bartsche, K. (1986). Infant search and object permanence: A meta-analysis of the A-not-B error. *Monographs of the Society for Research in Child Development* (Serial No. 214).

Wellman, H. M., Ritter, R., & Flavell, J. H. (1985). Deliberate memory behavior in the delayed reactions of very young children. *Developmental Psychology, 11,* 780–787.

Wender, P. H., Kety, S. S., Rosenthal, D., Schulsinger, F., Ortmann, J., & Lunde, I. (1986). Psychiatric disorders in the biological and adoptive families of adopted individuals with affective disorders. *Archives of General Psychiatry, 43*, 923–929.

Werner, E. E. (1979). *Cross-cultural child development: A view from planet earth.* Monterey, CA: Brooks/Cole.

Werner, E. E., & Smith, R. S. (1982). *Vulnerable but not invincible: A longitudinal study of resilient children and youth.* New York: McGraw-Hill.

Werner, H., & Kaplan, B. (1963). *Symbol formation.* New York: Wiley.

Wertsch, J. V. (1985). Adult-child interaction as a source of self-regulation in children. In S. R. Yussen (Ed.), *The growth of reflection in children.* New York: Academic Press.

Whaley, L., & Wong, D. L. (1989). *Essentials of pediatric nursing* (3rd ed.). St. Louis, MO: Mosby.

White, B. L. (1988). *Educating the infant and toddler.* Lexington, MA: Lexington Books.

White, M. A. (Ed.). (in press). *What curriculum for the information age?* Hillsdale, NJ: Erlbaum.

White, R. W. (1959). Motivation reconsidered: The concept of competence. *Psychological Review, 66*, 297–333.

White, S. H. (1985, April). *Risings and fallings of developmental psychology.* Paper presented at the biennial meeting of the Society for Research in Child Development, Toronto.

Whitehurst, G. J. (1985, April). *The role of imitation in language learning by children with language delay.* Paper presented at the biennial meeting of the Society for Research in Child Development, Baltimore.

Whitehurst, G. J., & Valdez-Menchaca, M. C. (1988). What is the role of reinforcement in early language acquisition? *Child Development, 59*, 430–440.

Widmayer, S., & Field, T. (1980). Effects of Brazelton demonstrations on early patterns of preterm infants and their teenage mothers. *Infant Behavior and Development, 3*, 79–89.

Williams, J. (1979). Reading instruction today. *American Psychologist, 34*, 917–922.

Williams, R. B., Barefoot, J. C., & Haney, T. L. (1986, March). *Type A behavior and angiographically documented atherosclerosis in a sample of 2,289 patients.* Paper presented at the meeting of the American Psychosomatic Association, Baltimore, MD.

Windle, W. F. (1940). *Physiology of the human fetus.* Philadelphia, PA: Saunders.

Winner, E. (1986, August). Where pelicans kiss seals. *Psychology Today*, pp. 24–35.

Winner, E., & Gardner, H. (1988). Creating a world with words. In F. Kessel (Ed.), *The development of language and language researchers.* Hillsdale, NJ: Erlbaum.

Witkin, H. A., Mednick, S. A., Schulsinger, R., Bakkestrom, E., Christiansen, K. O., Goodenbough, D. R., Hirchhorn, K., Lunsteen, C., Owen, D. R., Philip, J., Ruben, D. B., & Stocking, M. (1976). Criminality in XYY and XXY men. *Science, 193*, 547–555.

Witryol, S. (1971). Incentives and learning in children. In H. W. Reese (Ed.), *Advances in child development and behavior* (Vol. 6). New York: Academic Press.

Wodarski, J. S., & Hoffman, S. D. (1984). Alcohol education for adolescents. *Social Work in Education, 6*, 69–92.

Wolfe, D. A., Edwards, B., Manion, I., & Koverola, C. (1988). Early intervention for parents at risk of child abuse and neglect: A preliminary investigation. *Journal of Consulting and Clinical Psychology, 56*, 40–47.

Wolff, P. H. (1966). The causes, controls, and organization of behavior in the neonate. *Psychological Issues, 5*(1, Whole No. 7).

Wolff, P. H. (1987). *The development of behavioral states and the expression of emotions in early infancy.* Chicago, IL: University of Chicago Press.

Worobey, J., & Belsky, J. (1982). Employing the Brazelton Scale to influence mothering: An experimental comparison of three strategies. *Developmental Psychology, 18*, 736–743.

Worthington, B. S. (1988). Maternal nutrition and the course and outcome of pregnancy. In S. R. Williams & B. S. Worthington (Eds.), *Nutrition throughout the life cycle.* St. Louis, MO: Times Mirror/Mosby.

Wright, J. C., & Huston, A. C. (1985, April). *Developmental changes in children's understanding of form and content.* Paper presented at the meeting of the Society for Research in Child Development, Toronto.

Wylie, R. C. (1979). *The self-concept: Theory and research on selected topics* (Rev. ed., Vol. 2). Lincoln, NE: University of Nebraska Press.

Yardley, K. (1987). What do you mean "Who am I?": Exploring the implications of a self-concept measurement with subjects. In K. Yardley & T. Honess (Eds.), *Self and identity: Psychosocial perspectives.* New York: Wiley.

Yarrow, L. J., McQuiston, S., MacTurk, R. H., McCarthy, M. E., Klein, R. P., & Vietze, P. M. (1983). The assessment of mastery motivation in the first year of life. *Developmental Psychology, 19*, 159–171.

Yarrow, M. R., Campbell, J. D., & Burton, R. V. (1968). *Child rearing.* San Francisco, CA: Jossey-Bass.

Yussen, S. R. (1977). Characteristics of moral dilemmas written by adolescents. *Developmental Psychology, 13*, 162–163.

Yussen, S. R. (1985). The role of metacognition in contemporary theories of cognitive development. In D. Forrest-Pressley and G. Waller (Eds.), *Contemporary research in cognition and metacognition.* Orlando, FL: Academic Press.

Yussen, S., Mathews, S., Huang, S., & Evans, R. (1988). The robustness and temporal course of the story schema's influence on recall. *Journal of Experimental Psychology: Learning, Memory, and Cognition, 14*, 173–179.

Zahn-Waxler, C., Radke-Yarrow, M., & King, R. M. (1979). Child rearing and children's prosocial initiations toward victims of distress. *Child Development, 50*, 319–330.

Zajonc, R. B., & Markus, G. B. (1975). Birth order and intellectual development. *Psychological Review, 82*, 74–88.

Zamenhof, S., van Marthens, E., & Margolis, F. L. (1968). DNA (cell number) and protein in neonatal brain: Alteration by maternal dietary restriction. *Science, 160*, 322–323.

Zembar, M. J., & Naus, M. J. (1985, April). *The combined effects of knowledge base and mnemonic strategies in children's memory.* Paper presented at the biennial meeting of the Society for Research in Child Development, Toronto.

Zeskind, P. S. (1987). Adult heart rate responses to infant cry sounds. *British Journal of Developmental Psychology, 5*, 73–79.

Zeskind, P. S., & Marshall, T. R. (1988). The relation between variations in pitch and maternal perception of infant crying. *Child Development, 59,* 193–196.

Zigler, E. F. (1987, April). *Child care for parents who work outside the home: Problems and solutions.* Paper presented at the biennial meeting of the Society for Research in Child Development, Baltimore, MD.

Zigler, E. F. (1987, August). *Issues in mental retardation research.* Paper presented at the meeting of the American Psychological Association, New York, NY.

Zigler, E. F., & Farber, E. A. (1985). Commonalities between the intellectual extremes: Giftedness and mental retardation. In F. D. Horowitz & M. O'Brien (Eds.), *The gifted and the talented.* Washington, DC: American Psychological Association.

Zill, N. (in press). Behavior, achievement, and health problems among children in stepfamilies: Findings from a national survey of child health. In E. M. Hetherington & J. D. Arasteh (Eds.), *Impact of divorce, single-parenting, and stepparenting on children.* Hillsdale, NJ: Erlbaum.

Zucker, K. J. (1988). Toward a developmental sexology. *Contemporary Psychology, 33,* 197–199.

Credits

Illustrations and Text

Chapter 1

Figures 1.3, 1.4, and 1.5: From John W. Santrock, *Life-Span Development*, 3d ed. Copyright © 1989 Wm. C. Brown Publishers, Dubuque, Iowa. All Rights Reserved. Reprinted by permission.

Chapter 2

Figure 2.2: From John W. Santrock, *Psychology: The Science of Mind and Behavior*, 2d ed. Copyright © 1988 Wm. C. Brown Publishers, Dubuque, Iowa. All Rights Reserved. Reprinted by permission. **Figure 2.5**: From John W. Santrock, *Life-Span Development*, 2d ed. Copyright © 1986 Wm. C. Brown Publishers, Dubuque, Iowa. All Rights Reserved. Reprinted by permission. **Figure 2.7**: From I. Gottesman, "Genetic Aspects of Intellectual Behavior" in Handbook of Mental Deficiency, edited by Norman R. Ellis. Copyright © McGraw-Hill Book Company, New York, NY. Reprinted by permission of Norman R. Ellis.

Chapter 3

Figure 3.4: From K. L. Moore, *The Developing Human: Clinically Oriented*, 4th ed. Copyright © 1988 W. B. Saunders Company, Philadelphia, PA. Reprinted by permission.

Chapter 4

Figure 4.3: From L. Patten, *Human Embryology*. Copyright © 1933 McGraw-Hill Book Company, New York. Reprinted by permission. **Figure 4.4**: From M. M. Shirley, *The First Two Years*, 1933. Reprinted by permission of the University of Minnesota Press, Minneapolis, MN. **Figure 4.5**: From Esther Thelen, "Rhythmical Behavior in Infancy: An Ethological Perspective" in *Developmental Psychology*, 17:237–257. Copyright 1981 by the American Psychological Association. Reprinted by permission of the author. **Figure 4.7 right**:

Modified from John W. Santrock, *Life-Span Development*, 3d ed. Copyright © 1989 Wm. C. Brown Publishers, Dubuque, Iowa. All Rights Reserved. Reprinted by permission. **Figure 4.9**: From R. L. Fantz, "Pattern Discrimination and Selective Attention as Determinants in Infancy" in *Perceptual Development in Children*, edited by Aline H. Kidd and Jeanne L. Revoire. Copyright © 1966 International Universities Press, Inc. Reprinted by permission. **Figure 4.11**: From M. R. Gunnar, S. Malone, and R. D. Fisch, "The Psychobiology of Stress and Coping in the Human Neonate: Studies of Adrenocortical Activity in Response to Stress in the First Week of Life" in *Stress and Coping*, edited by T. Field, P. McCabe, and N. Schneiderman. Copyright © Lawrence Earlbaum Associates, Inc. Publishers, Hillsdale, NJ. Reprinted by permission.

Chapter 5

Figure 5.1: From A. F. Roche, "Secular Trends in Stature, Weight and Maturation" in *Monographs of the Society for Research in Child Development*, 44, ser. no. 179, 1977. Copyright © 1977 Society for Research in Child Development, Inc., Chicago, IL. Reprinted by permission. **Figure 5.3**: Reprinted with kind permission from J. M. Tanner, R. H. Whitehouse, and M. Takaishi, "Standards from Birth to Maturity for Height, Weight, Height Velocity, and Weight Velocity: British Children 1965" in *Archives of Diseases in Childhood* 41, 1966. Copyright © 1966 British Medical Association, London, England. **Figure 5.6**: Adapted from R. G. Simmons, D. A. Blythe, and R. L. McKinney in *Girls at Puberty: Biological and Psychosocial Perspectives*, edited by Jeanne Brooks-Gunn and Anne C. Petersen. Copyright © 1983 Plenum Publishing Corporation. Reprinted by permission. **Figure 5.7**: From C. A. Darling, D. J. Kallen, and J. E. VanDusen, "Sex in Transition: 1900–1984" in *Journal of Youth and Adolescence*, 13:385–399, 1984. Copyright © 1984 Plenum Publishing Corporation, New York, NY. Reprinted by

permission. **Figure 5.8**: From E. F. Jones et al., "Teenage Pregnancy in Developed Countries: Determinants and Policy Implications," *Family Planning Perspectives*, 17:53–63. Copyright © 1985 Yale University Press.

Chapter 6

Figure 6.1: From Morgan and King, *Introduction to Psychology*. Copyright © 1971 McGraw-Hill Book Company, New York. Reprinted by permission. **Figure 6.2**: From John W. Santrock, *Psychology: The Science of Mind and Behavior*, 2d ed. Copyright © 1988 Wm. C. Brown Publishers, Dubuque, Iowa. All Rights Reserved. Reprinted by permission. **Figure 6.5**: From A. Bandura, "Influence of Models Reinforcement Contingencies on the Acquisition of Imitative Responses" in *Journal of Personality and Social Psychology* 1:589–595. Copyright 1965 by the American Psychological Association. Reprinted by permission of the author. **Figure 6.6**: From John W. Santrock, *Psychology: The Science of Mind and Behavior*, 2d ed. Copyright © 1988 Wm. C. Brown Publishers, Dubuque, Iowa. All Rights Reserved. Reprinted by permission. **Figure 6.8**: From T. Field, R. Woodson, R. Greenberg, and D. Cohen, "Discrimination and Imitation of Facial Expressions in Neonates" in *Science*, 218:180–181, October 8, 1982. Copyright © 1982 American Association for the Advancement of Science, Washington, DC. Reprinted by permission. **Figure 6.9**: From Albert Bandura, *Social Foundations of Thought and Action: A Social Cognitive Theory*, © 1986, p. 24. Adapted by permission of Prentice-Hall, Inc., Englewood Cliffs, NJ. **Figure 6.10**: Data based on Hierarchy of Needs from *Motivation and Personality*, 3rd Edition by Abraham H. Maslow. Revised by Robert Frager, James Fadiman, Cynthia McReynolds, and Ruth Cox. Copyright © 1954, 1987 by Harper & Row, Publishers, Inc. Copyright © 1970 by Abraham Maslow. Reprinted by permission of Harper & Row, Publishers, Inc. **Figure 6.11**: From Mark R. Lepper,

"Microcomputers in Education" in *American Psychologist* 40:1–9, 1985. Copyright 1985 by the American Psychological Association. Reprinted by permission of the author. **Figure 6.12**: From M. Lepper, D. Greene, and R. E. Nisbett "Undermining Children's Intrinsic Interest with Extrinsic Rewards" in *Journal of Social Psychology,* p. 134. Copyright 1973 by the American Psychological Association. Reprinted by permission of the author. **Figure 6.A**: From K. W. Sower-Hoag et al., *Journal of Applied Behavior Analysis,* 20:136, 1987. Copyright © 1987 by the Society for the Experimental Analysis of Behavior, Inc., Lawrence, KS. Reprinted by permission.

Chapter 7

Table 7.1: From John W. Santrock, *Psychology: The Science of Mind and Behavior,* 2d ed. Copyright © 1988 Wm. C. Brown Publishers, Dubuque, Iowa. All Rights Reserved. Reprinted by permission. **Figure 7.2**: From John W. Santrock, *Life-Span Development,* 3d ed. Copyright © 1989 Wm. C. Brown Publishers, Dubuque, Iowa. All Rights Reserved. Reprinted by permission. **Figures 7.3, 7.4, 7.5, and 7.7**: From John W. Santrock and Steven R. Yussen, *Children and Adolescents: A Developmental Perspective.* Copyright © 1984 Wm. C. Brown Publishers, Dubuque, Iowa. All Rights Reserved. Reprinted by permission. **Figure 7.A**: Dennie Wolf/Josh Nove. **Figures 7.B, 7.D, and 7.E**: Courtesy of Dr. Ellen Winner, Project Zero. **Figure 7.C**: From Claire Golumb, *The Child's Invention of a Pictorial World: Studies in the Psychology of Child Art.* (Book in preparation.) Reprinted by permission.

Chapter 8

Figure 8.1: From Elaine Vurpillot, "The Development of Scanning Strategies and Their Relation to Visual Differentiation" in *Journal of Experimental Psychology* 6:632–650, 1968. Copyright 1968 by the American Psychological Association. Reprinted by permission. **Figure 8.2**: From Frank N. Dempster, "Memory Span: Sources of Individual and Developmental Differences" in *Psychological Bulletin,* 89:63–100. Copyright 1981 American Psychological Association. Reprinted by permission of the author. **Figure 8.3**: From Joel Levin et al., "The Keyword Method in the Classroom" in *Elementary School Journal* 80(4), 1980. Copyright © 1980 The University of Chicago Press, Chicago, IL. Reprinted by permission. **Figure 8.4**: From M. T. H. Chi and R. D. Koeske, "Network Representation of a Child's Dinosaur Knowledge" in *Developmental Psychology* 19:29–39, 1983. Copyright 1983 by the American Psychological Association.

Reprinted by permission of the authors. **Figure 8.5**: From S. Yussen, S. Mathews, S. Huang, and R. Evans, "The Robustness and Temporal Cause of the Story Schemics Influence on Recall" in *Journal of Experimental Psychology Learning, Memory, and Cognition* 14:173–179, 1988. Copyright 1988 by the American Psychological Association. Reprinted by permission of the authors. **Figure 8.6**: From P. Schank and R. Abelson, *Scripts, Plans, Goals, and Understanding.* Copyright © 1976 Lawrence Erlbaum Associates, Inc., Hillsdale, NJ. Reprinted by permission.

Chapter 9

Perspective on Child Development 9.1: From John W. Santrock, *Psychology: The Science of Mind and Behavior,* 2d ed. Copyright © 1988 Wm. C. Brown Publishers, Dubuque, Iowa. All Rights Reserved. Reprinted by permission. **Figure 9.2**: From John W. Santrock, *Life-Span Development,* 2d ed. Copyright © 1986 Wm. C. Brown Publishers, Dubuque, Iowa. All Rights Reserved. Reprinted by permission. **Figure 9.5**: From R. Brown, C. Cazden, and U. Bellugi-Klima, "The Child's Grammar from 1 to 111" in *Minnesota Symposium on Child Psychology* Vol. 2, edited by J. P. Hill. Copyright © 1969 University of Minnesota Press, Minneapolis, MN. Reprinted by permission. **Figure 9.6**: From J. Berko, "The Child's Learning of English Morphology" in *Word* 14:361. Copyright © 1958 International Linguistic Association. Reprinted by permission. **Figure 9.D**: Illustration by Roger Burkhart.

Chapter 10

Figures 10.1 and 10.A: From John W. Santrock, *Psychology: The Science of Mind and Behavior,* 2d ed. Copyright © 1988 Wm. C. Brown Publishers, Dubuque, Iowa. All Rights Reserved. Reprinted by permission. **Figure 10.2**: Adapted from Jerome M. Sattler, *Assessment of Children's Intelligence and Special Abilities,* 2d ed. Copyright © 1982 Allyn & Bacon, Inc., Needham Heights, MA. Reprinted by permission of the author. **Figure 10.4**: Item A5 from *Raven's Standard Progressive Matrices* reproduced by permission of J. C. Raven Limited.

Chapter 11

Figure 11.1: From *Psychology Applied to Modern Life,* W. Weiten. Copyright © 1983 Wadsworth, Inc. Reprinted by permission of Brooks/Cole Publishing Company, Pacific Grove, CA. **Perspective on Child Development 11.1**: From John W. Santrock, *Adolescence: An Introduction,* 3d ed. Copyright © 1987 Wm. C. Brown Publishers, Dubuque, Iowa.

All Rights Reserved. Reprinted by permission. **Figure 11.2**: From F. J. Bruno, *Adjustment and Growth.* Copyright © 1983 John Wiley & Sons, Inc., New York. Reprinted by permission. **Figures 11.3 and 11.6**: From John W. Santrock, *Life-Span Development,* 2d ed. Copyright © 1986 Wm. C. Brown Publishers, Dubuque, Iowa. All Rights Reserved. Reprinted by permission. **Figure 11.4**: From F. R. Harris, M. M. Wolf, and D. M. Baer, "Effects of Adult Behavior" in *Young Children* 20(1):13, October, 1964. Copyright © 1964 National Association for the Education of Young Children, Washington, DC. **Figure 11.5**: From John W. Santrock, *Psychology: The Science of Mind and Behavior,* 2d ed. Copyright © 1988 Wm. C. Brown Publishers, Dubuque, Iowa. All Rights Reserved. Reprinted by permission. **Figure 11.7**: From John W. Santrock and Steven R. Yussen, *Childhood Socialization/ Social and Personality Development.* Copyright © 1981 John Wiley & Sons, Inc. Reprinted by permission. **Figure 11.8**: From Ulrick Neisser, *Cognitive Psychology,* © 1967, pp. 17, 112. Adapted by permission of Prentice-Hall, Englewood Cliffs, New Jersey. **Figure 11.10**: J. Garbarino, "Sociocultural Risk" from Kapp/Krakow, *The Child,* © 1982, Addison-Wesley Publishing Co., Inc., Reading, Massachusetts. Chart on page 648. Reprinted with permission.

Chapter 12

Figure 12.2: From Jay Belsky, "Early Human Experience: A Family Perspective," in *Developmental Psychology* 17:3–23, 1981. Copyright 1981 by the American Psychological Association. Reprinted by permission of the author. **Figure 12.4**: From H. F. Harlow and R. R. Zimmerman, "Affectional Responses in the Infant Monkey" in *Science,* 130:421–432, August 21, 1959. Copyright © 1959 American Association for the Advancement of Science, Washington, DC. Reprinted by permission. **Figure 12.5**: From L. Matas, R. A. Arend, and L. A. Sroufe, "Continuity in Adaptation: Quality of Attachment and Later Competence" in *Child Development,* 49:551. Copyright © 1978 The Society for Research in Child Development, Inc., Chicago, IL. Reprinted by permission. **Figure 12.6**: From E. E. Maccoby and J. A. Martin, "Socialization in the Context of the Family Parent-Child Interaction" in *Handbook of Child Psychology,* 4th ed., Vol. 4, edited by P. H. Mussen. Copyright © 1983 John Wiley & Sons, Inc., New York, NY. Reprinted by permission.

Chapter 13

Figures 13.1 and 13.2: From R. M. Krauss and S. Glucksberg, *Child Development* 40:255–266. Copyright © 1969 The Society for Research in Child Development, Inc., Chicago, IL. Reprinted by permission. **Figure 13.4**: From Dexter C. Dunphy, "The Social Structure of Peer Groups" in *Sociometry*, Vol. 26, 236, 1963. Copyright © 1963 American Sociological Association. Reprinted by permission. **Figure 13.5**: From John W. Santrock, *Life-Span Development*, 2d ed. Copyright © 1986 Wm. C. Brown Publishers, Dubuque, Iowa. All Rights Reserved. Reprinted by permission. **Figure 13.7**: From K. E. Barnes, "Preschool Play Norms: A Replication" in *Developmental Psychology* 5:99–103. Copyright © 1971 American Psychological Association. Reprinted by permission of the author. **Figure 13.8**: From D. R. Anderson et al., "Television Viewing at Home: Age Trends in Visual Attention and Time with TV" from a paper presented at the meeting of the SRCD, Toronto, p. 18. Copyright © 1985 Daniel R. Anderson.

Chapter 14

Figure 14.1: From M. Lewis and J. Brooks-Gunn, *Social Cognition and the Acquisition of the Self*. Copyright © 1979 Plenum Publishing Corporation, New York, NY. Reprinted by permission. **Perspective on Child Development 14.2**: From John W. Santrock, *Adolescence*, 3d ed. Copyright © 1987 Wm. C. Brown Publishers, Dubuque, Iowa. All Rights Reserved. Reprinted by permission. **Table 14.6**: From John W. Santrock, *Children*. Copyright © 1988 Wm. C. Brown Publishers, Dubuque, Iowa. All Rights Reserved. Reprinted by permission.

Chapter 15

Figure 15.1: From John W. Santrock, *Children*. Copyright © 1988 Wm. C. Brown Publishers, Dubuque, Iowa. All Rights Reserved. Reprinted by permission. **Table 15.2**: From John W. Santrock, *Psychology: The Science of Mind and Behavior*, 2d ed. Copyright © 1988 Wm. C. Brown Publishers, Dubuque, Iowa. All Rights Reserved. Reprinted by permission. **Figure 15.A**: From J. S. Hyde, "Children's Understanding of Sexist Language" in *Developmental Psychology* 20:703, 1984. Copyright 1984 by the American Psychological Association. Reprinted by permission of the author.

Chapter 16

Figure 16.1: From A. Colby, L. Kohlberg, J. Gibbs, and M. Lieberman, "A Longitudinal Study of Moral Judgment" in *Monographs of the Society for Research in Child Development*. Copyright © 1982 The Society for Research in Child Development, Inc., Chicago, IL. Reprinted by permission. **Perspective on Child Development 16.2**: From John W. Santrock and Steven R. Yussen, *Children and Adolescents: A Developmental Perspective*. Copyright © 1984 Wm. C. Brown Publishers, Dubuque, Iowa. All Rights Reserved. Reprinted by permission.

Chapter 17

Figure 17.1: From T. Achenbach, C. S. Edelbrock, "Behavioral Problems and Compentencies Reported by Parents of Normal and Disturbed Children Aged Four Through Sixteen" in *Monographs of the Society for Research in Child Development* 46(1), Serial No. 188. Copyright © 1981 The Society for Research in Child Development, Chicago, IL. Reprinted by permission. **Figure 17.2**: Data from I. L. Gottesman and J. Shields, *The Schizophrenic Puzzle*. Copyright © 1982 Cambridge University Press, New York, NY. **Figure 17.4**: From *Illicit Drug Use, Smoking, and Drinking by America's High School Students, College Students, and Young Adults, 1975–1987*, by L. D. Johnston, P. M. O'Malley, and J. G. Bachman. (In press, 1988), Institute of Social Research, Ann Arbor, MI. Reprinted by permission.

Chapter 18

Figure 18.1: From L. L. Langley, *Physiology of Man*. Copyright © 1971 Van Nostrand Reinhold Company. Reprinted by permission.

Photos

Name Index

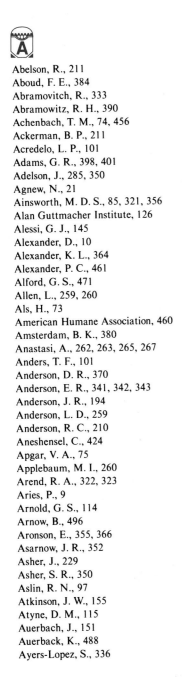
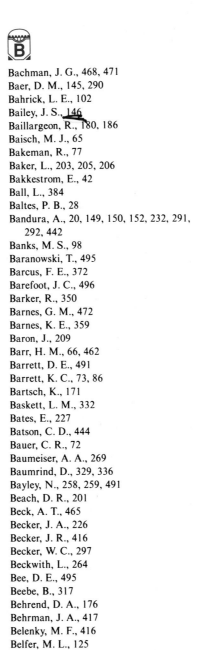

Brand, E., 343
Brannon, L., 482
Bray, H., 418, 419
Bray, J. H., 343
Brazelton, T. B., 75, 76, 84
Bremer, M., 369, 371
Bremner, R., 366
Brenner, A., 483, 485, 486
Bretherton, I., 86, 380
Brewster, A. B., 494
Brinker, R. P., 153
Brody, L., 423
Bronfenbrenner, U., 263, 304, 350, 437
Bronson, G. W., 300
Bronstein, P., 323
Brookman, R. R., 125
Brooks-Gunn, J., 118, 127, 363, 379, 380
Brown, A. L., 185, 197, 201, 203, 204, 205, 208
Brown, E., 349
Brown, J. D., 496
Brown, J. L., 88
Brown, J. S., 195
Brown, J. V., 77
Brown, M. M., 297, 350, 357
Brown, R., 223, 233, 234, 238, 355, 366, 444
Brownell, C. A., 349
Brumberg, J. J., 493
Bruner, J., 235, 317
Bryant, B. K., 21
Bryant, D., 264
Buchanan, N. R., 349
Buchsbaum, K., 297
Buckley, S., 350
Bukowski, W. M., 354
Bulcroft, R., 119
Bullock, M., 176
Burgeson, R., 369
Burish, T. G., 145, 292
Burns, K. A., 67
Burns, W. J., 67
Burton, R. B., 195
Burton, R. V., 297, 442
Buss, A. H., 50, 323
Buss, R. R., 211
Butcher, M. J., 101
Butler, R. A., 153

Cadigan, D., 364
Cairns, R. B., 10, 11
Calhoun, J. A., 468
Callan, J. W., 352
Callanan, M., 210
Camara, K. A., 342
Campbell, J. D., 297
Campbell, T. A., 371
Campione, J. C., 197, 205
Campos, J. J., 73, 86, 99
Candee, D., 443
Cannizzo, S. R., 201

Caplan, F., 84
Carasaniti, M. A., 341
Carey, S., 240
Carpenter, T. P., 206
Carper, L., 406, 423
Carton-Ford, S., 369
Case, R., 200, 201
Cassell, C., 123
Cassidy, D. J., 201
Cassidy, J., 318
Ceci, S. J., 462
Chalemian, R. J., 101
Chalip, L., 197
Chandler, L. A., 483
Chandler, M., 384
Chang, P., 77
Charnov, E. L., 323
Chase-Lansdale, P. L., 341
Chasnoff, I. J., 67
Chassin, L., 472
Cherry-Wilkinson, L., 235
Chess, S., 50, 51, 301, 323, 465, 475
Chi, M. T. H., 210
Chinsky, J. M., 201
Choi, H. P., 370
Chomsky, N., 227
Christiansen, K. O., 42
Chrousos, G. P., 22, 114
Cicirelli, V., 332
Clabby, J. G., 352
Clark, B., 366
Clark, D., 262
Clark, D. L., 415
Clark, E. V., 236, 237
Clark, H. H., 236
Clark, M. L., 366
Clark, M. S., 444
Clark, R. W., 155
Clark, S. D., 123
Clarke-Stewart, K. A., 319, 326, 362
Clevenger, M., 235
Clinchy, B. M., 416
Clingempeel, W. E., 343
Cohen, D., 151
Cohen, S., 260
Cohn, J. F., 317
Coie, J. D., 350
Colby, A., 433, 435
Coleman, J., 366
Coletta, N. D., 342
Collings, G. C., 416
Collins, W. A., 336
Condon, S. M., 337, 401
Condry, J. C., 350
Conger, J. J., 127
Contois, J. H., 490
Conway, B. E., 249
Cooney, T. J., 158
Coons, S., 89
Cooper, C. R., 336, 337, 399, 401
Corasaniti, M. A., 326
Corbin, S. B., 341, 342
Corboy, L., 488

Cornu-Wells, A., 186
Corrigan, R., 171, 172
Corter, C., 333
Cowan, C. P., 316
Cowan, P. A., 316
Cox, G. L., 202
Cox, M., 341
Cox, R., 341
Cratty, B., 105
Crimmins, D. B., 458
Crnic, K. A., 74
Croft, K., 383
Cronbach, L. J., 365
Cross, D., 171
Cross, K. P., 367
Crosswhite, F. J., 158
Crowder, R., 241
Cuban, L., 367
Culp, R. E., 315
Curtiss, S., 232
Cutler, G. B., 22, 114

Dachman, R. S., 145
Damon, W., 384, 401, 437
Dann, S., 349
Darby, B. L., 66, 462
Darling, C. A., 122, 123
Darlington, R., 363
Daro, D., 460
Davis, J., 366
Dawson, G., 457
Day, J. D., 208
De Caprona, D., 186
Deci, E. L., 156
DeFries, J. C., 51
DeLoache, J. S., 201
Delongis, A., 483
Demo, D. H., 391
Demorest, A., 185
Demoss, V., 489
Dempster, F. N., 200
Denham, S. A., 444
Depner, C. E., 342
Desimone, D., 410
Deutch, C., 363
Deutch, M., 363
de Villiers, J. G., 229, 233
de Villiers, P. A., 229, 233
de Vries, B., 437
Dewey, J., 445
Diamond, A., 172
DiLalla, L. F., 361
Dillon, R. F., 209
Dillon, R. S., 114
Dimsdale, J. E., 496
Dishon, T. D., 19
Dodge, K. A., 297, 350, 351, 357
Doehrman, M. J., 285
Doering, Z., 366
Dolan, R. S., 51

Dolgin, K. G., 176
Doll, G., 326
Dolloghan, C., 235
Domek, C. J., 349
Dorn, L. D., 114
Dossey, J. A., 158
Douvan, E., 350
Dove, A., 265
Downey, A. M., 497
Downs, A. C., 408
Dreyer, R. H., 122, 123
Dreyfus, H. L., 195
Dreyfus, S. E., 195
Dubow, E. F., 372
Dugdale, S., 155
Duncker, K., 207
Dunkel-Schetter, C., 483
Dunn, J., 233, 332
Dunphy, D., 356
Durand, V. M., 458
Durant, D., 472
Durden-Smith, J., 410
Durkin, K., 317, 417
Dwyer, C. A., 248
Dyer, K., 145

Eagleston, J. R., 496
East, P. L., 350
Eccles, J., 415, 416
Eccles, J. S., 422
Eckerman, C. O., 349
Eckert, E., 36
Edelbrook, C. S., 456
Edleman, M. W., 127, 128
Edwards, B., 461
Eger, M., 446
Ehrhardt, A. A., 410
Eichorn, D., 366
Eichorn, D. H., 381
Eidelman, A., 151
Eisenberg, N., 443, 444
Elias, M. J., 352
Elkind, D., 154, 178, 180, 183, 185, 186, 340,
    380, 382, 383
Elliott, J. E., 466
Elston, R. C., 497
Emde, R. N., 85
Emery, R. E., 318
Engen, T., 100
Enright, R., 438
Enright, R. D., 186, 439
Entus, A. K., 229
Entwisle, D. R., 364
Erikson, E., 320, 365, 379, 381, 386, 395,
    396, 410, 467, 475
Eron, L. D., 372
Escalona, S., 171
Eschel, Y., 364
Estes, D., 323
Evans, E., 384
Evans, R., 211

Fagan, J. F., III, 260
Fagot, B. I., 144
Falbo, T., 333
Falkenberg, S. D., 209
Fantz, R. L., 98
Farber, E. A., 269
Farnham-Diggory, S., 462
Faust, M. S., 116
Fein, G. G., 326, 358, 359, 360, 362
Feingold, A., 420
Feist, J., 482
Feldman, J. F., 72
Feldman, S. S., 484, 485
Ferrara, R. A., 197, 205
Feshbach, S., 371
Field, T., 151
Field, T. M., 72, 76
Fifer, G., 262
Fifer, W. P., 67
Fincher, J., 58, 73
Finney, J. W., 472
Fisch, R. O., 77, 101
Fischer, K. W., 185, 380, 381
Fischman, S. H., 496
Fisher, T. D., 127
Fishman, D. B., 292
Flavell, E. R., 361
Flavell, J. H., 165, 168, 171, 201, 205, 294,
    361, 383
Fleming, A. S., 315
Flett, G. L., 315
Fogel, A., 317, 444
Folkman, S., 483
Fontana, V. J., 460
Food and Nutrition Board, National
    Research Council, 489
Ford, M. E., 408, 409, 484, 485
Forrest, J. D., 128
Fowler, R. C., 466
Fox, L. H., 423
Fox, R. A., 65
Fraiberg, S., 94
Frank, G. C., 497
Frank, L. K., 360
Franklin, F. A., 497
Franks, C. M., 292
Freedman, J. L., 372
French, D., 350
Freud, A., 285, 349
Freud, S., 280
Friedman, M., 496
Friedrich, L. K., 370
Frisch, R., 114
Fritz, J., 86
Frodi, A. M., 325
Frommer, E., 298
Fucigna, C., 174
Fugua, R. W., 145
Fujimura, J. B., 490
Fulker, D. W., 51
Furstenberg, F. F., 342, 343
Furstenberg, J. J., 127
Furth, H. G., 182, 234

Gaensbauer, T. G., 85
Gage, N. L., 364
Gagne, E. D., 208, 209
Gagnon, J. H., 123
Gallup, A. M., 415
Galst, J. P., 373
Garbarino, J., 437, 461
Garcia, R., 229
Gardner, B. T., 230, 231
Gardner, H., 174, 185, 240, 256
Gardner, R. A., 230, 231
Gardner, W. P., 323
Garfinkel, P. E., 493
Garner, D. M., 205, 206, 493
Garrison, K. C., 116
Gaskell, J., 418
Gazzaniga, M. S., 228
Geffen, G., 199
Geis, G., 460
Gelman, R., 177, 180, 186, 241
Gesell, A., 92
Gesell, A. L., 11
Gewirtz, J., 85
Gibbs, J., 435, 436
Gibson, E. J., 96, 99, 102
Gibson, J. J., 96
Gilgun, J. F., 123, 124
Gill, S., 408, 409
Gilligan, C., 437
Gillum, R. F., 496
Ginsburg, H., 167
Gjerde, P. F., 341, 466
Glaser, R., 215
Gleason, J. B., 240
Glenn, C. G., 211
Glick, P. C., 338
Globerson, T., 262
Glucksberg, S., 351
Goelman, H., 185
Gold, M., 336, 467
Goldberg, B. D., 65
Goldberg, J., 201
Goldberger, N. R., 416
Goldenson, R. M., 360
Goldfield, E. C., 317
Goldhagen, J., 65
Golding, E., 324
Goldman, J. A., 490
Goldman, N., 128
Goldsmith, H. H., 50, 51, 73, 323
Goldstein, M. J., 460
Goldston, S., 264
Golman-Rakic, P. S., 94
Goodchilds, J. D., 124
Goodenough, D. R., 42
Goodlad, J. L., 367
Gordon, N. J., 371
Gordon, S., 123, 124
Görlitz, D., 35
Gorski, P. A., 76
Gottesman, I. I., 51
Gottesman, I. L., 459

Kety, S. S., 466
Keyes, M., 36
Kibbey, D., 155
Kidd, K. K., 51, 53, 113
Kifer, E., 158
King, R. M., 444
Kinsey, A. C., 124
Kirmil-Gray, K., 496
Kirshner, G. L., 66, 462
Klaus, M. H., 76, 77
Klein, P., 301
Klein, R. E., 491
Klein, R. P., 153
Klein, S. S., 415, 416
Klein, Z., 364
Klerman, G. L., 456
Knapp, H., 418
Knight, R. S., 445
Knopf, I. J., 199
Kobak, R. R., 336
Koegel, L. K., 458
Koegel, R. L., 142, 145, 458
Koeske, R. D., 210
Kogan, N., 271
Kohlberg, L., 295, 297, 411, 433, 435, 443, 447
Kohut, H., 385, 386
Kolbe, L. J., 495
Koperski, J. A., 85
Kopp, C. B., 72, 74, 475
Korner, A. F., 85
Koverola, C., 461
Kraemer, H. C., 85
Krantz, K., 315
Krauss, R. A., 351
Kreinberg, N., 416
Kreutzer, M. A., 205
Krogman, W. M., 106
Krowitz, A., 99
Krug, R. S., 297
Kuhl, P. K., 233
Kuhn, D., 186
Kupersmidt, J., 350
Kupfer, D. J., 466
Kurland, D. M., 201
Kuse, A. R., 51
Kutz, S. L., 349

La Barbera, J. D., 86
Ladd, G. W., 349
Lamb, M. E., 73, 144, 307, 323, 325, 414
Lambert, N. M., 464
Landesman-Dwyer, S., 67
Lane, H., 278
Lange, L., 415, 416
Langer, A., 99
Langlois, J. H., 408
Lapsley, D. K., 186, 379, 399, 435, 438, 439
LaRue, A. A., 413

Lawton, S. C., 208
Lazar, I., 363
Lazarus, R. S., 483
Lazerson, A., 185
Leboyer, F., 69
Lee, S., 158
Lee, V. E., 363
Lefkowitz, M. M., 372
Lehrer, R., 196
Leiffer, A. D., 371, 372
LeMare, L. J., 351
Lenneberg, E. H., 229, 236
Leonard, C., 205
Lepper, M. R., 155, 156
Lerman, R. H., 490
Lerner, M. J., 444
Lerner, R. M., 118, 119, 121, 186, 350, 462
Lesser, G., 262
Lester, B. M., 75, 76
Levin, J., 202
Lewis, J. M., 341, 342
Lewis, M., 153, 379, 380, 414
Lewkowicz, D. J., 102
Liberman, I. Y., 224, 241
Lieberman, M., 435
Liebert, R. M., 372
Lifshitz, F., 488
Lin, S., 338
Lincoln, R., 128
Lindauer, B. K., 198, 202
Lipkins, R., 467
Lipsitt, L. P., 100, 101
Lipsitz, J., 340, 367, 368
Lochman, J. J., 106
Locke, J., 9–10
Lockheed, M., 421
Lollis, S. P., 349
Long, L., 340
Long, T., 340
Lonky, E., 443
Lorch, E. P., 370
Lorden, R. B., 209
Lorenz, K. Z., 302, 320
Loriaux, D. L., 22, 114
Los Angeles Times, 248
Lovaas, O. T., 142
Lowell, E. L., 155
Lowrey, G. H., 104
Lueptow, L., 422
Lummis, M., 158
Lunde, I., 466
Lunsteen, C., 42
Luria, A., 415
Lykken, D. T., 36
Lyle, J., 370
Lynch, M. E., 338

McAdoo, H. P., 157
McAdoo, J. L., 157
McCall, R. B., 50, 260, 323, 381
McCandless, B. R., 384

McCarthy, M. E., 153
McCarton, C. M., 72
McClaskey, C. L., 297, 350
McClelland, D. C., 155
Maccoby, E. E., 77, 314, 317, 330, 334, 342, 378, 384, 394, 408, 411, 413, 414, 415, 420
Maccoby, N., 372
McDaniel, M. A., 202
MacFarlane, J. A., 100
MacFarlane, J. W., 259, 260
MacIver, D., 415, 416
McKnight, C. C., 158
McLaughlin, B., 242, 243
McLaughlin, L., 472
McMahan, C. A., 497
McNeil, D., 227, 234
McQuire, W. J., 372
McQuiston, S., 153
MacTurk, R. H., 153
McWhirter, D. P., 124
Maddux, J. E., 494
Mahler, M., 380, 381
Malatesta, C. Z., 86
Malone, S., 101
Maloney, J., 384, 401
Maltsberger, J. T., 466
Mandler, J. M., 212
Manion, I., 461
Maratsos, M., 231, 234
Marcia, J., 396, 398, 399, 401
Marcus, G. B., 264
Margolis, F. L., 490
Markman, E. M., 205, 206, 210
Marlow, L., 338
Marquis, A. L., 233
Marr, D. B., 260
Marshall, R. E., 101
Marshall, T. R., 85
Martin, D. C., 66, 462
Martin, E. E., 124
Martin, J., 366
Martin, J. A., 77, 317, 330, 394
Maruyama, G., 333
Maslow, A. H., 154
Massey, C. M., 177
Masters, J. C., 145, 292
Matarazzo, J. D., 482
Matas, L., 322, 323
Matheny, A. P., 51
Mathews, K. A., 496
Mathews, S. R., 211
Mayaux, M. J., 65
Mayer, R., 205
Mays, J., 366
Mednick, S. A., 42
Medrich, E. A., 350
Meece, J., 364
Meier, J. H., 458, 463
Meilman, P. W., 399
Melson, G. F., 444
Meltzoff, A. N., 151
Meredith, H. V., 104
Mervis, B. B., 210

Meschulach-Sarfaty, O., 151
Messer, D. J., 153
Meyer, C., 185
Meyerhoff, M. K., 331
Milberg, S., 444
Milham, J., 72
Miller, F. B., 125
Miller, G. A., 200, 223, 227, 229, 235, 240
Miller, G. E., 211
Miller, N., 333
Millon, T., 456
Minnett, A. M., 333
Minuchin, P. P., 366
Mischel, H., 443
Mischel, W., 291, 420, 442, 443
Miura, I. T., 421
Mizruchi, M., 467
Mnookin, R. H., 342
Moely, B. E., 201
Mollnow, E., 67
Monahan, J., 460
Money, J., 124, 410, 411
Monroe, R., 270
Montemayor, R., 336, 398
Moore, M. K., 151
Moore, M. S., 337
Moos, R. H., 472
Moosbrugger, L., 472
Morgan, G. A., 319
Morgan, S. P., 127
Morris, P. E., 195
Morrison, D. M., 123
Morse, W. C., 364
Moser, J. M., 206
Moses, N., 488
Mueller, E., 349
Murphy, M. N., 186
Murphy, R. R., 297
Murray, D. M., 496
Murray, F. B., 183
Muuss, R. E., 437

Nadar, P. R., 494
National Center for Health Statistics, 65
National Education Association, 418
Naus, M. J., 267
Neimeyer, R. A., 461
Neisser, U., 208, 298
Nelson, K. E., 212, 227
Newberger, C. M., 348
Newcomb, A. F., 354
Newcomb, M. D., 471
Nicholls, J. G., 157, 422
Nichols, I. A., 236
Nielson Television Index, 370
Niemark, E. D., 186
Ninio, A., 235
Nisbett, R. R., 156
Nottelmann, E. D., 22, 114
Nucci, L., 438, 439

Nucci, M., 439
Nugent, J. K., 75, 76
Nurcombe, B., 74
Nusbaum, H. C., 197

O'Connell, B., 227
O'Connor, M. J., 260
O'Connor-Francoeur, P., 494
O'Dell, M. C., 458
Offer, D., 389, 390
O'Hara, N. M., 495
O'Leary, K. D., 145
Olejnik, A. B., 413
Olson, F. A., 201
Olson, L., 438
Olweus, D., 357
O'Malley, P. M., 468, 471
Oppenheimer, M., 125
Opper, S., 167
Ortmann, J., 466
Oser, F. K., 446
O'Shea, G. 298
Osofsky, H. J., 315
Osofsky, J. D., 315
Ottinger, D. R., 66
Ourselves and our Children, 316
Ovelette, R., 444
Owen, D. R., 42
Oyama, S., 229

Page, D., 22, 44
Paivio, A., 202
Palincsar, A. S., 204, 205
Pallas, A. M., 364
Parcel, G. S., 494, 495
Pardes, H., 456
Paris, S. G., 198, 202
Parisi, S. A., 86
Parke, R. D., 324, 325, 442, 460
Parker, J. G., 353
Parmalee, A. H., 89, 260, 494
Parsons, J. E., 422
Parten, M., 358
Pasanella, A. L., 446
Pasley, K., 343
Patterson, C. J., 442
Patterson, G. R., 19, 468
Pavlov, I., 137
Pearson, P. D., 210
Pederson, D. R., 322
Pellegrino, J. W., 248, 249, 257
Penner, S. G., 233
Pepler, D. J., 333
Peskin, H., 118
Petersen, A. C., 113, 119, 121, 389, 390
Peterson, L., 72

Peterson, P. L., 365
Pettit, G. S., 297, 350, 357
Pfeffer, C. R., 467
Phares, E. J., 284
Phelps, E., 185
Philip, J., 42
Piaget, J., 92, 164, 167, 168, 171, 176, 358, 380, 431
Piatrich, P. R., 364
Pick, H. L., 106
Piers, E. V., 387
Pike, R., 388, 389
Pillow, B. H., 198
Pines, M., 380
Pinker, S., 227
Pipes, P., 489, 490
Pipp, S., 380, 381
Pittman, T. S., 156
Pleck, J. H., 323, 411
Plomin, R., 50, 51, 323
Plutchik, R., 467
Polit, D. F., 333
Polivy, J., 493
Pollack, W. S., 324
Pomeroy, W. B., 124
Porges, S. W., 101
Porter, F. L., 101
Posner, M. I., 199
Powell, M. C., 444
Power, C., 447
Power, F. C., 399
Prechtl, H. F. R., 88
Premack, A. J., 230
Premack, D., 230
Pressley, M., 202
Price, J., 371
Prineas, R. J., 496
Psychology Today, 441
Pugliese, M. T., 488

Quintana, S. M., 435

Rachford, D., 153
Radke-Yarrow, M., 444, 491
Rahman, T., 211
Ramey, C., 85, 264
Rasbury, W. C., 454, 458, 465
Raths, L. E., 446
Ratner, N., 317
Rauh, V. A., 74
Raynor, I. O., 155
Raynor, R., 138
Rebelsky, F. G., 236
Reid, D. K., 462
Reid, J. B., 19
Reilly, B. M., 101
Reinsch, J. M., 124

Rekers, G. A., 417
Rembold, K. L., 211
Resnick, G., 342
Resnick, S., 36
Rest, J. R., 435, 436
Revelle, R., 114
Ricciuti, H. N., 319
Rice, F. P., 64
Rich, C. L., 466
Rich, S., 36
Richardson, A., 418, 419
Richardson, J. G., 423, 424
Ricks, M., 299
Riedgeway, D., 86
Rimm, D. C., 145, 292
Ritter, R., 201
Roberts, D. E., 372
Roberts, M. C., 494
Robinson, H. F., 105
Robinson, N. M., 269, 270
Rode, S. S., 77
Rodin, J., 482, 492
Rogers, C. R., 386, 387
Romberg, T. A., 206
Roodin, P. A., 443
Roopnarine, J. L., 144
Rosch, E., 210
Rose, S. A., 72, 102, 103, 260
Rosen, B., 424
Rosen, J., 350
Rosenbaum, P. A., 497
Rosenberg, B. G., 333, 417
Rosenblith, J. F., 59, 69, 72, 76, 145
Rosenman, R., 496
Rosenthal, D., 466
Rosenthal, R., 268
Rosoff, J. I., 128
Ross, H. S., 349
Rotgers, R., 292
Rothbart, M. L. K., 50, 51, 323, 332
Rovee-Collier, C., 145
Ruben, D. B., 42
Rubin, K. H., 176, 351, 358, 360, 415
Rubin, V., 350
Ruble, D. N., 315, 384, 411, 422
Ruff, H. A., 102, 103
Rumbaugh, D. M., 231
Rutter, D. R., 317
Rutter, M., 341, 457, 458, 475, 483, 486
Ryder, N., 366

Sackett, G. P., 67
Sadker, D., 415
Sadker, M., 415
Salapatek, P., 85, 98
Sandell, R., 416
Sanders, S. A., 124
Sandman, B. M., 66, 462
Santrock, J. W., 263, 264, 294, 333, 336, 341,
    342, 343
Sattler, J. M., 253

Savin-Williams, R. C., 391
Sawin, D. B., 324
Scardamalia, M., 185, 203, 205
Scarr, S., 45, 51, 53, 113, 262, 265, 326
Scerry, A., 336
Schaffer, H. R., 234, 319
Schaie, K. W., 28
Schank, R., 211
Scheff, T. J., 456
Schefft, B. K., 145
Schiff, A. R., 199
Schneider, P. A., 85
Schnur, E., 363
Schopler, E., 457, 458, 483
Schorr, L. B., 126, 128
Schreibman, L., 142
Schulenberg, J. E., 389, 390
Schulsinger, F., 466
Schulsinger, R., 42
Schulz, H., 89
Schunk, D. H., 157
Schwartz, D., 65
Schwartz, M. A., 456
Scott-Jones, D., 366
Seebauer, E., 372
Segal, N. L., 36
Seigle, J., 369, 371
Seligman, M. E. P., 465
Selman, R. L., 294, 348, 353, 384, 385
Selye, H., 483
Senn, M. J., 11
Serbin, L. A., 415, 416
Serlin, R. C., 186, 439
Sexton, M., 67
Sexton, M. A., 199
Shakeshaft, C., 416
Shantz, C. O., 294, 352
Shantz, C. U., 176
Shapiro, E. K., 366
Shatz, M., 241
Shaul, D. L., 315
Sherif, C. W., 354
Sherif, M., 354
Sherman, A., 416
Sherwood, V., 317
Shields, J., 459
Shipstead, S. G., 383
Shore, C., 227
Shuey, A., 262
Siegel, J. D., 496
Siegel, L. J., 454, 459, 465
Siegel, L. S., 74
Siegler, R. S., 193, 197, 201
Sigman, M. D., 198
Simmons, J. E., 66
Simmons, R. G., 119, 369
Simon, M. L., 350
Simon, W., 123
Simons-Morton, G. G., 495
Simpson, C. H., 423, 424
Sims-Knight, J. E., 59, 69, 72, 76, 145
Singer, D., 181
Singer, D. G., 373
Singer, J. L., 280, 373

Sitterle, K. A., 343
Sizer, T. R., 367
Skells, H., 263
Skinner, B. F., 140, 142, 232, 290
Slavin, R. E., 204, 355, 366
Sledden, E. A., 494
Slobin, D., 238
Small, A. W., 422
Smenner, P. C., 226
Smerson, P. E., 319
Smetana, J., 438
Smiley, S. S., 185, 208
Smith, M. B., 65
Smith, P. B., 322
Smith, R. S., 474
Snarey, J., 435
Snow, C. E., 235
Snow, R. E., 365
Snyder, J., 468
Solovey, P., 482
Sophian, C., 172
Sorensen, R. C., 124
Sowers-Hoag, K. W., 146
Spearman, C., 255
Spelke, E. S., 102, 103
Spence, J. T., 407, 419
Spencer, M. L., 416
Sperry, R. W., 228
Sprafkin, J. N., 372
Srinivasan, S. R., 497
Sroufe, L. A., 77, 86, 322, 323, 356, 385,
    394, 475
Stafford, F. P., 334
Stage, E. K., 416
Stallings, J., 363
Stanhope, L., 333
Stanowicz, L., 233
Stearns, G., 65
Stein, A. H., 370
Stein, N. L., 211
Steinberg, J., 325
Steinberg, L. D., 336, 338, 340
Steiner, J. E., 101
Stenberg, C., 73
Stern, D. N., 317
Sternberg, R. J., 208, 209, 249, 260, 267
Sternglanz, S., 415, 416
Stevenson, H. W., 75, 158, 198, 460
Stevenson-Hinde, J., 16
Stigler, J. W., 158, 197
Stine, E. L., 233
Stipek, D. J., 422
Stockard, J., 408, 409
Stocking, M., 42
Stouthamer-Loeber, M., 468
Streissguth, A. P., 66, 462
Stunkard, A. J., 493
Suarez, T., 264
Sullivan, A., 337
Sullivan, H. S., 386
Sullivan, K., 337
Suomi, S., 51, 325
Suomi, S. J., 349
Susman, E. J., 22, 114

Sutton-Smith, B., 333, 357, 358
Swadesh, M., 235
Swafford, J. O., 158
Szasz, T., 456

Tangney, J. P., 371
Tanner, J. M., 116, 117
Tarule, J. M., 416
Tellegen, A., 36
Terman, L., 269
Terrace, H., 231
Teti, D. M., 74
Tetreault, M. K. T., 416
Thelen, E., 93
Thomas, A., 50, 51, 301, 323, 475
Thompson, A., 264
Thompson, L., 51
Thompson, P. J., 416
Thompson, R. A., 323
Thomsen, L., 493
Thoresen, C. E., 496
Thornburg, H. D., 127
Thorndike, R. L., 253
Thurstone, L. L., 256
Thyer, B. A., 146
Tiernan, K., 494
Timberlake, B., 65
Tobiasen, J., 315
Tobin, D., 423
Toda, S., 317
Tomlinson-Keasey, C., 466
Tonick, I. J., 415
Townsend, M. A. R., 208
Travers, K. J., 158
Trevethan, S. D., 437
Tronick, E. Z., 317
Trotter, R. J., 328
Trudel, M., 323
Tucker, L. A., 370, 495
Tuckman, B. W., 496
Tulkin, S. R., 307
Tuma, A. H., 460
Turiel, E., 435, 438, 439
Turkle, S., 421
Turner, T. J., 212
Turnure, J. E., 199

Utall, D. Y., 158

Vaillant, G. E., 486
Valdez-Ménchaca, M. C., 233
Vandell, D. L., 317, 326, 332, 333, 341, 349
Vandenberg, S. G., 51
Vanderberg, B., 358, 360

VanDusen, J. E., 122, 123
VanItallie, T. B., 491
van Marthens, E., 490
Vietze, P., 86
Vietze, P. M., 153
Virgilia, S. J., 497
Volkmor, C. B., 446
Voors, A. W., 497
Vorhees, C. V., 67
Vrazo, G. J., 145
Vuchinich, S., 318
Vurpillot, E., 198
Vygotsky, L. S., 359

Wachs, H., 182
Wachs, T. D., 153
Waddington, C. H., 46
Wagennar, A. C., 472
Wagner, D. A., 75
Walder, L. O., 372
Walk, R. D., 99
Walker, L., 436
Walker, L. J., 437
Wallace, I. F., 260
Wallach, M. A., 269, 270, 271
Wallerstein, J., 341, 342
Wallerstein, J. S., 341
Warren, J. V., 490
Warren, L. W., 466
Warren, M. P., 118
Warshak, R. A., 341, 342, 343
Washburn, K. J., 234
Waterman, A. S., 399
Waterman, C. K., 399
Waters, E., 86, 394
Watson, J. B., 12, 85, 138, 488
Watson, M. W., 361
Wearne, D., 206
Weaver, S. J., 21
Webb, W. B., 89
Webber, L. S., 497
Wechsler, D., 253
Weinberg, D. A., 484, 485
Weinberg, M. S., 124
Weinberg, R. A., 51, 262
Weiner, I. B., 457, 458, 464
Weinstein, N. D., 495
Weisberg, R. P., 352
Weiss, G., 464
Wellman, H. M., 171, 201
Wender, P. H., 466
Wenner, W., 89
Werner, E. E., 65, 474
Werner, H., 359
Wertsch, J. V., 203
Wessels, K., 364
Westoff, C. G., 128
Weyman-Daum, M., 488
Whaley, L., 41
Whatley, J. L., 349

White, B. J., 354
White, B. L., 331
White, M. A., 208
White, R. W., 153, 156
White, S. H., 10
Whitehurst, G. J., 233
Widmayer, S., 72, 76
Wiedenfield, S. A., 496
Wiggins, O. P., 456
Wilcox, K. J., 36
Williams, J., 241
Williams, R. B., 496
Williams, S., 408, 409
Wilson, G. T., 145
Wilson, K. S., 317, 349
Wilson, R. S., 51
Windle, W. F., 101
Winner, E., 174, 185, 240
Witkin, H. A., 42
Witryol, S., 143
Wodarski, J. S., 472
Wohlwill, J. F., 358
Wolf, M. M., 145, 290
Wolfe, D. A., 461
Wolff, P. H., 88, 151
Wolfson, J., 72
Wong, D. L., 41
Woodson, R., 151
Worobey, J., 76
Worthington, B. S., 65
Wright, H. F., 350
Wright, J. C., 371
Wright, L., 494
Wulf, D., 128
Wylie, R. C., 379, 387, 388

Yanof, D. S., 336
Yardley, K., 387
Yarrow, L. J., 153
Yarrow, M. R., 297
Young, D., 466
Yussen, S. R., 196, 203, 210, 211, 437

Zabin, L. S., 123
Zahn-Waxler, C., 86, 444
Zajonc, R. B., 264
Zamenhof, S., 490
Zelazo, P. R., 326
Zellman, G. L., 124
Zembar, M. J., 267
Zeskind, P. S., 85
Zigler, E., 327
Zigler, E. F., 10, 269
Zill, N., 343
Zimmerman, R. R., 319
Zucker, K. J., 417

Subject Index

moral development, 433–38
    authority and social-order maintaining morality, 434
    community rights versus individual rights, 434
    conventional moral reasoning, 433
    criticisms of, 436–38
    developmental course, 433–35
    extra-moral factors, 443
    females and, 437, 438
    good boy/good girl orientation, 433–34
    individual conscience, 434
    influences on moral development, 436–37
    Just Community (Cluster School), 447
    Moral Atmosphere Interview, 447
    naive hedonism or instrumental orientation, 433
    postconventional moral reasoning, 434
    preconventional moral reasoning, 433
    punishment and obedience orientation, 433
socialization, 295–97

L

Labeling, in language learning, 234, 235
Laboratory observation, 20
Lamaze method, 69
Language
    characteristics of, 223–24, 228
    definition of, 223, 224
    rule systems
        grammar, 225
        morphology, 224
        phonology, 224
        pragmatics, 226–27
        semantics, 225
        surface/deep structure, 225
        syntax, 225
Language acquisition device (LAD), 227
Language development
    animal language, 228, 230
    bilingualism, 241–43
    biological aspects, 227–32
    brain, 228–29
        language acquisition device (LAD), 227
    cognition and, 234–35
    early childhood, 239–41
        conversation, 240
        language rules, 239–40
        speech style, 241
    environmental aspects, imitation of language, 233–34, 235
    infancy, 236–38
        babbling, 236–37
        holophrase hypothesis, 237
        overextensions, 237
        telegraphic speech, 238
        two-word utterances, 238
        underextensions, 237–38
    reading, 241

Latchkey children, 340–41
Late childhood
    family interaction, 333–35
        coregulation, 334
    overview of, 507–9
    physical development, 106
Latency stage, 284
Learned helplessness, 465
Learning. See also Cognitive developmental theories; Motivation; specific topics
    classical conditioning, 137–40
    definition of, 135
    habituation, 145–47
    modeling, 134, 149–52
    nature of, 135–36
    operant conditioning, 140–45
    reinforcement, 134
Learning disabilities, 462–64
    attention deficit disorder, 462, 464
    behaviors associated with, 463
Leboyer method, 69
Longitudinal approach
    child development research, 26
    problems of, 26
Low-birth-weight infants. See Preterm infants

M

Macrosystem, 306
Malnutrition, 490–91
    effects of, 491
    studies on, 490–91
Mapping, in children, 106
Masturbation, 124
Maternal disease, and prenatal development, 63–64
Maternal employment, 339–41
    latchkey children, 340–41
Maturation
    and development, 16
    early/late maturation, 118–19
Maximally Discriminative Facial Movement Coding System (MAX), 86
Medical model, abnormal behavior, 455
Meiosis, 37
Memory, 199–202
    long-term memory, 201–2
    memory strategies
        imagery, 202
        keyword method, 202
        organization, 201–2
        rehearsal, 201
        semantic elaboration, 202
    short-term memory, 200–201
    social memory, 297–99
        ecologically valid memory study, 298
        research deficiencies, 297–98
        schema in, 298–99
Menarche, 112–13, 114
Mental age (MA), 252
Mental retardation, 268–69
    classifications by IQ, 269

cultural-familial retardation, 269
    organic retardation, 269
Mesoderm, 59
Mesomorphic, 106
Mesosystem, 306
Metaphor, formal operational thought, 185
Microsystem, 306
Middle Ages, view of child, 9
Middle childhood
    family interaction, 333–35
        coregulation, 334
    gender role development, 423–25
    overview of, 507–9
    physical development, 106
Minnesota Multiphasic Personality Inventory (MMPI), 22
Minnesota Study of Twins Reared Apart, 36
Minority-group children, achievement, 157–58
Miscarriage, 61
Modeling, 134, 149–52
    attention, 149–50
    behavior/cognition/environment relationship, 152
    incentive conditions, 150
    as information-processing activity, 151
    moral development, 435–36, 440
    motor reproduction, 150
    process of, 149
    retention, 150
    socialization, 291
Monozygotic twins, 46
Moral behavior, 439–42
    moral competence, 443
    moral performance, 443
    situation-specificity of, 440–42, 443
    social learning theory, 439–40, 442
Moral development. See also Kohlberg's theory; Piaget's theory
    care perspective, 437
    cognitive social learning theory, 443
    cultural factors, 437–38
    Defining Issues Test, 436–37
    Kohlberg's theory, 433–38
    meaning of, 431
    modeling, 435–36, 440
    moral reasoning, 438–39
    Piaget's theory, 431–32
    resistance to temptation, 442
    self-control, 442
    social conventional reasoning, 438–39
Moral education, 445–47
    cognitive moral education, 446
    direct moral education, 445
    as hidden curriculum, 445
    indirect moral education, 445
    Just Community (Cluster School), 447
    values clarification, 446
Moral feelings, 443–45
    altruism, 444
    empathy, 444
    guidelines for enhancement of, 445
    guilt, 443

Moro reflex, 83
Morpheme, 224
Morphology
    early childhood, 239
    language rules, 224
Mother-child interactions. *See also*
        Attachment
    individuation and, 381
    infant temperament and, 301
    reciprocal socialization, 317
    scaffolding, 317
Motherese, 233
Motivation
    achievement
        cross-cultural view, 158
        extrinsic motivation, 156
        intrinsic motivation, 156–57
        minority-group children, 157–58
        need for achievement, 155
    biological motives, 152–53
    competence motivation, 153–54
    hierarchy of motives, 154
    nature of, 136
    relationship to learning, 136
Motor reproduction, modeling, 150
Multimeasure/multisource/multicontext
        approach, child development
        research, 22–23
Multiple-factory theory, intelligence, 256
Musical intelligence, 256

N

Naive hedonism or instrumental orientation,
    433
Naturalistic observation, 20–21
Nature-nurture controversy, 16
    socialization, 300
Need, 153
Need for achievement, 155
Neglected children, unpopularity of, 350
"Neighborhood Walk," 21
Neurotransmitters, infancy, 94–95
Newborn
    assessment of, 74–76
        Apgar scale, 74
        Brazelton Neonatal Behavioral
            Assessment Scale, 74–76
    preterm infants, 72–74
New York Longitudinal Study, 475, 477
Nobel Prize sperm bank, 48, 49
Nonnutritive sucking, 85
Normal distribution, 252
Norms, tests, 251
Novelty-intelligence associations, 260
Nutrition, 488–90
    early childhood, 488–90
    fat consumption, 489
    infant nutrition, 488
    and prenatal development, 65
    sugar consumption, 489–90

O

Obesity, 491–93
Observation, 20–21
    laboratory observation, 20
    naturalistic observation, 20–21
Oedipal stage, 283–84
Offer Self-Image Questionnaire, 389
Onlooker play, 358
On-time/off-time development, adolescents,
    119–20
Operant conditioning, 140–45, 290
    behavior modification, 144–45
    definition of, 140
    punishment, 140, 144
    reinforcement, 140, 142–44
        and child's reinforcement history,
            143–44
        partial reinforcement, 142
        primary reinforcers, 143
        schedules of, reinforcement, 142–43
        secondary reinforcers, 143
    stages of
        baseline period, 140–41
        conditioning period, 141
        extinction period, 141
    successive approximations, 142
Oral stage, 283
Organic retardation, 269
Organization
    memory strategy, 201–2
    Piagetian, 166
Organogenesis, 59
Original sin, 9
Overextensions, language development,
    infancy, 237
Oxytocin, 71

P

Pain, infancy, 101
Parallel play, 358
Parental conflict, adolescence, 336–37
Parenthood, transition to, 315–16
Parenting
    and child's developmental maturity, 330
    recommendations for parents, 331
Parenting styles, 329–31
    authoritarian parenting, 329
    authoritative parenting, 329
    permissive indifferent parenting, 330
    permissive indulgent parenting, 330
Partial reinforcement, 142
Peers
    child/parent relationship and, 356–57
    children's groups, 354–56
    cognition and
        perspective-taking, 351
        social-information processing skills,
            351–52
        social knowledge, 352
friendship, 353–54
function of, 349
gender roles, influences on, 414–15
interaction, developmental course, 349–50
maladjusted children, 352
popularity/unpopularity, 350
Perceived Competence Scale for Children,
    388, 391
Perception, meaning of, 95
Perceptual development. *See also* Sensory/
        perceptual development
    early childhood, 105–6
Permissive indifferent parenting, 330
Permissive indulgent parenting, 330
Perseveration, 172
Personal fable, formal operational thought,
    186
Perspective-taking
    and peer relations, 351
    stages of, 384–85
Phallic stage, 283
Phenotypes, 45
Phobias, classical conditioning of, 138–39
Phonemes, 224
Phonics method, reading, 241
Phonology
    early childhood, 239
    language rules, 224
Physical development
    early childhood, 104–5
    late childhood, 106
    middle childhood, 106
Physiological research, 22
Piaget, J.
    background information, 164
    contribution of, 165, 186
Piaget's theory
    cognitive processes in
        adaptation, 165–66
        equilibration, 166
        organization, 166
    concrete operational thought
        basic features of, 180
        classification, 182
        conservation, 180–82
    criticisms of, 186–87
    educational application, 183
    emphasis of, 165
    formal operational thought, 432
        basic features of, 182–83
        egocentrism, 185
        hypothetical deductive reasoning,
            184–85
        imaginary audience, 185–86
        metaphor, 185
        personal fable, 186
    moral development, 431–32
        autonomous morality, 431–32
        heteronomous morality, 431–32
        imminent justice, 432
    play, 359, 360
    preoperational thought, 167, 172–80
        animism, 176
        basic features of, 172–73

centration, 178
conservation, 178–80
egocentrism, 176
intuitive thought substage, 177–80
symbolic function substage, 173–77
sensorimotor thought, 167–72
basic features of, 168–69
object permanence, 171–72
substages of, 169–71
Pictorial Scale of Perceived Competence and
Social Acceptance for Young
Children, 388
Piers-Harris Scale, 387–88
Pituitary gland, 115
PKU syndrome (phenylketonuria), 40–41
Placenta, 59
PLATO Project, 155
Play
associative play, 358
cooperative play, 359
functions of, 357–58, 359
onlooker play, 358
parallel play, 358
Piaget's theory, 359, 360
pretend play, 359–60
same sex play, 414–15
solitary play, 358
unoccupied play, 358
Play therapy, 357
Pleasure principle, 280
Polygenic inheritance, 44–45
Popularity/unpopularity, 350
Postconventional moral reasoning, 434
Postpartum depression, 315–16
Pragmatics, language rules, 226–27
Precipitate, 71
Preconventional moral reasoning, 433
Predictive validity, tests, 251–52
Pregnancy
adolescence, 126–28
marital relationship and, 316
Prenatal development
abortion in, 61–62
hazards to
age of mother, 65
drugs, 66–67
maternal disease, 63–64
nutrition, 65
stress of mother, 66
teratology, 63
miscarriage in, 61
periods of, 58–61
embryonic period, 59
fetal period, 60–61
germinal period, 58–59
organogenesis, 59
Preoperational thought. See Piaget's theory
Preschool. See Early childhood education
Pretend play, 359–60
Preterm infants, 72–74
conclusions about, 74
gestation period, 72
"kilogram babies," 72, 73

Primary circular reaction, sensorimotor stage,
170
Primary reinforcers, 143
Problem solving
steps in
checking solutions, 207–8
goal setting, 207
monitoring progress, 207
planning the approach, 207
Project Follow-Through, 362–63
Project Head Start, 362
Proximodistal pattern, physical development,
90
Psychoanalytic theories, 12. See also
individual theories
Erikson's theory, 284, 286–88
evaluation of, 288–89
Freudian theory, 279–84
Psychological scripts, 212
Psychometrics, 249
Puberty
determinants of, 112–14
hormonal changes, 114–15
individual differences, 117–18, 121
physical changes, 115–17
psychological aspects
body image, 118
early/late maturation, 118–19
on-time/off-time development, 119–20
Punishment, 290
operant conditioning, 140, 144
punishment and obedience orientation,
433
resistance to temptation and, 442

Q

Questionnaires, child development research,
21

R

Racial/ethnic factors
achievement, 157–58
intelligence tests, 262
Ratio schedule, 142
Reaction formation, 281
Reaction range, 45–46
Reading, teaching
ABC method, 241
phonics method, 241
whole-word method, 241
Reality principle, 280
Recasting, in language learning, 234
Reciprocal socialization, 317
Reciprocal teaching, 204, 205
Reductionistic theories, 293
Reflexes
infant
crying, 85
Moro reflex, 83

smiling, 85
sucking reflex, 84–85
prenatal, 61
Reflexive smile, 85
Regression, 281
to cope with stress, 485
Rehearsal, memory strategy, 201
Reinforcement, 134, 140, 142–44, 290
and child's reinforcement history, 143–44
partial reinforcement, 142
primary reinforcers, 143
schedules of reinforcement, 142–43
secondary reinforcers, 143
Rejected children, unpopularity of, 350
Reliability of tests
split-half reliability, 250
test-retest reliability, 249
tests, 249–50
REM sleep, infants, 89–90
Renaissance, view of child, 9
Repository for Germinal Choice, 48, 49
Repression, 281
Reproduction, human, 37, 39
Resistance to temptation, 442
Retention, modeling, 150
Rhythmic motor behavior
infancy, 92–94
blind infants, 94
theories of, 92–93
Ritalin, 464
Roger's theory of self-concept, 386–87
criticism of, 387
real self vs. ideal self, 386
self-actualization in, 387
unconditional personal regard, 386
Role-taking, socialization, 294
Rubella (German measles), and prenatal
development, 63

S

Satire, adolescence, 184–85
Scaffolding, 317
Schedules of reinforcement, 142–43
Schema, 210–11
in social memory, 298–99
Schools. See also specific topics
early childhood education, 362–64
elementary schools, 364–66
gender role influence on, 416–17
jigsaw classroom, 355
secondary schools, 366–69
Scientific method, steps in, 19
Scripts, 211–12
Secondary circular reactions, sensorimotor
stage, 170
Secondary reinforcers, 143
Secondary schools, 366–69
and back-to-basics movement, 366
effective school, characteristics of, 367
top-dog phenomenon, 369
transition to, 367–68

Subject Index

Television, 369–73
attention and, 370–71
gender role influence on, 416–17
guidelines for children, 373
influence on behavior, 372–73
social context of viewing, 371–72
time spent viewing, 370
views of, 369–70
Temperament
consistency of, 51
dimensions of, 50
heredity's influence, 48, 50–51
infant, and socialization, 301
infants, differences in, 50
shyness, 52
Teratology, and prenatal development, 63
Tertiary circular reactions, sensorimotor
stage, 170
Testis determining factor, 44
Testosterone, 114
Test-retest reliability, 249
Theories, 18
Token reinforcer, 143
Touch, infancy, 101
Trophoblast, 59

Trust versus mistrust, 287, 379–80
Turner's syndrome, 42
Twin studies, examples of, 36
Two-factor theory, intelligence, 255
Two-word utterances, language development,
infancy, 238

Ultrasonography, 43
Umbilical cord, 59
Unconditional personal regard, 386
Unconditioned response (UCR), 137
Unconditioned stimulus (UCS), 137
Underextensions, language development,
infancy, 237–38
Undifferentiated, gender roles, 407–8
Unoccupied play, 358

Validity of tests, 250
concurrent validity, 251
content validity, 251

criterion validity, 251
predictive validity, 251–52
Values clarification, moral education, 446
Variables, dependent/independent, 24
Visual perception in infancy, 97–99
depth perception, 99
infant vision, 98

Wernicke's area, 229
Whole-word method, reading, 241
Wild Boy of Aveyron, 278
Withdrawal, to cope with stress, 486
Writing ability, adolescents, 185

XYY syndrome, 42

Zygote, 37